W9-CLG-449

COLLECTED WORKS OF ERASMUS

VOLUME 8

THE CORRESPONDENCE OF ERASMUS

LETTERS 1122 TO 1251

1520 TO 1521

translated by R.A.B. Mynors

annotated by Peter G. Bietenholz

University of Toronto Press

Toronto / Buffalo / London

The research and publication costs of the
Collected Works of Erasmus are supported by the
Social Sciences and Humanities Research Council of Canada.
The publication costs are also assisted by
University of Toronto Press.

Toronto / Buffalo / London
Printed in Canada

Printed on acid-free paper

Canadian Cataloguing in Publication Data

Erasmus, Desiderius, d. 1536.
[Works]
Collected works of Erasmus
Includes index.
Partial contents: v. 8. The correspondence of
Erasmus: letters 1122 to 1251, 1520 to 1521 /
translated by R.A.B. Mynors; annotated by Peter
G. Bietenholz.
ISBN 0-8020-2607-9
1. Erasmus, Desiderius, d. 1536. I. Title.
PA8500 1974 876'.04 C74-006326-X rev

Collected Works of Erasmus

The aim of the Collected Works of Erasmus is to make available an accurate, readable English text of Erasmus' correspondence and his other principal writings. The edition is planned and directed by an Editorial Board, an Executive Committee, and an Advisory Committee.

ADVISORY COMMITTEE

Contents

Illustrations

Preface

The letters in this volume, written between 30 July 1520 and the end of 1521, cover the last fifteen months Erasmus spent in the Netherlands and his move to Basel. It was a period of high drama. The play in which he found himself compelled to act was neither of his making nor to his liking. He knew, however, that a great many people were watching him. Some believed that he alone could save the day; when Albrecht Dürer thought that Luther had been done away with, he called on Erasmus, the 'old manikin,' to take Luther's place.[1] Although Erasmus never saw this famous passage in Dürer's diary, he was painfully aware of the misconception that Dürer shared with many others.[2] His cause was different from Luther's,[3] and it had lost momentum, while Luther's grew stronger every day. He was still a champion, but a champion hamstrung and vulnerable – as Luther put it, like a 'ram with his horns entangled in a thornbush.'[4]

The world moved and Erasmus reacted. Since the imperial election of 28 June 1519[5] the French and the Hapsburgs had been on a collision course. In the summit meetings of Calais in June and July 1520[6] English diplomacy succeeded in reassuring the French while quietly siding with the emperor. While Charles v presented himself to the German nation, first at his coronation in Aachen, 27 October 1520, and subsequently at the Diet of Worms, January to May 1521,[7] Francis I went to war, initially by supporting dissident subjects and disloyal allies of the Hapsburgs.[8] Not without reason[9] he decided that his best defence was to attack Charles, especially when he saw Pope Leo x taking the emperor's side.[10] In August 1521 a new round of high-powered diplomatic meetings, with Cardinal Wolsey at their centre,[11] merely confirmed the demise of Erasmus' golden age of peace.[12] The crucial objective for both sides was the control of northern Italy and on 19 November the French lost it with the fall of Milan.[13] Meanwhile Luther pursued his reform of religious life and thought with unfailing devotion, eliciting cautious but vital support from his prince, the elector of Saxony.[14] His *De captivitate Babylonica* and *De libertate christiana* made an impact that

Erasmus could not fail to notice.[15] On the side of Luther's opponents perhaps only the papal nuncio Aleandro could match his will and his judgment. It was Aleandro who confronted the Netherlands and parts of Germany with the bull *Exsurge, Domine*,[16] who fathered and published the Edict of Worms, and had Lutheran books burnt wherever he went.[17]

Erasmus' reaction to the political events around him may be assessed on three levels. On the level of perseverance he continued to defend his ideals with undiminished vigour. The outbreak of war pained him, as he had always considered peace a precondition for the flourishing of literature and learning.[18] He predicted that the rulers, and especially Charles v, would later be sorry for their current course of action.[19] To Guillaume Budé, his touchy Gallic friend, he addressed a manifesto on the merits of education, especially girls' education, assuring him in the first place that 'these upheavals between the monarchs do not disrupt the bonds drawn by the Muses.'[20] Above all, Erasmus continued to defend himself with desperate determination against the charge that he was supporting Luther.[21] He still believed himself to be the victim of a conspiracy and still insisted that 'the fountain-head and the seed-bed of all this sorry business' was 'an incurable hatred of the ancient tongues and of humane studies.'[22] But this explanation had definitely lost its sparkle at a time when, on the one hand (as he correctly perceived) his fellow humanist Aleandro was at the centre of hostile agitation against him[23] and, on the other hand, Lutheran-minded priests began to marry[24] and to show in other ways that they were out to change society rather than just theology. Erasmus also continued his public protests against the plague of anonymous pamphlets,[25] of which there were indeed plenty, including one that appeared late in 1520 and was in part at least his own doing.

In fact, Erasmus' reaction to the changing circumstances combined consistency with a measure of pragmatism. There is good reason to believe that he helped produce the anonymous *Acta contra Lutherum*[26] with its crop of pointed slanders against the Louvain theologians, and, in the preface, against Aleandro. Whatever may have been the degree of his previous involvement in the *Julius exclusus*,[27] such denigration from the shelter of anonymity is unique in his writings and quite beyond comparison with the innuendo in his published letters, of which apparently he was not even aware.[28] His perception of the church was fundamentally unchanged. He did not suggest that he had formerly gone too far in his critique of religious practice, he only regretted that certain statements could now be twisted to resemble Luther's position.[29] As he revised his notes on the New Testament again, he made some changes[30] but did not touch his most outspoken notes on corrupt church practices and the abuse of papal powers.[31] In other cases too he would not sacrifice to his critics what he believed to be statements of historical fact.[32] Therefore one must ascribe a measure of pragmatism to the new respect he found in the course of 1521 for some exponents of the church like Adrian of Utrecht,[33] Jan Briart of Ath, Cajetanus,[34] and especially Aleandro,[35] all of whom he had formerly censured if not maligned. At the same time he began to promise, albeit with some provisos, that he would take up his pen against Luther. Yet it was in part to relieve himself of that promise that he moved to Basel by the end of 1521.[36] Doubtless Erasmus drew his sober conclusions from the changing religious climate in the Netherlands. Whereas in the early letters of this volume he reports on the strength of Lutheran sympathies all around him, his later letters regularly speak of their repression.[37]

Besides perseverance and pragmatism there is a third and truly original reaction to what Erasmus came to see as the most dangerous division Christendom had ever suffered.[38] A new theme had recently appeared in his work and is given rich and original orchestration in the letters of this volume. One of the ways in which the 1518 edition of Erasmus' *Annotationes* on the New Testament differed from that of 1516 was the commentary on Galatians 2:11–14. It had grown to considerable length, maintaining with Jerome against Augustine that Scripture offered many instances of pious deception. In a letter of July 1520 Erasmus wrote that 'the truth need not always be put forward, and it makes a great difference how it is put forward.'[39] He restated this thought a number of times and in May 1521 he found the perfect formulation for it: 'A prudent steward will husband the truth' after the example of Peter and Christ himself.[40] In order to husband the truth one may employ concealment, even deception and 'holy cunning.'[41] It must be noted that such advice was offered as an alternative to Luther's abrasive censure of the church. Erasmus still maintained that 'the truth must win';[42] in spite of the wholly unacceptable positions Luther had developed in *De captivitate Babylonica*, there still was a good deal of truth in his stand. It could not be otherwise – after all, Erasmus himself had often attacked the same abuses. He still found falsehood nowhere more prevalent than in the railings of conservative theologians and besotted friars. Erasmus continued to maintain essentially the same view he had formed in 1517, that Luther was right in his spirit and wrong in his language. Concealment and dissimulation, Erasmus' alternative to the verbal excesses of the Lutherans, was not to be an act of surrender, an abdication of responsibility,[43] but rather an active force – the force of moral superiority inherent in an informed, but unspoken, opinion. The pope himself would not be able to ignore 'the unspoken judgments of learned and pious individuals,' since they would 'retain their force even among posterity.'[44]

But how were Erasmus' 'silent judgments' to become operative? It has been argued that with this particular train of thought Erasmus had found the recipe for Nicodemism, the deception practiced by religious dissenters who continue to accept the ministrations of an established church in order to save their livelihoods or even their lives.[45] This could be how Erasmus was understood by many contemporaries; it was not, however, what he meant to advocate. If we are to assess his statements correctly, we must look at the way he acted and justified his actions. In Ep 1143, addressed to Leo x, he had launched a bold appeal in favour of Luther.[46] That was in September 1520. In the light of what has been said about his pragmatism, one might not expect Erasmus to use similar words a year later. Nor did he, but he then released Ep 1143 to the printer. He had initially questioned the authenticity of the bull *Exsurge, Domine*,[47] but understandably he did not publish under his own name any statement to this effect. At the same time, however, the purges he made in revising the New Testament and the letters already in print for new editions were far less substantial than he had announced.[48] The *Epistolae ad diversos* – principal source for both the earlier and the later letters translated in this volume – offers a number of declarations of loyalty to the church of Rome and hence was scorned in Wittenberg.[49] Yet it can be argued that if the *Epistolae ad diversos* moderately surpassed the earlier *Farrago* in its severity against Luther, it was incomparably more outspoken in attacking the friars and Louvain theologians, and attacking them by name.[50] If the readers of the *Epistolae ad diversos* were told a hundred times that Luther was not Erasmus' friend, they had every right to assume that Hutten and Jonas still were,[51] in spite of their firm support of Luther.

Thus on many specific issues Erasmus was far from mincing his words in the *Epistolae ad diversos* and this may explain his subsequent expressions of discontent with the collection.[52] As a whole, however, the book may be taken as a perfect example of the informed 'silent judgments' he wished to encourage. Truth would speak for itself. Erasmus trusted the readers, especially future generations of readers, to judge for themselves and to accept his case. Future readers would understand what he meant when he said: 'We need a sort of holy cunning; we must be time servers, but without betraying the treasure of the gospel truth from which our lost standards of public morality can be restored.'[53] Truth to Erasmus was still the gospel truth as he had sought to present it in the *Enchiridion* and the *Ratio verae theologiae*.[54] It was the truth for which he said repeatedly he was willing to die.[55] 'Should matters develop into a final conflict, so that the state of the church might go either way, I shall plant my feet firmly ... on that solid rock ... And your Erasmus will be found on the same side, whatever it may be, as the peace of the Gospel.'[56] In a concrete way, the solid ground on which

Erasmus remained anchored for the next seven and one-half years was the city of Basel, as yet undecided which way it would go in the religious conflict, and Erasmus will be found there, for the major part of this time, editing the Christian Fathers.[57]

Concerning the arrangement of this volume not much need be added to what has been said in the prefaces of its predecessors. Of the 134 letters translated in this volume, no fewer than 89 were published in the *Epistolae ad diversos*. Seventeen were first published elsewhere, although in Erasmus' lifetime; of these, Epp 1203 and 1228 were printed at first without authorization. Finally, 34 letters were edited after Erasmus' death by scholars of the sixteenth to the twentieth centuries. Only Ep 1232A has come to light after P.S. Allen's edition. Epp 1233A and 1241A were given new dates; in Allen's edition they were printed as Epp 1201 and 2680. In the case of Epp 1130, 1140, and 1170 we question the dates tentatively assigned by Allen but lack sufficient evidence firmly to propose another date. Very few letters in this volume, only 19 out of 134, are addressed to Erasmus rather than written by him. All but 4 of these were not printed until after his death. This imbalance goes back to the *Epistolae ad diversos* and is by Erasmus' own choice, as he explained in his preface to that collection.[58] An attempt has been made to compensate for this lack of dialogue by reporting in our notes the issues to which Erasmus reacted and the response his views elicited. This volume covers the months in which Erasmus, through a painful process of frequently rephrasing his thoughts, came to spell out his considered views with regard to Luther. In view of the crucial importance of this issue we have attempted to connect a number of related statements and expressions through cross-references in the annotation, but have also been aware that to do so consistently would be pedantic and cumbersome. Readers will find in this volume far more repetition than in its predecessors, but on the other hand they will be gratified by such impressive specimens of the art of letter-writing as Erasmus' Epp 1162, 1202, 1211, and 1233 or Hutten's Epp 1135 and 1161, and also by such letters as Epp 1183 and 1232, whose significance has perhaps not yet been fully recognized. For additional biographical information readers may turn to *Contemporaries of Erasmus: A Biographical Register of the Renaissance and Reformation* (CEBR).

The letters exchanged between Juan de Vergara and Diego López Zúñiga that follow Erasmus' correspondence in this volume were translated by Alexander Dalzell (Letters 1, 3, 4, and 5) and Erika Rummel (Letter 2), who wish to thank Gethin Hughes of the Department of Spanish and Portuguese in the University of Toronto for his helpful comments.

It was originally expected that this volume would be annotated by the late Wallace K. Ferguson, but failing eyesight did not in the end permit him to tackle this task, for which he would have been uniquely qualified. Any serious student of this volume, however, is bound to be aware of the debt Erasmus scholarship owes to the editor of *Erasmi opuscula*. Once again I must express my gratitude to the Library of the University of Saskatchewan, the Warburg Institute, University of London, and the Öffentliche Bibliothek of the University of Basel, and also to those who helped me generously with particular problems, Professor J.B. Trapp, London, Dr Frank Hieronymus, Basel, Professors Paul Grendler and John Munro, Toronto, and Professor P.M. Swan, Saskatoon. Some of Erasmus' references to classical authors have been identified by Erika Rummel and Alexander Dalzell. The index was prepared by Howard Hotson and the manuscript was copyedited by Mary Baldwin. CWE continues to receive vital financial support from the Social Sciences and Humanities Research Council of Canada.

PGB

Oxford
London
Rochester
Canterbury
Aldington
The Hague
Utrecht
Gorinchem
Groningen
Zwolle
Halle
Trzebiatów
Elbe
N
Calais
Bruges
Ghent
Antwerp
Thérouanne
Courtrai
Mechelen
Lille
Louvain
Tournai
Brussels
Liège
Aachen
Cologne
Wittenberg
Leipzig
Erfurt
Zwickau
Fulda
Schneeberg
Wrocław
Seine
Paris
Maas
Mainz
Kreuznach
Worms
Würzburg
Rhine
Nürnberg
Sélestat
Ettenheim
Ingolstadt
Olomouc
Altomünster
Augsburg
Znojmo
Memmingen
Danube
Basel
Lake Constance
Lake Geneva
Sion
Rhône
Milan
Pavia
Venice
Avignon
Florence
Siena
Rome
0 50 100 MILES
0 50 100 KILOMETRES

THE CORRESPONDENCE OF ERASMUS

LETTERS 1122 TO 1251

1122 / To Matthias [Meyner] Louvain, 30 July 1520

Epp 1122–8, dated between 30 July and 2 August, are all addressed to correspondents in Saxony and elsewhere in Germany. Most, if not all, of them were entrusted for conveyance to three visitors from Saxony who had called upon Erasmus in Louvain and were then ready to return home. Johannes Draconites, a young canon and lecturer from Erfurt, had brought Erasmus a message from the rector of the university and other tributes, including probably a collection of epigrams attacking his bitter critic, Edward Lee, composed by members of the Erfurt humanist circle (cf Ep 1123 n9, n12). Draconites took charge of Epp 1124, 1127. For an echo of his visit see *Jonas Briefwechsel* Ep 43, and for earlier callers from among Erasmus' admirers in Erfurt see Epp 870 introduction, 963:6n. Although personal contacts between Draconites and Luther probably did not begin before the spring of 1521 (cf Luther w *Briefwechsel* II Ep 410), Draconites no doubt shared the Lutheran sympathies of his Erfurt friends. It is possible that he left Louvain in the company of Johannes Egranus, priest at Zwickau, who had arrived there by way of Wittenberg and Basel and had brought Erasmus a message from Luther (cf Epp 1127A, 1141 n11). Erasmus' third visitor was Heinrich Eppendorf (cf n5), who had arrived with gifts from Duke George of Saxony and Matthias Meyner; the latter had also sent a letter (cf lines 21–2), now missing.

Matthias Meyner (c 1475–c 1523), of Karlmarxstadt (Chemnitz), held a master's degree from the University of Leipzig and from 1515 an administrative position at Schneeberg in ducal Saxony, a mining town in the Erz Mountains. Between 1470 and 1530 large quantities of silver were produced from an exceptionally rich mine at Schneeberg. Meyner's newly acquired interest in liberal studies (cf lines 4–5) may well have been inspired by his friend Petrus Mosellanus (cf Ep 1123), who dedicated to him in 1522 his edition of a work by Prudentius. In 1526/7 Meyner's widow married Georgius Agricola, who was later to become the most distinguished among Erasmus' correspondents in the mining towns of the Erz Mountains (cf Agricola *Ausgewählte Werke* II 301–4, 368–71).

This letter was first published by Adrianus Cornelii Barlandus in his *Epistolae aliquot selectae ex Erasmicis* (1520; cf Ep 1163 introduction) and subsequently in Erasmus' *Epistolae ad diversos*; cf Ep 1206 introduction.

ERASMUS OF ROTTERDAM TO THE EXCELLENT MATTHIAS, DECIMARIUS[1] OF HIS SERENE HIGHNESS GEORGE, DUKE OF SAXONY, GREETING

I am delighted to hear of your good fortune, honoured sir, in at length securing your release from the time-wasting and tedious business of the court and deciding to occupy your old age in liberal studies. Duke Albert,[2]

the famous warrior, I once knew by name only, in Holland when I was a boy. Long ago, when I was living in England, I had a wonderful picture of Duke George from his chancellor,[3] and what he told me was fully borne out by public repute. After that, I came lately to know of the more than heroic valour of Duke Frederick, not only from hearing our princes speak of him, but from a letter and a present that he himself sent me.[4]

Heinrich Eppendorf,[5] a gifted young man whose face already indicates a noble mind, brought me as a present from you three lumps of native silver[6] as they are dug out of your mines, the smallest reddish, the largest livid in colour, and the middle one pale. I never saw such a thing before, and was quite delighted. Though when you say that I had taken a great fancy to your veins of silver, I must tell you that the thought of your mines had never entered my head before. For the moment I have nothing at hand with which to return your generosity; all I can send is myself in lead[7] – and I myself am really clay or something still more worthless.

One other point: why you should keep your name from me, I cannot think; for I could find it nowhere in your letter. When I can learn it, I shall write you among my friends, and it will not be in the lowest class. Farewell.

Louvain, 30 July 1520

1123 / To Petrus Mosellanus — Louvain, 31 July 1520

Petrus Mosellanus taught Greek at Leipzig. On 3 January 1520 he was promoted MA as a first step towards his appointment to a regular professorship, in June he was made a fellow of one of the colleges, the 'Grosses Fürstenkollegium,' and on 1 May he took office as rector of the university for the summer term (cf lines 14–15). This letter, which was published in the *Epistolae ad diversos*, answers two from Mosellanus (cf lines 2, 20). Both are missing, but it can be assumed that the second had been carried by one of Erasmus' Saxon visitors; cf Ep 1122 introduction.

ERASMUS TO PETRUS MOSELLANUS, GREETING

I have a letter from you, in which you say you are sorry that your letter was printed.[1] For my part, this is not the only thing the printing of which I deplore; the enthusiasm of some of these Germans[2] does me more harm than the malice of my enemies. I ask you: what was the object of publishing the letter I had written to the archbishop of Mainz?[3] Our enemies show more sense than we do: they conceal everything and do their plotting in the dark, while on our side nothing is hid. I am preparing a second edition of my complete correspondence,[4] to discourage its reprinting in the form already printed; some things I shall cut out, and some I shall modify. The letter I wrote to Luther,[5] which they published in your part of the world, was reported to Pope Leo, and various extracts were sent to different people to arouse them against me. Who taught these diabolical characters this cunning method of propaganda? I congratulate you on your new dignity, and rejoice at the improvement in your fortunes. The news about Oecolampadius[6] I knew already from a letter from him. I will write to your duke,[7] if I can find the time.

I am getting ready to set out for Germany.[8] Lee[9] has left no stone unturned in his attempt to undermine me, but has had no success; every man of any standing in England is on my side. In your earlier letter you seemed to me to take a rather favourable view of Hephestius.[10] Remember he was solely responsible for stirring up Noxus[11] and is now playing the lead in all this melodrama, a really venomous and pigheaded character, as men tend to be who have crawled out of the dunghill. I have seen some epigrams attacking Lee.[12] He may be fit for the gallows, if you like; even so, I would rather the fellow were attacked with arguments by serious opponents than with scurrilities like this. Farewell.

Louvain, 31 July 1520

1124 / To Konrad van Thüngen [Louvain, c 31 July 1520]

This letter was inspired by Draconites and was taken back by him after his visit to Louvain (cf Ep 1122 introduction), and therefore it must be contemporary with Ep 1127. Draconites was born in the region of Würzburg, where Konrad von Thüngen (d 1540) had recently been elected prince-bishop by his fellow canons (15 February 1519). He is not known to have reacted to this approach by Erasmus, but after 1529 they corresponded for a while. An autograph rough draft of this letter in MS Gl. Kgl. Samling 95 fol, of the Royal Library at Copenhagen (cf Allen III 630–4), does not differ significantly from the text published in the *Epistolae ad diversos*.

TO THE RIGHT REVEREND FATHER IN CHRIST AND RIGHT HONOURABLE PRINCE KONRAD, BISHOP OF WÜRZBURG

Greeting, honoured Lord Bishop. Though I am by nature so modest that I do not often trouble even men of ordinary rank with an unsought letter, and am now too busy to have leisure to write to anyone at all, I have been pestered by Draconites, the bearer of this, to write a letter to your Highness. You take delight, I understand, in liberal and sacred studies, and at this time show a singular interest in those who pursue the better sort of literature – among whom I wish I might fairly include myself. At least I think I can be numbered among those whose efforts, for what they are worth, give fresh energy to other men, like those who sound the trumpet on the battlefield while remaining themselves outside the fray, or pour cold water on the competitors[1] without themselves competing in the race.

Up to now, it is true, a fresh supply of gifted men has come forward very well, provided we can avoid discord or at least conduct it in a more civilized fashion. If the old subjects could be united with the new in mutual amity,[2] each might be of service to the other. As it is, both parties take as their aim the utter rout of one faction or the other, and both suffer as a result. The blockhead battalions are banded together for the destruction of the humanities. Those with smaller wits have larger numbers, but the better side are winning. The risk is, as Livy puts it,[3] that the bigger party may defeat the better, unless we have the support of you and others like you. I would express gratitude to your Lordship's generosity, not only in the name of humane studies generally, but privately on my own account, for the open and friendly way in which you do not reject my trifling works, such as they are.

If you are offended at this brief letter of mine, this more than hasty scrawl, you must blame Draconites, one of the best young men I have yet seen, and also one of the most obstinate. May Christ almighty preserve your Highness for us in health and wealth as long as possible.

1125 / To Duke George of Saxony — Louvain, 31 July 1520

This letter, which follows an earlier exchange (Epp 514, 586) acknowledges the gift the duke had sent through Eppendorf (cf lines 57–60). It also shows that Erasmus continued to observe developments in the Saxon universities with attention, relying, apart from the information imparted by his current visitors (cf Ep 1122 introduction), probably on letters, now lost, from Petrus Mosellanus (cf n4). In the fifteenth century the University of Leipzig had gained a solid reputation in the field of scholastic theology, but it was slow to find room in its curriculum for the new learning of the humanists, although this had recently received considerable support from Duke George. Its professors stood divided, and in the eyes of the ebullient humanists of Erfurt the Leipzig theologians deserved to be ridiculed, as in fact they were in the *Epistolae obscurorum virorum* (cf Epp 363, 622). As for the relations between the young University of Wittenberg and Leipzig, Erasmus cannot have been unaware of the widening gulf after Duke George turned sharply against Luther in the wake of the Leipzig Disputation (cf Ep 1020 n9). In some ways the situation in Saxony must have reminded him of the University of Louvain, where continued feuding between conservative theologians and the advocates of the new learning could not fail to embarrass and worry him (cf CWE 7 preface; Ep

1174 n1). For some time he had argued that in Louvain as elsewhere traditional theology and the humanities might peacefully co-exist (cf Epp 950:21n, 1003:15n); now he emphasized the same point with regard to central Germany, here as well as in Epp 1124, 1127, 1127A, even as he commended the humanities with spontaneous warmth. Intentionally or otherwise, his letters show that he continued to view the Lutheran controversy as part of the older feud over academic methods (cf the preface and Ep 1238:45–8, 92–8).

This letter was published in the *Epistolae ad diversos*.

TO THE MOST ILLUSTRIOUS GEORGE, DUKE OF SAXONY, FROM ERASMUS, GREETING

Most illustrious Duke, the fame of your Highness' father, Albert,[1] as a warrior of no mean order was known to me long ago in Holland while I was still a youth; but your own comprehensive gifts of intellect and character, your lofty spirit worthy of a true prince, your rare wisdom, sobriety, and moderation, your astonishing powers of mind, your penetrating judgment – in a word, a kind of winning harmony of all the virtues, were first portrayed to me some time ago in England by that excellent and most modest man, your Highness' chancellor,[2] in such terms that I was kindled immediately into a warm feeling for you. You could not add lustre to your father's glorious name more effectively than by surpassing his most famous and outstanding qualities. And it will add no mean distinction to your glories in the eyes of posterity, that you have now undertaken the most honourable of all forms of competition with the illustrious Duke Frederick,[3] under whose auspices the study of the best literature flourishes in Germany with such success. How few are the years he has needed to raise that slumbering university to such a high reputation! Unless I am quite mistaken, this will be seen by posterity as not the least among his glories, that he has used the ancient languages and humane studies as material wherewith to adorn and strengthen Christendom.

And in this field of glory you run no risk of seeming less than your cousin. It is under your auspices and by your generosity that the University of Leipzig, which has so long been famous and a home of the traditional disciplines, has now thanks to you gained such fresh renown from the addition of humane letters and the ancient tongues that it scarcely yields to any other. It was your bounty that aroused and promoted the gifts of Petrus Mosellanus,[4] a young man of great learning and the very greatest promise. It was thus too that Heinrich Stromer,[5] long known for his complete integrity and unusual wisdom, was attracted to your city, to be both a glory to the university as an exceedingly skilled physician and also an influential councillor in the town. Thus Simon Pistoris[6] is honoured and supported as *professor ordinarius* of law, and Georg von Breitenbach,[7] a man not less distinguished for his legal knowledge than for his ancestors. And the example set by their excellent prince is followed by almost all the city council and the other magistrates, who do honour to liberal studies and to the virtues by all means in their power; far distant as they are from me, I have come to know them all from the letters of my friends and from their public reputation.

Indeed I would think the advancement of knowledge in a most happy state, were it not somewhat spoiled by discord. So it seems good to the Fates: there must be nothing in human affairs so fortunate at all points that it is disfigured by no defect. I perceive that there are faults on both sides. Those who cling tooth and nail to the older type of subject give an unfriendly reception to these new studies, and treat as enemies men who have a contribution to make of the highest value. Again, those who wish to restore the classical literatures would rather force their way in as though they meant to devastate everything than work their way by courtesy towards a kind and friendly reception. But though I agree that both sides are at fault, they show the greater discourtesy who furiously repel more liberal subjects, depriving themselves of great advantages; and their mouths are full of nothing but heresies, schisms, and Antichrists, as they arouse bitter controversy over trifles. Here also is a task for your wisdom, most illustrious Prince, to find a wise solution for this strife between the disciplines. It can be done, if every man will advance his own subject without despising the subjects of other people.

Heinrich Eppendorf,[8] a rarely gifted young man, has handed to me an unworked nugget[9] of silver dug up in your mines, which gave me no less pleasure than if you had sent me an Attic talent[10] of gold; though I should have found anything most precious that came from such a prince. I will endeavour to prove that you have not conferred this kindness on an ungrateful person. May Christ the almighty long keep your Highness in health and wealth as a blessing to us all and to sound learning.

Louvain, 31 July 1520

1126 / To Hermannus Buschius Louvain, 31 July 1520

The German humanist Hermannus Buschius had written from Mainz (Ep 1109) to pledge his participation in the German campaign against Edward Lee (cf Epp 1083, 1123 n9). This long and carefully structured (n17) reply gave Erasmus an opportunity to acknowledge Buschius' efforts in cautious language, as well as to direct attention to the stubborn hostility of two other critics (n5, n34), whom he suspected of acting in collusion with one another (lines 268–9) and with

Lee. Buschius was hardly expected to keep this letter to himself, and Erasmus had it published in the *Epistolae ad diversos*. It may have been sent to Germany with one of the Saxon visitors; cf Ep 1122 introduction.

ERASMUS OF ROTTERDAM TO HERMANNUS BUSCHIUS, GREETING

I am sorry for you, my learned Buschius, if you have wasted valuable hours on Lee's nonsense and my own. Among all the futile pamphlets spewed out for our benefit by the printing-houses, nothing – my life upon it – has yet appeared more ignorant and blockheaded and, what is worse, more venomous. The man is a laughing-stock, with his boastful book[1] he has been bragging of for so long, among scholars everywhere; he is anathema to all men of sense even in England; his own kinsmen[2] – and he has several who are elegant scholars – disapprove of him. Even those[3] for whose benefit he is acting this farce are dissatisfied. He is hissed off the stage by the whole theatre; and yet the man remains obstinately pleased with himself, he is the one person who applauds, and in fact he thinks it is a great stroke of luck for him that he has tried a fall with Erasmus and has roused the disgust of men of learning and sense and suddenly become known to the world at large. He has an abbot of egregious stupidity;[4] he has his Standish,[5] who has so many claims to fame, first a Minorite, then a theologian, and finally a bishop; and with the support of these two he is satisfied. The abbot's name shall still be kept a secret. As for Standish's metal, I will give you a sample. He cannot himself wish to conceal, I presume, what he laid down in public before a great concourse of people.

He was preaching in St Paul's churchyard in London.[6] Having started his sermon on the subject of charity, he suddenly forgot all decency and charity alike and began to rave against my name and reputation, maintaining that the Christian religion faced utter destruction unless all new translations were instantly removed from the scene. Things had become intolerable, he said, since Erasmus had the effrontery to corrupt the Gospel of St John; for where the church for all these years had read *In principio erat verbum*, he was now introducing a new reading, *In principio erat sermo*. He thought that in this way a weapon had been put into his hand which I could by no means escape. He added that Augustine somewhere approves of *verbum* rather than *ratio*,[7] and produces reasons why he should think so; 'but these reasons,' says he, 'are more than our miserable Grecian can understand.'

After much stupid ranting on this subject, which was entirely off the point,[8] our orator began to touch the hearts of his audience and to lament the lot of an old man like himself, a doctor of so many years standing, who hitherto had always read *In principio erat verbum* and was now reduced under compulsion to read *In principio erat sermo*, suspecting that such pitiful laments would leave not a dry eye. Then with touching eloquence he appealed to the lord mayor, who was present according to custom, and to the whole body of magistrates and the entire multitude of citizens to rally round the Christian faith in its hour of trial. He imagined his remarks were inspired, and yet they were to no one's taste. Everyone in the audience with even a moderate education was astonished at the man's stupidity; and among the common people anyone with any sense of the ridiculous laughed at the nonsense he talked, which had no connection with his text. Those who by nature had higher standards were indignant that the ears of the multitude should be filled with such rubbish, when they were expecting something very different.

It so happened that the same day (I think it was) he dined at court. No sooner has this been perceived by two men I know – one of them a bachelor[9] who, although well versed in the three tongues and in the doctrine of the Fathers, yields in the niceties of Scotism to none of those who have learnt nothing else and spend their whole lives on it; the other a married man,[10] but divinely gifted; courtiers both – but they promptly take their seats at the same table, though they were not the messmates Standish would have chosen. Their names shall be kept secret for the moment. Immediately, so as to lose no time, one of them began: 'I am delighted to hear that a godly man like you has been able to find some time to read Erasmus' commentaries,' setting a trap for the man of course, for had he denied reading them, the immediate reply would have been, 'How then can you condemn in public what you have not read?' Standish saw this coming; 'Maybe,' says he, 'I have read all I have a mind to read.' 'I have no doubt,' was the reply, 'that you have read him, for today you criticized explicitly a passage in his notes on St John.'[11] He again gave an ambiguous answer, but indicated somehow that he had read the book. 'That's splendid,' said the other man, 'for I long to know on what arguments or on which authorities he bases himself. For there can be no doubt that he must have had something to go on when he boldly altered the passage.' That had him on the hop, and this is how he shamelessly got out of it. 'I care nothing,' he said, 'for the authorities or the reasons of that man. I am content with what St Augustine says,[12] that the Son of God is more properly denoted by *verbum* than by *ratio*, though *logos* in Greek means both.' 'I agree,' said the other man, 'about *ratio*; but what has that to do with *sermo* for "word"? Erasmus does not translate *In principio erat ratio* but *In principio erat sermo*.' '*Sermo* and *ratio*,' says he, 'mean the same thing.' 'Not at all,' the other replied, 'and you show a lack of decent feeling in publicly attacking like this the reputation of a man who has done so much for the subject, when you have not read the passage and do not understand the point.' At this Standish swore that whatever he might have said had been prompted by genuine conviction; but that he could not remember any passage in Holy Writ where the Son of God was called *sermo*. 'I can,' says the second man, 'though I am neither a theologian nor a priest; let me refresh your memory.' And he produced 'Thine almighty word, O Lord'[13] and what follows. The man admitted that *sermo* was used in 'Thine almighty word,' but not in 'In the beginning was the Word.' The whole dinner-party made merry over his exquisite distinction.

After that, he diverted the conversation into a philosophical argument, in which he was at once taken up by my other friend, who is as far ahead of Standish in this branch of learning as Standish is behind him in the humanities. So when he had taken a fall from this man too even in his own particular field, imagine how he changed his tactics! 'If you feel so strongly about it,' he said, 'why not go up into the pulpit and answer me in a sermon?' To which the reply was: 'I am not such a fool as to wish to pour out stuff like this in front of foolish women and an ignorant mob. But if I chose, I should demonstrate in public without hesitation that what you said in your sermon today is half-way to heresy.' At this word Standish was horrified; and the other man went on, 'To bring an open suggestion of heresy against something the supreme pontiff has twice approved in an official document,[14] does this smack of heresy itself, or no?'

In spite of such a reception, the man showed neither repentance nor regret. On the contrary, some time later, in the presence of that unusually intelligent king and of a queen[15] who is as sensible as she is godly, with a large party of learned men and nobles standing round, he fell piously upon his knees.[16] Everyone looked for something remarkable from one who was a monk, a divine of so many years standing, a bishop, and last but not least an old man. Thereupon, using his mother tongue, in which he has some fluency, he praised the forbears of the king and queen for the stand they had always taken so piously on the side of the Catholic church against heretics and schismatics, and exhorted them – adjured them indeed by all that is holy – to continue in the image of their ancestors: a time of far the greatest peril was at hand, new books by Erasmus had appeared, and unless they were boldly resisted, it was all over with the religion of Christ. Then, raising hands and eyes to heaven, he besought Christ graciously to aid his spouse himself, if no mortal man should come to her assistance.

All this and more of the same sort he uttered with a wonderful air of saintliness; and it so happened that both the men who had previously dealt with him at dinner were standing by. So the one who was a layman started off as follows. After praising the reverend father's pious and saintly utterance, and reproducing with humorous mimicry something even of Standish's attitudes, he besought almighty God that the man might mean what he said, and that there might be no discrepancy between his thoughts and words. 'But I fear,' he said, 'that if we looked into it carefully, we should find his actions very different from what appear to be his sentiments.' And with that he told him that after arousing this anxiety in the minds of eminent princes, he ought at the same time to show what there was in Erasmus' books that made him fear destructive heresies and disastrous schisms. At once the man confidently promised to do so; and counting the points out on his fingers,[17] 'First,' says he, 'Erasmus does away with the resurrection. Secondly he makes the sacrament of matrimony worthless. Last but not least he holds false views on the eucharist.'

This statement at first somewhat shook those most religious princes; but my defending counsel, after praising Standish generously for putting his points so clearly and distinctly for all to see, observed that it only remained now for him to prove what he had so elegantly set forth. Without a moment's delay Standish assured them that he would do this likewise. And beginning with his thumb, he said: 'Point one. That he does away with the resurrection I prove like this: Paul in his Epistle to the Colossians' – for this elderly theologian is so familiar with St Paul that he imagined what is in 1 Corinthians to be in Colossians – 'writes as follows: "We shall all rise again, but we shall not all be changed."[18] Erasmus has done away with this text, which is accepted by the church, and follows those Greeks of his in reading "We shall not all sleep, but we shall all be changed." It is clear therefore that he does away with resurrection.'

Who could suppose this man to have any brains? In my annotations[19] I pass in review the variant readings and reject none of them, since the most approved authorities differ in their choice and the same men sometimes make different choices. In the continuous text[20] I translate the only reading found in the Greek copies. Now, with Paul confirming the resurrection in so many passages, what could be more crazy than to say that the resurrection is done away with, if in one passage the words 'rise again' are altered? When the Christian creed asserts the resurrection of the dead, does it thereby oblige all men to die in order that they may rise again? As though the canon law, when it rules that the man on whom a bishopric has been conferred must lay down his office, meant that any man on whom a bishopric has been conferred in Rome must acquire an office if he does not already hold one in order to be able to lay it down.

But when that champion of mine had clearly explained the whole thing and set out the man's stupidity for all to see, so that even uneducated men and mere women[21] could see that I had said nothing wrong, while the theologian himself, for all his impudence, could not open his mouth in reply, that was not the end. Following Lucian's principle that it is discreditable to hold one's tongue,[22] and anxious not to throw in the sponge[23] without saying a word, he admitted that it was true, and that this reading is taken into account by early and orthodox Fathers, especially by Jerome; 'but Jerome,' says he, 'restored what we have out of the Hebrew.'[24] This eminent scholar had heard of Jerome's emending some readings in the Old Testament out of the Hebrew sources, and thought that the same held good for the Pauline Epistles.

What Standish said was not suffered to pass unnoticed by the bachelor theologian whom I mentioned earlier. With a slight bend of the knee and a respectful address, which was not in character, 'Pray, Reverend Father,' he said, 'be so good as to repeat what you have just told us; I was not attending as I ought.' So he produced his idiotic opinion even more clearly and at greater length, promising himself great credit from this observation. My friend, to secure greater attention from the whole company, began: 'This is no light argument that the reverend father puts forward. I would however try to make some sort of answer to it, if his Majesty would not find it tedious to listen.' After that, the queen[25] plucked the king by the sleeve, and told him to attend. Whereat, putting on a serious face, so as to look thoughtful and not a little puzzled, my friend began: 'Really I do not quite see what arguments can be put forward against this position, or what answer should be given to do the worthy bishop justice. For I cannot think the reverend father so much at sea that he supposes the Epistles to have been written first in Hebrew, when every schoolboy knows that Paul wrote them in Greek. What could have been Jerome's idea in altering the current reading out of books written in Hebrew, when it is the normal practice to do that from the sources, and there is no record that anyone has seen these Epistles in a Hebrew text?' And this point, which by itself was foolish and absurd enough for anybody, he repeated and emphasized and enforced and rubbed in to such a tune that the king, with his noble kindness of heart, was sorry to see such colossal stupidity pilloried in such exalted company, and came to the man's rescue in his embarrassment by starting another topic that led in a different direction. Such was Standish's triumph under his first heading. Of the others we heard no more.

Tell me, in the name of all the Muses, my excellent Buschius, do you suppose there is any misdemeanour they will not attempt, if they are not afraid to show such brazen effrontery in accusing a man falsely on no ground at all, and to do so in the presence of the most eminent princes, before whom libel uttered ought to be a capital offence,[26] and in a circle of unusually well educated men? Anyone who heard it said that I do away with the resurrection supposed me to deny something which in very many places I maintain to be the foundation and the summit of our faith. On no point do I dwell with more emphasis than in upholding the resurrection of the body. The man had no lack of the desire to hurt, but his judgment was at fault. He had foolishly chosen these three weapons with this in mind: once he had proved that my views were unsound on the eucharist, he would rouse the clergy to a man against me; on matrimony, he would excite husbands and wives, and indeed the laity as a whole, to pelt me with stones; on the resurrection, he would mobilize all princes and peoples who call themselves Christians to destroy me. But his libels about the resurrection are proved by the facts to be not merely lies but lunacy. As for matrimony, so far am I from speaking against it, that in Louvain in a public lecture[27] in the theology faculty I was criticized in fairly unpleasant language because I was supposed in a brief declamation of the hortatory kind to have given matrimony too much importance. For the question which I have raised elsewhere,[28] whether divorce can be used as a relief for the unfortunate parties in a marriage which has come to grief, does not tell in the least against the solemnity of matrimony. As for the eucharist,[29] heaven forgive me if I have ever been able to guess what Standish means, seeing that no thought has ever entered my mind that was unworthy of that most holy mystery, so far am I from ever having said or written anything amiss. And he dares to behave like this as one priest to another, one theologian to another, one old man to another, besides which he is a professed follower of the way of life of the apostles, and last but not least is a right reverend father in Christ.

The laws of the Caesars prescribe that the spreader of scandals who brings a false accusation shall be liable to the same penalties as his victim would have paid had he been guilty.[30] This man brings three such accusations simultaneously which are as outrageous as they are false, and he brings them in the presence of princes before whom it would be right to speak with scrupulous accuracy even of established facts. Hence it is easy to guess what nonsense he must have talked[31] among his cronies as they drank their wine. Suppose a man were to follow Ajax' example and loose his fury with insults and with weapons on a herd of pigs,[32] addressing one of them as Agamemnon, another as Ulysses or Menelaus. Nobody would ever thereafter put any trust in a person who had once so abundantly gone off his head. But this man, after such a fit of insanity before such an audience of eminent witnesses, actually admires his own performance as though he had done well, and pompously lays down the law on questions of the faith. What difference does it make whether insanity stems from bodily illness or from a disorder of the mind – in other words, from humours which impair the organs of the mind – or from hatred, stupidity, pride, jealousy, and other evil qualities which impair its judgment? And in my experience nearly all the enemies of the humanities are men like that; their pretext may be now

Reuchlin,[33] now Luther, now the pope, and different names at different times; but it is the same piece they play with changes of cast and scenery, and I find them not merely ignorant but demented.

In this Standish story I have not invented a syllable, and some things I have discreetly suppressed. I could tell you hundreds of tales of the same sort. But I will add one just now, which is not wholly irrelevant. The man's name I will keep secret for the moment,[34] although when I told him to give up slandering me by name he went on being his true self. Nor will I mention his order; for he is one of those who are commonly called mendicants. I observe the whole order is up in arms if one criticizes a Carmelite or a Preacher; and I do not know whether this is more foolish or more unjust. Why should not the whole priesthood be equally indignant if someone says he has been injured by a priest, actually suppressing his name? And yet they declaim daily against the priesthood in most subversive language before public audiences, while not allowing their own orders to be mentioned except in the most honourable terms, so that if I complain that I have been swindled by a Carmelite, the whole order would accuse me of slander. Some of them I could name behave like this even if one speaks the truth, or indeed part of the truth, not making public all one knows and courteously withholding the man's name meanwhile.

But to return. I had observed in the presence of this man, who was a theologian and a professed religious (he will silently agree that I speak the truth), that I wondered very much why Standish should have taken it into his head to accuse me on the subject of the eucharist when there was nothing in my books that could provide a handle for such slanders; and he promised that he would show me a passage.[35] From this I understood at once that they were carrying out a prearranged plot. I promised in return – and kept my promise – that I would prove he had not understood the passage if he could show me that he had read it. He read it through at a hand-gallop in such a way that no one could hear it but himself. Then he closed the book and put it away, as though it was now established that I had said in print that one could not assert the real presence of Christ's body in the communion. He then began to argue with me, saying that he had written some pamphlet or other on this very subject,[36] from which he hoped for a great reputation. I said I was not prepared to fight the empty air like a show-boxer, unless I had first proved to him that he had not understood the passage. He swore that it was just as he said. I was all the less ready to believe him, especially because I already knew from the most certain evidence that the man was an egregious numbskull.

One or two examples of this may perhaps not be out of place here. I have many grounds for suspicion that this man was entrusted by fellow spirits in his order with the business of noting down out of all my books things they could get their teeth into.[37] He threw himself into it, this man who knows absolutely no Latin and in theological reading has the most meagre equipment, no judgment, great arrogance, and such wits as, did not his cowl speak for him, might lead him to be taken commonly for a zany, for his whole countenance proclaims what a numbskull he is by nature. Well then, in one particular passage, excusing a slip by St Thomas, I had added that he did not deserve[38] to live in such times, meaning of course, and saying it too, that Thomas was worthy of a happier intellectual climate, since he himself lacked neither brains nor energy. What does our theologian do but complain of me bitterly, protesting that it is intolerable to say that Thomas, that great and saintly man, was 'undeserving.' I suppose, if I had said that he himself was worthy to labour in the mill with slaves, he would have claimed credit for the fact that I had called him worthy. And there was no end to his complaints until he fell in with a theologian who knew some Latin and, suspecting what in fact had happened, asked to be shown the passage. When he was shown the place, he laughed heartily, and the story became a well-known anecdote and almost proverbial.

He also protested to me in person with all seriousness, because in one place I appeared to approve of defamatory libels. This struck me as absurd, for I object to such things as much as anyone in the world, and I demanded to know what made him say this. He produced a passage from a letter of mine to Thomas Lupset,[39] I think it was, in which I wrote that a defamatory libel sometimes can plead necessity as an excuse. He thought I was defending the defamatory libel under the pretext of necessity, although (the courteous man that he is!) he admitted that my adding the word 'sometimes' lent a certain colour to this view. He had failed to understand, this blockhead set up as a critic, that in order to make my point clear by exaggeration I was comparing the behaviour of certain detractors, who actually use falsehoods to attack other men's reputations both privately and in public, with the publication of defamatory libels, as an example of an outrageous crime worse than many capital offences; and I show from the circumstances that their rabid defamation is to some extent harder to excuse than a defamatory libel, because sometimes this is excused by necessity, for example when someone has to instruct or threaten a despotic ruler whom it would not be safe to instruct openly, however much this may be in the public interest. These men could safely tell me where I go wrong; but they neither instruct me nor listen to me, they attack my reputation with their falsehoods. So in that context I am no more a supporter of defamatory libels than a man would be in favour of murder who in comparing it with seduction took the point of view that in one way a seducer is worse than a homicide because murder damages only one half of a human being, and that his less valuable half, while seduction corrupts both mind and body.

Next he undertook to point out a passage where I stated that the Blessed Virgin was conceived without original sin.[40] I again promised to make clear that he had read the place wrong if he could show that he had read it at all. And he pointed out a passage in which, after adducing two or three quotations from Chrysostom and Augustine in which they seemed in some way to attribute sin in deed to the Virgin, I conclude what I say with the words 'Yet we hold her to be entirely free from all sin.' This he took to be a statement of fact, whereas I was making an inference that we must be wrong in holding her free from original sin, if such great names are right in attributing sin in deed to her. And on this point he gladly admitted his error, differing of course from the followers of Scotus.

After this we passed on to a passage far more full of peril than any other,[41] which occurs in 1 Corinthians chapter 11. With great difficulty I at length extracted from him permission to inspect the passage. He showed it to me, but covered the margin with his hand. I pushed his hand away, and found a note which ran, 'Note how dangerously he writes here on a point on which the church has ruled so often.'[42] 'Note,' said I 'how foolish are your comments on a place you have not understood,' and full of surprise, I proceeded to ask him what he objected to. The first part of the passage said that Thomas held the opinion of those who denied that Christ's real body is present in the eucharist to be heretical, while he rejected the opinion of those who denied that Christ in the consecration had used the words 'This is my body' but did not call it heresy. I asked him whether he had any objections to this part, and he said no. It goes on, 'In all points we should accept the judgment of the church, although this seems the language not of one consecrating but of him who offers bread which is already consecrated.' I asked him whether he disapproved of this, and he said no. It goes on, 'To me it seems *in totum*, altogether wiser in matters of this kind, where clear instruction on the basis of evidence from Holy Scripture is not available but all depends on human interpretation, not to make such absolute statements that we wish to give our own opinions oracular force.' I asked him whether he felt any difficulty here, and he hesitated. When I pressed him he at length replied that there was poison in that *in totum*. Wondering what underlay this, I at length got out of him on examination that he did not know what the Latin words *in totum* meant. When I gave it as my opinion that one should refrain from all asseveration not only on this topic but on all others 'altogether,' he imagined that *in totum* meant 'in both the preceding parts,' and that I was throwing doubt on the opinion of the church, which had laid down that Christ's body is really present in the eucharist. For my part, seeing what a numskull the man was, I told him to go away and learn Latin, and to desist from criticizing books which he fell so far short of understanding.

This is an average specimen of those who rant against the humanities and dismiss everything they have not learnt themselves as 'poetry.'[43] Their natural stupidity is remarkable, their ignorance of good literature profound, their judgment nil. If they have a spark of intelligence or a scrap of knowledge, they are so blinded by jealousy and spite that they see no more than moles.[44] And these are the reverend rabbis,[45] the salt of the earth, the light of the world,[46] whose opinion decides whether we are Christians or not, who in succession to the apostles dictate to us new articles of faith, who hand us down oracles like divine beings and do not deign to give us mere mortals any reason for their opinions. They are content to say 'This is an error,' 'This is suspicious,' 'This is heresy.' And this they dare to do, relying on their sworn bands of henchmen, on the stupidity of the public, on the state of the world in which effrontery now passes for wisdom as it never has before, on corruption in the minds of leaders in both church and state, most of whom have their eye on absolute power[47] and would rather hear smooth words than what will do them good, preferring advice which suits their own desires above what is sound. These are the supports on which the kingdom of those blockheads rests; and would that learning were the only likely victim! If their attempt succeeds, it will be all over with the gospel teaching; Christ's people will be enslaved to the lawless desires of men without shame or sense.

The greetings of your host,[48] whose reputation equals his courtesy, I accept with gratitude, not like a supreme pontiff, as you humourously suggest, but as a mere man of no great position in the world whose will to forward Christian learning is greater than his power. Nesen[49] is so sick of the idiotic trouble which some men stir up here for him without ceasing that he has set off for you and yours. Dorp[50] is working on the best subjects and enjoying himself. I do the same as often as I can. Farewell, dear Buschius, learned friend.

Louvain, 31 July 1520

1127 / To [Ludwig Platz] Louvain, 31 July [1520]

The original letter, entirely in Erasmus' hand, was until the second world war in the Burscher collection at Leipzig (cf Ep 1067 introduction). It was published, with some immaterial additions, in the *Epistolae ad diversos*. It answers a complimentary message conveyed to Erasmus – orally perhaps, for when Erasmus replied he was apparently unable to find the rector's name – by Johannes Draconites (cf Ep 1122 introduction).

Ludwig Platz (d 1547), of Melsungen near Kassel, received his MA at Erfurt in

1504 and subsequently his licence in theology. He was elected rector for the summer term of 1520. So great was the admiration for Erasmus at the University of Erfurt that this letter was deemed worthy of a summary in the matriculation register following the notice of Platz's appointment; cf *Acten der Erfurter Universität* ed J.C.H. Weissenborn et al (Halle 1881–99) II 314). Platz, who continued to teach in the university, held a benefice at Walschleben near Erfurt, but subsequently joined the Reformation and married at an advanced age.

TO X, RECTOR MAGNIFICUS OF THE FAMOUS UNIVERSITY OF ERFURT, FROM ERASMUS OF ROTTERDAM, GREETING

Honoured sir, it is impossible for me not to entertain warm feelings towards a man like yourself who, as I learn from Draconites, a most reliable young man, are not only a good scholar in your own right but a zealous supporter of liberal studies, and by incorporating them in the University of Erfurt, over which you preside with such distinction, have given it fresh lustre. It says much for your wisdom – and in this you stand alone – that you can effect this without the disorders which we see arising elsewhere[1] from the imprudence of some men that I could name. This is how good literature should make its way into our universities: not with the air of an enemy who will lay waste all before him, but rather as a guest who will grow gradually into union with his fellow-citizens. I have never liked disorder, and, unless I am quite blind, a moderate policy is more effective than uncontrolled violence. Indeed, I think it the duty of all good men to wish to benefit their fellows in such a way that they hurt very few, or none at all, if that is possible. Theology, frigid and quarrelsome, had sunk to such a pitch of futility that it was essential to recall it to the fountain-head. Even so, I would rather see correction here than destruction, or at least toleration, until some better approach to theology is forthcoming. Luther has rendered a great service by pointing out so many abuses, but I wish he had done so in more civil language. He would have more supporters and more champions, and would reap for Christ a richer harvest. And yet it would be quite wrong, where he has said what wanted saying, to leave him quite without support, or in the future no one will dare to speak the truth. It is not for one in my position or with my endowments to pass judgment on his teaching. Hitherto, there is no doubt, he has done a service to the world at large. Many people have been driven to study the works of the early divines, some to establish their own position and some to develop a case against Luther.

I would commend Draconites to your kindness, were not his character and his pure and gentle nature such that he cannot fail to be acceptable to every man of good will. I know how little power I have. Were there, however, anything in which I might contribute to the needs or to the fame of your university, I would so act as to prove, if nothing else, my keen desire to be of use. Farewell.

Erasmus of Rotterdam (signed with my own hand)
Louvain, 31 July

1127A / To Martin Luther — Louvain, 1 August [1520]

This letter is known only from a manuscript copy made by Johannes Poliander, who died c 1541 as pastor at Kaliningrad (then Königsberg in eastern Prussia). Poliander's copy was discovered by Otto Clemen, who published it in 1930. In Allen's edition it is printed among the preliminary pieces of volume VIII. Its accuracy need not be questioned in view of many close parallels to Ep 1126 and other letters of this period.

Erasmus wrote this letter after the visit of Johannes Egranus (cf Ep 1122 introduction), who had evidently brought a message from Luther. Egranus almost certainly took this letter back with him to Wittenberg, which he visited again on his way home to Zwickau. Erasmus had thus decided to continue his epistolary dialogue with the Wittenberg reformers (cf Epp 1041 n16, 1113 introduction), albeit with a heightened sense of caution. Luther is asked to refrain from mentioning Erasmus in his polemical writings (lines 77–9). While an admonition that Luther should write with more restraint is attributed to Henry VIII (lines 66–9), Erasmus himself encourages him to devote his effort to Scriptural exegesis (lines 98–9, cf Ep 1143:16–18).

Luther probably answered this letter in the first half of November. His answer is missing, but one statement is reported by Erasmus in Ep 1166:99–101. On 17 November Luther wrote to Lazarus Spengler (cf Ep 1141 n11) that he had never harboured any ill will against Erasmus, that he quite approved of Erasmus' request to refrain from mentioning his name, and that he had written to Erasmus to this effect. 'With God's help Erasmus and I will surely continue to stand united' (Luther w *Briefwechsel* II Ep 353).

Greeting. I had long known Egranus from his books,[1] and it was a pleasure to meet him in the flesh. Edward Lee[2] has stuck, and still sticks, at nothing to secure my undoing, but has had no success so far. While he tries to drive a wedge between me and my friends, he loses his own. All men of education are on my side, on his only an ignoramus or two, and those are men of bad character. They had done something to unsettle the minds of the king and queen,[3] but my arrival blew the clouds away. I see clearly that those who promote this uproar against humane studies produce stuff which is not only ignorant but, if you examine it closely, insane.

Here is a sample of it for you. In the presence of the king and queen of England a Spanish Franciscan,[4] who has been invited there to teach Scotus[5] (for by now it is the general policy over there that Scotus must be taught, or it will mean the end of Christianity), challenged a certain doctor of divinity, who is the king's chaplain,[6] to 'defend Erasmus.' He replied that I needed no defending, and told the friar to put forward something of his own choice. He propounded, as worse than heretical, that passage *In principio erat sermo*, which he attacked as follows: '*Sermo* does not mean an unspoken concept in the mind, and so this proposition "In the beginning was the *sermo*" is false,' imagining, I suppose, that 'word' (*verbum*) is not used except of an unspoken concept in the mind, and that that is the only way in which Christ is called the Word. In support of this view he produced a torrent of nonsense before those eminent princes and a large company of learned men and councillors in their gold chains.[7]

After the queen had given him leave to go, for she was sorry to see him in such a fix,[8] he was succeeded by that well-known madman Standish,[9] who is now bishop. Falling on his knees and raising his hands to heaven, he proceeded to beseech their Majesties to follow the example of their ancestors and crush the numerous heresies and schisms which Erasmus' books would breed. Thomas More[10] was there, and told him to produce the passages he called heretical. The poor lunatic begins to count the thing off on his fingers. 'First,' says he, 'he abolishes the resurrection. Second, he makes nonsense of the sacrament of marriage. Thirdly, he is all wrong about the eucharist.' At this the king and queen were somewhat shaken, but More, having praised him for the clarity of his exposition, observed that it only now remained to prove the individual points; and this he promised to do. 'Where we,' he says, 'read "We shall all rise again," Erasmus reads "We shall not all sleep"; he thereby abolishes the resurrection.' When More had replied to this lunacy so clearly that even a beginner could not miss the point, and the stupid man was left unable to say a word, at length he found a loophole; he said that Jerome had reinstated the current reading out of the Hebrew, imagining that the Epistles had been written in Hebrew. Pressed on this point by one of the theologians present, he was a sorry sight, and the king took pity on the bishop, turned the discussion onto another topic, and broke it off. If such things were said at a drinking-party, would not they seem quite mad? Now, when they say them with sublime confidence in front of monarchs and scholars of the highest standing, who can suppose they have a grain of sense in them?

I could tell you plenty of stories of the same sort. A theologian called Jan Turnhout[11] has been refuting your propositions for some months now, but without making any personal attack. Latomus[12] is now doing the same, and does not restrain himself from breaking into abuse from time to time. I am not the right man, my dear Luther, to give you advice; but if you entirely reject all philosophy, you will have on your hands not only all universities but all the Ancients and even your favourite Augustine whom you follow so readily. Even granted that philosophy were to be entirely rejected, it will be unwise to take on so much at once. Hair by hair gets the tail off the mare.[13]

I am delighted to hear of the peace in your university,[14] of which you speak; the important thing is that it should last, and then that it should include many individuals, everyone if possible. I cannot tell you the conspiracies that go on everywhere against the authors of the 'new learning,'[15] as they are pleased to call it. They have seized upon all the courts of princes. What happens at the French king's court you can easily guess, the reigning power there being Guillaume Petit,[16] a Dominican; in our own court, there is more than one Hoogstraten.[17] The king of England is mild and well disposed, but even so he listens every day to men such as I have just described. He asked me what I thought of you.[18] I replied that you were too good a scholar for a man with too little learning to be able to form an opinion about you. He expressed the wish that you had written some things with more prudence and moderation. That wish is shared, my dear Luther, by those who wish you well. It is a serious matter to challenge men who cannot be overthrown without a major upheaval. And I fear upheavals of that kind all the more, because they so often burst out in a different direction from what was intended. If a man lets in the sea, it is not in his power to control where it should go. If an upheaval is required by the state of things, I would rather someone other than myself took the responsibility. But I shall not oppose your policy, for fear that, if it is inspired by the spirit of Christ, I may be opposing Christ. But this at least I would beg you: not to bring my name or my friends' names into what you write in an unpleasant way, as you did in your answer to the condemnations at Louvain and Cologne.[19] In that way you deprive them of any power to assist you, by casting suspicion on men who could be more use to you if they were left alone. Your enemies seek every opportunity to make us unpopular with princes. In England they laid a complaint against me as the author of that pamphlet *Julius exclusus*.[20] Some time ago they sent the bishop of Liège[21] a letter of mine to you, having printed it at Leipzig, in which some prominence was given to him by name. At the time I satisfied the bishop somehow. Just lately the same letter has been shown to the pope, who was somewhat indignant with the bishop of Liège for lending his support to an opponent of the Holy See while himself enjoying the pope's favour in so many respects. He has set his heart on an abbey, and on the archbishopric of Valencia too, and I dare say on a cardinal's hat as well;[22] and such men need the favour of the pope. On this

Martin Luther
Engraving by Lucas Cranach the Elder, 1520
Lutherhalle, Reformationsgeschichtliches Museum, Wittenberg

subject he[23] had received an unpleasant and even hostile letter from my friend Girolamo Aleandro.[24] On this occasion likewise I somehow pacified the man concerned. Now they have printed a letter in which I tried to mollify the cardinal of Mainz,[25] who was, I kept on hearing, very angry with you.

The purpose behind all this I do not know. Undoubtedly it harms me and does your cause no good. You have had quite enough controversies with Eck,[26] and with everybody else. I wish you would write a treatise on some part of Holy Scripture, and keep personal feelings out of it. It may be that in the mean time this turmoil will calm down. Your commentary on the psalter[27] has reached me, but after a six-month wait. I have not yet read it right through, but what I have read, I like very much indeed. Give my greetings to Melanchthon (to whom I wrote the other day[28]) and to your colleague Karlstadt.[29] Farewell, dearest brother in the Lord.

Louvain, 1 August

To the Reverend Dr Martin Luther, the eminent theologian

1128 / To Johann Lang — Louvain, 2 August [1520]

The text of this letter was first printed in 1743. The original letter, in Erasmus' own hand, was reproduced in facsimile in 1860; by 1911 it was in a private collection in Wilhelmshafen. Manuscript copies had circulated among Lang's friends and two such contemporary copies were examined by Allen; for all details and also for information on other editions, see his introduction.

Johann Lang was the prior of the Augustinian friars of Erfurt and a personal friend of fellow Augustinian Martin Luther. He had probably sent a letter with Draconites (cf Ep 1122 introduction), who was likely expected to take this short reply back to Erfurt.

TO THE WORTHY THEOLOGIAN JOHANN LANG

Greeting, honoured sir. I should feel very sorry for Lee,[1] if he had not conducted the whole business with so much venom: he is being so roughly handled, even by his fellow Englishmen. Spain too has a second Lee. His name is Zúñiga,[2] and he has published a book, I hear, with venomous attacks on Lefèvre and myself. The late cardinal of Toledo[3] had vetoed it, but now he has died, the man has brought his poison out into the open. I have not seen the work yet; they are taking good care not to let the book get into my hands.

I do not know what will be the end of all this tumult. Things now look altogether like civil strife, which I have always abhorred. If it must needs be that offences come,[4] I would much rather they did not start with me. The conspirators[5] show great enthusiasm: they are laying siege to great kings' courts, and I fear they may carry them.

The news about Philippus[6] and Oecolampadius[7] had already reached me in letters from other people. Both your letters[8] have now arrived. Farewell, beloved in the Lord.

Your sincere friend Erasmus
Louvain, 2 August

1129 / To John Fisher Louvain, 2 August [1520]

This letter was first printed in the *Epistolae ad diversos*. The year 1519, added to the date in the *Opus epistolarum*, can be corrected in view of the vicissitudes of Reuchlin. As a result of the events reflected in Epp 923, 986 he left Stuttgart for Ingolstadt on 9 November 1519. As Erasmus is accurately informed on his academic appointment, effective 1 March 1520, he may also have learnt that the old scholar lived in a house belonging to his own opponent, Johann Eck (cf Ep 1127A:97–8; RE Epp 285, 290–1; Geiger *Reuchlin* 460–2). At any rate, the account in this letter of Reuchlin's motives for leaving Stuttgart was later criticized by Hutten as a deliberate denigration (Hutten *Opera* II Ep 310.97). Replying to Hutten in his *Spongia* (ASD IX-1 144–5) Erasmus named as his informant the Austrian physician Dr Johannes Salzmann (cf Ep 1120 n3), whom he had met, he said, at the court of Charles V – presumably at Bruges (cf n1) and no doubt before writing Ep 1148, which answered a letter carried by Salzmann.

ERASMUS OF ROTTERDAM TO THE RIGHT REVEREND JOHN, BISHOP OF ROCHESTER, GREETING

Right Reverend Father and my good Lord, when I was in Bruges[1] a doctor of civil and canon law who was once a councillor of the emperor Maximilian, and was a learned and sensible man, told me that our friend Reuchlin is now living in Ingolstadt, where he has a salary of two hundred gold pieces for lecturing in Greek and Hebrew. This arrangement was made for him by his friends, since it was not safe for him to live at home. The reason, if we may believe what they say, is this. When there was a danger that the duke of Württemberg,[2] who has been attacked by Hutten, would retake Stuttgart, Reuchlin persuaded several of his fellow-citizens to move elsewhere, planning to do the same himself. They made their escape; Reuchlin changed his mind and stayed behind to look after his possessions. Afterwards, when the duke had been beaten back again, some of Reuchlin's friends secured that the victorious troops should not pillage his house. However, the townspeople whom he had let down made trouble for the old man on their return. So now he has safely removed all his property, and is living peacefully in Ingolstadt. I thought you ought to know this.[3]

Germany is in a proper frenzy against Lee, there has been such an outburst of pamphlets.[4] Lee deserves the worst that can happen to him; but all the same, I wish they would keep quiet. They say frankly in writing that they will not do as I ask,[5] except to the extent that they will refrain from abuse of the English as a nation. I have threatened to become a Frenchman,[6] unless they desist from a devotion to me which does so much harm. For my part, I shall do all I can. But it would be wise of Lee by publishing something himself to try and pacify the people he has made so angry.

I hear preparations are on foot for war[7] against the Dominicans and the Roman party in general. I am afraid that these fireworks will develop into a large-scale conflagration. They will declare war on the Preachers and the Romanists, and before we know where we are, there will be savage attacks on priests of every kind, as happened with the Bohemians.[8] Farewell.

Louvain, 2 August [1519]

1130 / To Jan van Merleberghe [Louvain, c 1518–20]

This letter and poem (Reedijk no 111) are known only from the two copy-books of Erasmus' friend Maarten Lips (cf Ep 750 introduction), who was a canon regular at the Augustinian convent of St Maartensdal in Louvain. In one of his copy-books, now at Brussels, Lips prefaced each letter he transcribed with a short argument. In this case he identified Merleberghe as a native of Diest in Brabant and an older member of the St Maartensdal congregation, who had entreated Erasmus to compose an inscription for a painting representing Sts Mary Magdalen and John. Merleberghe lived in St Maartensdal from 1497 until his death in 1533.

A general indication of the date is supplied by the reference to Lefèvre's book (n1). Allen inserted this letter here because in Lips' other copy-book it is followed immediately by two other epigrams belonging to the summer of 1520 (Reedijk nos 109–10; cf Ep 1106 introduction). He also noticed that the word *oestrus* 'gadfly, urge' (line 10) reappears in Ep 1132:16 and surmised that the picture might perhaps have been erected on St Mary Magdalen's day, 22 July 1520, when Erasmus was probably away from Louvain (cf Ep 1129 n1).

It should be noted that Erasmus' poem uses elements from Luke 7:36–50, 8:2 and John 12:1–8 and thus reflects the popular belief that the three women mentioned in these places were one and the same, the Mary Magdalen represented in the picture. The opposite view, that they were not, was argued forcefully in Lefèvre's books, and caused a great deal of controversy. This letter reflects Erasmus' attitude (cf Ep 1030 n2). He thought that Lefèvre was right, but wished to remain neutral. Acrimony between scholars may have seemed to him a high price for striking at a devotional tradition which was in this case as harmless as Merleberghe, the ageing monk, who stood for it.

ERASMUS OF ROTTERDAM TO JAN MERLEBERGHE OF DIEST, CANON OF ST MAARTENSDAL, LOUVAIN

The verse is trochaic tetrameter catalectic. In each line take the first letter, and the last letter before the caesura (which is marked with a stroke), and similarly the first and last in the second half of the line, and so on with all of them, and you will have what you want: IOHANNES MERLIBERCH A DIEST.

In Honour of St Mary Magdalen

In the driving urge of love, IO / Here the blessed MagdalenA
Nard the precious ointment pours oN, / Eye his feet with weeping washeS,
Makes dry with her tresses, look yE. / Ruler of the sky eternaL,
Instant once to spurn and to snuB / Every trick, accepts her offeR
Charmed by her devotion, her faitH. / As the devil Eve defeateD
In his first and fatal malicE / She with tears has paid for the forfeiT.

I have written this poor stuff to give you pleasure, for I would rather err in that direction than seem unfriendly. At the same time I am sending you the three Magdalens[1] as they are represented by Jacques Lefèvre. Farewell, Reverend Father, and remember me too sometimes in your prayers.

Erasmus

1131 / To Haio Herman of Friesland — Louvain, [c August 1520]

Haio Herman, a Dutch student at Paris, apparently wrote Erasmus a letter, now missing, which referred to Thomas More's controversy with Germain de Brie (cf Epp 620, 1045). This reply presents a stance similar to the one Erasmus had taken in a recent letter to Brie (Ep 1117). In the mean time, however, More had shown him his rejoinder to Brie (n3) when they met at Calais (cf Ep 1184:22–3). Although More's defence was actually in print, Erasmus was still confident that More had not changed his intention to suppress the pamphlet (cf Epp 1087 introduction, 1096:129 and n10, 1133:21–2).

This letter was published in the *Epistolae ad diversos*. When it was reprinted in 1529 the year date of 1521 was added, but this should be ignored. The letter was apparently written after Erasmus' return from Bruges (cf Ep 1129 n1) and was perhaps sent to Paris together with Ep 1133.

ERASMUS OF ROTTERDAM TO HERMAN OF FRIESLAND, GREETING

I showed More the passage in your letter, my learned young friend, which referred to him; he caught the flavour of your style, and at once read the whole letter and conceived a great affection for your gifts. I have an uncommon warmth of feeling for Brie's gifts, and I admire his style; but I wish he would employ both on a less unpromising subject. He has a low opinion, as you say, of More; but I fear he may discover too late that More should not have been underrated. Brie must take care to control his pen, if he wants to be thought not only clever but honest and fair-minded. I wish he would take advice from his serious and scholarly friends like Budé, Deloynes, Ruzé, and Du Ruel,[1] instead of following his own youthful enthusiasm. Brie understood something I said in a note to Bérault[2] as meaning that I thought his reputation for learning was the higher of the two. I am not so ill informed or so blindly devoted to More that I cannot see the difference between them; much rather I wished Brie to strive in the services he could render the Muses than in personal abuse. And I am confident that I can persuade More on his side to suppress some things he has already finished[3] which are more biting than in my view is suitable, either to More as their author or to Brie as their target. I beg you urgently to encourage Brie to employ his gifts on some other subject; this will be better for his reputation. Farewell. Mind you give my greetings to Bérault.

Louvain [1521][4]

1132 / To Thomas Wolsey Antwerp, 7 August 1520

When Erasmus attended the meeting of the monarchs at Calais in July (cf Ep 1106 introduction) he found no opportunity for a talk with Cardinal Wolsey. This letter is intended to be an introduction for its bearer (cf n3), but it also gave Erasmus a chance to remember himself to the powerful cardinal and chancellor. It was printed in the *Epistolae ad diversos*.

As he had done in the preceding year (cf Ep 999 introduction), Erasmus visited Antwerp at the time of the summer vacations, probably staying with his good friend Pieter Gillis, at whose table he was to meet Albrecht Dürer in February–March 1521 (cf Ep 1199 introduction). The first of Dürer's encounters with Erasmus dates from about the time of this letter, however. He took the portrait of Nikolaus Kratzer (cf Ep 515:3n), who was then in Antwerp and recorded that he was present when Erasmus sat for Dürer. Dürer himself noted that 'herr Erasmus' gave him a Spanish 'mantilla' and three male portraits. This patron could be either Erasmus of Rotterdam or Erasmus Schets, who subsequently became a good friend of the former and his banker. Schets had close personal and commercial ties to the Iberian peninsula and also to the

Erasmus
Charcoal drawing by Albrecht Dürer, 1520
The Louvre, Paris

Portuguese factory in Antwerp, to which Dürer was repeatedly invited (see CEBR III). In early September Dürer noted that he gave 'Erasmo Roterodamo' in Brussels a 'Passion' (a set of his sixteen engravings on the Lord's Passion, executed in copper at Nürnberg, 1507–11) and 'once more' took his portrait (the charcoal drawing now in the Louvre); see Dürer *Diary* 59–60, 65, 83; H. Plard 'Erasme dans le journal du voyage aux Pays-Bas d'Albrecht Dürer, 17 mai 1521' in *Colloquium Erasmianum* (Mons 1968) 255–73; cf also Ep 1221 n8.

ERASMUS OF ROTTERDAM TO HIS EMINENCE THOMAS, CARDINAL OF YORK AND LORD CHANCELLOR OF ALL ENGLAND, GREETING

I have made all that long journey to Calais, and stayed there for so many days, in hopes of enjoying the society of your Eminence; but you were too busy for this to be possible. I know the pressure of business is always very great, but just then I saw that it was so great that I did not dare after paying my respects to interrupt you with a longer conversation. For the exceptional favour which your Eminence has always extended to me, I am grateful, though I know that this is meant not so much for my own benefit as for the good of liberal studies, to which my sleepless nights are all devoted. I was in hopes of proving by some concrete evidence that I am neither forgetful nor ungrateful, but hitherto there has been no opportunity to do as I would wish. In the mean time, however, I have done what I could to indicate my feelings, by the modest offering of a book,[1] which I hope you will be ready to accept with your habitual courtesy.

Germany seems to have felt the bite of some sort of gadfly, and shows her rage and fury against Lee in a hundred pamphlets.[2] I write letters to discourage this as far as I can. They reply that they will never spare Lee himself, but that they will refrain from attacking his fellow-countrymen, and to that extent will listen to me. I think Lee would be wise if he published something to appease the Germans, whom he has aroused by his unpleasant attacks on me. I will endeavour in my turn to see that we hear no more of this tragic fuss.

The bearer of this letter, Christophorus Palaeologus,[3] is a monk of Mount Sinai, by the common consent of reliable judges a man of good family and a thorough Christian, and (as I have learnt from the familiar intercourse with him) upright, modest, and not without wit. He is anxious to collect funds for the relief of his monastery, which experiences the truth of Hesiod's dictum[4] that a bad neighbour is a great evil, so often is it harried by the Saracens in its vicinity. In this part of the world his harvest has proved most unproductive, either because we are a close-fisted lot, or because the whole system of indulgences begins to be everywhere exceedingly unpopular. He hopes that in your country he will do better, nor do I doubt that he will, if he enjoys the support of your Eminence. And you will support, I hope, either such an excellent cause or such a worthy man, for I would not venture to ask that the recommendation of one so obscure as myself should have any weight with a great man like you. My respectful best wishes to your Eminence, to whom I am cordially devoted.

Antwerp, 7 August 1520

1133 / To Guillaume Budé — Antwerp, 9 August 1520

This letter to Guillaume Budé, secretary to the king of France and celebrated Greek scholar, is another effort on the part of Erasmus to compose the quarrel between Thomas More and Germain de Brie after his recent meetings with More (cf Epp 1131, 1145 n1). It was published in the *Epistolae ad diversos*.

ERASMUS TO HIS DEAR FRIEND BUDÉ, GREETING

Best and most learned of my friends, if More and Brie were perfect strangers to me, it would still distress me on behalf of good literature that two such distinguished devotees of the Muses should go for one another in such virulent pamphlets, to the great discomfiture of the humanities and the great glee of those who have long been waging war on liberal studies. As it is, both are my friends and one of them most intimately, and I cannot say what pain it gives me that this discord should have arisen between two people, when I admire the gifts and am jealous for the reputation of both alike. Each has a decided contempt for the other; but what can mutual contempt produce except a rift that steadily gets worse? I have pleaded earnestly with More to pass the thing over in silence, and I should have succeeded, had not Brie put such a malicious interpretation on that passage where praise of the king is coupled, according to Brie, with criticism of his father.[1] It is no laughing matter to be concerned with Jupiter,[2] whom it was fatal to address with wrongly worded prayers. Not that More has anything to fear from his own master, who has a very high opinion of his gifts; but it does show that Brie has made up his mind to ruin More.

What Brie has written against More is by common consent already too much, but his malice is not satisfied. He seizes every occasion of attacking More. Nothing of his comes out without a long attack on him, though More has so far not replied. I wonder very much what provokes Brie to do this. In the Muses' name, pray use all your authority to control this young man's fury. I am not thinking only of my friend More; take my word for it, if this strife continues, Brie may find himself – notorious, yes, but glorious? No. Farewell, dearest Budé.

Antwerp, St Lawrence's eve 1520

1134 / To Sebastian von Rotenhan

Louvain, 13 August 1520

Sebastian von Rotenhan (1478–1532) was born at Rentweinsdorf near Bamberg. From 1493 he studied at Erfurt, Ingolstadt, and subsequently Bologna, before obtaining a doctorate of laws from Siena in 1503. He set out in 1512 for several years of travelling in western Europe as well as in the Orient. On 25 September 1514 he was created a knight of the Holy Sepulchre at Jerusalem. Erasmus met him at Mainz, presumably in 1518 (line 5), by which time he had probably entered the service of Archbishop Albert of Brandenburg. From the beginning of 1523 he was marshall at the court of Konrad von Thüngen, bishop of Würzburg (cf Ep 1124). He was a friend of the Erfurt humanists and of Ulrich von Hutten, to whom he was related through marriage. In February 1520 Hutten dedicated to him his dialogue *Vadiscus* (Mainz: J. Schöffer April 1520), which called for a literary campaign against Rome. This letter indicates Rotenhan's eagerness to join the battle against Edward Lee, which had then become a prominent cause for militant and patriotic German humanists, who viewed Lee's attack on Erasmus as a slight to the national genius (cf Epp 1083 introduction, 1123 n9, n12). While he dissociated himself before long from these friends on the question of church reform, he retained his humanistic interests in geography and history.

This letter was published in the *Epistolae ad diversos*.

ERASMUS OF ROTTERDAM TO THE HONOURABLE SIR SEBASTIAN VON ROTENHAN, KNIGHT,[1] COUNCILLOR OF THE CARDINAL OF MAINZ, GREETING

Your characteristic letter[2] called back the memory of those most delightful days I spent in your society in Mainz,[3] for I shall always think of you as a man much more distinguished for learning of widest range than by pride of ancestry, although in ancestry you rank among the first. Indeed this itself struck me as typical of exceptional sincerity of feeling, that, burdened as you are by the affairs of princes and surrounded by the noise of arms, you should remember a modest friend like myself. I only wish you had had some better-favoured reason for writing to me than Edward Lee. You may think him shameless; he must think himself exceptionally fortunate in having acquired fame by so little work! Poor fellow, he had such a passion for it that 'Twere death, could he not somehow vent his spite.'[4] I am the more surprised at the zealous obstinacy of some people,[5] who abandon all else and try everything they can, leaving no stone unturned, to suppress the humanities, which now show such a promising revival, and all the time neither maintain their old learning with sufficient energy nor learn anything new. And they work, what is more, by such tricks, such underhand methods, putting up one stalking-horse after another! Not but what even those people do not support Lee, except as wishing ill to me in any way they can. With that end in view no hireling comes amiss. What benefits I get from philosophy I am not prepared to say; but this I do get from a good conscience, that the crazy efforts of such men I am more ready to endure than imitate.

And now a man of your high standing promises me assistance against Lee under your own name, if I need help from Germany. I appreciate your incredible generosity; your kind help I absolutely refuse. God forbid that such men as you should show Lee so much respect that they should make a concerted attack on him in writing. I wish they might find some grander subject! I myself have already lost a whole month and a half[6] on this topic, and that seems to me more than enough; for he wrote in such a way as to give least satisfaction to those who most wished for his success.[7] This was all the praise he got, even from my worst enemies! Never were ignorance and arrogance so wedded. And yet he calls this a dispute!

You promise me an immortal name in those lines of Seneca:[8] but what posterity will think of me is a matter for a higher power, if only these studies may flourish by which I hope to commend myself to Christ. Surely all must perceive that the world is hastening towards some barbarous tyranny. It has long been in the throes, and what the birth[9] will be I know not. I wish to play a helpful part, if I can do so, but I am not willing to be one of those who stir up trouble. Farewell, and make my humble duty to your prince.

Louvain, 13 August 1520

1135 / From Ulrich von Hutten — Steckelberg, 15 August 1520

The original letter, sent by Hutten but not written in his own hand, is in the Öffentliche Bibliothek of the University of Basel, MS Fr.-Gr. I 19 f 38. It was not published until 1832, and there is no evidence of earlier circulation in manuscript (cf lines 28–30). It does not seem that Hutten's frank admonitions were taken amiss by Erasmus (cf Ep 1195:157–61) and Hutten himself did not repeat them in Ep 1161. He had recently defended Erasmus against Edward Lee, and when writing to Reuchlin on 8 August used the phrase 'Erasmus and our other friends' (Hutten *Opera* I Epp 166, 183). That Hutten should write so freely is perhaps another indication that his recent meeting with Erasmus was untroubled and congenial (cf Epp 1114 introduction 1119:38–9, 1129 n7). Hutten appears to be taking issue with some of Erasmus' statements in the ill-fated Ep 1033 and in some letters published in the *Farrago*, which he must have seen before his visit to Louvain. Moreover, he may have seen Ep 1041, but otherwise Hutten's statement (lines 22–5) that Erasmus had 'just lately' done all he could to persuade Luther's opponents that he was not going to defend him (cf Ep 1127A n18), while borne out soon enough by such letters as Epp

1143–4, can hardly be supported by anything that Erasmus is known to have written 'just lately.' If Erasmus was troubled by the frank tone of this letter, he did not permit his irritation to show in any statement known today until much later (cf Ep 1161 introduction).

This letter also served to bring Erasmus up to date on recent developments following Hutten's journey to the Netherlands. He did not afterwards return to Mainz (lines 14–17). In letters to Cardinal Albert of Brandenburg (Hutten *Opera* I Epp 176, 179, 5 and 12 July) Leo X and one of his officials had requested Hutten's dismissal from the court of Mainz. Hutten himself wrote on 8 August of two letters in which the pope demanded his arrest and extradition to Rome (Hutten *Opera* I Ep 183). In letters to Albert and Rotenhan (cf Ep 1134) he continued to plead his cause, but Albert had severed all ties with his former protégé; see Hutten *Opera* I Epp 180, 191–2, and cf also Ep 1182 n2.

ULRICH VON HUTTEN TO ERASMUS OF ROTTERDAM, GREETING

Did you ever hear of anyone in such a state of frenzy, so stark staring mad, as this man who now calls himself Leo the Tenth? He has sent a series of letters to instruct the cardinal of Mainz –with the most violent threats thrown in if he fails to comply –to send me in custody to Rome. I do not know which is more astonishing in the fellow, that he dare make such a demand, even if he expects it to be successful, or that he should make it of such a great and good man. There is nothing for it: we must recognize that he is blind, and now we know it is mental rather than physical. He has a legate too at Charles' court,[1] who is indefatigable in his efforts to get me into trouble. This is the scheme that I heard they were hatching, those slippery customers. They suppose me for my part to be badly frightened, though they have been lately heard to suggest that quite respectable conditions are available, if I am willing to receive overtures of peace. They are trying this line, now they see that I have given them the slip. Warned by my friends and suspecting something in my own account, I left Mainz a little before they had made up their minds, I dare say, what steps were proper for them to take.

This is what I want you to do. Hold your fire entirely, write nothing; we need you safe and sound. I want to tell you something, which I can only say in full reliance on our friendship. When the Reuchlin business was at its height, I thought you showed more weakness[2] than was worthy of you in your respect for the other side. And over Luther, just lately, you did all you could to persuade[3] his opponents that you had not the faintest intention of defending the common cause of Christendom, while they knew all the same that your real feelings were quite different. I did not think this did you much credit. I say this because I know the friend I am writing to, and how wrong and unlike you it would be to take my criticisms in bad part. I did not enjoy listening to what people said, but I stood up for my friend's reputation at a moment when I was not much pleased with him on that score myself. Now, since no one but myself is concerned, I am perfectly frank. So do please do this for me, as for a man who has always been most deeply attached to you, and would still like more than anything else to earn your good opinion if I possibly could: do not put out anything in an unguarded moment like what you wrote in Luther's case and Reuchlin's, the effects of which were all too clear. You know with what triumph those gentry still pass round certain letters of yours in which, while you side-step the ill will yourself, you divert it pretty invidiously onto other people.[4] This was the way you slit the throat of the *Epistolae obscurorum virorum*,[5] of which you once thought so highly; and in Luther you condemn his readiness to rouse what is better left unroused, though you yourself have set your hand to that same Camarina[6] in various places in your own books. Even so you will not get them to believe that all your dearest wishes are not on the other side. Thus you do us harm, and do not make friends with them; you provoke them all the more and arouse their hostility by trying to conceal what is so obvious.

And so, as concerns my side of the case, though it would be the most splendid piece of luck if it could have the support of what you write, yet if you are afraid of burdening yourself with any unpopularity, do grant me just this: do not let the fear of anything force you into making light of it – better pass it over in perfect silence. I know what harm can be done me by one word from your pen which seems either to attack my position or even simply not to accept it.

I have written this frankly, as one friend to another. With best wishes, from the stronghold of the Hutten family,[7] 15 August 1520

To Desiderius Erasmus of Rotterdam the divine, my very dear friend

1136 / To Leontius — Brussels, 1520

Erasmus dated letters from Louvain on 13 August (Ep 1134) and again on 31 August (Ep 1137); in the interval he must have spent a few days at Brussels at the same time that Charles v's court was there. He met Luigi Marliano (Ep 1198:17) and the Łaski brothers (Ep 1242 n5), who were with the emperor, and it was at Brussels that Dürer made another drawing of Erasmus (cf Ep 1132 introduction). As Dürer was at Brussels from 27 August to 2 September and Charles v spent 23–4 August at Louvain and 25 August–17 September at Brussels (cf Gachard II 28), it appears likely that Erasmus accompanied the court from Louvain to Brussels.

Nothing certain can be said, however, about the date and the recipient of this letter. It was published in the *Epistolae ad diversos*, but 'Brussels, 1520' was added only in the *Opus epistolarum* of 1529. Although such late additions are frequently unreliable, Allen placed this letter here, arguing that perhaps in this case Erasmus' memory might be relied upon as he did not often go to Brussels. Leontius was perhaps a schoolmaster (lines 15–17) who had apparently proposed to write a pamphlet in praise of Erasmus and in defence of the new learning against its opponents, conceivably the theologians at Louvain (cf Ep 1126:247–389). Allen drew attention to one Nicolaus Leontius of Leiden, described as 'grammaticus' by Erasmus' friend Gerard Geldenhouwer (cf Ep 1141) in his *De Batavorum insula* ed P. Scriverius (Leiden 1611) 69, a treatise which was completed on 19 September 1520; in another source that Nicolaus Leontius is called a 'rhetor.' On the other hand, Erasmus may have wished to conceal rather than reveal the identity of the man he addressed.

ERASMUS TO HIS FRIEND LEONTIUS, GREETING

I will gladly excuse your rashness in writing to one you have never met and to whom you are unknown, but you in turn must excuse me if, overwhelmed with business as I am, I send such a brief answer that it is almost no answer at all. That you are a devotee of the Muses I highly approve; that you should fight continually with their enemies, I cannot agree. On those who cannot be defeated one should waste no time; and in recommending these humane studies of ours, it is important not to breed ill will by condemning studies which other people may find more attractive.[1] It can never be a good plan to stir up the hornets' nest.[2] In any case, anything I have written was not written to be laid up in some sanctuary, but to be taken home and read. Your excessive enthusiasm can have no result except to make me unpopular. I deserve no honours of the kind you suggest, and in any case shrines are not set up even to those who have earned them until after the funeral,[3] as the saying goes. In my opinion you will do more good if the efforts you devote to squabbling with opponents who are maybe already past hope are expended on educating boys or young men of outstanding promise. Humane letters will make progress more successfully by stealth than by brute force, and will take root more easily if they make their way in courteously like guests than if they rush in like enemies. As for me, I do what I can, and gladly make it public, without recompense; if anyone will produce something better, I give way without resentment. Further, I undertake no struggle with these noisy scoundrels except under compulsion, or rather, not even then. Furthermore, my life contains nothing worthy of record, except that I am (I suppose) the most consistently unfortunate man who ever lived.[4] Consequently, if you will take my advice, you will choose another subject; indeed you will choose any subject in the world rather than this. Farewell.

Brussels, 1520

1137 / To Johannes Thurzo

Louvain, 31 August 1520

Johannes Thurzo, bishop of Wrocław, had been dead for several weeks (cf Ep 1242:3–11) when Erasmus wrote this flattering reply to Ep 1047, acknowledging the gifts sent with the bishop's letter. Both were published together in the *Epistolae ad diversos*.

ERASMUS OF ROTTERDAM TO THE RIGHT REVEREND JOHANNES THURZO, BISHOP OF WROCŁAW, GREETING

Why did the powers above think fit to set such a great barrier of mountains and rivers between men united by such great affection of one mind for another? Your letter took six months to reach me, and the presents with it, every one of which would have been highly welcome had it cost very little as coming from so great a prelate, if for no other reason, but far more as coming from such a gifted man; as it is, they have their intrinsic value, their actual novelty, and the giver's name to recommend them. Even so, nothing about them seemed to me so desirable that it was not eclipsed by your letter; which is the second I have now received,[1] written with your own hand and composed by your distinguished intelligence, so that it gives one all the more an image of your mind. And what a mind, in heaven's name! Would it might please God to make many bishops and princes emulate a heart like yours, that they may enrich their ancient lineage with a new distinction and enhance their authority by an increase of goodness and wisdom.

What a burning love of goodness breathes in those letters of yours, what a thirst for Christian learning! Besides which, what friendliness, what modesty they display! Who would suppose this was written by so great a prelate and so great a prince? For your mind seems to me no less admirable, though you think far better of me than I deserve, for this is an error in respect of the person, not of the thing itself. Your error lies in supposing me to be what I am not, but you do not err in admiring and seeking after the things that you wrongly suppose to be found in me. I have tried hard to recall a world too far sunk in sophistical quibbling to the sources in Antiquity, and to arouse a world that places too much trust in Jewish ceremonies[2] to a pursuit of true religion. And I only wish these efforts of mine may bring as much benefit to others as they have brought ill will on me. I should bear my own losses far more easily, if I could see that they were linked with gain for the majority. But this we must leave to Christ himself who, unless I am gravely wrong, will approve the spirit that inspires me.

And now if I may indulge in some reflections on your presents, I count you most fortunate in possessing dominions in which veins of such pure and brilliant gold are worked; but you are more blessed, inasmuch as you yourself so eagerly search the far richer veins of Holy Scripture for the gold of gospel wisdom, that you may use it to enrich the flock entrusted to you like a rich householder who brings out of his treasure things new and old.[3] How different from so many bishops, who hand over the noblest portion of their duties to mean men whom they have neither proved nor tested, though no one should be admitted to perform that function unless he is recommended by Christian learning, high character, experience in business, and more common wisdom.

Two of the timepieces were inscribed 'Make haste slowly,'[4] and the second half of this inscription is obeyed by the sand that pours slowly through its tiny hole as I write this. But it is with great speed that our life hastes away, and death hastens towards us, not slackening its pace even though that trickle of sand should cease to run. The other had 'Make haste slowly' written on its upper surface, but when you turn the thing over it portrays a death's head; and, O my honoured Thurzo, would that it might come slowly upon you! – for you fully deserve to be not merely longlived but immortal, if the jealousy of Fortune were not such that she removes most promptly from the scene the most excellent things in human life. May this threat remain as far from you as possible, for as I read your letters and hear what others say of you I perceive that you possess such copious and precious gifts of mind as make your lineage, your wealth, and your high rank as a bishop only a small part of your endowments.

The fur cap I can only wear at home, for it is too grand for a man of no account like myself (perhaps here again we have your error of supposing that Erasmus counts for something), and a little foreign to the practice of this country. The Ancients had a proverb[5] that everything suits a good man; now, only the powerful get nothing wrong. But I shall preserve it, for one purpose in particular, to refresh my memory of your noble self.

The gold coin[6] puzzled many people. Some conjectured that it was Noah's three sons coming down out of the ark, with the dove bearing home the olive-branch on the other side; others that it was two victorious generals leading a captive between them, and an eagle carrying a branch of bay bent into a wreath. The inscription no one has yet been able to read, neither Grecians, Latinists, nor Hebrew scholars.

How ungrateful I am! For all your presents and for such a brilliant and yet friendly letter, I send you no return but this uninspiring note. But there will be another opportunity, and in the mean while best wishes for your health, my honoured Lord.

Louvain, 31 August 1520

1138 / To William Burbank

Louvain, 1 September 1520

This is the first letter we know of that Erasmus wrote to Burbank, an old friend and patron, who may have sent Erasmus a gift after a decade had passed without direct contacts (cf lines 7–11). At the same time Erasmus wished to record his affection for some other friends at the English court. The letter was published in the *Epistolae ad diversos*.

William Burbank (died c January 1532) was registered at Cambridge in 1496 as a student of civil law. In 1509 he went to Rome in the service of Christopher Bainbridge, archbishop of York, and there apparently met Erasmus (cf lines 6–7). After Bainbridge's death in 1514 he returned to England and by 1516 was chaplain and secretary to Cardinal Thomas Wolsey. He held a canonry at Lincoln (1517–27) and degrees in canon and civil law from Cambridge; see Emden BRUC.

ERASMUS OF ROTTERDAM TO WILLIAM BURBANK, SECRETARY OF HIS EMINENCE THE CARDINAL OF YORK, GREETING

He truly loves, and he only, who loves without reward. Your friend Erasmus does nothing to deserve it, and yet you show such warm affection for him, that one could scarcely find anyone ready to show more sincerity, more constancy, more warmth to some benefactor. It was in Rome, when I had done nothing for you, that you started to be so kind to me, and ever since then your quite uncalled-for generosity has shown no sign of cooling, although for so many years there has been no interchange of kindness between us of the kind that usually feeds and refreshes affection between friends that otherwise might languish from neglect. Truly you were born for friendship and open dealing! – and did I not love you in return, I could not complain if all men said I had an adamant in my bosom or anything harder there may be.

And here too, as the proverb has it,[1] one favour begets another. Mountjoy[2] inspired you with something of his feeling for me, and it was the support of you two that won me so many friends in one household, if I mistake not. For what other cause can I conjecture? It was no gifts of mine, nothing I did for him, that kindled such affection for me in Thomas Lovell,[3] doctor of canon law. What was it that won me no ordinary good will from that excellent scholar Robert Toneys?[4] To what do I owe the great kindness towards me of that most promising young man Franciscus Philippi?[5] Why need I mention one who was no new friend, and all the more reliable for that, Francis the physician?[6] Or the incomparable Doctor Sampson,[7] whose nature is as open and as friendly as anything one could wish to see? Or

Gonnell,[8] not so much a friend as half of my own soul? Or Clement,[9] in whom More has kindled some sparks of his love for me? Or Richard Pace,[10] who not only promises to be my Pylades but is as good as his word? Or Cuthbert Tunstall,[11] a man to be compared with any hero of the olden time, whose match Antiquity itself could not so very often find? How rich I am, how noble and how blest that household! How truly magnificent the cardinal, who has such men as his advisers and such luminaries round his table!

Yet if they love their Erasmus more than he deserves, so do other people I could name greet him with undeserved resentment. And would that malice did not breed the faster! But I would rather be acceptable to fewer men, and those of outstanding merit, than to many men of their sort, stupid as a rule and ignorant, or clearly suffering from some disease of envy and ill will, or with minds so distorted that they wish well to nobody and almost hate themselves. But as for our detractors, let us pray that they may see the light. Among my friends, please be a sort of social secretary and give each one by name my special greetings. Farewell, most faithful of friends.

Louvain, 1 September 1520

1139 / To Willibald Pirckheimer — Louvain, 5 September 1520

In Ep 1095 Pirckheimer, patrician and scholar of Nürnberg, had expressed the opinion that Erasmus should have answered Edward Lee either more aggressively or, even better, not at all. With this reply Erasmus chose to take Pirckheimer's friendly suggestion more seriously perhaps than it was intended. No doubt he remembered Pirckheimer's defence when taken to task by Erasmus for writing too harshly against the opponents of Reuchlin (cf Epp 694, 747). This letter, which was published in the *Epistolae ad diversos*, also shows that Erasmus was not aware of the degree to which he continued to attack Lee's reputation at the same time that he claimed that he wished to maintain a truce; cf Epp 1100 introduction, 1123 n9.

ERASMUS OF ROTTERDAM TO THE HONOURABLE WILLIBALD PIRCKHEIMER, GREETING

I had plenty of people, my honourable friend, to give me the same advice that you now offer me, wisely and helpfully enough but too late in the day. God forbid that any man's malignity should so far disturb the balance of my mind that I give free rein to invective and rage against other people's reputations. This would be simply to join the madman in his lunacy,[1] and to seek revenge for the wickedness of other men in a way that could only make one wicked oneself. I wish I were man enough to follow the Apostle's teaching[2] and overcome evil with good! I had at least decided to hold my peace, but two or three things persuaded me to change my mind. For one thing, I was afraid that if I myself had overlooked the offence, many would rise up in place of my one self who would have given Lee a much rougher welcome than I have. Even if they had attacked him more severely or with more learning, I doubt whether they would have treated the situation as appropriately as I; some of them perhaps, not knowing how little common sense Lee has and how much he is despised even by his own party,[3] might have taken him more seriously than he deserves. And such is the man's nature that he would have judged it a splendid triumph if he had succeeded in enraging a number of well-known scholars. I myself knew the man's whole nature and all the background of the business intimately.

Then again, as he tunneled away for two whole years (for Lee is a master engineer at this sort of thing), it had been his one object to raise everyone's expectation of his *Annotationes*[4] to prodigious heights. He used to write hundreds of letters – had several clerks doing nothing else. He was the first person to entertain any visitors, especially Englishmen, and would win their confidence with his hospitality; then he used to fill them up with his ingenious falsehoods, all the time pretending to be wonderfully modest, so that he could ruin his neighbour's character with more conviction. When they left, he sent them away loaded with every kind of lie. Some of them were even shown anything in his *Annotationes* that looked rather plausible at first sight. The good opinion of the monasteries was purchased with presents or food and drink, especially of those that he knew enjoyed a public reputation for uprightness. Everywhere he had agents among whom he had allotted the scenes of this play, all of whom were actively engaged. In these ways he at length succeeded in arousing anxiety even among those who knew me well,[5] and thought they knew Lee. And so, had I not replied, there was a risk that in a few months' time I should have lost the confidence of many people, and with it some of the good results I was expecting from so much midnight oil. The loss of my own reputation would have moved me very little. While I sacrifice a good part of my life to Christian studies, why should I fear to sacrifice to them some part of my reputation? And so I answered Lee in such a way as to strip him of the glory he so foolishly expected without losing my old reputation for self-restraint.

This, my excellent Willibald, was the reasoning behind my plan, and I have as yet not much reason to regret it, although I never grudged any time lost more than the month and a half[6] in which I read and refuted Lee's nonsense, which was as dreary as it was uneducated and venomous. Furthermore, when you express the fear that my mildness may encourage invective from many other quarters, I think there is a more serious danger that invective may provoke invective until there is no end to the madness of it – and they have all nearly gone mad already. This was God's purpose in forbidding everyone to exact punishment from Cain,[7] for fear that a vendetta actively pursued on both sides would never end. However this may be, I took the risk of being overwhelmed by a crowd of malevolent scribblers, rather than lose my reputation for never having blackened any man's character in anything I have written.[8] Let Lee have only himself to thank if people think ill of him. Moreover, when you suspect that Lee is a hired actor, put up by monks and theologians to play their game for them, I could indeed easily believe that his behaviour has given satisfaction to certain enemies of liberal studies; but I think it more likely that in this he follows his own bent, in the main, which is naturally prone to such behaviour. He was always like that, according to those who knew him as a boy[9] – always savage and vindictive, jealous of everyone else, intolerant of any equal, much more of any superior; he wished to be the only figure of importance, had a great thirst for petty reputation, and held obstinately to his own opinions. He was like that as a boy, as a youth, and as a young man; he is like that now that he is of full age, except that faults tend to increase with years. We can only hope that in old age at least he may some day turn over a new leaf.

When you say how fortunate I am in having so many friends who are as learned as they are influential, and in the immortal name I have earned by work well done, and that I am above jealousy, it is very kind of you of course, my dear Willibald, to revive, as you suppose, with amiable consolation a friend who is in danger of malignant underhand attacks from every quarter. But the immortality of which you speak means nothing to me. I do not know what you mean by work well done; my sole object has been my efforts should serve to some extent the public advancement of learning, and to arouse men's minds to embrace the pure teaching of Christ. But I fear that things will end by going the opposite way. Heretofore, religious minds were chilled and sickened by a scholastic and argumentative theology, and they soon began to grow more cheerful when they tasted the gospel truth; but so active was the conspiracy of those who set their own glory above the glory of Christ, that I fear that things will end by going the opposite way. And the moving spirits in this are those who are commonly accounted the light of the world and the salt of the earth.[10] It is now a good and pious thing to fill your sermons with shameless falsehoods in the cause of gospel truth, and to rant like a fishwife[11] against the good name of your neighbour. And what perverse villains they are! – to make certain persons unpopular and to please the princes whose favour they seek to win, they preach in public what they condemn among themselves at home. New books they spurn; but it is new books flavoured with the liberal studies which they hate worse than dog or viper.[12] What all the time they are setting before us in their own new books, I have at the moment neither leisure nor stomach to recount; and yet I am ashamed to remember what they are not ashamed to write.

Of Luther I will say nothing except the only thing that it is at the moment safe to say, that I am heartily sorry to see a man of such gifts, who seemed destined to be like a great trumpet for proclaiming the gospel truth, embittered like this by certain men's frenzied uproar. Your story[13] of the attack on my eating of chickens gave me a hearty laugh, and I admit that I owe you a present for defending me so well.

Of the sweet and blessed leisure that Lee enjoys you make very good fun;[14] but seriously, I wish he would return, even now, to his accustomed leisure, having tasted the hazards of war. But he is said to be making great efforts to renew the campaign, relying on a certain abbot,[15] a proper blockhead, the only man who has yet called that nonsense of his 'his saintly annotations.' Who could believe he has a grain of sense in him, if he is not ashamed after such a disgraceful defeat to take the field again? If he does so, I have made up my mind not to contend in future with such scum. A number of scholars in Germany have sent some bundles, or more truly volumes, of letters, in which they cut Lee up into little pieces. I have kept them very dark and given them to no one to read,[16] partly because I long to see an end of this sad business, partly because I do not wish Lee to seem important enough for so many men of such standing to sharpen their pens against him. And so your threat[17] that Germany will make an annual bid for his favour with a panegyric I not only regard as a joke, I most sincerely hope it is one; for if this came off, he would simply think he was God.

In getting ready to set out for Germany,[18] I am being a regular Callipides.[19] I shall eagerly look forward to a sight of that palace of yours, if it can be managed without too great a detour. To me the merest cottage would be finer than any palace if it contained my Willibald. You say the plague will cease on the arrival of Prince Charles. What wiseacre told you that?

What you tell me Oecolampadius[20] has done, I already suspected would happen from his letter. Whether he did it wisely or under some delusion, it cannot be altered now, and we must pray it may turn out as well as possible for him and us. I see society so much corrupted everywhere, that down the centuries I would think that effrontery and stupidity and villainy had never had more scope. Sometimes I think of getting away from it somewhere; but I fear that wherever I turn the trouble will pursue me. And so I think it safer to seek a remedy for the evil in my own spirit rather than in some change of place or way of life. Thank heaven that Christ, in this dark night of wickedness, has left us some glimmers of the gospel teaching. Farewell, my distinguished friend.

Louvain, 5 September 1520

1140 / To Maarten Lips [Louvain? June–September 1520]

This letter is known only from the copy-book of Lips now in Rotterdam (cf Epp 750, 1130 introductions) where it precedes Epp 1116 and 1130. Allen conjecturally placed it among the letters of September 1520 because of the departure of Edward Lee (line 18). When Erasmus met Lee at Calais (perhaps 10–14 July, cf Epp 1106 introduction, 1123 n9) the latter was probably on his way home to England. At any rate his presence in Louvain is no longer suggested in subsequent letters (cf Epp 1123, 1134, 1139). If Lee had indeed gone to Calais to attend the court of Henry VIII, who was there from 31 May, and returned to England at the close of the royal visit, it is difficult to assume that Erasmus was not made aware of his intentions when he too was present at the meeting of the courts of Henry VIII and Charles V. Thus it would be rather before than after the Calais meeting that he had to surmise Lee's destination as he does in this letter. Also, if Lee did not return to Louvain after Calais, the as yet unconfirmed information given in this letter would be welcome to Lips, who knew Lee well, in June–July, but in September would no doubt be obsolete. It may be preferable to read this letter in the context of Ep 1116, but a later date cannot be ruled out, as there is no firm evidence for Lee's presence in England before December (cf Ep 1165:28). By December he was probably one of the king's chaplains (LP III page 1543), but rumours of this appointment must have reached the German author of the *Hochstratus ovans* (cf Ep 1165 n11) a little earlier, as in this pamphlet (Hutten *Operum supplementum* I 465) Lee is made to say that he got himself recalled to England to be the chaplain of the queen.

DESIDERIUS ERASMUS OF ROTTERDAM TO HIS FRIEND LIPS

If there is no other inconvenience except that the Origen[1] is such a bulky volume, there is no danger. I never had any suspicions of the prior of St Agnes;[2] only of the brothers at Zwolle,[3] though that too did not amount to much. About Listrius' wife[4] and the dropping of Greek[5] I realized that the letter had misinformed me, and I protested to the writer, for he is a great friend of Listrius.

The prior remarked to me about Augustine,[6] but in the most courteous manner, and I am not so prickly[7] as to object to remarks of that kind. If I have not yet given him full satisfaction, I am not in the fortunate position of being able to please everybody. That particular passage did not call for a panegyric on Augustine. I would rather some people thought me a little less than fair to Augustine than that I should have to prove to them that I am much better disposed to him than they seem to think. The prior's feelings are perfectly honourable; he is supporting his founder. In the same way, no one can praise St Thomas enough[8] to please the Dominicans. And in any case, I have so many supporters and so many opponents, that I hardly have time to concern myself with either of them.

Lee has now left, I believe, for England after a distinguished campaign. Farewell.

1141 / To Gerard Geldenhouwer — Louvain, 9 September 1520

This intense letter, addressed to the secretary of Bishop Philip of Burgundy, was published in the *Epistolae ad diversos*.

The first paragraph acknowledges a gift from the bishop, for which Erasmus had so far thanked him either only by word of mouth or indirectly. In 1524 he recalled that after he had dedicated the *Querela pacis* to the bishop, Philip offered him a prebend (cf line 7) and when Erasmus declined, gave him a precious ring instead (cf Allen I 43). This ring, which was evidently not offered at once (cf Ep 758), is probably the gift here mentioned, unless the more recent dedication of the shorter Pauline Epistles to Philip (cf Ep 1043) was rewarded by another present.

ERASMUS OF ROTTERDAM TO GERARD OF NIJMEGEN, CHAPLAIN TO THE RIGHT REVEREND BISHOP OF UTRECHT, GREETING

In Bruges[1] I did not much like the look of you. I should like to see you with your old, fresh, cheerful face again. I beg you particularly to use all your eloquence to persuade his Lordship[2] that his gift was most welcome, though I have not yet had time to thank him. I wish I could do it in some book that will live. I had told him that I have a certain fear of prebends;[3] I do not want to have to deal with chapters. But now I seem to have found a way of solving this problem too.

I am filled with forebodings about that wretched Luther; the conspiracy against him is strong everywhere, and everywhere the ruling princes are being provoked against him, especially Pope Leo. If only he had followed my advice and refrained from that offensive and seditious stuff![4] He would have done more good, and been much less unpopular. One man's undoing would be a small matter; but if they are successful in this campaign, their insolence will be past all bearing. They will not rest until they have overthrown all knowledge of languages and all humane studies. They are now mounting a new attack against Reuchlin,[5] merely out of hatred for Luther; against my advice he brought Reuchlin's name into his own business,[6] made him most unpopular, and did himself no good at all. Eck held a disputation;[7]

Hoogstraten had promised to produce some sort of syllogisms,[8] to which everyone would be obliged to capitulate. There were disputations and even pamphlets at Louvain.[9] Everyone was waiting for a verdict from the University of Paris;[10] and now, lo and behold, the thing suddenly looks like issuing in a bull and a cloud of smoke.[11] A bull is in print – a terrific affair, but the pope forbade its publication. I am afraid all this will end in serious disorders. The pope's advisers in this give him, in my opinion, counsel which may or may not be religious, but is certainly full of danger. This business started from the worst possible beginnings, and it was the worst possible policy that brought it to its present state. Hatred of liberal studies and the stupidity of monks – they were the prime sources from which the whole tragic story sprang. Gross recrimination and venomous conspiracy brought it to its present pitch of madness. Their ultimate object is clear to all: to overwhelm the literature of which they are ignorant and reign unquestioned in their native barbarism. I am having nothing to do with this miserable business. Otherwise, there is actually a bishopric waiting for me,[12] if I will attack Luther in print. It grieves me to see the doctrine of the Gospel so lost to sight, and ourselves exposed only to compulsion and not taught; and that what they do teach should be repugnant alike to Scripture and common sense. Farewell, dearest Gerard, and let me have an account of your health.

Louvain, 9 September 1520

1141A / To Jan Dirksz van der Haer — Louvain, 9 September [1520?]

The original letter in Erasmus' hand is preserved in the Bibliothèque Nationale, Paris, MS Dupuy 699 f 3, and was first published by Allen among the preliminary material of volume V. Assuming that Gerard (line 5) is Gerard Geldenhouwer, this letter was no doubt dispatched together with Ep 1141; otherwise it could also be assigned to the year 1519. In it Erasmus acknowledges an invitation extended to him by Jan Dirksz van der Haer (or Harius), canon of Gorinchem (Gorkum); cf Ep 184:19n.

Greetings, my more than ordinary friend. Your letter gave me all the more pleasure, coming as it did after a long interval, so that it refreshed the memory of our association. A visit to Holland,[1] even were it not precluded by my work, is not recommended by the approach of winter. Otherwise I would come and survey your magnificent library[2] with particular pleasure. Gerard[3] gave you a taste of his poetical imagination. In actual fact I am extremely busy in promoting scholarship; though the most unpleasant conspiracies are on foot against Luther and Reuchlin, and I see clearly enough that they are tending to a head-on collision with the whole of the humanities. Farewell, dearest Jan.

Louvain, 9 September

Your sincere friend Erasmus

To Canon Jan Dirksz, my especial friend, in Gorinchem

1142 / From Georg Schirn — Milan, 10 September 1520

The original letter, preserved in the University Library of Wrocław, MS Rehdiger 254 no 136, was first published in 1904. On the same date, 10 September, Schirn also wrote to Beatus Rhenanus (BRE Ep 178), explaining that he had just written this letter when a rumour reached him that Erasmus had died (cf Epp 854:7n, 1008 introduction). Schirn asked Beatus to forward his letter if Erasmus was, none the less, alive, but if the rumour was true, to let him know what he thought of the point raised in this letter. The letter to Beatus Rhenanus is another indication of Schirn's fervent admiration for Erasmus, but beyond the two letters no information on Schirn, a Cistercian monk of Chiaravalle (cf n12), has come to light.

Greeting. Never have I meant to write to anyone and for so long put off doing so, Erasmus, prince of scholars; never has my reason for writing made it more difficult to start than I find it now. When I thought whom I should be writing to if I were to write to you, and how great and rare and various is the learning of the man to whom what I write must present itself, more or less barbarous as it is, or at least devoid of all charm and all importance that might recommend it, I lost heart all at once, and with it went all my resolution to write; my mind's feeble eyes were overcome with fear at the mere thought of your glorious reputation, as though I had seen Moses when his face was horned.[1] And in this (if I mistake not) I am to be forgiven rather than blamed, if I have been so terrified of the critical eye of a man whose supreme abilities and many-sided knowledge of all fields of study have made all admire him as something unique; whom all – not only Germans to whom (whether other men will or no) he really belongs,[2] but Italians and foreign nations – agree in extolling as the fountain-head of learning that never fails, whence new rivers of paper pour every day in generous measure to refresh the parched palates of all who wish to learn. And yet that very great kindness of heart which is known everywhere, both from your letters, pamphlets, and books and from the unanimous witness of all living men, and your many-sided virtues have driven away all the fear that made me pale; and what my own skill (skill I have none) could not accomplish has been vouchsafed me by your own goodness which, like wine, maketh glad the heart of man.[3] And so pray let the patience and kindliness with which you receive what all men write give a hearing to this letter of mine whatever its defects, as a continuing token of my affection for you; for, as God is my witness, no sound strikes more sweetly on my ear, no sight so gladdens my eye, nothing is more deeply rooted in my heart, than the name Erasmus. For if Philip of Macedon thought it a sign of great good fortune that Alexander was born in the lifetime of Aristotle the philosopher,[4] we shall all boast – all we who wish to learn – that it was at any rate a most happy omen to have had Erasmus as a contemporary, from whom we receive in its perfection everything in literature that is honourable, all that is recondite and profitable and apposite and worth the knowing, as though from an oracle of Apollo. Yes indeed, we really possess in this present age something we can admire; we need not always look up to the genius of the Ancients. For you, Erasmus, are the leading champion of both humane and sacred studies, and your books are the most beguiling, elegant, well-nourished, authoritative, lucid, divine thing we have – the most desirable from every point of view from which literature can be an object of desire. No wonder that, when I play truant from the pointless jingles of the questionists[5] (if I may use the word) and their barbarous syllogisms, and betake myself to your books as to some delightful pleasure-ground, it is remarkable how much I am refreshed everywhere by the sweetness of your style as though by some delicious fruit.

But lately, when I had taken up the small book you call your *Ratio verae theologiae* and had opened it just at the passage where you vigorously set about those who misuse sacred theology, and among them you mention that most saintly of doctors St Bernard,[6] the most glorious founder of my order, I stopped on the instant and, as though I had tasted some fruit that was new and unknown, my blood froze in my veins.[7] Now it is a very common experience for a man to dislike at first the taste of something new that he has never eaten before, but once he has acquired the habit of eating it and has learnt from those who are familiar with it what it is good for, he not only eats it but develops a passion for it. Exactly this happened to me (for my letter must not be wholly serious) with melons. When they were first set before me in Italy, I did not know how to eat them and had no practice, for most of Germany, as you know, has no melons; but now hardly anything appears on our table that I enjoy more. It nearly always happens like that, my dear Erasmus, in one's programme of reading: when we do not really understand the style and sentiments and purpose of authors, we constantly form the wrong opinion of what we have not understood and of the writers, but once everything is properly understood, it is not a rare experience to approve and praise and think most highly of what we did not like at first.

Now for my part, of all the books of yours which I have seen, I have never been troubled, not to say offended, by any sentence as I was by that. Who ever found any matter for criticism in such a good man, who is still better as a philosopher, and best of all as a theologian? And yet somehow, as I read your remarks about Bernard, my mind, diminutive as it is, seems to abandon its usual habit, and to disagree. As far as it can form a view of that most saintly father and his works (and I hope filial affection and the solidarity of my vows do not affect my judgment), it never finds him dealing with Holy Scripture except in a serious and fitting and proper spirit and with the greatest veneration. And then, besides this, his works are open to all. The writers of his life, surely no ordinary men, and those who knew him when he lived on earth almost from infancy, and through friendship and occasional correspondence, contradict you flatly. These words, if I remember right, are to be found in his life:[8] 'The canonical Scriptures he used to read in all simplicity and in their due order, frequently and with enjoyment. He used to say that he understood them best in their own words, and maintained that any ray of divine truth or virtue that came to him from them had more flavour for him in the first fountain-head than in the rivulets of commentary that flow from it. Yet, as he humbly read the saintly and orthodox commentators on Scripture, he never pitted his own interpretations against theirs, but put them forward to be reshaped; and treading loyally in their footsteps, he would often drink himself from the spring whence they had drawn.'

Do you think, my most honoured friend, that this venerable father did not know that remark of St Augustine on Psalm 48,[9] where he says: 'All Holy Scripture brings salvation to those who rightly understand it, but peril to such as would rather twist it to match the perversity of their own hearts than correct their own hearts by the straight rule of Scripture; and this is a great and widespread error. For though they ought themselves to live according to the will of God, they prefer a God to match their own will; while they are reluctant to be set right themselves, they are willing that he should go wrong, thinking that the right is not what he wills but what they want themselves.'

It cannot be that our most saintly father used the Scriptures in such form as he might have wished to support his own meaning rather than God's. That would be an offence that no victims could expiate, that no sanctity could atone for. But I would not suggest that in your words you either meant or said this (though in my judgment they mean something like that), for the last part of the opinion you there expressed includes an ample and laudatory tribute to him. Nor do I criticize your intelligence, but my own, my own slowness and ignorance, which so impede me that what you mean in those same words I cannot understand at all. I urge beg and beseech you therefore, as our modern father in all humane and sacred studies and our master in all learning: send me (little as I deserve it so far) a friendly letter; express yourself more clearly, and lighten my lack of understanding. Where or in what passages, or at least in what work and how, did that same most saintly father use the sacred text 'with elegance but irresponsibly'? – that the taste of the wild gourds set before me, as in the story of the prophet,[10] may be seasoned with the salt of your learning and become delicious. For I am a novice in theology, the veriest tyro, and am very anxious to discover some way by which it is possible to make progress in it. If under your guidance I secure such a way more easily, I shall never cease to love and honour you perpetually as my teacher, my master, and my father. I would also most seriously beseech you, my honoured Lord, to add my name to the list, I will not say of your friends (for such a garland hardly befits my head) but of your disciples, and indeed among the last of them.

If you have decided to send me an answer as, knowing your kindness, I do not doubt you will, arrange for it to go to the monastery of Sant' Ambrogio in Milan for presentation to the abbot or the cellarer;[11] and do not take offence, most learned of men, if an unknown person like me approaches you by letter, with more audacity perhaps than suited my lowly station or befitted a great name like yours. Nothing more desirable could come my way – pray believe this without hesitation – than to see and admire face to face a man whom I know only from your letters and your world-wide reputation, and to take in those words, so delightful and so entirely impressive, not from correspondence, not from the reports of others, but as they fall from your golden lips. Farewell, O glory of our age, saviour of literature, and treasure-house of every kind of learning.

From Chiaravalle,[12] a famous house of the Cistercian order near Milan, 10 September 1520

Georg Schirn, a German, of the order of Cîteaux[13]

To Erasmus of Rotterdam, glory of the German people, prince of theologians and master of the two ancient tongues, his most revered master

1143 / To Leo X Louvain, 13 September 1520

Epp 1143–4 were evidently sent to Rome together and both were published by Erasmus in the *Epistolae ad diversos*. In writing them, he endeavoured to counter curial criticisms of his stand with regard to Luther, especially the sympathetic stance reflected fifteen months earlier in his Ep 980. That such criticisms had reached the ear of Leo X is confirmed by his answer to this letter, Ep 1180.

Erasmus had learnt this as early as July through a letter written by Aleandro (cf Epp 1123:10–13, 1127A n24), and no doubt also through another from Francesco Chierigati (cf Ep 1144:88–9).

While this letter is largely apologetic, Ep 1144 is mostly an attack on Erasmus' critics; both reflect courage and self-confidence. In a sense the concrete proposals towards a solution of the Luther problem put forward shortly afterwards in the *Consilium* complement these letters; cf Ep 1149 introduction.

TO THE MOST BLESSED FATHER LEO, TENTH OF THAT NAME, FROM ERASMUS OF ROTTERDAM, GREETING

Though I had no fear, most holy Father, that in your goodness you might be moved to hurt an innocent man or in your wisdom you might lend an ear to vicious calumny, yet when I see you assailed by so much business flooding in from all parts of the world, and consider that the unparalleled effrontery of certain sworn foes of the humanities never sleeps, sticks at nothing, and leaves no stone unturned, I thought it of some importance for myself that I should send your Holiness a sort of antidote like this to protect you, for though you have keen sight you are very busy. I observe that, in order to strengthen their own faction, some have attempted to connect the cause of the humanities, Reuchlin's case, and my own with the case of Luther,[1] although they have nothing in common. And this I have always maintained both in conversation and in what I have written and published.[2] Luther I do not know,[3] nor have I ever read his books except maybe for a mere ten or twelve pages, and those in snatches. From the samples I then tasted, he seemed to me admirably equipped as an expositor of the mystical Scripture in the ancient manner,[4] while this age of ours was spending more time than it should on problems more elegant than necessary. I therefore supported the good qualities in him and not the bad; or rather, through him I supported the glory of Christ.

I was almost the first person to detect the risk that the affair might issue in public strife,[5] a thing I have always detested more than anybody. And so I actually used threats to dissuade Johann Froben the printer from printing any of his works.[6] I wrote both often and with emphasis to friends,[7] urging them to tell him to remember the mildness proper to a Christian in what he wrote, and always to promote peace in the church. And when he took the initiative in writing to me two years ago,[8] I told him in friendly fashion what I wished him to avoid. How I wish he had followed my advice! That letter[9] has, I hear, been reported to your Holiness in order, I suppose, to get me into trouble, though it ought rather to secure me your Holiness' good will. What advice do I there fail to give him? I do it in courteous terms, I know; but that is more rapidly effective than severity, and I was writing to a stranger. After laying down a code of behaviour, a sort of rule for the man, I added, to avoid giving offence by the freedom of my admonitions, 'I write this not in order to tell you what to do, but to encourage you to continue doing what I know you do already,'[10] picturing him of course as behaving already of his own accord as I wished him to behave. Had I been satisfied with the style of writing Luther used before, why need I in so many words prescribe him a new method? And yet I know that this passage has been shamelessly wrested to my discredit by many people, and still more the phrase I added, that where I was then he had many supporters.[11] When I wrote that, it was true. Many men supported his good qualities just as I did. This I wished him to know, not to encourage him to publish more sedition, but to make him moderate his manner to the style I had suggested if he wished this support to be permanent.

How the name of the bishop of Liège[12] came to be mixed up with this in Leipzig, where for some reason unknown they published this private letter, when it was not added in Basel,[13] I cannot think. One thing is absolutely certain; he never had anything whatever to do with Luther, any more than I did. Indeed, even had his name been added, it could have been added with nothing else in mind than the sense I have just explained. I wrote the letter nearly two years ago,[14] when things had not yet reached their present bitterness and the challenge had been issued to that debate. If anyone ever heard me defending Luther's opinions even in my cups, I would not object to being called Luther's supporter.[15] But, they say, I never published an attack on the man. For one thing, I could not refute him unless I had first read him carefully two or three times; and for that I had no leisure, being more than sufficiently occupied with my own work. And then I saw that the business went beyond the limits of my learning and my brains,[16] besides which I did not wish to forestall the credit of the universities which were engaged on it.[17] Last but not least, I was afraid of arousing the resentment of so many powerful persons, especially as no one had entrusted me with this as a duty. And so if among those around you the enemies of the humanities accuse me falsely, your wisdom and my own innocence are my sure defence. I am not mad enough to make some bold move against the supreme vicar of Christ, I who would be reluctant to withstand even my own proper bishop.[18] I am not ungrateful enough not to do my best to respond to the more than fatherly kindness you have shown me. The small gifts I have, such as they are, shall all be devoted to the glory of Christ and the tranquillity of Christ's flock. Whoever is his adversary shall be mine too.

I lent no countenance to Luther, even in the days when one was more or less free to support him. I only objected to the methods by which he was attacked, thinking not of him but of the authority of the theologians. I saw that the business took its rise in hatred of the classical languages and what they call liberal studies.[19] I saw that it was carried on with bitter strife and seditious clamour in public, the only result of which was to make Luther's works famous and arouse the common run of men to read them eagerly. Had they first refuted Luther and taken him out of men's minds,[20] and then burnt his books, they might have done away with the whole of Luther without setting the world by the ears, if indeed he deserved what they say he did. A free and generous mind loves to be taught but will not take compulsion.[21] This policy favoured the theologians against Luther, did not certain persons misinterpret it.

I had decided to pass the winter in Rome,[22] to consult your Holiness' library in certain passages; but these conferences of princes have delayed me.[23] I hope to come next winter. May Christ the almighty guard and keep your Holiness.

Louvain, 13 September 1520

1144 / To Francesco Chierigati — Louvain, 13 September 1520

For this letter, which was printed in the *Epistolae ad diversos*, cf Ep 1143 introduction, and for Erasmus' acquaintance with Francesco Chierigati, a papal diplomat, cf Epp 639, 1080, 1183 n9. A letter to Chierigati from Christophe de Longueil, dated from Padua, 21 November [1520], shows that Chierigati had sent this letter for Longueil to read; see Christophe de Longueil *Orationes … epistolae* (Florence: heirs of F. Giunta 1524; repr 1967) f 112 verso.

ERASMUS OF ROTTERDAM TO FRANCESCO CHIERIGATI, ENGLISH DOCTOR OF CIVIL AND CANON LAW,[1] GREETING

Your attitude is so fair-minded, so well disposed, so frank and open, that did I not welcome it I should be more uncivilized than any Goth. Few men, perhaps, feel the pain of all this uproar over Luther as much as I do. If only I had had the power to suppress it when it started or could pacify it now! But the whole business had an ill-starred beginning,[2] by way of certain monks who were pursuing their own ends, and an ill-starred series of events brought it to its present state of frenzy. That man would be no Christian who did not maintain the honour of the Roman pontiff; but I with the pope knew how much it suffers from the acts of certain blockheads who think that they defend it admirably. Believe me, if my word is worth anything, nothing has done more to bring Luther into people's hearts than the stupid clamour these men make before the people. And all this time not one of them has published a book to prove Luther wrong,[3] as I have always urged them to do. I could see that this was the sole way to suppress Luther, if he were the sort of man they falsely said he was. Those who have written against Luther hitherto do not satisfy even Luther's worst enemies. Let me show you the criminal designs of some I could name, who hate me worse than they hate Luther himself! – not because I support him, which they know to be false, but because I support the humanities, with which they have been doing battle for a long time now, because I recall theologians to their sources, and because I point out to them where true religion has its roots.

When the bull had appeared which commands them to preach against Luther,[4] two or three of these barefoot bullies passed a decree in their cups[5] to this effect, that they would couple me with Luther and defame me too in public. There is a certain Preacher here,[6] a man whose name does not deserve recording, an ignoramus, a natural booby and stupider than Morychus[7] himself, devoid of human feeling, all effrontery, and as noisy as any fishwife. Abandoning all other subjects, this man confines himself to prating against me, and neither shame nor weariness can stop him. A second man there is, with a white habit and a black heart,[8] a dull, furious blockhead, and so spiteful that the whole university finds him a burden. When he was publishing the bull, this man said more about me in his sermon than about Luther. In a public lecture he glanced at Lefèvre d'Etaples,[9] for after saying that we do not agree, he added 'Heretics never do.'

Following this man's lead, two members[10] of the Dominican gang held forth against me by name before a public audience in such a scurrilous fashion that things were heading towards public disorder, although I did nothing about it; and the leading men of the university, though in other ways not very well disposed towards me, were obliged to silence them. The same thing happened in Antwerp.[11]

In Bruges there was a certain Minorite,[12] a suffragan of the bishop of Tournai, blear-eyed with drink, who ranted before the public whole hours at a time against Luther and myself, calling us beasts, donkeys, storks, and blockheads,[13] but not proving that anything we said was wrong. When in a second sermon he had openly stated that some things in my books were heretical, one of the magistrates, who is an educated man, went up to him and asked him what there was in my books of that description. And this is the answer he got from the buffoon of a bishop! 'I have not read Erasmus' books,' says he; 'I meant to read the paraphrases, but the Latin was most lofty, so I am afraid he may be able to slip into some heresy, with all that lofty Latin.'

Such are most of the men here who declaim against Luther and, as it seems to them, defend the Roman see; the honour of which no one will fail to support, but no intelligent man will ever tolerate these noisy blockheads. If the pope knew them as well as I do, they would be the chief targets of his

Frans van Cranevelt
Portrait medal by Janus Secundus, 1533
Bibliothèque Royale Albert I / Commissie voor Numismatiek, Brussels

indignation. I only wish I had as much influence with the pope as I have genuine zeal to maintain his honour! I would have given him advice more profitable to himself and more salutary for the world at large.[14] Uproar and threats will maybe secure one result, the temporary suppression of the evil; but it will break out again and do greater damage. The upshot of these measures will be not to reduce the support for Luther or to increase the popularity of the Roman pontiff, but to make men more careful to conceal their views.[15] Thus far at any rate we have seen it happen: their threats and bawling have irritated men so much that those who before were Luther's lukewarm supporters are now keen, and those who were prejudiced against him before now begin to support him.

As for me, there is nothing to fear. I shall never be a leader in falsehood or a captain in civil strife. And yet you would hardly credit through what channels I have been invited to involve myself even slightly in this business of Luther;[16] and had I been willing to give them any hope of this, Luther's position would be very different from what it is. But may such a thought never enter my head! Hitherto I have preached peace and concord, hitherto I have laboured for Christ. The end of my life approaches; I will not abandon my principles, I will not lose my crown. These noisy wretches, who are a disgrace to their order, I leave to the judgment of Christ, though they do themselves more harm than they do me, such is the popular reaction against them everywhere.

I am now editing the entire works of Augustine,[17] revised and illustrated with brief notes. When that is finished, I shall display my dislike of men who talk subversion and my heartfelt devotion to the see of Rome,[18] though Rome needs no support from a mere worm like me. To that see all men of good will will be more seriously devoted, if in turn it shows a sincere devotion to the glory of Christ. No ornaments ought to confer splendour on Christ's supreme vicegerent, other than those which distinguished Christ himself.

Your letter[19] reached me after being opened; so pray be careful what you write. Next winter you will see me in Rome,[20] if life and health hold up. Farewell, best of patrons. Pray commend me warmly to the bishop of Worcester.[21]

Louvain, 13 September 1520

1145 / From Frans van Cranevelt — Bruges, 19 September 1520

This letter was published in the *Epistolae ad diversos* together with Erasmus' answer, Ep 1173. Frans van Cranevelt, of Nijmegen (1485–1564) was educated in Louvain, receiving a doctorate in civil and canon law in 1510. In 1515 he was appointed pensionary or legal consultant to the city of Bruges, and in October 1522 he moved to Mechelen as member of the Grand Council. His duties did not prevent him from translating St Basil and Procopius of Caesarea. He also composed verses and befriended many scholars. He may have met Erasmus for the first time at Louvain in August 1514 and in the following years he remained his friend and supporter; see de Vocht *Literae* xlviii and passim.

FRANS VAN CRANEVELT TO HIS FRIEND ERASMUS, GREETING

I cannot fail to thank you, most learned of men in every way, though it be only in one of my foolish letters, for the kindness you have lately done me, which I shall keep in memory for ever, and value so highly that I would not exchange it for all the wealth of Croesus. What kindness is this, you ask? Your introducing me to your – I may now say, our – delightful friend More,[1] of whose society I saw much after your departure, at his invitation. His more than Sicilian dinners[2] I value highly, but much more his learning, his kindliness, his generosity. So I acknowledge a very great debt to you, and wish I may be able to give you some evidence of my gratitude. And then it grieves me to think how seldom I visited you while you were in Bruges, being taken up with business of no importance, so that the opportunity to learn so much and such interesting things slipped from me, and I did not get my teeth into it as it went by. I do not forget what you said about Flemish habits,[3] but I beg you to believe that I am entirely on your side, and have escaped the contamination entirely.

When he left, More gave my wife a gold ring,[4] on which was written in English 'All things Doth measure still good will.' To me he gave two ancient coins,[5] one gold and the other silver; one with a head of Tiberius and one with the deified Augustus. I tell you this, because I shall always admit that I owe these likewise to yourself. Farewell, and let me know if there is ever anything I can do for you.

Bruges, 19 September 1520

Our friend Fevijn[6] is well, and wished to send you greeting.

1146 / To Johannes Alexander Brassicanus Antwerp, 26 September 1520

In the second half of September 1520 Erasmus paid another visit to his friend Pieter Gillis, secretary of the city of Antwerp. His stay in Antwerp may have coincided with that of another friend, the English envoy Cuthbert Tunstall, c 23–28 September, and of Charles V (cf Gachard II 28, LP III 991–2). He also met a brilliant young Swabian, Brassicanus, who was attending the court with his master Maximiliaan van Bergen, lord of Zevenbergen (cf Epp 953:27n, 1119 n1). A snippet of their conversations 'at Antwerp in the house of Pieter Gillis, 27

September 1520' survives in a note Brassicanus sent Joachim Vadianus (*Vadianische Briefsammlung* II Ep 219). Brassicanus had asked Erasmus how one could become learned. The answer was that one should live with, and listen to, learned men, read and memorize learned works, and never think of oneself as learned. Brassicanus took his advice to heart and by the end of the year he could claim to have enjoyed familiar contact with Erasmus first in Louvain and later in Cologne (cf BRE Ep 189; below Ep 1155 introduction).

Johannes Alexander Brassicanus (1500/1–39) studied and taught until 1519 in Tübingen, his native city. In 1522 he received a doctorate in law and became Reuchlin's successor as professor of ancient languages at the University of Ingolstadt. Bishop Johannes Fabri recommended him to Ferdinand I, and in 1524 he was appointed to the chair of rhetoric in the University of Vienna, where he subsequently advanced to a professorship in law. Brassicanus published this letter of recommendation as a preface to his *Musae et Gratiae* (Vienna: J. Singriener 9 July 1524) and continued to correspond with Erasmus.

DESIDERIUS ERASMUS OF ROTTERDAM TO THAT LEARNED YOUNG MAN JOHANNES ALEXANDER BRASSICANUS, GREETING

I congratulate you, my dear Brassicanus, on having already in the flower of your youth made such progress in rhetoric and poetry as falls to the lot of few men full of years; and I congratulate this age of ours, which produces many persons like you in almost every part of the world. Your learning is indeed graced by the crown of bay[1] awarded to your gifts by the emperor Maximilian, whose practice was to bestow this honour as a gift and not to sell it, and to do so not at random but after rigorous choice; in fact he never conferred the honour on anyone to whom he did not also make a present. How I wish that our prelates would follow in holy things the example he has set them in the things of this world! Though everything is holy that pertains to honourable studies; in any case the fair crown of bay, the crown of glory, which you will continue to deserve by what you write, will never fade from age to age.

With all this praise[2] of Erasmus you load him rather than laud him, and you will be well advised to find a more fruitful subject for your eloquence. You write that you are entirely of Erasmus' school; are you quite sure you have not chosen a less than excellent model? There may perhaps be something in Erasmus for other men to imitate; but he would be foolish, in my opinion, who tried to reproduce him entire.[3] Even this age of ours will provide a more finished pattern; so true is it that there arise everywhere 'many pupils who outstrip their teachers.'[4] What feelings others may have, I know not, who were the first to struggle against the cohorts of barbarism; for my part, I am happy to be outstripped in this field,[5] and am all the happier, to be sure, when I think how in Italy in the old days scarcely any man taught the humanities whose intellectual gifts were not stained by grievous vices of character,[6] whereas now scarcely anyone has a higher or more religious character than the devotees of the more elegant of the Muses.

Farewell, most learned Brassicanus.

From Antwerp, 26 September 1520

1147 / To Petrus Manius — Louvain, 1 October 1520

At a time of familiar contacts and promising co-operation with one member of the Dominican order (cf Ep 1149) Erasmus was reminded of the friendly and admiring letter written by another, Petrus Manius. It had reached him several months earlier and then been misplaced (lines 5–11, 15–16, n2), so he decided to answer it from memory (lines 14–15), publishing this reply later in the *Epistolae ad diversos*.

The Dominican addressed with this letter, perhaps a Hollander (cf n2 and lines 30–50) has not been identified so far. Manius may perhaps be a Latin form for Man, a name quite common throughout the Netherlands, but in the absence of earlier connections between Erasmus and the Dominican (cf lines 13–14, 27–8) further conjectures would be hazardous at this time.

ERASMUS OF ROTTERDAM TO PETRUS MANIUS OF THE DOMINICAN ORDER, GREETING

Your letter was most welcome, dear sir, on more grounds than one, but a chain of accidents deprived me of it at one moment and restored it at another, and that is why I have not answered it until now. To begin with, when it reached me, I hardly had the time to read it. Later, when I was allowed some leisure, it lay hidden among bundles of letters so effectually that for some months after long and careful search it could not be found. At length it came to hand of its own accord unlooked-for and, as Ovid[1] puts it, not so much was found as turned up. I put it on one side once more to await my first free moment, and it was again lost – how, I cannot guess. And so, lest you should suppose that your letters are not appreciated or that I am so difficult to please that I dislike having to answer a letter from someone who may be unknown to me but is, as I can guess, a man of integrity and learning, I will seek to recover from my memory what I should have rediscovered in your letter.

In the first place, if I remember right, you reported the enthusiastic reception and applause given to Maarten van Dorp by the whole congregation, and especially by educated people, for a public sermon,[2] and you tried to divert some part of this success to my account as though his development into the man he is owed not a little to my published work. Then you related that there are many very keen readers of my work in your part of the world, but that there are some on the other side who detest both Erasmus himself and his books, and that you yourself were of this number before you had read anything of mine; but that reading my books and thinking them over had made a new man of you so entirely that you enjoy no one else's work so much, and now have a quite special affection for that same Erasmus whom you used to abominate. Whereupon, as though you and I were already in some way old friends, you make two requests of me – first, that I should quote no Greek in what I write, so as not to put off the reader who knows no Greek; and secondly, that I should not allow myself to be claimed by France,[3] but openly admit that Batavia is part of Germany,[4] presumably that Germany may not lose such a distinction.

To give you a brief answer, and inverting your order: in the first place, I do not think it makes much difference where a man is born, and it seems to me a mere empty boast if some city or people prides itself on having produced an individual who owes his eminence and fame to his own efforts and not to any support from his native country. Credit would more justly be due to the place that made him great than to his birthplace. In saying this I speak as though there were something in me on which my native country might pride itself. Personally I am satisfied if she is not ashamed of me; although the great Peripatetic[5] does not wholly reject credit of this kind, because it may stimulate rivalry in honourable pursuits. If there were anything of the sort in me, I should wish that not only France and Germany should claim me for themselves, but that individual regions and cities should vie with one another to secure me. This error would have its value, in spurring on so many to honourable competition. Whether I am a Batavian is not yet wholly clear to me; that I am a Hollander I cannot deny, born in a district which, if we may believe the drawings of geographers, tends more towards France than Germany, though it is beyond controversy that the whole of that area is on the boundary between the two.

If I sometimes mingle a certain amount of Greek with what I write, I not only follow in this the example of almost all scholars, whether you consider ancient or modern, but I do this, I think, much more sparingly than all the rest, and at least never without good reason. There are some things which must be expressed in Greek, or the force of emphasis, the elegance of allusion or the charm of some rhetorical figure is lost. There are even things now and again which I should not wish to be intelligible to the first comer.[6] It may well be desirable too that a touch of Greek should be added here and there to bring more pressure to bear on everyone to learn a language which in so many ways is essential. For if you think it reasonable that I should abstain from Greek entirely just because some people cannot understand me, you will forbid me at the same time to write in Latin because there are so many to whom Latin is unknown. And yet I do not deny that there are places where charity must stoop to match the understanding of simple folk; but how far one should go to oblige them this is not the moment to enquire. They ought always to be trying to raise themselves to higher things.

And then the fact that many are violently hostile to me and my work is fully brought home to me by common report every day, even had you not written. It is not only in your part of the world; everywhere, in nearly every town, and even here in Louvain, the brethren of your order and their allies the Carmelites[7] rave so stupidly in front of the uneducated public against liberal studies and even against me by name that I am ashamed to repeat what they feel no shame in uttering. And this I would attribute to the personal stupidity of a few individuals, did they not do it so universally that they can be seen to do it by arrangement, and with such impunity that their actions probably have the agreement of the senate and people. For if they feel no shame in spewing out this tedious nonsense and these baseless and outrageous scurrilities in these sermons which are dedicated to teaching the Gospel, what rubbish do you suppose they utter in front of silly women, doting old men, superstitious people of no education, and simple-minded youths with whom they enjoy all the prestige of an oracle? How I wish, my dear Petrus, that they might all have the experience which you say happened to you! It would benefit not so much me privately as your whole order, which acquires no little unpopularity from these tub-thumpers; not to mention for the moment that they infect the public with the plague of evil-speaking, which is among the most fatal of wasting diseases, and undermine the authority of the pulpit.

It is good that, as you say in your letter, you are now conquered; your defences have been stormed, and you have become a new man. But meanwhile this is a pretty way to treat me, for my reputation, innocent as I am, has I suppose suffered indiscriminate attacks[8] from you. Those who profess a perfectly religious life ought to take all the more care to refrain from bitter language, for in that way it is very easy to do harm and very hard to mend it. And yet we often see men who think it wicked to eat meat or to vary what they wear round their waist, and regard this most criminal of all disorders as a mere game. There are two of your brethren here,[9] one a member of the theological faculty and the other an aspirant thereto; and if I wished to treat them as they deserve, no way could be more fitting than to enshrine in writing the clamour they direct every day, with astonishing self-satisfaction, against me by name and against my field of studies, of which they do not possess a tincture. There is also a certain Carmelite,[10] a leader of the theological faculty, who feels no embarrassment although he sees himself daily a public laughing-stock. Then my friend Dorp: it is true I have a high opinion of his merits, and he is so gifted and so learned and writes so well that I could not dislike him even when bad influences were poisoning him against me;[11] but I do not see what credit I deserve on that score, except perhaps that long ago when he was a young man I encouraged him to pursue more liberal studies and my writings either kindled to some extent or aided his own. Either I am mistaken, or he will succeed where my efforts have not been very happy. And so farewell, and pray commend me to Christ in your prayers.

Louvain, 1 October 1520

1148 / To Konrad Frick and Lorenz Effinger — Louvain, 1 October [1520]

In Ep 1120 two abbots of Benedictine houses in the Breisgau had asked for Erasmus' support of their appeals to the Hapsburg court. Their letter had probably reached him quite recently (cf Ep 1129 introduction). Having just returned to Louvain, where Charles v and his court were stopping from 1 to 8 or 9 October (cf Gachard II 28), he sent this answer, which was printed in the *Epistolae ad diversos*. The wrong year was added to the date in the *Opus epistolarum*.

ERASMUS OF ROTTERDAM TO THE VERY REVEREND KONRAD, ABBOT OF SCHUTTERN AND LORENZ, ABBOT OF ETTENHEIM IN THE PROVINCE OF BREISGAU, GREETING

This is no new thing in our friend Zasius,[1] that he should praise my humble self everywhere, until he has made the fly greater than the elephant,[2] and thus impose not only on you but on many besides. He was himself the first victim, imposed on by his own enthusiasm. Unfortunately in this regard he quite misunderstands my position. No man on earth refrains from contact with the court more readily than I. And no one can have any influence there who does not play his part, with the support from time to time of his own hangers-on. Not for me to canvass the various factions,[3] to thrust myself forward, and elbow some other man out of my way. With your experience, you must already know what a monster is the emperor's court, a beast of uncounted heads, so much so that if I had any business to be done there, I would rather face the financial loss and preserve my freedom than go through with it.

I have, it is true, been admitted to the roll of councillors,[4] but on the understanding that I do not attend even when summoned, let alone put myself forward. Yet I shall not hesitate to advance your case to the best of my ability, if opportunity arises; though I do not doubt of its success without my help, being a most just cause submitted to a most just prince. For Charles possesses, in addition to his other outstanding gifts, an asset specially appropriate to imperial rule, that he has a most firm grasp of justice and equity – mistaken he may be, but never corrupted. I feel the more confidence that this will be so, since, as you say, his clemency has begun already to give you some protection against the violence of the man who causes you so much trouble.[5] Farewell, most honoured and respected Fathers.

Louvain, 1 October [1519]

1149 / To Jakob Villinger — Louvain, 3 October 1520

Epp 1149–52, 1156 were written as introductions for a new acquaintance. In Louvain and subsequently in Cologne Erasmus spent considerable time in the company of the Dominican Johannes Faber of Augsburg, who attended the imperial court (cf Epp 1148, 1155 introductions) in pursuit of both private and public concerns. He had been a councillor and confessor to Maximilian I, who promised him the nomination to the see of Trent when it should fall vacant; Faber now sought to have his appointments confirmed by Charles V (cf Ep 1150:11–14). He also wished to gain support for the Conventual branch of his order, to which he belonged. After Maximilian's death the more conservative Observants had succeeded in gaining control of some houses formerly under Faber's rule. They also persistently opposed his efforts at promoting scholarship and teaching; cf N. Paulus *Die deutschen Dominikaner* (Freiburg 1903) 299–303. Erasmus recalled later in the *Spongia* (ASD IX-1 156) how at Louvain Faber had talked persuasively of his plans for a trilingual college at Augsburg, showing him Maximilian's charter for such an institution, and also that they had discussed Luther and that he had given Faber some letters of recommendation. In turn Faber seems to have admonished Erasmus' critic, the Dominican Vincentius Theoderici (cf Ep 1196:139–51). Talk about Luther was resumed at Cologne, where according to the *Spongia* Faber produced an admirably fair memoir on the question (see V.L. von Seckendorf *Commentarius*, Frankfurt-Leipzig 1692, I 145), which he also showed to Cardinal Albert of Brandenburg. It was largely identical with a *Iudicium* that was subsequently presented to Frederick the Wise (see *Reichstagsakten* J.R. II 484). Faber had lengthy discussions with Erasmus (cf Ep 1156:10–12); both believed that the ecclesiastical authorities had failed to give Luther a fair hearing (cf Epp 1033:61–94, 1141:23–8, 1143:76–81) and that the only hope for peaceful solution lay with an independent commission of inquiry and arbitration. The result of their consultations is commonly thought to be an anonymous pamphlet, printed five times in 1521 or soon after and also translated into German, *Consilium cuiusdam ex animo cupientis esse consultum et Romani pontificis dignitati et christianae tranquillitati*. Soon Cologne was named as the place of publication and Erasmus as the author. Luther attributed it to him without hesitation (Luther w *Briefwechsel* II Ep 410). Erasmus preferred to attribute it to Faber, but he endorsed its views (cf Epp 1199:36–43, 1217:41–63), and in Ep 1156 he himself published an extensive summary of them. In fact, some statements reappear in his letters almost verbatim (cf the index and W.K. Ferguson's critical edition in *Opuscula* 338–61). The *Consilium* lends early expression to the irenic views which later became synonymous with the name of Erasmus, but as a concrete proposal it was soon rendered obsolete by Luther's own intransigence (cf Ep 1203:23–32) and by the condemnations of him issued by both the pope and the emperor (cf Epp 1192 n8, 1197 introduction, cf also Ep 1180 n3). Even the friendship between its co-authors eventually lapsed.

Johannes Faber of Augsburg (c 1470–1530) probably studied at the University of Freiburg from 1489 and apparently taught there in 1512 after having obtained a doctorate in theology in Italy. He visited Italy again in 1515 and travelled elsewhere with Maximilian I, whose funeral oration he delivered. But the centre of his activities was Augsburg, where he had been appointed prior of the Dominican house in 1512, being at the same time vicar-general for his order in Upper Germany. In 1524 his opposition to Luther forced him to leave Augsburg, and little is known about his remaining years.

Jakob Villinger (d 1529) of Sélestat attended the famous Latin school of his native town at the same time as Beatus Rhenanus, who was perhaps his kinsman. In 1500 he is first mentioned as a financial official in the service of the Hapsburgs, and in 1510 he was chief treasurer to Maximilian I. Working closely with the banking house of Fugger, he played a crucial role in the financing of the imperial election of 1519 (cf Ep 1009 n6), but afterwards his influence gradually declined. Erasmus published this letter in the *Epistolae ad diversos*; it did not, it seems, lead to any further connections with Villinger.

ERASMUS OF ROTTERDAM TO THE HONOURABLE JAKOB VILLINGER, TREASURER OF THE KING OF ROME AND SPAIN, GREETING

If I write to your Excellency, though unknown to you except by name, you must not ascribe this to effrontery on my part but to your universal reputation for courtesy. If you cannot acquit me of effrontery, your condemnation will, I know, be less severe, if you consider that my importunity has its source in good will. This bold step was forced on me by pressure from the excellent Johannes Faber, the bearer of this, or rather, by his merits. When I perceived his many excellent gifts – his rare integrity, learning of no common kind, keen judgment, incredible reliability and courtesy – I thought your Highness might even feel in my debt, if I brought such a man to your knowledge, or made him better known if you knew him already; for with your habitual uprightness and your devotion to the prince, you always view with special favour those whose virtues will be at the same time an ornament and a buttress to the throne. Among such, I give you my word, you may count this man, Johannes Faber, who is, if my judgment is worth anything, no ordinary credit to his order; without a word from me, once you have seen him at close quarters, he will commend himself to the full by his own gifts. As for myself, I do not see what I am in a position to offer, but at least I can offer loyalty and willing zeal, if in anything you wish to test the devotion of my humble self. Farewell.

Louvain, 3 October 1520

1150 / To Mercurino Gattinara — Louvain, 4 October 1520

This letter was published in the *Epistolae ad diversos*. It was written to introduce Johannes Faber (cf Ep 1149 introduction) to the powerful Gattinara. Erasmus' acquaintance with the chancellor was still slight at this time (cf lines 17–18), but in years to come he would find in Gattinara a faithful admirer and protector.

Mercurino Arborio di Gattinara (1465–1530) was descended from Piedmontese nobility. He studied law at Turin, counting Claude de Seyssel among his teachers. With the marriage of Duke Philibert of Savoy to Margaret of Austria, he entered her service and moved with her to the Netherlands when in 1507 she was appointed governor after the deaths of her husband and her brother. He became the president of Margaret's private council and in 1518, when Jean Le Sauvage died, Gattinara was hastily sent to Spain to succeed him as the grand chancellor of young King Charles. A year later he persuaded the young monarch to seek the succession of his grandfather Maximilian I as emperor.

TO THE HONOURABLE MERCURINO GATTINARA, CHANCELLOR OF CHARLES, KING OF ROME AND SPAIN, FROM ERASMUS OF ROTTERDAM, GREETING

My most honoured Lord, the bearer of this, Johannes Faber, a Dominican, is – as I have learnt from several intimate conversations with him – a man of many excellent gifts, sincerely religious, of sound judgment and wisdom, and of solid learning; all of which recommended him to the special esteem of the emperor Maximilian, who was not only a generous supporter but a strict judge of excellence of every kind. It is but fitting, I think, that as our present prince Charles has succeeded to his ancestral empire, he should also take up the inheritance of those ancestral virtues.[1] Furthermore, what this man asks for is not only perfectly equitable, but very easy to grant: that he should be allowed to retain under the reigning emperor the position he held under Maximilian.[2] That he should do so is, in my opinion, conducive to the public benefit of Christendom and to the dignity of the Holy Roman Empire. What this amounts to, you will learn better from himself.

I know that I have not the privilege of much acquaintance with your Highness, but my confidence stems in part from your known accessibility to all who have an honourable purpose of any kind; in part from my belief that as the successor of the excellent Jean Le Sauvage,[3] a man equal or more than equal to any distinguished station, you will so far reproduce his virtues as to be a supporter of my humble self, for I have no other aim in this life except to promote by my researches the glory of Christ and the cause of humane learning. If at any point I can do anything useful or ornamental for yourself or his Imperial Majesty, I will refuse nothing that I can fairly undertake. May I offer my best wishes to you, as a pattern of every excellence, and commend myself most warmly to your good will.

Louvain, 4 October 1520

1151 / To Erard de la Marck — Louvain, 8 October 1520

This is another letter of recommendation for the Dominican Johannes Faber (cf Ep 1149 introduction), published in the *Epistolae ad diversos*.

ERASMUS OF ROTTERDAM TO THE PRINCE-BISHOP OF LIÈGE, GREETING

Greetings, my most honoured Lord Bishop. The bearer of this letter, Johannes Faber, a distinguished theologian of the Dominican order, desires a recommendation to your Highness, and in my opinion deserves it. He was particularly appreciated by the emperor Maximilian on account of his unusual gifts, as a man of recondite learning, a ready and supple intelligence, a most happy style in writing, of easy and agreeable manners in society, and (so far as I can see) of complete integrity. He is viewed with favour by many of the German princes; and yet he has his ill-wishers, for excellence is never free from jealousy. He has a very great respect for your Highness, with whom he supposes me to have some influence. If I can do anything, I owe it entirely to your kindness, not to any merit of my own. I hope, however, that the man's good qualities will secure him what he asks, even if my letter fails to do so.

An annuity has been obtained from the prince,[1] through no efforts of my own; but this makes the generosity of an excellent prince all the more acceptable, and increases my debt to you and others like you. The unbridled licence of certain persons is being curbed,[2] I rejoice to say; but my joy is

19

Eras. Cardinali Moguntino.
post. Non. Octob. Anno. 1520.

S. P. Rx^me D. ac princeps longe clarissime, gestientem aduolare isthuc in tuos
complexus, hactenus aliquot negociola detinuerunt Verum si posthac coelum dabitur
commodius, adero breui Coloniae. Epistolam, quam tuae Celsitudini de Luthero
scripseram, editam doleo Ego certe bono animo scripseram, sed non in hoc scripseram
ut ederetur. Neque cuiquam a me fuit exemplaris copia. Utinam hic Joannes Faber ordinis Dominicalis Tuae Celsitudini tam esset commendatus, quam merentur hominis
eximiae dotes Ingenium promptum & expeditum, iudicium excussum, eruditio
solida et abstrusa, lingua felicissima, mores candidi facilesque Video tyrannidem
quorundam nimium succedere. Nec aliud mihi succurrit, quam precari ut res tota
cedat in gloriam Christi, utcunque cedet nobis. Bene vale meum decus. Louanii
postrid. Non Octobr. An. M. D. 20.

Erasmus Roterodamus
E. R. D. T. addictiss.

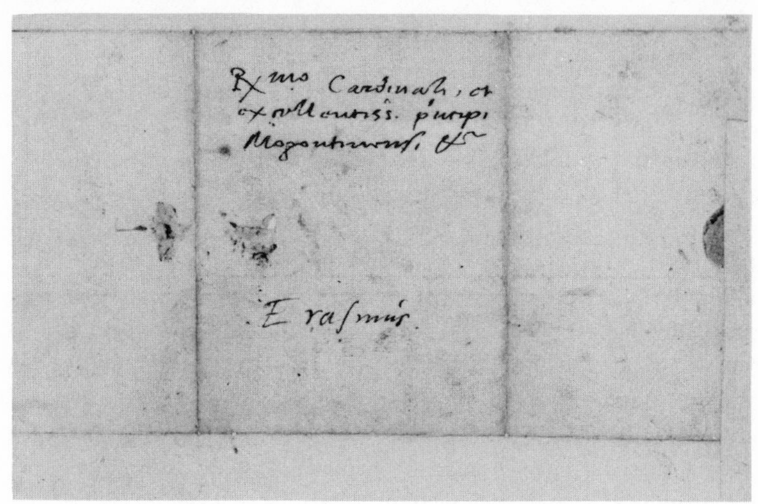

Rx^mo Cardinali, et
exellentiss. princ.
Moguntinensi &c

Erasmus

Letter from Erasmus to Albert of Brandenburg, Ep 1152
Öffentliche Bibliothek, University of Basel
Only the signature and address are in Erasmus' own hand.

tempered by the fear that this success will inspire those who hate humane letters to suppress studies of the better sort; for I will not say, to suppress the teaching of the Gospel. My respectful greetings to your Highness.

Louvain, 8 October 1520

1152 / To Albert of Brandenburg — Louvain, 8 October 1520

The original letter actually sent is preserved in the Öffentliche Bibliothek of the University of Basel, MS Fr.-Gr. I 19 f 19; only the signature and address are in Erasmus' own hand. Johannes Faber's desire for letters of recommendation (cf Ep 1149 introduction) offered Erasmus an opportunity to resume his efforts (begun with Ep 1101) at appeasing Albert after the unauthorized publication of Ep 1033. Erasmus had this letter printed in the *Epistolae ad diversos*; the important middle section (lines 8–13, however, blaming Hutten for the publication of Ep 1033, is not in the original and was not added until the *Opus epistolarum* of 1529. At the time this letter was written Erasmus' friendship with Hutten was still intact; cf Ep 1135 introduction.

ERASMUS OF ROTTERDAM TO THE MOST REVEREND CARDINAL OF MAINZ

Greeting, most reverend prelate and most illustrious prince. I long to hasten to your side, but hitherto some minor matters of business have detained me. After this, if the weather improves I shall shortly be in Cologne.[1] I regret that the letter[2] I wrote to your Eminence about Luther has been printed. I certainly wrote it with the best intentions, but with no intention of its appearing in print. Nor did I give anyone access to a copy of it. I had enclosed it in a sealed letter to Hutten, asking him, if he thought this a good plan, to give it to you at a suitable moment; but if not, to keep it to himself or destroy it. So I wonder all the more what purpose was served by having it printed, and by not delivering it to you. If this was an accident, it was a most unfortunate one; if bad faith, it was more than Punic treachery.[3]

I could wish that your Eminence might form as high an opinion of the bearer of this, Johannes Faber,[4] a Dominican, as his exceptional gifts deserve, – his ready and fluent wit, his experienced judgment, his solid and recondite learning, his excellent style, his easy open ways.

I see the dictatorial ways of certain people I could name are achieving undue success; nor have I anything to suggest, except to pray that the whole affair may tend towards the glory of Christ, whatever it may mean for us. Best wishes, source of such distinction as I have.

Louvain, 8 October 1520

Your Eminence's humble servant, Erasmus of Rotterdam

To the most reverend cardinal and right excellent prince-archbishop of Mainz etc

1153 / To Godschalk Rosemondt Louvain, 18 October 1520

Godschalk Rosemondt, of Eindhoven in Northern Brabant, matriculated at the University of Louvain in 1499 and remained there until his death in 1526. A doctor of divinity in 1516, he succeeded in 1520 to the chair of theology formerly held by Jan Briart of Ath. Like Briart he was a personal friend of the future Pope Adrian VI. His prominent position in the theological faculty notwithstanding, he retained an open mind towards humanistic studies and a measure of sympathy for Erasmus. This letter is addressed to him in his capacity as rector of the university for the winter term of 1520–1 (cf *Matricule de Louvain* III-1 637). It was published in the *Epistolae ad diversos*.

In preparation for a confrontation with the theologian Nicolaas Baechem Egmondanus, to be held in the presence of the rector, Erasmus launches an elaborate protest against his opponent, who had attacked him from the pulpit of St Peter's church on 9 and 14 October; cf Ep 1162.

ERASMUS OF ROTTERDAM TO THE DISTINGUISHED THEOLOGIAN GODSCHALK ROSEMONDT, RECTOR OF THE UNIVERSITY OF LOUVAIN, GREETING

I do not suppose it necessary that I should remind you of your duty. It is your business, not merely to ensure that you yourself hurt no man, but to see that no one else has licence to injure one of his colleagues. That Nicolaus Egmondanus, either on your instructions or under the authority of the papal diploma,[1] should frequently have attacked Luther is no business, I conceive, of mine. But he has gone beyond his instructions and against the intentions of the pope, who is so far from wishing any outsider to be involved that he desires to win over even men who have hitherto been on Luther's side; and he has delivered almost more attacks on me, attacks as false as they are undeserved. I therefore believe that both your official authority and your personal honour oblige you to restrain this man from this kind of impudent language, the more so as this is a very dangerous precedent, and in my opinion a very considerable disgrace to the faculty of theology and to this celebrated university; unless perhaps you hold your office not so much for the public benefit of this learned institution as for the private gratification of a few individuals. In that case, you are a servant and not a rector.

On St Denis' day[2] he was preaching in St Peter's, and had opened on the subject of charity,[3] when suddenly in the most indecent manner he began to direct his remarks against me (for by chance I had just entered), saying to my face among many other things that I was a keen supporter of Luther, while I have consistently maintained from the beginning,[4] what is indeed the truth, that I have no relations whatever with Luther except what any Christian must have with any other person of the same profession. The teaching of the Gospels and the apostles is what I recognize. Beyond that, there is no man of whom I think so highly that I should be ready to become a devotee of his opinions in all respects; so far am I from taking up at my own risk the defence of a man whose books I had not read, and the content of whose future writings was still quite unknown. As I had gone on record to this effect in published books,[5] no one could be in any doubt about it. The impression I received, when I sampled rather than read a few pages of Luther, made me admire certain gifts he has; from which I inferred that he has the power to become a notable tool in Christ's service if he would learn to use those gifts for the glory of Christ. When many outrageous things were commonly said of him, of which some were clearly false, I wished that, if he was not as good as he ought to be, he might be set right rather than destroyed.[6] If this is support for Luther, I openly confess myself one of his supporters even now, and in that sense, I suppose, the pope supports him and so do all of you, if you are truly theologians or even truly Christians; for the pope allows him a considerable space of time[7] and invites him to amend his ways. But of course the public, when they hear the word support, think it means merely that I share his opinions on questions where others condemn him.

He added something even more outrageous, that I had not merely supported Luther but had tried to defend him with all my might, and had held himself personally up to ridicule, great man as of course he is. The point was this. Luther had written[8] that the duty to confess one's sins to a priest extends, not to all capital sins but only to those which are manifest, meaning by manifest, of course, not such as are public knowledge but those of which the man who committed them is in no doubt: manslaughter, for example, and adultery and theft and (what has now ceased to be regarded as a sin) the spreading of malignant slanders.[9] In a letter written to the cardinal of Mainz[10] I mentioned a certain Carmelite who had brought up this remark of Luther's before a public audience as though he had maintained that it is permissable to say nothing in confession about certain criminal offences which you have committed. And I did not make that up; I was told of it by a leading member of your faculty,[11] whose name I will give you when necessary. To this day they declare that what I wrote was perfectly true.

Does a man defend Luther who points out that some passage in his works has been misunderstood? If it is a pious duty to refute Luther, surely it is needful to understand him first. I recognize that I have only moderate, indeed meagre abilities. I do not suppose myself learned enough to pronounce on another man's faith, nor do I claim sufficient authority to be willing to do so, nor have I sufficient leisure to find time to read Luther's books. Nor am I sufficiently deranged to be ready to approve or disapprove in a field so fraught with ill will, without carefully reading and rereading all his books, as they say, from cover to cover.[12] A hasty verdict is always condemned, and specially so when it points to a man's destruction. Nor, finally, am I fool enough to involve myself voluntarily in such an invidious business, to which I should be a slave for the rest of my life, when I am allowed to be a spectator at my leisure. Even so, I offered you my pen as an instrument,[13] if you would supply me with suitable arguments. Though what this business needs is not a practised pen, it needs good judgment and a faultless understanding of the Scriptures and above all a spirit free from all human weakness.

This being so, you can see how irresponsible it was of Egmondanus to say so much about me rather than about Luther. Nor was that enough. When he was reciting some articles condemned in the bull, and had reached the article on confession, he suddenly left the track,[14] as the saying goes, and observed, 'Some men say that this confession was instituted not by Christ[15] but by the Fathers. This,' says he, 'is false.' He was no doubt pointing at me, for in the defence in which I reply to Lee[16] I argue that this system of confession is of human origin; and argue it in such a way that Egmondanus will not prove me wrong, although I lay down nothing definite. Later, after exaggerating Luther's errors in the most outrageous language, he returned to his interrupted remarks about myself. 'Into such prodigious errors,' he says, 'has Luther fallen because of his passion for novelty.' And after ranting on about 'things new and old' until many people felt sick, 'Cleave to the old ways,' he says, 'shun that which is new, hold fast by the ancient Gospel,' hinting quite openly at my New Testament as though I had produced a modern Gospel, and had not rather given the old one new life and light. Need I say more? He waxed so warm during all this, this eminent man and pillar of religion, that his whole countenance displayed the fury in his heart. Nor would he have brought this raving madness to an end, had he not observed that some of his audience were laughing, some catcalling in indignation, some muttering in protest among themselves.

Was not this a pretty comedy, fit to be acted by such a mountebank in his white habit[17] in a sacred place and before a scholarly audience? But even this did not satisfy him, and the following Sunday[18] he said much the same again, after I had left for Antwerp,[19] adding a pretty postscript: 'These men too,' he says, 'will come to the stake one day, unless they desist.' I say nothing here of the nonsense he talked in the theology faculty, both in his ordinary courses and in public lectures, about Lefèvre and myself; you would have thought the speaker not a professor on his rostrum but some drunkard on a wagon.[20] You have enough sense to see how irresponsible all this was, even had I been a supporter of Luther; and this at a time when in any case it was permissible to support him, the case against him being not yet decided. As it is, no one has ever heard me even over the wine defending any of Luther's opinions, although there was no lack of eminent theologians[21] not afraid to affirm that there is nothing in Luther that cannot be defended out of standard authorities.

But what rouses their spleen is two letters,[22] one of which I wrote to Luther himself and the other to the cardinal of Mainz. But what, I ask you, is there in that first letter except some courteous advice? – and if only he had followed it, things would not have developed into this present uproar. But, they say, I told him in that letter that he had several supporters here.[23] And it is true that he had many, but their support was like mine: not that they approved everything he said, but much of it, and wished that the whole might prove pure and innocent. This I wrote with no intention of encouraging him to subversive writing, from which I deterred him in that same letter, but to persuade him to try and satisfy these people when he wrote by avoiding the faults I pointed out to him. Had he done this, he would have had the pope himself on his side. In my later letter, my only object is to have Luther dealt with on moderate principles rather than with violence and cruelty, and that he should not be handed over to the Jacobites[24] to do as they would with him, but be overcome by due process of law: for I observed that the cardinal was being urged by some people to suppress him by his own authority, when it was more expedient that he should be shown to be wrong. There were many other reasons why I thought this the right course, which it would be better to explain to you in person.

This implied no approval of what Luther writes, only disapproval of the method and procedure by which they were trying to suppress him. I am of the same opinion today. I never have approved, and I never shall, the suppression of a man in this way by public uproar, before his books have been read and discussed, before a man's errors have been pointed out to him, and before he has been refuted with arguments and with evidence from Holy Scripture. If this is support for Luther, he has the support of great men, but men of intelligence; who none the less have taken up the case against him. I will give you their names too, when it proves necessary. In fact, the pope seems to have lent him some support in the bull (although the bull smacks more of the cruelty of certain barefooted bullies than it does of our beloved Leo's kindly nature[25]); for he allowed him time,[26] and instructed them to preach against Luther, not with any intention that they should call him Antichrist, but to have them expound the opposite case with evidence from Holy Scripture if his teaching proves to have been erroneous. For this, I take it, is what preaching means to theologians, not climbing into the pulpit and calling someone a beast or an Antichrist at the top of your voice, which does not need a theologian, for any buffoon can do it.

That my design was not wholly bad may perhaps be proved by the outcome. It is not for me to give an account to God for what you have all done; whatever the plan on which the campaign was started, I pray that it may turn to the glory of Christ. My advice was,[27] that for a start Luther's books should be read with proper care; that he should then be refuted in published books and in disputations; that strife should be left out of it, and truth be the only consideration; and that the public should not be admitted to the theatre where this piece is being played. What really happened, you yourselves already know. With all these thousands of rabbis,[28] these thousands of men who think themselves gods, not one was found to give Luther a sober and scholarly reply, whether the reason was ignorance or laziness or fear, none of which should apply to a true theologian. Of those who have written against Luther hitherto, I know that you approve no more than I do: Silvester[29] first, then some Minorite,[30] the third anonymous,[31] although he flaunts the Dominican order and does not conceal his receipt of an annual salary from the king of France. There are others too,[32] whose pieces have not been published. I suppose the cardinal of Tortosa[33] to have been of the same opinion, when he gives instructions for Luther to be resisted on doctrinal grounds – that he should be put down, not by clamour and subversion but by all the resources of theology, if he will not or cannot be put right.

A noble nature desires to be instructed, and will not endure to be coerced. Merely to use coercion is for tyrants; merely to suffer it, for donkeys.[34] In war not every kind of victory is creditable. I was thinking of the honour and high standing of theology, I wished to see theologians win a true victory that should deserve applause. Had I been the keenest supporter of your faculty and Luther's most bitter opponent, what advice could I have given other than what I gave? The burning of his books will perhaps banish Luther from our libraries; whether he can be plucked out of men's hearts,[35] I am not so sure. This was possible, had my advice been accepted. This policy of mine may not have appealed to you, but it ought not to count against me, for I proposed it with the best intentions to a cardinal who had been good to me,[36] and to whom I thought I owed this as a duty. And I made my proposal in a sealed letter; the last thing I expected was that it would be published, and I am told it was published before it ever reached the cardinal. That it was not published just as I wrote it is clear from this, if nothing else, that in it (so they tell me) I refer to Luther as 'my friend,'[37] and those words were certainly never added by me; I should not have added them even had we been acquainted.

But to return to our Carmelite. There was much empty prating about avoiding what is new and clinging to the old, and how we must be suspicious of every new thing and cleave to the old and hold fast by the ancient Gospel. What all this meant puzzled the uneducated multitude; of the educated no one failed to see that he was attacking the ancient tongues and the New Testament as revised by me. In fact, as far as the tongues are concerned, he notably insults the pope, who is so keen to secure the teaching of Greek in Rome.[38] As for the New Testament, it should have been enough for him that Leo x approved the fruits of my industry,[39] for he wishes the pope's authority to be given supreme weight when it coincides with his own feelings. If the pope's authority means so little when he approves my work, why think it so important when he condemns Luther? – to say nothing meanwhile of this most foolish prating about old and new, at which most people could not refrain from laughing. He applies the word new to everything unfamiliar to him personally. He will call Hilary new and Cyprian new and Jerome new and Augustine new. Nothing is old except the opinions repeated parrotlike in the classroom, and the *Glossa ordinaria*[40] with the additions thereto. In reality, to him what is new counts as old, and the old is new. All I do is to restore the old; I put forward nothing new. People were disgusted at his brazen falsehoods when he said that Luther had derived those horrible errors of his from new texts, whereas it is from ancient authors that he has derived anything derivative in his work, as we are told by those who have read his books. But perhaps he will deny that he did me any wrong, because he did not mention me by name. At any rate he pointed to me so clearly that no one familiar with the subject could fail to identify me. Whatever Luther may deserve, I cannot think it right that clamour of this kind should be used to rouse the common people to violence, when the question could be dealt with between learned men.

But your decision on this point I leave to your own wisdom. In any case, to use a sacred building and the privilege of a sermon before a miscellaneous throng to publish lies about a man who has done nothing to deserve this – has in fact done good service – seems to me nothing but an attack on the authority of the pulpit, which ought to be as far above such pollution as the liturgy itself; it deprives the public of the benefit they have a right to expect and darkens the fair fame of this university. I think that all my labours deserve a very different reward. Suppose indeed that I were somehow at fault: even so, here I am, I can be refuted without risk, and I ought not to be falsely accused before the public. But this is a form of revenge of which Egmondanus is too fond already. Someone recounts perhaps over the wine what someone or other has said about him. Next day he takes his revenge in the pulpit; and as the bottle goes round next time he celebrates his victory to the plaudits of a few boon companions of the same kidney. Not but what, as far as the injury I have suffered is concerned, it does not much distress me. What you ought to consider is this: Can it be good for public standards that people should grow used to such scurrilities, for which they even acquire a liking as the poison spreads? Can it be for the general good of this university, in whose prosperity I take more interest perhaps than many who regard themselves as its keenest supporters? The generosity of our prince did not found this university that three or four men might live in it a life of ease, but that it might benefit all his dominions as a place where all honourable studies flourish.[41] No doubt, to please Egmondanus, *poetria*[42] must be sent packing (for so he calls what we call *poetice*; he knows so little of it that he cannot even get its name right); and a home will be found for the gentle art of slander, and a college founded for it too.

But I must not burden you, Rector magnificus, with a longer letter. If you silence this sort of stupid clamour, you will promote not my own interests so much as the public peace essential to our studies, the standard of public morality, and the authority of the pulpit, which is profaned by such foolish ranting, whatever may be thought of me personally. If you either will not or cannot do this, I may perhaps attempt a remedy of my own. I think I have suffered this man's frenzy long enough, and I know that none of you approve of it. But there are people who use his personality for their own ends, like those who take a crooked wedge to a crooked knot.[43]

I thought it better to send this in writing, as more convenient for us both. Tomorrow,[44] if you have the leisure and your health[45] permits, let us meet, and I shall have more both to say and to hear. Farewell.

Louvain, 18 October 1520

1154 / From Arkleb of Boskovice — Znojmo [c October? 1520]

This letter was written by the nobleman Arkleb of Boskovice (d 1528) while he occupied the office of governor (*supremus capitaneus* Allen line 73) in the margraviate of Moravia. His family estates also lay in Moravia and he was a member of the Utraquist church (cf Ep 1021:110–12). His purpose in writing this letter appears to have been twofold. In the first place, he wished to hear Erasmus' opinion concerning the Czech Brethren, who are mentioned in this letter not without sympathy (lines 19–21). Conceivably Arkleb was aware of, but had not been able to see, Ep 1039, in which Erasmus dealt with the religious situation in Bohemia. Secondly, Arkleb wished to state his favourable opinion of Luther, apparently believing that Erasmus was in general agreement with the German reformer (cf lines 33–4, n6).

The original letter, in the hand of a secretary but signed by Arkleb, is in the University Library of Wrocław, MS Rehdiger 254 no 36. It was first printed by Jean Leclerc in LB. An approximate date can be assigned from Erasmus' answer, Ep 1183, which seems to indicate that considerable time had passed between the visit of the two Czech Brethren (cf Ep 1039 introduction) and the arrival of this letter; see Ep 1183:7–8, cf Ep 1177 n5.

Greeting. Such, reverend and beloved Father, is the reputation of your name and works even in our country that, layman though I am, I have been moved by them these many years; and now the accounts of you that are on the lips of all learned men are such that it is small wonder if in this age of ours all Christendom is illuminated by the transparent sincerity of what you write, while at the same time the two famous kingdoms of my master, his most Serene Majesty,[1] the king of Hungary and Bohemia, learn their lesson. For these reasons I thought it would not be a waste of my time to send you the manifesto and rule[2] of life of the sort of men who in our country commonly call themselves Brethren.[3] They form an uncounted multitude of every class and of both sexes, which has made surprising progress and grows day by day. There are, it is true, some communities of priests and colleges of lawyers who launch attacks every day upon their way of life, who regard them as an evil and dangerous class of men and would reject and outlaw them for heresy, and who reduce them to great hardship in reliance on papal censures and sometimes on the authority of the crown; yet all the time their numbers are irresistible nor is their doctrine properly torn up by the roots. This seems to me not very surprising for this further reason, that we have in our midst few men who can answer their doctrines, which are drawn in any case from the Scriptures, with solid argument from Scripture, and these same men also cannot match them with evidence of a more holy way of life.

And so, dear sir, I thought it right to beg and pray you to spare a little time to read this manifesto, for you will contribute to the happiness and peace of many, and at the same time exercise your powers in what is clearly an important work of Christian charity. When you have a sufficient knowledge of the details, think the whole question over and consider it carefully; then decide what you think most useful and necessary, and finally show us the rules of Christian piety as they apply in our case too. For pray take it as certain that, whatever opinion you come to, people in my country will easily and gladly agree with you, and will value what you say far more than if one were to confront them with decrees of the supreme pontiff or any thunderbolts of opposition launched by men.

The books and pamphlets of Martin Luther are currently in circulation here and are much read,[4] along with yours. You would hardly believe their universal popularity, and almost none reject them except those who profess the religious life and follow the rules of the cloister. And though in some places they provoke not a little envy, some people none the less go so far as to conceal them – though that multitude does not really understand either the teaching or the purpose of the saintly man, and so are carried away by an unreasoning enthusiasm and even lay on him the charge of heresy.

But did he not trounce that Romanist[5] recently as he deserved – very much as long ago he had smitten other men of the same way of thinking? If, however, as one hears commonly in our country, it should be his misfortune to be condemned unheard (which God forbid), clearly his writings and his teaching cannot be confined, and will be valued none the less for that by everyone; in fact that would much more be the occasion for many and great evils. Who knows whether they may not some day rebound upon the heads of those responsible for them? Luther undoubtedly has friends, and there is a constant story here that one hears everywhere, that our doctors of divinity gladly admit and tolerate empty fables and the most foolish fabrications; but that if anyone meanwhile puts forward the gospel truth and the law of God in their purity, they all end by finding him an abomination, but he is thought particularly insufferable by those who arrogate to themselves as their own property the name of the religious life.

May God almighty bring it to pass, I pray, that the seed you sow,[6] which by God's help falls on good ground, may daily be multiplied and bring forth fruit as it deserves. Only do you keep on as you have begun, and write and tell us what you think will be the best course. Spread it abroad, scatter your seed, and in turn bring it aid and comfort, that the seed-corn of Christ, now trampled under foot and suffocated,[7] may under your guidance grow into a crop. Diligently as you have done this in the past, there is the future: do not falter now! Nor will your labour be in vain: first you will earn immortal honour among men, and then you will receive a reward worthy of your efforts.

It remains for me to ask you to take in good part my plan of writing to you and to put the best interpretation on it that you can; remember that I have had no other purpose in doing so except that under your lead and guidance I may learn to hold the right opinions and do all I can to set them before the eyes of other men. If you are willing to answer this – and do answer, I beg –you can send your letter to the Fuggers[8] in Augsburg; from there it will go to Vienna, and so reach me quite easily. Until then I commit myself to your prayers, most excellent and saintly Father. Farewell. From my castle of Znojmo.[9]

Arkleb of Boskovice and Czernahora,[10] lord of Vranov,[11] captain-general of the margraviate of Moravia, with his own hand

1155 / To Johann Reuchlin   Cologne, 8 November 1520

Since the spring of 1520 Erasmus had been planning to go to Germany, to work at Basel (cf Ep 1078 n15), visit Nürnberg (cf Epp 1085:12–14, 1095:163–75) and eventually proceed to Rome where he might have spent the winter (cf Ep 1143:89). In July he expected to leave soon (cf Ep 1123:18) and even hoped to see his friends in Saxony in the autumn (cf Ep 1119:24–8). But in early September he still tarried, partly for fear of the plague (cf Ep 1139:117–21). On 8 October he expected to leave shortly for Cologne, having been detained by business and bad weather (cf Ep 1152:3–5). In a letter dated from Basel, 8 November 1520, Beatus Rhenanus is quite specific in stating that Erasmus was in Cologne by the time Charles V was crowned King of the Romans in Aachen on 23 October (cf AK II Ep 749). There has been much speculation that Erasmus attended the ceremonies in Aachen in his capacity as a councillor, but neither he himself nor any contemporary seems to have said that he did. Had he in fact been there, this silence would be all the more surprising in view of numerous references to his presence at the meeting between Charles V and Henry VIII in July (cf Ep 1106 introduction; indexes CWE 7 and 8). It is true that Erasmus' visit to Antwerp late in September (cf Ep 1146 introduction) as well as his subsequent return to Louvain coincided with the presence of Charles V's court in these two cities, but when the monarch left Louvain on 8 or 9 October after a visit of eight days (Gachard II 28), Erasmus stayed behind. By then he expected to see Cardinal Albert of Brandenburg, a leading figure in the coronation ceremonies, at Cologne rather than Aachen (cf Ep 1152:3–5). His continued presence in Louvain is documented for 9, 14, and 18–c 20 October (cf Ep 1153 introduction and n44). In 1524 Erasmus recalled that he had spent three weeks in Cologne (cf Allen Ep 1512:18–19), a statement that bears out the assumption that he was there from c 23 October to c 13 November, while the imperial court, attended by many princes, remained in Cologne from 29 October to 15 November (cf Gachard II 28). On his return journey to Louvain he stopped in Aachen with his friend Leonardus Priccardus, whom he seems to have left on a Sunday (cf Ep 1169:15); if so, presumably 18 November.

On 4 November the papal envoys Aleandro and Caracciolo caught up with an evasive Frederick the Wise, elector of Saxony, and handed him a papal brief (cf Ep 1166:84–90) demanding the extradition of Luther to Rome and the burning of his books. On the following day, 5 November, the elector summoned Erasmus to a momentous interview. It was the first time that they met, and their talk inevitably turned to Luther. Erasmus reportedly told the elector that all Luther's sins consisted of striking out against the crown of the popes and the bellies of the monks. Frederick's chancellor, Georgius Spalatinus, who was present at the meeting, recalled that afterwards his master entertained Franz von Sickingen and Philipp von Dalberg for dinner. It can be assumed that Erasmus also stayed for the meal (cf Ep 1166:79–81). Afterwards Spalatinus walked him back to his quarters in the town house of count Hermann von Neuenahr. There Erasmus sat down and summarized for the benefit of the elector his views on the Luther question. He gave the sheet to Spalatinus on condition that it would be returned to him. On the following day Frederick rejected the papal requests. Despite Erasmus' precaution, his advice to the elector was sent to Luther (cf Luther w *Briefwechsel* II Ep 378) and printed soon afterwards at Leipzig as *Axiomata Erasmi Roterodami pro causa Martini Lutheri* (n p, n d; *Opuscula* 329–37). For details see Allen's headnote to this letter and Irmgard Höss *Georg Spalatin* (Weimar 1956) 180–3. Among some other encounters Erasmus is known to have had in Cologne the most important was no doubt with Aleandro (cf Ep 1167 n20). He also met Capito (cf Ep 1158 n5), Riccardo Sbruglio (cf Ep 1159), Hieronim and Jan Łaski (cf Ep 1242 n5), Rudbert von Mosham, and perhaps Mosham's master, Cardinal Matthäus Lang (cf Epp 1450, 1512), and Cardinal Schiner (cf n1).

There is no evidence of direct exchanges between Erasmus and Reuchlin since November 1517 (cf Ep 713). The testimonial for the aged scholar contained in this letter was probably prompted in part by his recent condemnation at Rome (cf n2), which put him in the same position as Martin Luther, whom Erasmus had just defended before Frederick the Wise (cf n5). This letter was printed in the *Epistolae ad diversos*.

ERASMUS OF ROTTERDAM TO THE HONOURABLE JOHANN REUCHLIN, GREETING

His Eminence the cardinal of Sion,[1] when I was dining with him lately, told me that you were dead. I was unwilling to believe this for, if true, it was such bad news for the humanities. But soon better tidings reached me from other people, which I hope will always be true, for you are a good scholar as well as a good man. You can see what a desperate tragedy is now being enacted, and what will happen in the last act is uncertain. Whatever the outcome, I pray it may tend to the glory of Christ and profit the truth of the Gospel. I would rather be a spectator of this play than one of the actors; not that I refuse to undergo some risk for Christ's sake, but because I see clearly enough that the business is too big for a small man like me. I only wish my ability to do what is best were equal to my desire. I do not doubt that you have reliable friends at hand to console you and relieve all your bitter feelings,[2] if you have conceived any, so that you need no consolation from me. You are too deeply seated in the affections of all men of good will to be torn thence by any insinuations on the part of the Jacobites.[3] The truth must win. And the unspoken judgments of men of good will[4] acquire an authority which will retain their force even among posterity.

It has always been my aim to separate the question of Luther from your cause, which is also the cause of the humanities,[5] because the confusion exposed us equally to the risk of sharing his unpopularity and did not assist him in the least. But others think differently. I too have been loaded by them with so much ill will, that I narrowly escaped being attacked myself by those creatures who have conspired against the humanities and the gospel teaching. There is nothing obscure in their intentions. To promote their success, they give their programme splendid names, they arouse the feelings of a most pacific pope to feather their own nests at his expense. I only wish the devotees of the humanities (for they are the target of these men) were as much united in defence of their honourable cause as these men are devoted to the overthrow of all civilized studies. If only our fellow Germans had accepted the civilized restraint which I have always urged them to adopt,[6] perhaps things would not have moved so far towards the edge of chaos.

That English bishop,[7] who is the best scholar of his nation and its most saintly prelate, is so much attached to you that he will not listen to anyone who praises you in moderation. He has it in mind to visit you next summer. Farewell, dearest Reuchlin.

Cologne, 8 November 1520

1156 / To Konrad Peutinger — Cologne, 9 November 1520

As early as 1512 Konrad Peutinger had written praising Erasmus' *Moria*, in a letter published by Reuchlin and therefore known to Erasmus (cf *Peutingers Briefwechsel* Ep 103). But despite some common friends (cf Epp 318:3, 611:54) they had apparently not corresponded, and they had not met until quite recently when the presence of the imperial court at Bruges brought them together (cf Epp 1129 n1, 1247:10–18; LP III 925). On 26 July Peutinger greeted Charles V in the name of the city of Augsburg.

This letter, published in the *Epistolae ad diversos*, was given to the Dominican Johannes Faber (cf Ep 1149 introduction) to serve as his introduction to the influential Peutinger (cf lines 118–22). It sums up the ideas Faber and Erasmus had developed together in the *Consilium* in such a way as to present Faber as its sole author. Erasmus makes it clear, however, that he fully endorsed the

Consilium and that was probably the point of the introduction, for Faber and Peutinger, who both lived in Augsburg, were bound to know each other. According to Ernst-Wilhelm Kohls (*Reichstag zu Worms* 422–4) Peutinger did not fail to act in Worms in the spirit of the *Consilium*; cf Ep 1217 n16.

TO THE DISTINGUISHED DOCTOR OF CIVIL AND CANON LAW, KONRAD PEUTINGER, COUNCILLOR OF HIS IMPERIAL MAJESTY, FROM ERASMUS, GREETING

I know, honoured sir, that you have no spare time for reading letters from casual correspondents, nor have I much more leisure in which to write; but I have been impelled to do so by Johannes Faber, a theologian of the Dominican order (though the nearer my acquaintance, the more I find him very unlike certain members of the same society). For besides solid learning, and integrity, and even charm of character, I have found him a man of no mean value in judgment and counsel. We have often discussed between ourselves a means of ending this sad business of Luther without a world-wide conflagration. For everyone who wishes well to the human race must be moved by the first scene of this tragedy, which may issue, unless steps are taken to prevent it, in a climax most dangerous to the Christian religion. Quite trifling beginnings have sometimes led to horrible divisions of the world; and in my opinion this is another situation in which Cicero's words are very true, that even an unjust peace is preferable to the most just war.[1] Already this sad business has been going on for longer than I could wish, and yet I still think the trouble can be cured; certainly it is easier to deal with now than if it were to progress still further at its first rate of increase. But if it is to be dealt with, I wish it might be in such a way that the evil is not suppressed at first only to break out more violently afterwards, as often happens when doctors drive out a fever with some medicine without first clearing up the veins in which the fever breeds or let a scab form over a wound before they have properly drawn off the infected matter.[2]

Some think it the best course to suppress the whole thing by rigorous measures; and Faber does not much dissent from this view, if he were not afraid that severity might be unsuccessful. He says that it is not enough to move forcibly in the direction in which one's wishes call one. There are so many things to be kept in mind. First, that in maintaining the dignity and authority of the Roman pontiff, who as Christ's supreme vicegerent rightly enjoys the support of all who sincerely love Christ, one must see to it that the gospel truth suffers no loss. Nor do I doubt that our Pope Leo is of this mind, and will not think he has deserved his glorious position until he has seen his Master's teaching flourish everywhere. Faber says the question is, not merely what do Luther and his supporters deserve, but what will contribute to the public peace of the whole world. It matters greatly who they are who take up the remedying of this disorder, and what remedies are used to heal it. For certain people are meddling in the business whose ill-judged enthusiasm can only embitter the situation and double the evil, as they think not of the pope's authority but of their own personal advantage; in a word, who act in such a way as to damage the humanities and the ancient languages no less than to injure Luther. Nor is it fair because of this business of Luther to do harm to studies which are quite innocent, and indeed deserve all reverence; and it is imprudent to involve more people without good reason in the Luther affair.

Faber used to add that one ought to consider from what source this entire tumult arose – from hatred of humane studies, which with malignant cunning they now try to drag into the Luther affair, obviously in hopes of finishing off both with the same weapon, although they have so little in common. As a result, he says, many are hostile to those who attack Luther, for no reason except that his enemies use the same underground tactics against the humanities; and hatred of such methods arouses many to support Luther who otherwise were not likely to be on his side. He demonstrated with considerable feeling how widely the infection of this evil has spread in how few years. He knew, he would say, the German mentality:[3] they are more easily led than driven, and the situation will be fraught with peril if their natural ferocity is excited by the cruelty of certain other people. 'We can see,' he says, 'how obstinate Bohemia still is, and things are not very different in the countries round.' Attempts have often been made to deal with this by force, and no progress has been made. One must use different remedies. Hatred of the name of Rome is deep-rooted, he thinks, in the minds of men of many nations, I suppose because of the stories commonly told of behaviour in the City, and through the wickedness of certain people, who conduct the pope's affairs sometimes to suit themselves rather than him, and act in their own interests and not his, while even the pope himself should do nothing, except in so far as his authority can serve Christ and Christ's flock.

I perceive that things have been handled hitherto in a very different way from that which commended itself to men of sense. Even if every word Luther wrote were true, he has written in such a way as to prevent the truth from doing any good. On the other side, those who have rushed into this business headlong have behaved before the public so badly, that even if they had an excellent case, they could only do it harm by the clumsiness of their support. Luther was told to change his style and moderate his violence;[4] he writes more ferociously, they tell me, every day. The other lot were told to conduct their campaign in a more moderate spirit; some of them have behaved in such a way that they seemed to be trying to beat him at his own game. But there is a class of men, my dear Peutinger, who grow fat by public mischief and only suffer in time of peace. They desire nothing more than a state of utter confusion in human affairs. Then 'in civil war, even Androclides is a general.'[5] It is the policy of those people that this question should be buried under atrocities rather than settled, nor do they care how much the world loses, provided they themselves gain.

In my opinion, no good will be done in this business, if those who have the matter in hand set before themselves any object other than the glory of Christ. There is a great rock here, which may be pounded on this side and on that, but removed from its place it may not be; and on it is written the mysterious words 'The Lord knoweth those that are his own.'[6] Whatever arises from the spirit of Christ cannot be suppressed by human measures, however hard it may be pressed; whatever is attempted by human policy is only temporary, however great the enthusiasm behind it, however much toil is devoted to fortifying it to last for ever. It is not for the likes of me to pass judgment on papal bulls.[7] But there were some people who found the bull brought recently by the papal nuncio to be lacking in that Christian charity proper to him who is the chief lieutenant on earth of Christ the all-merciful, and proper to the spirit of the present Pope Leo, who has shown himself so mild hitherto; this they ascribe not to him, but to those who have put him up to issue this. 'Even supposing,' says Faber,[8] 'that this severity is quite successful, that Luther's books are abolished and he himself removed from the scene, even so we must fear that the trouble would be exacerbated rather than ended, and that in place of one man removed more would arise, until the thing issued in open conflict and in schism.'

In short, these stormy times need some great master of exceptional skill to guide the course of the affair, so that it is neither overwhelmed by the billows nor driven on to a shallow shore; one who can avoid Scylla (as the saying is) and yet not be sucked into Charybdis,[9] who can cut down this evil monster in such a way that it does not grow afresh hydra-headed. Faber's plan therefore is to commit the whole question to arbitration by some learned and upright men who are above all suspicion;[10] not that the Roman pontiff should be reduced to the ranks and forced to do as he is told, but because he thinks that the pope, as a true Christian, will do this willingly and of his own accord, once he has realized that it will lead to the public peace of Christendom.

But the stages of this plan he will himself expound to you at greater length when he sees you; and if you approve of it, you will add the support of your own sound judgment, so that some decision may be come to in the Diet of Worms,[11] which all men of good will can approve. Though I do not doubt that Johannes Faber, the bearer of this, will be most acceptable to you for his own merits, yet I beg you earnestly to think yet more highly of him as a result of my recommendations. You can do nothing for your friend Erasmus which would oblige him more. Where now are those who complain that I am unfair to his order? Such a spirit, such learning, such a character delight me under any habit, no matter what. Farewell.

Cologne, 9 November 1520

1157 / To Justus Jonas — Cologne, 11 November 1520

Of various friends and admirers in Erfurt Jonas was the one most dear to Erasmus' heart (cf Epp 876, 1202, 1211 introductions). This short letter to him, which shows Erasmus' desire to keep in touch with the Erfurt humanists, was printed in the *Epistolae ad diversos*.

ERASMUS TO JODOCUS JONAS, GREETING

The letter attacking Lee[1] I have decided, my good friend, to suppress, even if he does deserve more severe treatment; and this for various reasons, but principally in order not to provide him with a party of supporters, since even my opponents do not recognize his existence. Girolamo Aleandro has arrived,[2] a fairly good scholar in the three tongues, but made, it is clear, for troubles of this kind. He has burnt several of Luther's books,[3] first in Louvain at the moment of the emperor's departure, then again at Liège, and he is preparing to do the same in Cologne tomorrow. They are as indignant with me as they are with Luther himself, supposing me the only obstacle which prevents Luther's complete and universal destruction; whereas for many reasons I have never let myself be mixed up in the Luther affair. My heart is set on the humanities, it is set on truth as truth is found in the Gospel; and there I will pursue it in silence,[4] if I may not do so openly. One day Christ will grant us better times.

I have written these few lines, my dear Jonas, rather than write nothing, since a letter-carrier presented himself,[5] who was once a companion of your wanderings. Give my warmest greetings to Kaspar Schalbe, Draconites, Hessus,[6] and my other friends.

Cologne, Martinmas 1520

1158 / To Johannes Oecolampadius — Cologne, 11 November 1520

This letter was published in the *Epistolae ad diversos*. Oecolampadius was now in the abbey of Altomünster (cf Ep 1102). He had written Erasmus a personal letter, accompanied by a longer statement (cf lines 3–4), neither of which is extant. The longer text probably offered a careful explanation for his hard-won decision to enter the monastery. An analogous statement had been sent to Pirckheimer, but is also missing; cf Ernst Staehelin *Das theologische Lebenswerk Johannes Oekolampads* (Leipzig 1939) 114. It is clear that Oecolampadius had read Erasmus' Ep 1102, especially the last sentence, as a veiled criticism of the monastic way of life and his own decision to adopt it. Although often critical of monasticism, Erasmus had intended nothing of the kind when he wrote Ep 1102 and he now hastened to reassure Oecolampadius.

ERASMUS OF ROTTERDAM TO THE WORTHY DR JOHANNES OECOLAMPADIUS, GREETING

Your missive, your treatise rather, I have not yet read right through, and your sealed-up letter (which gave me very great pleasure) must be content with three words in reply, as I am extremely busy. Heaven forbid, dear brother, that I should seek to deter anyone from the religious life, let alone you, who are old enough to know your own mind and were not ignorant what that life is like.[1] At that stage I wished sincerely that whatever you undertook should be successful, for I suspected from your letter[2] that you had something of the sort in mind; and now I am delighted that all goes well. What a truly blessed principle of life, and in the spirit of the Gospel, to devote yourself seriously to clearing and liberating your mind of all worldly desires, that it may be free to take wing and follow the summons of Christ!

As for the Pharisees,[3] you go too far. I meant the men who under the pretext of religion attack the religion that is truly such, and give me so much tedious extra work by the strange tricks they play. I am so tired of them that I would gladly settle, if I might, in some deserted place; and so I would, if my physical weakness did not prevent it. So pray drive that suspicion entirely out of your mind. Nor have I any doubt that in your wisdom you have chosen a community that is pure and sincere.

Your *Metaphrasis* on Ecclesiastes has come,[4] but I have not read it yet. In my next letter I will tell you what I think of it. Capito[5] is the complete courtier,[6] and is getting on very well; but I am a little afraid that he may be enticed away by this world, which is as perverse here as it has ever been anywhere. I can do nothing for the moment except hope for the best. Farewell, dearest brother in Christ.

Cologne, Martinmas 1520

1159 / To Riccardo Sbruglio — Cologne, 13 November 1520

Sbruglio, a little-known humanist from Friuli, went north to seek his fortune as a neo-Latin poet. He produced verses for many occasions and was admired by some and despised by others, but failed to gain a permanent footing. In 1507 he attracted the attention of both Maximilian I and Frederick the Wise of Saxony. On his wanderings he had met many friends of Erasmus, including Pirckheimer, Zasius, and Bonifacius Amerbach, who showed appreciation for him. Nothing is known about his visit to Louvain (cf line 8), which preceded his meeting with Erasmus at Cologne (cf Ep 1155 introduction). Sbruglio succeeded in obtaining this flattering letter, which was published without delay by Adrianus Cornelii Barlandus in his collection of Erasmus' letters (cf Ep 1163 introduction), and subsequently in the *Epistolae ad diversos*.

ERASMUS TO HIS FRIEND RICCARDO SBRUGLIO, GREETING

He would seem hardly courteous who was angry with a friend for loving him even to excess! And so, most learned Sbruglio, I am bound to forgive your verses for the falsehoods they contain about me, elegant indeed but affectionate to a fault. Nor do I doubt that the open friendliness of your poems is matched by the same quality in your heart. Your happy vein in this regard, as genuine as it is fruitful and pleasing, I first learnt to know from the poem you left behind at Louvain,[1] which you threw off, like this, extempore. Each of us had already learnt to know the other's mind, though neither yet knew the other by sight. But the acquaintance which arose between us in Cologne made no small addition to my opinion of you, though meetings often bring with them some loss of esteem.

But, my dear Sbruglio, hold! Love your Erasmus as immoderately as you please, but pray moderate your language. You know that old maxim of the Roman lawyers:[2] 'Not everything, not everywhere, and not from everybody.' It is not unpleasant, to be sure, to receive praise from a man who is praised himself;[3] but it is not expedient to proclaim in any casual company what your affection for me has dictated to your heart, not to say for the moment that some of it was quite unsuitable. The man who suppresses what good qualities we have lays on us less of a burden than he who ascribes to us what we have not. Sometimes under the gadfly promptings of affection you hold forth with all your powers and fight with every sort of weapon against those who think Erasmus less important than you with your kind heart would have them think him. Consider: what is the result, except to rouse them to speak more harshly of me than before, and lay a burden of ill will upon me, some of which perhaps may brush off on you? I have long grown used to criticism, and no less am I sated with praise and glory. Admitting openly that I know nothing, I do what I can. If my attempts are unsuccessful, at least in honourable and difficult enterprises one is normally given credit even for the attempt. If my foot slips, I have my consolation: I am a man, I share this fault with all my fellows. If anyone does better, I do not grudge this addition to the public stock of learning; nor do I think it to my discredit if, after I have outstripped many men myself, someone arises who in turn can outrun me. It will not make me one hair's breadth[4] the better scholar, if I claim to know everything; nor am I any the less learned if, with Socrates, I profess to know nothing at all. Though, when all is said and done, how small a part of knowledge is comprised in all we know! for of what I know myself I will not speak.

I have acted out my play almost to the end, and it only remains to add the 'Farewell, and give me your applause.' I rejoice to see men arising here and there who will put my reputation, if I have any, in the shade.[5] I pray for the success of all of them, and especially for you, my warm-hearted Sbruglio, and I shall hope to see you gilded by the sun of our emperor's favour. Farewell.

Cologne, 13 November 1520

1160 / To Paulus Ricius — Cologne, [November] 1520

Erasmus had met Paulus Ricius in 1506 in Pavia and again in 1517 at Antwerp (cf Epp 548–9): now they apparently met again at Cologne. A converted Jew, Ricius had been appointed physician to the late Emperor Maximilian and was now serving Prince Ferdinand in the same capacity. Of a possible exchange of letters between Ricius and Erasmus this is the only one known today. It was first printed by Adrianus Cornelii Barlandus at the end of the final sheet of his collection of Erasmus' letters (cf Ep 1163 introduction), which was published in December 1520. It was then reprinted in Erasmus' *Epistolae ad diversos* and in the *Opus epistolarum* of 1529, where the place and year date were added for the first time.

Ricius was involved in more than one controversy, but Erasmus' references to a book on the Cabbala, written in defence of a friend against his detractor (cf lines 14–15), point to Ricius' *Apologeticus adversus obtrectatorem Cabalae sermo*, which is a defence of Reuchlin's study of the Cabbala against Jacob of Hoogstraten's *Destructio Cabalae* (Cologne 1519; cf Ep 1006 n13). Erasmus may have been shown this text at Cologne in manuscript, as the earliest known printed edition dates from 1523 (*Apologetica ... oratio* Nürnberg: F. Peypus 1523). The text was later incorporated in Ricius' *De coelesti agricultura* (Augsburg: H. Steiner 1545, ff 70–85).

ERASMUS OF ROTTERDAM TO PAULUS RICIUS, THE DISTINGUISHED PHILOSOPHER, GREETING

Your book, most learned Ricius, has made me a little more well disposed towards this business of the Cabbala, though before that I was not notably hostile,[1] for I think one must excuse it as a human failing, if someone is prejudiced in favour of a subject to which he has devoted a great deal of time and in which he knows he is in a specially strong position. In any case, how insufferable those people are who persecute with such bitter and undying hatred whatever they cannot understand! Nor had I only one reason for liking the book. The learning, which you always show, was at this stage no surprise. What I found most enjoyable was the sincerity and clarity with which you lay the whole topic open so that a blind man could see it clearly. I enjoyed that spirit of yours, formed for the Graces and for friendship, here zealously defending the innocence of a very good scholar against the most shameless and malicious attacks. And I enjoyed the moderation, so worthy of a complete and genuine philosopher like yourself – boldly defending your friend, but in such a way as to refrain from abusing your adversary, for you were thinking more of what was unworthy of you than of what he deserved. You were short: and that I was rather sorry for, for busy as I am, I read your book right through and was still hungry for more. Farewell, my learned friend.

Cologne, 1520

1161 / From Ulrich von Hutten Ebernburg, 13 November 1520

This letter follows Ep 1135 and like it was never published by either Erasmus or Hutten. There is no indication that Erasmus ever received it; in fact Ep 1225:302–6 suggests that he did not. It was first printed by J.J. Moser in his *Patriotisches Archiv für Deutschland* 7 (Mannheim-Leipzig 1787) 23–32. Moser had before him a copy of what appears to have been the original letter, written by a secretary, with signature, postscript, and address in Hutten's own hand. There is no trace today of either the original or the copy.

Hutten expresses his hope that Charles v, even though at present unduly influenced by Aleandro (cf lines 77–83), might still come to support, and even take the lead in, an armed struggle against the church (cf lines 38–40, Ep 1129 n7). In September 1520 Hutten had defended his cause in open letters to Charles v, Albert of Brandenburg, Frederick the Wise of Saxony, and the German nation (cf Hutten *Opera* I 371–419) and in his other writings of this period (cf n12, n16) he also attempted to exploit the traditional antagonism between emperors and popes. Hutten is still convinced of Erasmus' sympathy (cf lines 40–2) and genuinely concerned for his safety. In a bitter letter of 22 February 1521 he was going to blame Reuchlin for not following Erasmus' example of ostensible neutrality (RE Ep 299). On his part Erasmus continued to avoid any direct censure of Hutten; cf Epp 1184:26–8, 1217:25–6, 1244 n5.

TO ERASMUS OF ROTTERDAM FROM ULRICH VON HUTTEN, GREETING

Whatever it may be, dear Erasmus, that I have set out to do at such personal risk in this moment of time, may it end in disaster if I am not more concerned for your safety, best of men, than for what may happen to me. You can see well enough what things are heading for: I cannot think what you are doing in the place where our party is more unpopular than anywhere else,[1] and orders from Number Ten[2] are active now, I hear, frightfully. They have burnt Luther's books: do you think you can stay in peace where you are? – as though his condemnation were not a precedent for your own case, or one could suppose that the men who have condemned Luther would spare you. Escape, man, escape! – we want you safe. I myself am in plenty of danger, infinite danger I dare say, but I can match it with a spirit that is hardened to danger, and I have private means to support me; your case is quite different. Escape, dear Erasmus, escape while you can, in case, if things go wrong (which God forbid), it may by then be no longer open to you and you may be obliged to say what no wise man ever said: 'I never thought it could happen here.'[3] Those fellows are already clamouring openly that it was you began it all, that you were the fountain-head of all Leo's present troubles; you showed us the way (they think), you taught us, you first kindled men's minds with zeal for liberty, you are the man on whom the rest of us depend. Of course this isn't true; but you know the kind of men we are dealing with, and you ought not to harbour such hopes as might make you think you are safe where you are. In this business liberal studies have got a bad name; how much worse the man who introduced them, who filled Germany with sound learning? Why, this letter from the cardinal of Tortosa[4] to Number Ten, taking him severely to task for suffering you, the master-mind of all this, to remain in Germany: what weight do you give to that? I think you simply must escape – if you are not concerned for your own fate, then to save the humanities from losing their great leader and literature from becoming a fatherless orphan. If you still had any doubts, you ought to learn from Aleandro[5] at any rate that there is nothing we can trust; who would have thought he could be hired with money from the priests to fight against us? And yet he is just now the most bitter opponent we have. As for you, you have treated the pope gently all these years and buttered him up and sung his praises; and what have you got for it except that he hates the thought of you and longs for your destruction? And he will wish still more he could destroy you, when he sees armed forces mobilizing against his insane proceedings. It would have happened already if Franz's policy[6] had not been to try the king first, hoping that the king would do this himself, or at least connive at our doing it. And I think it as good as done, unless that Slavonic scoundrel[7] turns everything upside down by offering the crown to

Caesar,[8] Luther and myself being demanded as the price.[9] So get yourself out of there; for I have to take to the sword, of which, that you may not suffer from it, I give you fair warning now.

If you do not approve my design,[10] yet the reason why I attempt all this you cannot disapprove – the liberation of Germany; for then liberal studies will flourish and the humanities will be held in honour. 'This is a hard thing to achieve,' you say. Very hard indeed, but the attempt is honourable whatever the outcome, and to fight with the outcome of events is not my affair. Let fortune have the last word; that is where I shall spend all my efforts heart and soul. If I hit the right moment, who can stop our project from going through as we desire? If it should turn out otherwise, the pope is not enough of a statesman to have any hope of putting out this blaze once we have lit it. Things will catch fire all right in your part of the world for all their efforts, even if they are too strong for us; for out of our ashes will spring fresh champions of liberty still more desperate than we are. I know this will happen, and it makes me all the more active now; I mean to try everything, I shall seize every chance wherever I can, I shall leave nothing untried; and no threats, no perils are enough to deter me. My heart is set on liberty and I will not suffer it to be diverted. How could I endure it when I see such dishonour, such slavery in store for me unless I rebel? Am I to cringe to these epicene priestlings? Must I keep my hands off these mincing sodomites and worship these lecherous popes and run errands for men who are utterly worthless, when I know how my forefathers refused to do the like for the greatest emperors and my nature was not made to bear such indignities? I will make all split first.

And to leave you in no doubt of the spirit in which I act, I am now convinced that this is the moment of destiny, when one of my name is in peril for his country's sake; and this purpose is so fixed in me that I think no death more glorious than to die for the liberty of us all. Forward then, all citizens of good will! Stand up, you who love your country! Let us drive those vile despots out of Germany, let us break out of our dishonourable servitude and throw off their shameful yoke. Let us not forget that we are Germans, and let there be no one among us who would care to live if he cannot live in liberty. We shall be cut off from some things, not everything, if a proclamation by the king intervenes,[11] as these men hope; for he will not succeed in stopping up all our places of refuge and depriving us of all support. But I think he has for the moment been swayed by very bad advice, and will not maintain even this position very long. Soon he will come to his senses, and not let himself for ever be betrayed by the advice of these Romanizing spaniels, partly because it is easy to show him by countless examples that nothing in Rome can be trusted,[12] partly because the time seems to be at hand when this tyranny shall be done away with. It may be impossible for this to be achieved by me, but it can make a start with me; and then what becomes of those people who would bid me hold my peace? Is it holding one's peace for a brave man, such as I strive to be, to submit to despicable servitude, and that at a time when this humiliation has reached its peak; when they think they can do exactly as they please; when everything sacred and profane is in godless confusion as never before; when lies and chicanery are a mark of kings and popes, rapine and robbery are actually sanctified? From these practices you have tried to wean them away with fair words; your attempt was well meant, but their lunacy was too much for you, and your flattery got you nowhere. Has not the time now come to give up all hope of cure, of which they are perfectly incapable? to cast out these stinking carcases and burn them and make an end? Suppose we try by force of arms to give these furies a taste of their own medicine, will someone insult our courage and label it rashness? Let him! We shall think it glory; not that glory is what we seek, it is the zeal for liberty that brings us gladly face to face with danger. We cannot be slaves; we can hardly endure to see others in Germany living like slaves; and it may be we shall bring them their freedom against their will. I have written this to you at such length to make you realize, when you know what is brewing here, how far from safe you must be where you are, where resistance to the long-delayed resurgence of liberty is at its greatest and slavery has its deepest roots.

My advice therefore is, not to value that precious ease of yours where you are, so highly that you think you will remain in peace in a position of great peril. Your friends in Basel are longing to see you;[13] what holds you from moving to join them as soon as you can? – especially as nowhere do men enjoy more liberty[14] (that has always been their nature) and at the moment moreover they are wonderfully excited by what Luther writes[15] and by a poem I have written in German.[16] In a word, get out of where you are, and have the sense to avoid an obvious risk.

Such is my advice to you; and I have been persuaded to offer it, since they themselves could make no impression on you, by the great affection of our common friends. Give some weight to the prayers of us all, even if you have no care for your own safety; you will do yet another public service. Yield to our appeals, though you despise their threats; give way before your friends' desires, if you do not yield to the violence of the enemy. I cannot believe Erasmus values Louvain so much, that for its sake he would deprive the whole of Germany of what it gets from him; it would set too high a value on your love of one town, to put it above the wishes of your whole people. Do not forget that poison works in secret; remember there are daggers, though you do not fear what you can see. This is what those who love you urge upon you; do, do give way before their appeals, and save yourself for the public good. And so, my very best wishes.

From the Ebernburg,[17] by a secretary, 13 November 1520

What you have done for my servant, please consider as done for me. I will repay you. I shall not send him back from here, for I cannot spare a servant I can trust.

To Desiderius Erasmus of Rotterdam, the great Christian theologian and his beloved friend, greeting. At Mainz, or Cologne,[18] or wherever he may be

1162 / To Thomas More — Louvain, [c November?] 1520

This letter gives a spirited account of a confrontation between Erasmus and Nicolaas Baechem Egmondanus before the rector of the University of Louvain, Godschalk Rosemondt (cf Ep 1153 introduction and n44). Printed in the *Epistolae ad diversos*, it was no doubt composed with a wider public in mind; Thomas More, to whom it is addressed, need not have been told at length an episode of which he was himself a protagonist (cf n24). Erasmus also described the confrontation with Baechem in Ep 1173:29–109.

ERASMUS OF ROTTERDAM TO THE RIGHT HONOURABLE THOMAS MORE, GREETING

The story that has reached you about my little dispute with Nicolaus Egmondanus in the presence of the rector of this university is not wholly true, and yet not quite devoid of truth; such is the way of rumour, which likes to enhance the facts and tell the story with a difference. Nor are he and I so much at variance that I would willingly see him the victim of false reports. So here is the true story, since I see that in your part of the world you are so idle you can find time to follow the silly things we do here.

I had written to the rector of the university to protest against the attacks made on me by Egmondanus in the pulpit,[1] and he wrote back that if I was prepared to listen in person while he did his tale unfold, we might perhaps come to some agreement. I replied that I had no objection, though well aware that no lasting good would come of it.[2] So we met, and the rector took the chair, with me on his right and Egmondanus on his left. This arrangement was not without point. He knew Egmondanus' temperament, and of me he had quite the wrong idea: he thought I was capable of losing my temper. So he sat between us, to keep the combatants apart, in case our contest of words should warm up into assault and battery. Thereupon the rector opened the subject in a few words, and then, with a countenance of wonderful and comical gravity Egmondanus began: 'I have spoken ill of no man in my sermons. If Erasmus thinks he has suffered an injury, let him declare it, and I will answer him.' I asked him whether he thought there could be a more atrocious injury than to traduce an innocent man in a public sermon with a string of lies. That roused him at once; dropping the mask he had assumed, and almost purple in the face (his face was red already, for it was after dinner), 'And why, pray,' says he, 'do you traduce me in your religious books?' 'In my books,' I replied, 'your name is never mentioned.' 'Nor has yours,' he retorted, 'ever been uttered in my sermons.' I denied that my books were religious books, for in them I sometimes set down my own imaginings and write whatever comes into my head – a thing, I added, which is not allowed in the pulpit. 'Besides which,' I said, 'I have written far less about you than the facts warrant. You have told lies about me in public, calling me a supporter of Luther,[3] whom I have never supported in the sense that the public reads into your words and you mean yourself.' By this time he was not merely excited, he was like a madman. 'No, no,' he shouted, 'you are behind the whole lot. You are the slippery customer, the double-dealer; you can twist everything somehow by the tail.' And he spewed up, rather than uttered, much more of the same kind, which glittering bile[4] at the moment put into his head.

I felt my own hackles rising, and had already let out a word which was the forerunner of rather intemperate language, not exactly 'Thou fool'[5] but something of the sort that would smell worse than it sounds. But I controlled myself instantly, thinking it better to respect my own health (for I was poorly) and that of the rector, who was also in the doctor's hands;[6] besides which, it seemed both foolish and undignified to answer a madman in his own language. So I turned to the rector with a smile and said, 'I could bring evidence of his outrageous calumnies, and I could well return his abuse. He calls me slippery; I could call him in my turn a fox. He calls me a double-dealer; I could call him doubly double. He says I twist everything by the tail; I could reply that he poisons everything with his tongue. But all this is unworthy of grown men – almost of women too.[7] Let us resort to argument. Imagine I …' Here he burst in at once with his loud bargee voice: 'I do not imagine, I will not imagine; I leave that to you. You poets are all imagination, and all falsehood.' By this time I felt more like laughing than losing my temper. 'If you are not prepared to imagine,' I said, 'then grant …' 'I grant nothing,' he said. 'Suppose,' I said, 'that it is so.' 'I won't suppose,' quoth he. 'Assume it is so,' I tried. 'I won't assume anything.' 'Then let it be so.' 'But it is not so,' he said. 'Then what do you want me to say?' I asked. 'Say that it is so,' he said.

The rector could hardly persuade him to let me speak. 'Suppose it is true,' I began, 'that in my books I have set down some things otherwise than I should have done, yet it was not your business, in order to satisfy your spleen, to abuse the sacred authority of church and pulpit and the credulity of simple folk. You could have attacked me in print in your turn, you could have laid a formal complaint against me. As it is, you injure not simply me, but this whole university, the whole public, the sanctity of the pulpit, which is reserved for far other themes than this.' Whereupon, being gravelled for an answer, he tried, as usual, a new tack. 'Ah,' he says, 'don't you wish you enjoyed a position of such authority?' 'What position?' I replied, 'the right to preach?'[8] He nodded. 'Well,' said I, 'I have preached before now, and I think I could still say things more worth hearing than what I hear you sometimes produce.' 'Then why don't you?' he asked. 'Because,' I replied, 'I think I make a better use of my time by writing books; though I would not undervalue the work you put into your sermons, if only you would teach what contributes to amendment of life.' At this point he recalled my having said in my letter to the rector,[9] which he had seen, that it was monstrous to give this treatment to a man in my position who had done no wrong and had positively done good. 'Where,' says he, 'have you done good?' 'Many people agree,' I replied, 'that I have not given bad service to the cause of good literature.' 'Ah!' he retorted, 'so you call it, but it's not good; it's bad.' 'And in the Scriptures,' I added, 'I have made many corrections.' 'Not corrections,' he said; 'corruptions.' 'Why then,' I replied, 'has the pope approved them in a formal brief?'[10] 'Brief, indeed!' he snorted. 'Who has ever seen your brief?' (suggesting that I had forged it). 'What do you want?' I asked. 'Am I to hawk my brief around from man to man or pin it up in the market-place? I have shown it to Atensis; Dorp has seen it.' 'Dorp, indeed!'[11] says he, and was about to add something uncomplimentary about him too, but the rector gave him a look that shut him up. 'You shall see it too, if you wish,' I went on. 'I don't want to see anything of yours.' 'Then how dare you condemn it?' I said. 'How is it that when he condemns Luther[12] the pope carries so much weight with you, and when he approves something of mine he is lighter than a feather?'

So he dropped that topic, and began to recall, as though to appeal to the emotions in the best rhetorical style, all the honours which the theologians in Louvain had lavished on me before my attacks on them began. 'We did all we could for you,' he said. Of the venomous attacks with which Egmondanus had torn me to shreds even before I set foot in Louvain,[13] not a word. I replied that it was not my custom to make light of kindness done me by anyone, but that hitherto I had not experienced much from the theological faculty. At this he cooled down somehow. 'True,' he said, 'there was little we could do.' 'In that case,' I retorted, 'you must not expect gratitude for what you have not done. What you could do to hurt me, I know from experience; of kindness I have received nothing, except that you have invited me to some of what you call your acts,[14] and to certain solemn feasts which no one dislikes more than I do; so far am I from thinking myself much indebted to you under this head. You took the first steps in offering me friendship; this I have never sought, but equally I have never offered any excuse to break it off.'

These words reminded him of the reconciliation arrived at between us,[15] in which he was the only person not yet really content, though nobody had done more damage by his stupidity than he. They think it the last word in Christian behaviour that people should go to them on bended knee even after intolerable ill-treatment, so far are they from making it up of their own accord or doing good to the man who has wronged them, as the Gospel teaches us to do.[16] 'That reminds me,' he said, 'you make much of an agreement supposed to have been made between us.' 'Well, was it not made?' I replied. 'Did we not have a splendid wine-party in Falcon College?'[17] (This dinner had cost the principal[18] of the college a pretty penny. And as it was a Wednesday, as much fish had been cooked for Egmondanus alone as would have been enough for four prize-fighters.) 'Surely peace was proposed, on the basis of an amnesty, all grievances on both sides to be wiped out?' He denied this emphatically, though it had taken place before so many witnesses. Here the rector interrupted, and called the dispute to order by making him admit that a certain degree of agreement subsists between all Christians; but it was said that peace on that occasion was not ratified at all points.

I asked with a smile how many pints were required to conclude a binding peace in the theological domain; for a simple soul like myself supposed that peace could be concluded between men of good will with no liquor at all. This put him again on another tack. 'That reminds me,' he said, 'you hold us up to ridicule with the monstrous suggestion that we drink too much.'[19] I demanded when it was that I had said he drank. 'You put it in writing,'[20] he replied, 'that I was tipsy after a heavy dinner; and how does that differ from calling me a heavy drinker?' 'When I wrote that,' I said 'your name was not mentioned, and I told it on other men's authority; for your Carmelite friends' (and I used the second person singular) 'were saying by way of excuse that no one should take too seriously what you had said when tipsy after a heavy dinner.' 'Your friends!' he snorted, furious no doubt at my not using the second person plural. 'And suppose I *had* given your name,' I went on, 'why was it so criminal if I took the liberty of reporting what you had had the face to say in public? As it is, I suppress your name out of respect for you, and give a courteous report of outrageous behaviour. You had said about Lefèvre and me,[21] that we might be fighting one another now, but the time would come when we should be fighting in the depths of hell.' 'Ah,' said he, 'you heard that from other people.' 'Yes, and more than one,' I said, 'but dare you deny you said that?' He was silent; and I had a new cause for astonishment – the man was ashamed of himself.

He then proceeded to range over a new field, and declared he would never cease declaiming against Luther until he had put an end to him. I replied that he was welcome to declaim until he burst, provided he stopped ranting against me; what I resented was not his abuse of Luther, but of myself, and that he could go on attacking the other man if he had such a passion for it, though he would gain nothing by it except to become the laughing-stock of all men of any judgment, for during that sermon of his I had seen people everywhere grinning.[22] 'Ah! I daresay,' quoth he, 'but they were all your people.' 'How far they are my people,' I said, 'I have no idea; most of them I did not even know by sight.' Among other accusations, he charged me with citing the *Epistolae* of famous men as paying me some sort of tribute,[23] his suggestion being that I had made them up, and that no one existed who thought well of my work, although I suppress almost all letters of the kind, while at the same time he hinted that nothing should be considered acceptable that did not carry his own imprimatur. This will give you a good idea both of the modesty of the man, who has such a low opinion of himself, and of his straight-forward and purely Christian spirit, which is ready to think any and every evil of his neighbour.

Among other things I had said that it ought not to seem surprising if I complain of theologians in my books now and again, seeing that John Standish,[24] a Minorite theologian and bishop of St Asse, in front of the king and queen of England, with many magnates and learned men standing by, accused me most outrageously on three counts, one that I abolished the resurrection, another that I attached no value to the sacrament of matrimony, and the third that I held unsound opinions about the eucharist; whereas in all my books there is nothing I defend more loyally than the resurrection, I have so much exalted marriage in a published declamation[25] that theologians have regarded it as an error in theology to give it undue importance, and of the eucharist I have never either written or spoken except in the proper way, which means with great reverence. When I said this, 'Aha,' said he, 'I expect it's all true.' What a remark! –from a man who has lost all self-control, and allows himself any liberties he thinks fit! Why should this be more true of me than if anyone were to say of Egmondanus that he had robbed the treasury of a church, or put a spell upon men on their deathbeds to make them defraud their heirs and leave him everything,[26] or betrayed the secrets of the confessional for private gain? It is perhaps more likely that these charges would apply to him than that those he wished to seem somewhere near the truth would apply to me. There's a saint for you, to whom let parents entrust their children that they may acquire the seed of true religion!

Need I now go into details? Every single chance remark was seized upon for some foul slander, as is the way of quarrelling schoolboys and saucy fishwives; everything I had said was thrown back at me inside out. He brought up a letter I had written to Luther.[27] 'In that letter,' I said, 'I tell him what he ought to avoid.' 'On the contrary,' he replied, 'you show him how to write.' Even that, it seemed, would have been unwelcome, had there been less error in what Luther wrote; so anxious was he to see him destroyed, not set right. The thing he could not swallow was my having added 'I am not telling you what to do, but to continue doing what I know you do already.'[28] When I explained that this was the courtesy of the speaker who disclaims any wish to instruct just when he most wishes to, he flared up again. 'How right!' he cried. 'This is just like you rascally rhetoricians – all soft soap and falsehood and lies!' I admitted with a smile that speakers do lie sometimes, but that even doctors of divinity have been known to do so too. Again, when I said I was thinking of the reputation of the theological faculty, 'You leave that to us,' he said. 'We will take care of that.' And when I added that by burning Luther's books one might get them out of the libraries, but not out of men's minds,[29] 'Ah! men's minds!' he retorted. 'It was you put him there.'

So we completely failed to agree – if I spoke of good literature, he instantly called it bad; what I called a sound text, he called corrupt; if I said I was outside all party politics, he at once dubbed me leader of a party, and would have denied that there was anything hard inside the olive or outside the walnut,[30] had I suggested that there was. The rector then cut short our dispute, which had already gone on far too long, saying that it was unworthy of two theologians, and that he would prefer to listen to proposals for making peace. 'Well then,' said I, 'if you think peace cannot be concluded at a single drinking-party,[31] what more must we do to complete it?' Encouraged by the rector, he replied, 'If you repair the damage you have done to our reputation.' 'Where?' I said, 'In my letters?'[32] He nodded assent. 'For those that are already published, I cannot do what you ask,' I said, 'although in them I have damaged no man's reputation.' 'Then issue a recantation,' he replied. 'What do you mean?' 'State it in print that in Louvain the theologians are sincere,' (*synceres*[33] was the form he used) 'and honourable.' 'That,' said I, 'is a thing I have never denied; and as for those I have criticized, if they will provide me with the right material, I will pay them a splendid tribute.' That annoyed him: 'You too,' he said, 'you give us a chance of speaking well of you, and we will do so. You have the pen; we have the spoken word. You complain of us for barking at you behind your back; but I dare say all this to your face.' 'Nothing odd in that,' I retorted. 'With your character, you would be ready to spit in the face of an honourable man.' He said he was no longer so obstreperous.

The rector interrupted this exchange, and told us to concentrate on Luther, which was the main issue. 'Right,' he said; 'you have written in support of Luther, now write and attack him.' At this I denied that I had written to support him, but rather to support the theologians against him,[34] and excused myself on many grounds[35] – I was too busy, too little qualified, too fearful – and among other reasons said I was afraid of being thought vindictive if I published a savage attack on a man who was brought low and defeated. 'No, no: that's just what you ought to write,' he said. 'Say that we have defeated Luther.' I answered that there were plenty of people to say that at the tops of their voices even if I kept silence, and that it was more appropriate for those who had won it to celebrate their own victory; besides which, it was not clear to me that they had won, because none of their books had yet appeared. At this he lost heart, turned to the rector, and said, 'Did I not tell you that we should be wasting our time? As long as he refuses to write against Luther, we shall continue to regard him as a member of Luther's party.'[36] 'On that showing,' I retorted, 'I shall reckon you one of Luther's men, for you write nothing against him, and not only you, but countless others too.' And so without taking his leave – only a parting gesture to the rector, and not to me – he went his way, like the man in a school for gladiators who has received a wound not allowed for by the rules, and gives his hand to all the others but not the one who wounded him.

That gives you a rough summary of our famous discussion, which none the less he thought a very courteous performance, his object being to win me over by his eloquence to publish an attack on Luther. Nor did he risk the loss of any credit that might be won from this confrontation, for he boasted to his colleagues over their cups how boldly he had withstood Erasmus face to face. The rector, telling the same story to his own friend with a good deal of amusement, said he would never have believed I could keep my temper like that; not that I claim any credit for that, for I should have been quite mad to have struggled with him. And yet there are two or three more criminal than he is.[37] Tiresome and obstinate as he is, at least he is less deceitful, and always his true self. They say he was always the same – as a boy, as a candidate, as a bachelor, as a doctor of divinity, always what he now is as a Carmelite. Vulcan could not reshape him on the anvil, Mercury could not remould him into something new. In his own eyes he is the principal pillar of Christian religion, and the glory of the order of Carmelites. He is as much comfort to this university as a sty in the eye;[38] but this is a boil that nobody can lance.

Farewell, my dear More.

Louvain, 1520

1163 / To Adrianus Cornelii Barlandus — Louvain, 30 November 1520

This letter, like Ep 646, is known only from the *Epistolae aliquot selectae ex Erasmicis per Hadrianum Barlandum* (Louvain: D. Martens December 1520; NK 820). This is a selection of Erasmus' letters edited by his friend Barlandus for use in the schools. Erasmus had clearly given his consent to Barlandus' undertaking (lines 2–7), but he probably did not intend this letter to be included and never published it himself.

ERASMUS TO HIS FRIEND BARLANDUS, GREETING

No doubt you have been careful to choose only those letters which have nothing prickly about them, for you can see how certain people nowadays take offence at the slightest opportunity. All the same, I could have wished that you had thought of something else; for I am afraid they will be annoyed by the very fact that they see something of mine prepared to be read in schools.

I persuaded the printers with some difficulty not to reprint the *Farrago*.[1] I have revised it, removing a few things and toning down others, so that it can appear in this form rather than as it was printed before; this was not my idea, but I did it to satisfy the wishes of my friends.

It is a pity that Dirk[2] has refused to print Dr Turnhout's book.[3] For one thing, it would have been better not to indicate his own opinion; and then there are many reasons why I like to see this work published. He is a first-rate theologian, and I do not doubt that in writing it, as in his public disputations, he has used solid argument and not abuse. I did not approve of Luther's being silenced by clamour and conspiracy, but I should much like to see him refuted on the evidence of Scripture and with sound reasons.[4] Even if we give the pope's bull great weight,[5] yet such a course would have more effect on the learned, and even on the intelligent public. So please persuade him not to refuse hereafter, and I as far as I can will try to do so too. Farewell.

Louvain, St Andrew's day 1520

1164 / To Godschalk Rosemondt

[Louvain, c December 1520]

This undated letter follows Ep 1153 and Erasmus' visit to Cologne (cf line 48); it also reports an event that took place on 25 November (cf n13). It was published in the *Epistolae ad diversos*.

ERASMUS TO THE DISTINGUISHED THEOLOGIAN GODSCHALK ROSEMONDT, MODERATOR OF THE FAMOUS UNIVERSITY OF LOUVAIN, GREETING

I have no desire to interrupt you so often with a letter, and yet this is better for us both. We had enjoyed silence for a time from that Frisian Dominican[1] who put a gloss long ago on my *Moria* and since then on my *Antibarbari*,[2] pouring every sort of rant and calumny on my name and reputation. And he supposes that he is doing right, for this reason if no other, that I have touched on monks in what I write, although I always refrain from the outrageous tales told of them all too often – and let us hope, without foundation – by common report, and repeated of late at the crowded dinner-table of the cardinal of Sion,[3] and have always avoided names of men and even of orders.[4] Or do they think perhaps that the whole Dominican order suffers, if anyone complains that some one Dominican has done him wrong? Look at Jerome:[5] does he not depict the faults of monks and nuns, although a monk himself? If it is unlawful to mention the faults of monks in any form, it will not be permitted to mention those of priests or courtiers either. But these men habitually declaim against them, like roisterers on a wagon,[6] with the greatest freedom. In my *Antibarbari* what else does Batt (whom I make the speaker) accuse them of except a hatred of any liberal education?[7] Do they not proclaim this themselves, even if I kept silence, by the bitterness of their constant attacks on the ancient languages and on good literature? In which at least they differ widely from the Holy Father, who in his briefs addressed to me says it is called good and deserves the name,[8] and from the last Lateran Council,[9] which allocates five whole years to these studies and does not forbid them thereafter, provided there is some admixture of more serious subjects.

But when he admits that his savage attacks on me are provoked by my mention of monks, does he not make it perfectly clear that he does this in a vindictive spirit? But what could be more disgraceful than for a personal vendetta to misuse the house of God, the pulpit intended for the preaching of Christ's glory, and the simple faith of common folk? And these actions are the more discreditable because they are done in this famous university and before your very eyes, as though you authorized or at least approved them.

What can one trust in any longer, if we turn the word of God into a weapon with which to cut our neighbour's throat? It is a heinous offence if a man partakes unworthily of the Lord's body; but greater disaster results for many people if a man adulterates the words of the Gospel. If they have suffered damage, there are other means of righting their wrongs without impairing the sanctity of the pulpit. Even this, I suppose, will give some people pleasure, if they feel that I have to some extent been hurt. For my part, I have faced worse than this, and still can face worse; but it would be a lie if I said that all this left me unmoved. I should take it less hard if I were attacked by a mule, or by a raving lunatic; but I would prefer not to be attacked at all. He who values not his own life can command the lives of others, and it is the same with reputation. It is within any man's reach to hurt another. And heaven forbid that I in my turn should wish to discover what I can do in this field. Though I spent so many days in Cologne,[10] I never uttered a word of complaint to anyone, relying on your assurance that you hoped Egmondanus would keep silence in future. As for this Frisian, I never expected fresh storms from that quarter. These troubles can be ended by one word from a man in your position. Whether you ought to do so is for you to say; personally I think you ought, if not for my benefit, at least for the sake of the public peace.

Before this letter was finished, I dined with Abbot Maximilian of Middelburg;[11] and as he was in my vicinity I took the opportunity to approach the prior of the Dominicans.[12] He disclaimed all knowledge of what the man had said; but his face and bearing and our whole conversation left no doubt that this was done with his connivance and approval. Next day the Frisian came to see me, as though to clear himself – a young man of astonishing self-confidence who seemed to think every word he uttered was a jewel, a bright flower, a proper oracle. He admitted that on St Catherine's day[13] he had said more than had been reported to me. And by way of clearing himself he brazenly put forward some propositions so foolish that it would have been the height of folly to reply to them, though I did reply in two or three words. Egmondanus, in his opening lecture on St Paul,[14] prayed that, just as Paul after persecuting the church had become a Doctor of the church, so we might one day see the conversion of Luther and Erasmus. What will become of men like them? They would like nothing more than somehow to make mischief. They cannot forgive me for not being of Luther's party; to which in truth I do not belong, unless he were to think of nothing but Christ's glory.

I know that I speak rather freely, but no man ever heard me approve of Luther's teaching. His books I have never had much desire to read, except for a few pages, and those I sampled rather than read. Your public arguments against Luther have always had my unwavering support,[15] and even more what has been written, especially by Dr Jan Turnhout,[16] who has argued (they tell me) in a scholarly way and without heat. When his books were burnt, no one saw me downcast.[17] I have consistently admitted that there are very many things in him I do not like. I have written at length to him privately and have argued with him at length in hopes of repressing his provocative style of writing – and I am called a member of Luther's party! If this type of humour satisfies your university, I am capable of bearing it; for I would rather bear it than take reprisals. But in my view it would be better to deal with the situation quite differently. Vincentius[18] lays the uproar in Holland at my door, because after a most foolish sermon that he preached there he was nearly stoned by the crowd; while I have never written to any Hollander either for Luther or against him.

Farewell in Christ, dear Rector magnificus.

Your sincere friend Erasmus

[1519][19]

1165 / To Wolfgang Faber Capito Louvain, 6 December 1520

The letter actually sent and written in Erasmus' own hand – some of its contents were highly confidential – is in the Öffentliche Bibliothek of the University of Basel, MS Ki.Ar. 25a 1 no 98. It was first published in 1790 by Salomon Hess. After his recent encounter with Erasmus at Cologne (cf Ep 1158 n5) Capito had now returned to Mainz.

Greeting. Our Hollanders have firmly rejected this bull from the pope,[1] or rather, from Louvain. The president[2] has replied that he is waiting for something in writing from the pope when he is better informed, and that he has not yet received any proclamation from the prince;[3] but that if it arrives, he knows by what means to give the prince satisfaction. The bishop of Utrecht[4] is said not to have accepted it either.

A man called Vincentius,[5] a doctor of divinity and a confounded numbskull, who is always barking at me, was preaching at Dordrecht against Luther, and had scarcely come down from the pulpit when the pastor mounted it and urged the people not to tolerate those who undermine the teaching of the Gospel. The women tore the other man's gown when he tried to interfere. Vincentius escaped with difficulty. On his return to Louvain the blockhead maintained that this was arranged in a letter from me. The theologians wished to propel Egmondanus the Camelite[6] in that direction; but he lost his nerve and refuses to be made into a martyr. The Louvain people almost regret the whole thing. Latomus[7] and Turnhout[8] dare not

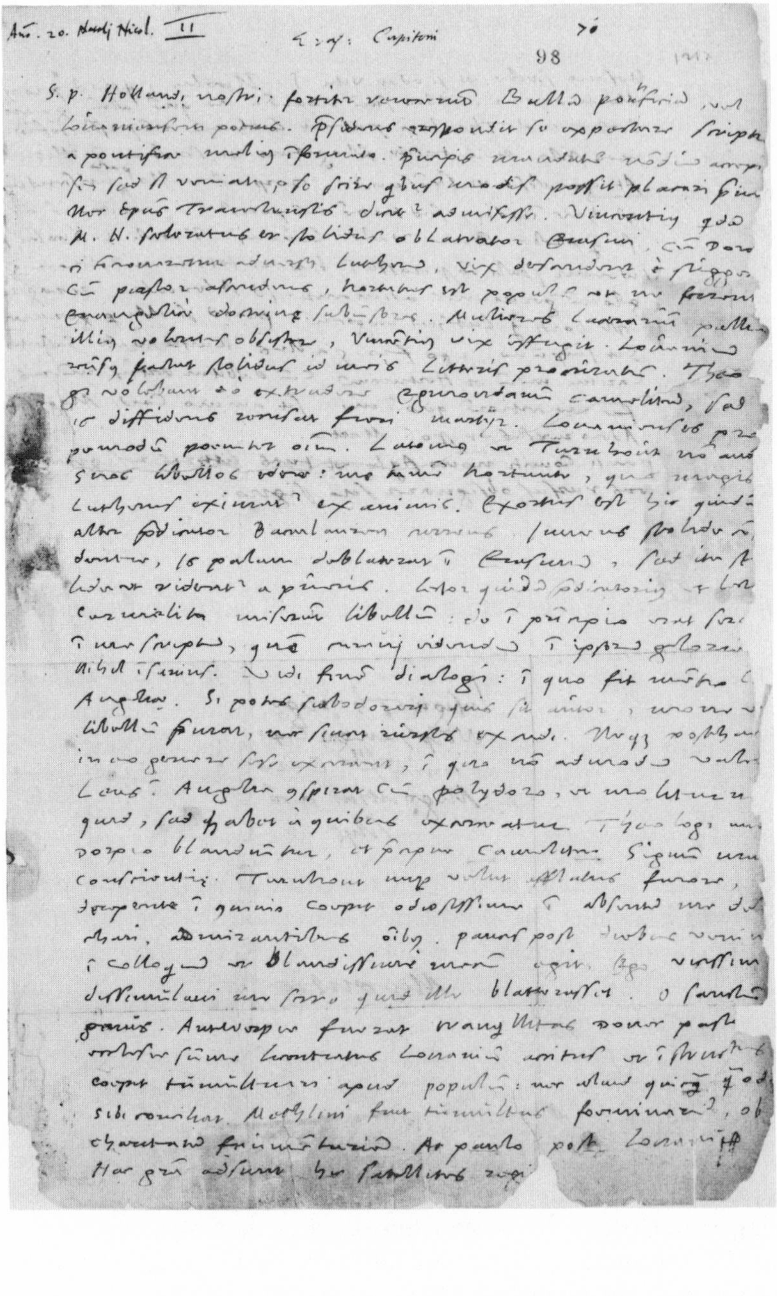

Autograph letter from Erasmus to Wolfgang Faber Capito, Ep 1165
Öffentliche Bibliothek, University of Basel

Vehementer probo ut si edat vitā S. Nicolai, quod promi-
sit ille nescio quis, addat suū nomē. ne quā ille grauius
suspitionē. Theologi putant Lutherum nō posse cōfici ni-
si uno stilo. Et a tertio flagitant ut scribam in illū.
At ego absit ut scribendo corpus ullo [pacto] discindam
est huic studio, sed mens nō potest animaduertere se
se ī pectore. Bene vale Louanij. Natali S. Nicolai 1520
Videmus fatali cōspiratione hoc ut totum conditionis
gloriā germanis adimunt. Ab Aleandro nescio
sit concitati Lutheri negotiū. Quod si ille germanus
sit suspectus, ego sum gallus. Rursū vale. Saluta
Carum meū et Hartmannū, cū dabitur, verbis meis,
[illegible] quo animo sit animo Card. Moguntinus
[illegible] et [illegible] Martio.
[illegible] Comitis nostri Agli ut tuas litteras resignare, et
nos rursus obsignare suo signo.

Insigni Theologo
Wolphango Capi-
toni Rmi Card
Moguntini a cō-
silijs

Moguntiae

publish their books, though I encourage them: we must get Luther out of people's heads.

A second Dominican[9] has sprung up here, a bachelor in course, quite young, and a self-confident blockhead. He holds forth openly against me, but in such a stupid fashion that children make fun of him. A lecturer who is a Dominican and another who is a Carmelite have sent me a pamphlet on *In principio erat sermo* attacking me,[10] which I have arranged to have published to bring them glory. It is the maddest thing you ever saw.

I have seen the conclusion of a dialogue in which the cardinal of England is mentioned.[11] If you can sniff out who the author is, tell him to suppress his piece and not let it be reprinted, and in future not to try his hand at this kind of thing, at which he is not much good. Lee in England[12] is conspiring with Polidoro[13] and is preparing I know not what. But there are people who will give him a run for his money. The theologians, and the Camelite in particular, are now making up to Dorp[14] – sure sign of a bad conscience. Turnhout the other day, as though some frenzy had come over him, began suddenly at a party to rant against me in my absence in the most offensive way, which left everyone gasping. A few days later we fell into conversation, and he was most friendly. On my side, I pretended to know nothing of his outpourings. What a saintly lot they are! In Antwerp all was peace, until the pastor of the Groote Kerk,[15] a licentiate, was summoned to Louvain to receive his instructions and began to make an uproar before public audiences; he got nothing but odium for his pains. At Mechelen the housewives have rioted over the price of grain,[16] and the same a little later at Louvain. In view of this we have royal guards here.

Write and tell Nesen,[17] if he published his life of St Nicholas, which the subject richly deserves, to put his name to it, so as not to lay suspicion on other people. The theologians think that nothing but my pen can polish off Luther, and are silently bringing pressure on me to attack him in print.[18] Heaven forbid that I should be so mad! Dorp[19] must at all costs be kept out of this unpleasantness; in spite of all, he could not show himself more friendly than he does.

Farewell, from Louvain. St Nicholas day 1520

The Italians seem to have made a conspiracy with the object of depriving the Germans of all credit for scholarship. This is nearer to Aleandro's heart than the Luther business.[20] If the Germans let him do this without reprisals, I become a Frenchman.[21] Farewell once more.

Give my greetings to my friend Carinus[22] and to Hartmann.[23] When you have a reliable courier, let me know the attitude of the cardinal of Mainz towards me.[24] I shall appear again,[25] I hope, in March. I gave the count of Neuenahr[26] leave to open your letter and seal it again with his own seal.

To the distinguished theologian Wolfgang Capito, councillor to his Eminence the cardinal of Mainz. In Mainz

1166 / [To a patron, perhaps in The Hague] [Louvain, c December 1520]

This long fragment of a letter was published by Jean Leclerc in LB from an unknown source, perhaps a rough draft or copy added at one time to the Deventer Letter-book (see Allen I 609). The contents show that it must have been written shortly after Erasmus' return from Cologne, and some parallels to other letters leave little doubt that it is authentic.

The beginning of the text indicates that it was addressed to a person of some standing who was a good friend of Maarten van Dorp. It further appears that he was interested in men who, like Erasmus and Dorp, came from the northern parts of the Netherlands, that he could be trusted to be discreet, and was sympathetic to Luther. Various names have been proposed. Cornelis Hoen, a lawyer in the Council of Holland, Gerrit van Assendelft, another councillor (cf Ep 1044 n5), and especially the council's president Nicolaas Everaerts (cf Epp 1044:17–34, 77–83, 1165:2–5, 1186) seem plausible recipients of this letter.

The more I reflect how little there is in the part fortune has allotted me that has ever deserved your support or ever can deserve it in the future, the more I admire the sincerely open and friendly nature which leads you not only to mention me frequently in your letters to Dorp, but even to write to me personally, especially while you are continually immersed in such a sea of business. I was raised to the rank of councillor three years ago now.[1] Only a patent from the prince was not forthcoming, and in its place Jean Le Sauvage, the former chancellor, had pledged his own responsibility; but death did not let him redeem his pledge. All this however is not, as I see it, a matter for much congratulation; I have not much in common with the court,[2] nor the court with me. In the promotion of the humanities I think I have done my share. I shall not abandon them, however, though I shall gradually withdraw from the field, unless there is a pronounced change in human affairs; of which up to now I see no acceptable gleam of hope in any quarter, such is the success achieved by those who under the pretext of religion are battling for their own bellies[3] and their despotic power against liberal studies and the genuine teaching of the Gospel. The great men at court have other business in hand; the great men in the church are hunting mitres and red hats. Theologians of the ancient fashion align themselves with Dominicans and Carmelites, who are ready to say or do anything without a tremor. There is a Carmelite here by the name of Egmondanus who constantly launches the most fatuous attacks on me in public sermons and in his regular lectures;[4] he is laughed at by his hearers as a lunatic, and yet the old man[5] can see nothing wrong in all this nonsense.

Some months ago a Frisian Dominican called Laurensen[6] made his appearance here, a young man of no accomplishments but almost beside himself with conceit. For several weeks he gave a public exposition of some passages in my *Moria*, with most scurrilous attacks on me; in the end, without my doing anything about it, his ranting was officially silenced by the university.[7] He kept quiet for some time, but has lately resumed his ravings – who put him up to it, I do not know – nor can anyone's authority suppress him. He is ignorant and stupid and spoiling for a fight, and has no lack of supporters to stimulate him if he flags.[8] If I go to law with them, I shall have war with monsters and mobs on my hands; if I answer them in print, they lost all sense of shame long ago. I know what they think: 'Let him write for the learned; there are not many of them. And we will bluster away before the public.' If you press them hard, their final step is to transfer the offender to another convent; so it pays to leave the uproar where it is. To all this our grave doctors of divinity turn a blind eye; not a few of them have been against me for some time now – why, I do not see. They do not confront me personally, and there is no appeasing them; they are constantly irritated by fresh suspicions, which they have discovered already once and for all to be entirely false.

There is a man here called Vincentius,[9] a Dominican from Alkmaar, a doctor of divinity, no scholar, and a booby by nature. After he had been ranting against me for a long time everywhere – and there was no end to it, though he had been warned more than once – I eventually approached him,[10] and urged him to speak out if he had anything to complain of. He showed me certain passages he had marked in my books, none of which he had understood in the least. There is also some sort of prior,[11] a man of no education but with all the virulence of a prostitute, who comes from the convent in your part of the world, and he is the man behind this sort of nonsense. If these men are allowed with impunity to abuse the authority of a sacred building and a sacred occasion to air their feelings if they have any resentment or any suspicions, clear though it is what manner of men they are, where I ask you will all this end?

As for Luther, you will know that there was some burning at Louvain,[12] this being a favourite project of the theologians who produced the bull,[13] and afterwards at Liège with the connivance of the bishop,[14] who has his eye on a cardinal's hat; later with more bitter hostility in Cologne,[15] where Hoogstraten rules the roost. But though Luther's writings are not liked by everyone, everybody disapproved of the way it was done and of such savage and tyrannous behaviour. Nor would they have done it with impunity in Cologne, had not the king's presence stood in the way. As it is, Luther sells there as he did before. Here, two people have written attacks on him, Latomus and Jan Turnhout,[16] but neither seems likely to publish a book; I suppose they do not trust their own case, and it is much easier to win the day with bulls and burning than with arguments. I have never embroiled myself in Luther's case, though the clamour they make has never been to my taste any more than the pamphlets of those who have resisted Luther hitherto.[17] And this they resent. If I were to support Luther, they would attack me too with the same devices; if I opposed Luther, they would use the hatred of the Germans which I should call on my own head as a means to undo me – these men with all the mildness and simplicity of the Gospel! With these falsehoods they have made a case against me to the apostolic nuncio[18] as the one man who upholds Luther's business so as to prevent his destruction; for that is their only object; they have no wish that he should mend his ways.

Duke Franz von Sickingen[19] was telling how he had protested to the emperor Charles about the proclamation he was reported to have issued,[20] and Charles replied that he had issued nothing of the kind. Duke Frederick of Saxony, when he raised the question of Luther with him, received the reply that Luther shall not be condemned unheard. The bishops were obliged to conceal their feelings. Of his own accord the duke, when shown the brief in which he was ordered to throw Luther into prison until some further decision should be taken in his case,[21] expressed surprise that the pope should ask him to do anything of the kind, since he was a layman and it was not yet established that Luther deserved such treatment, and said that therefore the question must be postponed to the Diet of Worms.[22] This reply is most unpopular with the nuncio.

It is known that the pope has forbidden the publication of the bull.[23] Aleandro, who brought it, has made public no instructions except that he is to confer with the universities. He is a good scholar in the three tongues, but everyone affirms he is a Jew;[24] everyone agrees at least that his life is above all reproach. His mission in Lower Germany has been performed in Upper Germany by a certain Eck, a valiant theologian. The Germans play their part with scurrilous pamphlets.[25] How extraordinary that no living man can find any way of pacifying this uproar! Luther writes more bitterly every day, and seems plainly to be heading for civil strife, though discouraged by me.[26] He writes[27] that he himself wished entirely to ignore the papal bull, but that on the advice of his friends he has lodged a renewed protest. A brief was exhibited in Cologne to the cardinal of Gurk, in which he was told to summon Staupitz,[28] the vicar-general of the Augustinians, on the ground that he had supported Luther, and oblige him to abjure all Luther's doctrines; and if he refused, to put him in chains, or punish him in some other way at his own discretion.

There is much in Luther's books that is worth reading, with an admixture of some things that would have been better omitted; and the whole is too bitter in tone, not to say revolutionary. Had he put the things that are really important in a more moderate tone, even though he had freely criticized the intolerable faults of the Roman curia,[29] he would have had everyone on his side; and even so it happens, I know not how, that those who write against him produce nothing worth reading. If he has shown crass folly in what he writes, they are far worse in their answers. And among those who wish for Luther's destruction, I do not see one single man of principle. The letters of Cardinal Adrian of Utrecht[30] are full of the most extraordinary virulence; he supports his own disciples, who are just what he deserves, tedious, artificial, ambitious, and vindictive. The bishop of Liège is all out for a red hat, and has with difficulty secured an abbey in Antwerp.[31] I have seen a letter from Hutten,[32] in which he complains that the pope has written to say he is to be put in chains. He never appeared while I was in Cologne; he is said to beset the roads with a party of forty men in hopes of cutting off the emissaries of Rome, against whom he has declared war.[33] What end there can be to these things, I know not. I take no part whatever in this business. 'The Fates will find a way.'[34] The Observant Franciscans have been told by their superiors to keep their mouths shut;[35] on Luther they are sensible. The Dominicans are their true selves, always setting some mischief on foot in the world; that order will overthrow Christianity, if ever it is overthrown ...

1167 / To Lorenzo Campeggi — Louvain, 6 December 1520

Written for the benefit of a sympathetic cardinal and probably other members of the papal court (cf n24), this letter continues the long succession of Erasmus' complaints against his opponents. Like Ep 1143, it offers a long account of his attitude towards Luther, dealing in particular with Ep 980, which had aroused suspicion in Rome (lines 150–277). Erasmus also risks a cautious defence of Johann Reuchlin (lines 85–104). It is particularly interesting, and symptomatic of Erasmus' vacillation at this time between support for, and critique of, the German reformers, that this letter, intended for circulation at the curia and published in his *Epistolae ad diversos*, often closely resembles an anonymous pamphlet as savage as the *Acta contra Lutherum* (cf Ep 1166 n24). At about the time he was writing this letter Erasmus must also have revised Ep 1062, the dedicatory preface of his paraphrase of Ephesians, likewise addressed to Campeggi; cf n5.

TO HIS EMINENCE LORENZO CAMPEGGI, CARDINAL OF SAN TOMMASO IN PARIONO, FROM ERASMUS OF ROTTERDAM, GREETING

I had decided to spend the winter in Rome,[1] for other reasons as well, but principally in order to use the riches of the papal library on several passages, for among us there is a great shortage of religious texts in Greek, the Aldine press not having given us much as yet besides pagan authors.[2] But these frequent conferences between monarchs,[3] which it was important for me not to miss entirely, have delayed me here; and so what has not been possible now I shall attempt with God's help next year. I shall be happy to spend all the life that heaven may be willing to remain for me in Rome, where liberal studies not only find tranquillity but are held in honour. This country, though it grows more civilized every day, cannot yet quite slough off all its native rudeness,[4] and the ranks of ancient barbarism have most obstinate champions at their head.

And in my opinion there are faults on both sides. The supporters of the humanities would rather force their way in like enemies than grow gradually into friendship and amity as guests; they would rather drive the old tenants from their holdings than share their advantages, and so do what is best for both.[5] Those on the other hand who have so foolishly convinced themselves that they will lose a great part of their reputation with the multitude unless they entirely suppress the subjects which they have not the good fortune to have learnt themselves and have no time to learn now, rant at them with such bitterness and such stupid obstinacy, in public and private and even in the pulpit, that I should be ashamed to describe what they feel no shame in outlining before large mixed audiences in their attacks on the ancient languages and liberal studies in general. And this, though those studies are so highly valued not only by all the pick of our princes but by Leo himself,[6] the supreme champion not only of religion but of those subjects too from which he sees how much the Christian philosophy has to gain in lustre and width of range and depth of foundations. This is the purpose of a conspiracy of fanatics, and – what is more criminal – they misuse the pulpit for their nefarious purposes; and for the state of public morals the purity of the pulpit is more important than the sacred liturgy. He who handles the liturgy unworthily puts no man in jeopardy but himself. But he who misuses the authority of the place and credulity of a public who believe what they hear from it, not for the glory of Christ but to satisfy his own ambitions, defrauds the hearts of many who expect to be fed with sacred doctrine and infects them with his own poison, while robbing the sacred office of preaching of its authority. But these men, not content with pouring truth and falsehood indiscriminately on the humanities, often have no fear of attacking from the sacred pulpit the reputation of those whose efforts they suppose to promote such studies, among whom they place the name of Erasmus among the first. Were I to deny that I support the cause of good letters, I should be a liar; but my support is always coloured by the wish to see them serve the glory of Christ.

The principal actors in this play are some men I could name of the society of St Dominic, an order which has always had, and I think still has, many men distinguished for learning and piety; nor ought it to seem strange if among so many thousands there are some of quite a different description. These men have enlisted the aid of some members of the company who call themselves Carmelites, I know not why, and imagine me to be their enemy, although no one is more devoted to true religion. I have the greatest respect and affection for Christian piety, whatever be the dress or habit in which it gives true evidence of itself, black or white, linen or woollen, dark or tawny. If any reference is ever made in passing to the faults of monks, it is no more reasonable for them to be indignant than for the order of priests to be indignant when someone depicts the ideal of a good priest and shows how far the common run of priests fall short of it, or princes when someone glances at the faults of princes. And yet, if there is any order of men that deserves to be gently handled, it is above all the priests, whose order was instituted by Christ himself, and he was himself a member of it; and princes one should handle gently, for their majesty, if provoked too often, brings great disasters upon mortal men.

In principle, I am determined to give offence to no order whatever in a subversive spirit; but at the same time those people claim too much who allow themselves complete freedom in attacking others, openly and publicly using lies to blacken other men's reputations, and labelling heresy, or at any rate attacking in the most offensive way, what they do not even understand, while they do not allow their own order to be mentioned except in most respectful terms. The whole Dominican order would combine against a man who complained among his private friends that his money had been stolen or his wife debauched by a member of the order. Yet think of the passages where St Jerome depicts the faults of monks, and he a monk himself! – the satiric wit with which he castigates the lives of nuns and godly virgins, and yet no protests from Paula, no protests from Eustochium![7] Not that I ever claim for myself the freedom claimed by Jerome. I never attack an order, I criticize no man by name,[8] while they themselves often will not leave my name alone. All I do is to show in a number of passages where true religion is to be found; nor do I ever touch on those disgraceful features which are commonly retailed by many people, to the embarrassment of those who really wish well to their profession.

So this is the fountain-head and the seed-bed of all this sorry business – an incurable hatred of the ancient tongues and of humane studies.[9] From time to time the scene, the characters, the actors change; the play never changes. Hence came that storm of protest against Johann Reuchlin, those claims that they were defending the faith, when the only true motive behind it all was to obtain satisfaction for one man's resentment.[10] Their project was not yet going as they had hoped, when there appeared some pieces by Martin Luther, written, it would seem, in an unhappy hour, and their spirits rose at once: here was a weapon, put into their hands, with which they could finish off the tongues and the humanities, and Reuchlin and Erasmus into the bargain.[11] I do not say that all theologians thought like this. But that such was the plan of those first authors of this play is clear from this if nothing else, that a number of men of that kidney soon began, in different places and as if at some prearranged signal, to deliver the most astonishing tirades against liberal studies, making them share the burden of odium attached to Luther's name, which they were trying to make as hateful as they could, and proclaiming that liberal studies are the source of heresies, of schisms, and of Antichrists. Whereas we can plainly see what they have contributed in strength and splendour to the faith, as our Holy Father Leo himself confesses in his briefs;[12] and did he not say so in writing, his actions would speak for him none the less, for there are none whom he more readily singles out for honour and preferment than men who have distinguished themselves in this field of studies.

In fact, as the object towards which they were heading did not escape my notice – I mean, the inclusion under one label of things by nature quite distinct – I made it clear in speech and in writing, privately and publicly, that Reuchlin had nothing in common with Luther's case, and that I had nothing in common with either; though a little more with Reuchlin,[13] with whom I had had two or three discussions,[14] and shared the same zeal for encouraging the ancient tongues and the humanities, and in old days I learnt not a little from his books. Whereas Luther I have never known even by sight, nor is he so far advanced in knowledge of the tongues or of elegant[15] scholarship to provide supporters of such studies with any interest in his case.

All this, I conceive, was not unknown to these gentlemen, but they were looking for a handle to gratify their private spite; and not having secured one, they resent this, and invent anything that may involve me in hatred or suspicion among those who do not know the facts. To begin with, two or three prefaces mixed in with Luther's books in rather better Latin than his usual were enough evidence to satisfy them that Luther had had help from me in the writing of his pieces,[16] in which there is not one letter that belongs to me. As though Wittenberg had no one who could write Latin, to say nothing of the rest of Germany! On this point they know themselves that I am not inventing; and many things I pass over in silence for fear of irritating some who are too easily provoked. On top of this there appeared a letter from me to Luther,[17] and soon thereafter another to the cardinal of Mainz,[18] both printed. In this regard I cannot express my astonishment at the policy of certain persons who rush into print with something that I had written under seal for the eye of a single reader. It makes me suspect a deliberate move by my enemies, searching everywhere for some means to do me harm. For the letter I had written to the cardinal of Mainz was circulating in print before the sealed original had come into his hands. That earlier letter was in circulation here[19] first among bishops and members of the court, with the idea that it should prove me clearly to be a supporter of Luther's teaching. Later I heard in a letter from Girolamo Aleandro and in conversation with him that it had reached the pope,[20] though its tenor was much more to show that I do not support what Luther writes, unless one first misinterprets everything.

Out of all Luther's books I have not read a dozen pages through, and even those in snatches; and yet, from what I have dipped into rather than read, I seemed to detect rare natural gifts and a nature finely adapted to expound the mysteries of Scripture in the classical manner[21] and blow the spark of gospel teaching into flame – that teaching from which our public standards of morality and our universities, with their excessive devotion nowadays to minor questions more ingenious than relevant, seemed to have fallen so very far short. I heard men of high character and acknowledged scholarship and piety rejoicing that they had come upon this man's books. I perceived that the higher a person's character and the nearer he came to the simplicity of the Gospel, the less opposed he was to Luther. His way of life moreover was highly spoken of, even by those who could not endure his views. In any case, as regards the spirit that moves the man, of which none but God can judge with certainty, I chose the reasonable course of leaning towards the good side rather than the bad. Last but not least, the world, as though already weary of this teaching which lays so much emphasis on petty human inventions and human rules, seemed to me to thirst for the pure living water drawn from the conduits of evangelists and apostles; and to fulfil this need I thought he had both the natural endowments and the necessary zeal.

In these terms then I thought well of Luther;[22] I thought well of the good things which I either saw in him or thought I saw; in fact, it was not of him I thought, but of the glory of Christ. And yet I saw in him at the same time enough to cause me some anxiety and suspicion. And so, when he took the initiative in writing to me,[23] I seized the opportunity at once, and warned him in detail of the things I thought he should avoid, in hopes that, once corrected and reformed, his gifts might restore for us, to our great profit and to the glory and also the advantage of Christ, that gospel philosophy which is now almost cold. Had he done this, I did not doubt that he would find Leo himself among the chief supporters of his enterprise; for I believe he values nothing so much as the glory of Christ, whose vicegerent he is for the time being, and the salvation of the flock committed to his charge. Pray consider[24] whether this letter of mine is the work of one who supports Luther, if Luther has written anything contrary to Christian doctrine or Christian piety.

In his writings it was not long before I stumbled on something rude and harsh, which did not properly reflect the gentle spirit of the Gospel; and I warned him to take example by Christ and the Apostles and teach with all gentleness the elements of true piety. To increase his chances of doing this to good purpose, I warned him not to attack the Roman pontiff, for it is in the general interest that his authority should be sacrosanct, and not to attack the majesty of princes,[25] for when they are the targets of abuse or ill-timed warnings, not only do they not become better but sometimes they are embittered and give rise to dangerous storms. Then the man who issued the warning loses all his influence, and sometimes his life, and its recipient loses the benefit he should have had. Indeed, while it can never be lawful to go against the truth, it may sometimes be expedient to conceal it[26] in the circumstances. And it is always of the first importance how timely, how opportune, and how well judged your production of it is. Theologians are agreed on some things among themselves which it is not expedient to publish to the common herd. And a correction that is well timed, gentle, and courteous often puts people right who would be driven into perdition by a severe and ill-timed rebuke. I will not mention (what Plato seems to have perceived so clearly[27]) that a mixed and uneducated multitude cannot be retained in its allegiance unless it is sometimes misled by artificial colouring and well-intentioned falsehood. But this requires a man not only of the highest character, but of exceptional wisdom.

I warned him not to condemn the universities or the monastic orders out of hand, but to point out courteously what changes he would wish to see made; and that in things which are accepted more from tradition than from sound judgment, he should use close-packed and solid arguments rather than mere asseveration.[28] Knowing as I did the German temperament,[29] and being aware that he was irritated by the excessively hostile tone of certain persons' attacks upon him, I urged him not to answer one insult with another,[30] but either to ignore the whole thing or to reply with argument, refraining altogether from common abuse. Besides which, as I feared that so much freedom of speech would end in civil strife, I told him to avoid arrogance or faction in all he said or did. Last but not least, I advised him to examine his own heart (on which it is not for me to pass judgment) to ensure that he was not tainted with anger or hatred or vainglory, which so often lies in wait for a man even when he is fully engaged on works of mercy; for he who was a prey to these emotions, I said, would not be thought an ideal champion of the Christian philosophy. I ask you, was anything omitted here of which Luther ought to have been warned?

All this I wrote in a sincere and friendly spirit; yet even so there was no lack of Germans who used this letter as a stick to beat Luther, because they thought it attacked his teaching, while the other party falsely declared it was the work of a supporter. Some people even resented my answering the man at all. As though it should be held against me, if the sultan[31] were to write to me and I answered him – especially since he would not try to make me share his beliefs. Others resented my sending such a courteous answer. But such men fail to observe what a favourable view every man has of himself, and how essentially unpleasant it is to be given good advice. Luther was unknown to me personally, as he still is; I had not opened his books, except for a few pages. Things had not yet reached the present level of hostility, except for complaints from a few men whom everyone supposed to have ulterior motives. People were demanding that there should be a confrontation, and a panel of judges.[32] And with what self-confidence could I, to begin with a man unknown, and then in no position of authority, and furthermore a very superficial scholar,[33] have taken on myself a critic's lordly air at his expense? What hope could there have been that he would let me do so, and what result could be expected, except that by criticizing him I should finally turn his pen against myself? To go no further, it was barely courteous to offer my advice to a man who did not seek it. Nor was I unaware how much more one can usually achieve by courteous and friendly advice than by savage protests.

I lay no claim to the ability or the learning required to decide upon another man's faith, unless he openly rejects the tenets universally accepted. What claims others make is their own affair. Some people deny that I am anything but a schoolmaster. Whether I am more than that, this is not the place to discuss; but at least it is beyond controversy that they are. But to the point: would such men have endured to see a schoolmaster laying down the law on heresy? And had I had all the needful learning, I could not refute his books without reading them through two or three times, and without careful consideration of the passages in the authors from which he derived his opinions. And he has drawn most of them from ancient sources;[34]

had he cited them everywhere by name, he would not have been nearly so unpopular. But I had scarcely leisure enough to read what I write myself, and if there were any time left over, I would rather devote it (to speak frankly) to the reading of the Ancients. Besides which, many scholars and even some universities[35] were undertaking the task of refuting Luther, and it would have required great impudence to rush in headlong and deprive others in advance of their authority as judges and of the credit of a successful outcome. In any case, those who find fault with me, after I have told him how he ought to instruct us, for adding 'I am not instructing you to do this, only to do what you do always'[36] seem to me quite unfamiliar with the polite formulas with which it is normal to soften the edge of a rebuke. Surely such rhetorical devices are common knowledge.

But all this time I am telling you what you already know, and instructing the instructed, like Minerva and the sow.[37] The point is that I already imagined him to be doing of his own accord what I wanted him to do. Otherwise, had there been nothing in him to disapprove of, it would have been foolish to spend so many words on telling him how he ought to write differently. And these men suppose me to have meant 'Continue as you are, writing subversion and heresy.' And yet, however much that might be a fair description of Luther, it was not even possible for what I said to be understood except in the light of the style of writing I had told him to adopt. There is also another point which they explain quite wrongly – adding that both here and in England there are not a few people who think well of his books[38] – as though I meant to encourage him to fresh effrontery, whereas my object rather was to urge him to write with greater moderation and caution, in order to win more approval from men of good will, and to choose his subjects and control his style so as to earn the continuing support of religious and scholarly readers. We encourage athletes with signs of our support, not to make them try less hard, but to evoke a response to the good will of their supporters. And all the time some people do not sufficiently observe that in that letter I pursue a double theme: one, the noisy attacks on the humanities and those who teach them, the other the uproar directed at Luther. On the first, I differ entirely and openly from that party. On the second, I set myself up neither as judge nor as prosecutor nor as defending counsel;[39] I merely point out what I should wish Luther to avoid.

Again, in my letter to the cardinal of Mainz,[40] I have no purpose except to prevent his being forcibly silenced before his case has been heard, for fear that this might open the door to the condemnation by some persons I could name of what they do not refute, and I dare say cannot even understand. Even so, I openly admit in that letter that there are some things in Luther that I do not like. I supported Luther up to a point of not wishing to see him handed over to the tender mercies of men who were ready to seize any pretext to undermine the humanities; but I did not support him to the extent of not wishing to see him disproved with evidence from Holy Scripture and refuted in argument, if he deserved to be refuted. Noble natures desire to be instructed, and will not endure to be coerced. Instruction is for theologians, merely to use coercion is for tyrants.[41] I supported Luther in that I would rather see him set right than destroyed, recalled from his errors rather than extinguished, if he has erred. And no one who has ever written, down to the present day, is free from error, the canonical Scriptures alone excepted. In this spirit I believe that even today all honourable theologians wish Luther well. Indeed, this is the spirit which I see in Pope Leo himself. Cyprian admired the writings and the genius of Tertullian; he did not agree with his views.[42] Jerome admired Origen's genius, but kept clear of those of his opinions which had been condemned.[43] Augustine seems delighted with Tychonius' books and his genius, while all the time keeping his party at a distance.[44]

Yet in saying this, I do not wish it to be used against Luther. I pass no judgment on him either way; he has his proper judges. Praise from me would do nothing for him; but by the same token I should be sorry for it to count against him if I express an unfavourable view. I merely wished to show how far I am from the position they place me in. I was the first person to regard his work with suspicion for fear it would breed discord. I was the first to oppose its printing in Basel,[45] and my opposition was serious, first in speech and in menaces when I was there, and later in letters after I left. I told him frequently and in detail, sometimes by letter, sometimes through friends,[46] of the things I wished he would avoid, and I did this with such freedom that my friends warned me[47] in their letters not to make myself unpopular with the majority in Germany by talking freely in the language I used in my letters – while nothing of the sort was done by the theologians, who supposed themselves powerful opponents of Luther. None of them gave him brotherly advice, no one deterred him, instructed him, proved him wrong.[48] They contented themselves with outcries: a new heretic had arisen, who taught that it was unnecessary to confess all one's capital sins[49] and that the advent of Antichrist is upon us.[50]

On his case I have never expressed an opinion; it was the method of attacking him, and no more, that I disapproved of as hasty, unbecoming, unmerciful, and fruitless. Is a man instantly in favour of murder, if he does not wish a man on trial for murder to be condemned before his case has been heard? Is a man on the side of the enemy who shows how he can be overcome with the least loss of life, or even points out that one should test whether he cannot be forced to surrender without risking a battle? If a man pursues the best interests of a commonwealth who would rather see its enemies survive than be destroyed, how have they the effrontery to blame a man who would like to see theologians do the same? In saying this, I am supposing for the moment something of which I was not convinced, that Luther is a master in error. Even so, in pointing out what I thought would be the best course, I left it none the less open to others to follow their own ideas if they found greater favour. I observed that this is a sore point which cannot be touched on without peril in front of a mixed audience, in which there are many people who resent the burden of confession; for there is no burden they will more readily throw off once they find that a theologian and a man of exemplary life is of this opinion. And yet it is uncertain even now whether Luther has expressed this opinion in his writings. Again, the sole result of this kind of clamour has been to make his books famous, which previously were known to very few, and to spur people on to read them who otherwise would never have opened them – greatly to the profit of the booksellers, who sold off their stock to all the more advantage, the more unrestrainedly those men declaimed against him. And all the time they taught the people nothing, and they taught Luther nothing. How can they glory in this title of doctor, which means teacher, if they do not mean to teach?

Let Luther be what he will, it must at least be more civilized to cure him than to snuff him out. In the old days bishops used their authority to intercede even for convicted criminals; which shows how far churchmen should be from a wanton lust for destruction. Augustine appealed on behalf of the Donatists,[51] pernicious heretics and pitiless robbers – I know not which aspect was worse – he knew they were plotting against his life, and yet he appealed on their behalf to the imperial governors not to subject them to physical torment. That excellent man, of course, wished them to repent; he had no wish to see them perish. He wanted them to be allowed to live because they might repent, and he wanted them to live in spite of the risk to himself personally. In the old days a heretic was listened to, even with respect, as is clear from what Augustine writes; and yet in those days the penalty of a convicted heretic who persisted in his error was no more than expulsion from the community of the orthodox.[52] Nowadays no proscription is more brutal than an accusation of heresy, and yet no word comes so easily to the lips of those persons, whoever they may be, who usurp what was the business of bishops; some of whom I know to be men of such character that I should not regard myself as better by one hair's breadth,[53] if they pronounced me orthodox in their opinion – to say quite frankly what I think.

The policy of certain wise men has found approval, who wished to see even the most abandoned criminals forgiven, thinking that one should consider not what men deserved for whose crimes no adequate punishment could be invented, but what was demanded by the dignity of the Roman name[54] and recommended by the good of the commonwealth. Paul everywhere lets false apostles go, for fear that if provoked they might do even more serious damage to the gospel teaching, which was still in its infancy.[55] How much less appropriate is this instant resentment against a man whose purity of life was highly spoken of by everyone, and whose books gave pleasure to so many eminent magnates, and to so many learned and religious readers! Had Luther really been the man they wanted him to appear, no policy could be put forward more likely to bring him low and give the theologians a glorious victory. They wished to see Luther entirely extinguished. Had the man either by his errors or by his contumacy deserved those ultimate remedies which are normally applied as a last resort, when all else has been tried and a limb is despaired of, of course in this way Luther could have been completely abolished; but first he must have been removed from men's minds and then from libraries too,[56] and all this without setting the Christian world by the ears. He might have been removed from their minds, had his opinions first been refuted with solid arguments and evidences from Holy Scripture by those qualified for the task by more than common learning and well-known integrity,[57] able to protect them from any hint of corruption.

Great weight attaches in the eyes of all Christians, and rightly so, to the authority of the Roman pontiff; but the greater its importance, the more need for care that it does not give too much scope to some men's private feelings, and the less it should overlook the unspoken judgments of learned and pious individuals.[58] Indeed, I should not be afraid to say that in principle no one does more harm to the honour of the pope than he whose support for him is either foolish or corrupt. Everyone knows that the pope has means of either destroying or terrifying whomsoever he pleases; but was ever any supreme power so well provided that fear alone sufficed to render it permanent? God himself desired to be loved as well as feared. And so, as I was about to say, the more weighty and wide-ranging is the pope's authority and the more outrageous the question at issue, the greater the need in my opinion to move slowly and with moderation. Had I been the only man to propose this, it would not, I think, have been reprehensible. As it is, I see that all intelligent men are on my side and think as I do, not only here but in Rome, not only among laymen but even among professional theologians and indeed among the Dominicans themselves.[59] Some of them would gladly see Luther condemned, but not condemned like this. I will not analyse here what sort of men are the leaders in this business,[60] I will not recount what they inflict upon us in place of the opinions of Luther which they condemn – much safer things perhaps, as human affairs are now conducted, but far more pernicious if one has a thought for the cause of gospel piety, and intolerable even to theologians who in other respects are ready to use any kind of artillery against Luther.

And so this policy of mine has supported Luther only to this extent: I think he should not be suppressed undeservedly, illegally, by popular clamour, or at the price of setting the world by the ears. But I thought it supported much more the dignity of the papacy and the authority of professional theologians, whose judgments should deserve to carry great weight, and whose character should be steady and well-balanced and as far removed as possible from any suspicion of folly or jealousy or avarice or ambition or spite or flattery and all the other appetites which deprive us of impartiality. No one gives the pope less support than he who supports him unwisely or from interested motives; and likewise no one does more damage to the reputation of theologians than those who make it their business to turn theologians into flatterers or tyrants. Moses did not hesitate to follow the advice of Jethro his father-in-law;[61] and yet they are angry with me for giving them honest advice, which as far as I was concerned they were at liberty not to take. If we wish to be told the truth, everyone must be free to utter his opinion, and even the man who gives bad advice must be forgiven, provided he was doing his best. But if one man is rewarded with a mitre and the other gets into serious trouble, what hope is there of hearing the truth? Out of so many universities only two have condemned some of Luther's peculiar opinions,[62] and even these do not agree – indeed the theologians of one of them are not entirely agreed among themselves.[63] Everyone was waiting for the opinion of the University of Paris,[64] which has always held the chief place in theological matters, much as the church of Rome has chief place in the Christian religion. While its judgment was still awaited, ought it to count against me, even if I did express approval of some of Luther's principles? As things are, I have never defended anything of his, even when it was permissible to do so; I merely disapproved of the turbulent and headstrong judgment of men who were not popular even with Luther's opponents.

This truly is a new kind of supporter for Luther![65] I was the first person to condemn Luther's books,[66] at least to the extent that they seemed to envisage public disturbance, which I have always consistently abhorred; I was the first to put obstacles in the way of his books being published. I am almost the only man who has not read his books, the only man who has never attempted to defend any of his opinions, even at some drinking-party, when the nonsense talked tends to be written in wine.[67] I have always urged that those who can should dispute against Luther and write against Luther.[68] When they began to do this in Louvain, I consistently approved, and only wish they had not begun at the wrong end. Out comes the preliminary verdict of two universities, hostile to Luther. Then a terrifying bull[69] is published under the pope's authority. Luther's books are burned. Noisy appeals are made to the public. The thing could hardly be done in a more spiteful way. Everyone thought the bull more merciless than suited the mildness of our beloved Leo, and the cruelty of it was not a little enhanced by those who carried it out. And no one all this time saw me either uneasy or more melancholy[70] than my wont.

What Silvester Prierias[71] had written against Luther has so far, from what I hear, found favour with nobody, even of those to whom Luther is anathema. Augustin the Minorite[72] found even less acceptance than Silvester. Of Thomas Rodaginus,[73] having only sampled him, I shall say nothing for the moment. There was one man in Louvain with an uncommon knowledge of scholastic theology and not ignorant of the theology of the Fathers, by name Jan Turnhout,[74] and he disputed for many days against some of Luther's principles – disputed as a theologian should, without personal abuse. He also wrote a pamphlet on this subject, and I do not doubt that he wrote with the same moderation that he showed in disputation. Nobody strove with more zeal than I to have that pamphlet published. Would a man do this who supported Luther in his errors? What connection have I with Luther, or what can I hope from him in the way of reward, that I should be willing to take his side against the teaching of the Gospel? or against the Roman church, which does not differ, I conceive, from the Catholic church? or against the Roman pontiff, head of the whole church, I who would not be willing to oppose even my own diocesan bishop?[75] I am not impious enough to dissent from the Catholic church, I am not ungrateful enough to dissent from Leo, of whose support and exceptional kindness to me I have personal experience. Last but not least, I am not imprudent enough to resist a power which even kings resist at their peril, even did I not much approve of his cause, especially since there would be no hope of doing any good.

If the corrupt behaviour of the Roman curia demands some great and instant remedy, at least it is not for me or men like me to take this province on ourselves. I would rather keep the present posture of human affairs, with all its faults, than see the rise of fresh disorders, which often tend in the opposite direction to what was expected. Those who admit the sea into pools newly built often make mistakes, for the water once admitted does not go in the direction designed by the man who admitted it, but breaks out where it pleases to the great loss of all within reach.[76] I have never knowingly been nor will I be, a leader in error; I have no intention to be a captain or coadjutor in civil strife. Let others court martyrdom;[77] it is an honour of which I find myself unworthy. I know that some people hate me, not because I am one of Luther's party[78] – this is the very thing that moves their anger, that I am not one – but it is those of whom no one approves except silly women, the uneducated, and the superstitious. Nor indeed are there any others who do not like me, except those who do not like the humanities and the truths of the Gospel, those (that is) who are fed and fattened by the folly of the public.[79]

I have written this to you at such length that, if there are any in your part of the world who bring me under suspicion,[80] you may not be moved by their false accusations. Pray be quite certain and perfectly convinced that your friend Erasmus always was and always will be a zealous supporter above all else of the see of Rome, to which I know myself indebted on so many grounds, and shall count any of its enemies my personal enemy. And how I wish the Germans had chosen to think out some prudent way of bringing this business of Luther to a peaceful close, preserving the pope's honour and the public peace, instead of aggravating a sore place already serious enough in itself, with impudent and subversive pamphlets. To many weighty and wise judges things looked like coming to a happier outcome had they been taken in hand with greater moderation and less ferocity by weighty, learned, and wise men; in other words, if Pope Leo had chosen to follow his disposition in this case and not give free rein to other men's prejudices. But however the trouble began, I pray that Christ the almighty may bring it to a solution which will mean happiness for all men, glory for himself, honour and renown for your Eminence, whose glory I shall never fail to defend to the best of my ability, if what I write has any value. Farewell.

Louvain, St Nicholas' day 1520

1168 / To Christoph Hegendorf — Louvain, 13 December 1520

This letter was published in the *Epistolae ad diversos*. The letter it answers was not selected to appear with it and has not survived. Christoph Hegendorf (1500–40), of Leipzig, received his MA at Leipzig at about the time he wrote to Erasmus. In 1521 he taught at the Leipzig faculty of arts while studying law. A prolific author, he moved to many places and although sympathetic to the reformers, was content to live in Catholic jurisdictions until later in his life. He was for a short time professor of law at Frankfurt an der Oder and died as Lutheran superintendent of Lüneburg.

ERASMUS OF ROTTERDAM TO CHRISTOPH HEGENDORF OF LEIPZIG, GREETING

I am as unlike Ulysses, whom you make me out to be in your letter, as you are unlike Thersites,[1] to whom you compare yourself. The repute of being a learned man, which you lavish on me to the limits of the tolerable, is a thing I reject over and over again, without effect. A reputation for courtesy and friendliness I would gladly accept, if my commitments and the jealousy of fortune allowed me to do as much as I would wish. For learning, I willingly give place to the first comer; in the obligations of courtesy I sometimes take second place, but this comes by necessity, not by nature. If Philippus Melanchthon has married a wife,[2] what else can we do except wish him happiness? What's done cannot be undone. So what is the point of collecting his friends' opinions now?

What Eck is doing[3] in your part of the world is being done by certain people here with even greater zeal. But this is a play in which I am resolved to be always a spectator; if it goes well, I shall claim no credit, and I cannot be blamed if it does not. 'The Fates will find a way.'[4] In any case, this making game of Eck by posting up placards[5] I dislike for many reasons. First, it is a dangerous precedent, which might rebound at short notice on anybody. Secondly, what could be more foolish than to provoke those whom you cannot control? And finally, what could be less creditable to the Germans, whose chief claim to fame used to be warlike valour,[6] than to fight with anonymous pamphlets? – which for the time being lay a load of suspicion on many innocent people, while they make the adversary's case even stronger.

The use of arms, except in urgent necessity, is not my policy, and in the same way I think poster warfare quite foolish and unworthy of grown men. It was more to the point to look about for some policy by which this whole business could be settled without disturbance.[7] As it is, Luther is taking on people who, even if their cause were bad – which I do not think it is – could not in any case be put down. And all the time he lays a burden of unpopularity on the humanities, against which he stirs up these hornets;[8] hardly tolerable even when things are going badly for them, they will be unendurable when flown with victory. Unless I am quite blind, they have another target besides Luther – they are in a hurry to storm the citadel of the Muses. I shall be quite content to look a fool if the facts do not bear me out. Farewell.

Louvain, 13 December 1520

1169 / To Agostino Scarpinelli — Louvain, 13 December 1520

Agostino Scarpinelli of Naples was at this time an attendant of Luigi Marliano, bishop of Tuy. From 1522 to 1532 he was Milan's ambassador at the court of Henry VIII of England. Erasmus acknowledged receipt of a letter from him in March 1535 (cf Ep 3005); nothing is known of him after that date. This letter, which seems to reflect a recent meeting (cf n1), was printed in the *Epistolae ad diversos*. It may not have reached Scarpinelli; cf Ep 1198 n6.

ERASMUS OF ROTTERDAM TO THE HONOURABLE AGOSTINO SCARPINELLI OF NAPLES, GREETING

I could wish such a journey reserved for my enemies as fell to my lot when I hurried back here.[1] The wind, the rain, the floods! Even in the hills we narrowly escaped shipwreck, for we had to take to the water on horseback. My servant's horse swam safe to shore with some difficulty; for I preferred to learn wisdom at other people's expense. The queen of Aragon[2] had proceeded a mile and a half from Aachen, when she and her company were forced to return to the city. But I was brave. It seemed cowardice to return defeated to my starting-point, and be laughed at by my host, the kindest man alive – Leonardus Priccardus,[3] I mean, who had begged and prayed me in vain to spend one more day with the friends who were so eager for my society. So I continued on my way. I should never have heard the last of it, if wind and rain had extorted from me what I had refused to concede to a great friend, and other friends with him too, and to Sunday,[4] when even farmers take a day off. We rode almost the whole way by ourselves, without seeing a single bandit, though there were many terrifying rumours.

What about you? How goes it in your part of the world? Are you picking up the true German spirit? How do you fancy those German stoves?[5] Happy man, who are blessed with summer in midwinter! And how, pray, goes your darling Cicero?[6] What hope have you that the whole of him may some day come to life again? But be very, very careful not to be so devoted to your Tully that, like Jerome,[7] you end up with your shoulders black and blue with the strap. You laugh, you think it was a dream; but he, who experienced it, says it was not a dream. Seriously though, my dear Agostino, I applaud the zeal with which you devote yourself wholly to Cicero. If I had done the same, perhaps our more fair-minded spirits would have shown more gratitude than I now get from certain persons I could name, to whom you render a service at your instant peril.

I shall shortly return to your society.[8] Meanwhile please give my greetings to that gentle spirit, your old friend Saeverus,[9] and to that leader of men, Luigi Marliano, bishop of Tuy. Farewell.

Louvain, 13 December 1520

1170 / To Leonardus Priccardus — Louvain [or Basel, 1520–c 1523]

This letter is addressed to a friend in Aachen (cf Ep 972), who had extended hospitality to Erasmus on his return from Cologne in November 1520 (cf Ep 1169:9–16). It was written, possibly tongue in cheek, to explain away the somewhat biting humour of Erasmus' account of a visit with the canons of Aachen in September 1518 (cf Ep 867:114–53), but was not printed until the *Opus epistolarum* of 1529, where the year date given is clearly wrong and the place may not be correct either. As Allen has pointed out, this letter is not likely to have been written prior to the publication of Ep 867 in the *Farrago* of October 1519, even though Ep 867 circulated widely in manuscript. By the time the *Epistolae ad diversos* followed the *Farrago* (cf Ep 1206 introduction) Erasmus must have received protests from the canons which caused him to make changes in Ep 867 when it was reprinted (cf n3, n4). Perhaps the protests were voiced during his recent visit and the changes made shortly thereafter. This letter too might have been written in preparation for the *Epistolae ad diversos*. It is not printed there, however, and Erasmus states that the wound Ep 867 had caused to the pride of the Aachen canons had 'already healed over,' but had now been 'rubbed up' again (lines 7–9). A date after Erasmus' move to Basel and the publication of the *Epistolae ad diversos* may therefore be preferable. A later date is more likely to explain the reference to Johann von Vlatten (line 52), who is not otherwise mentioned in Erasmus' letters before 1523, when he became a regular correspondent. Vlatten studied from April 1520 to October 1521 in Orléans (cf *Matricule d'Orléans* II-2 67–8) and is therefore less likely to have been present during Erasmus' recent visit to Aachen, where he too held a canonry. As it does not seem possible to date this letter more precisely, Allen's placing has been retained.

ERASMUS OF ROTTERDAM TO LEONARDUS PRICCARDUS, CANON OF AACHEN, GREETING

Dear Priccardus, my most learned friend, how well Aristophanes puts it![1] 'But for the tooth of slander there's no cure.' Against the poison of asps men have discovered charms, for the bite of vipers and mad dogs the physicians have invented remedies, but for the tooth of calumny no remedy exists. I hear that a certain theologian in your part of the world has rubbed up an old sore, or rather, has made a serious wound out of a place that was already healed over. He says it is my doing that your canons are a laughing stock in the universities on account of a letter I wrote to Beatus Rhenanus.[2] To begin with, as far as my intentions are concerned, nothing was ever further from my thought than that words of mine should cast the least aspersion on such men, to whom I owe so much; on the contrary, I shall stop at nothing if I can render any service that may tend to their honour or their well-being. I should be the most discourteous brute in the world, if I had wished to repay consummate courtesy with insult.

This much about my intentions is the first thing I wish to record. But what is there, I ask you, in the thing itself, that could reflect on their reputation? Was it my saying that the party was prolonged far into the night?[3] Why, we had sat down very late; and this too was courtesy on their part, because by inviting some people for my benefit they made their party last longer. There was not a touch there of the drinking-party,[4] and not a soul showed more of the effects of drink than I did myself. As for the dean's[5] dragging me to the party against my will, what am I complaining of except distinguished courtesy on his part? In the same way did not the two disciples constrain Jesus to stay all night?[6]

And how does it reflect on the vice-provost[7] if, at a time when stormy weather kept the fishermen from fishing, he had nothing on the table but eels and fish dried in the wind? As if the same thing did not sometimes happen in Rome to the grandest of the cardinals! And yet I am by nature very partial to this dried fish. Furthermore, if some pieces were mixed in that were not properly cooked, I suspected the reason was that more guests flocked in than he was expecting. At any rate, I thought that vice-provost a young man of exceptional courtesy and most abstemious. In short, I hardly ever fell in with any society which I should have found more attractive, had I had my health. And what kind of insult lurks in my mention of the rotation? As if the custom did not exist among most bodies of canons – and were not admirable on many grounds – of dining in rotation and acting as host in turn, either to avoid the regular habits of laymen, so that familiarity may not breed contempt, or to reduce expenses, which are less when a larger number meet together. And all the time one learns something in such a party, one talks a little business, sometimes even certain mistakes are set to rights. Hence it is that Plato,[8] most strait-laced of philosophers, approves moderate parties of the kind, and does not disapprove even of the Greek habit of inviting others (in moderation) to drink with you, provided the principle of moderation in all things remains intact.

I beg you therefore, my dear Leonardus, if my traducer has told the story badly and got it wrong, explain it properly and put it right; and promise my masters on my behalf all that they have a right to expect from a grateful man with a good memory. And if they do not trust what I say, let them put me to the test. I will shrink from nothing, be it ever so laborious. My greetings to Vlatten[9] and all the rest.

Louvain, [1517]

1171 / To Matthäus Schiner — Louvain, 16 December 1520

Erasmus continued to paraphrase the apostolic Epistles (cf Epp 710, 916, 956, 1043, 1062, 1112) and had now produced his rendering of the Epistle of St James. Like most of the preceding paraphrases it was first printed in Louvain: *In epistolam Iacobi paraphrasis* (Louvain: D. Martens December 1520; NK 2958) and reprinted in *Paraphrases in omnes epistolas Pauli germanas et in omnes canonicas* (Basel: J. Froben March, and again in July 1521; cf CWE 42 xxii–xxiii).

This letter is the dedicatory preface addressed to Cardinal Schiner, an old patron, who continued to take a special interest in the paraphrases of the New Testament; cf n11, Epp 1179, 1248.

TO HIS EMINENCE THE RIGHT REVEREND MATTHÄUS, CARDINAL BISHOP OF SION, COUNT OF THE VALAIS,[1] FROM ERASMUS OF ROTTERDAM, GREETING

I thought I had already reached the end of my race, and was intending to give myself a rest, at any rate from studies of this kind, having now explained all the Epistles which I thought genuinely Pauline; to which I have added Peter's two and one by Jude,[2] because they not only stand close to the Pauline Epistles in the force of their gospel teaching but are even more involved in darkness[3] than they are. As for the so-called Epistle to the Hebrews,[4] not only can it be gathered from many indications that it is not Paul's, but it is written in a rhetorical style unlike the Apostle's, and therefore does not present nearly so much difficulty. The same is true of those ascribed to James and John.[5] John writes with such fullness that he virtually explains himself, and James almost confines himself to commonplaces, for example: For Christ's sake we must bravely endure adversity and therein rely principally on support from God; Men become wicked through no fault of nature or of God but by their own fault, whether fortune be cruel or kind; One should not speak rashly or give rein to one's anger; It is not sufficient to profess the Gospel in word alone, unless we express it in our actions and affections; That religion is empty which is combined with lack of control over the tongue; True piety is found in the services whereby in mercy we relieve the needs of our neighbour; No man's worth should be gauged by his external wealth, but by the true wealth of the mind; Profession of the faith is useless, unless it is evidenced by pious actions; No man should take up the task of teaching unadvisedly; The chief plague of life springs from an unbridled tongue, just as on the other hand nothing is more useful than a good and well-governed tongue; There is a great difference between worldly and Christian wisdom; Peace cannot last unless human desires are driven out of the heart; There can be no agreement between this world and God; Those who are elated by their own resources and trust in them are abandoned by God, while he is good to those who distrust themselves and depend upon him; He does wrong to God who condemns and judges his neighbour; Short-lived and fleeting is the felicity of this present life; The powerful, who can do as they please with impunity here, will be bitterly punished hereafter; Revenge for wrongs suffered must be left to God as the judge; Good men's prayers have great weight with God; The virtuous action which most inclines God to forgive our sins is that we should forgive our brother when he sins against us and that when he wanders we should lovingly recall him to the right way – and much else of the same kind, which cannot present very much difficulty in the exposition, though they are most difficult in the performance. And yet there are certain passages which I had to wrestle with, such as the one which puzzles Augustine:[6] 'Whoso offendeth in one thing is guilty of all.'[7] Again, where he says that faith is of no value without works, while Paul argues on the other side that it happened to Abraham not by works but by faith that he was accounted just before God and was called the friend of God.[9] There also seem to be some gaps,[10] so that I have had some trouble in establishing connections.

Be that as it may, when I first took this labour in hand, I did not propose to pay this attention to any except those two great chiefs of the apostles and of the gospel philosophy, Paul and Peter. And behold, as I reach my goal and look forward to my rest, your voice calls me back onto the course,[11] urging me over and over again to leave no portion of this task to others, not only because you judge that this activity will be exceptionally useful to seekers after the gospel philosophy, but also since, though the tooth of slander in these days leaves almost nothing intact, yet this work of mine alone has not yet been bedevilled[12] (so to say) by all the demons of criticism. I obey the summons of your Eminence. It is no secret from me, your heartfelt love of truly Christian teaching, in which you spent not a few successful years yourself; nor your sincere support for me, your perspicacious mind, your clear and independent judgment. If the Catholic church possessed more such men, we should see Christianity far more flourishing and somewhat more peaceful.

What spirit hounds them on, those men who, at the risk of their own reputation and authority and to the detriment even of their sacred duty of preaching, endeavour so persistently to reduce the profit that the studious may hope to find in my work? This question only they can answer. I am myself more swayed by the judgment of other men whose more than common scholarship and high integrity clears them of all suspicion of envy or ill will. I stand in the way of no man's reputation, I chase no man from his professorial chair, I interrupt no man's researches; I seek no promotion, I do not hunt for gain, but what little talent I have I contribute to the common good. The man who does not like my work is free to leave it alone; I make this gift to the public without reward. Should anyone wish to do better, I will vote for him with both hands.[13] I have never worn the badge of any faction, and what I write has left no man blacker by a single hair.[14]

In every age it has been permissible to dissent now and again from the most eminent authorities. If I disagreed only with Thomas,[15] I might be thought to have a prejudice against him. In fact, I disagree with Ambrose and

Jerome and Augustine not seldom – always with great respect; towards Thomas I have a more open mind than commends itself to many excellent and learned men. But this respect I do not think I owe to Hugo and Lyra[16] and to all their like, although to Lyra I do acknowledge a debt. In every generation, however blessed, the best things have always appealed to the minority. But was there ever a generation that gave more scope to ignorance, effrontery, shamelessness, stupidity, and abusive language? Write books they dare not, for these must undergo the silent criticism of educated men;[17] their weapons are words steeped in venom, and their audience the unlettered multitude and poor credulous women. This innocent credulity offers them their only hope of winning. What heroes! – these doughty performers with one single weapon, which they share with fishwives. After which they think it my fault if their own reputation suffers, if fewer recruits come forward to join their holy flock;[18] while they themselves make it clear, even in public, from the facts, how much closer they are to impious blackmailers than to devotees of true religion. And their nemesis will one day descend upon them, as they bring disaster upon themselves with their own horse and cart,[19] and from some source or other will come the proper wedge to split that knot.[20] Nor do I think it sensible to fight against a conspiracy of potbellies,[21] without eyes or mind. It is more in keeping for a true Christian to endure mountebanks than to imitate them. For myself, encouraged by you and others like you, but above all with Christ as my lodestar, I shall continue by sleepless toiling in this field to urge myself and others on to better things. Farewell, my most respected benefactor.

Louvain, 16 December 1520

1172 / To Godschalk Rosemondt

Louvain, [between 16 and c 25 December] 1520

Following Epp 1153, 1164 Erasmus appealed once again to the rector of the University of Louvain. This letter was published in the *Epistolae ad diversos*; an approximate date can be assigned in view of line 23 and n1.

ERASMUS OF ROTTERDAM TO THE DISTINGUISHED THEOLOGIAN DR GODSCHALK ROSEMONDT, RECTOR OF THE UNIVERSITY OF LOUVAIN, GREETING

You know, I doubt not, Rector magnificus, for it is common knowledge, of the seditious rancour unloaded on me by a second Jacobite,[1] a worthy successor of the previous rascal,[2] who draws the line at no abuse and from time to time spreads obvious falsehoods. Have these men no sense of decency? Having spouted rubbish till he was sated and his audience were feeling sick, this merry mountebank ended by bidding them pray to God for me, that some day I might be turned to a better frame of mind. Unless some theologians either instigated or winked at this, they would not dare use such insulting behaviour in a university so famous, and that in church sermons, and interminably too. It does not surprise me that Jacobites should display such audacity; I am surprised that it should commend itself to the faculty of theology. The faculty could not endure the single word 'vain talker'[3] launched obliquely against Egmondanus; yet all this seditious and worse than scurrilous stuff they placidly tolerate and, if I am not mistaken, encourage. This is the method they have adopted for putting an end to their Erasmus. If only I were as mad as they are, what a splendid set-to we should see.

At this stage, a clear conscience can endure all this, and worse; but all the time what an example of spite they are setting! And where will it end? A pretty piece of Christmas play-acting![4] I have no wish to take on the whole tribe of Preachers: I am not as mad as that. For better or for worse, I leave them to the judgment of God. I am no enemy of monks, or theologians either, unless perhaps he is to be regarded as an enemy of all Christians who disapproves of some things in their behaviour. If the theological faculty has anything against me, let us have it out; let them put forward what they wish. I am ready to give an account of my work to all men in their right mind; for discussion with Egmondanus is not discussion at all.[5] Well said that old moral maxim[6] 'He talks to the wind who takes a sot to court'; much more so he who takes a raving lunatic. This scurrilous uproar is too much even for laymen; all the less reason to doubt that it is too much for a man of the highest standards like yourself. But your mildness is tantamount to cruelty towards me, and indeed towards the whole university. It was your duty, even if I said nothing, to order the whole monastery, and indeed preachers everywhere, to refrain from such provocation. His predecessor was warned off under threat of the severest penalties;[7] and no one took any steps against him whatever. A child could tell what that means.

Henceforward I shall not make myself a nuisance to your Magnificence. I hope that you will do your duty; and if you do not, my temperament is such as can make light of these things. But if a riot does break out, it will be laid at the door of those who either pretended they did not exist, or encouraged their early stages. You certainly cannot so pretend. Farewell, Rector magnificus, and if you wish me to do anything, let me have your commands, and you will find me most ready to obey.

Louvain, 1520

1173 / To Frans van Cranevelt

Louvain, 18 December 1520

This letter, whose first paragraph is an acknowledgement of Cranevelt's Ep 1145, was published in the *Epistolae ad diversos*. It was given to a young Louvain scholar (cf lines 13–14) to serve him as an introduction to the influential pensionary of the city of Bruges. Primarily, however, it offers another account of Erasmus' confrontation with the Carmelite Nicolaas Baechem Egmondanus (lines 27–109) and repeats Erasmus' complaints against some Dominicans (lines 110–23, 141–67).

TO THE DISTINGUISHED DOCTOR OF CIVIL AND CANON LAW FRANS VAN CRANEVELT, COUNCILLOR OF THE CITY OF BRUGES, FROM ERASMUS OF ROTTERDAM, GREETING

This is, to be sure, what the current proverb calls acquiring two sons-in-law with a single marriageable daughter.[1] You thank me as the person responsible for your having made friends with such an open-hearted man as More; and he in turn thanks me, through whom he has been blessed with the acquaintance of Cranevelt. I knew from the start, given your kinship in character and gifts, that you would make friends if only you could get to know one another. To own such friends is one of the most precious things there is, and very rare, especially in days like these, which makes it the more important to acquire and keep them too.

There has lately moved to your part of the world one Petrus surnamed Amicus,[2] a young man whose character and abilities are wholly admirable. He spent several years with Gilles de Busleyden,[3] whose children he taught, and who loved him like a son as an upright man whom he could trust. He is now in search of a somewhat more lucrative position, and in my opinion deserves a very good one. He is an elegant Latin and Greek scholar, besides which he has spent some years not without success in the study of law. Last but not least, he is a reliable secretary. I do not doubt that his own gifts will fully recommend him; but he thinks none the less that he will be even more acceptable to all men of good judgment if added to your company of friends. For myself, I am most ready to have my name entered afresh in your list of debtors, if you can do any service to a man to whom I am so much attached; but I think it more likely that, as has happened before, it will be both of you who are grateful to me.

Our old friends here do not cease to be their true selves, caballing, muttering, yelping, threatening; they think it is my doing that Luther's business is not such an appalling failure as they would like.[4] Egmondanus the Carmelite throws a stone at me from time to time in a sermon or a public lecture,[5] and is laughed at all the time even by his fellow Carmelites. When I laid a complaint and he appeared some time ago before the rector of this university,[6] he piled so much falsehood and scurrility on me face to face that he was prepared to make me out guilty of sacrilege, parricide, peculation, or anything else you please, had the words occurred to him. In this way he thought himself a hero, while the rector and I rightly thought he was mad. It was monstrous to hear such outrageous language from a theologian, a monk, and an old man. At the first of his outrages I began to get very angry; but soon I thought it better to laugh at the man than to try to correct him.

At length our prolonged altercation ended like this. If I were willing to testify in print that at Louvain there are worthy and honourable theologians, if I were willing to use my pen to cut Luther to pieces,[7] then we should be brothers, but on no other terms could there be peace. I replied that they had better prove themselves to be in fact what they wished to appear; and as to Luther, I replied that I had no intention of meddling now in a case so fraught with ill will, in which I had never meddled before. True, I did not approve of the clamorous attacks on him in public places, thinking that people ought to publish books in order to refute him; but this policy, I said, told against Luther and favoured the theologians, for this would be absolutely the end of him if he had first been put out of men's heads, whereas now all that happens is the removal of his books from libraries, and the man himself remains fixed in their hearts.[8] The bulls of popes, I said, carry great weight, but among scholars there is much more force in a book that seeks, with sound arguments and evidence from Holy Scripture, to convince and not to compel; for noble natures are easily led by reason, and not so easily driven by absolute rule.[9] For the point to be considered, as I told him, was not simply what Luther deserves, but how best we can remedy this evil.

And it did not seem right, I went on, for me to meddle on my own initiative in an affair that did not take its rise with me; it was more appropriate that the same people who had begun to act this play should play it out, that they should finish weaving the piece of cloth they themselves had started, and empty the mortar with all the garlic they had pounded in it.[10] In any case, why should I write against Luther rather than anybody else?[11] If it is a mad idea to set all the theologians to write against one man, and few are capable of doing so, it was most fitting, I said, that he should be refuted in print by the men who had argued against him, who had torn him to pieces in their sermons, who had made up their minds in advance and passed judgment on him before the pope himself could. If I had any ability with the pen, this was not peculiar to me, I said, and what this case needs is not fine writing but solid learning, of which they claimed a near monopoly. Besides which, I added, it might be thought brutal for me to attack with my pen a man who was laid low already and routed and even committed to the flames. Nor indeed would it be safe to rouse against my own person the resentment of a man who lacked neither teeth nor muscle and, as his books show, really has hay on his horns;[12] nor would it be prudent for me to inflame for no good reason the hatred of so many German princes and so many learned men. It would moreover have been rash of me to take upon myself a task which no one could have entrusted to me with any authority, especially as I saw so many orders of monks and so many universities preferring to be spectators rather than actors in this play – perhaps because they were doubtful what the end would be. For the danger is not over that the action of the piece may culminate in uproar, unless milder counsels can find some way to peace. But whatever the outcome may be, I pray that it may tend towards the glory of Christ. Some perhaps may say that it was thirst for glory made me come up at speed after the battle was over to claim for myself the credit of other men's exploits.

My last point was this. I know myself too well to suppose that as a light-weight theologian – a schoolmaster,[13] rather, as they love to call me – I could assume such an arduous task, which would need a divine of the first rank and of great authority. For I do not choose to think that some of them were playing a double game and purposed, once I had written against Luther and roused the anger of the Germans,[14] to use their hatred forthwith as a means to destroy me. I added that my labour would be wasted; what weight could my judgment carry with men who remained unmoved by the opinion of two universities[15] and an official statement by the pope?[16] Even were there no truth in all this, it was impossible to refute anything that one had not read two or three times from cover to cover; and Luther had written a great deal. Indeed, I scarcely had the leisure to revise my own books. Let them for preference publish their own, I said; for Latomus and Turnhout had books ready now,[17] and both are good scholars, while one of them has some idea how to write.

In the end Egmondanus would have been satisfied if, though unwilling to do battle against Luther, I would at least go on record that he had been defeated by the university of Louvain.[18] I said that there were plenty of people to publish that fact, and it was not yet clear to me that he had been defeated, before their arguments were published. It was not, I suggested, a very glorious victory or one that should be widely published, especially by theologians, if it was earned from bulls and burning books. And so I quit that interview, having narrowly escaped being spat upon.

And now something has roused them again, and there seems to be a plot to finish me off from the pulpit. When I was at Calais for the meeting of monarchs,[19] a certain Jacobite,[20] a youngish man, conceited and self-confident, a regular Phormio,[21] held forth against me in Louvain for several weeks, raining abuse on me by the cart-load. He was commenting on my

Moria before a public audience according to the vituperative sense.[22] At length, while I did nothing about it, he was ordered to be silent, but not before he had spewed out all the nonsense that came into his head. Just lately he has begun again worse than ever, provoked by my *Antibarbari*,[23] which he does not understand; again, he has been repeatedly told to stop, but has not yet recovered his self-control. Finally, two days ago another Jacobite,[24] newly returned, they say, from France, came forward to preach and piled all the abuse you can think of on me by name with such impudence that everyone, even the laity, was disgusted. Admire the new-found tolerance of our theologians! They take this without comment, while the one expression 'vain talker'[25] aimed indirectly at the Camelite[26] Egmondanus roused them to fury. No one fails to understand when this happens that there are certain theologians who partly wink at it and partly give it encouragement. A pretty weapon for theologians! They do not protest face to face, backbiting for them and caballing in corners; and this is the sort of buffoon who does their work for them. That eminent doctor Nicolaus Egmondanus, beginning public lectures on the Pauline Epistles,[27] brought in a charming pleasantry. Paul, he said, who had been a savage persecutor, became the mildest of preachers of the Gospel; 'and in the same way,' he went on, 'we must pray for the conversion of Luther and Erasmus,' as though I had any more connection with Luther than Egmondanus himself has. They thought this a pretty trick (but they were hardly sober at the time) to put Luther and Erasmus in double harness – like yoking an ox with a fallow deer.

You have been wondering for some time, I dare say, why I inflict this sad nonsense on you. The fancy took me to gossip with a friend and to pour my trifles, such as they are, into your sympathetic ear. But I do wonder why an order,[28] to which I wish well above all others, and perhaps in a truer sense than they do themselves, should take special pleasure in this kind of tragic upheaval, as though after all the tumults they have aroused – first over the conception of the Virgin Mother of God,[29], then in Florence at the hands of Girolamo Savoronella, after that in Bern through criminals far more abandoned,[30] again in the attacks on Johann Reuchlin led by Jacob of Hoogstraten,[31] and yet again in the opposition to Hermann, count of Neuenahr, a man much loved all over Germany – as though, I say, after all this they had not made themselves sufficiently unpopular without a fresh campaign of such seditious clamour aimed at me to rouse still more the hatred of all men of good will; for good men cannot approve such impudence, even those who may not approve of Erasmus. And they make me out to be an enemy, though I never did anything to hurt them; it would be truer to say that I have done them services for which I get very poor thanks. When

Reuchlin was attacking them so fiercely, I sent him two or three letters[32] telling him not to harm the order, but to confine his ferocity to the man who had done him wrong. Again, when Hermann, count of Neuenahr was angry for very good reasons, and debarred all the Jacobites from collecting their cheeses,[33] I urged him strongly in a letter[34] to let them do it, and he, as one would expect of a man of truly high and noble heart, overlooked their offensive behaviour and did not retaliate. And now see the gratitude I get! They think the whole order is insulted if one says a word against unprincipled monks, exactly as though such men did not exist, while they would do better to keep their indignation for those whose characters are a disgrace to their order. In fact, if one were to draw a pattern of a good monk, they take it as a personal reflection.[35]

If they have any right to do this, they will rightly be angry with Chrysostom,[36] who in his fiftieth homily and several that follow depicts the ideal of the monastic life in language that will give everyone plenty to think about who has had to do with the monks of our own day. 'Shunning the market-place,' he says, 'and cities and all their turmoil, they have chosen a life in the hills that has nothing in common with the present and does not suffer the lot of common men, the sadness of this world and grief and care, the dangers and the pitfalls, the ill will and the jealousy, the foolish passions and all else of the kind.' Then, after speaking at length of the modesty of their food and clothing, their industrious labours, their hospitality, their sacred studies, he gives the following picture of their conversation at table: 'And should you wish to learn of their customs at table, come nearer, and you will find their talk all of the same kind, all mild and cheerful and full of a sweet spiritual fragrance; no unworthy language could ever pass those lips, no scurrility, no rudeness, but all is worthy of heaven.' Later on, after mentioning the virulent hostility of laymen, Chrysostom adds, 'Their tongues may be likened to rivers that flow with honey and pure welling streams.' And again, in the next homily, 'Let us then,' he says, 'betake ourselves to them, and there we shall learn to know a table loaded with countless good things, that never fails, free from anxiety, immune from envy and jealousy and all the plagues of life, full of good hope, and proud of many victories. There is no tumult there, no sickness, and no wrath; all is tranquillity and all is peace.' These men will have to scrape his words out of their books, unless they prefer to become unrecognizable; and not these words only, but all that Jerome and all that Bernard[37] have written about the true religious life. 'It is expedient,' they say, 'that the public should have the highest possible opinion of monks.' This may perhaps be true, if they are good monks; but it is still more expedient that they should be what they wish to seem to be. Otherwise, it is a great calamity if under the mask of a religious life they impose upon the world. It is expedient that the people should have a high opinion of their pastors, their bishops, their magistrates; yet these are the targets, whenever those men choose, for their unlimited vituperation.

But I have already said too much on this subject. Take my advice, and mingle in all this tragic business as little as you can. Farewell, best of men.

Louvain, 18 December 1520

1174 / To Maarten Lips — Louvain, 20 December [1520]

This letter was copied by Lips into the copy-book which is now in Rotterdam (cf Ep 750 introduction), and was not published until 1882. The year date can be established by comparison with Epp 1166 and 1189–90.

ERASMUS OF ROTTERDAM TO MAARTEN LIPS OF BRUSSELS, GREETING

I have no doubt, my dear Maarten, that you have long been thinking me uncivil; but my behaviour is dictated not by nature but by inescapable necessity. I have by now become hardened to all rumours. Things have issued in sheer madness.[1] The potbellies,[2] and their shameless scurrilities under the cloak of religion – these now rule the roost. Satan is already singing his song of triumph. As for me, I shall busy myself here in the philosophy of Christ, that I may not give rise to any faction or disturbance. And if the world shows itself ungrateful, may Christ out of the abundance of his riches recompense the poor fruit of my nightly labours.

I was put on the roll of councillors three years ago, but owing to the death of Le Sauvage my patent was never issued.[3] And I pressed for it with the air of a man to whom it had no value. Now it is ready, but what importance it has, I do not know; I certainly am not greatly moved by it.

The volume containing both Testaments in Greek,[4] when you asked for it, was with the Franciscans;[5] now I need it in the revision of the New Testament.[6] I will see, however, whether it can be found on sale here; but I fear the price will be high, and it cannot be divided. I am engaged in revising the text of Augustine. If your library has anything in the way of old copies, let me know.[7] Farewell, and best wishes for your enjoyment of your sacred studies.

Louvain, 20 December

1175 / To Polidoro Virgilio — Louvain, 23 December 1520

This letter exposes a touchy moment in the course of a friendship of long standing (cf n4). Polidoro Virgilio and Erasmus had both produced collections of ancient proverbs. While Polidoro's *Proverbiorum libellus* (Venice: C. de Pensis 10 April 1498) predated the first edition of Erasmus' *Adagia* (Paris: J. Philippi 15 June 1500) by a good two years, at the time of this letter each scholar was unaware of the first edition of his rival's work and believed that its second edition actually was the first (cf n9, n17). As a result Polidoro had all the more ground to claim priority in the preface to the second, enlarged edition of his collection, now entitled *Adagiorum liber* (Basel: J. Froben July 1521), which occasioned this reply by Erasmus. The relevant sections of Polidoro's preface, addressed to Richard Pace (cf n2 and Ep 1210), are reprinted in Allen's headnote to this letter. At no time was Erasmus prepared to admit that Polidoro's book had been the first to appear (cf Ep 531:456–62) and in the preface to the 1533 edition of his *Adagia* he still claimed priority for himself (cf Allen Ep 2773:69–76). At the time he wrote this letter Erasmus was also piqued by the suspicion – again unjustified, it would seem – of collusion between Polidoro and Edward Lee (cf n28).

Bonifacius Amerbach, who had left Basel in May 1520, mentioned the arrival of the copy for Polidoro's enlarged collection in the first letter he wrote to Andrea Alciati after his return, 11 June 1521 (cf AK II Ep 791). We may assume that the copy had arrived during his absence, and this is confirmed by the date of this letter, which was first printed in the *Epistolae ad diversos*. When Erasmus wrote it he had evidently seen Polidoro's two prefaces (lines 126–9, cf n2) and actually states that he had sent them back. In Ep 1210 he writes that Hieronymus Froben had taken the entire copy of Polidoro's collection to Antwerp in order to return it to the author. By January 1521 Hieronymus met Erasmus in Louvain or Antwerp (cf Ep 1226 introduction). We may perhaps assume he had arrived shortly before this letter was written and that Erasmus had intervened right then to reverse Froben's refusal (cf lines 5–9). At any rate, that the friendship with Polidoro was not seriously threatened is shown also by Erasmus' letter (Ep 1210) to their common friend, Richard Pace.

Polidoro Virgilio (cf Ep 531:456n), often known by his Anglicized name, Polydore Vergil, was appointed archdeacon of Wells in 1508 in recognition of his diplomatic services. He remained in England until 1553, when the growth of Protestantism and a desire to spend his last years in his native Italy prompted him to leave. His principal works are a history of England, *Historia Anglica* (Basel: J. Bebel 1534, reprinted with a continuation in 1555) and *De rerum inventoribus*, a historical encyclopaedia of ancient culture, originally published in 1499, but now reprinted by Froben together with Polidoro's *Adagiorum liber*; cf Ep 1210:5–6. This new edition of July 1521 contained five books, not previously printed, on the development of Christian institutions, which earned Polidoro a place on the index of prohibited books.

ERASMUS OF ROTTERDAM TO POLIDORO VIRGILIO, GREETING

What a heartless man you are! Not content to see Edward Lee deprive me of the credit of revising the New Testament,[1] you must needs proceed to deprive me of a good part of the praise due to me from my book of proverbs. For that seems to be the object you pursue at great length in the preface in which you commend to the reader your half-pagan and half-Christian book,[2] the success of which is so far from making me jealous that, when Johann Froben objected with great force to printing it, it was I who forced rather than persuaded him to produce it with his most elegant type and paper.[3] For it is perfectly untrue, my dear Polidoro, that I look askance at your reputation and your books; on the contrary, you and I have known each other for so long,[4] and I so much admire your talents and your wit, that there is hardly another person to whom I wish so well. But it is even more heartless that, in claiming for yourself the credit of being the first to treat of this subject in Latin, you should at the same time try to involve me in the suspicion of being a vainglorious and jealous man; though you would be hard put to it to find a more unselfish or more whole-hearted supporter of the devotees of good literature. It is a pleasure, even if they throw one in the shade[5] – so far am I from trying to stand in the way of any man's reputation. Besides which, my affection for you is such that I should not hesitate actually to give you a larger part, out of my own stock, of the credit of which you say I claim more than my fair share.

In any case, if there is no mention of your name in the first edition,[6] this is not surprising, for at that time the name Polidoro was still unknown to me, except for the character in tragedy[7] whom Polymnestor 'by violence cuts down and takes the gold.' On this point, you suppose me to be dissembling,[8] for you assert that what I say is most unlikely, since Matthias Schürer's preface bears witness that before he printed my book of proverbs, he had already printed yours.[9] What Schürer may have said, I do not know; what cannot be denied is that my book of proverbs had been printed ten years earlier in Paris by Johannes Philippi,[10] before I had ever heard the name of Schürer. Though what you say is pointless, for since Schürer did not produce the first edition of either your book or mine, this argument has no more force in deciding which of us came first than the proverbial 'white line on a white stone.'[11]

And yet, when a dispute once arose between us on this point at dinner,[12] I pointed out where you could look for a decisive test – the very place where I had myself found the evidence that I was first, I mean, the date of publication. In the days when you and I were still strangers to one another, my book, such as it was, had already been thumbed by the studious young for several years, when the plague, which raged continually in Cologne as well as in Paris,[13] obliged me to take refuge in Louvain.[14] Why I always disliked Louvain, though a most agreeable place, as though it gave me a feeling of trouble to come, I now at length understand.[15] It was there that a certain Sarmatian called Lukas,[16] a theologian with whom I was on pretty familiar terms while I was there but who was prejudiced against my work, for no other reason (I suppose) except that he had himself wooed the reluctant Muses for many years without success – this Lukas had started a widespread rumour among his boon companions that I was a jackdaw and dressed myself in peacock's feathers; for long ago, says he, a certain Polidoro wrote a capital book on this subject, and Erasmus is nothing but a sedulous ape and plagiary.

When I heard this and did not know what he was talking about, I gave some of the young men the task of seeking out the book of this Polidoro Virgilio. This was not on sale anywhere, for it had not yet (I suppose) been imported from Italy; but at length I found a copy by chance in the library of that distinguished man Jérôme de Busleyden,[17] which he, being a great buyer of books of all kinds, had brought with him from Italy. Delighted with my unexpected prize, I compare the day and the year, which publishers commonly put on record, for my book was printed in Paris while I was away. And I discover that it appeared from the printing-house of Johannes Philippi in 1500 on 15 June, as is shown by the letter of Fausto[18] (which the printer had extracted from him to recommend the book to the public, though it must have been written before the book was finished), whereas yours had appeared in Italy three months later. Even were someone to produce an edition of your book earlier than Johannes Philippi's of mine – which I know no one will succeed in doing – there will still be no reason for anyone to accuse me of theft or plagiarism.[19] For it was quite possible – and I have no doubt this is what happened – that the same idea came into both our heads at about the same time, while you never dreamt of Erasmus nor I of Polidoro. So that if any credit is to be gained from having invented the subject, each of us can claim it without being unfair to the other. I having said this in jest at the dinner-table – for I quite believed that you were jesting – it was incumbent on you in all seriousness to compare the first edition of your book with the first of mine before you wrote that preface accusing a friend and an innocent man and a supporter of your reputation of jealousy combined with plagiarism.

But look here: suppose that your publication came first, suppose it was not unknown to me, suppose I have such a thirst for glory that I have no shame in stealing from a friend – what credit was there, I ask you, in inventing this subject? for we do not create proberbs, we collect them. In medicine or astronomy, those who make discoveries become famous; how little praise is due to a man who plucks a few ordinary blossoms accessible to anyone in a public meadow and puts them in a basket! In the treatment there may perhaps be some credit to be won, in the collecting there is very little to be proud of. If there is any glory, it is due to the Greeks, who left us collections of proverbs many centuries ago. Besides which, since you had made your collection out of the most obvious authorities, why should I have cited you rather than those on whose stores the men had drawn whom you normally follow? Beroaldo[20] I never quote; I quote Poliziano,[21] because he had read some authors I had not yet read.

Here is another argument for you: if I had read your collection, so great a plagiarist as myself would have overlooked none of your material. As it is, there are things in your collection by no means to be despised, which were not in mine.

But when you say that I added nothing except bulk,[22] I do not really know what you mean. In my first edition there were about eight hundred proverbs, while you stopped short of two hundred. Nor did I ever enlarge that tiny *Collectanea*[23] book except once, in 1506, when I was in Paris and preparing for a journey to Italy. At the request of my friend Bade, who was proposing to republish the book, I added twenty proverbs, more or less, of no special interest; and I did so out of the mass of proverbs that I had collected for an edition in Venice. Your collection was reprinted in Milan the same year by Johannes Anglus.[24] As for the Aldine edition, in which I produce some thousands, I do not see why the 'bulk' should be despised, especially in a subject where industry in collecting is more than half the battle; all the more so, as I have got together most of them either out of Greek sources or from authors not so common or familiar as Perotti[25] or Beroaldo. In any case, whether in the treatment I am in no way better than you is for others to judge. I could wish to see such a fresh blossoming of the humanities that everyone, and not only Polidoro should leave me behind.

But since all this is too obvious to be denied, what has become of that 'truth' which you say in your preface 'shines out afar'?[26] – in reliance on which you take it in good part that such a cunning pretender as I should have tried to insinuate myself into reputation which belongs to you. My affection for you is such, my dear Polidoro, and such my desire for your good name, that I should not object to presenting you with at least half of all the credit if you really take this so much to heart – if only you did not claim this in such a spirit that you would not thank me for it, while I should be thought by posterity to be not a man unselfish towards his friends but a petty thief of other men's reputations, – always supposing that posterity will read what we write. I only wish the serried ranks of the learned might approve your work as much as I do. I certainly liked many things in it, especially in your essay *De rerum inventoribus*.[27]

How far I was from being unfair to your book, you may judge from this too, that when Froben, as I said, was reluctant to publish it, I persuaded him. Your preface, in which you criticize me, they had sent me as something intolerable. I sent it back, and told them to print it faithfully, just as you had written it. They had cut out a mention of Lee,[28] to whom you refer in most polite language; I told them to put it back. Is this the behaviour of a friend, or no? You are a sensible man, and need no advice from me. Yet there is one thing I would suggest, my dear Polidoro: that in future, when you publish what you have written, you should seek the advice of Thomas More, Cuthbert Tunstall, Thomas Linacre, William Latimer, really good scholars and friends. Farewell, learned Polidoro, and do all in your power for the cause of good letters.

Louvain, 23 December 1520

1176 / To Thomas Bedyll

Louvain, 31 December 1520

This letter was printed in the *Epistolae ad diversos*; it is addressed to the secretary of William Warham, archbishop of Canterbury.

ERASMUS TO THOMAS BEDYLL, SECRETARY OF THE ARCHBISHOP OF CANTERBURY, GREETING

What you tell me of his Grace's feelings towards me is the best news in the world, though it is by no means new; but when you upbraid me so often for asking nothing from him, you are a little unkind, my dear Bedyll. Why, I have long prayed that he would steer some fat prebend in my direction. No doubt he will survive me in my present enfeebled state;[1] but in human affairs one can take nothing for granted. Still, I must show just a touch of effrontery, so let me say how much I wish my annuity for the coming year might again be paid me in advance,[2] or at least that I might be sent a bill of exchange against which I could draw it either here or in Italy. For I am getting ready to set out this coming Lent, with the idea of spending the summer in Basel; whence I shall perhaps revisit Italy,[3] unless something arises in this congress of princes[4] to detain me.

St Paul was stoned once only;[5] here I am stoned daily with a hail of abuse from Dominicans and Carmelites, and that too both by name and in public sermons. They achieve nothing however, except to make even the common people realize that they are hounded by the Furies.

Give my most hearty greetings to his Grace the archbishop, my supremely great benefactor; after him to Dr Welles[6] and to your major-domo, the kindest of men. Farewell, my dearest Pylades.[7]

Louvain, eve of the Circumcision 1520

1177 / To Andreas Knopken Louvain, 31 December 1520

This letter, published in the *Epistolae ad diversos*, is Erasmus' answer to the repeated approaches of Andreas Knopken or Cnophas (d 1539), born near Kostrzyn (the former Küstrin in the Brandenburg Neumark). He studied at Frankfurt an der Oder and was a chaplain at Riga, 1517–19, before moving to Trzebiatów (Treptow in Pomerania), from where he had probably written to Erasmus. In 1521 he returned to Riga and soon was the leading pastor to the Lutheran part of the population, although he always maintained a moderate stance.

ERASMUS OF ROTTERDAM TO THE WORTHY FATHER ANDREAS KNOPKEN, GREETING

Of the three letters you say you have written me,[1] I have received only two. At first, there was no sign of anyone by whom I could send an answer. Then at last, when I was in Cologne,[2] somebody offered to take one, but after he had called on me two or three times in vain, he never came back, having I suppose lost hope. Yet this was not my fault: I was never idle, and I was never alone. Also, to be perfectly frank, as I saw nothing in your letters that much needed an answer, I should not have written back if you did not call me to account with all this asking and protesting.

Your religious habit of mind and your enthusiasm for Christian learning I cordially welcome, for both are evident in your letter. And this does you all the more credit, since you follow this course among people who are more interested, you say, in their bellies than their books, besides being so close to the Ruthenians,[3] whom you call uncouth and shaggy, I suppose because of their barbarous character and manners. For it has been truly said that it takes a really honest man to be honest in Athens;[4] and similarly anyone who does not swerve from the Catholic faith though his neighbours are heretics,[5] and who lives a life of devotion to liberal studies in the midst of barbarians who are devoted to eating and drinking, and contrives to be infected by none of it, must be an outstandingly good man. So, if you ask me for advice, you will get none, except to press on manfully on the path you already follow; for you seem to me to have adopted the very course which will lead to true felicity. Nor do I doubt that you will do your level best to bring as many others as you can to your way of thinking. Indeed it surprises me that, with so many shepherds everywhere, not one arises to imitate the example of the Good Shepherd, who did not hesitate to endure so many evils for the sake of one stray sheep. Those who hunger for tithes are two a penny; but I see almost none who thirst for the salvation of souls. Here every place is full of monks, where there is no risk to be run and the harvest is plentiful. Why do they not go to the Ruthenians, and by their learning and their holiness of life recall them to the church's fold? Here they are pillars of the church, to which they are more burdensome than useful. But where the situation calls for a simple and genuine Christian, who is to win some gain for Christ at the risk of his life, they are nowhere to be found. So, while each of us is devoted to his own advantage, Christ's people are neglected.

And it is, alas, our own characters which are, at least in part, the reason why so few come over to our side. They read the teaching of the evangelists and apostles, and see that our way of life differs from it far and wide. I am not thinking now of the common folk, who are usually much the same as those who lead them, but of the princes of the church, the priests and the monks. A great many of us are slaves to money or food or reputation or our personal power; the faith of which we speak is a mere pretext. This drives away the people whom they ought to attract by gentleness and tolerance and service. All the same a touch of hope comes into my mind, when I see that even in your part of the world there are people fired with love for the teaching of the Gospel.

I have finished paraphrases[6] on all the Epistles except the one called Hebrews, and have added a paraphrase on the two Epistles of Peter, on Jude, and on James, with the intention of publishing the remainder of the Epistles of the apostles shortly, for so my learned friends thought would be best. I rather liked the verse in which you prayed for my welfare; and in return I pray in plain prose, but from the depths of my heart, for your immortal life. Farewell, dear Father, and commend me to Christ in your prayers.

Louvain, 31 December 1520

1178 / To Godofredus Rhodus Stegrius Louvain, 1520

This letter, which was printed in the *Epistolae ad diversos*, is addressed to an admirer of Erasmus who has not so far been identified. 'Stegrius' may perhaps indicate that he was a native of Estaires, between Hazebrouck and Lille. His admiration for Erasmus was enduring. The only thing known of him in addition to this letter is a Latin elegy which he wrote after Erasmus' death, praising his achievements and describing the welcome he was given in heaven. It was first printed in *Catalogi duo operum D. Erasmi Roterodami* (Antwerp: widow of M. de Keyser for J. Coccius c 1 May 1537; NK 2858) and may also be found among the preliminary material in LB I. Allen mentions a marginal note in handwriting on the page containing this letter in his own copy of Erasmus' *Opera* III (Basel 1538) which may indicate that Rhodus died on 2 October 1545.

The date of this letter cannot be confirmed or indicated more precisely. Allen mentioned in connection with it a new year's gift (cf CWE 5 preface) made to Erasmus on 1 January 1521 by one Hugo Bolonius, probably a native of Lille, for whom see CEBR I.

ERASMUS OF ROTTERDAM TO GODOFREDUS RHODUS STEGRIUS, GREETING

If I have been rather slow in acknowledging what you wrote, my dear Rhodus, the reason was a crowd of people interrupting me with letters and even books; so do not suspect for a moment that I am discourteous or hard to please. You dwell upon my publications; I only wish they were as useful to the world or as profitable to their author as they are numerous. But if I was dissatisfied with myself as seen in your mirror, I was no less impressed by your abilities. For I had as good a view of you as of myself, and found your image more agreeable to contemplate than my own. I liked your mind, so sensible, so fertile, sober, and free from any trace of affectation; I liked your unselfishness and modesty, your style stripped of tiresome fancy and of needless verbiage. There was another thing I greatly admired: how you can use a metre bound by stricter laws than almost any other and yet express your meaning so easily, especially since you treat of a subject both scanty and unattractive. I almost think you chose such sterile and unpromising material on purpose to win greater glory for your gifts by showing you can make an elephant out of a gnat.[1] For I took it very hardly that with these undeserved and excessive eulogies you should merely lay a heavy burden on my humble self. I must admit, though, that this is such a regular practice in poetry, that poets seem to have a regular licence to do so.

Had not Fortune treated me so unkindly[2] that no one could expect me to do anything for him, there might perhaps be people whose suspicions would rest as heavily on you as on myself: on you for praising with an ulterior motive, on me for taking pleasure in such praise as that. You have my sympathy all the more, for having undertaken so much work without reward; for you will not get from me even the return that beasts of burden make when one scratches another.[3] But lest I give you no return at all for such unselfish enthusiasm on my behalf, I give you a piece of advice: devote your leisure hours henceforth to better books, and never take up some trifling piece by Erasmus unless you have access to nothing better. Furthermore, if you ever wish to practise your pen and give your talent exercise, choose a more promising subject. Farewell, dear Rhodus – the more you do for the cause of good letters, the more you can rely on my support.

Louvain, 1520

1179 / To Matthäus Schiner Louvain, 6 January [1521]

This dedication of Erasmus' paraphrase on the two Epistles of John is a sequel to Ep 1171. For the paraphrases Erasmus wrote before his move to Basel (cf Ep 1242 introduction) first editions printed in the Netherlands are known in all but two cases; this is one of the exceptions (for the other see Ep 1062 introduction). The text of this letter is based on Froben's composite volume of the paraphrases on the apostolic Epistles, published in March 1521, cf Ep 1171 introduction.

TO HIS EMINENCE MATTHÄUS, CARDINAL OF SION, COUNT OF THE VALAIS, FROM ERASMUS OF ROTTERDAM, GREETING

I lately offered you St James, speaking Latin and more lucid than of old, and now here is St John. Thus I take my labour in stages piece by piece, and I do not overwhelm your Eminence when you are fully occupied with the business of the empire[1] – if, that is to say, I may assume that you have any time to spare for looking over what I write. My best wishes to your Lordship.

Louvain, 6 January

1180 / From Leo X Rome, 15 January 1521

This papal brief answers Ep 1143. Composed by Bishop Jacopo Sadoleto, apostolic secretary (cf Ep 1511), it shows appreciation of Erasmus' concern for 'peace and concord' (line 7), but it also reflects the conflicting views of Erasmus within the Roman curia, with the sympathetic one eventually gaining the pope's endorsement. At the same time the brief leaves little doubt that such excuses as Erasmus had made in Ep 1143:56–63 for not taking up his pen against Luther would not be acceptable in future. Before long Erasmus was again to be reminded of his duty to 'battle vigorously' (Ep 1213:44) against him (cf Ep 1228 n11).

This letter is known from a manuscript copy in the Vatican Archives (MS Nunziatura di Germania 50 f 44, the heading and signature in Sadoleto's own hand), which must have duplicated the original sent to Erasmus. The Vatican manuscript is preserved in a volume of papers concerning the nunciature of Girolamo Aleandro (cf Ep 1135 n1). It was dispatched to Aleandro, then in Worms, together with instructions dated 19 March 1521 (Balan nos 49, 53), and was first printed in 1754; for further details see Allen's headnote. In his preserved letters Erasmus does not mention the brief, nor his reaction to it (but cf Ep 1213 n5). Aleandro, however, had learnt about its dispatch by 12 February and, although he was not sent his copy until later, voiced his alarm in view of such unwarranted encouragement given to Erasmus; see Balan nos 21, 32.

TO DESIDERIUS ERASMUS OF ROTTERDAM

My beloved son, greeting and so forth. Your letter was most welcome, for it established a point upon which we had begun to have some doubts, not only from the testimony of certain persons[1] of great wisdom and integrity but even more from sundry products of your pen which are in circulation:[2] to wit, that your loyalty is none the less unimpeachable and unshakeable both to us and our apostolic see and towards peace and concord in general and in particular the public polity and law of Christendom.[3] This consorts admirably both with the intellectual gifts which by divine benevolence you have applied in full measure to the most exalted subjects, and with the religious studies which you have always set before you. Thereupon we, who had the thought of you often in our mind despite your absence, and had formed the idea of recognizing your outstanding merits by some suitable reward,[4] but had been somewhat deterred from this intention, acknowledge with much satisfaction that thanks to your dutiful and careful letter our original wish to regard you with affection is now reinstated.

And it would be well if we might see all other men no less certainly convinced than we are ourselves of your loyalty and good will towards this Holy See and our common faith in God. Never was the time more opportune or the cause more just for setting your erudition and your powers of mind against the impious, nor is anyone better suited than yourself – such is our high opinion of your learning – for this praiseworthy task, wherein very many men by their labours past and present have earned the highest repute for religion and scholarship. But it was God who directed their hearts aright; and your own course of action we are content in the same way to leave to your discretion. For our part, armed as we are against sedition and its calumnies with help and patience from on high, we are much more distressed when we see no small portion of the wholesome crop corrupted together with the tares, and the loss of any creature from the flock committed to our charge fills our heart with concern. How can we fail to grieve at the loss of men of excellent understanding drawn into error, seeing that we desire the salvation even of those very men who are the authors of error and impiety. But God will not desert us, nor shall we desert our bounden duty.

As concerns your letter, we are now convinced of your perfect good will, and your arrival in this city, when that moment comes, will be welcomed with pleasure and satisfaction.

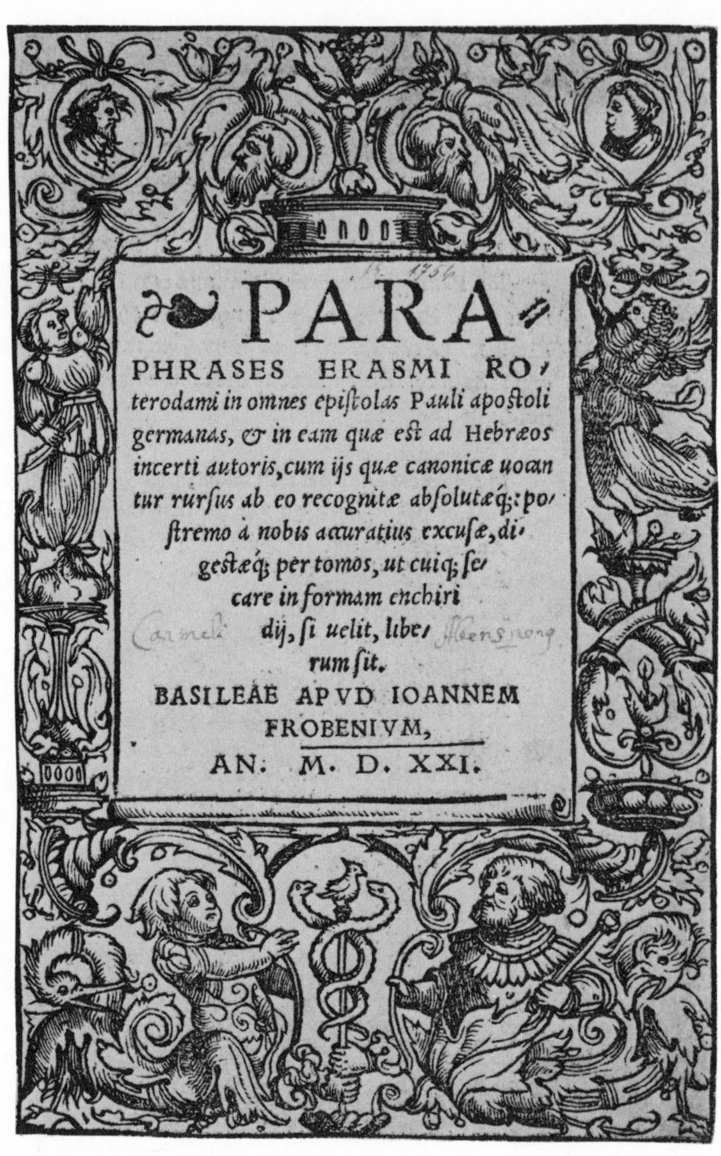

PARA-

PHRASES ERASMI RO-
terodami in omnes epiſtolas Pauli apoſtoli
germanas, & in eam quæ eſt ad Hebræos
incerti autoris, cum ijs quæ canonicæ uocan
tur rurſus ab eo recognitæ abſolutæq; po-
ſtremo à nobis accuratius excuſæ, di-
geſtæq; per tomos, ut cuiq; ſe-
care in formam enchiri
dij, ſi uelit, libe-
rum ſit.

BASILEAE APVD IOANNEM
FROBENIVM,
AN: M. D. XXI.

Erasmus *Paraphrases in omnes epistolas Pauli* title-page
Basel: Froben 1521
Centre for Reformation and Renaissance Studies, Victoria University, Toronto

Given at Rome, this fifteenth day of January 1521, being the eighth year of our pontificate

Jacopo Sadoleto

1181 / To Silvestro Gigli — Louvain, 17 January 1521

Erasmus' *Paraphrasis in Hebraeos*, to which this letter is a preface, was first printed in Louvain by Dirk Martens in January 1521 (NK 2959) and reprinted with a separate title-page at the end of Froben's edition of all the paraphrases on the apostolic Epistles (March 1521; cf Ep 1171 introduction). Since the copy for the other Epistles had reached Basel before the middle of January (cf AK II Ep 764) and Froben repeated Martens' title exactly, he may have used a printed copy rather than a manuscript. In 1532, when the Froben press reprinted all the paraphrases on the New Testament together, this preface was omitted. Its recipient, Silvestro Gigli, had from his post at the papal court assisted Erasmus in securing papal dispensations (cf line 10). He died on 18 April 1521.

An interesting aspect of this letter is Erasmus' attribution of the Epistle to the Hebrews to Paul, which is repeated in Martens' title and on Froben's internal title-page. This represents a clear change in Erasmus' position. Formerly he had rejected Paul's authorship (cf Epp 1062 n15, 1064), and he had repeated this rejection most firmly in Ep 1171:9–12, which was reprinted in Froben's collection. Perhaps on account of this contradiction Froben's next reprint of the same collection of paraphrases appeared in July 1521 with a title-page reversing the attribution: *Paraphrases ... in omnes epistolas Pauli apostoli germanas et in eam quae est ad Hebraeos incerti autoris ...*

TO THE RIGHT REVEREND SILVESTRO, LORD BISHOP OF WORCESTER, PERMANENT ENVOY OF HIS MAJESTY THE KING OF ENGLAND TO HIS HOLINESS LEO X, FROM ERASMUS OF ROTTERDAM, GREETING

It is only right, my Lord Bishop, that for your goodness and your distinguished support of liberal studies your name should be commended to posterity by everyone who writes; not that your modesty cares for any praise from men, but because many will be encouraged to pursue higher studies if they see that eminent persons who have deserved well of the Christian polity are not deprived of the fame which they have not sought and thereby deserve all the more. It was right, in return for all that you have done for me,[1] that there should be no page in my books that does not display the name of Silvestro. So far, however, it has been possible for me to entertain proper feelings of gratitude towards your Lordship, but not to show them. I would have preferred to produce something rather later, provided that it might be on a larger scale; but now that I see myself overwhelmed by a mass of work that increases daily and, as Varro puts it,[2] becoming more like a bubble every day, I thought it right to dedicate this short work to you, not with a view to paying off my debt with this small offering, but as an acknowledgment that I am indebted to you on so many counts that I have no hopes of ever being able to repay you. And yet, if I am hereafter granted life and opportunity, I shall attempt, not to get my name crossed off in your ledger, which I should be sorry to do, since there is no one in whose debt I would rather be, but to escape the stigma of ingratitude.

Herewith Paul, who with my assistance has learnt to write at greater length and more clearly and, what is more, in Latin. Not that I have any fault to find with the way he writes; but our sluggish wits could not keep pace with him as he soared upwards. I have certainly made it possible for him to be well thumbed by readers as he never was before. Previously, he was scarcely accessible to scholars, working hard; and now he is intelligible even to those with only a tincture of learning, provided they are not wholly ignorant of Latin. For this no credit may be due to my brains and none to my scholarship, but something I do claim for industry. During the time that I was thus lightening the labours of others by my own, I might have taken my ease, I might have slept or sipped my wine or hunted for promotion or indulged in other avocations; in such things some men pass their time away, except for what they devote to criticizing the work of others. The classical languages and liberal studies have almost reached a stage at which we may hope that their future is secure, though even now there is active opposition from the champions of ancient ignorance. If only we had the same hope of seeing the teaching of the Gospel restored to its purity and simplicity! But here a bloody battle rages still. Yet we have a good hope of victory, if Christ will help us through you and men like you. And help us he will, if we do his work in sincerity of heart. Towards both ends it will make the greatest contribution if Leo, the supreme head of our religion, works unfailingly for the glory of him whose vice-gerent he is. Farewell, my most distinguished Lord.

Louvain, 17 January 1521

1182 / To Willibald Pirckheimer — Louvain, 26 January [1521]

This letter was first printed in Pirckheimer's *Opera* (Frankfurt 1610; repr 1969) 272. The year can be assigned from Pirckheimer's summons to Rome; cf n2.

Greeting, my eminent Willibald. A letter from you has lately arrived,[1] in which you protest that I have not sent you an answer. This surprises me, for a long reply from me was printed long ago in Basel. I am amazed that you should have been summoned to Rome,[2] for I know the pope gave them strict instructions not to molest any harmless person, but rather to try by all possible means to get hold of those who are privy to heresy and, to use their own word, supporters of it. But some of these raving theologians have thought otherwise. I hope you are in good health and escape them successfully in the sequel.

I myself here have stones thrown at me daily[3] by the Dominicans in their sermons, and am coupled with Luther, with whom I have nothing to do; but they bungle their business so badly that the public, however stupid, can see through it. They will find it difficult to do more harm to the pope or to secure more popularity for Luther.[4] At long last they are becoming his supporters! I wish Leo knew how things are managed here. He would go for them for the first time like a lion. Farewell, dear friend. Louvain, 26 January

Your sincere friend Erasmus

To the honourable Willibald Pirckheimer, councillor of the famous city of Nürnberg

1183 / To [Arkleb of Boskovice] Louvain, 28 January 1521

This letter clearly answers Ep 1154. When it was printed in the *Epistolae ad diversos*, Arkleb's name and titles were not available, probably because of a corresponding gap in Erasmus' rough draft due to his lack of familiarity with them; cf n35.

ERASMUS TO X, A MAN IN HIGH POSITION, GREETING

Honoured sir, your Highness' letter found me fully occupied with my literary labours, and it was delivered by a man quite unknown to me of whom the letter made no mention. And yet I had to make good the loss of his journey-money, for he assured me that he had been stripped by robbers somewhere or other. For these reasons I send you a somewhat brief reply,[1] and will write soon at greater length through the Fuggers,[2] if I am allowed any leisure and if I find that this would be acceptable. The book[3] I had already received six months before by way of two Bohemians,[4] though I have not yet found time to read it through; and on the schism I had had a detailed letter from Jan Šlechta.[5] This business has caused me no little anguish of mind, for I have always been a supporter of peace and concord between all mortals everywhere, so far as possible, and especially between Christians. For since God, as the prophet bears witness,[6] rejoices to rule over the people far and wide, while we see the boundaries of Christianity contracted to such narrow limits,[7] who would not be tormented at the sight of what little remains vitiated by so many diseased opinions and so much corruption of morals, and divided and torn asunder by so many sects? I made some proposals on this lately to Cardinal Campeggi,[8] who is a well-read and civilized person, when he was with us, and afterwards to a papal nuncio;[9] and both gave me a friendly reply and offered good hopes of restoring peace. Personally, I derive still greater hope from the mild and peace-loving nature of this Leo of ours, if only he would choose to follow his own natural bent instead of favouring the prejudices of certain people who in my opinion do not consider his great position as they should,[10] and think more of their own private advantage than of the interests of the world at large.

Furthermore, that you should ask me to give you some kind of rule, which will carry more weight, you say, with your own people than if the Roman pontiff were to brandish his thunderbolts, makes me, who have hitherto given this business a wide berth (for I neither carry the needful weight nor possess the knowledge),[11] still more reluctant. And I doubt whether you could find any argument more likely to deter me from what you try to persuade me to do. Who am I to issue pronouncements about other men's beliefs or make any decisions beyond what has already been decided and is now followed by the Catholic church? If I were certain that something had been wrongly decided by the church of Rome, I might perhaps ask a question or issue a respectful warning, given a suitable opportunity; heaven forbid that I should boldly decide anything for myself. In all my work my sole object has been to resuscitate the humanities, which lay almost dead and buried among my own people; secondly to arouse a world which allowed too much importance to Jewish ceremonial[12] to a new zeal for the true religion of the Gospel; and finally to recall to its sources in Holy Scripture the academic theology in our universities, too deeply sunk in the quibbling discussion of worthless minor problems.[13] I have never made any assertions, I have always shunned the character of one who lays down the law, particularly on topics which are already accepted among the articles of our religion; though I admit that some theologians I could name have handed down decisions on some points which, at least in my opinion, might be left undecided without prejudice to the religion of the Gospel.[14]

And so, my honoured friend, I have no rules to lay down; I have some wishes. I could wish first that all that region of yours might come together in Christian unity, and then that it could enjoy perfect peace and fellowship with all other regions beyond the reach of controversy. Already indeed the best part of the realm,[15] if not the largest, accepts the public unity of the church; besides which, the monstrous faction of the Nicolaites[16] is, I hear, already the abomination of the common people in your part of the world. That leaves only one faction still to be reconciled, the Pyghards.[17] And I see good hope of achieving that, if you yourself and the pope and a number of princes entrust this question to a number of learned men and men whose integrity is beyond doubt[18] but there must be excluded from this panel the men who have a finger in every pie though they profess quite other motives.[19] Not that I am against them, if only they would do what they profess to do; but we see some among them everywhere who support the pope's cause (as they themselves see it) with such uproar and rioting and such fawning, that in my opinion no one does more damage to the pope's authority. They bawl away to such a tune that even the uneducated think they must be mad. No one has done more to endear Luther to the heart of the people than those who have ranted so noisomely against him. They fear I know not what, and that is why they leave no stone unturned to prop up their personal rule. Such men I should therefore like to see kept quite outside this arbitration. If the question could be decided by argument, in a spirit of mildness and moderation, I should hope to see Pope Leo win praise as a merciful shepherd of his people,[20] and those for whom you speak get the praise, or rather the profit, of obeying as a Christian ought.

For it is wholly impossible to approve of those who either embitter the Roman pontiff by their scurrilities or travesty him with their vulgar abuse. For if Peter rightly rebukes those who despise the powers that be,[21] which means those in public positions of authority, even if they are gentiles, how much less ought he to be attacked to whom almost all the churches ascribe the supreme authority? I cannot now discuss the source whence this authority was originally conveyed to him; to say the least, just as in the early days out of many priests who were still all equal one bishop was chosen for the prevention of schism, so now it is expedient for one pope to be chosen out of all the bishops, not only to rule out divisions but to restrain the despotism of other bishops, should any one oppress his own flock, and of secular princes. I know well enough the complaints that are commonly directed against the see of Rome; but just as it is unwise to give immediate credence to popular rumour, so it is clearly unfair to blame the pope for everything that happens in Rome. Much is done without his knowledge, for one man cannot know everything; much that he dislikes, and against opposition from him. And in the present posture of human affairs, if Peter himself were to preside in Rome,[22] he would be compelled, I suspect, to connive at some things which in his heart of hearts he could not possibly approve. But be that as it may: far more would be achieved by reasonable requests or argument or courteous complaints than by slander or virulent pamphleteering. If this is what our sins deserve, that the world must be set right by some great upheaval, and if it must needs be that offences come,[23] at least I will take pains that they shall not come through me. No man shall have me as his authority in error or his leader in civil strife.

That Luther's books should be in circulation among you, as you say they are, does not greatly distress me, provided only that your people read them as I am wont to do myself.[24] If there is anything of value in them, I pluck it out; if anything wrong, I pass it over. Nor will I say at this present time what I think of this man. I will say just this: the greatest part of all this tragic business has arisen from the inordinate greed of certain theologians, mainly Dominicans and Carmelites,[25] of whom at the moment I cannot bring myself to write more. One thing I will say: if Leo knew the things I see and hear, either my estimate of him deceives me or he would be somewhat less than grateful to them for their devoted efforts. Between Luther and myself there is nothing except Christian friendship; this is the absolute truth, and I have often said so.[26] I am neither his inspiration nor his patron, neither his advocate nor his judge.[27] The matter of what we write is not the same, I should suppose, nor is the manner. On the spirit in which he writes I am reluctant, nor is it my business, to express an opinion. Nor have I read very much of him, being in any case at full stretch in my own work. Nothing of his have I ever attacked or defended, except that now and again I have wished to see in him rather more of the mildness of the Gospel.

At the same time, I have never approved the savagery and the uproar of those who before they have even read his books declaim against him so foolishly before public audiences, using words like donkey and stork and blockhead[28] and heretic and Antichrist and universal pest, while all the time they neither show him how to do better nor prove him wrong; the sole result of all their uproar is to make more people buy Luther's books and read them more readily. And now a bull has appeared,[29] which could not by itself divert popular support from Luther although it is unusually full of threats; and there is a conspiracy of men who have formed an alliance in their cups always to couple my name with his in their public harangues, in order to overwhelm me under the ill will he and I are to share. And me they regard as an enemy because on occasion I have criticized those who are so devoted to Scotist niceties that they never reach the true springs of divine wisdom;[30] because I sometimes differ in my *Annotationes* from Thomas;[31] because I have pointed out that young men ought not to be inveigled into the bonds of monastic life before they have learnt to know themselves and understand what the life of religion is;[32] because I have pointed out that true piety lies not in ceremonies but in a state of mind and heart; because I defend the humanities on which they long ago declared war. When they are asked after a sermon what they have found in my books that is heretical, they reply that they have not read them,[33] but that they are dangerous because the Latin is so difficult. This is the reply you get from theologians and monks equally, and from buffoons and sometimes from bishops. This is the sort of noisy rascals who defend the majesty of the papacy and are pillars of the church. But the public in several places are beginning to be sensible, and unless they use better arguments I do not see what they can hope to achieve.

When you urge me to join Luther, this will be easy, once I see him on the side of the Catholic church. Not that I would pronounce that he is estranged from it, nor is it my business to condemn anybody. It is by his Master that he stands or falls. Should matters develop into a final conflict, so that the state of the church might go either way, I shall plant my feet firmly until further notice on that solid rock,[34] until peace is restored and it is clear where stands the church. And your Erasmus will be found on the same side, whatever it may be, as the peace of the Gospel.

So much, my excellent friend, for my present thoughts, lest the man who brought your letter should go away quite empty-handed. Your letter had no day or year written on it. Farewell.

Louvain, 28 January 1521

To the honourable Arkleb of Boskovice and Czernahora, lord of Vranov, captain-general of the margraviate of Moravia[35]

1184 / To Guillaume Budé Louvain, 16 February 1521

This letter was published in the *Epistolae ad diversos*. It was no doubt sent to Paris together with Ep 1185 by a man named William; cf n10.

ERASMUS TO GUILLAUME BUDÉ, GREETING

See, dearest Budé, as though we wanted misfortunes, how envious fate has snatched from us the chief of all the company of Williams![1] Guillaume de Croy,[2] as you will have heard, has left us, the archbishop of Toledo – left us like some precious flower cut down in its first blooming, and so reads us a lesson to rely on nothing placed within the range of Fortune's caprice. But on this subject I learn from the man who brings this letter that you have already written a book.[3] What could a man ask of Fortune that she had not willingly given him in full measure? Lineage most ancient and distinguished; an uncle[4] who stood so high with our Prince Charles that the whole empire almost seemed to be within that one man's grasp; life in its prime, for he was not yet past twenty-three; a strong and active frame; distinctions of every sort, such that even the majesty of his cardinal's hat scarcely added to their lustre; such courtesy, such frank simplicity of character! With his whole heart he loved liberal studies, nor had he any aversion from my humble self. I fear our friend Vives[5] has lost a patron for whom he will be hard put to find a match.

He showed me your recent letter to him.[6] Were Brie and More alike unknown to me, I should still be sorry to see scholarship in such parlous state. As it is, each is my friend, and I admire the gifts of both; I cannot without great unhappiness be a witness of their confrontation, which will I fear grow all too warm. For More's letter,[7] which I think you saw before More showed it to me at Calais when it was already printed, is such that in comparison with it myself, who am thought by some people to have rather sharp fangs, seem positively toothless; and yet he almost promised me that if Brie kept quiet, he would suppress it. I thought Hutten[8] too had a delightful wit, and now it is lost to literature,[9] being swept away by this whirlwind of Luther.

The man who brings this letter is a member of the fraternity of Williams who are indulgent friends of mine,[10] and as soon as he had heard from me what sort of person you are, he conceived a great desire to make your acquaintance. I do indeed believe him to deserve your friendship: he has a lively intelligence, spotless character, great skill in business, he is devoted to humane studies and by no means unacquainted with them – in short, his resemblance to you is not confined to the name.

Look after your health properly, my dear Budé, for in this wretched climate, with all this toilsome research, and all the inconvenience of noisy wretches and fish-eating[11] days, it is hardly possible to keep well.

Louvain, 16 February 1521

1185 / To Nicolas Bérault — Louvain, 16 February 1521

This letter, addressed to an old acquaintance of Erasmus' and a good friend of Budé's, was clearly sent with Ep 1184; it too was printed in the *Epistolae ad diversos*.

ERASMUS TO NICOLAS BÉRAULT, GREETING

To judge by Budé's letter to Vives,[1] nothing can prevent a conflict between More and Brie. I love and admire them both, and would much rather see any other two people come to grips; but what is outside our control, we must leave to fate to settle. I was encouraged by your letter to write to Hué,[2] the dean; not a word in reply, as though my overtures had given offence. If so, I must ask you to recreate the friendship which you were trying to create between us.

Such is the fanatical opposition to liberal studies of some of the monks here,[3] that one feels more like retching than researching. I am daily pelted with showers of abuse by the Dominicans, even in their public sermons; and if I must endure these for the advancement of the true faith, I should scarcely fall short of St Stephen himself, the first of martyrs.[4] He was stoned once, and his troubles were at an end; and he was attacked with nothing but stones. But I am pelted often and in different places, with lies and calumnies dipped in deadly poison; and all the time, in so doing, they are betraying their real selves and showing their true colours to the mob. Such is the character they display that, had I described them, scarcely anyone would have believed me; but now they make the truth credible. Yet such is their blindness that they prefer to make mischief, even if they themselves are the losers by it.

Luther is piling on both liberal studies and myself a massive load of unpopularity. Everyone knew that the church was burdened with tyranny and ceremonies and laws invented by men for their own profit. Many were already hoping for some remedy and even planning something; but often remedies unskillfully applied make matters worse, and the result is that those who try, and fail, to shake off the yoke are dragged back into slavery more bitter than before. Oh, if that man had either left things alone, or made his attempt more cautiously and in moderation! Luther means nothing to me; it is Christ's glory that I have at heart; for I see some people girding themselves for the fray to such a tune that, if they win, there will be nothing left but to write the obituary of gospel teaching.

Farewell, most learned Bérault. Give my greetings to our mutual supporters, Ruzé and Deloynes;[5] Budé[6] I have written to. And give my warmest regards to that promising young man, Herman of Friesland.[7]

Louvain, 16 February 1521

1186 / To Nicolaas Everaerts Louvain, 25 February 1521

Allen was the first to publish this letter from the original manuscript, autograph throughout, which is now in the Gemeentebibliotheek of Rotterdam, MS 94 d 1. The letter is addressed to Nicolaas Everaerts, the influential president of the Council of Holland at The Hague, who had known Erasmus for many years (cf Ep 1092 introduction). At this time Erasmus evidently expected him to be quite critical of Rome's handling of Luther's case and equally opposed to those Louvain theologians and their allies who inclined to throw Erasmus and Luther into one pot; cf Epp 1165:2–5, 1166 introduction, 1188.

Greeting, my distinguished friend. What a load of unpopularity Luther is piling both on liberal studies and on true Christianity![1] As far as he can, he brings everyone into this business of his. Everyone was ready to admit that the church is burdened with the tyrannical government of certain persons, and many people were already planning some remedy for it. And now this man has appeared, and handled things in such a way that the yoke is heavier

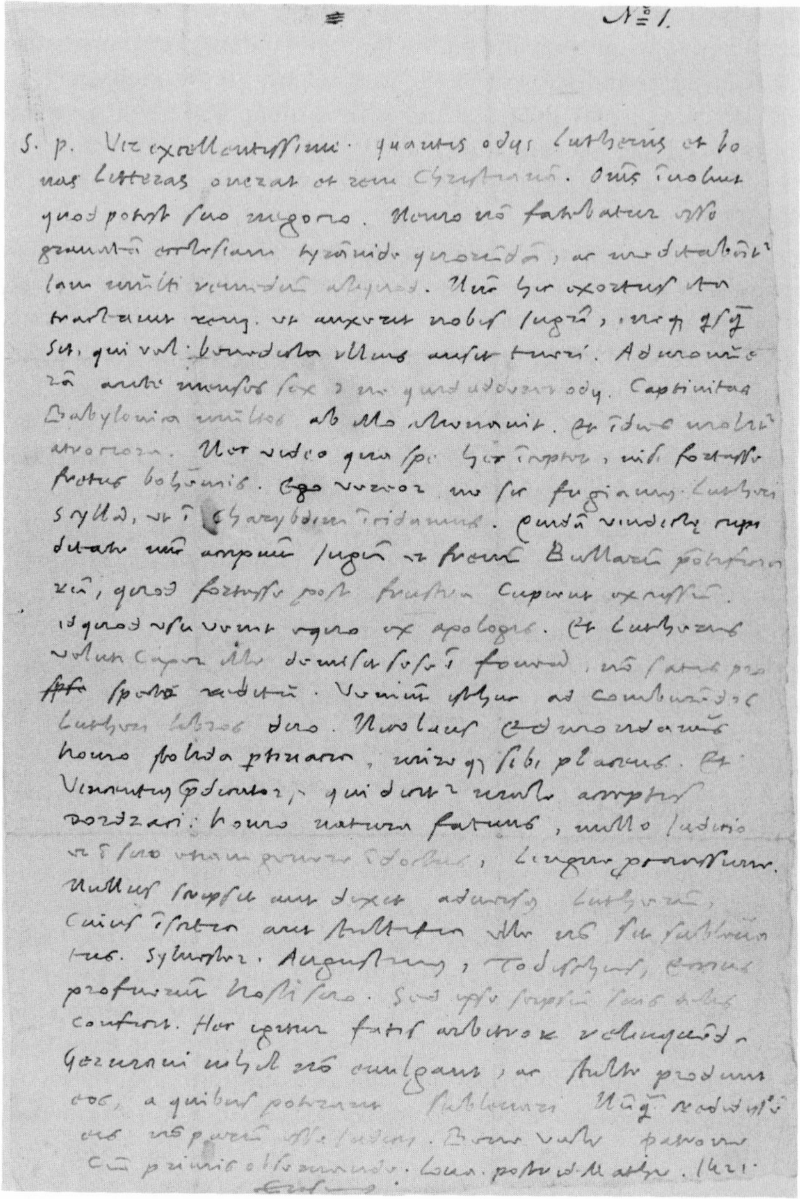

Autograph letter from Erasmus to Nicolaas Everaerts, Ep 1186
Gemeentebibliotheek, Rotterdam

than ever, and even when he says what needs saying, no one dares support him. I warned him six months ago not to add to the ill feeling.[2] His *De captivitate Babylonica*[3] alienates many people, and he is proposing something more frightful every day. I do not see what he is hoping for in setting this on foot, unless perhaps he is relying on the Bohemians.[4] My own fear is that we may escape the Scylla of Luther only to fall into some worse Charybdis.[5] Some men in their eagerness to get the better of him are ready to take the bit and submit to the yoke of papal bulls, which (who knows?) they may hereafter vainly wish they had thrown off, like the horse in the fable.[6] And Luther like the he-goat has got himself into the pit without stopping to think how he is to get out.[7]

Two men are on their way to your part of the world to burn Luther's books,[8] Nicolaus Egmondanus, an obstinate fool who is wonderfully pleased with himself, and Vincentius,[9] a Dominican, who is said to have got himself into trouble at Dordrecht, one of nature's numskulls, a man of no judgment and ignorant even by the standards of his own class, but a scandalous talker. No one has written or preached against Luther without doing him more good than harm by a display of ignorance or folly. Silvester, Augustin, Todischius,[10] and Eck[11] have all done their adversary good service. But Luther destroys himself with his own weapons.[12] So I think all this must be left to fate. The Germans publish everything,[13] and stupidly betray the very people who might help them. I would not have believed they could show such bad judgment.

Farewell, my most respected patron. Louvain, morrow of St Matthias 1521

To the honourable Nicolaas Everaerts, most worthy president of Holland

1187 / To Lorenzo Bartolini — Louvain, 1 March 1521

With this letter, published in the *Epistolae ad diversos*, Erasmus attempted to renew his contact with a potential patron. Lorenzo Bartolini Salimbeni (c 1494–1533) belonged to a Florentine family who were staunch supporters and protégés of the Medici. Better known than Lorenzo are his brothers Zanobi and Gherardo. In 1502 Lorenzo succeeded the latter as commendatory abbot of the Augustinian house of Entremont in Haute-Savoie. He is also said to have figured on a list of candidates for imminent appointment to the college of cardinals when Leo X died in 1521; see Marino Sanudo *I Diarii* (Venice 1879–1903; repr 1969–70) XXXII 188, and cf Ildefonso de' San Luigi *Istoria genealogica delle famiglie ... Bartolini Salimbeni*, appended to his edition of Gherardo Bartolini *Del Magnifico Lorenzo de' Medici cronica* (Florence 1786)

Nicolaas Everaerts
Portrait medal by Janus Secundus, 1528
Bibliothèque Royale Albert I / Commissie voor Numismatiek, Brussels

355–61. There is no evidence that Erasmus' letter led to further contacts with the abbot.

ERASMUS OF ROTTERDAM TO ABBOT LORENZO BARTOLINI, GREETING

I have more than once felt great dissatisfaction, excellent Bartolini, at my failure to give a warmer welcome to a man of your character, born for honourable actions and liberal studies, when you were here in company with Longueil.[1] For social duties of this kind it is leisure that I lack more than good will. Who would not feel an affection for your lively mind, so eager for knowledge that, for all your Italian blood, you were willing to engage in the long pilgrimage through so many barbarous countries, not so much like Ulysses, who 'knew the cities and the ways of men,'[2] to acquire experience of some definite kind, as to make the acquaintance of men known to be of repute for their learning. Among whom someone had persuaded you that Erasmus was one. But though in this respect I know full well that your expectations were disappointed, yet you did I suppose make one small gain: you will not in future lend so ready an ear to either my panegyrists or my detractors. In the mean while, I salute this Italian fair-mindedness, which is ready to think well of men of intellect in other countries, while we are jealous of one another. When you took your leave, you asked that we might continue our converse when far apart by the interchange of letters. I therefore take the initiative, although for the moment I have little leisure to write and nothing serious to say. Have a care to your health, and let me know how you are.

Louvain, 1 March 1521

1188 / To Nicolaas Everaerts Mechelen, [c March 1521]

This letter was first published by Pieter Burman in *Gudii epistolae* (Utrecht 1697) and soon afterwards by Jean Leclerc in LB. The early editors knew it no doubt from the same collection of autograph letters as had supplied Epp 949 and 1092. While the autograph of this letter is now missing, that of Ep 949 exists and attests to the reliability of Burman and Leclerc. Thus the unusually unguarded statements of this letter (cf lines 45–7) may be accepted as authentic, all the more so as many points are repeated in other letters of this period.

This letter probably follows the more restrained Ep 1186, also addressed to Everaerts, and possibly responds to an encouraging reaction received to the latter. In passing through Mechelen on his way to Antwerp (cf Ep 1199 introduction), or from Antwerp back to Louvain, Erasmus may have taken advantage of the availability of a trustworthy messenger going to The Hague. The year date proposed in LB is clearly correct.

ERASMUS OF ROTTERDAM TO NICOLAAS EVERAERTS, PRESIDENT OF HOLLAND, GREETING

If Luther had written with more moderation, no matter how freely, he would have won more credit for himself and done a greater service to the world; but fate thought otherwise.[1] Nothing astonishes me more than that the man should continue to maintain his position. He has aroused great hostility to Reuchlin,[2] greater still to me and, what is worse, to liberal studies, to the best of his ability. On the other side, the tactics of his opponents are so crass, one might think they were in collusion with him.[3] If I were a sworn foe of certain of these Jacobites[4] and Carmelites, I could not wish their behaviour any different from what it is now. At Antwerp[5] the other day a Minorite who had been induced to join the faction started raving before a public audience – a Hollander; his name is Matthias.[6] The authorities instructed him to preach the Gospel. In his next sermon says he, 'The Gospel is what your parish priest teaches you, even if he spent last night in bed with a whore.' These monstrous brutes are kept by the world, which makes pets of them, and even tyrants. Against such men I see no steps one can take except to cut off the contributions they receive[7] and refuse them admittance to decent society. Let the young go to their parents for instruction and wives to their husbands, and let them confess to the parish priest. Let the preachers be deprived of an audience; or rather, when they start ranting in this fashion, let nearly everyone get up and go home. These steps will soon make them rave with more moderation.

They assure me here that an imperial proclamation has been drafted which is much fiercer than the papal bull,[8] but they have some misgivings about issuing it. Now this too is most extraordinary, that the pope in such a business should act through such men, some of them quite uneducated and all certainly of uncontrollable self-will. What could be more arrogant, more raving mad, than Cardinal Cajetanus?[9] Or Karl von Miltitz,[10] or Marino,[11] or Aleandro?[12] All have adopted that childish principle[13] 'My little finger is thicker than my father's loins' and so forth. Aleandro is obviously a maniac, a wicked, stupid man. Antonio Pucci[14] in Switzerland is amazingly choleric and uncontrollable. In Paris Luther has two principal opponents, a Norman called Duchesne,[15] a little oldish man full of venom, and Béda of Standonck,[16] who is a blockhead and not a human being. They are now using poison, I hear; in Paris several of Luther's most outspoken defenders have been put out of the way.[17] Perhaps this is included in their instructions: if the enemies of the Holy See (as they call everyone who does not do exactly what these vampires tell him) cannot be overcome by other means, they are to be removed by poison under papal benediction. Aleandro is a master at this. In Cologne he invited me most pressingly to dine with him, and the more he pressed the more obstinately I refused.[18] Against indulgence[19] the remedy will be to give nothing, until a better opportunity offers to hound this godless traffic off the stage altogether.

I have let myself go rather freely in writing to you, my excellent friend. You will be careful not to let this letter go astray into the hands of too many people; for the Germans publish whatever they can get hold of.[20] My best wishes to you and yours. Give my greetings to Master Jacob Mauritszoon and to Sasbout.[21]

From Mechelen. Written in a hurry in my inn, having by good luck found this man who can take a letter

1189 / To Maarten Lips [Louvain, March 1521]

This letter follows Ep 1174 and precedes Ep 1190, all three of which were copied by Lips in this order into his copy-book, now at Rotterdam. For the date cf lines 8–9.

DESIDERIUS ERASMUS OF ROTTERDAM TO MAARTEN OF BRUSSELS, GREETING

My especial friend, for certain definite reasons I have put off my journey[1] for a few weeks. I do not doubt that with your usual kindness you will blame the pressure of business if I seem to have forgotten you. I have three philippics[2] for you; they shall be laid out on such purposes as you may wish. The Greek Bible is not to be had for less than ten florins,[3] nor are there at the moment any copies in Antwerp. I send you my own copy, but shall ask for it back soon after Easter;[4] for I shall need it, if you do not want it very badly. Some of the Minorites were insistent to have it,[5] but I would prefer to oblige you, especially if you have set your heart on it. I am sending back the Augustine *Contra Faustum*.[6] Write and tell me, if you have any other copies in a fairly early hand, for this one I found most useful. Farewell, my dear Maarten, and commend me to Christ in your prayers.

1190 / To Maarten Lips [Louvain, c March 1521]

Cf Ep 1189 introduction, and for the date, line 11.

DESIDERIUS ERASMUS OF ROTTERDAM TO MAARTEN LIPS, GREETING

Dearest brother in Christ, your illness greatly distressed me, and I am all the more delighted to hear you are better. Now it remains to make sure you do not relapse; you must not work so hard. I have given the three philippics[1] to the bearer of this, if you will please to accept them. Pray give copious thanks on my behalf to Jan Aerts,[2] the venerable head of your institution, for his present. I will consider how to requite him, when opportunity offers. My paraphrases have not arrived yet.[3] I would have come to see you, but these winds have given my whole body a touch of some sort of fever. When I am a little better, I will pay you a visit. About my journey, it is not yet quite fixed up. I am waiting for a letter from Worms.[4] Farewell, my dear Maarten. The Lord Jesus, who is the author and restorer of all health, strengthen and confirm you in spirit and in body.

1191 / To Louis of Flanders — Louvain, [January–May] 1521

This letter was written to express Erasmus' appreciation for the friendship shown him by a nobleman of high standing, although it bears out Erasmus' candid admission that he had nothing much to say (lines 13–14). Louis of Flanders, lord of Praet (1488–1555) was descended from the ancient house of the counts of Flanders. From 1501 he studied at Louvain, where Erasmus became acquainted with him (line 15). In 1515 he was appointed grand bailiff of Ghent and two years later named to Charles' privy council. Subsequently he was entrusted with a number of important diplomatic missions and military commands. He continued to take a lively interest in literature and scholarship and to show genuine admiration for Erasmus.

This letter was written after the death of Cardinal Guillaume de Croy (6 January 1521, line 63–4) and before Erasmus' departure for Anderlecht (cf Ep 1208 introduction). It was printed in the *Epistolae ad diversos*.

TO THE HONOURABLE LOUIS VAN PRAET, PREFECT OF GHENT, FROM ERASMUS OF ROTTERDAM, GREETING

My honoured Lord (with honours indeed of many kinds), Antonius Clava[1] writes to me often and, whatever the subject, is never deserted by that wonderful gift of persuasion which was planted in him by nature and improved by experience and wide reading; but never has he put forward any cause with more fire and force than in his last letter, in which he takes issue with me seriously for having forgotten my ancient promise[2] and written nothing to your Highness, to whom I have owed, and daily owe, so much. I take it kindly that he should provoke me to write; not that there was any need of provocation, did the unmeasured toil of my researches leave me free to satisfy in this way either my own feelings or the wishes and deserving of my friends; it would have been kinder still, had he furnished me with the subject of the letter. I know your truly noble spirit, full worthy of your distinguished ancestors; I had a taste of it in Louvain in my youth, and now I learn of it frequently from the reports of many of my friends. Scarcely anyone visits us from your part of the world but he recites a long story of the zeal, the eloquence and the energy with which on every occasion you support the cause of my humble self.

The greatest and best patrons tend to be called in when the cause is really bad, and a man in high place might not be unsuitable as patron of a highly placed rogue. Now I am a man of no standing in society, and my cause is so good that those who make trouble for me owe me a great debt of gratitude for the very same activities for which they seek to put me in jeopardy; yet such is the wickedness of my adversaries in their serried ranks, such the unhappy state of our society, which gives open licence to effrontery, impudence, hypocrisy, avarice, ambition, and servility, that great and noble persons are obliged to maintain the cause, however self-evident, of their followers, however humble. Once upon a time, as the fable has it,[3] the members of the body conspired against the belly. Now we have changed all that, and the bellies[4] of society are in league to wage war against the rest of the body politic; and, however great my ill will, I could hardly wish them anything worse than their present state of mind. The louder that party blusters against liberal studies, the more those studies flourish everywhere.

As for Luther, I never had any business with him, except what one has with any fellow-Christian.[5] No one does more to advance his cause than those who attack him with every weapon they can command;[6] and it is extraordinary how, while they vilify him atrociously, they secure for their enemy a warm corner in the hearts of the public and cover themselves with obloquy. If only Luther did not wound himself with his own weapons[7] by writing more atrocious things every day, he would owe a great debt to the stupidity of his enemies. One thing is clear: if we escape this Scylla, Charybdis is waiting for us,[8] waiting to engulf all at once the entire liberty of the people of Christ, and to extinguish the last spark of gospel teaching.[9] For who will endure this stupid sort of men, who up to now by tricks and treachery have held despotic rule over Christ's flock, and whose greed, pride, lust, and avarice nothing can satisfy? Would that God might either give them a change of heart or remove them from the scene, so that they may cease to make this uproar against the Gospel of Christ. As for me, my spirit is unbroken; I do what I have always done – advance as best I can the cause of liberal studies and true piety, without however taking any part whatever in this hateful strife. My wish is to be of use, and if there is no prospect of success, I would rather hold my peace.

But I must finish my letter. Let me assure you that I know well how much I owe to the spirit you have always shown towards me, and that I shall make it clear, when the right time comes, that such great kindness was not entirely wasted on an ungrateful or forgetful object. May Christ our Lord and Master long preserve you for the benefit of us all, and in you preserve that spirit.

Pray give my greetings to all my friends, especially to Antonius Clava, most frank and friendly of them all, and Willem de Waele,[10] who fully deserves inclusion in my list of Williams.[11] From which the envious Fates have lately removed one, in the shape of the cardinal de Croy.[12] In that one brief example Fortune made clear how great her power is for good or ill: we saw him swiftly raised to the pinnacle of dignity, and suddenly cut short, like some flower plucked by the finger of fate. Farewell, my honoured Lord. I write this on the spur of the moment, to escape more and even more forcible rebukes from Clava.

Louvain, 1521

1192 / To Alexander Schweiss — Louvain, 13 March [1521]

This letter was first edited by Paulus Merula in *Vita Des. Erasmi* (Leiden 1607) after a manuscript copy made from the original, which may have remained in the possession of Maximiliaan van Egmond (cf line 92 and Allen's headnote).

Alexander Schweiss (d 1533–6), of Herborn in Hesse, was probably in the service of the landgraves of Hesse from 1504. In 1516 he was secretary to Henry III of Nassau and, having gone to Spain with his master in 1522, there became an influential secretary at the court of Charles v. His acquaintance with Erasmus may have dated from the summer of 1520 (cf Ep 1119 n1). This letter was no doubt directed to reach him at Worms (cf lines 90–2). Henry of Nassau was attending the diet (cf Ep 1197 introduction), but left around 19 March to take command of Charles v's army in the Netherlands, primarily against Robert de la Marck (cf Ep 1228 n12; *Reichstagsakten* J.R. II 826).

ERASMUS OF ROTTERDAM TO THE HONOURABLE ALEXANDER, SECRETARY TO THE ILLUSTRIOUS COUNT OF NASSAU,[1] GREETING

The bearer of this, a kinsman of mine,[2] makes trouble for me by his repeated appeals, and now in my turn I trouble you. May I beg you, if he has no hope or very little hope indeed, to extinguish this hope that does him no good. For I have other things to think about.

Luther's books I do not read, nor have I any relations with the man, except such as one has with any fellow-Christian.[3] It is true that I would rather see him set right than put down altogether,[4] and if he is sowing poison of any kind among the common people, no one will get rid of it better than the man who put it there.[5] No objections from me if they prefer their Luther either roast or boiled.[6] The loss of one man is bearable. But it is the public peace they must consider.

I only wish that those who are in charge of this business, and whose policy has more heat than healing in it, would support the dignity of the pope with as much intelligence as they seem to show devotion. In these parts, I am sure, no one does more harm to the standing of the Holy See than those who are Luther's loudest and most offensive opponents, and no one does more to commend him to the emotions of the multitude: with such stupidity, such demagogy do they go about it, these monks,[7] none of whom has the reputation of an honest man. The bull instructs them to preach against Luther,[8] which means to prove his opinions false by the evidence of the Scriptures and teach something different and better. As it is, no one takes up his pen to refute him, though everybody is clamouring for it; no one proves him wrong; they simply abuse him, and that often with a pack of lies. They say[9] he wants to abolish confession, wants to abolish purgatory, is publishing blasphemous attacks on the Deity – so they say. There is a Jacobite in Antwerp who declares that Luther has stated in writing that all Christ's miracles were performed by the black art.[10] And a Carmelite preaching before the king of France declared that the coming of Antichrist is at hand, and that he already has four precursors, some Minorite or other in Italy, Jacques Lefèvre d'Etaples in France, Reuchlin in Germany, and Erasmus in Brabant.[11]

In Bruges, a Minorite, who is a suffragan of Tournai,[12] preached for a whole hour in St Donatian's against Luther and me – for this is the policy worked out by the monks over their liquor;[13] though I have no connection with Luther, they always bracket us together – without establishing a single point; he merely called us storks, donkeys, beasts, blockheads, Antichrists,[14] until the whole congregation thought he was off his head. In another sermon he declared that Erasmus' books contain certain things that are heretical. After the sermon he was asked what these were by one of the city council who is an educated man.[15] He replied that he had never read my books; he had tried to read the paraphrases, but the Latin was so profound, he was afraid I might fall into some heresy. There's effrontery for you! – and this ranting hack is a bishop. Even worse rubbish is poured forth by the Jacobites in Antwerp,[16] in such an inflammatory style that a councillor who is far from stupid foresaw that it might end in a riot, and warned them that in their public sermons they must neither approve of Luther nor attack him, but must preach the Gospel of Christ. Next up gets a Minorite called Matthias,[17] a very fluent preacher, and says: 'If you want to hear the Gospel, you can hear that from your parish priests, even if they have spent the night in bed with a whore.'

In Louvain a Carmelite called Nicolaus Egmondanus[18] in his regular theology course said that Paul after persecuting the church had become an honest man, and 'we must pray that the same thing may happen to Luther and Erasmus.' In another lecture he said there was disagreement between Erasmus and Jacques Lefèvre; 'and no wonder,' says he, 'for heretics never agree.' And this is our leading university theologian, stupid and choleric and astonishingly obstinate.

These are a few examples out of many, from which you can gauge what the rest are like. If only the Holy Father knew the way things are done here! These monks, I do assure you, have their own interests at heart rather than his. Whatever ought to happen to Luther, it is certainly time for Charles to do something for the peace of Christendom.[19] It would be best if complete silence could be imposed on both sides in public, and if Luther ceased to write books of this kind, or rather, were obliged to purge the books he has written of everything that acts as a cause of strife. Those who hope to win credit out of public misfortunes would like to see the whole thing brought to an end by violence. And would it were brought to an end, but in the right way, so as to advance the glory of Christ! But no one would believe how widely he has made his way into the minds of many nationalities, and how deeply he has taken root in books which are circulating in all directions and in every language. There is talk here of a threatening proclamation by Charles.[20] I devoutly hope that every action of our excellent prince may prove a blessing to the Christian world; but this will not, I fear, meet with the success that some people expect.

You may be wondering, my most enlightened friend, why I write all this to you. For this reason alone, that some steps may be taken to counter the perilous disorder which seems to me inevitable, as long as princes prefer to be guided by the passions of a few whom I could name, rather than take thought for the body politic. I hold no brief for Luther, though it makes a difference what steps are taken to punish him; it is the public peace that I am concerned for, and you know well that in any disorder it is the rascals who get most advantage. I am a supporter of the Order of Preachers,[21] and have nothing against the Carmelites. But among them I know several whose character is such that I would rather be a vassal of the Grand Turk[22] than submit to be governed by them. We depend on the wisdom of the pope and on the foresight of princes to see that men of this kidney are not turned loose upon the fortunes and the lives of right-thinking people.

Farewell, my dear Alexander, and be sure to give my greetings to the noble count.[23] If you have the opportunity, remember me to Floris, heer van Ysselstein,[24] whose son[25] came to see me yesterday; he does this from time to time, and can render his Greek Homer with admirable readiness. May God preserve the boy to be a great ornament of his native country.

Louvain, 13 March

1192A / To Georgius Spalatinus — Louvain, 13 March 1521

A contemporary copy of this letter was traced by Otto Clemen and edited by him in the *Archiv für Reformationsgeschichte* 27 (1930) 260–1. It was then part of a private collection in Hannover. The letter is also among the preliminary pieces in Allen VIII.

Erasmus had met Spalatinus at Cologne in November 1520 (cf Ep 1155 introduction). The influential secretary was now with his master, Frederick the Wise, in Worms for the diet (cf Ep 1197 introduction), and Erasmus no doubt wished to inform them that he no longer expected to go there.

Greeting. I was always afraid this would happen, when I saw Luther taking on so many things at once, and with such ferocity. It was better to put up with what was wrong than try to mend it so clumsily. As it is, I fear we shall suffer the fate of those who try to shake off their fetters and, if things do not go as they wish, have a still heavier burden to bear. It is scarcely credible how much the common people are attracted to Luther,[1] and most educated people too. A certain number of Jacobites and Carmelites go on bawling at the public in a way that does them the greatest discredit and could hardly do more harm to the papal cause and more increase Luther's general popularity.[2] If only Leo, and Charles too,[3] knew what is really going on! They would keep their loudest thunders for such people. As it is, he knows nothing, except what he learns from the letters of certain persons who are more devoted to their own interest than the pope's.

The loss of one man is perhaps not very serious;[4] but if anything were to happen to Luther, I can foresee the victors behaving with great cruelty, and ordering us to believe things they do not believe themselves. In God's name, how can posterity be expected to believe that such theologians ever existed as some of these we now see? We must pray that Christ himself will defend his spouse, and put into the minds of princes counsels that may save the day.

I have decided to put in an appearance in your part of the world, but apart from many other things, my health was too uncertain for me to risk the journey and Lent as well.[5] Mind you give my warmest greetings to the duke. I do not forget how much I owe to him. If only all princes had the same spirit, and set the good of their peoples above their own personal ambitions! Christ have you in his keeping.

In haste, from Louvain, 13 March 1521

Erasmus

To Georgius Spalatinus

1193 / To the Reader

Louvain [c March] 1521

This is the preface to the *Progymnasmata quaedam primae adolescentiae Erasmi* (Louvain: D. Martens 1521; NK 855), an authorized reprint of some of Erasmus' early poems, all devoted to various themes of Christian ethics (Reedijk nos 23–6, 85, 88; cf Ep 175 and below n4). An approximate month can be assigned to Martens' *Progymnasmata* and this preface from a dated reprint, undertaken probably without Erasmus' knowledge and enlarged through the addition of *De ratione studii: Progymnasmata* (Deventer: A. Pafraet May 1521; NK 854).

ERASMUS OF ROTTERDAM TO THE YOUNG WHO WISH TO LEARN, GREETING

Those who publish my works in printer's type while I am still alive are impudent enough;[1] more impudent those who put out trifles from my student days. But the greatest impudence of all is theirs, who set my name to other men's rubbish, as someone (I know not who) has recently done in publishing a book about a method of letter-writing,[2] none of which is mine except for a few stolen words. Nor have I ever been acquainted with anyone called Petrus Paludanus.[3]

Long ago, when I was a boy, being but an indifferent performer in elegiac verse, I began to exercise myself in a kind of short declamatory piece in that metre, and these I perceive have been published once or twice.[4] What there is in them that is thought to merit publicity I do not understand, unless the object is, by exhibiting the work of one callow youth, to encourage other youths of some intelligence to practice on subjects of a better sort, instead of the long-winded love-poems which some learned men regard as admirable. Still, trivial though it is, I have revised the material, and allowed it to be reprinted, for there was nothing else I could do.

Farewell, dear reader, and if you take my advice, you will spend your time on something more worth having.

Louvain, 1521

1194 / To the Reader

[Louvain, 1521]

Erasmus wrote this preface for the first edition of his *De contemptu mundi epistola* (Louvain: D. Martens 1521, NK 2907). The circumstances of its composition – Erasmus apparently wrote it in the name of another man (lines 13–15) – are explained in this letter and repeated in Allen I 18:16–19, cf 37:2–7. The work is a declamation in praise of monastic seclusion from the world; for the popularity of this theme see Allen's headnote and Sem Dresden's introduction to his edition of *De contemptu mundi* in ASD V-1 1–86.

The date of 1521 appears in the colophon of Martens' edition, and a more precise date cannot be assigned to this letter. Allen placed it here in view of its similarity to Ep 1193.

ERASMUS OF ROTTERDAM TO THE FAIR-MINDED READER, GREETING

I have often complained, gentle reader, of what I suffer from the zeal of my friends, who publish in my lifetime and against all my protests the most trifling pieces, which I threw off as a boy for practice in writing; nothing was further from my thoughts than that they should pass into circulation. And under this head I am the more unfortunate in that they come out in these days, when we are so much blessed,[1] and would have been much less exposed to public scorn had they been put out when they were first written. As it is, they are taken by their readers for the work of a man of some seniority, though I wrote them as a youth, and even so did not write them with this in view, and their readers belong to this age of ours, which is so rich in critics of exquisite taste.[2]

Long ago, when I was scarcely twenty, I yielded to the importunity of one Theodoricus,[3] who is still with us, and wrote for him a letter by which he hoped to persuade his nephew Jodocus to share his form of life. This was often copied and passed from hand to hand, and my name was attached to it, although I have no nephew called Jodocus. I wrote it against the grain and, as the piece itself proclaims, without much care, making play on the spur of the moment with commonplace reflections, for in those days I had no equipment of solid reading. Then the printers openly threatened that they would publish it unless I published it myself. I read it through again, changed a word here and there,[4] and allowed it to be entrusted to the press. In this way, I suppose, the time will come when I cease to have any love for my youthful effusions.

Farewell, dear reader, and if you read this book, read it in charity, and remember as you read that it was written against the grain.

1195 / To Luigi Marliano — Louvain, 25 March [1521]

This letter – and no doubt others dispatched to Worms at the same time – was written to counteract the machinations of Erasmus' enemies at the imperial court (lines 4–8), express his loyalty to the church of Rome (lines 33–6, 47–8, 117–20), and to announce his decision not to travel to the diet (lines 165–7). It is known in the version Erasmus authorized for printing in the *Epistolae ad diversos*, where Marliano's bland answer, Ep 1198, was also published.

In a carefully worded paragraph (lines 56–71) it criticized Aleandro for his unwise handling of the Luther issue rather than for his attacks on Erasmus, although the papal nuncio was the man Erasmus feared most at the imperial court (cf Ep 1167 n20). If we can trust Aleandro, Erasmus' enemies at court, however, included Marliano, the recipient of this letter (cf n3). Despite an ominous conversation they had had at Brussels (cf Ep 1198:17–22) Erasmus' trust in Marliano's friendship evidently continued undiminished (cf n37).

In 1523 Erasmus recalled (Allen Ep 1342:54–61, ASD IX-1 150) that to exculpate himself he had sent his own messenger to Worms with a whole bundle of letters addressed to prominent members of the court, including Chancellor Gattinara, Cardinal Schiner, Marliano, and Aleandro himself, all of whom answered in writing; only Bishop Erard de la Marck was content to send an oral message. Despite a slight confusion in the chronology (Allen Ep 1342:51–2) it seems clear that of these letters of Erasmus this is the only one known today, while Epp 1197–8 were among the answers he received.

ERASMUS OF ROTTERDAM TO THE RIGHT REVEREND LUIGI MARLIANO, BISHOP OF TUY AND MEMBER OF THE EMPEROR CHARLES' PRIVY COUNCIL, GREETING

Letters from several friends,[1] no ordinary men and persons of some authority, though their affection makes them perhaps unduly anxious, inform me that in your part of the world I have secret enemies, I know not who, who continually spead fresh rumours and suspicions that I am a supporter of Luther.[2] I understand also that sundry scandalous pamphlets are attributed to me,[3] of which I hear you have a constant supply, some from one source and some from another. I know that in these days calumny reigns supreme, and that there never was a time when unbridled scurrility was allowed more licence; but among scholarly and intelligent persons of good judgment, among whom I place your Lordship in the very first rank, there should be no scope for this sort of underground attack. Long ago you warned me[4] with your usual wisdom (though you were, as they say, preaching to the converted[5]) not to involve myself in Luther's business. So far have I been from doing so, that I have devoted the greatest efforts to prevent matters from reaching this stage, which was the last thing I wished. Only at the very beginning, before I saw which way Luther was heading, I discouraged public clamour that might be subversive. I urged that discussion should be conducted in print by learned men.[6] I hoped to see Luther put right rather than put down;[7] or, if his destruction was inevitable, I hoped he would be stopped without setting the world by the ears. This policy would even now be approved by the pope, if he really knew how this question is being handled here, and the enthusiasm so many nations feel for Luther. But all that was the invention of certain monks, who have no more love for me than they have for the humanities – to involve me in the Luther business whether I would or no.

Those who appear to support Luther have done all they possibly can to lure me into his camp.[8] Luther's persecutors have tried to drive me into his party, raving against me by name everywhere in their public utterances somewhat more offensively than they do against Luther himself. None of their tricks, however, have succeeded in moving me from my position. Christ I recognize, Luther I know not; the church of Rome I recognize, and think it does not disagree with the Catholic church. From that church death shall not tear me asunder, unless the church is sundered openly from Christ.[9] Subversion I have always loathed; and would that Luther and the Germans one and all were of that opinion! I perceive that in most regions this side of the Alps there are many who support Luther from a kind of destiny,[10] and it happens in an extraordinary way that Luther is helped by his enemies and helps them in turn, as though there were collusion between them. No one does Luther more harm than himself,[11] with this stream of new and progressively more offensive pamphlets. Again, there are men who bawl away in public with such ignorance and folly and such a tendency to subversion, that they make themselves universally detested while securing a public welcome for Luther, and damage the pope's cause[12] as an incompetent lawyer damages his clients. I think highly of the supporters of the Roman pontiff, who has the support of every religious person; who would not support him who is Christ's closest follower, and devotes himself utterly to the salvation of Christian folk? – but I wish his champions were more intelligent. They have no ideas except to eat Luther alive, and it is not my business whether they prefer him boiled or roast.[13] At any rate, when they drag me into business that is nothing to do with me, their behaviour is both ungodly and unwise; for they would dispose of Luther sooner if they left me out of it.

And in this respect I feel bound to say that Aleandro, a man who is in other ways uncommonly civilized and singularly learned, shows a lack of the wisdom necessary in such a perilous business, if what one reads and hears about him is true. He and I were once very close friends.[14] I gave him letters of introduction when he was setting out for France, and spoke of him most highly everywhere in any company and even in print.[15] I respected his scholarship and found his character congenial, though he is not like other people; and the two of us seemed by nature to get on very well. It was part of his instructions that he should use every means to win over even those who had previously been of Luther's party;[16] so far was the Holy Father from wishing to alienate any innocent man. But though by nature he himself was not uncivilized, pressure from other people I could name[17] has driven him in a different direction. Yet he would have been more successful, I believe, in this business of Luther, if he had adapted his sense of values to my own; he would have had a supporter in the cause of religion, and in the pope's cause at least not an opponent.[18]

They say freely that Luther has drawn heavily on my books.[19] This is a shameless invention, and the very first of his articles[20] gives the lie to their obvious falsehood. Where do I suggest that whatever we do is sinful? Not to speak of countless other points which have nothing the least like them in my books, even when I am writing humorously. And yet in the old days heretics went to the writings of evangelists and apostles to extract poison for their own use. For the moment I speak as though he had written something heretical, and had drawn that from what I have written. He is said not to admit the authorship of certain pamphlets. He would be wiser perhaps if he admitted none of them, provided he could get people to believe that; but whatever assistance he may have in his writing, at any rate, in all the books that circulate under his name, there is no syllable that comes from me. I would not hesitate to swear this with all possible solemnity.

For many years now I have been familiar[21] – and not I alone – with your singular wisdom, familiar likewise with your open and friendly attitude towards myself; and the influence you exert is common knowledge. I therefore urge you to defend my innocence against false and malicious charges of this kind. Let them examine every word which even in my most private letters I have poured into the bosom of my friends, with more freedom perhaps (such is my nature) than is sometimes expedient; let them examine even the casual words I often let fall over the wine. They will find nothing, except that I would rather have seen Luther put right than put down,[22] at a time when there was still hope that he would turn towards better things. Even now I would rather see the matter laid to rest than grow more and more bitter and set the whole world by the ears. I would prefer to see a distinction made between good and evil, rather than that hatred of some things that seem evil should mean the destruction of what is very good. Last but not least, I urge that in avoiding the Scylla of Luther we should not fall headlong into the Charybdis of the opposite faction.[23] If they think these views deserve to be punished, they have a culprit who pleads guilty. I at least have acted with no purpose in view except to promote the honour of the Roman Pontiff and of theologians, and the public peace of Christendom.[24] Not one of Luther's books, however small, have I yet read right through;[25] not one of his unorthodox opinions have I defended, even in jest. The ignorant and subversive clamour of some men I could name I cannot accept, nor can any honest and intelligent man here accept it. What they are heading for is clear enough – to destroy the humanities and make their own dictatorship secure. Avoid Luther as I may, I cannot all the same approve of men like this. They are few in number, but they rouse many more. It is not the order I condemn;[26] it is they themselves who do their own order great disservice.

Such, Reverend Father, is the whole picture of my mind. If anything is bandied about in your part of the world which is contrary to the Christian religion or disturbs the public peace or attacks the honour of the see of Rome, you may be absolutely certain that it does not come from me, under whatever name it circulates. That this is true, Time, who brings all things into the open,[27] will one day make clear; and I am ready now to demonstrate by any proof they wish that I have no mind to differ by one hair's breadth[28] from those who agree with the Catholic church. I know that one should endure anything rather than upset the general state of the world and make it worse; I know that sometimes it is a good man's duty to conceal the truth,[29] and not to publish it regardless of times and places, before every audience and by every method, and everywhere complete. Every educated man is well aware that some things are generally accepted, through the gradual growth of custom, through complaisance towards modern legal authority, through hasty pronouncements by academic philosophers, or even through the arts and craft of princes, things which would be better done away with. But the wisdom of the Christian required that if a remedy is to be applied, it should not be applied so clumsily that it makes the disease more acute instead of ending it, and even replaces the disease by an early death. For I would not dare to determine whether there is any way in which Christians can approve Plato's opinion,[30] when he allows those wise guardians of his to deceive the people with lies for the public benefit; for sound philosophical reasoning has no power to restrain the mingled throng of men from lapsing into something worse.

One thing I have always been on my guard against: I would not be a cause of disorder or an asserter of doctrinal novelties. I was invited by many eminent persons to ally myself with Luther, and wrote back that I would be Luther's man if he were of the Catholic party. They invited me to lay down a rule of faith,[31] and I wrote back that I know no faith but that of the Catholic church.[32] I urged them to seek a reconciliation with the Roman pontiff, and took the substance out of their complaints. I was the very first person to resist Luther's pamphlets to prevent their printing.[33] Not long after, I made an approach to him,[34] to make him refrain from writing in a subversive fashion, for that was the outcome I always feared; and I would have

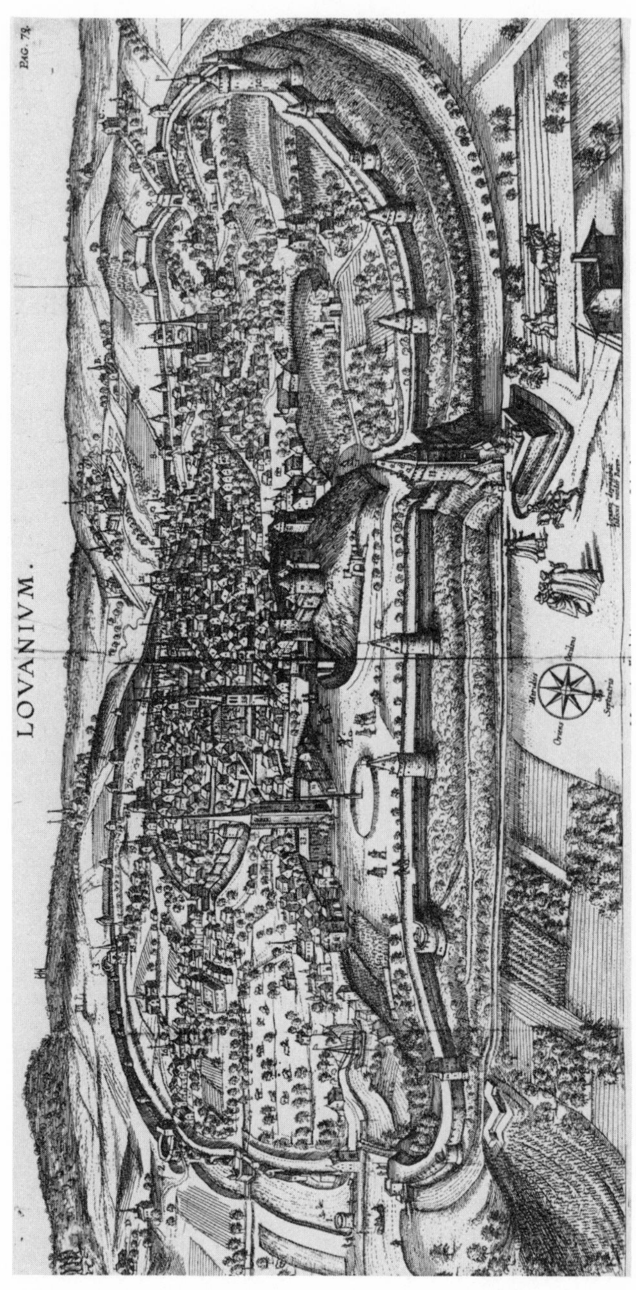

View of Louvain
Engraving by Josse van der Baren (fl 1600)
Courtesy of Memorial Library of the University of Notre Dame, Indiana

attempted something more, had I not been deterred, among other things, by a kind of superstitious fear[35] that I might be unconsciously resisting the spirit of Christ.

I have urged many people, and still I urge them, to refrain from libellous pamphleteering,[36] and anonymous pamphlets especially, with which they do so much to rouse men's passions, doing great harm not only to the peace of Christendom but to the man whom they are supposed to support. Warn them I can, compel them I cannot. The world is full of printing-houses, full of bad poets and rhetorical scribblers. The uproar they arouse is not within my control, and it is the height of injustice to hold me responsible for other men's rashness. And on this point I am less inclined to think ill of Hutten,[37] though it pains me beyond measure to see all those gifts, and that happy vein in both prose and verse, not consecrated to happier subjects; for he maintains his own style and his own name everywhere, and the resulting burden of ill will is his and no one else's.[38] The others forfeit all claim to our confidence, being so unsure of their case, it seems, that they dare not put their real names to it; and at the same time they lay a burden of ill will on innocent people, and many of them.

I should already be with you, in the company of the illustrious Ferdinand,[39] had I been able to discover for certain that you were still at Worms. But it is astonishing how little is certain here, even among the great men at court. Farewell, O leading light of prelates, who are not least among the glories of the imperial court.

Agostino Scarpinelli I wrote to some time ago.[40] Pray give my greetings to him, and also to Severus,[41] that gentlest of men and so unfitly named.

Louvain, 25 March [1520]

1196 / [To Vincentius Theoderici] [Louvain, c middle of March 1521]

This very long letter was published in the *Epistolae ad diversos*, although much of what it contains is also set forth in other letters (eg Epp 1126, 1162) printed earlier in that volume. It must have been obvious to many of its early readers to whom it was addressed, even though the retention of Theoderici's name in one spot is probably not intentional but due to an oversight (cf n48). In Allen Ep 1821:19–20 Erasmus explicitly named Theoderici as the addressee. The approximate date is indicated by lines 166–7.

The first part (lines 11–176) presents a roughly chronological (cf lines 136–7) account of Erasmus' troubles with Theoderici from the time they both arrived in Louvain in 1517. A confrontation over dinner in the Augustinian monastery of St Maartensdal (line 24) was followed by a trip Theoderici made to his native Holland (lines 25–6). After his return they met again in his lodgings, presumably at the Dominican priory (line 37), for an exchange already reported at great length in Ep 1126 and thus prior to 31 August 1520. At least one other meeting followed (lines 96, 122–3) before Erasmus' friend, the Dominican Johannes Faber, mediated a temporary end to their mutual recriminations (lines 139–42) in the autumn of 1520. A little while later Theoderici preached at Dordrecht in the course of another trip to Holland (before 6 December, lines 159–60). Finally on 7 March 1521, a few days before the composition of this letter, Theoderici stage-managed, or so Erasmus claimed, another attack on him in the course of a solemn function to commemorate St Thomas Aquinas (lines 166–76). It was not by any means the last (cf Epp 1217:16–17, 1233 n28).

After this chronicle of his grievances against Theoderici Erasmus turns to a more general defence, aiming his shafts at other friars as well. After line 339, however, the letter consists mainly of admonitions addressed to Theoderici in a personal, almost homiletic tone. While this may well be the most original aspect of the letter, it also lays Erasmus open to the charge of self-righteousness he so continually levelled against his opponents. Although the letter reveals once more Erasmus' sensitiveness to criticism – he may well have felt 'that no one for many centuries has been more unpleasantly attacked than I' (lines 503–4) – nothing really is known of Theoderici that would contradict Erasmus' contemptuous assessment of his intellectual calibre (lines 714–17).

Vincentius Theoderici (1481–1526) was born at Beverwijk, north of the city of Haarlem, where he entered the Dominican priory. He studied and taught at Paris until 1517 when he was sent to Louvain. There he obtained on 13 October a doctorate in theology. In his Paris years he did some editorial work in the field of Thomistic theology; cf line 296.

ERASMUS OF ROTTERDAM TO HIS MOST OBSTINATE OPPONENT, GREETING

It is the duty of all those who have given in their names to Christ in baptism to follow to the best of their ability the example of their Prince and teacher, who when he was reviled reviled not again, but in return for bitter railing offered the teaching that leads to salvation; and this is especially true of those who profess the learning and life of theologians. But what a great gulf separates from that ideal, my good X, those who return evil for good and harrass one of the brethren without ceasing, even though he has done them service, with their deadly venomous tongues!

Ever since you moved to Louvain,[1] you have never ceased to deliver wild attacks on my reputation at every opportunity, although never provoked by any injury, however slight. And at first I was unwilling to believe this. Such conduct seemed unworthy, I will not say of a priest, of a preacher of the Gospel, of a theologian, or of a monk, but of a man. It is a habit of women,[2] and of impudent and foolish women, to use their tongues as a weapon in order to relieve their feelings. Later, when so many reports arrived from all quarters of what you had said, at dinner in one place, in monasteries at another, at another in some tumbrel or hoy,[3] I believed what I was told, but with the limitation that the whole thing, whatever it amounted to, was clearly negligible. And all the time, when we met you were all smiles, all friendly greetings, evidently supposing that what you scattered everywhere would never reach me.

At length, at a solemn dinner in the Augustinian house,[4] when you asked me with a most friendly expression whether I had any wishes as you were just leaving for Holland,[5] I wished you might have a little of the fraternal charity to which hitherto you had paid too little attention, warning you of course, in a courteous and friendly way, to desist from the offensive language which did you more harm than me, and from poisoning the minds of simple folk with venom which you could not afterwards withdraw. For a scorpion, when applied to the wound it has made, sucks up the poison that it has injected from the sting in its tail,[6] nor is anyone at risk in any other way except the man who was stung; but here, once you strike someone with your venomous tongue, you cannot cure him, and the plague spreads far and wide, as the contagion ever seizes on fresh victims.

When my well-meant warnings were followed by worse behaviour, Christian charity made me approach you in your lodgings,[7] not a thing I often did, as you yourself admitted. I advised you in private, and without restraint but in a friendly spirit, to turn that eloquence of yours to better use. In the course of that conversation you know how much evidence I uncovered of your impenetrable and utterly disgraceful ignorance, although you spent your whole time in listing my dangerous errors, even to the point of making a charge of heresy, while all the time you did not even understand what I had written. Clearly things had come to such a desperate pass that X was obliged to lend a hand to the Christian religion in its peril. When, for instance, finding excuses for St Thomas or, more truly, expressing a high opinion of him, I had said that he did not deserve[8] to live in such times, meaning of course that his intellect deserved a happier climate, you called heaven and earth to witness that I had said of a great Doctor of the church, and what is more one who had been canonized, and above all a professed Dominican, that he did not deserve to live.

In another place,[9] where my object was to magnify the disease of malicious accusation, I had adduced the example of a defamatory libel, as being a capital offence, in order to show by the comparison what a serious crime it is to conspire together to attack the reputation of an innocent man; and you thought that I approved of defamatory libels, just as if a man approved of murder who, when arguing against adultery, taught that in certain circumstances this could be a graver sin than murder. Again, after quoting several passages from Augustine and Chrysostom in which they appear to attribute human emotions, akin to some kind of sin, to the Blessed Virgin,[10] I had added, 'And we make her absolutely exempt from all sin,' meaning of course that we were wrong in exempting her from original sin if the Fathers are right in attributing sin to her which she has herself committed. You supposed me to be laying down that the Blessed Virgin was exempt from the contagion of our first parents. Had I laid down something of the sort, there was no danger in it, for that opinion is not only more favourable to her, it is, in my view at least, more likely to be right. But all the time, sharp-witted as you are, you did not understand that I was arguing the opposite case. Here you were very easily satisfied, and were prepared to forgive me even if I disagreed with the judgment of the church, provided I accepted the opinion of St Thomas.

I had cited[11] from the commentaries of St Thomas that he called heresy the opinion of those who denied the presence of Christ's true body in the eucharist, while the view of those who denied that Christ consecrated with the words 'This is my body' he refuted, but called erroneous and not heretical; and I later added that it seemed to me on the whole (*in totum*) safer if the leaders of the church, when dealing with things which could not be demonstrated either by the explicit testimony of the Scriptures or by solid arguments, would not lay down the law as though they wished their opinion to be accepted as an oracle. Your verdict was that this was extremely dangerous; you went astray, of course, through ignorance of Latin, for you took *in totum* to mean 'wholly,' referring to both the views which had preceded, while in Latin *in totum*, 'on the whole' means 'generally speaking' – not only, that is, in the matter before us but in similar things as well; referring of course to the second part of what was then under discussion, which cannot be demonstrated either by arguments or explicit evidence. And you had added in the margin in your own hand, 'Note pernicious comment on a point on which the church has pronounced so often,' clearly suggesting that I denied the real presence. And when I protested that you wrote such a monstrous falsehood against a passage which you had read but not understood, you countered with the most witty reply, that you had a right to write what you liked in your own book. As though others did not have the same right to jot down what they please in their own notes, or as though a man charged with defamatory libel is brought to court because he wrote it in someone else's notebook! And yet you thought so well of this brilliant epigram that in our next conversation you repeated it over and over again, on the old principle that you can't have too much of a good thing.[12]

These examples of egregious folly I came upon in one short conversation, while you were putting them forward consciously as very pretty and quite irrefutable. Nor do I doubt that you would have put forward things even more idiotic, had I not preferred to correct you in friendly fashion and not fish cunningly for what I wanted.

And yet what you had previously done was enough to dissolve the closest friendship; while I, who had no relationship with you except that which exists between any two Christians, did you a service in return for so much malevolence, in hopes that you would one day repent. I gave you serious advice, as one brother to another, to spend the effort you devote to picking to pieces other men's books which you do not understand, on learning grammar and reading some of those classical authors your ignorance of whom fills your work everywhere with foul mistakes and blinds you to things that any child can see. I advised you, if there was anything you did not like, to complain of it to me in person, severely if you so wish, but not to accuse me falsely in front of other people when I do not deserve it. And you seemed not to reject my advice, which was friendly rather than agreeable.

Not long afterwards the bull was published which was supposed to be against Luther.[13] On this subject I never said a word to any mortal man; but you suddenly returned to your true nature, and began loudly to protest that I was against the papal diploma, put up to do this, I suppose, by an individual whose heart I could wish not so black as his habit is white.[14] By this time I had Paul as my authority for giving you up as by nature past praying for, for I had warned you two or three times without effect;[15] but since Paul equally tells us that 'charity hopeth all things,'[16] I went to see you again and protested, just the two of us, rather more freely, for the case required it, but even so in friendly terms. You there denied what I knew to be perfectly true, and produced another objection, that I had written a letter to the cardinal of Mainz in which I had criticized your order.[17] Nor were you ashamed to confess that you had not read the letter which made you so indignant. You showed no more decency than your colleague Nicolaus Egmondanus the Carmelite. He had declaimed without restraint against the New Testament which I had edited;[18] and when I had moved to Louvain, and asked him several times after dinner to show me in person what he did not like in my work, the man innocently replied that he had never read it.[19] I said nothing, supposing that he must know enough dialectic to be aware what I could infer from such premises. He had declaimed in the most spiteful way that Antichrist is upon us, and had never read what he was damning.

But I will return to the letter;[20] for the moment I will pursue the order of events. At that time, after reminding you of your duty, I came away, not much hoping that you would improve but not giving up hope altogether. A few days later Johannes Faber,[21] a member of your order (and I only wish you were as like him in learning, character, and wisdom as you are in cowl and habit), told me how he had warned you on this subject, or rather, taken you to task; for as it happened I had told him the state of the case. Your answer was, if his report was true, that henceforward you would be a most faithful friend to Erasmus, if I would let fall this trouble between us. When Faber added that he did not want to return to me with something vague instead of certain, you seized his right hand and confirmed that it should be as you promised. Faber, having persuaded me that all this was true, began to beg me in the name of Christian charity to let myself be persuaded to relent and to make it up with you. And I, who have always been very ready to make up a quarrel,[22] answered that I was very ready not only to forgive what had been done amiss but to forget it.

If this is not true, at least not a syllable of it is my own invention; this is what I was told by a man advanced in years,[23] a priest, a theologian very well qualified in his own field, a select preacher before the emperor and prior of the monastery at Augsburg. He himself can write me down as a man of straw if there is a word in this that is not true. But although there was no change on my side, you soon slipped back into your native bent, in season and out of season continually using your poisonous tongue against the man who had given you such friendly warnings and so mercifully forgiven you. When you had had to face some sort of riot at Dordrecht[24] after a sermon, and had retreated to Louvain in a fast carriage, not yet being ready to face a risk to your life on behalf of the faith, you kept protesting, they told me, that this too you owed to me and to my writings, although at Dordrecht I do not know a soul, and at that time I had written to no one in Holland[25] about Luther either for good or evil.

Nor was your poisonous mind content with this. A few days ago, on St Thomas Aquinas' day,[26] a young member of your order was put up to make a fine hash of abuse of me and glory for St Thomas. The youth had learnt by heart what was more of a hotch-potch than a speech, and meant to recite it like a parrot without understanding it. How well he understood it you can judge from this, that when he quoted Horace's *feriuntque summos fulmina montes*,[27] he produced it at the top of his voice with *feruntque*; and later for *illi antistites* he recited *illi antistes*, like the good people of Praeneste saying *conia* or Plaustus' rustic turning *arrabo* into *rabo*. And to leave the rest in no doubt who was the author of this pretty show, there were you standing under the pulpit, telling him to say *feriunt* and *antistites*.

It was a wonderful and most happy glorification of St Thomas. Eloquence was ascribed to him and denied to me. Anyone can see that this was pure rhetoric. This is like Plutarch comparing the great of Greece with their Roman counterparts,[28] or the way one might compare an ant and a camel.[29] And what could be more impudent than for a young man who hardly knew his letters to pronounce how much theology I knew and whether I could write? 'X is an eminent theologian, a champion of the faith; and Erasmus knows no theology. What an imposter Erasmus is! He writes paraphrases on the Epistles and annotations on the New Testament. He publishes replies to sundry theologians; but he does not know a word of theology.' For my own part, I lay no claim to eloquence, and think little of myself in theology. But I have not such a low opinion of my own learning, my good X, that I should be willing to exchange mine for yours; how much good you are even in the subject you profess you yourself made sufficiently clear, when we heard you in the schools reading most of your material off a sheet of paper, and even that with some difficulty, and making some very unfortunate answers.[30] As a disciple of St Thomas you celebrate his festival on the same system used by the people of Lindos[31] in making a sacrifice to Hercules or the Greeks to Bacchus: they did not think the rites were duly performed unless there was plenty of public abuse. And after all this you wonder why intelligent men and rich matrons do not send their children to join your society, where in their early years they learn such arts as these with you to teach them, and learn to speak evil of their neighbour when they have hardly learnt to speak.

If however St Thomas is as much a saint as you wish him to appear, there is no doubt he must hate personal abuse, which is offensive to God and to all pious souls; and if you think he appreciates the sort of panegyric in which he is glorified by dragging his brother's name in the ditch, you must surely have a very low opinion of him. This irreligious performance did not please the rest of your audience, as they showed by stamping with their feet, but neither you nor your disciples, who profess the religion of the Gospel, were at all put out. They were beaming on one another as though things had gone very well, even before that parrot of yours gave his distinguished and well-memorized address, just so that everyone could see that there was a common plan behind it all. You are indignant with me because I sometimes differ from Thomas; why are you not more indignant because I differ sometimes from Jerome or Ambrose or Augustine? If Thomas is hurt because I occasionally think differently from him, why do you not rather prove me wrong and vindicate his reputation? Not to do this is sufficient confession that you cannot. And how can you have the face to declaim that a man knows no theology, who in several passages knows better than Thomas himself, who in your opinion is not only first of them all but the next man is a long way behind? At this point therefore, when you have shown no wish to conceal that you were the producer of this play, no one can have any doubt who it was inspired your other colleagues to rave as they do in their public sermons, commenting on my *Moria* and my *Antibarbari*,[32] advertising their own folly while they try to make mischief for mine.

But I must now return to the letter I wrote to the cardinal,[33] which irritated you so much that, whereas before you confined your noisy attacks on me to dinner-parties, boats, and wagons,[34] you now seem possessed and display your true self everywhere, assisted by several hirelings as if, when it came to abuse, you were not a host in yourself. First of all, the one topic in the whole of that letter is that Luther should be set right rather than extinguished,[35] and refuted rather than overwhelmed by conspiracies, and the world be instructed rather than dragooned and nothing else. This would contribute to the dignity of theologians everywhere, to the honour of the papacy, and the tranquillity of Christ's people.[36] At that time the pope had not yet interposed his authority; and I was well aware what certain persons were after who aim at nothing short of despotic rule. I therefore warned a prince who was friendly and had earned my lasting gratitude, in a sealed letter, not to let anyone misuse his authority. As for the men who published that letter, whether they meant to do me harm I do not know, but at least the result was harmful. The same advice I should not have been afraid to give to Pope Leo himself, had I had the opportunity, and I do not doubt that he would have found it acceptable. At least the facts show that it was not foolish or useless, and I fear we may find that more and more true in the future.

But this only moved you slightly. What you thought intolerable was that I had glanced at your order and had mentioned Bern.[37] Nor could I restrain a smile when you said that your order had existed for so many years, as though I intended to put an end to it. As far as I am concerned, I hope your order will continue, yes, and will flourish, until the world comes to an end. Is the whole order hurt because I said that some of its members were aiming at despotic rule?[38] You have thousands of houses, and tens of thousands of men; and must they all be called to the colours if one utters a complaint for some particular reason against two or three of the society? If a man were to discover that his priest had gossiped about something he learnt in the confessional, and warned his friend not to trust in anyone indiscriminately, because men are found who do not keep confidences as they ought to do, will all priests complain that they have been insulted? And yet what I wrote is so far from being a secret that men both know this commonly and complain about it. Moreover, if I mentioned Savaronella[39] and the outrage at Bern, I did not do this to make the order unpopular, as I say explicitly, nor do I do it offensively or at length; but it was necessary to the point I was then making. What would have happened if I had mentioned it, given the opportunity?

Would the world have known nothing of it, if I, and I only, had held my tongue?

Things would be different if it was forbidden to glance at any body of men. You yourselves attack princes, magistrates, bishops, and abbots openly and freely, and sometimes in subversive language, and you do not think it fair that anyone should seek to have the law on you, because you say you attack the thing in question and do not touch the people. Against none do you hold forth more readily than against the shepherds who are set to mind the Lord's flock. Not many days ago in Antwerp a certain monk[40] (I will have pity on his order), when told by the magistrates to preach the Gospel and abstain from subversive clamour, said in a public sermon, 'They tell me to preach the Gospel; but that is a thing you can hear from your parish priest, even if he slept the night before with a great whore.' A remark like that, as indecent as it was subversive, they give themselves licence to make, and do not consider that they have insulted a body of men instituted undoubtedly by Christ himself. And you contemplate an action for high treason if for good reason anyone glances at a Dominican or a Carmelite? If any name deserved to be respected, it would be the name of Christian; and the reason is no light one – not to give the godless a handle to cast our faults in our teeth. And yet the histories of Christianity record the disgraceful acts of Christians, not even sparing their names. Why does the order of nuns not tear Jerome's books to pieces because of the picture he gives of vicious virgins?[41] Why do the bishops not tear up the books of Cyprian, who attacks the bishops of his own day so severely, accusing them of making disgraceful profits and even of usury? Or will it be like the old days, when it was ill omened even to name certain gods – and shall we be forbidden to mention Dominicans or Carmelites without some honorific introduction?

It was said by that disciple of yours that even if these things were true they ought not to be mentioned, for the honour of the order. Why then do certain people, who wish so much honour paid to their own order, tell such lies about other orders by name and publicly? I have many examples to prove this is perfectly true. Personally, for all the attacks I have suffered, I have never mentioned a Dominican or a Carmelite by name in my books.[42] The Dominican order I even approve of above the rest,[43] for this reason if no other that it is less burdened with ceremonies. I would not concede even to you in person, though you swear to believe every word St Thomas says, that you are a keener supporter of true Dominicans than I am. Nor am I so unfair as to attribute the faults of individuals to the order. So far am I from doing so, that I often have mercy even on those from whom I have had most spiteful provocation, for fear of doing damage to an innocent order, being confident that their behaviour will be disapproved of by all the best men in the order. And yet this is done by so many and with such impunity, that a suspicious man might well think they are told by their superiors to behave as they do. And after all this do you still pretend that I am an enemy of your order, when I support it in a truer sense than you and your friends? Will you have cleared the honour of your order if you dishonour me, or make it white if you have made me black? If you are really keen to recommend your order to all men of good will, work for a renewal of the same gifts by which long ago it came into being and spread and won its standing in the world: integrity of life, holiness without feigning, disdain for the world, the teaching of the Gospel, and the gentleness of the true Christian. Follow these ideals, and all men will support you and praise you and wish you well. As things are, what shocking tales, continually new, are told of you! What complaints we hear! What crimes are committed! And would that they were either false or at any rate less creditable!

Moreover, how far I am from wishing to see any order in disgrace, you can tell from this example among many. There was bitter resentment against you in the heart of that excellent prince Hermann, count of Neuenahr,[44] because he had been undeservedly reflected on in something written by Jacob of Hoogstraten. Had the count persisted in the spirit in which he began, it looked as though no small peril to your order might be involved. I wrote a most careful letter in hopes of persuading my friend to relax his indignation; and so he did, though it was his own truly generous and gentle nature that made him do so. Hermannus Buschius,[45] a good scholar and a good writer, had indicated to me that he had in hand a work which would be, as I guessed from the title, a fairly severe attack on your order. I begged him seriously to change his mind, and when the work appeared it had been revised and was much more moderate, and the title too had been changed. I know another man[46] who writes so well and is so well read that I foresaw that anything he writes would clearly live. He had begun to write an account of the egregious scandals of the Dominicans and Carmelites. I did not rest until I had weaned the man from his purpose, partly because it seemed unjust to convert the misdeeds of one or other group of men into disgrace for the order as a whole, and partly because there seemed little purpose in spreading such stories and making the world a more unpleasant place. For there are some crimes which it is not safe to put on record: for example, unnatural vices, magic, poisoning,[47] soothsaying, and others of the kind, which your colleagues sometimes learn from the confessional, and which some of them practise.

You can see, my good Vincentius,[48] what my hostile attitude to your order really amounts to. You will say perhaps in reply that these are inventions; in fact there are men alive who can refute me. And yet posterity will discover that I tell less than the truth, when letters are published which my friends now keep dark. But you complain that two or three men have drawn back from your way of life as a result of reading my books,[49] and well-endowed men too. Whether there is truth in this, I do not know. It may be that when they watched some men's lives at close quarters, they changed their minds, perceiving that character and costume do not always correspond; that this has happened lately to men of high position and high character is too well known to need recounting. One thing I admit: I point out in several places[50] that the smallest element in religion lies in food or dress or similar ceremonies, and the greatest part in purified desires and in works of charity.[51] The most sacred vow, I hold, is the vow we take to Christ in baptism; the vow that is most worth keeping is the vow which everyone takes. If a man lives up to this, there is no great reason why he should long for any other religious profession.[52]

I have warned young men not to be in a hurry to throw themselves into the labyrinth of the religious life, before they know themselves and understand where true religion is to be found.[53] I have condemned those who range over land and sea, seeking to get as many as they can into their net, for profit, for ambition, or for some other reason more discreditable even than those. If someone has been made more cautious by my warnings and refrained in time, to speak quite frankly, I do not regret it. Had anything I have written turned a man away from Christ, I should, to tell the truth, be inconsolable, and should hate my own books. But if a man has abstained from a way of life of which, had he adopted it, he would soon have repented, I see no reason to be sorry; and it was your duty to impress the warnings I have given on your recruits. If you are honourable men, you must, I suppose, prefer fewer of them, provided they are truly religious, to a large and indiscriminate number. I will say no more for the moment. I would rather see ten abstain for good reason as a result of my warnings, than be responsible for one who has mistakenly fallen into the net. If only this could be dinned into the ears of you all, there might be fewer whose characters disgrace their monastic profession, and we should not hear so many fruitless complaints from those who have put their necks into the noose. It may be that even you would not be a member of your order, but would have the plough-tail in your hands instead of books, or some other instrument more suited to your mind and body.

No: if you wish to attract as many as you can into your society, see to it that you move and look and speak and behave and act in a way that has about it the marks of true religion. Let us often hear examples of your sober life in the midst of luxury, of your courageous rejection of the pleasures that come so easily, of your preferring piety to pelf and Christ's glory to your own, of your enduring wrongs with Christian gentleness, overwhelming one who has done you a disservice by your kind actions, and exposing yourselves in the defence of truth to the hostility of wealthy men and princes. See to it that he who falls into conversation with you leaves that encounter a better man, that he who meets you at dinner carries away an example of self-restraint, that he who has to conduct with you any of the business of human life feels that you are better men than the common run, less greedy, less hard to please, less artificial, less deceitful. Let them, in a word, recognize the simplicity of the Gospel in all you do and all you say.

This is not the moment I would choose to recount how different from this is the account commonly given of you. And these facts might be concealed, did not certain persons give themselves away in their public sermons. Do you think that ordinary people do not have the common feelings of mankind? Do you gauge everyone's nature by yourself and others like you? Even common folk have acquired some wisdom – by nature, by experience, by intercourse with educated men, by reading books. What do you suppose comes into their minds when they see a theologian distinguished by his religious vestments and standing in that sacred place, the pulpit in a church, from which we expect to hear the teaching of the Gospel; and he holds forth with uncontrolled spite and in virulent language against the good name of his neighbours, with blazing eyes and frothing lips and roaring voice, and with the whole posture of his body evincing bitterness and spite? If every word they said were true, the public is not too stupid to understand that this is not the place to say it; they understand that there can be no religion in the heart that utters such offensive words. As a result, they may preach sound doctrine, but they are not listened to. Who would believe a man whom he can see to have lost his self-control, and to be the slave and victim of his passions? What when, as not seldom happens, they actually hear what are plainly lies? For even to these lengths are some men carried by their blindness.

I wish you could hear the murmured comments of women as well as men, who are not a little wiser than preachers such as these. 'What?' they say. 'Is this why we came to church, to sit here and listen to this man or that man raging against someone else? We leave our busy life at home, and come here that we may hear Christ speaking to us from the heart of the priest, that we may return home better people, that we may take back with us something in the way of pious teaching and precious consolation; and in church we are taught to blacken our neighbour's reputation, and what we take home is a lesson in hatred, jealousy, and bad language. At dinner and round the fire strife is renewed, as we all take different sides. What need was there to go to church to get what grows plentifully at home? Why do they keep on telling us that there are men who correct the Magnificat, who correct the Lord's Prayer,[54] who correct the Gospel of St John?[55] If there is anything wrong with these, why cannot they put it right among themselves, instead of calling on us to start throwing stones and rousing subversion among those who are at peace? We pay for their victuals that they may strengthen us in the faith; and must they fill us with doubt? We pay them that thanks to them we may unlearn our faults and learn instead the teaching of the Gospel; and what we learn from them is the worst thing there is, the language of virulent abuse. If this is what they are like, I shall not entrust my children to them, nor shall I confess to them the secrets of my heart. They cannot be trusted to keep silence, and they do not give good advice if they are not led by judgment but swept along by blind emotion.'

This is what we hear said every day, my good X, by bargemen, carters, and uneducated women. There is no man of intelligence and good will who does not see that their complaint is perfectly justified. Thus the result is the opposite of what you intend: you attack another man's reputation, and ruin your own. What else can you gain from this kind of prating except the hatred of every honest man? Think of the friends, by no means to be despised, whom you have lost by this impudence! – and you will lose more unless you change your ways. Look round you, pray, and see whether you can find any man of education or high character who likes impudence of this kind. Abuse has this peculiar quality that, even if it carries conviction, the hearer forms a lower opinion of the man who produced it, just as a prince must hate a traitor, although he may think that the man who was betrayed deserved it. But these decrees of yours originate over the wine,[56] and you think the world will accept what was acceptable to two or three good fellows drinking. You have a very low opinion of the human race if you think everyone will like this. The world has not yet grown so deaf to all the common feelings of nature, not yet so lost all affection for the piety of the Gospel. If you were to teach the truth of the Gospel with sincerity and freely, and were hated in return for the good deed you had done, Christ's consoling words would apply to you: 'Blessed are ye when men hate you.'[57] As it is, all good men are estranged from you by your bad example.

You would think of this, X, for yourself, did you not prefer to be guided by hatred and not reason. When you travel from one monastery to another, Carthusian houses too,[58] and after their kindly reception are under a duty – and they expect it – to give them something in return out of the sacred studies which you profess, something from those secret hours of contemplation in which they suppose theologians sometimes to converse with God, which may kindle them to love of the heavenly life, fill them with spiritual consolation, and implant some seed, some spark, of gospel charity – when that moment comes you, a priest, a Friar Preacher, a theologian, tell them a long rigmarole about Erasmus, mingling truth with falsehood and pouring out in a disgusting fashion whatever can be either invented or related about his worldly position, his manner of life, and his teaching. Nor does it restrain you from your scurrilities even when you see them received with frowns by everyone, when in fact you hear them all protesting. What suspicions do you suppose those pious fathers to form about you when they hear all this, and what complaints to exchange among themselves?

My worldly position is such that I both can and often do complain of it with good reason. But it is in no man's hand to make his own position as he pleases. And I think there is more credit in fighting one's way through to virtue in despite of Fortune,[59] and even in rejecting her when she smiles, than if an ample position in life had come my way while I slept. There was no lack of opportunity, and I knew the way, to get myself more generous provision, had I been ready to pay the price for it which I see many people pay. Nor do I count my way of life free of all faults, especially the life I lived as a young man. Of learning I give myself a very small share, though I will not suffer you and your like to judge how much I have. You think it a grievous insult to call me an orator or a poet. I accept neither title; but those who know how much recondite knowledge, how much genius, how much power of expression goes to the making of a poet or an orator, consider your remarks more worthy of pigs than men. Despise as much as you like what you call *poetria*,[60] which is so unfamiliar to you that you cannot even get its name right; out of the same block of wood you will find it easier to make two distinguished Thomists than one tolerable poet or orator.

But this is the kind of remark that is wasted on those who have the Muses all against them. And yet, if you were to devote the time which you spend on speaking ill of your brother to reading good authors, or if you would at least open the volumes of Ambrose, Jerome, and Augustine, you would be much less satisfied with your own attainments and less disposed to criticize those of others. I in my turn could inquire into your worldly fortune, your manner of life, and your standard of learning; I could scent out whether you had ever been sick over the dinner-table or had violated a nun or had planned any other outrage long ago as a young man or even were planning one now. But heaven forbid that I should fall so far short of the teaching of Christ; heaven forbid that I should so put off all Christian decency, and do something which even gentiles would not do who have somewhat more healthy natures. Some people are shameless enough to accuse me of a too sarcastic style. But men of taste and sound judgment agree that no one for many centuries has been more unpleasantly attacked than I have, and yet that no man's pen has been so slow to wound, nor anyone been more courteous in his criticism of human faults, or mentioned fewer names and persons, although many have had no mercy on my own name or person.

But if the reason for your attack is some offence given to your order, this is a confession in the first place that you are driven by desire for vengeance and not led by reason, though it is part of your religious profession to render good even for evil. Besides which, the kind of revenge you choose is the most damnable of all and even such as men should not stoop to. There was a gentile prince[61] who flogged the man who cursed his enemies, when he had been hired to fight them. And your only weapon is the railing tongue with which disreputable women show such skill. When it comes to writing edifying books you have no hands; when asked to preach the philosophy of Christ you have no voice; but in railing at me your eloquence is inexhaustible. And all the time you imitate Saul,[62] Saul before his conversion: you give aid and encouragement to others who cast stones at me in their sermons. And this is the disgraceful thing, that to relieve your personal feelings you misuse the sanctity and authority of the preaching of the Gospel, and would rather mingle earth and heaven[63] in conflagration than fail to wreak your spite.

But this is merely godless; another point is also unwise, that in your efforts to inflict a small prick on me, you deal a much more serious blow to your own reputation. I know certain people who began to think better of me, as soon as ever they saw how much your colleagues dislike me. You at least have gone down in everyone's opinion, whatever their view of me. There is a theologian who really deserves the name,[64] so good in the scholastic field that at Paris he deserved first place purely on his reputation of the learning, and yet on top of that he is equipped with the resources of the humanities and the ancient tongues; and when you visited him lately to pay your formal respects to a man so unlike yourself, your hatred was so much out of control that you had hardly greeted him before you burst out in furious attacks on me. What had I done to deserve this? – because the man in his usual courteous way had supped with me the day before, though neither at supper nor in the fairly long conversation I had with him had there been any mention of you. It was really good manners to give your first greeting this sinister force with your evil-speaking, which augured so much ill for the future. Nor did it occur to you what a bad effect you were making on two great experts in that field of literature of which I have always been a supporter and which I have done something to promote. Nor did this satisfy your spite. You flavoured the whole dinner with your tasteless scurrilities, until even your own colleagues had all had enough; for they too complained that your conceited and unbridled talk was quite ungovernable.

Would you care to hear what progress you made with your impertinence? Those scholars were so much disgusted with you that they said they would not have believed that your virulent abuse could be so uncontrolled, had not you in fact convinced them. I asked them whether they would not have believed me either. 'No,' they said, 'no living man could have convinced us, had not the facts themselves done so.' And all they could do was to pray that you might recover your sanity. There was a similar result at Antwerp. In a large dinner-party there, that worthy Jacobite who gets his name from honey[65] though his remarks are nothing but bitter aloes, declared that there was no more accursed heretic anywhere in this part of the world than Erasmus; and what sort of a reception do you suppose he got? Everyone was disgusted by his mad folly, especially those who had read my books. Who would not be equally disgusted by that remark of yours? – 'Luther is pestilential, but Erasmus more so, for Luther sucked all his poison from Erasmus' teats.'[66] Those who have read the books of both of us can come to no conclusion, except to think you the most brazen coxcomb, the most abusive liar, and the most ungovernable madman among living men. Indeed, those who do not know you, and have heard you disputing about the Catholic faith in some barge or wagon,[67] ask who is this Dominican with the shining face and the sardonic laugh, who talks so loudly and says such silly things, and is so eloquent in denouncing Erasmus.

The answer they usually get I wish you could hear sometime, and you would see yourself painted in your true colours. You regard me as an enemy of your order because I point out the places where someone should take thought for the dignity of the order, while you, who dishonour your order by your language and behaviour, and do so indiscriminately with no regard for time or place or persons, are a pillar of the order. I have absolutely no feelings against any order, Franciscans, Carmelites, Dominicans, bargemen, and wagoners,[68] for I know that worthy men can be found in each of them. No matter what the habit or the name, piety and integrity are always welcome; and all good men dislike a rascal everywhere. Suppose I were a most bitter enemy of your order, I could wish it nothing worse than more members like yourself. Tell me, are you the man whose voice decides whether we are Christians or no – you who have never seriously considered what a true Christian is? Everywhere you display your ignorance, the gulf between your profession and your behaviour, and the festering matter in your heart; and do you say it is my fault if the world's opinion of you sinks? We often see your colleagues refuted by uneducated people, even by women, and silenced to their great disgrace so that they cannot utter a word in reply. And considering how you hold forth against other men's way of life, it is fair exchange if they often reveal the mysteries of your Bacchanalia,[69] a subject almost too promising!

In Antwerp,[70] while your subversive clamour was rousing that city with its international population to the pitch of riot, though the magistracy repeatedly said this must stop, consider how much support you secured for Luther[71] and how much hatred for yourselves. As for me, no friend of mine became more distant as a result of your efforts, and several new ones were added to the old by your attacks on me. But you – how many substantial and educated supporters did you lose? How many men repented of their generosity towards you? How much higher Jacob of Hoogstraten would have stood, had he had not attacked anyone, or not attacked them so bitterly!

I ask you, what good did Nicolaus Egmondanus do by holding forth against me so often with so little self-control and so little sense?[72] And how discreditable for a priest, a theologian, a Carmelite, and an old man to hold forth so offensively against a work which he admitted he had never read, and perhaps would not have understood if he had! There was not a child but laughed at the man as he so often and so foolishly tiraded in his sermons against *poetria*, as he called it,[73] and against rhetoric and those ancient tongues which our most valued men so greatly value and wish to acquire. What an advertisement for his white habit that, when all the other theologians were making overtures for peace,[74] he alone preferred discord! When asked what his objection was, he replied that I had written my New Testament. And when asked 'Why, what follows from that?' his reply was 'Then all we do amounts to nothing.' A pretty piece of logic! All theology, it seems, is undone if, without encroaching on the ordinary version, some things are made more correct or more lucid. And he puts it about that, when he thus begs the question, I do not deign to reply, while he himself does not deign to read the defence in which I dispose of such objections of this sort as can be made.[75] Apparently it was not enough to write what everyone may read; I must spend whole days disputing at leisure with litigious individuals, say rather, with windbags and blockheads.

What a testimony to the religious life it was, when in a theology lecture, his ordinary lecture as a professor, he said publicly that Lefèvre and I were fighting, and would be fighting one day in the depths of hell![76] He had no misgivings as he poured this venomous filth on Lefèvre, a man stricken in years, a scholar, and universally respected for his consistent holiness of life; and even so he did not understand what the point at issue was between Lefèvre and myself, as he himself showed by what he said. Who in that audience was so much on his side that he could tolerate such outrageous words? Could anyone suppose him in his right mind? His best friends defended him on the ground that he had said it after dinner[77] – an excuse one might perhaps make for a brothel-keeper but hardly for a theologian. But though every man of judgment was disgusted with him, he could have no misgivings about himself. Indeed, to give his audience an exhibition of what they call the camel dancing,[78] he added, in his opening lecture on the Pauline Epistles,[79] that Paul had once persecuted the church of God, but was turned from a wolf into a sheep. 'And we must pray,' says he, 'that the same thing may happen to Luther and to Erasmus.' There's Attic wit[80] for you! and mud-slinging that would be at home on any dunghill![81] Braving the widespread laughter and the catcalls, there was scarcely a lecture in which he did not aim some coarse jest at me, and he took to doing it in his sermons too. When he was publishing the bull that was put out against Luther, and saw me, as it happened, in the audience, he suddenly broke off the topic on which he had started and said more about me than he did about Luther himself.[82] There was no end to it and no limit. Now and then he resumed his interrupted sermon, and while his audience were making signs to one another everywhere and laughing, his whole countenance showed that he had lost control of his resentment, so that he did not so much finish his sermon as break off the torrent of abuse.

When I protested to him about this in the presence of Godschalk,[83] the rector of the university, he ranted away to my face with such insults, or rather, such lies, that Balatro[84] would hardly have treated Nomentanus to the language he used, as one old man, one priest, one theologian to another, and that moreover in front of the head of his university. He called me a slippery customer and a double-dealer, responsible for all the uproar over Luther and capable of inventing anything; it was I had implanted Luther in men's hearts, and in many passages falsified the New Testament. He hinted that the papal letters I used were forgeries,[85] and that I had forged the *Epistolae eruditorum virorum*[86] written to me by way of compliment, although I suppress the majority out of modesty. In a word, like women wrangling, he seized on everything that was said as the basis for an insult. I happened to say, 'Imagine I …,'[87] meaning 'Suppose it to be the case.' This upset him: 'I will not imagine,' he said. 'I leave that to you; you people are all imagination and all falsehood.' I happened to mention the rhetorical use of courtesy,[88] the way in which sometimes we tell people what to do while disclaiming any wish to tell them. This gave him, he thought, a weapon. 'Ah!' he said. 'These experts in rhetoric are all lies and falsehood and concealment.' One could say nothing without his making it the basis for an insult.

At length, when he was tired of ranting and had let himself go to the top of his bent, spitting invective in my face to his heart's content – at length, under pressure from the rector, he proposed two conditions of peace. One was that I should recant what I had written against the theologians of

Louvain and, following the example of Stesichorus,[89] state in print that in Louvain the theologians are sincere (*synceres*[90] was the form he used) and honourable men; as though, if I said that, he would at once be taken to be a changed man himself. The other was that I should attack Luther. If I accepted these and carried them out, we should be brothers; if I refused, he would permanently regard me as a member of Luther's party[91] – as though there was not equal reason to regard him as Luther's man, because he wrote nothing against him.

His disciple the prior of Antwerp,[92] a doctor of the violet cap, when defending himself before the magistrates on a charge of subversive clamour against Luther, declared that he had not read Luther's books, but had been told in a letter from Father Nicolaus Egmondanus to say what he had said. At the same time the leaders of the Dominican monastery behaved so improperly that they set all decent people against them. One of their society said in the hearing of a number of the laity, 'I wish I could chew Luther's gullet between my teeth! I should say mass without hesitation with my mouth still bloody.' Is there any honourable man so incensed against Luther that he would not be disgusted to hear a priest vomiting such filth?

I told you to your face the story of Standish,[93] and how he made such a fool of himself in front of the most intelligent king of England and that very wise lady his queen, that the prince himself was embarrassed by such a display of lunacy. But why number the grains of sand?[94] Every day and everywhere certain members of your order say such foolish and impudent things that, if they did not force themselves upon the eyes and ears of many people, no one who was told the story would believe it. With this behaviour they are religious in their own eyes, and frequently appear at God's holy table; and then they are surprised if men dislike them, as though all the inhabitants of the world were brute beasts. They simply behave as though they would rather be feared for their villainy than become popular by modesty and true religion, forgetting that fear is a poor protection for anything that is meant to last.

But I must sometime bring this long epistle to an end. Although I have suffered attacks from you, my good X, of so many kinds, I have experienced the Lord's mercy towards my sins, and will do my best to follow his example. Let me urge and exhort you most seriously to give up your passion for abuse and learn to speak well of people – this will be good for yourself and for your order. Consider for preference what Christ's teaching tells you to do and not the instructions of your boon companion Egmondanus; what will win the approval of intelligent and honourable men rather than the plaudits of two or three kindred spirits in their cups. But the unbridled impertinence of your language is detested even by members of your own society who have no fondness for me, but know how much disgrace and disadvantage it can bring upon their order.

My own feeling for you is pity rather than resentment, and I pity you the more if you have still no pity for yourself. A large element of health lies in diagnosing one's disease. If nature has denied you the brains to become a great scholar, the eloquence to be an effective preacher, the skill to write so that you might publish books for the general good, you must at least try to become a good man. And he begins to become a good man who has ceased to be a bad one. He is a bad man who speaks ill of his neighbour; doubly bad if he speaks ill of one who has done him some good. If you cannot do good to others for want of brains, eloquence, learning, common sense, and judgment, do what you can at least to do them no harm. Some forgiveness perhaps is due to those who have done good in many ways, but in some places done ill. But it is a desperate kind of wickedness, when you do not good at any point, to turn all your efforts to do harm to others. That Luther whom you proclaim as 'pestilent'[95] has yet in some ways done even you no small benefit. You have been forced to read his books, and these have taught you a good deal; you have been forced even to open some ancient authors. Thanks to him, the world has learnt to recognize those Sileni turned inside out,[96] who seemed to be pillars of religion, who were thought to know everything, and were a very long way from both. And if I may speak the truth in jest, many men owe him a better position in the world; you yourself, maybe, have hopes of some trifle in the way of a mitre as a reward for all your shouting.[97] You owe something too to that 'more pestilent' Erasmus; for while you read his books with an earnest desire to find fault, you have corrected some of your inability to express yourself, and learnt quite a few things of which you were unaware, master doctor though you may be.

This advice, springing as it does from brotherly feeling, will do me at least some good in the eyes of Jesus Christ. It is for you to try to make it useful for you too; and so it will be, if you obey the man who gives it you with the best intentions. Farewell.

1521

1197 / From Mercurino Gattinara — Worms, 5 April 1521

Summonses to a diet at Worms, the first imperial diet Charles v was to hold, were issued on 1 November 1520. The emperor himself arrived in Worms on 28 November, and the diet was opened without undue delay on 27 January 1521. Although it continued for three months and tackled constitutional, juridical, fiscal, and military matters of considerable importance, it is remembered primarily for the ten days of Luther's presence, 16–26 April. The stage for Luther's appearance had been set on the one hand by his burning on 10 December of the bull *Exsurge, Domine* (cf Ep 1141 n11) and the books of canon law, on the other by the issuing on 3 January of the final bull of Luther's excommunication (cf Ep 1192 n8). On 17 and again on 18 April Luther stood before the emperor and assembled estates. A proclamation of the imperial ban against Luther, the famous Edict of Worms, was drafted by Aleandro and ready by 8 May. As it lay outside the regular business of the diet it was not presented to the estates, but was proclaimed by Charles V on 26 May, the day after the final session, which took place in the absence of many princes who had already left Worms; see *Reichstagsakten* J.R. II and *Reichstag zu Worms*, especially 148–54.

The diet was a matter of great concern to Erasmus (cf Ep 1217 n16). He had sent his own messenger to Worms with a bundle of letters (cf Ep 1195 introduction). Of the answers he received only Epp 1197–8 survive. He had also pondered visiting Worms in person, perhaps on his way to Basel and eventually to Rome (cf Epp 1143 n22, 1242 introduction), but in the end decided otherwise (cf Ep 1095:165–7).

This letter is the last one published in Erasmus' lifetime. It is found in a small collection of unpublished letters appended to his exposition of Psalm 14 (15), *De puritate tabernaculi* (Basel: H. Froben and N. Episcopius [c February] 1536) 116–17.

MERCURINO GATTINARA, CHANCELLOR OF THE EMPEROR CHARLES, TO DESIDERIUS ERASMUS OF ROTTERDAM, GREETING

Honoured sir, your letter reached me yesterday, in which you show some fear that falsehoods may have been put into circulation against you by your opponents, and defend yourself against them as far as you can. My first reply must be to thank you warmly for your good opinion and your confidence in me. It must always, I suppose, have been easy for you to gather what my sentiments were towards you, and certainly they have always been such that no man could presume to hope for a friend with warmer feelings. I assure you that, so far as I am concerned, not only do I gladly accept your defence, but as a result of it, though I could never before have any idea of you other than of the kind you outline, I now seem to see the truth itself. You are the chief luminary of liberal studies in Germany, and have employed all your labours and life itself in the glory and elucidation of the orthodox faith, toiling away at this night and day. Never was there any reason why I should suppose you to deviate a hair's breadth[1] from its sound principles, or think differently in any respect; and I am in a position to say that I have found all right-thinking men to be of the same opinion.

If anything had perhaps aroused any suspicion against you – and I am not entirely sure that this was so – it might have been the style of some books I could name,[2] which seemed to come very close to yours; but it was quite uncertain who was responsible for their publication and, to put it briefly, there was nothing heretical in their contents. You can therefore set your mind at rest: to all right-thinking men you are free from any breath of suspicion, and I shall take particular trouble to see that, if any vestige of suspicion had taken root in the minds of certain persons, you emerge daily more independent of it, while I shall always be one who values you and your work at a price which I would rather you learnt from facts than words. Farewell.

Worms, 5 April 1521

1198 / From Luigi Marliano — Worms, 7 April 1521

This letter answers Ep 1195 and in turn is answered in Ep 1199, all published in the *Epistolae ad diversos*. It probably reached Erasmus together with Ep 1197 and other letters dispatched from Worms; cf Ep 1195 introduction.

LUIGI MARLIANO, BISHOP OF TUY, TO ERASMUS OF ROTTERDAM, GREETING

How much I value you, and wish others to do so too, you know well enough, and so do all who are in any relationship or daily contact with me. I set such store by the friendship between us, which sprang from your singular qualities and my great devotion to you, that I have overlooked no opportunity of advancing your interests and reputation; for I thought that all my future prosperity was linked with yours. So when I was in Spain,[1] I arranged with a common friend and admirer, Barbier, to write and tell you,[2] now that you are retired and in a secure position, not to go down every day to fight in the arena and not to take risks so often with your reputation, when you have already done all you need do to secure honour and glory; and you promised in your reply that you would do so. For it grieved me to see you sometimes entering the lists against people to whom it was an honour to be defeated by you, and exposing yourself to the stormy seas of common and ignorant men.

When he had returned from Spain and I met you in Brussels,[3] I begged you to have no dealings with Luther; for at that time there were many men (foolish men no doubt) who thought that you were clearly not out of sympathy with him. And you promised you would do what I asked, in such terms that I promised other people this would happen, in your name no less than my own. Since then, this disastrous calamity of Luther has gained in strength day by day, and has taken root in many men's minds to such a tune that I think there must be few left who can still be infected by it; it makes me feel that the days in which we live are past praying for, when we see the troubles so much greater than the remedies. We can neither endure the evils nor find cures for them, for people nowadays are in such a state that they are more easily carried away by old wives' tales than kept straight by right reason.

My friend Aleandro, who is, I think, closely connected with you by common interests and the things you have done for one another, and who is a friend of long standing, has never said anything of you[4] in my hearing that he would not wish to be said of himself. He is very modest, which I admire in someone who knows so many languages and is at home in so many branches of learning, a kindly man, and has great charm of character; besides which he has such an equable temper, if I mistake not, that he never speaks more slightingly of other people than he would wish them to speak of him. You say you have deterred Luther and many Germans, so far as you could, from writing, and this is what I should have expected of you, for you have shown that your only wish is to do everything in your power to support the common weal and true religion. What others have done I approve no more than you would, for their remedies have merely driven him mad. He should have been tackled in quite another way.

For my part, you must not think I have been idle; for I have written two speeches against Luther,[5] one fairly mild and the other – written after the publication of his latest books – more severe. Not that I wish to see the man condemned; his cause I would condemn. I should like to see the common weal and religion safe and sound, and him safe too. I would send them to you, were I not proposing to return; and on my return, you and I will talk over many things which I may not write and do not wish to. Until then, I will take as much care of your interests and your reputation as I could wish to take of my own, or you of yours if you were here. If however you can do anything either to restrain this turbulence or to quiet this sedition, use all the influence and authority you have; for the immortality which you seek and which your writings promise you will easily be yours if you add to them this work of piety.

I gave your greetings to Agostino Scarpinelli and Severus, who marvel that you have written to them as you say you have,[6] and take it hard that the letters never reached them, for they wanted them above all things. In any case you have in them two very keen champions of your reputation.

Farewell, from Worms, 7 April 1521.

1199 / To Luigi Marliano

Antwerp, 15 April 1521

Erasmus seems to have visited Antwerp repeatedly in the spring of 1521. Between 11 February and 16 March he met Albrecht Dürer at the dinner-table of his friend Pieter Gillis (cf Ep 1132 introduction). This letter and Ep 1205, dated 24 May, point to two more visits, of which we have no further information.

This answer to Ep 1198, printed in the *Epistolae ad diversos*, is the final letter of the correspondence with Marliano, who died at Worms of the plague the night of 10–11 May 1521; cf *Reichstagsakten* J.R. II 903.

ERASMUS OF ROTTERDAM TO THE RIGHT REVEREND LUIGI MARLIANO, BISHOP OF TUY AND COUNCILLOR TO THE EMPEROR CHARLES, GREETING

My Lord Bishop, I should be the most ungrateful man alive all the world over, did I not acknowledge your kindness towards me and your zeal for my welfare. I should moreover be very stupid, if I were reluctant to follow your advice, since there is no one whose advice is followed more readily or with better success by the emperor himself. The disasters of our own day I feel obliged to ascribe to fate,[1] nor do I see any remedy, unless some god should arise from the machine to put an end to the whole tragic story. Aleandro's feelings towards me have been reported to me from sources so numerous and so reliable that I cannot altogether disbelieve them. And yet his scholarship tells against it, and so does our long-standing friendship; nor do I readily admit into my mind anything that might loose the ties of the Graces.[2] I rejoice that you share my disapproval of those who attack Luther for such stupid reasons, and in such a manner that they can only do harm to their own cause and give themselves away, putting the pope in a very unfortunate position,[3] harming many innocent people and, most serious of all, provoking the multitude to rebellion. You would subscribe even more readily to my point of view, if you could see with your eyes and hear with your ears the idiotic designs they publish every day.

I shall look forward eagerly to reading your speeches, on which I have already had a first opinion from Cuthbert Tunstall.[4] I have no doubt that you display in them, as you do in all your other works, a marriage of capital learning and no less capital prudence.

My friends' letters give me to understand that the man who wrote to warn me[5] of a growth of suspicion in your part of the world was needlessly anxious on my behalf. They tell me that there was no cause to suspect anything untoward, except from a speech the title-page of which bore the name Didymus Faventinus.[6] The brilliance of the style and the occasional sallies of wit made some people claim it as my work, but only as a suspicion without foundation. It was later sent to me, and I laughed outright at men's suspicious nature, for it gave away its author's true name at the end; only it was in Greek. Though even had the name not been given, I should never have had any doubt as to the author.

A man I know has put me on notice of the publication in Cologne of a *Consilium*[7] made by someone who thinks it possible to settle things in such a way that the pope should get credit for clemency[8] and Luther for obedience; and some people, he says, suspect that it comes from me. The thing was indeed shown me while the emperor was in Cologne, but in manuscript, and before the publication of the books which have set so many men against Luther;[9] it was said to be the work of a certain Dominican.[10] To tell the truth, at the time I rather liked it. If however the princes prefer severe measures to deal with the situation, I pray that what seems better to them may also turn out better – better, I mean, for the Christian cause, and not for the private interests of certain persons whose heart is set on the things of this world. Farewell, my patron beyond compare.

Antwerp, 15 April 1521

1200 / To Willem Frederiks — Louvain, 30 April 1521

Willem Frederiks (d 1527) studied in Cologne and Ferrara, where in 1475 he obtained a doctorate in medicine. From 1485 he was among the clergy of St Martin's church at Groningen, which was presumably his native town. Four years later he was one of the two principal pastors of St Martin's. A frequent visitor to Wessel Gansfort's academy at nearby Aduard, he also played a leading role in the secular affairs of Groningen.

This letter was printed in the *Epistolae ad diversos*.

ERASMUS OF ROTTERDAM TO WILLEM,[1] PASTOR OF THE TOWN OF GRONINGEN, GREETING

There is no call to thank me, my dear sir, for the recall of the young man.[2] For what I did I earn no praise; but I should have been brutal and forgetful of Christian charity had I not helped the boy when I had the opportunity. The gilt cup[3] was delivered to me on your behalf by that most sincere and friendly person Gozewijn[4] and of course it was a most acceptable present, being given me by one admirable man and carried by another. The only thing I fear is that he may have prompted you[5] to do this out of his affection for me, for I never even dreamt anything of the kind.

From his letter and from what he told me I learnt of the zeal with which you perform all the duties that fell in old days to those who were bishops in far more than name. You outshine all others in holiness of life, you feed your flock continually with the doctrine of the Gospel, and you gather round you priests who by their innocence of life and sacred learning can adorn your church and take your place among the people. Thus there is no call for this new sort of preachers,[6] not instituted by Christ, but brought into the world by the idleness of the shepherds of His flock. If only they had been all like you, the world would not now be holding a wolf by the ears[7] which it cannot tolerate and sees no means of shaking off. The people see in you no boon companion; they find by experience one who can teach them, comfort them, exhort them, give them instruction and advice in the most faithful and loving way. So far are you from despoiling your flock that you even give generously from your own store to those oppressed by poverty; nor do you pile up wealth for your own benefit, but hasten with fervent zeal towards that prize of immortality which you will certainly receive from the great Shepherd, the Prince of all shepherds, who freely laid down his life for his sheep. However great the treasure that a man may have piled up in this life, he cannot fail to pass hence penniless, for he may take with him absolutely nothing of his hoarded wealth. He, and he alone, is rich as he leaves this world, who at the time of his departure is well fortified with letters of credit. We must live on credit for the time being; but he is trustworthy upon whom we are to draw. Nor is there any risk if our indebtedness rises to great heights; for he from whom we expect to receive our reward is rich enough to suffice for all men.

To my thinking it is further evidence of your true piety, that you are building up a library in your church,[8] filled especially with those authors who breathe the spirit of Christian charity, such as Origen, Chrysostom, Cyprian, Ambrose, Augustine, Jerome. From the reading of such men we feel our hearts fired with the love of heavenly things, taught to despise those things, a blind desire for which turns human life upside down; while from the study of those whom we owe to the regular schools we rise cold-hearted, and sometimes with our faith less firmly founded than it was when we began. Your table, again, is crowned with frugality, and, what is more, derives a relish from the stories taken out of Holy Writ to feed minds hungry for that sort of feast. Each man contributes to the common store some blossom plucked from the meadows of Scripture; another brings forth something sweet as honey which he has sucked like a bee working over all the blossoms in the innermost parts of Holy Writ. Nor do you allow your table to be defiled by venomous gossip, which reeks of hatred and ill will.

With what authority you have lately put to silence two men who boast that they are ordained preachers of the Gospel,[9] when they had begun to rant with as much impudence as malignity against the name of Erasmus! To interrupt their pestilent talk, you asked them whether they had read my books; and they confessed that they had never done so.[10] You then added that you wondered at the effrontery with which they held forth against the teaching of a man whose books they had not read. When even this rebuke failed to constrain the blockheads, whom the wine by now had made more offensive, you told them that you did not care for guests who befouled your table with such rubbish, and invited them to change either their conversation or their place of entertainment. And these are the men who stir up trouble by declaiming in front of the people against what they are pleased to call secular priests; from whom they would do better to borrow an example of sobriety and moderation.

May Christ almighty grant that men such as you may abound everywhere, until either the world has had enough of this irregular sort of itinerant teachers, or they themselves are compelled to leave their easy luxury and luxurious ease and return to the pursuit of true piety. Farewell.

Louvain, 30 April 1521

1201 / To Bonifacius Amerbach

This letter has been assigned a new date and is Ep 1233A in this edition.

1202 / To Justus Jonas

Louvain, 10 May 1521

This letter – without doubt one of the finest of this period – was printed in the *Epistolae ad diversos*. It reflects Erasmus' great fondness for Jonas (cf lines 304–11, Ep 1157 introduction) and his corresponding alarm at seeing him side with Luther (cf n1). The letter was probably sent to Erfurt, but it was meant not so much for Jonas alone as for a whole group of German humanists ready to commit themselves irrevocably to the Lutheran cause, especially Melanchthon in Wittenberg (cf lines 313–15, 321–2). This letter is intended as a plea lest Erasmus' 'philosophy of Christ' be sacrificed to national pride and opposition to Rome, however justified; as such it would soon be given a sequel in Ep 1211. With special care Erasmus develops his theory that truths ought to be advanced in a measured way, which is to say concealed at times, as was done, he believed, by St Paul and recommended by Plato; cf lines 52–154 and the preface.

ERASMUS OF ROTTERDAM TO JUSTUS JONAS, GREETING

There has been a persistent rumour here for some time, dearest Jonas, that you gave Martin Luther steadfast support at Worms,[1] and I do not doubt that as a truly religious man you did as I should have done had I been there, in hopes of laying this tragic business to rest by moderate measures in a way that may prevent its breaking out again later with more disastrous results for the whole world. Personally, I am surprised that this did not happen; the best men[2] had it very much at heart for, as befits truly Christian spirits, they wanted steps to be taken for the peace of the church, which if not held together in concord has ceased to deserve the name of church. For what is our religion, if not peace in the Holy Spirit? Moreover, the church of Christ, inasmuch as she still holds good and bad fish in the same net and is compelled to endure tares mixed with the wheat,[3] suffered even in the old days from great faults, as orthodox Fathers testify, deploring from time to time the gross corruption of the ranks of society whence models of simple piety ought to proceed. And how far the church of Rome fell away even in the old days from its zeal for the purity of the Gospel, Jerome of himself is a sufficient witness when he calls her the Babylon of the Apocalypse,[4] or St Bernard in his book *De consideratione*;[5] not that there has been any lack even among the moderns of celebrated authors to demand the public restoration of church discipline.

But I doubt whether the princes of the church have ever displayed such a passionate and unconcealed appetite for the good things of this world, which Christ taught us ought to be despised, as we see today. The breakdown was no less in the study of Holy Scripture than in morality. The word of God was forced to become the slave of human appetites, and the simple faith of the multitude was distorted to the profit of the few. Well might religious souls lament all this, who set Christ's glory above all else. This was the reason why to start with Luther had such a favourable reception everywhere as has fallen to the lot of no other mortal, I suppose, for many centuries. We readily believe what we strongly wish to be true; and people thought a man had arisen who was unspotted by all this world's desires and would be able to apply some remedy to these great evils. Nor did I myself entirely despair of this, except that at the very first taste of the pamphlets which had begun to appear under Luther's name, I was full of fear that the thing might end in uproar[6] and split the world openly in two. And so I sent warning letters both to Luther himself and to friends of his[7] who might, I thought, carry some weight with him; what advice they gave him, I do not know; but at any rate the affair was handled in such a way that there is some danger of remedies wrongly applied making our troubles twice as great.

And I wonder very much, dear Jonas, what god has stirred up Luther's heart[8] to make him write with such freedom of invective against the Roman pontiff, against all the universities, against philosophy, and against the mendicant orders. Had all he says been true – and those who examine what he has written declare that the case is quite otherwise – once he had challenged so many people, what other outcome was to be expected than what we see now? Luther's books I have not yet had the leisure to read;[9] but to judge by the samples I have taken, and from what I have sometimes picked up in passing from the accounts of others, though it was perhaps beyond my meagre attainments to pronounce on the truth of the opinions he put forward, at any rate his method and the way he sets to work I could never approve. For seeing that truth of itself has a bitter taste for most people, and that it is of itself a subversive thing to uproot what has long been commonly accepted, it would have been wiser to soften a naturally painful subject by the courtesy of one's handling than to pile one cause of hatred on another.

What therefore was the point of dealing in paradoxes,[10] and putting some things forward in language that was bound to give even more offence at first sight than when regarded steadily at close quarters? For some things are rendered offensive even by a kind of wilful obscurity. What was the point of a savage torrent of invective directed against men whom it was unwise to treat like that if he wished to make them better, and impious if he did it to provoke them and set the whole world by the ears? Furthermore, when a prudent steward will husband the truth[11] – bring it out, I mean, when the business requires it and bring it out so much as is requisite and bring out for every man what is appropriate for him – Luther in this torrent of pamphlets has poured it all out at once, making everything public and giving even cobblers a share in what is normally handled by scholars as mysteries reserved for the initiated; and often a sort of immoderate energy has carried him, in my opinion at least, beyond the bounds of justice. To give an example: when it would have sufficed to point out to the theologians that they mix in too much Peripatetic, or rather, sophistic philosophy, he calls the whole Aristotelian system[12] the death of the soul.

That spirit of Christ in the Gospels has a wisdom of its own, and its own courtesy and meekness. That is how Christ attuned himself to the feelings of the Jews. He says one thing to the multitudes, who are somewhat thick-witted, and another to his disciples; and even so he has to bear with them for a long time while he gradually brings them to understand the celestial philosophy. With this in mind he bids his followers preach first repentance and the impending kingdom of God,[13] and keep silence about Christ. So Peter in the Acts of the Apostles preaches without upbraiding but in a mild and affectionate style, when he adds that great multitude as first-fruits to the church.[14] He does not declaim against those who had put Christ to death; he does not exaggerate their impious madness in savage language, although it is likely that in his audience there were men who had hounded Christ to his death. No: as though he wished to encourage them, he says that all this was done by the divine wisdom, and later even puts the responsibility for this impious crime on the world itself, urging them to save themselves from this untoward generation.[15] He does not return insult for insult upon those who said that the apostles were drunk with new wine,[16] but mildly finds reasons to excuse their mistake: it was the power not of new wine but of a new spirit. He produces the testimony of Joel,[17] because he knew that with them it would carry great weight. And he does not yet declare that Christ is both God and man; this mystery he reserves until its proper time. For the present he calls him a just man and declares him to be the Lord and the Messiah, and does this on the authority of God,[18] whom they too scrupulously worshipped, so that the recognition of the Father might win acceptance for the Son. Besides which, when he demonstrated that what they understood of David was really said not of David but of Christ, he begins by softening a remark which will give offence with the words 'Men and brethren, let me freely speak unto you of the patriarch David.'[19]

Thus does Paul become all things to all men, that he may gain them all for Christ,[20] training his disciples to teach with all gentleness, without estranging any man by harshness of behaviour and language, but by their gentleness winning over even those who are stubborn and hard to please. With what courtesy he preaches Christ to the Athenians, casting the responsibility for their sins on the age in which they lived! 'And the times of this ignorance,' he says 'God winked at,'[21] addressing his audience with a respectful and acceptable opening as 'men of Athens.'[22] Nor does he use harsh words in rebuking their impious worship of demons,[23] but in courteous language charges them with superstition, because they worshipped more than they ought. Having by chance observed the inscription on an altar,[24] he twists it into evidence for their faith, with the alteration and omission of several words; nor does he as yet call Christ anything but a man,[25] by whom God had ordained that salvation should be conferred on the whole race of mortals. Nor does he produce before that audience the testimony of the prophets, which would have carried very little conviction, but uses the witness of Aratus[26] in his argument with them. Think of the courtesy with which he conducts his case before Festus and before Agrippa![27]

It is the same with Augustine. When he refutes the crazy Donatists, and the Manichaeans who are worse than madmen, his indignation stops short of what the facts deserve, and everywhere there is an endearing admixture of charity,[28] as though he thirsted for their salvation and not their destruction.[29] It was this gentleness in teaching, this prudence in husbanding the word of God that conquered the world and made it pass under the yoke of Christ as no military force, no subtle philosophy, no eloquent rhetoric, no human violence or cunning could ever have done. All the more is it our duty, if we wish to do good, to refrain from all abusive language, especially if our target is men high in public authority. Paul would have honour paid to magistrates, even when they are gentiles,[30] and offers as it were a recantation because he had used severe language of a Mosaic and openly criminal high priest.[31] He wishes servants who are initiates of the mysteries of Christ to obey their gentile masters even more strictly than they did before.[32] He would have wives, after they have made their profession to Christ, be still more obedient to their unbelieving husbands, solely in order that by their compliant behaviour they might win them all over to love the teaching of the Gospel.[33] The man of a religious mind will in any case desire nothing but to do good to others, either holding his peace if there is hope of making progress, or bringing the truth out of his store and husbanding it, for fear lest instead of healing the evil it may make it more violent.

Brutus[34] is indignant with Cicero for infuriating in his speeches and writings men whose fury once roused he cannot put down. Plato[35] does not disapprove of pretence and concealment of the truth in a philosopher who has to govern the commonwealth, provided he uses these tricks for the good of the people. A Christian, I admit, ought to be free of all pretence; but even so an occasion sometimes offers when it is right for truth to remain unspoken, and everywhere the time, the manner and the recipients of its publication are of great importance. Reliable physicians do not take refuge at the outset in their ultimate remedies; first they prepare the patient's body with less powerful drugs, and they adjust the dose to cure and not to overwhelm.[36] Nor will I listen to people who say that the distemper of our generation is too serious to be healed by the gentler remedies. It is better, as the Greek proverb has it,[37] to let the evil lie that's well disposed, than by unskilful physic to arouse its full force.

I do not of course deny that sometimes God uses war, pestilence, and distress to correct his flock; but religious men have no call to introduce war or suffering contrary to their religion, although God sometimes turns the ills of other men to the good of his own people. The cross of Christ brought salvation to the world; and yet we abominate the men who crucified him. The deaths of the martyrs shed lustre on the church of God and strengthened it too; and yet we condemn the wickedness of those to whom we owe these advantages. Many bad men would be less bad if deprived of their wealth; but it is not a good man's business to rob anyone of his property in order to make him better. And furthermore, since every novelty causes an upheaval, even if it is a summons to better things, any proposal that diverges from what men are used to should be put forward in such a form as to make that divergence seem as small as possible.

But they say that sometimes, when Luther's teaching is no different from other people's, he tries, it seems, by his actual choice of words to make it seem very different. Now men are inclined by nature to go wrong, and their faults should be corrected in such a way as not to give others a handle to err with greater freedom. Paul preaches the liberty of the Gospel as against the baneful slavery of the Law, but adds this limitation, 'not to use liberty for an occasion to the flesh.'[38] His discouragement from the cold works of the Law goes closely with a ceaseless urging to works of charity. There were perhaps men who with no ulterior motive were in favour of summoning the orders and the princes of the church to mend their ways; but I rather think that some people are encouraged by this opportunity to covet the worldly wealth of churchmen, and nothing, I think, can be more criminal or more dangerous to the public peace than that.[39] For if they think it lawful to lay hands on the property of priests, just because some of them use their resources for a life of luxury or for purposes which are unworthy in other ways, many of our citizens and noblemen alike will find that their hold on their possessions is precarious. And it would be a pretty service to mankind to rob priests impiously of their property in order that military men may put it to worse uses; for the way in which they squander their own possessions, and sometimes other people's too, is of no benefit to any mortal man.

No more will I listen, my dear Jonas, to those who say that Luther has been provoked by the intolerable impudence of his opponents until he was unable to maintain the modesty of a true Christian. However others might behave, the man who had undertaken to play that part ought to have overlooked all else and stood by his principles. And then he should have foreseen the outcome before he let himself fall into this pit, for fear of suffering the same fate as the he-goat in the fable.[40] Even in religious undertakings it is foolish to attempt what you cannot carry through, especially if an unsuccessful effort brings in its train not the benefits you hoped for, but infinite loss. We now behold things brought to such a pass that I for my part can see no happy issue, unless Christ uses his skill to turn certain men's rash folly to the public good.[41]

Some people I could name make excuses for him because it was, they say, under compulsion from others that he first wrote so outrageously and then refused to trust himself to the judgment of that most merciful Pope Leo and to the honour of the emperor Charles, who is far the best and mildest of princes. But why did he choose to listen to those advisers rather than to his other friends, who are neither ignorant nor inexperienced, and who invited him to take a very different course? Look at the majority of his supporters: what sort of weapons had they with which to try and defend him? – ludicrous pamphlets, empty threats. As though their kind of nonsense could either frighten their opponents or satisfy the men of good will, to whose judgment the whole business should have been adapted, had they really wished their play to have a happy ending. As it is, the great army of evils unleashed by their temerity lays no mean burden of unpopularity on the study of good literature and on many good men who to start with were by no means hostile to Luther, either because they hoped he would handle things differently, or because they and he shared common enemies. For it happened by some accident that those who stirred up trouble for Luther in the beginning were enemies of good literature; and for this reason its devotees were less opposed to Luther, for fear that if they aided the party of his opponents, they would strengthen their own enemies against themselves. Although, whatever the state of affairs, religion should have come first in people's thoughts, before their favourite studies.

And on this point, my dear Jonas, I have sometimes been obliged to long for an example of the gospel spirit, on observing how Luther, and still more his supporters, use a kind of cunning to secure that others may be involved in this unpleasant and perilous affair. Why need they burden Reuchlin, who already had enough to bear, with a still heavier load of ill will?[42] Why need they so often mention me by name in a tendentious way, when this was quite uncalled-for? I had sent Luther warning in a private letter under seal; it was soon printed in Leipzig.[43] I had warned the cardinal of Mainz, in a letter under seal,[44] not to abandon Luther unadvisedly to the hostility of certain persons, when his case still had much to be said for it in the eyes of most men of good will; it was published in print even before it reached him. Willibald complains in a letter to me[45] that certain letters are circulating in printed form which no one has ever delivered to him. In these he is urged to continue on the course he has adopted, no doubt in order to drive him willy-nilly into membership of their own faction.

From my own books, written before I ever dreamt of Luther's appearing, they have made a selection of troublesome statements and published them in a German translation,[46] that they might be thought to approximate to some of Luther's opinions. And the men who do this wish to be thought my friends, although an enemy set on one's destruction could do nothing more hostile. My worst enemies used not to have such a genius for making mischief. This weapon they have put into the hands of my opponents, so that now they can hold forth in their public sermons on the points of agreement between me and Luther. As though falsehood were not very close to truth on either side if you overstep the line. Somewhere maybe I point out that vows should not be undertaken unadvisedly, nor do I approve of those who leave at home the wife and children whose life and morals are their first concern, and go running off to Santiago[47] or Jerusalem, where they have no business. I point out that young men ought not to be inveigled into the shackles of the religious life before they know themselves

Die göttliche Mühle
Zürich: Christoph Froschauer, 1521

and know what that life is;[48] Luther,[49] they say, entirely condemns all vows. Elsewhere I complain that the burden of confession[50] has been made heavier by the traps laid by certain people; Luther, they say, teaches that all confession should be rejected as pernicious. Elsewhere I have laid it down that the best authors should be read first, adding that the books of Dionysius do not yield as much profit as their titles seem to promise;[51] Luther calls the man a fool, I hear, and entirely unworthy of a reader's attention.

A pretty form of agreement indeed, if given an opportunity I say something true and reasonable, and another man kicks over the traces[52] and distorts it! How can I do business on such outrageously unfair terms, if I am expected to guarantee that no one shall misuse what I have written, even after my time? – a piece of good fortune that even the Apostle Paul never enjoyed, if we may believe his colleague Peter.[53] Not but what (to be quite frank) had I known that a generation such as this would appear, I should either not have written at all some things that I have written, or should have written them differently. For I wish to be of use to all men, in such a way that if possible I hurt no one. Pamphlets are bandied about, the work of conspirators, in which I too am depicted;[54] whereas there are no words I hate more than conspiracy and schism and faction.

The whole of this performance, whatever one thinks of it, was started against my advice, or at least I steadfastly disapproved the form it took. What I write has never been in the service of any party; I serve Christ, who belongs to us all. What my brains or my pen can achieve, I do not know; at least, all my efforts and my desires have been and are devoted to the good not only of Germans but of Frenchmen, Spaniards, Englishmen, Bohemians, Ruthenians,[55] and even Turks[56] and Saracens, if I can – so far am I from ever having wished to take a hand in a faction so fraught with peril. And all the time I find a lack of common sense in men who think that anyone can be attracted into their camp by tricks of this kind. If they wished to set an intelligent man against them, what better way could they find to do so? They make it clear enough what broken reeds[57] they depend on, when in so perilous an enterprise they rely on resources such as these. And I am dreadfully afraid that this business will bring great discredit on our native Germany[58] in the eyes of all other nations, seeing how prone the ordinary man is to attribute the folly of a few to a whole nation.

And so, with all these outrageous pamphlets, all this deception, all this formidable threatening and bombast, what I ask you has been achieved, except to take what has hitherto been discussed in the schools as an acceptable opinion and make it for the future into an article of faith? – to make it hardly safe to teach even the Gospel, now that everything is inflamed and everything is seized upon as material for calumny? Luther might have done wonders for Christ's flock by teaching the philosophy of the Gospel; he might have done great service to the world by publishing books, had he refrained from things that could not fail to end in strife.[59] My own work has lost a great part of the good effect I hoped for, thanks to him. Even disputations in our universities are not free,[60] which ought to be as free as air. If it were lawful to hate any man in return for wrongs suffered personally, no one has suffered more from Luther's party than myself. And yet I could wish to see him safe and sound and these our divisions ended, which are far the most dangerous we have ever suffered – ended in such a way that they may not break out again later in an even more dangerous form, like wounds not properly healed.

You will ask me, dearest Jonas, why I spin this long complaint to you when it is already too late. For this reason first of all, that though things have gone farther than they ought to have, even now one should be on the watch, in case it may be possible to still this dreadful storm. We have a pope most merciful by nature, we have an emperor whose spirit is mild and placable. If it proves impossible, I would rather you had nothing to do with it. I have always admired the precious talents Christ has given you, and they make me wish all the more that you should be spared for the service of the Gospel. The more I admired the streak of genius in Hutten, the more I regret that he has been torn from us by these tumults.[61] Who would not suffer torment if Philippus Melanchthon,[62] a young man of such outstanding gifts, were carried off by this tempest, and the hopes of scholars everywhere frustrated? If there are things we do not like in the men whose judgment governs human affairs, my view is that we must leave them to their Lord and Master.[63] If their commands are just, it is reasonable to obey; if unjust, it is a good man's duty to endure them, lest worse befall. If our generation cannot endure Christ in his fullness, it is something none the less to preach him so far as we may.

The points I put to you now, my dear Jonas, I should like you to put to Philippus,[64] and to any others like him. Above everything I think we must avoid the discord which must be disastrous to every man of good will. We need a sort of holy cunning; we must be time-servers, but without betraying the treasure of gospel truth from which our lost standards of public morality can be restored. Someone may perhaps ask whether my attitude towards Luther is the same as it used to be. It has not changed. I have always wished that some things could be altered which I never liked and that he could then devote himself entirely to the gospel philosophy from which the standards of our generation have so lamentably fallen away. I have always wanted to see him put right rather than put down.[65] I used to wish that he would treat Christ's business in such a way that the leaders of the church might approve, or at least not disapprove. I wanted Luther to be loved in such a way that it might be safe to love him openly. Nor do I feel any differently about the wretches who attack me than I do about him. If they show the same energy in the virtuous preaching of Christ that they have in their vicious attacks on me, I shall forget what I have suffered from them and welcome their new zeal for Christ. The noisy fellow who becomes Christ's harbinger I shall no longer hate. Farewell.

Louvain, 10 May 1521

1203 / To Ludwig Baer — Louvain, 14 May 1521

This letter is addressed to Ludwig Baer, the leading member of the Basel faculty of theology. Before Erasmus published it in the *Epistolae ad diversos* it was seen by a number of people in manuscript. On 15 July Udalricus Zasius stated in a letter to Bonifacius Amerbach (AK II Ep 801) that it was condemned by men who had formerly praised Erasmus to the skies. By the beginning of September a manuscript copy had reached Wittenberg (cf *Melanchthons Briefwechsel* I Ep 163) and began to circulate among Luther's Saxon friends. Probably in October it was printed anonymously at Leipzig (for details see Ep 1228 introduction). This translation gives precedence to the Leipzig edition, whose variants are listed in Allen VI xx–xxi.

TO THE ACCOMPLISHED THEOLOGIAN LUDWIG BAER, PROVOST OF ST PETER'S IN BASEL, HIS INCOMPARABLE PATRON AND FRIEND, FROM ERASMUS OF ROTTERDAM, GREETING

Luther has served us a pretty turn, most learned of men, by putting into the hands of certain raging madmen who detest the humanities just exactly the weapon they hoped for, with which they can let fly against the security of honourable men who were supporters in simple faith of the gospel teaching and the liberal arts. Either I am quite mistaken, or up to now he has had a capital part and played it very badly – an outstanding champion indeed of the liberty of the Gospel,[1] which he has assailed to such a tune that I fear we shall have two yokes to bear instead of one: we shall share the experience of those who after trying unskilfully to break out of jail find their irons doubled, or who take the wrong medicine and make their sickness worse. He himself perhaps is in safe keeping;[2] but all the more savagely do these fanatical monsters, these passionate enemies of liberal learning vent their fury here on all our best people.[3] For they think everyone belongs to Luther's party who supports the gospel philosophy or the humanities. I am their target: in all their sermons, at the dinner-table and in conversation they rain scandals on me like a shower of stones, until Stephen himself,[4] it seems, must look to his laurels. He was overcome once and for all and found release from his sufferings; but I am pelted without ceasing by so many swarms of ruffians, though all the time I do them service.

Things have been brought to such a pass by the bitterness of Luther's party and the stupidity of some who try to mend this evil with more zeal than sense, that I for one can see no way out, short of great tumult and confusion in human affairs. What evil spirit[5] spread this frightful seed through the world of mortals? I did my best, when I was in Cologne, to arrange that Luther should earn credit for obedience and the pope for clemency,[6] and there were certain monarchs who thought well of the idea. Lo and behold, he burns the decretals,[7] publishes his *De captivitate Babylonica*,[8] issues those over-emphatic assertions[9] – and has made the evil to all appearance incurable. Luther seems to me to behave as though he did not wish to be kept alive; on the other side some people handle their case in public so clumsily that you might think they are in collusion with Luther[10] and only pretending to be advocates for the pope. One thing remains, my dear Baer: I pray that Christ the almighty may turn all things to good effect, for he alone can do so.

I had for some time been wishing to come your way,[11] but there were and are things that detain me still. I hope to be with you this coming autumn. Meanwhile may Christ preserve you and yours in health and wealth.

Louvain, 14 May 1521

1204 / To Adrianus Cornelii Barlandus [Louvain, c May 1521]

The latest of Barlandus' school-books was an epitome of Erasmus' *Adagia*, made from the Froben edition of October 1520 – *In omnes Erasmi Roterodami Adagiorum chiliadas epitome* (Louvain: D. Martens June 1521; NK 2844). The volume was prefaced with a dedicatory letter from Barlandus to his friend Pieter Zuutpene (cf Ep 1005), followed by this letter by Erasmus, no doubt specifically composed for publication in that place. Erasmus had supplied similar prefaces in the past (cf Epp 602, 635, 842, 1082). Barlandus' epitome was reprinted several times and other epitomes followed in its wake. Writing on 13 July 1527 from Bruges, Juan Luis Vives sent one of them to Henry VIII, noting that he had not found any for sale in London; cf Allen's headnote.

ERASMUS OF ROTTERDAM TO ADRIANUS BARLANDUS, GREETING

Really, my excellent Barlandus, you deserve to be a most popular figure among young people everywhere, for your efforts are always devoted to the production of something that will assist them in studying the best subjects, rather than bring profit or distinction to yourself, and you would rather choose some useful field where you can promote the interests of the young than a more splendid theme which will advance your own reputation. It is of course a mark of your truly exalted and truly Christian spirit to be of service freely and without reward not only to your country, which (as Plato rightly says[1]) justly claims a share in what we are, but to the whole race of mortals. A sample of your labours seemed to me wholly admirable. You do me no less a service than Florus[2] did to Livy, if Livy and I could fairly be compared. My *Chiliades* was too large a volume to be within the reach of those in modest circumstances, or to be read in the grammar schools, or to be carried round with them by those who like strolling players are always on the move. And now your epitome at its very low price can be bought by anyone however ill endowed, and thumbed by schoolboys, and will add little weight to a traveller's baggage. And then those who teach your compendium in schools will be able to use my longer work as a commentary. One thing I would ask you, which you will no doubt have thought of for yourself: first, to include what is most worth having and not everything,[3] and secondly that if you light on anything improper (for most proverbs are drawn from human behaviour) either leave it out, or treat it in such a way that no infection may pass from it into those of tender years; for if I wish them to be brought up on good literature, it is with this proviso, that they are not inspired to bad behaviour. And some faults are of such a kind that ignorance of them is more than halfway to innocence.

Should you wish to know what my Muses are engaged on at the moment – for idleness is something quite outside their ken – my great object is an edition of all the works of St Augustine,[4] in a revised text with illustrative notes, labelling and not excising what is wrongly current under his name. In such a great enterprise I am obliged to seek the help of other scholars, but on condition that none of them loses his share of the credit. On such a point I would rather be deprived myself than seek more than my due. Some people suppose that all his works are to be had in good and accurate texts; but I would never have believed there were so many prodigious blunders as what I now discover, partly from more attentive reading and partly from comparison of the text with ancient copies. Farewell.

1205 / To William Warham — Antwerp, 24 May 1521

This letter to Warham, one of Erasmus' most dependable patrons (cf Ep 188), was published in the *Epistolae ad diversos*.

TO WILLIAM ARCHBISHOP OF CANTERBURY, PRIMATE OF ALL ENGLAND, FROM ERASMUS, GREETING

Your feelings towards me have been carefully reported to me in a letter from Zacharias of Friesland,[1] once my servant and pupil, and now your Highness' protégé, who is an honest and trustworthy young man and fully deserves any advancement at your kind hands. I extorted the money at length from that Italian,[2] though not without effort and expense. He refused to give me gold and would only produce stuivers,[3] and those reluctantly, most of them substandard coin. He cut the total by a tenth, giving me ninety of our florins for every hundred, and forty-five instead of fifty, so that I lose fifteen florins.[4] He is no broker; he's a procurer, the most rascally class of men. He himself is now suffering from the French itch, and in the hands of a bad doctor, not without some danger to life itself. His deputy[5] has the itch too, in mind as well as body. I have had to deal with a most unpleasant complaint.[6] All the same, with the help of friends I have got part of the money out of their grasp. In your wisdom, I hope that henceforward you will consider narrowly to whom you should entrust the money; for this remittance was put very much in the wrong hands.

That first hot spell gave me a severe fever,[7] but at least it was a single attack. I have not yet found time to be ill, or to consult the doctor: so much am I rent by labours I cannot escape.[8] The emperor's court has made a first payment of my annuity,[9] for the past six months. This is a most promising beginning; for it is a great sign that one is in favour when the court gives one anything beyond words. Not that I am without supporters at court; but it is better to go on as I am. And my health gets more feeble every day, though my mind is as good as ever.

Luther has caused very great trouble, nor do I see any end to it, unless Christ converts our headstrong folly[10] in the same way as the owl, they say, brings the unwise decisions of the Athenians to good effect. I wish Luther had either kept his mouth shut on some points, or had put them quite differently. As it is, I fear we shall escape this Scylla only to fall into some far more disastrous Charybdis.[11] If those who will stick at nothing to be bullies with full bellies[12] win the day, nothing remains but to write R.I.P. for Christ, who dies to rise no more. Farewell to the last spark of gospel charity, farewell to the twinkling light of the gospel star, to the true vein of heavenly doctrine: so foul is their flattery of princes, and of everyone from whom they hope for some personal gain, to the immeasurable loss of Christian truth. As for me, I manage the whole business so as not to be wholly useless to wholesome learning and to the glory of Christ, and yet not to get myself mixed up in civil strife. Some gleam of hope is cast by the justice of our Holy Father Leo: it may be that he will hold Christ's glory more precious than his own, or rather, will perceive that there can be no glory for him as pontiff unless and until he offers everything to the glory of Christ and Christ alone.

In your thoughtful inquiries whether I am in any degree of need,[13] I recognize your paternal affection towards me. But a man who has learned to live content with very little is not easily oppressed by want. Not but what I now feel a regular grandee, keeping as I do two horses who are better cared for than their own master and two servants[14] better turned out than he is. As for your kind promise about a benefice,[15] I fear that the harpies will prevent it; there are so many vultures in your part of the world who smell out any prospective carcass[16] many months ahead. I wish I could be given the opportunity just once more to enjoy a sight of your Highness and to converse with you; and perhaps it will happen one day. I do not pray to be spared a longer life, if Christ so please, nor do I anxiously desire it. I should like to be granted length of days sufficient to record for posterity my gratitude towards you, and to rouse the minds of men still further to the genuine philosophy of Christ. In this spirit I think to earn more merit with Jesus our Prince than by crawling thrice on my bare knees over the threshold of St Peter. My respectful best wishes to your Grace, whose good opinion I so much desire.

Antwerp, 24 May 1521

1206 / To Beatus Rhenanus — Louvain, 27 May [1521]

This is the preface to the *Epistolae D. Erasmi Roterodami ad diversos et aliquot aliorum ad illum per amicos eruditos ex ingentibus fasciculis schedarum collectae* (Basel: J. Froben 31 August 1521, according to the date on the title-page). Source of most of the letters included in this volume of CWE, the *Epistolae ad diversos* combine such new letters with the contents of the collections previously released by Erasmus; cf Allen I 595, 600 and L.-E. Halkin *Erasmus ex Erasmo* (Aubel 1983) 97–117.

Even as the *Farrago epistolarum* (cf Ep 1009 introduction) was being printed to catch the Frankfurt fair in the autumn of 1519, Erasmus spoke of another edition with new letters added and others revised (cf Ep 1013A:10–12). Some revisions were indeed indicated (cf n3, n5, n6), but Erasmus' repeated remarks that he would have preferred not to see any more letters printed ought to be taken with a grain of salt (cf lines 17–21, 56–7, Ep 1163:10–11). Meanwhile the *Farrago* sold so well that as early as February 1520 Erasmus had been asked to revise it for a second edition (cf Ep 1066:93–7). The last thing he desired was a straight reprint of the *Farrago* either by Froben or by another publisher. So in the summer of 1520 he was going through all his letters (cf Ep 1123:8–10) and in November the review of the *Farrago* was apparently completed (cf Ep 1163:8–11). Before the middle of January 1521 the revised copy together with a substantial number of new letters had reached Basel (cf AK II Ep 764). When he sent the first part of the revised New Testament shortly afterwards (cf Ep 1174 n6), he apparently asked to have all letters, old and new, back for another

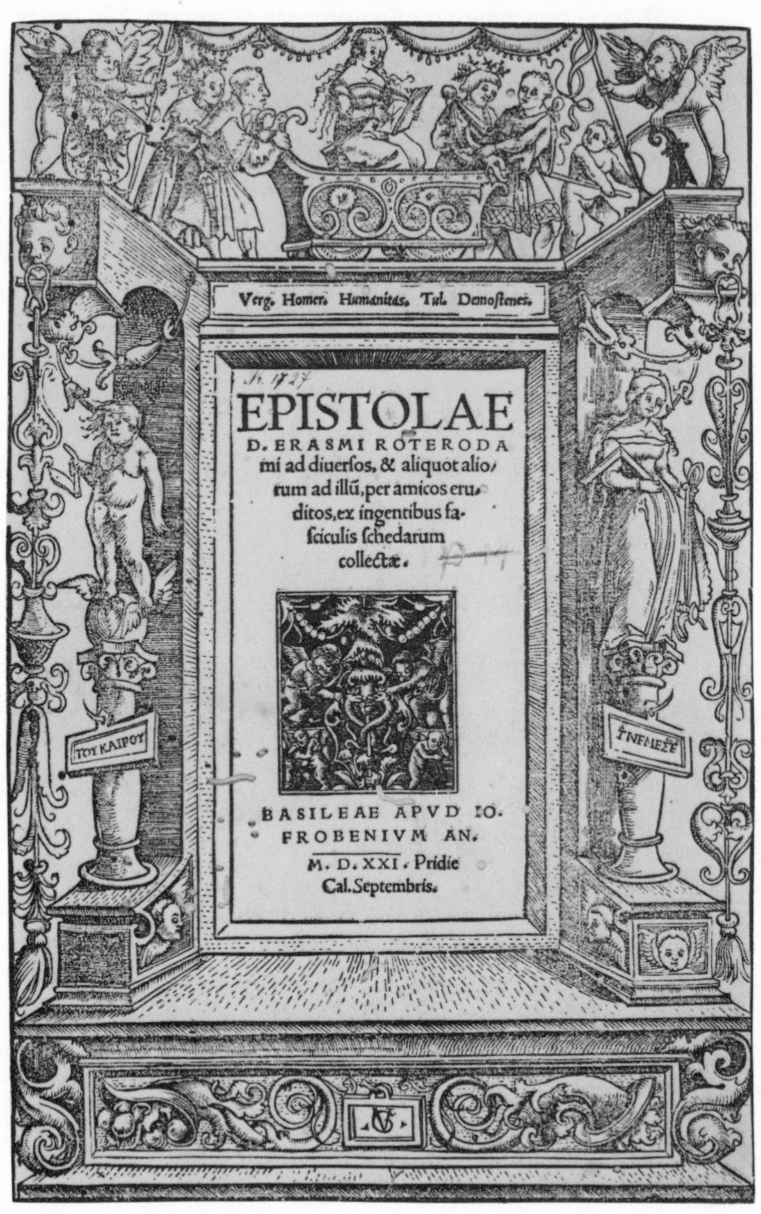

Verg. Homer. Humanitas. Tul. Demostenes.

EPISTOLAE
D. ERASMI ROTERODA
mi ad diuersos, & aliquot aliorum ad illũ, per amicos eruditos, ex ingentibus fa-
sciculis schedarum
collectæ.

BASILEAE APVD IO.
FROBENIVM AN.
M. D. XXI. Pridie
Cal. Septembris.

ΤΟΥ ΚΑΙΡΟΥ

ΝΕΜΕΣΙΣ

Erasmus *Epistolae ad diversos* title-page
Basel: Froben 31 August 1521
Centre for Reformation and Renaissance Studies, Victoria University, Toronto

review (cf lines 71–4), but was sent none and told instead that a volume of 41 quires (pages 1–490) was set in type, lacking only a preface and an epilogue (cf lines 61–3). So he wrote this preface as well as probably dispatching more letters to Basel (see Ep 1207 introduction). Froben next prepared a preliminary quire containing the title-page (dated 31 August), Epp 1206, 1225, and, to fill some space left over on the last page, Ep 1239. All was printed and ready to be launched at the Frankfurt autumn fair, but with the certain prospect of Erasmus' return to Basel (cf Ep 1242 introduction) a delay was indicated. As Froben now preferred his volume not to reach the public and his rivals until the time of the spring fair of 1522, Erasmus could add more letters including the last in time, Ep 1243, dated from Basel, 22 November 1521, which appears on page 639 but is followed by thirty more pages of letters. Presumably as a result of Erasmus' review of the printed volume, over three pages of corrigenda were added at the end.

On 20 March 1522 Heinrich Eppendorf ordered a copy of the book, which was then for sale (cf AK II Epp 855, 857). Subsequently he added to his copy some interesting marginal notes (see Allen IV 615–19). Luther had seen the new collection by 15 May (cf Luther w *Briefwechsel* II Ep 490). Like others, he retained for it the convenient name of *Farrago*, a habit that was perhaps encouraged by Froben's use of the same woodcut frame for the title-pages of the *Farrago* of October 1519 and the *Epistolae ad diversos*. In this preface Erasmus was able to state cogently the policy he observed in releasing some of his correspondence for print, but he was not optimistic that readers would do justice to the spontaneous quality of each letter (cf lines 51–5). The contents and the reception of this collection are discussed in the preface of this volume; for a manuscript copy of this letter see Ep 1225 introduction.

DESIDERIUS ERASMUS OF ROTTERDAM TO BEATUS RHENANUS OF SÉLESTAT, GREETING

What you say in your letter, my excellent Beatus, I perceive to be more true than I could wish. What surprises me is that my friends in Germany should be demanding particularly the very things that make me most unpopular.[1] You know what unfavourable omens attended the birth of the letters of which you supervised the first edition;[2] but how much worse they were for the *Farrago*! That book I was forced to publish, partly by the importunity of my friends and partly by sheer necessity, for I saw people all ready to publish such letters of mine as they possessed, whether I would or no, and they were already writing to me with open threats that they would do so. It was to prevent this that I sent you a bundle, entrusting the choice to you and even giving you the right to alter anything in it that you might think would damage my reputation or rouse passionate resentment in anyone. Nor do I doubt that with the kindness you have always shown me you took care to do all that a true friend should. And yet there too things were found which made some people furiously angry.[3] I had therefore resolved to refrain entirely from this kind of composition, especially as universal confusion is now the order of the day, and many men are so embittered in spirit by hatred that, however conciliatory and simple and cautious you may be, you can write nothing that they will not seize upon as an excuse for calumny.

As a young man, and even when I came to man's estate, I wrote many letters, but scarcely one with the intention that it should be published. I practised my pen, I whiled away an idle moment, I gossiped with friends, I gave rein to my feelings – did little in fact but amuse myself, expecting nothing less than that such trifles would be copied and preserved by my friends. It was when I was in Siena that Piso,[4] the kindest of men, who was then his king's envoy to Pope Julius, found on sale at a bookseller's a volume of letters from Erasmus, but in manuscript; this he bought and sent me. In this there was much that perhaps might seem worth keeping; but I took fright at such an unexpected chance, and for better or worse I burnt the lot. On my return, I found similar collections preserved here by several people, of which a number of copies had been made; and these, whenever I could extract them from my acquaintances, I consigned to the flames. But experience at length taught me that I was confronted with a hydra-headed monster.

And so my idea in permitting certain letters to be published has been either to satisfy the demand and put an end to requests for more, or at least to discourage others from their idea of publication when they saw that I have set my hand to this task myself. It was a further object that there might at least be some selection before they appear, that they should be less corrupt than the manuscript copies that were in many people's hands, and lastly that they might contain less bitter aloes. With this in mind I have revised the *Farrago*, making some things explicit on which a sinister interpretation had been put,[5] removing some things which I had observed to give offence,[6] especially to over-sensitive and irritable readers, and toning some things down. But once again the times are such that I repented of my undertaking. There had long been a deep strain of bitterness in everything written both by the supporters of the ancient tongues and of the humanities and by those blockheads who are convinced that any progress in liberal studies must weaken their own position. Then this sorry business of Luther blazed up into such a controversy that it is safe neither to speak nor to keep silence. Everything is wrested into the opposite sense, even what one writes with unimpeachable intentions; no notice is taken of the time when a man was writing, but what was entirely correct when it was written is transferred to a date which it does not fit at all.

I had written therefore to our friend Froben telling him to suppress this portion of my work permanently, or to keep it for a later occasion, or at least to postpone it until my return, and to press on with my paraphrases,[7] which I had not as yet heard that anyone had taken offence at. But he, misguided as he so often is,[8] in my opinion, dropped everything else (as I learn from my correspondents) and hastened to print the volume of my letters; and this without my knowledge has already reached the forty-first six-leaf quire, nor does anything delay publication except the need of a preface and epilogue. And he says that he will not keep the work by him any longer, even though I may perhaps be reluctant to add anything; he would rather issue the book without top or tail than face the loss of all that he has spent on it. Of course I must fall in with his wishes, and perhaps accept some loss of reputation myself in order to suit his convenience. But since the thing I wanted is not to be had, you of your kindness, dear Beatus, must see to it that the publication may do my name as little harm as possible. I do not quite remember what letters I have sent; and that was why I gave instructions that he should send back with the young man whom I dispatched with the first part of the New Testament[9] everything in the way of my letters that had been printed. What he had in his head that made him reluctant to do this, I cannot conceive.

And so in this business I implore you in the name of our friendship, dear Beatus, the most learned of my friends, to be in truth my second self and do for me what I should have done myself had it been possible; do all you can to make it seem as though Erasmus had never left your part of the world. Do not be moved by the small financial loss that will have to be faced in the alteration of some leaves; I wish the whole expense, whatever it may be, to be charged to me,[10] and my instructions are that Froben is not to suffer. I regard as profit any loss of money incurred to safeguard my reputation. The small sum involved can easily be made up from some other source; but a slur on one's name is not remedied so easily. And though my name might not even be at risk, I regard it as in the spirit of a Christian to do all in our power to satisfy all men,[11] with this proviso that we offend no man even unawares. Now it so happens, by some evil genius of mine,[12] that I am deflected by fortune from the things for which I seemed fitted by nature into other and very different fields, whether you consider the life I lead or the subjects I am engaged on. Not to go into details, though I seemed born for the flowing, untrammelled style commonly displayed in sermons, in theoretical disquisitions, and in set pieces too, I have wasted a great part of my endeavour on collections of proverbs, on commentaries, and on notes.

Be that as it may, for the writing of letters I might perhaps seem not wholly ill equipped; but in other respects there were many things which discouraged me from adopting this form of composition. To begin with, letters which are deficient in true feeling and do not reflect a man's actual life do not deserve to be called letters. Of this sort are Seneca's letters to Lucilius; and indeed, among the letters written at one time by Plato and those which Cyprian, Basil, Jerome, and Augustine wrote in imitation, it would seem, of the apostolic Epistles, there are very few that could not be called pamphlets with more propriety than letters. Again, what can we call those left to us by anonymous authors under the names of Brutus and Phalaris,[13] and the letters of Paul and Seneca,[14] except small-scale declamations? At the same time, the kind of letter that displays like a picture the writer's character and fortunes and sentiments, and the state of affairs both public and private –such, for example, as the letters of Cicero and Pliny and in more recent times those of Aeneas Pius[15] – have somewhat more risk about them than writing the history of recent events which, as Horace says,[16] is 'a task with dangerous hazard filled.'

And so, if things of this sort are to be published, I should not wish to encourage anyone to publish in his own lifetime, but to find some Tiro[17] and leave the task to him; though in publishing his master's work Tiro is thought to have shown more zeal than discretion. Whether you praise a man or criticize him, there will be no lack of people to take offence; not to mention some who cannot even endure to be well spoken of in print, either because they are too grand to be mentioned by anyone at random, or because they fear some may suspect them of enjoying a little incense. Which makes me the more surprised at St Bernard's publishing his letters, in which so many men are given a black mark.[18] Nowadays, if one mentions a Jacobite or a Carmelite even anonymously without plenty of butter for a start, they think it time to start throwing stones. There is the further drawback that, with the affairs of mortals changing as they do, one's dearest friends sometimes turn into deadly enemies and vice versa, so that one regrets one's praise of the first class and one's attacks on the second. Last but not least, it does no good to the author's reputation either, for many people judge a man's whole genius from a single letter, whereas one may write sometimes only half sober and sometimes half asleep, now weary, now ill or with one's mind full of other things, sometimes against the grain, and frequently in a style that is adapted to the intelligence or the taste of one's correspondent. As a result, inexperienced readers suspect one of inconsistency, whereas the variation should be attributed to various changes in age and sentiment, in persons and circumstances.

Such thoughts might well deter another man, however happily circumstanced, from publishing his letters; but I had a special reason to discourage me. My position in life has always been not only humble but consistently unfair, nor has the course of my life been such that I either could or would defend it against all aspersions; and so I had no reason to wish to preserve much record of either aspect. The same feeling might also affect those to whom I write: they might be unwilling for all the nonsense poured as it were into their private ear in letters from their friends to be made public, for there are people cursed by the Graces in the cradle who can put a discreditable sense on anything. It is a common experience that something which is popular at the dinner-table or between private people without prejudice may cause bitter resentment if repeated in an unsuitable place. This is why I have included so few of the letters I am answering; but I have added a certain number, especially letters from learned men, partly because I could not face the labour, which Angelo Poliziano generally takes upon himself, of providing a summary of the letter to which he replies, and partly because, even if you add a summary, there is some loss of clarity and life unless you read first the letter that is being answered.

So there, dear Rhenanus, are the principles behind my plan. Nothing is left except, first, to ask you to show yourself a true friend in the choice you make, and secondly, to pray that heaven may send a blessing on your judgment and on my readiness to comply, not only for me who find obstinate resistance to my friends' wishes impossible, but also for those who with more zeal than discretion have secured my compliance. Farewell.

Louvain, 27 May [1520][19]

1207 / From Basilius Amerbach — Basel, 30 May 1521

This letter, preserved among the Amerbach papers (Öffentliche Bibliothek of the University of Basel, MS G II 13a f 12; cf AK II Ep 786), appears to be the original actually sent or at least ready for dispatch. Written in Basilius' own hand, it has to do with the third edition of Erasmus' New Testament (cf Ep 1174 n6), which caused a flurry of communications between Louvain and Basel. The first part of Erasmus' copy for the new edition was sent to Basel with a young man who must have returned to Louvain before 27 May (cf Ep 1206:71–3). He must have been followed by the carrier of Ep 1203, dated 14 May, presumably the man who also took Erasmus' letter to Basilius (cf lines 23, 27) and was waiting while he wrote this reply (cf line 34). But in the mean time Erasmus seems to have dispatched the rest of the New Testament copy, accompanied probably by Ep 1206, dated 27 May, and additional letters for the *Epistolae ad diversos*. Whether or not he was eventually given this letter to carry, Erasmus' messenger seems to have gone from Basel to Anderlecht and from there to Louvain (cf Ep 1209 n5). He has not been identified, nor have the other messengers; cf Epp 1205 n14, 1209 n4.

This is no way to treat me, my dear Erasmus, sole glory of our age! Here am I, rendered immortal by mention in your immortal works;[1] yet you set so high a value on the trifle of attention which I was able now and again to contribute towards supervising the second edition of your New Testament[2] that, though as in the famous exchange between Glaucus and Diomede[3] you have given me gold in return for bronze, you yet seem to yourself to have returned no thanks at all. What am I supposed to do now, who am your debtor on every count? Ought I to admit my debt? I shall certainly be declared a bankrupt, and be myself responsible for bringing the bailiffs in; for I have been given immortal currency in exchange for mortal, rare coin for ordinary, very much for very little. But this I would attribute to the courtesy in which you surpass even the Graces themselves. So I will submit to defeat on this point, for I am only one of the many people who in generous actions of this kind cannot compete with you and do not wish to. Not that meanwhile there will be any falling off in my desire to repay you what I can by such services as I can render. And if I cannot, you must please accept a heart entirely devoted to you, for the attempt is sometimes to one's credit.

This one thing I would have you believe with all the solemnity of a Delphian oracle,[4] that there is nothing I would not do for your sake, were I ever given an opportunity. That it should not be open to me to do anything now in respect of your New Testament[5] causes me more regret than I could express in a few words. For I have made up my mind to go abroad,[6] and was almost packed up for the journey when your letter came. It is a grief to me, a great grief, that your New Covenant should have been sent to us precisely at this moment, when I absolutely must leave Basel, whether I will or no. And so, dear and learned Erasmus, please take my unavoidable departure in good part; otherwise, if I were able to remain in Basel or if your letter had reached me sooner, I would have left no stone unturned[7] in correcting your work as it goes through the press, so that you might have learnt by experience of my devotion to you, which is most sincere; for you have a perfect right to ask anything of me. Farewell, Erasmus, pillar of learning and the pride of Germany.

Bonifacius[8] returned from Avignon a month ago, but he has gone to Freiburg and cannot write, not knowing your courier is here. But he is bound to you by every possible oath of fealty which I can underwrite on my brother's behalf with a clear conscience. Remember, dear Erasmus, that we are both of us devoted to you and ever shall be.

Basel, 30 May 1521

Yours most sincerely, Basilius Amerbach

To the most admired and learned Dr Erasmus of Rotterdam, his celebrated teacher

In Louvain

1208 / To Maximiliaan van Horn

Anderlecht, 31 May 1521

This letter first appears in LB, where it was edited by Jean Leclerc from an unknown source (cf Ep 1166 introduction).

As in years past (cf Epp 963:6n, 1117 introdution), the heat of the summer interfered with Erasmus' health (cf Ep 1205:19) and drove him away from Louvain. In this year, however, the heat was rendered doubly unbearable by the festering animosity against him. For some time he had planned to go away (cf Ep 1174 n1) but had been held back by his work. But now, with the copy for the New Testament and the *Epistolae ad diversos* recently dispatched (cf Epp 1205 n8, 1206 introduction), he was free to leave. Not content with one of his usual short vacations at Antwerp, he took his books along, planning to stay away for three months (lines 9–10). In the autumn he knew he would have to go to Basel (cf Ep 1242 introduction).

In Anderlecht, now among the western suburbs of Brussels, Erasmus' host was canon Pieter Wichmans (cf Ep 1231). He found the rural setting unexpectedly charming, healthy, and completely congenial (cf Epp 1215:3–5, 1216:86–7, 1223:2–16, 1233:202–5, 1238:11–15, Allen Ep 1342:19–22, 62–9). So he stayed until the middle of October (cf Ep 1239) in Wichmans' hospitable house, which is now part of a museum dedicated to Erasmus.

Maximiliaan van Horn (d 1543), a courtier, occasional diplomat, and Knight of the Golden Fleece, owned family estates at Gaasbeek, situated in the same direction as Anderlecht but a few miles farther away from Brussels. His wife, Barbara van Montfoort (cf line 16), bore him four sons.

TO THE HONOURABLE MAXIMILIAAN, COUNT OF HORN AND OF GAASBEEK, FROM ERASMUS OF ROTTERDAM

My honoured Lord, this charming place and my host's unheard-of kindness are so refreshing that they really seem to have made a new man of me. There is also the agreeable society of Leonard,[1] who is bringing up your son[2] and teaching his boyish mind in the spirit, one might say, of a father. From his tutor's conversation I often gather[3] that your Lordship is well disposed towards me; and the greater my debt to you in this regard, the less I deserve it. I wish there were something I could do to show my gratitude in return. I shall spend perhaps three months here, for I have brought my whole library with me. During that time, if I can assist your son's studies in any way by advice or action on my part, I shall not fail to do all that a grateful man should. Your son has a delightful nature; it is of the first importance among whom and by whom he is educated. I pray that your intentions may be blessed with the fortune they deserve. My respectful best wishes to your Lordship and to the honourable lady your wife.

Anderlecht, on the morrow of Corpus Christi 1521
Erasmus
Written in my own hand, in haste

1209 / To Conradus Goclenius [Anderlecht] 8 June 1521

This letter was first printed by Paulus Merula in the appendix of his *Vita Des. Erasmi* (Leiden 1607) 86.

Conradus Goclenius, a Westphalian, had studied and taught privately at Louvain before his appointment in 1519 as professor of Latin at the Collegium Trilingue (cf Epp 1050–1), a position he held with great distinction to the end of his life. By now he had become an intimate friend of Erasmus, who deposited money with him on three occasions; cf Allen x 406.

ERASMUS OF ROTTERDAM TO CONRADUS GOCLENIUS, GREETING

Please remember about renting a house for me[1] which will suit me and has a garden. You can have a word about this with Dorp. For though I shall go to Germany this fall to work on the New Testament,[2] I should like to have a nest among you ready for me. I send the book which Rutgerus[3] is asking for. Please return the letters to our Swiss friend.[4] Farewell.

8 June 1521

This rascal[5] will give you an unfinished shirt, which Froben's wife sent me. He seems to have thought it was his own property.

1210 / To Richard Pace Anderlecht, 11 June 1521

This letter was printed in the *Epistolae ad diversos*; Richard Pace was an English courtier and diplomat with humanistic tastes.

ERASMUS OF ROTTERDAM TO RICHARD PACE, GREETING

News from the Froben press from some of my learned friends there is that Polidoro's proverbs[1] is being printed in large format, and on such splendid paper, that Froben has never shown any other book such respect and attention as he does to this. He will add his work *De rerum inventoribus*[2] in equal splendour. This he does as a result of encouragement and even pressure from me. For he had actually sent the book back to Antwerp with his son Hieronymus[3] and could by no means be induced to take it on. They will both appear at the next Frankfurt fair, and all promises well. Now let Polidoro go and believe the gossips who keep on saying that I am jealous of his reputation!

I understand that More has been promoted from privy councillor to treasurer,[4] a post which is full of honour with a far from negligible salary. As far as I can see, he is such a success at court that I am sorry for him. But I am refreshed by his having held out some hopes of my seeing him again in August.[5]

But there is one thing, my dear Pace, that distresses me: I have still no news of those notebooks left behind in Rome.[6] I beg you not to let expense stand in the way of their being sent back here. It will cost you nothing; the outlay shall be defrayed to the uttermost farthing. If only the second book of the *Antibarbari*[7] would find its way home, I shall easily bear the loss of the others. Farewell.

From my country retreat in Anderlecht, 11 June 1521

1211 / To Justus Jonas — Anderlecht, 13 June 1521

This admirable composition, printed in the *Epistolae ad diversos*, consists of portraits of two friends Erasmus had deeply respected, Jean Vitrier and John Colet. Colet had died on 16 September 1519; the date of Vitrier's death is not known. The letter is a sequel to Ep 1202, also addressed to Jonas. If Ep 1202 was intended to explain and defend Erasmus' own position in the religious controversy, a position characterized by compromise and occasionally concealment, this letter presents two men who did not compromise and whom Erasmus may well have considered to be more perfect Christians than himself. Without breaking away from the traditional and highly imperfect church, both had succeeded in always remaining truthful to themselves and 'the law of Christ' (line 39) or, as Luther's friends might have preferred to say, of the 'spirit of the Gospel' (line 682). In the final analysis Erasmus concluded that of the two Vitrier was the more saintly and also the more perfect for having willingly submitted to the uncongenial bonds of monastic life.

According to Erasmus this letter was written in reply to Jonas' request for a life of Colet, a request conceivably made in a missing answer to Ep 1202. Jonas may have heard about Erasmus' intention to commemorate Colet (although Epp 1026–7, 1030 were not printed until the *Epistolae ad diversos*), and he must have read Ep 999 in the *Farrago* (cf Ep 967A introduction). Thus it could have been in analogy with Hutten's request for a description of Thomas More (cf Ep 999:20–1) that Jonas asked for a life of Colet. If Erasmus had invented Jonas' request for the sake of epistolary style, one might have expected it to extend to Vitrier as well. But the analogy with Ep 999 could also mean that in giving this composition the form of a letter, Erasmus again wished to honour a young and brilliant German for whom he had taken a special liking, as he had for Hutten. If this letter was sent to Erfurt, it did not reach Jonas there. On 31 May he had moved to Wittenberg, where he was installed as provost of All Saints' on 6 June. His transition to the Lutheran camp was thus complete. No reaction of his to this letter is known, and for Erasmus there remained only the sad conviction that Jonas was lost to his cause (cf Epp 1258, 1425).

There are two previous English translations of this letter. One, with extensive and careful annotation, by J.H. Lupton in Erasmus *The Lives of Jehan Vitrier ... and John Colet* (London 1883) and another, also annotated, by J.C. Olin in his *Christian Humanism and the Reformation* (New York 1965). There is also an exhaustively annotated French translation (with the Latin text on opposite pages) by André Godin (Angers 1982).

ERASMUS OF ROTTERDAM TO JUSTUS JONAS OF ERFURT, GREETING

You beg me earnestly, dear friend, to write you a short life, a portrait in miniature[1] as it were, of John Colet; and I will do so the more readily because I suspect you of seeking some outstanding example of piety which you can use as a model for your own way of life. For my own part, dearest Jonas, I admit that I have enjoyed the society of many men whose integrity I greatly admired; but I have never seen anyone in whose character I did not still feel the lack of some element of the pure Christian, whenever I compared anyone with the two faultless figures of whom I am now to speak; one of whom I had the good fortune to know in the town in Artois they call Saint-Omer,[2] when the plague (which proved a blessing to me in this respect) had driven me thither from Paris, and the other in England, to which I had been drawn by affection for my friend Mountjoy.[3] You will find you have a bargain, and I know how much you like bargains: I will give you two men in the place of one.

The first, Jean Vitrier,[4] was a Franciscan, for he had happened in youth upon that way of life; and in my judgment he was in no respect second to Colet, except that as the servant of his order his sphere of benevolence was more limited. He was about forty-four when I first knew him, and at once he conceived an affection for me, though a man much unlike himself. His opinion carried very great weight with those whose approval was worth having, and he was most acceptable to many in high place; he was tall and well built,[5] gifted by nature, and with such high standards that nothing could be more civilized. The niceties of Scotist philosophy[6] he had imbibed as a boy, and neither wholly rejected them (for there were clever things in it, he thought, though expressed in inelegant words) nor again did he set much store by them. In any case, once he had the good fortune to sample Ambrose and Cyprian and Jerome, he thought wondrous little of the scholastics compared with them. In sacred studies he admired no one more than Origen;[7] and when I said, not very seriously, that I wondered he could enjoy reading a heretic, he retorted in the most lively way, 'There can be no doubt that the Holy Spirit dwelt in a heart that produced so many books with such learning and such fire.'

The regular way of life into which he had slipped or had been drawn in the ignorance of youth[8] by no means appealed to him. He used to say in my hearing that it was a life for idiots rather than religious men to sleep and wake and sleep again,[9] to speak and to be silent, to go and to return, to eat and to stop eating, all at the sound of a bell, and in a word to be governed in everything by human regulations rather than the law of Christ. Nothing, he said, was more inequitable than this equality among men so far from equal, especially because in those places men with heaven-sent gifts and born for better things were often buried by ceremonies and petty man-made constitutions, or even by jealousy. But, none the less, he never suggested to anyone that he should change his way of life, nor did he attempt anything of the sort himself; for he was ready to endure everything rather than be a cause of stumbling to any mortal man, following in this as in other things the example of his favourite, Paul.[10] Nothing was so unfair that he would not endure it with the greatest readiness in his desire for peace.

The Holy Scriptures, and especially the Pauline Epistles, he had got by heart, and no one knew his own fingers and toes[11] better than he knew every word of Paul his master. Had you started him off anywhere, he would promptly have finished the whole Epistle without a slip. Large parts of Ambrose he knew by heart, and it is scarcely credible how much of the other orthodox Fathers he had stored in his memory. This he owed partly to a memory that was naturally good, and partly to constant and thoughtful reading.

I asked him once in familiar conversation how he prepared his mind when setting out to preach, and he replied that he usually opened Paul, and went on reading him until he felt his mind take fire. At that point he paused, praying to God with passion, until told that it was time to start. As a rule he did not divide his sermons under heads as the common run of preachers do,[12] as if it were not permitted to do anything else; which is often the source of very tedious subdivisions, though all that painstaking organization takes the warmth out of an address, and because it sounds artificial, it make the speaker carry less conviction. But Vitrier used as it were a continuous flow of language to connect the Epistle with the Gospel, so that his hearers went home not only better informed, but kindled with a new desire for a pious life. There was no purposeless gesticulation, no noisy ranting;[13] he was entirely concentrated, and brought his words out in such a way that you felt they came from a passionate and simple but yet sober heart, nor did he ever dwell on any point till he was tedious or make a parade of citing various authorities, like those who cobble up an insipid patchwork at one moment from Scotus or Thomas or Durandus,[14] at another from the civil and canon law, or from philosophy or the poets, that the public may think there is nothing they do not know. Every sentence he produced was full of Scripture, nor could he utter anything else. His heart was in what he said.

He was absorbed by a kind of incredible passion for bringing men to the true philosophy of Christ, and from labours of this sort he hoped to win the glory of martyrdom. And so, as I have heard from his most intimate friends, he had long ago obtained permission from his superiors to voyage to countries in which Christ is either unknown or worshipped falsely, thinking that he would be fortunate if in this service he could win a martyr's crown. But he was recalled in mid-course, hearing as it were a voice from heaven, 'Return, Jean; you will not fail of martyrdom among your own people.' He obeyed the oracle, and found that what that voice had foretold was true. There was in those parts a small house of humble nuns,[15] in which the whole discipline of the monastic life had so far collapsed that it was more truly a brothel than a nunnery. And yet there were some among them who both could be rescued and wished to be. While he was recalling these women to Christ with constant exhortation and encouragement, eight desperate creatures among them formed a plot: they lay in wait for him and dragged him to some distant place, and there they strangled him with scarves, nor did they make an end of it until by some chance they were interrupted and their wicked crime brought to a stop. By now unconscious, he was with difficulty revived so that he could breathe again. Yet he never uttered any complaint even to his closest friends, nor did he fail to do everything for them that he was accustomed to do to further their salvation; in fact, even the look they saw in his face was never more severe than was his wont. He knew the man responsible for this conspiracy. He was a Jacobite theologian and a bishop,[16] a suffragan of the bishop of Thérouanne,[17] and a man of openly irreligious life. To him too he never uttered a single word of rebuke, although he detested no class of men more than those who profess themselves teachers and examples of godliness and then by their impious character and teaching turn the multitude away from Christ.

Sometimes he preached seven times in a single day, nor was he ever short of matter for a well-studied sermon, when Christ was his subject. Not but what his whole life was a sermon in itself. In company he was cheerful and the reverse of gloomy; but in such a way that he never gave any impression of levity or silliness, much less of self-indulgence or intemperance. He would introduce learned topics into the conversation, religious topics for the most part, and such as promoted piety. Such was his talk if anyone paid him a visit or if he went to call on anyone. If he were on a journey, he had influential friends who would supply him sometimes with a mule or a horse as he went,[18] to make conversation with him easier; and then the excellent man would produce with a more cheerful heart sayings worth more than any precious stones. He used to send no one away downcast; indeed there was no one but went away a better man and kindled to a greater love of piety.

There was nothing in which you could feel that he was acting in any way for his personal advantage; he was immune against the pleasures of the table, against ambition and avarice and self-indulgence, against spite and jealousy and all inordinate desire. Whatever befell, he used to give God thanks, nor did he know any joy like that of kindling others with zeal for the religion of the Gospel. Nor were his efforts fruitless. Many were the men and women whom he had won for Christ, and how much they differed from the common run of Christian was shown by their deathbeds. There you might have seen his disciples meeting death in the most cheerful spirit and, like swans that sing before they die,[19] uttering words that proved how the divine spirit had touched their hearts; while the rest, after ceremonies duly performed and the familiar solemn declarations made, breathed their last believing, doubting? – who shall say? A witness to this is Ghisbert,[20] the worthy physician of that town and a keen devotee of true religion, who attended on their deathbeds many persons of either school.

He had won over also a certain number of members of his own society, but not many, just as Christ could not perform many mighty works among his own people.[21] What they like as a rule is a man whose learning brings plenty of business to their common kitchen, rather than those who win plenty of souls for Christ. And while his spirit, pure as it was and in truth Christ's hallowed temple, hated all vices and lust in particular, so that he was profoundly upset even by the smell of such persons, he was equally far from being able to endure improper language. He never held forth tediously on the faults of ordinary people, nor did he ever produce anything he had learnt in the confessional; but he presented such a picture of honourable conduct that every man silently recognized his own faults. In giving advice, his wisdom, his integrity, his skill were alike remarkable. He was never very willing to hear secret confessions, but in this too he did his loving duty; anxious and continually repeated confessions he openly abominated.[22]

To superstition and ceremonies he attached very little importance. He used to eat what was set before him soberly and with thanksgiving. The clothes he wore were no different from other brethren's. He had a habit of making a journey sometimes for the sake of his health, if he felt his body was weighed down by humours. One day, when he was finishing his allotted stint of prayer at matins with his companion, he felt sick, perhaps as a result of fasting the day before, so he went into the nearest house and got something to eat; then made his way back and proceeded with his prayers. At this point his companion supposed that they must repeat everything from the beginning, because he had eaten something before saying prime; but he cheerfully denied that he had done anything wrong, in fact he said God would profit by it. 'To start with,' he said, 'our prayers were languid and lazy; but now we shall repeat our spiritual hymns with cheerful, active spirits. And God delights in offerings of this sort, which are made by a cheerful giver.'[23]

I myself was staying at the time[24] with Antoon van Bergen, the abbot of St Bertin's where no one ever dined till after midday, and my stomach could not endure to go so long without food – and it was Lent – especially as I was working very hard; so I used before dinner to fortify my digestion with a small hot drink to enable it to hold out till dinner-time. On this point I consulted him to know if I was breaking the rules; and after looking round for his companion, who at the time was a layman,[25] for fear he might be shocked, he said, 'On the contrary, you would be doing wrong if you did not do this, and if through the need of some quite unimportant food you had to break off your sacred studies and damage your health.'

When Pope Alexander had made two jubilees out of one[26] to increase the profits, and the bishop of Tournai[27] had purchased the right to sell the resulting indulgences in return for a cash payment at his own risk, his commissaries worked really hard to ensure that the bishop did not lose his capital, and for choice that he might make a far from negligible profit. The principal persons summoned to act a part in this play were those known to be popular preachers. My friend, perceiving that money was going into the bishop's coffers that used previously to relieve the poor, did not speak against the papal offer, but he did not recommend it, all the same. In any case, what he did speak against was the sight of the poor people cheated of their usual relief; and he condemned the foolish confidence of those who after throwing a coin into a coffer supposed themselves to be free from sin.[28]

At length the commissaries offered a hundred florins towards the building of the church – for at that time a new church[29] was going up in his monastery – so that, if he would not recommend the papal indulgence, at least he might stop saying things that spoilt the sales. At which, as though struck by divine inspiration, he cried: 'Depart from me, ye workers of simony, and take your money with you! Do you think I am the man to suppress the truth of the Gospel for money? The truth may stand in the way of your gains, but I must think more of souls than of your profits.' The men, who knew they were doing wrong, gave way before the power of the Gospel in his heart; but all the same, quite unexpectedly, at daybreak a notice of excommunication was nailed up – only one of the townspeople tore it down before many men had seen it.

Not in the least frightened by these threats, he continued in perfect peace of mind to teach the people and to offer sacrifice to Christ; nor did he show any signs that he was afraid of an interdict aimed at him for preaching Christ. Shortly afterwards he was summoned to the bishop of Thérouanne. He obeyed the orders of his diocesan, and appeared with one companion. He himself had no misgivings about his future; but unknown to him, the townspeople had posted men on horseback to protect him on the way, for fear that he might be caught in an ambush and thrown into some dungeon. Nothing is too outrageous for 'the accursed appetite for gold.'[30] The bishop put several points to him which they had collected from his sermons; to which he gave answers without flinching, and satisfied the bishop. Some time later he received a second summons, and more objections were put forward. After replying to these as well, he asked why his accusers were not present, to take the responsibility for their charges. He had come twice, he said, out of respect for the man who summoned him, because he was his bishop; but he would not come a third time if sent for in the same way, because he had more important work to do at home. So he was left to his own devices, either because they lacked a handle by which to do him harm, or for fear of a popular uprising, for his high character had earned the devotion of all honourable members of the public, although he aimed at nothing of the kind.

You will have been wondering for some time, I am sure, how he met his end. He was unpopular not only with the commissaries but also with some of his own brethren, not because they did not approve his way of life, but it was of a higher standard than they found convenient. He was entirely devoted to the winning of souls; but in equipping a kitchen or building walls or attracting well-endowed young men he was less active than they wished, though this too that excellent man did not neglect, at any rate if there was any question of relieving distress. He did not, however, like most people, attend to such things in the wrong order. In fact he had also lost a large fish. The man concerned[31] was a member of the court and had just the character you would expect of a courtier, roaming abroad from one bedchamber to another, defiling other men's marriages at random and treating his own wife as a castaway, although she was of noble birth and the mother of several children. As luck would have it, the time came when she too was corrupted; and he instantly rejected the poor woman for her first fault, although he had allowed himself to commit so many. At length she sank even lower, and reached the ultimate of calamity, for besides the disgrace of it all, she was infected with what they call the French pox. Vitrier tried all he could to reconcile the wife and the husband, but in vain; the hard-hearted brute remained quite unmoved by respect for his kindred, by affection for their common children, or by his own bad conscience, for he had given her the occasion to go astray by his own constant adulteries and his neglect; and so he abandoned the man as hopeless. A little later the man, as the custom was, sent him a shoulder of pork or a flitch of bacon. Jean had however instructed the porter – for he was then warden – to receive nothing without sending for him first. When the present arrived, he was summoned. Whereupon he said to the servants who brought the gift in their master's name 'Take back your burden where it came from. I do not accept gifts from the devil.'

And so, knowing as well as they did that his life and teaching were an outstanding nursery of the religion of the Gospel, all the same, because he was not equally successful with the profits of the kitchen, he was instructed to lay down the office of warden (which he did[32] with the greatest readiness), and a man was chosen to succeed him whom I know,[33] an outsider, of whose character I will say nothing, nor of the difference between him and his predecessor; but to put it briefly he seemed to me a man to whom no prudent person would be ready to entrust his sheepfold – whether he was foisted onto them by those who wished to get rid of him, or whether he seemed more suitable for the job. Moreover, since living in our man's society was encouraging the growth of two or three others who were carried away by a similar spirit to put first the Christian religion rather than an increase in their victuals, they banished the man to a small house of nuns at Courtrai.[34] There, as far as he could, he remained what he had always been, teaching, comforting, encouraging; and there he peacefully breathed his last, leaving behind him a few short books in French,[35] which he had got together out of religious authors, which resemble, I do not doubt, the life and conversation of their compiler. Even so, I hear that some people now condemn them, thinking it most dangerous for ordinary men to read anything except foolish fables and stories and the dreams of monks. A spark of his teaching still glows in the hearts of many, compared with whom you might say that other people are not Christians but Jews. Such was the contempt with which this outstanding man was treated by his own colleagues; though had he fallen to Paul's lot as a companion, I do not doubt that the Apostle would have valued him above his familiar Barnabas or Timothy.

Such was my friend Vitrier, that jewel of a man, unknown to the world but popular and famous in the kingdom of Christ. Now let me tell you about Colet, who was very like him. I had described each of them to the other, and both had a burning desire to meet; indeed Vitrier had crossed over to England for this purpose. And Colet told me afterwards that he had had a visit from a Minorite whose wise and pious conversation would have been a great delight to him; but another member of the same order, a Stoic, was introduced, who seemed to disapprove of their Christian conversation and interrupted it. And Colet perhaps deserves the more credit for this reason, that neither the indulgence of fortune nor the force of a nature that urged him in quite a different direction could turn him from his passion for the life of the Gospel. For he was born of well-known and well-to-do parents, and in London; his father twice held supreme office in his native city, and was, as they call it, lord mayor.[36] His mother,[37] who is still alive, was a woman of the highest character, who bore her husband eleven sons and as many daughters.[38] Colet was the eldest of them all, and therefore would be in English law the sole heir, even had the others survived; but of them all he was the only one still alive when I first knew him. To these advantages of fortune he added a tall and elegant figure.

As a young man he acquired a thorough knowledge of scholastic philosophy, such as it is, in his own country, and earned the title which indicates proficiency in the seven liberal arts.[39] Indeed there was none of these which he had not practised with energy and success; for he had greedily devoured the works of Cicero, had perused the books of Plato[40] and Plotinus with strict attention, and left no part of mathematics untouched. After this, like a keen businessman in search of valuable goods, he set off for France, and then for Italy.[41] There he devoted himself entirely to the reading of sacred authors; but first he went with great energy on a pilgrimage through literature of every kind, and took particular delight in the early Fathers, Dionysius, Origen, Cyprian, Ambrose, Jerome. Among the ancient authors there was none to whom he was so unfair as Augustine.[42] Yet he did not fail to read Scotus and Thomas[43] and others of that kidney when circumstances required it. With the literature of both civil and canon law he was actively familiar. In short, there was no book containing either history or constitutional principles which he had not read. The English possess authors who did for their own people what Dante and Petrarch did for the Italians.[44] By reading the writings of these men as well he acquired a facility of speech, preparing himself even then to be a herald of the gospel message.

On returning from Italy, he left his parents' house and chose to live in Oxford. There he gave public lectures without fee[45] on all the Epistles of St Paul.[46] It was here that I first knew him,[47] for some good fortune had brought me there at the same time; he was then about thirty, and two or three months younger than I. In academic theology he had taken no degree whatever,[48] and had no desire to do so; but there was no doctor there of theology or of law, and no abbot or holder of any other dignity, who did not go to hear him, even carrying books along with them, whether this distinction was due to

John Colet
Portrait by Sir William Segar, 1585/6, which appeared on the cover of the statutes of St Paul's School
The Worshipful Company of Mercers

Colet's authoritative words or to the keenness of his audience, who were not ashamed to learn, old men and doctors though they might be, from a young man who was not a doctor – though later they offered him the title of doctor,[49] which he accepted more to please them than because he wished for it.

From these pious labours he was recalled to London by the favour of King Henry VII, and made dean of St Paul's,[50] thus becoming head of a society dedicated to the saint whose letters he loved so dearly. The deanery is the leading position of its kind in England, though there are others with a larger income. Here that excellent man, as though summoned to work and not to enjoy preferment, restored the discipline of his chapter, which was in decay, and introduced the innovation of preaching every festival in his cathedral, besides the special sermons which he preached from time to time in the Chapel Royal and other places. Moreover, in his own church he did not choose a text at random from the Gospels or the apostolic Epistles, but put forward some one subject, which he pursued in several sermons until he finished it, for example the Gospel of St Matthew, the Creed, the Lord's Prayer. And he had a large audience, including most of the leading men in his native city and in the king's court.

The dean's table, at which hospitality had been an excuse for devotion to luxurious living, he reduced to the level of frugality. Some years before, he had given up supper entirely,[51] and therefore did without entertaining in the evening. Moreover, as he dined rather late, he had fewer guests then too; and they were fewer also because the entertainment was modest, although nicely served, and the time spent at table was short, while the conversation was such as would suit only educated and serious people.[52] After grace, some boy read out clearly in a loud voice a chapter from the Pauline Epistles or the Proverbs of Solomon. From this he himself often chose and repeated a passage and made it the subject of conversation, asking the learned and clever people present, and sometimes even the uneducated, what this or that expression meant. And he so managed the conversation that, though religious and serious, it was never tedious or pretentious. Again at the end of the meal, when they had somehow had all they need if not all they might have fancied, he introduced another topic, and sent his guests away so refreshed in mind and body that they went away better men than they came, and never departed with stomachs replete with food.

He took the greatest delight in conversation with his friends, which he would often carry on until far into the night; but all his talk was either of books or of Christ.[53] If someone that he liked to talk to was not available, – for he was not satisfied with the first comer – a boy used to read something out of the Bible. I myself was sometimes invited to go with him on pilgrimage.[54]

On such occasions he was the most cheerful companion; but he always had a book with him, and Christ was the only topic of conversation. He was impatient of everything slovenly, and thus could not stand language that was ungrammatical and defiled with barbarisms. All his household gear, the service of his table, his clothes, his books – all must be neat; for splendour he did not trouble himself. He wore only dark clothes, though in that country priests and theologians commonly wear purple. His outer garment was always made of wool, and plain; if cold weather demanded it, he kept himself warm with an undergarment of fur.

The proceeds of his benefices he left to his steward to spend on household expenses; his patrimony, which was more than ample, he distributed himself on charitable objects. After his father's death, when he had inherited an immense sum of money, for fear that if he saved it up it would have a bad effect on him he built a new school[55] in St Paul's churchyard dedicated to the boy Jesus, a noble building; by it was a splendid house, in which two schoolmasters were to live, for whom he established ample salaries, that they might teach without demanding fees, but with the proviso that the school should take only a definite number. He divided it into four parts. The first form takes as it were the catechumens, for no one is admitted unless he has already learnt to read and write. The second contains those who are taught by the under master, the third those taught by the high master. Each is divided from the other by a curtain, which can be drawn or drawn back at pleasure. Above the high master's desk sits a remarkable representation of the boy Jesus in the attitude of a teacher,[56] which is greeted by the whole body with a hymn when they enter or leave school. Above is the Father's face, saying 'Hear ye him';[57] for he added these words at my suggestion. In the last place there is a chapel, which can be used for divine service. The whole school has no nooks and corners, so much so that there is neither sitting-room nor study. Each of the boys has his allotted place on steps that rise gradually, with their spaces marked out. Each class contains sixteen, and the head boy in each class has a stool a little higher than the rest. Nor do they admit anyone at random, but choose boys for character and brains.

Being a far-sighted man, he saw that the greatest hope for a commonwealth lies in the education of its young. Immensely expensive as this is, he allowed no one to share the burden.[58] Some person had left a hundred pounds of English money towards the building. When Colet realized that by this benefaction laymen were claiming some sort of rights in the school, he secured leave from his bishop,[59] and used the money to buy vestments for the cathedral.[60] In charge of the finances[61] and all the business side he set, not priests or the bishop or the chapter, as they call it, nor eminent laymen, but a certain number of married citizens of approved reputation.[62] When someone asked him the reason, he replied that nothing was certain in human affairs, but that this was the class of men in whom he had found the least corruption.

And while this work won universal approval, many people wondered greatly why he was building a very splendid house[63] within the walls of a monastery of Carthusians not far from what is called Richmond Palace. He used to say that he was preparing that retreat for his old age, when he might be past work or broken in health and be obliged to retire from the society of men. There it was his intention to devote himself to philosophy with two or three special friends, among whom he was accustomed to include myself; but death forestalled him. For having been seized a few years before by the sweating sickness,[64] a disease which is peculiarly rife in England, and attacked by it for the third time, he made some sort of recovery, but from the aftermath of that complaint contracted a wasting disease of the intestines which proved fatal. One doctor diagnosed it as a dropsy. Autopsy produced nothing new, except that the fibres at the extremities of the liver were found to be rough with projecting hairy growths. He was buried on the south side of the choir of his cathedral, in an unassuming grave which he had chosen for the purpose some years before, with the inscription IOAN. COL.[65]

I will make an end, my dear Jonas, but first I must say a few words about the manner of man he was, then of his paradoxical opinions, and lastly of the storms by which his simple piety was put to the test, piety which was only to a very small degree the result of his natural disposition. For he was born with an exceptionally lofty spirit, most intolerant of any wrong, strongly disposed towards female society and self-indulgence and sleep, unusually inclined to joking and pleasantry (he told me this himself), and not entirely immune from the love of money.[66] Against these temptations he fought so successfully with the help of philosophy and sacred study and watching, fasting, and prayer, that he passed his whole life unspotted by the defilements of this world. As far as I could gather from his manner of life and his familiar conversation, he preserved his chastity to the day of his death. His wealth he distributed on charitable objects. His lofty spirit he fought against by the power of reason, and learnt to endure correction even from a child. Sex, sleep, and luxury he put to flight by habitual abstention from supper, unbroken sobriety, unwearying study, and religious conversation; and yet, if an opportunity had ever presented itself of joining in the merriment of a festive company or of conversing with the female sex or of taking his place at a grand dinner-party, one might have seen some traces of his natural bent. For this reason he usually abstained from the society of laymen, and particularly from dinner-parties; and if he was obliged to attend them, he used to take me or someone like me with him, that by speaking Latin he might be able to avoid lay conversation. And all the time he would eat a little of one sort of food only, and was satisfied with two or three draughts of beer, refraining from wine; though he enjoyed wine when it was good, but drank it very sparingly. As he thus had himself always under suspicion, he avoided everything in which he might give offence to others; for he was not unaware that all men's eyes were upon him.

I never met a more fertile mind, and for this reason he took especial delight in minds like his own; but he preferred to restrict himself to such topics as prepare us for immortality in the life to come. He would find a moral in everything if ever he relaxed under the charm of story-telling. In boys and girls what delighted him was the purity and simplicity of nature which Christ calls on his disciples to imitate;[67] and he would often compare them with angels.

To deal now with my second topic,[68] in his opinions he differed widely from the majority, but in this matter showed great wisdom in adjusting himself to others in order not to give offence or incur a stain on his reputation; for he knew how unfair men's judgments are, how ready they are to believe evil of anyone, and how much easier it is to hurt a man's reputation by malicious gossip than to mend it with praise. In the company of friends and other scholars he most freely admitted what he thought. Scotists,[69] who are thought by ordinary men to have minds which are somehow specially acute, seemed to him, he used to say, dull and slow-witted, and anything rather than gifted. To argue all the time about other men's opinions and language, gnawing away first at one point and then at another, and cutting everything up into fragments, was the mark of a barren and ill-furnished mind. But to Thomas he was for some reason more unfair than to Scotus. When I once praised Thomas[70] in his hearing as no negligible figure among recent philosophers, because he did seem to have read both sacred literature and the old authors (so I had come to suspect from what they call the *Catena aurea*[71]) and showed some sensibility in what he wrote, Colet concealed his feelings two or three times and said nothing. But on another occasion when I made the same remarks with more emphasis, he looked carefully at me, as though to see whether I meant it seriously or was pretending; and when he saw that I meant what I said, he broke out as though some spirit inspired him: 'How can you praise that man in front of me? Had he not been most arrogant, he could never have been so rash and so self-confident as to lay down definitions for everything; and had he not been touched by the spirit of this world, he would not have mixed up the whole of Christ's teaching with a gentile philosophy of his own.' I was surprised at the force with which he spoke, and began to read Thomas with more attention; I need not enlarge upon it – but I certainly formed a lower opinion of him than before.

Though no one was more devoted to Christian piety, he none the less had very little affection for monasteries, a name most of them now do not deserve; he contributed either nothing to them or very little, and even on his deathbed gave them no share. It was not that he disapproved of the orders, but that their members did not live up to their profession. It was his own dearest wish to extricate himself from this world, if he could have found a society that had truly sworn to live the life of the Gospel. And he had given me this task on my setting out for Italy, saying he had heard that among the Italians there were monks who were truly wise and pious.[72] For he did not think the religious life to be what is commonly supposed, since there is sometimes a lack of intellectual life. He used also to praise certain Germans,[73] among whom vestiges of the ancient religious life were said still to remain. He used to say that he never found more uncorrupted characters than among married couples;[74] for their natural affection, the care of their children, and the business of a household seemed to fence them in, as it were, so that they could not lapse indiscriminately into sin.

Although he lived a most virtuous life himself, yet among those whom he could not approve he was least hard on men whom although they were priests or even monks, committed nothing worse than sexual offences, not that he did not abhor the fault of unchastity, but that he found them by experience much less evil men when compared with others who were proud, jealous, tale-bearers, critical of others, dishonest, vain, ignorant, wholeheartedly abandoned to money or ambition, and yet seemed to themselves to be something; while the others, once they recognized their weakness, became more humble and more modest. He used to say that avarice and pride were much more to be abhorred in a priest than if he had a hundred concubines. Let no one distort this to show that he thought unchastity in priest or monk was a venial offence; let him understand that offences of the other class are much further from true piety.

There was no class of men to whom he was more hostile than bishops who behaved like wolves instead of shepherds, and none of whom he spoke more harshly, because they appealed to the people with liturgy and ceremonies and solemn benedictions and indulgences while serving the world, which means glory and gain, with all their hearts. He had learnt certain things from Dionysius[75] and from other very early theologians. He was not so much in favour of them that he would ever contend against the legislation of the church; but they made him less opposed to those who did not approve of the present indiscriminate adoration of images[76] in churches, whether painted, or made of wood, stone, bronze, gold, or silver; likewise to those who doubted whether a priest who was an open and notorious evil-liver can accomplish anything by his sacramental function.[77] It was not that he was the least in favour of their errors, but he was indignant with those who by the open and widespread corruption of their lives provided a reason for such suspicions.

The colleges[78] which have been founded in England at great expense and with such spendour were, he used to say, a hindrance to good learning, and nothing but an invitation to the lazy, nor did he attach much value to universities, on the ground that the ambition to hold a chair and make money ruined everything and undermined the integrity of every subject.

Secret confession he approved emphatically, saying that nothing else gave him so much consolation and encouragement, but anxious and continually repeated confessions he disapproved of just as much.[79] Though it is the custom in England for priests to say mass almost every day, he was content to celebrate on Sundays and festivals, or at least on very few days besides them; either because he was occupied with the sacred studies with which he used to prepare himself for preaching, and by the business of his cathedral, or because he discovered that he celebrated with more lively feeling if he did it at intervals. But he was far from disapproving the practice of those who prefer to approach the Lord's table every day.

Although himself a man of great learning, he did not approve the meticulous and laborious wisdom which seeks perfection from a knowledge of all subjects and the reading of all authors, as though to lose no approach; he used to say that this wore down the natural health and simple vigour of the human mind, and made men less healthy and less adapted to Christian innocence and pure and simple love of others. He gave great weight to the apostolic Epistles, but so much reverenced the wonderful majesty of Christ himself that, compared with that, even the writings of the apostles somehow lost their lustre. He had reduced almost all the sayings of Christ with great ingenuity to groups of three, out of which he had intended to write a book.[80] That priests, even busy priests, should be compelled to go right through such long prayers every day, even when at home or on a journey, surprised him greatly, for he was strongly in favour of making divine service a splendid thing.[81]

Countless opinions are most thoroughly accepted nowadays in our universities with which he strongly disagreed. He would sometimes speak of them among his intimate friends; in other company he did not mention them, to avoid the twofold trouble of simply making matters worse and of damaging his own reputation. No book was so heretical that he did not read it with attention, saying that he sometimes got more profit from them than from the books of men who define everything in such a way that they frequently pay a fulsome tribute to the leaders of their school, and sometimes to themselves. A fluent and accurate style should not, he held, be sought in the rules of the grammarians, which he declared to be a hindrance to good writing,[82] for it could only be derived from reading the best authors. But he himself suffered from this opinion; for though eloquent by nature and from his reading, and gifted while speaking with surprising fluency, he did from time to time make mistakes while writing of the kind that are blamed by the critics. This was, if I mistake not, the reason why he refrained from writing books.[83] And how I wish he had not refrained! – for I would gladly read the thoughts of such a man, whatever the language.

And now, that you may not think that there were any shortcomings in Colet's piety, let me tell you of the storms by which he was shaken.[84] He had never got on very well with his diocesan,[85] of whose character I will say nothing but that he was a fanatical and invincible Scotist[86] and thought himself a demigod on that account. I have known several people of the kind whom I should hesitate to call bad men, but I have never yet seen one whom in my opinion you could call a true and unblemished Christian. Nor was he[87] very popular with most of the members of his chapter, who found him too much of a disciplinarian; and from time to time they complained rather shrilly that they were being treated as monks, although their body was Eastminster[88] in the old days and is so called in ancient charters.

But when the dislike felt by his aged bishop, who was already not less than eighty, became so strong that it could no longer be concealed, he sent for two bishops of similar intelligence and no less virulent, and began to make trouble for Colet, using the same weapon that such men always use when they wish to destroy someone.[89] He reported him to the archbishop of Canterbury,[90] with a list of points which he had selected from Colet's sermons. One of these was that he said we must not worship images.[91] The second point was that he had deprived Paul of his well-known hospitality,[92] for in explaining that passage[93] in the Gospels 'Feed my sheep' three times repeated, he agreed as to the first two with other interpreters that it meant 'Feed them with examples of good life' and 'Feed them with the word of sound doctrine,' but had differed on the third, saying it could not be right that the apostles, who in those days were poor men, should be instructed to feed his sheep with material help in this world, and had substituted in its place some other meaning. The third point was that by saying in a sermon that some people read their sermons off sheets of paper, as many do in England with depressing effect, he had obliquely criticized the bishop, who was accustomed to do so from old age. The archbishop, who was perfectly familiar with Colet's gifts, took up the case of the innocent man, becoming defending counsel instead of judge, while Colet himself disdained to reply to these and other yet more foolish charges.

The old man's dislike, however, was not pacified. He tried to rouse the king's court against Colet, and first of all the king himself. They had now acquired another weapon, for Colet was reported to have said publicly in a sermon that an unjust peace was preferable to the most just of wars[94] – and preparations were already making for a war with France. Not the least part of this play was performed by two Minorites,[95] one of whom was a firebrand in the cause of war and earned a mitre; the other had a powerful voice and held forth in his sermons against the poets[96] – for so he labelled Colet, who, though not ignorant of music in other ways, had not a scrap of poetry in him. At this point that admirable young man the king gave clear proof of that intelligence so worthy of a crown, and urged Colet privately not to desist from using his learning freely to come to the rescue of a generation whose standards were so badly corrupted and not to deprive an age of such thick darkness of his peculiar light. He knew, he said, what had provoked those bishops to attack him, and was not unaware how much he had done for the English people by his life and his sacred learning. He added that he himself would suppress their efforts to such a tune that it might be clear to others that anyone attacking Colet would not go scot-free. At this point Colet thanked him for his truly royal spirit, but begged him not to do what he offered, saying that he did not wish any man to be worse off on his account and that he would rather resign from his position.

But a little later they were given such a handle as made them hope that they could put an end to Colet. Preparations were making for an expedition after Easter against the French.[97] On Good Friday[98] Colet delivered a marvellous sermon before the king and his court about the victory of Christ, exhorting all Christians to fight and conquer under the banner of their King. Those who fought with evil men in a spirit of hatred and of desire for evil, with mutual slaughter of each other, fought under the standard not of Christ but of the devil; and at the same time he showed how hard it is to die a Christian death, how few enter upon a war without being poisoned by hatred or by greed, how difficult it was for one man at the same time to love his brother – and without that no man will see God – and to plunge a weapon into his brother's entrails. He added that they ought to imitate Christ their King rather than characters like Julius and Alexander.[99] He made many other eloquent points to the same effect, so much so that the king was somewhat afraid that this sermon might demoralize the soldiers whom he was leading into battle. At this point the forces of evil began to gather like birds mobbing an owl,[100] hoping that it would now be possible to poison the king's mind against him. Colet was sent for at the king's command. He came, and dined in a small house of Franciscans[101] attached to the palace at Greenwich.[102] When the king knew that he was there, he came down into the monastery garden, and on Colet's appearance sent away all his entourage.

When the two of them were alone together, he told Colet to cover his head and talk to him informally; and thus that most civilized young man began: 'Do not be in a hurry to suspect anything, Mr Dean; I have not sent for you in order to interrupt your most sacred labours, of which I have the highest possible opinion, but to clear my conscience of some scruples, and ask your advice how I may do my duty more effectively.' But I must not repeat the whole conversation, which was prolonged for about an hour and a half. Meanwhile at court Bricotus,[103] a Franciscan turned bishop, was in a fever, thinking that Colet now really was in peril, while in fact he and the king were in agreement on all points; only the king expressed the wish that what Colet had said, which was perfectly true, might sometime be repeated more clearly for the benefit of the unlettered soldiery, who might interpret it in a sense he had not intended – that for Christians there can never be a just war.[104] Colet, being a sensible man and a man of singularly well-balanced mind, not only satisfied the king, but increased the king's original esteem for him. When they returned to the palace, the king, preparing to dismiss Colet, sent for a cup of wine and drank to him; then embraced him in the kindest way, and dismissed him with all the promises that could be expected from the most loving prince. The crowd of courtiers were now standing round, waiting to see the outcome of this conversation. And there, in the hearing of them all, the king said: 'To every man his own teacher, and let each man back up the teacher of his choice. This is the teacher for me.' So some of them departed, like wolves in the proverb,[105] gaping because they have lost their prey, and Bricot in particular; and from that day forward no one dared attack Colet any more.

You have before you, dear Justus, not a portrait but such a sketch as fits the narrow limits of a letter, of two men born in our own day who were in my opinion truly and sincerely Christians. It will be for you to choose out of them both what seems to you to help most towards a really religious life. If you now ask which I prefer, they seem to me to deserve equal credit, when one considers their different surroundings. It was a great thing that Colet in his station in life should have followed so steadfastly the call, not of his nature, but of Christ; yet Vitrier's achievement is more remarkable, in that he developed and demonstrated so much of the spirit of the Gospel in that sort of life, like a fish that lives in stagnant water and yet has no taste of the marsh about it. But in Colet there were some things which showed that he was only human; in Vitrier I never saw anything which in any way had a flavour about it of human weakness. If you take my advice, dear Jonas, you will not hesitate to add the names of both to the calendar of saints, although no pope may ever write them into the canon.

O blessed souls, to whom my debt is so great, assist by your prayers your friend Erasmus, who is still struggling with the evils of this life, that I may find my way back into your society, never thereafter to be parted from you.

Farewell, my dear Jonas. I am content if I have done justice to what you wanted; for I know that I have by no means done justice to my subject.

From my country retreat at Anderlecht, 13 June 1521

1212 / To Louis Guillard — Anderlecht, 17 June 1521

This letter presents the sequel to an earlier, indirect approach to the bishop of Tournai, with whom Erasmus is not known to have had any previous connections. The first appeal had evidently been made through the good services of Pieter de Vriendt (cf lines 3–4) and had induced the bishop to redress Erasmus' complaints, but perhaps not as firmly as the latter would have liked (cf lines 24–9). This letter was published in the *Epistolae ad diversos*.

ERASMUS OF ROTTERDAM TO THE RIGHT REVEREND LOUIS, BISHOP OF TOURNAI, GREETING

Indeed I was most fortunate, my Lord Bishop, in that letter of mine to Pieter de Vriendt,[1] for it produced a result I would scarcely have dared to hope for in the shape of a most kind letter from your Lordship, which was evidence of your good will towards me and gave me, as it were, a lively picture of your unusual good nature and that zeal for true religion of which reports from many people had not left me in ignorance.

Your suffragan[2] I would gladly forgive for having been misled by others into his public attacks on my reputation, had the insult been a light one or had his position entitled him to be excused. As things are, what could be more outrageous than in a public utterance – a sermon, no less – to use obvious fabrications and actual falsehoods to attack the honour of a man who has done nothing to deserve it, in fact quite the opposite, and to charge him with heresy, the most odious word one Christian can bring against another? And the man who does this is a monk, of mature years, a theologian, and a bishop, and, what is more, the vicegerent of so highly respected a prelate as yourself! And is any buffoon shameless enough to outdo the impudence of his answer, when asked what heresy in my books had offended him? 'I have not read Erasmus' books' says he. 'I had it in mind to read the paraphrases, but the Latin looked so abstruse that I was afraid he might possibly slip into some heresy.' This was the excuse offered by that superb theologian to a man of great intelligence and no common learning.

Be that as it may, by the severity of the letter in which you told the man not to rant so shamelessly in future against the reputation of those who are doing some service to biblical studies you did your duty as a worthy prelate; but this approach does more for other people than it does for me. If only that scorpion could withdraw into himself the venom[3] he has implanted in the minds of his unlettered hearers! In letters from friends I am told that in a sermon before the most Christian king of France a certain monk[4] gave an even more crazy exhibition, declaring that the approach of Antichrist was now at hand, for we have seen his four forerunners, some Minorite or other in Italy, Luther in Germany, Jacques Lefèvre in France, and Erasmus in Brabant. Do men of such effrontery regard great princes as such blockheads that they understand nothing and swallow everything, or such rascals that venomous falsehoods give them pleasure? Or do they just despise them?

But these things happen almost every day, and I ought to have grown hardened to them long ago, especially since I see that the only result of these insane disorders is to advertise their compound of stupidity and ignorance and malice to the world. As for me, whether I have made any useful contribution to sacred studies, I do not know; at least I have tried with might and main, so that if I am thought to deserve no credit, at any rate I cannot be thought to deserve this abuse. The subject of the work which in your zeal for religion you suggest to me would certainly appeal to me very much, but at the moment I had no leisure to undertake it, being fully occupied in preparing the third edition of my New Testament[5] and revising the works of St Augustine.[6] But I will think about this later when I have time. In the mean time, I am surprised that your Lordship should ask this of an old cistern like myself, when you have at home a most copious fount of excellence in Josse Clichtove.[7] You offer me all the aid and service in your power; but for the moment I ask nothing except that you should continue your support of the humanities and of sacred studies, and enter Erasmus' name among your well-wishers. You will find him a humble and affectionate dependant who will be no trouble. Farewell.

From my country retreat at Anderlecht, 17 June 1521

1213 / From Paolo Bombace — Rome, 18 June 1521

This is one of the few letters addressed to Erasmus that were published in the *Epistolae ad diversos*, in this case together with his answer, Ep 1236. Bombace, an old friend, was attached to the papal court, where Erasmus now needed much good will (cf Ep 1180 introduction, below n8). In the first paragraph he cautiously invites Erasmus to spend his remaining years with him in Rome, although lines 67–9 discount any expectation that Erasmus might come soon, while in the third paragraph he urges Erasmus to write against Luther. Above all he answers an inquiry stemming from Erasmus' continued preoccupation with the Greek New Testament.

PAOLO BOMBACE TO HIS FRIEND ERASMUS, GREETING

If I write to you so carelessly and so seldom, dear Erasmus, you must not suppose there is any reason except a continuous and confused mass of business which is very foreign to our studious life of long ago,[1] and which for several years now has so broken up my time that it has almost divorced me from all learning and literature and reduced me to a sort of exile from the Muses. In all this I try as best as I can not only to perform my task, though it goes against the grain, but to give satisfaction; and to this I am driven by a kind of misplaced sense of shame, for fear that, when I have so great an opportunity to do things well, the critical public may judge that I have not done my best and think me of no account; while all the time I get older, as you see, nor do my resources increase beyond the point where I need not be concerned about them and they can make up by themselves for my sacrifice of the humanities. Though I am not so badly treated that I need fear a return to teaching.[2] For I have brought up my annual income to four hundred ducats[3] with no religious obligations attached, which I owe not to fortune but to my own efforts; and this I could never have expected, never even have dreamt of, from the leisured literary life of the old days. If I could someday enjoy this freely in your company, I should not envy Croesus his riches, and should secure a formal release from these tedious and illiberal preoccupations. And so, as Hercules did to set Theseus free,[4] I beg and pray that you, to release your Bombace from his chains, will betake yourself, not like Hercules to the nether regions, but to the light of this place which is more unconfined and more brilliant than it is elsewhere, provided you think me the sort of person whom you would not be sorry to have as a companion in your studies or at least an admirer of the result.

There are several great men here, let me tell you, who are great supporters of your reputation and defend you against all comers. Leo x you have very much on your side; and whenever he is shown a letter from you to anyone, he reads it eagerly and praises it without reserve. Your last letter to me[5] was shown to him by the cardinal my master,[6] and having read it he asked for it again a few days later and gave it to Sadoleto[7] and other scholars to read. In which, at least in my opinion, you seemed to make this one mistake, that there was too much about a certain person,[8] though your reputation is now so great that you can afford to ignore any remarks made about you that smack more of prejudice than judgment, especially as Pope Leo thinks so well of you that, when some Spaniard[9] made a wanton attack on your work, he told the man, I understand, not to publish anything attacking your reputation in future, and if he took a fancy to champion the truth, he must do so with moderation and show that he had allowed no room for hate and jealousy.

If then you have him so well disposed to you while you say nothing in defence of his just and holy cause, what result might you not expect if you were to take up arms and do battle vigorously,[10] as you know so well how to do, in his behalf, or rather in behalf of truth itself, which your supporters of Luther, with their zeal for revolution and their ill-timed revival of heresies long since exploded and extinct, are striving to uproot by godless methods and entirely overthrow? This is what most people expected of you, speaking as though those monsters had been provided by some destiny for you alone as a road to greatness and immortality. Against which I would advise you, if I thought I knew anything, especially in such a well-known business, that is concealed from you. One thing at least I do know, that all the other labours which you have undertaken hitherto with your nightly vigils and all your writing have been absolutely barren when compared with what this piece of work would be. I am not unaware what particularly discourages you from doing this; I do not mean the risk of offending many people,[11] which there would be some danger in undertaking, but the unfettered licence of certain idiots who seem to go astray on purpose[12] and while trying to defend what is in itself an admirable cause do it very serious damage and discourage all the really good people who have carefully to watch their own position for fear they may be thought to partake of their idiocy, from defending it. I should not myself suppose their foolish raving to be so important that I might be thought to forget where my duty lay. When you say that it was expedient that this question should be dealt with by other people and on other lines, many now agree with you, and I always was of this opinion. But let us not go through it all again, rather than discover some remedy.

When I hear that you have reached Basel,[13] I shall try to arrange my work so that it is possible for me to approach you, indeed interrupt you, with more frequent letters. All this time, while you were in Louvain, I reflected how much space lay between us, and could scarcely bring myself to write to you. Now I must do my best to see that you never grow tired of the nonsense which, however busy I may be, I mean to rain upon you until you can take no more.

The first Epistle of John written in very ancient characters I have at last found in the Vatican library;[14] the verses in chapter 4[15] run as follows:

> *᾿Αγαπητοί, μὴ παντὶ πνεύματι πιστεύετε, ἀλλὰ δοκιμάζετε τὰ πνεύματα, εἰ ἐκ τοῦ Θεοῦ ἐστιν, ὅτι πολλοὶ ψευδοπροφῆται ἐξεληλύθασιν εἰς τὸν κόσμον. Ἐν τούτῳ γινώσκετε τὸ Πνεῦμα τοῦ Θεοῦ. Πᾶν πνεῦμα ὃ ὁμολογεῖ Ἰησοῦν Χριστὸν ἐν σαρκὶ ἐληλυθέναι, ἐκ τοῦ Θεοῦ ἐστι. Καὶ πᾶν πνεῦμα ὃ μὴ ὁμολογεῖ τὸν Ἰησοῦν, ἐκ τοῦ Θεοῦ οὐκ ἔστιν. Καὶ τοῦτό ἐστι τὸ τοῦ ἀντιχρίστου. ᾿Ακηκόατε ὅτι ἔρχεται, καὶ τὰ λοιπά.*

and again in chapter 5:[16]

> *Ὅτι τρεῖς εἰσιν οἱ μαρτυροῦντες, τὸ Πνεῦμα καὶ τὸ ὕδωρ καὶ τὸ αἷμα, καὶ οἱ τρεῖς εἰς τὸ ἕν εἰσιν. Εἰ τὴν μαρτυρίαν τῶν ἀνθρώπων λαμβάνομεν, ἡ μαρτυρία τοῦ Θεοῦ μείζων ἐστίν. Ὅτι αὕτη ἐστὶν ἡ μαρτυρία τοῦ Θεοῦ, ὅτι μεμαρτύρηκε περὶ τοῦ υἱοῦ αὐτοῦ. Ὁ πιστεύων εἰς τὸν υἱὸν τοῦ Θεοῦ ἔχει τὴν μαρτυρίαν ἐν αὐτῷ· ὁ μὴ πιστεύων τῷ Θεῷ ψεύστην πεποίηκεν αὐτόν, ὅτι οὐ πεπίστευκεν εἰς τὴν μαρτυρίαν ἣν μεμαρτύρηκεν ὁ Θεὸς περὶ τοῦ υἱοῦ αὐτοῦ. Καὶ αὕτη ἐστὶν ἡ μαρτυρία, ὅτι ζωὴν αἰώνιον, καὶ τὰ λοιπά.*

How this differs from the printed editions,[17] you do not need me to tell you. If there is any point on which you need my opinion, not so much in this question as in many others over which doctors dispute, there shall be no concealment or hesitation; I shall speak out, as you know I do. Farewell, and give my greetings to the scholars in your society.

From the City, 18 June 1521

1214 / To Lieven Hugenoys — Anderlecht, 21 June 1521

Lieven Hugenoys (d 1537), the Benedictine abbot of St Bavo's, Ghent, had renewed his earlier acquaintance with Erasmus (cf n2) by sending him a gift and offering him his friendship in the accompanying letter. Erasmus released this answer, but not the abbot's letter, for publication in the *Epistolae ad diversos*.

ERASMUS OF ROTTERDAM TO THE VERY REVEREND LIEVEN, ABBOT OF THE MONASTERY OF ST BAVO IN GHENT, GREETING

What comes unearned is all the more highly valued; what comes quite unexpected often gives the greater pleasure. Sometimes too the giver's high position adds value to his gift. But nothing is in itself of so little worth as not to be sure of a warm welcome if it has its origin in friendly feelings. Imagine then how many reasons I had to enjoy your gift, my lord Abbot, which you sent by that excellent man Cornelis,[1] the treasury counsel, when I was so little expecting it that had it fallen from the sky it could not have been more of a surprise. What is sent unasked to one who has done nothing to deserve it and has never even dreamt of expecting it can only come from a heart full of good will. The present itself is most acceptable, and your words make it more so. You say it is no present, but a symbol of what you feel; you say it is not sent to enrich me but to bring your greetings. And so I gratefully accept your attitude, and I acknowledge my debt. Though I give you equal friendship in return, you will still have the advantage, because you first issued the invitation to be friends. For in the intercourse I had with you at Ghent and Termonde,[2] I showed such bad manners that more than once I was afraid that I had quite hurt your feelings. A man who can take such provocation and still be friends deserves, I think, to be loved in return with one's whole heart.

Now Marcus Laurinus,[3] the dean of St Donatian's, has promised me a very ancient manuscript from your library, which is said to contain St Jerome's commentary on the Psalms.[4] If this cannot conveniently be sent me, I should wish at least to have two or three pages copied out, in hopes of discovering by the comparison whether the commentary we possess in print is spurious or mutilated, or no. If to do even that is not convenient, I think I shall return to Bruges[5] about the beginning of August. So then I shall be able to greet you, Father, at least in passing. Farewell, most truly reverend Father in Christ Jesus.

From Anderlecht, 21 June 1521

1215 / To Karl Harst — Anderlecht, 22 June 1521

This letter is addressed to a young man who would later as a councillor at the court of Jülich-Cleves occupy a prominent position in the circle of Erasmus' friends there. Karl Harst (1492–1563) had studied in Cologne and subsequently in Orléans as a contemporary of Adolf Eichholz (cf Ep 866) and the future chancellor of Jülich-Cleves, Johann Gogreve (cf Ep 2298). He was now in Louvain and studying with Conradus Goclenius. Later in the year he demonstrated his admiration for Erasmus by accompanying him on his journey to Basel as far as Koblenz (cf Ep 1242 introduction, Allen Ep 1342:176–7).

This letter was printed in the *Epistolae ad diversos*.

ERASMUS OF ROTTERDAM TO HIS FRIEND KARL HARST, GREETING

So I owe you a double debt, my dear Karl, for wanting to come and see me, and for not coming in case you interrupted my work. You congratulate me on this country retreat of mine;[1] at any rate, nothing I have done for many months now has turned out a greater success. I was done for, had I not left behind the stench of cities. I was already beginning to be involved with the physicians, and those I consulted had all prescribed different medicines. I took none of them, the only reason being that I had no leisure to be ill, with fresh business constantly summoning me elsewhere. Not but what the beggar-bullies[2] find their way even here; is there any place they cannot reach? And every day I hear foolish stories from my neighbours.

What you suggest about Carinus[3] I put in train some time ago. I directed it to Nesen, but the man to whom I had entrusted the letter told me he gave it to Capito. Conradus Goclenius is a man richly endowed with learning of every kind. Do all you can to pick his brains, and return home like a keen and enterprising merchant loaded with goods of the highest quality. Above all, learn how to sharpen your pen, that some day you may take these noisy fellows who so stupidly resist sound learning and paint them in their true colours. Farewell.

From my country retreat in Anderlecht, 22 June 1521

1216 / To Pierre Barbier — Anderlecht, 26 June 1521

Barbier, an old friend, was now in the service of Cardinal Adrian of Utrecht, the future Pope Adrian VI, who was Charles V's regent in Spain. Erasmus' attitude towards the cardinal was becoming more sympathetic (cf the preface and Ep 1166 n30); no doubt he hoped that this letter and subsequent ones to Barbier (Epp 1225, 1235) would be reported to Adrian.

Published in the *Epistolae ad diversos*, this letter shows many analogies, some of them literal, to the introductory section of Erasmus' first *Apologia* against López Zúñiga; cf n1.

ERASMUS OF ROTTERDAM TO PIERRE BARBIER, GREETING

At last[1] I have secured a copy of Diego López Zúñiga's attack on me, and find him a much better scholar and less spiteful, if judged by the standard of Lee and his falsehoods. I have no wish to damage his reputation; in fact I even wish him a double portion of what he so generously allows himself, although he is so mean towards me that he strips me of everything – brains, memory, judgment, scholarship, familiarity with Scripture, knowledge of the tongues, and even of grammar – while claiming for himself charmingly enough a kind of horn of plenty[2] overflowing with them all. At least he has provided a pretty counterweight to the excessive admiration of some people, who extol me until they make an elephant out of a fly;[3] he finds me a pygmy and leaves me a gnat. That he should think so much of himself causes me neither surprise nor envy. But I do wonder what could have so embittered him against me; for I never hurt him by so much as a word, nor can I believe that a spirit of gentle birth (and I am told that he combines a distinguished pedigree[4] with his scholarship) could harbour so much ill will, unless some rascal were at hand to instigate it. I now hear that the cardinal of Toledo,[5] of blessed memory, who has again, alas, been followed by our own de Croy,[6] advised him to send his work to me before publishing it; if my reply should be satisfactory, it would be better for Zúñiga, he thought, to suppress the book than to publish it; but if I did not answer, or sent an impudent and ignorant reply, he could publish his labours, and good luck to them. The moment the cardinal was dead,[7] however, he sent his work to the printers, although at that time he could not be unaware that a second edition of the New Testament either had just appeared or would appear shortly.

Whatever the answer to this, I at least am happy to think that the ancient tongues and the humanities are flourishing in Spain as well; and of Zúñiga's gifts I have considerable expectations. But I fear that among intelligent men and good scholars he will gain less glory than he seems to promise himself from this book which is his first bid for fame. Let him by all means convince us[8] that he is exceptionally well equipped in all languages and literatures and in long and diligent study of the Fathers, and knows very well what concessions to make to a translator who sometimes makes a slip in the most obvious places. Let him show it was only yesterday or the day before that I began to read the patristic commentators, and that I have no understanding of Jerome, though it is twenty years since I wrote my *Enchiridion*, in which I adduce such a mass of testimony in some disorder (as he rightly says), with no assistance all this time from indexes,[9] in which he has been more fortunate than I. But who will believe him when he says he began this work with no desire to speak ill of anyone and 'with a mind entirely free from controversy'[10] – when the whole thing from beginning to end is nothing but lordly mockery of me and criticism and abuse? He imputes to me the mistakes of others – the printers, for instance, or Oecolampadius[11] – in the most unpleasant way, and sometimes stirs up an outrageous fuss over some quite straightforward statement,[12] such as that Naples is now occupied by Spain, and that *Spania* is used for Spain by St Paul. From time to time as a great insult he calls me a Dutchman, as though it ought to be held against me if I were born in Sogdiana,[13] or as if any region of the world could despise Holland, whether you consider its level of culture, its large and famous cities, its material wealth, or its reputation as the nurse of gifted minds – which are so gifted and so common there, that compared with them I really might seem what Zúñiga makes me out to be!

And not content with an introduction[14] to his work written in such a spirit that it contains almost as many jibes at me as it does words, almost every note is supplied with a new opening and a conclusion which give him a chance to abuse me. And again, as though that were not enough, he adds marginal summaries which are more prickly than the text itself. So difficult was it to satisfy that modest spirit that was 'entirely free from controversy.'

I rather wonder whether it will be thought truly wise to affirm that his translator[15] made a neat and elegant version of the New Testament. At any rate, he will not be thought to honour his undertaking to defend his translator against all attacks, if he makes no reply at all on the many bad mistakes I have pointed out. Such is the damning effect of his silence on the author whom he so grandly undertook to defend; though it was no part of my purpose to attack his translator, for what good would that do me? All I do is to make notes in passing of anything which might, I thought, be useful to a careful reader. How much damage Zúñiga may have done to my reputation, I do not know; but at any rate I could wish he had taken more thought for his own. I can easily take in good part anything that promotes the cause of learning. And reasonable discussion does indeed sharpen our wits; but this virulence which now, by some strange dispensation, exacerbates everything, I could wish to see banished from all honourable studies, and particularly from theology.

As for you, my dear Barbier, you have tormented me far too long with hopes of seeing you, for you deceive me continually with some fresh expectation.[16] My own departure[17] has been delayed by several other things, but the principal reason was a very great desire to see you. If you have the same wish to see me, you must hurry; for I am so bombarded here every day by the abuse[18] of these noisy ruffians that there is some danger that this rain of stones on my solitary head will prove the death of me. The tragedy of Luther is finished among us here;[19] and how I wish it had never appeared upon the stage! The one thing certain people are afraid of is that having so eagerly avoided Scylla we may be swept into Charybdis,[20] and that some men may make a more cruel use of this victory than can be good for the health of Christendom. Farewell, my patron without peer.

From Anderlecht, which has turned me from a townsman into a countryman,[21] and this I find quite agreeable, 26 June 1521

1217 / To the Theologians of Louvain — Anderlecht, [June–July] 1521

At an unspecified date during his stay at Anderlecht (cf Ep 1208 introduction) Erasmus launched this further protest against his critics in Louvain, especially Vincentius Theoderici and Nicolaas Baechem Egmondanus. In contrast to earlier complaints addressed to the rector of the university, who at that time was himself a theologian (cf Epp 1153, 1164, 1172), this one is addressed to the theological faculty collectively. At the end of February the theologian Godschalk Rosemondt had been succeeded as rector by Joost Vroye of Gavere, doctor of arts and law (cf *Matricule de Louvain* III-1 646), who was close to Erasmus (cf Ep 717:22) and therefore not suited to act in this matter or to appear associated with it in a programmatic letter intended for publication and actually printed in the *Epistolae ad diversos*.

Allen was no doubt right to place this letter with Epp 1216, 1218. The activities of Aleandro in Louvain (c 21–7 June, cf Ep 1216 n19) and subsequently in other cities culminated on 13 July with the burning of Luther's books at Antwerp, where popular resistance ran strong. Baechem was the preacher on that occasion and earned the nuncio's praise (cf Ep 1186 n8; Balan no 108). To Erasmus this raised the spectre that the campaign against him too might reach a new pitch; cf Epp 1218:7–17, 25–7, 1228.

ERASMUS OF ROTTERDAM TO THE THEOLOGIANS OF LOUVAIN, GREETING

Reverend and honourable Fathers, with my humble duty. When I consider the responsible behaviour to be expected of a faculty of theology, and my own innocence, or rather (if I may speak with some self-assurance) the services I have rendered to students of Christian literature, I would rather not believe what I am told. Yet I am told it by so many people, and by people of such standing, that a thing cannot seem wholly baseless which rests on the testimony of so many witnesses of such high character. It was in the interests of us all that this sorry business, which has now continued between us for some years to your great loss and mine, should at last be brought to an end. What good I have done with all my labours is best left to the impartial judgment of posterity; what I have suffered in Louvain from the poisonous tongues of certain persons I could name, must by now be common knowledge.

I now hear that trouble is breaking out again, the ringleaders responsible for this being Vincentius[1] and Latomus, one of whom resents a letter to the cardinal of Mainz in which he thinks I criticize the Dominican order,[2] while the other has taken offence at a plan for making peace in this sad business of Luther,[3] which has been published anonymously and is said by some over-suspicious people to come from me. Let me say first that the letter, which was written before either your adverse verdict or the papal censure had been promulgated,[4] has no object in principle except to put Luther right,[5] in preference to destroying him and setting the world by the ears. This letter I had sent under seal to a member of the Cardinal's household,[6] authorizing him to deliver it, if he thought it would do any good, but if not, to burn it. He waited some time before delivering it and, before doing so, had it printed with, I am told, some changes in the wording; for where I had written 'Luther,' he substituted 'my friend Luther.'[7] That the question should be abandoned without more ado to the disorderly clamour of casual public opinion seemed wrong to me then, and seems wrong now; and this gives more weight in all men's thinking to the condemnation of the Paris authorities,[8] which will prove to have been belated. No religious order has ever been criticized by me or aroused my dislike.[9] Bad men I dislike, under whatever garb they may be concealed. For an order to achieve the highest standing in public affairs lies in its own hands and not in mine. If they have set their hearts on popularity, let them develop the qualities which earn a high reputation and influence and good will. If they find themselves less highly valued than they would wish, let them reform those faults from which they feel that their loss of reputation takes its rise.

So much for the letter. The plan did not come from me, but from a Dominican theologian of no mean learning.[10] It was shown to a certain prince[11] to see whether he approved, and this was done before the publication of *De captivitate Babylonica*,[12] when the situation was as yet more capable of remedy. This too by some chance was published by the Germans, who seem to have some sort of policy of keeping nothing dark.[13] As far as I am concerned, it was shown to me at that stage[14] by the Dominican I speak of, who will not deny that it is his; and, to speak frankly, I did not entirely dislike it. His object was not to secure the withdrawal of the papal censure, or of your own, but to get satisfaction for the convictions of those who protested loudly, and still protest, that Luther is being suppressed by authority; nor would the pope's authority suffer in any way if he willingly relaxed his severity to some extent in the cause of public peace. And this plan found approval with kings as well, had not *De captivitate* and other pamphlets like it alienated the sympathies of most of them. When one is formally asked one's opinion, anyone is free, I imagine, to say what he thinks; and a religious man will do what he can for the public peace, provided the pope's dignity is unimpaired.[15] If this is not lawful, how could exactly this policy be followed with enthusiasm, when Luther was at Worms, by men of the highest reputation,[16] and that too with public applause? And so, if this famous plan were my work, which it is not, I still do not see why this tragic uproar should be aroused for my benefit. As it is, it has its proper author, who will not be ashamed to own it.

You may remember all the tragic storms that blew up for me from the entirely groundless suspicion,[17] when Luther's works first appeared, and there was a bit of preface in rather better Latin; though it is perfectly true, and I have often asserted it, that in all his books there is not a syllable that was written with my knowledge or consent. On the contrary, this is the outcome I have always feared, and therefore I have tried in all possible ways to deter the man from writing in this fashion. It is now for you in your wisdom to take care that from suspicion you do not do fresh evil to your neighbour. It is a form of manslaughter to attack a man's reputation.[18] This makes me wonder all the more what object Vincentius can have in mind, who never ceases to abuse me most grossly in season and out of season, to tear my reputation in pieces, and to rain scurrilities on me like stones.[19] Even were I the sort of man that he falsely says I am, such abusive language would be a disgrace to a priest and a monk and a theologian, and fraught with peril too for your university; for his example may encourage its members to rant like this even against those who have done no harm. He could hardly do his order a greater disservice. Virulent and unbridled malevolence does not commend itself even to those who wish to see me in trouble. In fact, those who are already strangers to me it cannot estrange further, and those who wish me well find it objectionable. And everywhere I have well-wishers not a few, not because I have set myself in any way to win their favour, but they are bound to me by the value they set on my work. Were I willing to use my pen with the same licence he allows his tongue, what then? Surely the outcome would be raving madness, and we should be a scandal both to Christians and to the enemies of Christianity. But he despises me – as though I had not far more reasons to despise him in my turn, if mutual contempt were permitted to a Christian heart; or as though I would allow myself to do battle with a man like him, if the contest were a matter of our intellectual gifts. If we are to compete in poisonous scurrility and shameless insolence, it will be easy to find some women[20] who can take on this kind of men.

But let us say no more of Vincentius, by whom, be he what manner of man he may, I shall not let myself be defeated if he competes with me in anything good – if, that is, he contributes something which can do more for Christ's glory and for true religion. With Latomus I am sorry to find myself in disagreement, for his learning is by no means to be despised and he has some acquaintance with the Muses of literature; and I am sorry to believe what I hear none the less from many quarters, especially as I have never done him wrong. One thing we must avoid, even at this late hour: we must not snap at each other till each proves the other's undoing. Civil strife has never been to my taste. I have never had a hand in any faction, neither Reuchlin's nor Luther's;[21] the glory of Christ I have always supported to the best of my power. To your university I have been no disgrace and no embarrassment. Luther's pamphlets I have done more to resist than any mortal man,[22] not that I am unaware that much of his advice is sound, but because I see that an honourable silence[23] is better than an ill-starred attempt at reform. In all the things that truly or falsely pass under his name, there is not one letter that belongs to me. As to the spiteful pamphlets that appear in crowds everywhere,[24] I wish I could stop them, for my own sake if nothing else. All of them increase my burden of unpopularity and some traduce me as well; and the praise in them does more harm than the abuse. One thing is absolutely certain – in all of them there is nothing of mine.[25] Of the authors of some of them I have my suspicions; but of the majority I cannot even guess the source.

I have been approached by many men,[26] even men in high place, to come into the field on Luther's side. I have felt certain other pressures, of which this is not the place to speak. All this I have rejected with every fibre of my being.[27] His opponents, monks especially, have attacked me so savagely, that even had I previously been Luther's enemy, their hostility might have driven me to join him. On the other side, I observe that Luther's supporters have done all they could to drag me in by force whether I would or no. None of this has made me abandon my position. Examine everything I have written, every word even that I have uttered light-heartedly over the wine: you will find nothing except my dislike of sudden and violent uproar in public places and my preference for settling questions without setting the world by the ears. If other people prefer a different method, I pray it may prosper in the cause of Christ; but up to now what the outcome will be, I know not.

If it lay with me, this tempest would be stilled tomorrow. If my friendship with you is not intimate, this is not my fault. We made a start in the Falcon;[28] we had agreed to let bygones be bygones, although all that had gone wrong before had fallen on my head. Johannes Atensis[29] would not have been anxious for a reconciliation, had he not been aware how groundless were the suspicions which had deceived him into stirring up this trouble for me. Nor do I see what prevented that agreement from remaining in force, except that Egmondanus was not really satisfied. Nor do I see what should have set him against me, except that for the abuse which he piled on me before he had even seen me I did not show proper gratitude. If this is certain people's policy, to attack me in any way they can, with no holds barred[30] and their charges all false, let them observe first of all that this may not be such plain sailing as they think; and if they are successful, let them observe that the outcome may not be so happy as they promise themselves. Lastly, if they have made up their minds to destroy Luther, they will find that this will go a little better if they leave me out of it. None the less, whatever other men may set on foot, no one shall separate me from the rock that is Christ, none shall involve me in any faction. Had I been of Luther's party[31] –

I will go this far – his affairs would be in better case. But heaven forbid that I should be of any party save only Christ's.

Hitherto I have not written against him. True enough. If I get no credit for my fear of the dangers; if, besides countless other reasons, my lack of leisure, my age, and my indifferent health are not in my favour, let me at least plead my lack of skill in theology,[32] which they attribute to me in such great measure and which I largely admit. And in the end, now that three universities have condemned Luther,[33] now that the supreme pontiff himself has launched his thunderbolt against him, now that the emperor has added his,[34] what further weight can my censure carry, who am a worm and no man? – especially now that so many learned men (as you think them) come forward to attack Luther in print? And yet as far as in me lies, I will not abandon the peace of the Catholic church, the truth of the Gospel and the dignity of the roman pontiff, while this is possible.[35] And perhaps I may carry more weight than those who think that this uproar can settle the question. Of one thing we must be careful, that if we hate Luther we do not by so doing lose the things that really matter; that if we are the slaves of our own personal authority we do not undermine the authority of the gospel truth; that if we are supporters of human glory, we do not stand in the way of the glory of Christ. In the mean while, if you have anything against me, do not pursue it with scurrilities, as Egmondanus lately did before Rosemondt[36] your rector, and as Vincentius does all the time. Produce your arguments, and I will satisfy you on every point. Nay, if you are willing to compete with me in friendly actions, I shall not let myself be beaten; but if any prefer to strive with me as enemies, I shall make no effort to win in that line of strife, but I shall endeavour to defend my innocence, and am confident of the help of Christ and of all good men. My reverend Lords and honourable brethren in Christ, I wish you farewell.

Anderlecht, 1521

1218 / To Richard Pace Brussels, 5 July 1521

Allen's text here translated is based on the original letter, in Erasmus' own hand throughout, preserved in the British Library, London, MS Harley 6989 f 5. The letter was first edited in 1699 from the transcript of a seventeenth-century copy, which is now f 6 of the same Harleian volume; for details see Allen's headnote.

Epp 1218–20 were perhaps sent to England together. With the first two Erasmus evidently intended to clear himself of allegations circulating at the English court that he stood behind Luther (cf Ep 1219:6–9). Such a vindication of his orthodoxy seemed all the more indicated as he was expecting shortly to meet many of his English friends in the entourage of Cardinal Wolsey (cf Ep 1223 introduction).

In view of the proximity of Anderlecht to Brussels (cf Ep 1208 introduction), Erasmus' visits to the capital city were bound to be frequent, especially after the return there (on 14 June; cf Gachard II 28) of Charles V and his court; cf Epp 1221:4, 1233 n28, 1248:17, Allen Ep 1342:64–5.

Greeting. If only this tragedy which Luther has begun with such bad omens for us might be given a happy ending by some god from the machine![1] He himself has offered his enemies a weapon with which they can deal him a fatal wound,[2] and has behaved as though he had no wish for his own safety, though in letters from me and advice from his friends he has been constantly warned to keep his pen, that lethal weapon, under control.[3] There is such bitterness in him that, even if all he has written were perfectly true, the business cannot have a happy outcome. But I fear that the Jacobites,[4] and certain theologians I could name, will make a far from moderate use of their victory, especially the Louvain people, who are engaged in a sort of private vendetta against me.[5] For this they have acquired the most appropriate possible tool in Girolamo Aleandro. He is mad enough by nature, even without any encouragement; and he now has men to encourage him who might drive even the most balanced mind quite mad. The most poisonous pamphlets come pouring out everywhere,[6] all of them fathered on me by Aleandro, though I did not know that many of them existed until I heard of them from him.[7] Luther has acknowledged his own productions before the emperor;[8] and yet one of them, *De captivitate Babylonica*, he[9] still says is mine. What a ready pen I must have, to be able to run off all these tracts! – though all the time I am burdened with the great difficulty of revising my New Testament[10] and correcting the works of Augustine,[11] as well as other sections of my research. My life upon it, in all Luther's books there is not a syllable of mine, nor has any defamatory work appeared which I had anything to do with;[12] in fact I continually discourage them.

At the moment their object is to show that Luther has taken some things out of my books,[13] as though he had not taken more out of the Pauline Epistles! Now at length I perceive that it was the policy of the Germans all along to drag me willy-nilly into this business of Luther. An idiotic idea, I must say! Was anything more likely to antagonize me? Or what could I have done to help Luther, had I made myself his partner in peril, except to provide two candidates for disaster instead of one? The spirit in which he has written I find quite astonishing; at the very least he has laid a heavy burden of public hostility on all lovers of the humanities. Much of his teaching, many of his denunciations are admirable, if only he had not spoilt his good qualities with intolerable defects. Even had all he wrote been religious, mine was never the spirit to risk my life for the truth.[14] Not everyone has the strength needed for martyrdom. I fear that, if strife were to break out, I shall behave like Peter.[15] When popes and emperors make the right decisions I follow, which is godly; if they decide wrongly I tolerate them, which is safe. I believe that even for men of good will this is legitimate, if there is no hope of better things. Then again they father that pamphlet about Julius[16] on me; so ready are they to leave nothing untried which may damage not so much me as liberal studies, the present revival of which they deplore.

But Christ must take care of me, for my poor writings will always be in his service. When Luther is in ashes,[17] and the Preachers and certain theologians who are not very sound at heart can claim the credit for it, intelligent princes must see to it that there is no extension of their right to rage against the innocent and those who have done the Christian religion some service; let us not be so carried away by our hatred of the falsehood in Luther's writings that we lose the benefit of the good things he has written.

All else you will learn from More's letter.[18] Commend me as warmly as you can to my lord cardinal,[19] my incomparable patron. Farewell, dear Pace, my distinguished friend.

Brussels, 5 July 1521
Your sincere friend Erasmus

1219 / To William Blount, Lord Mountjoy Anderlecht, [c 5 July?] 1521

This letter, which was published in the *Epistolae ad diversos*, serves the same purpose as Ep 1218 and may well be contemporary with it (cf n17, Ep 1218 introduction). It was written in reply to a letter from Mountjoy, which is now missing. Against Mountjoy's wish for decisive opposition to Luther (cf lines 125–7), Erasmus pleads once again the wisdom of silence in situations where protest seems fraught with danger; cf the preface.

ERASMUS OF ROTTERDAM TO THE RIGHT HONOURABLE WILLIAM, LORD MOUNTJOY, GREETING

The sincerity of your feelings towards me, my honoured Lord, and the true friendship you have shown me as my Maecenas, make me regret all the more that I do you less credit as a friend than your readiness to think the best of me deserves. You write that in your part of the world some people, I know not who, are spreading a rumour that I am not only a supporter of Luther's faction but his collaborator and almost his moving spirit, and you urge me to clear my name by publishing a book against Luther. As this is a shameless falsehood – they might equally say that Erasmus has sprouted wings – I will briefly explain the source from which this rumour stems.

There are a number of people here who bear me mortal hatred because they think it was I who introduced the classical languages and the humanities into their reign. These men, even before the world first heard the name of Luther, were seeking everywhere for some weapon with which they could satisfy their resentment. And so the first begetters of this rumour are not yet convinced of its truth themselves, though they have tried to convince others. They have also approached Girolamo Aleandro the apostolic nuncio, a scholar of high quality whose friendship I have long enjoyed,[1] and tried with astonishing falsehoods to rouse him against me. There were sundry scandalous pamphlets issuing from both sides.[2] To escape from the suspicion of having written these, certain Germans diverted it onto me. To cut a long story short, they had persuaded their victim, who has a penetrating and straightforward mind but is easily misled, that my feelings and my language about him were unfriendly. Nor was there any lack of people, when our friendship began to heal again, to rend it asunder from time to time with fresh innuendoes.

Be that as it may, you must take as nearer the truth than all the Sibyl's leaves,[3] that in all the books of Luther and his followers there is not one syllable that is mine or written with my connivance.[4] Nor have I supported him[5] – unless he supports a man who urges him to abandon his plans and does his best to prevent the publication of his books.[6] I foresaw before anyone else that this business would end in severe and world-wide disorder. I have made no secret agreement with Luther or with any member of his party; and so far am I from giving anyone encouragement, that both in speech and writing I have deterred everyone I could from following a perilous course. All I did was to disapprove of the over-hasty uproar created by certain people, especially before public audience, when it was not yet clear enough which way Luther was going.

No one can fail to admit that the discipline of the church has sunk far below the purity of the Gospel, that Christian people have had many burdens laid upon them, and that men's consciences are caught in a net of perplexities of every kind.[7] For these evils Luther was thought by many good and learned men to offer some sort of remedy. And while he was winning support everywhere, I alone stood up and counselled him to change his tune and approach the problem in the gentler spirit of the Gospel. No man knows better than you how my heart has always been set on peace and how much I have hated war.[8] And so, had every word Luther writes been true, I should object strongly to the subversive licence he allows himself. Personally, I would rather go wrong on some points than fight valiantly for the truth and set the world by the ears. And in contests of this kind, when the turmoil and the bloodshed are over and the facts are clear, we sometimes find that both parties held the same opinion, and the struggle was only over words. The teaching of the Gospel, the glory of Christ – these I have always supported, and I have been a supporter of the humanities so far as they might serve Christ's glory. It grieved me to see too much importance given to argumentative theology; it was painful to see the ancient sort quite done away with.[9]

This was the target of all my exertions, nor have I any reason to regret this course. How could I guess that a Luther would arise to put my work to such bad use? For it is common talk that he has taken some things from my books.[10] Yet how can I undertake that no one shall misuse my writings, when so many men have made a wrong use of the Gospels themselves? And yet, had some deity forewarned me that this age was on its way,[11] there are certain things I would not have written at all, or would have written differently; not because what I wrote could do harm, but because at any given moment some things are better left unsaid. My own spirit is such that I should wish not to offend even the Turks,[12] if that were possible. The Germans are indignant with me as being, they say, an opponent of Luther; and in your country, I perceive, I am of his party, am I? I must be a proper weathercock, one thing here and something quite different with you. Neither the tricks of some men I could name, nor the promises or hostility of others, have ever been able, or ever shall be, to make me a member of any party but Christ's. A curse on all who rejoice in these factious labels! If he is a Luther man who defends all that Luther has written or will write in future, I must be a lunatic if I wish to be thought a Luther man[13] when I do not read his books. And what reason could I have for throwing myself into such a dangerous faction? I laughed aloud at that critic you speak of,[14] who detected from hearsay that Luther is nothing but a blockhead and a dunce who knows no theology. I only wish that man had as much moderation in him as he is learned in divinity! And that he had devoted as much effort to Christian unity as he has to showing his paces in biblical scholarship! What has become meanwhile of the verdict of the man who is held to be, and is, the most accomplished theologian among you,[15] who openly declared at court that Erasmus is as far outstripped by Luther in knowledge of the Scriptures as Luther is surpassed by him in style? And how can they now have the face to match me against Luther, who have been talking nonsense hitherto about my being no better than a schoolmaster?[16]

But suppose Luther is an ignoramus: what then? That was a pretty piece of reasoning, when the man of whom you write looked you calmly in the face and suggested that if Luther is uneducated his books must come from me! Germany is well supplied with very many good scholars who can write; and I who live so far away am the one man who helped him as he wrote! What need to answer such stupid stuff? But, you will say, they are men in high place who say this kind of thing. Yes, but neither pedigree nor gold chain gives a man sense. Those men would be better advised to confine their conversation at dinner to the hunting-field, rather than these subjects which they do not understand. Luther acknowledged the authorship of all his books in front of the emperor.[17] I on my side have never published anything without putting my name on it.[18] I have never claimed other men's works as my own, nor fathered my own on someone else. Indecency, subversion, reckless and perilous assertion I have always shunned. I have always submitted what I write to the judgment of the church,[19] and listened willingly to the advice of other scholars, being ready even now to mend what learned and wise men may take exception to. I except a few who have given clear indications of their unbridled hatred and distorted judgment. I never had any desire to fight against the leaders of the church. If they will define what will promote Christ's glory, I shall cheerfully accept it. If it should be something that I rightly dislike, I shall endure it, provided it is not clearly impious. They have their Master, in whose eyes they stand or fall. And I suppose it is lawful to keep silence concerning the truth if there is no hope of its doing any good. In this way Christ kept silence before Herod.[20] Nor am I so headstrong that I wish to fight against the decrees of powerful princes, being the mere worm I am. If they ask my advice, and are willing to let me give it with impunity, give it I will forthrightly; perhaps not wise, it shall at least be sincere. It is not for nothing that this feeling has taken hold of the minds of so many peoples and that the evil is continually breaking out afresh. Perhaps it would be more prudent to imitate those careful physicians who clean away all the purulent matter from a wound before they encourage a scab to form over it, or who expel the material cause of a disease from the patient's veins rather than those who forcibly drive off a fever that will soon come back.[21] If they do not ask my advice, I shall hold my peace and, as far as I may, shall serve the interest of the Gospel; and if anything is done otherwise than I could wish, I shall pray to Christ that he may turn those men's hearts to better things.

Furthermore, when you say in your letter that it was in my power to bring all this disorder to an end, how I wish that what your Highness says were true! This sorry business would never even have started. They protest here that I have no pen. I have a pen indeed, but there are countless reasons that dissuade me from using it. To call Luther a booby is easy enough; to defend the cause of the faith with the proper arguments I at least find very difficult, and hitherto others have not had much more success.[22] And yet I should gird up my loins for this business much more readily, if I were certain that some of those who pursue the purposes of the world under the pretext of the faith were likely to use their victory to further the Christian religion. None the less, I shall go to Basel[23] with this in mind, that when I have finished what I have in hand[24] I may attempt something that may help to heal this discord,[25] or at least may prove my will to do so. For all that, I do not see how far it is my business to take up such a formidable task, when there are men of great learning,[26] great place, great wisdom and authority, who have already attempted something in this field. An eloquent argument is put forward by those who say that silence gives consent. If those who do not write pass for silent, there is a great body of consent. And yet my own silence has had the effect of rousing all Luther's party against me.

But I must conclude. Most excellent Maecenas, you have no cause to doubt your old friend Erasmus. Neither piety nor religion, neither public morality nor the public peace will suffer from anything I write. For my own innocence I can answer; men's tongues are not in my control. Those who talk such nonsense will render their account to God as thoughtless if not venomous. If I cannot win the approval of men for what I try to do, at least I am confident that Christ will approve; and if this generation is less grateful than it should be for my labours, posterity will prove a fairer judge. In the end of all, it is something to have, if no one else, Christ on one's side.

I have written this in haste, on the chance offer of a courier, and will write with more care another time.

From Anderlecht, 1521

1220 / To Thomas More — Anderlecht, [June–July 1521]

This letter, which is printed in the *Epistolae ad diversos*, was written in anticipation of Thomas More's visit to the Netherlands (cf Ep 1223 introduction), with a view to introducing Erasmus' friend Conradus Goclenius to him. It might have been sent to England either with Ep 1210 or with Epp 1218–19. In Ep 1218:51 Erasmus implied that he was writing to More by the same courier on matters evidently not mentioned in the following text. Thus either he must have written to More twice in a short interval, without releasing the other letter for publication, or this letter, as it was actually sent, contained some additional sections (in fact, both hypotheses could be correct). The first paragraph of this letter reads rather as if Erasmus had earlier congratulated More on his appointment as under-treasurer (cf Ep 1210 n4) and was now replying to More's reaction.

ERASMUS OF ROTTERDAM TO THE RIGHT HONOURABLE[1]
SIR THOMAS MORE, TREASURER OF HIS MOST SERENE MAJESTY
THE KING OF ENGLAND, GREETING

I most heartily approve and applaud your attitude, dear More, my most distinguished friend, if no new wealth gives you more joy than an increase in sincere and faithful friends, and you think that the chief delight of this life is to be found there and nowhere else. Other men may take the greatest care not to be deceived by imitation gems;[2] but you, despising such resources, think yourself rich enough if you have added to your assets a friend in whom there is no guile. Nor can any man take more delight in gaming[3] or checkers, in hunting or in music than you do in unfettered conversation with a scholarly and honourable friend.

In wealth of this kind you are extremely well endowed; but knowing as I do that a miser is never satisfied – and both you and I have often been successful in this way before – I shall invite you to take delivery of a man whom in all points you can love with all your heart and take to your bosom. He is Conradus Goclenius, a Westphalian by birth. It is true that Westphalians are commonly thought rather uncouth; but they have given us many most gifted men and scholars of no common learning. No other race of men work harder; trustworthy and honourable people, their simple wisdom and wise simplicity is their greatest recommendation. You know that a college of the three tongues[4] has lately been founded in Louvain. In this college he teaches Latin publicly with remarkable success and to the great profit of the whole university, with such uprightness and such courtesy that he makes the subject that he teaches popular even among those who were previously repelled by it. He has a keen mind, which has successfully proved itself even in those subjects which are traditionally taught in public schools. He has wit, real Attic wit,[5] and could compete even with you in elegant conversation. In poetry he possesses a grace of his own; he is always limpid, always musical and charming, nor is there a subject so unlovely that it is not tamed when he treats of it. In prose he is so like himself – so unlike himself, perhaps I should say – that when you read him in prose, you would think he might be quite averse from poetry.[6]

For friendship he seems clearly made,[7] and if you once make him your friend, you need have no fear that any chance may separate you. That happens in men who are either disloyal by nature or unable to control their feelings, for such people are inclined to leave one when some occasion arises; they neglect the laws of friendship and follow their own bent. This man is not ambitious, he is not much given to avenging an injury, or more than moderately fond of any pleasures. What jealousy means he has never understood even in a dream, his nature is so open, so prone to think well of others. In the converse of daily life, nothing could be more easy or less temperamental. For the rest, nothing could be more averse than he from filthy lucre,[8] although his position is still modest and supports no more than plain living and equipment in the way of books. If only our princes, both in the world and in the church, had learnt to render their due to men of outstanding gifts, as is done in Italy, my friend Goclenius would be hung with gold.

But they are waking from their sleep. Already there is hardly one among the nobles who does not take the trouble to have his children diligently taught in liberal subjects,[9] although among the chief men at court none is at home in literature[10] with the sole exception of Joris van Halewijn;[11] whose literary pursuits have so far gained for him nothing except envy, though if I mistake not they will soon put high promotion in his way. I hope now that, as soon as you have made Goclenius' closer acquaintance, you will both of you be grateful to me, as happened lately with Frans van Cranevelt,[12] who has now such a hold over you that I am almost jealous of him. Farewell.

From Anderlecht, [1520]

1221 / To Daniël Tayspil — Anderlecht, 5 July 1521

This letter, which was printed in the *Epistolae ad diversos*, is addressed to Daniël Tayspil (d 1533), of Nieuwkerke near Armentières in Flanders, who was from 1516 suffragan to the bishop of Thérouanne, with the titular see of Byblos (biblical Gebal, modern Jebeil). A Premonstratensian, he became abbot of the Austin canons of Voormezele near Ieper in 1524. His brother, Pieter, was president of the Council of Flanders in 1527. Nothing apart from this letter seems to be known about his connections either with Erasmus or with Agazio Guidacerio; cf n3.

ERASMUS OF ROTTERDAM TO THE RIGHT REVEREND DANIËL TAYSPIL, BISHOP OF JEBEIL AND SUFFRAGAN OF THE LORD BISHOP OF THÉROUANNE, GREETING

Right reverend Father, as soon as your letter reached me in Brussels,[1] I asked Gilles de Busleyden[2] to come and see me; he is such a devoted supporter of the humanities that he supports them even to his own hurt. He welcomed the spirit in which you sincerely wished to advance both liberal studies and the glory of the name of Busleyden. He read both your letter to me and what Agathius[3] had written to you. He thought well of the man's abilities, and would like him to be sent for, especially as his character also is highly spoken of, and that too by someone so highly spoken of by all men of good will as yourself. And so in writing to him about the state of affairs, he must be told exactly what it is.

The University of Louvain yields in popularity at the present time to none except Paris. Numbers are roughly three thousand, and more join every day. The college maintains very few: one president, who is responsible for the business side, three professors, and I believe twelve young men; and these it maintains free. Besides them, the house holds a few others, who board with the president and the professors at their own expense. There is a lecture-room, of a fair size by the standards of this university, which sometimes takes not less than three hundred. He will enjoy this climate of ours,[4] and will not find the friendliness of the people uncongenial. The situation of the college is respectable, and it is quite a seemly building. The salary,[5] which is fairly generous in proportion to the revenues, is – to speak frankly – too low when set against professorial standards; but in the light of a person's standing and how hard he works it can be somewhat increased at the discretion of the executors. And he will be allowed to teach outside his regular courses, in Greek or Hebrew as he may prefer. He will be dealing with excellent colleagues of the highest character. And there is good hope that soon, thanks to the liberality of the princes, the college's income may increase, especially if you and men like you add their support. It is a pious undertaking, and will be a great ornament in future both to this university and to Prince Charles. The chief credit is due to that great man Jérôme de Busleyden, who devoted to this enterprise all that he possessed, even depriving his brothers of their share.[6] But they will not be deprived of their share of the credit, for they assisted this splendid foundation with additional funds. A thing cannot be hid from posterity that will be celebrated with the eloquence of three languages; and not the least share of the glory will belong to those who first began the teaching that will one day be so celebrated. And if a man is not moved by thoughts of glory among men, at least it is a pious thing to seek approval from Christ. So you must encourage your Agathius to come here with all speed, and good luck go with him.[7]

The baseless rumour that Luther had been ambushed and killed[8] reached us too. Every effort was made at Worms, partly by threats and partly by entreaties, to have his books, all of which he acknowledged, submitted to the emperor; and when that could not be secured, he was taken back to Wittenberg under safe conduct by an imperial herald, for which twenty days were provided. Then on the instructions of the emperor – who is violently hostile to Luther, either because others have put him up to it or from a serious and genuine devotion to the Christian faith – his books were burnt at Worms.[9] A fearsome proclamation announcing penalties for any refusal to obey the emperor's wishes has also been printed at Louvain.[10] Farewell.

From Anderlecht, 5 July 1521

1222 / From Juan Luis Vives — Bruges, 10 July 1521

The correspondence between Erasmus and Vives has been preserved only in part. Four letters preceding this one were released by Erasmus for publication

(Epp 927, 1104, 1108, 1111), but from then on neither he nor Vives published any further letters, in part perhaps, as Allen suggests, because of the strains to which their friendship was subjected by the omission of Vives' notes on Augustine's *De civitate Dei* from Froben's great Augustine of 1528/9. Some of Vives' letters, however, must have remained among Erasmus' papers in the possession of Bonifacius Amerbach. Presumably from that source this letter and many subsequent ones were printed – rather carelessly – in the earliest edition of Vives' collected works (Basel: N. Episcopius the younger 1555). Perhaps as a result of that edition the originals have disappeared from the Amerbach papers, just as Erasmus' letters to Vives have also perished.

JUAN LUIS VIVES TO THE DISTINGUISHED SCHOLAR DESIDERIUS ERASMUS OF ROTTERDAM, HIS MUCH RESPECTED TEACHER, GREETING

This moment Dean Laurentius[1] sends me word for the first time that Etienne Lecomte[2] is setting out for your part of the world, and that if I want to send anything he will be leaving here tomorrow shortly before sunrise. So you will get from me whatever comes into my head just now. I had in mind to write you a proper long-winded letter, as the man says,[3] if I could have found a courier to give me reasonable notice.

In Louvain, the day before I left, I gave the regent of the College of the Lily[4] a letter addressed to you with some more proverbs,[5] which I expect you have had. And I told you I was going next day to Antwerp, where I found your man Johannes[6] on the merchants' exchange. Shortly afterwards I sent for him, so that I could write to you, but he was no longer to be found, and I was surprised that he brought me nothing from you. As I got no better[7] in Antwerp, I came to Bruges, thinking I should not stay here more than two weeks, and it is now the sixth, this illness had taken such a deep hold of me. But it is mostly gone, and what is left does not much frighten me. But having settled here so far, I shall await the king and More,[8] in hopes of seeing how I am to live henceforward. So far I have maintained myself on the queen's money, and still do. I wrote to More that I should have a long talk with him on his arrival. He can suspect what I mean, but I put nothing openly; I did not want to without consulting you, though I pretty much know your advice – to secure leisure for a life of study from whatever source I can. I can take the responsibility for everything else, but this is beyond my powers; and if fortune is to be found in that alone, no man is the architect of his own fortune, as Appius said.[9]

So much for what I have done hitherto and for what I expect to do shortly. I know the thought that comes into your mind: what about Augustine? I have six books already – revised, that is; for many others are written out. These six I could send, if I had anyone to make a copy of them. Anyhow, if they are not sent this August, they will be, I hope, before the winter. God knows how sorry I am; but would you have me right against heaven? I thought it better to postpone Augustine than to work myself to death, or end up useless for anything else, laid low by sickness and with nothing to live on. For I could hardly recover the other things once I had lost them; but Augustine, if he is put off, I can easily pick up again whenever I please. I beg you urgently, if you do not think the blame for this lies with time or fate or destiny, at least to forgive this mistake, if I really was mistaken.

I send you some further proverbs which have turned up during my reading. Be sure and send me an answer by the bearer of this letter, provided you have the time; and if you either cannot or will not do so in writing, at least let me know by word of mouth the state of your health and how things are going, for I am so deeply concerned and interested in your affairs as in my own. Farewell, my dear teacher, the dearest of men.

Bruges, 10 July 1521

1223 / To Conradus Goclenius — Bruges, 12 August [1521]

This letter was published in the *Epistolae ad diversos* with a year date that can easily be corrected. It is printed there immediately following Ep 1220. Taken together, these two letters are a strong public endorsement of Goclenius (cf Ep 1221 n3), who must have been all the more gratified as at the time of his appointment to the Collegium Trilingue of Louvain Erasmus had supported a rival candidate (cf Ep 1046 n5).

The first paragraph of this letter is another tribute to the delightful ease Erasmus experienced in the rural environment of Anderlecht (cf Ep 1208 introduction). It is possible that the letter was begun there, although it is dated from Bruges, where at the time world politics were being shaped. Charles v was at Bruges from 7 to 25 August (cf Gachard II 30) and on 14 August he received Thomas Wolsey. The English cardinal had come over from Calais (where he had landed on 2 August), leaving behind him a French delegation that awaited the outcome of the Bruges meeting with great anxiety (cf Ep 1233 n3). Wolsey left Bruges at about the same time as the emperor but did not return to England until 28 November. With the war between France and the Hapsburg empire in full progress (cf Ep 1228 n12), the purpose of the Bruges meeting was the conclusion of a formal alliance on the basis of the friendly entente created during the summit meetings in the summer of 1520 (cf Ep 1106 introduction), and a secret treaty to this effect was signed on 25 August (cf LP III 1352, 1443, 1458, 1503, 1508, 1513, 1810, and passim).

Wolsey was accompanied by some of Erasmus' good friends, in particular Mountjoy (cf Ep 1219), Tunstall, and More (cf Ep 1220), who had brought his own fool (cf Allen IV xxx). Erasmus, who had gone to Bruges to see them (cf Ep

1228:3–4 and Epp 1227–30 for echoes of their conversations), was present when Charles v rode out to greet Wolsey's party on their approach to the city. Frans van Cranevelt (cf Ep 1220:56–7) delivered an address of welcome. Erasmus, who was staying with the faithful Marcus Laurinus (cf Ep 1227:43–4), could now have a talk with Wolsey (cf Epp 1227:33–4, 1233:2–6), having missed the chance of doing so in the preceding summer (cf Ep 1132:4–6). He also enjoyed special attentions from King Christian II of Denmark, the emperor's brother-in-law (cf Ep 1228 n6), and found the time to consult the manuscripts of St Donatian's (cf Ep 1174 n6) before returning to Anderlecht by the end of August (cf Ep 1232). For a detailed account of the Bruges meeting see Gerard Geldenhouwer's *Collectanea* ed J. Prinsen (Amsterdam 1901) 116–20.

ERASMUS OF ROTTERDAM TO CONRADUS GOCLENIUS, GREETING

I used to think in the old days that it was merely for the pleasure of it that the Ancients spoke so highly of life in the country. Experience has now taught me that it is not so much enjoyable as healthy. Your friend Erasmus had nearly been done for in cities: so endless was the trouble with my digestion. Already I was involved with more than one physician; physic was prescribed for me and pills and enemas, powders, ointments, baths, poultices – everything. And all the time I had no leisure to be ill, so constantly was I called away now here now there by business suddenly arising. And so I packed up my traps and mounted my horses. 'Where are you going?' my servant asks me. 'Wherever we are greeted by a friendly and health-giving climate,' was my reply. Scarcely had I spent two days here and my fever had departed to the devil, and my digestion was sound again. I really seemed in this country to grow young again; my stomach was ready to digest anything, after a long spell of weakness. My dear Goclenius, I never did anything in my whole life of which I had less reason to repent.

I am delighted with you for all the energy you show in the teaching of Latin, and the way in which your learning and ability are equally ornaments of Busleyden College.[1] Happy are those of our young men who have chanced to be born into this generation![2] Really I should be jealous of them, were I not a whole-hearted supporter of the public weal. The more the old frogs creak, the warmer grows the enthusiasm of the young men who have spurred the knowledge that is ignorance writ large and are pressing on to better things. I can see what those men's selfishness deserves. But you must save time you might have wasted, or at least misplaced, in quarreling with these noisy wretches, and devote it to the promotion of liberal studies. Will you let me show you a noble and glorious form of punishment? Do this: show yourself a man of spotless character and a diligent and painstaking teacher of all that is best in literature. You could not find a quicker way of driving them to hang themselves, a fate, to be sure, which they richly deserve, tormented as they so sorely are by public benefits, which they would keep if they could not only from others but from themselves. There is something to be said for jealousy 'between neighbour and neighbour as both hurry to get rich'[3] but these men have it within their power to enjoy the benefits which they are tortured to see others sharing. One thing above all else has always seemed to me admirable in the two of you:[4] not only is your personal character free from all stain, your teaching too is innocent, and not innocent only but self-restrained. What will intelligent men think, when they hear that in Louvain the teaching of poetry and rhetoric is free from every trace of impropriety or personal rancour, while lectures on theology and even sermons are so soured with falsehoods[5] and with scandal that even unlettered folk abominate them?

I had given More a picture of you,[6] being so careful not to add from my own imagination that I left much unsaid. I would rather that that should be the grounds of his complaint, when you have seen more of one another and are better acquainted. He seems to have a very great desire to see you. When you write to him, congratulate him on his rise in dignity and position. In the old days he was only a member of the king's council, but lately, without seeking or wanting it, and solely from the personal preference of that most civilized prince, he has been knighted,[7] and holds an office of great distinction among the English which carries a salary not to be despised and is called the treasurership.[8] Farewell.

Bruges, 12 August [1520]

1224 / To William Thale — Bruges, 13 August 1521

Published in the *Epistolae ad diversos*, this letter is addressed to an old acquaintance from Erasmus' days in Italy (cf lines 6–8). Their friendship was eclipsed for some time when Thale disposed of some of Erasmus' papers that had remained in the care of Richard Pace (cf Epp 244:7n, 1210 n6) and published *De ratione studii* at Paris (cf Ep 66) without authorization from Erasmus. Thale's life is little known otherwise, except that he later followed up Erasmus' suggestion in this letter and enrolled at the University of Louvain on 3 December 1522 (cf *Matricule de Louvain* III-1 688), becoming a friend of Juan Luis Vives.

ERASMUS OF ROTTERDAM TO HIS WORTHY FRIEND WILLIAM THALE, GREETING

When will you cease to complain that I have removed your name from my list of Williams?[1] There may be no Thale in the list, if you like; but the name at any rate has never been out of my mind. Whenever I go, I carry round with me the record of your affection for me. I only wish it might some day be my good fortune to return to our old intimacy, and add a happy ending to what began first in Ferrara[2] and later was renewed in England. I wish some chance might send you – for your own advantage, of course – on a visit to this Brabant of ours. The climate of Louvain[3] you might prefer even to your old love, Italy; it is delightful, and healthy too. Nowhere could you find a more peaceful place for study, or a more flourishing output of able men; nowhere a larger or more accessible staff of professors. If these advantages do not lure you over here, at least it is worth coming to escape your British plague,[4] which they tell me spares nobody in your part of the world. Farewell.

Bruges, 13 August, 1531

1225 / To Pierre Barbier — Bruges, 13 August 1521

This letter and Ep 1206, which preceded it on a preliminary quire of the *Epistolae ad diversos*, are also found in Gouda MS 1324 (cf Allen I 609–13). While not discounting the possibility that the Gouda scribe copied the text printed in the *Epistolae ad diversos*, Allen inclined to think that he rather had a manuscript before him and therefore gave precedence to his variants. If the Gouda copies were based on a manuscript, the latter could have derived, as did the text of Epp 1203, 1228, from Erasmus' own study about the time the letters were dispatched. Like Epp 1216, 1235, this letter was probably intended to come to the attention of Barbier's master, Cardinal Adrian of Utrecht; cf n1, n5, n47.

ERASMUS OF ROTTERDAM TO PIERRE BARBIER, GREETING

You show true affection, my dear Barbier, in urging me from time to time[1] to piece up my friendship with the theologians of Louvain; but I assure you that you spur a willing horse, as the saying goes.[2] No living man is more keen to form friendships than I am or to retain them; but some evil spirit, I know not how, sees to it that with them either I cannot make friends or it does not last. In my own nature I am a straightforward person; I love my friends more than I court their notice. Of this you can well bear witness, who have seen how little trouble I took to court that excellent man Jean Le Sauvage, chancellor to the emperor, and a Maecenas whom I shared with you. It was the same with the archbishop of Canterbury,[3] with Mountjoy, and with the cardinals who were my warmest supporters in Rome.[4] And yet, should an occasion arise when my services are required, I am likely to refuse nothing for the sake of my friends. But in the party of whom we speak there are men with whom it would be far more difficult to make friends than with some mighty monarch; and yet their avowed way of life should have the greatest friendliness of disposition as its natural ornament, and courtesy, and a readiness to think well of all men, if their character did but answer to their costume. With Johannes Atensis[5] and with the rest of them agreement would have been easy, had it been possible to placate two or three theologians of the Carmelite and Dominican faction.[6] The slightest suspicion, or some remark made elsewhere and truly or falsely reported, and they reopen the whole tragic business. And, to confess the truth quite frankly, I am by nature more prone to humour than is perhaps appropriate and speak more freely than is sometimes wise. I measure other men's feelings by my own; and though I have been wrong so often, I cannot escape from my natural bent. I ask you, what could there be in my edition of the New Testament to make some of them declaim against it so ferociously and put up Maarten van Dorp[7] against me to write an attack on Erasmus?

I moved, as you know, to Louvain,[8] for such was at that time the emperor's wish. For my part, I desired to be friends with all men, but pursued no man's friendship in particular. The efforts of Atensis[9] secured me an invitation to be friends with the theologians. I accepted it frankly, overlooking all that had been done or said against me before. So things were pretty tranquil for some time, until the rise of the College of the Three Tongues.[10] This gave offence to some I could name, especially to Nicolaas the Carmelite.[11] And in my opinion they would have entirely overthrown an institution that promises to be such an ornament to our prince's dominions and of such value to the general state of learning, had not their attempts been suppressed by his Eminence the cardinal of Tortosa;[12] or so I am told. This enterprise at least I supported openly and freely, and I did so solely as a supporter of the public advancement of learning. Apart from that, none of the harvest in that field was mine, though some of the seed was of my sowing.

However, having discovered that they objected mainly to the New Testament, I devoted many months to the effort of correcting it.[13] Seeing also that Johannes Atensis outshone them all in judgment and scholarship as much as he surpassed them in authority, so that by him one could gauge all the rest, I proposed to him, in the presence of Nicolas of Mons[14] with whom we had then been dining, that he, being so accurate and so widely trusted, should help me in this undertaking, assuring him that I was determined to issue the work in a form at which no scholarly and pious reader could reasonably take offence; that my efforts and intentions were pious but my strength unequal to so great a task, so that he would lay me under the greatest obligation if he would tell me what he thought should be corrected. I dwelt on this at great length, and he replied that he had already bought the book but had not yet read it through; but read it through he would, and deal with me exactly as he would with his own brother – those were the words he then used. And he repeated them two or three times. Again, in the first conversation I had with Nicolaus Egmondanus,[15] I asked him to tell me freely if there was anything in the book he took exception to, and he would be doing me a very great service. He gave me no answer, except that he had never read the book. I made the same suggestion several times to Latomus, and more frequently to Dorp as well.

At length the time was approaching when for the second edition I must go to Basel.[16] Shortly before that, Atensis invited me to supper.[17] Egmondanus and Luis Vives were there. After supper I remarked to Atensis that in a few days' time I should be leaving for Basel. I asked, begged, and besought him to be so kind as to tell me if he thought anything should be altered, especially if anything might harm public morality or the Catholic faith. He answered that he had read the whole work, and it seemed to him equally religious and scholarly. 'I would rather be corrected than commended,'[18] was my reply. 'Correction will be good for me, but that praise of yours will not have done me any good. At the moment I can still make corrections; later, there will not be the same opportunity.' Whereupon he repeated the praise he had already uttered. 'If you are sincere in your remarks,' said I, 'why did some people attack this work with such ferocious clamour when it first appeared?' 'Before I had read it,' he replied, 'many points had been reported to me; but when I read it through, I found the facts were quite different. What you have written, I like very much; what you intend to write, I do not know.' To which my answer was that if he approved the first edition, I had no doubt that he would like this one much more. And he ended by urging me to press on with my sacred labours (those were his words) for the advancement of the Christian religion.

Relying on these words from a man of such high standing, I set off for Basel. I finished the part of the work in which there was the greater risk – the annotations, that is. I returned.[19] Atensis hastened to see me, and so did Dorp, although the surgeons had judged me to be suffering from the plague.[20] This was evidence of friendship as yet unimpaired. I gave Dorp the part of the volume that was in print, on condition that if he found anything he did not like, he would tell me; it was still open to me to alter it, I said, though with some financial loss, as long as the work was confined within the walls of the printing-house.

Soon a rumour reached me about Lee, who was said to criticize hundreds of passages in the New Testament as appalling and fraught with peril. I invited him to a discussion, offering this stipulation among others, that if he had any point connected with a risk to either morality or the faith, he must tell me and I would correct it (for the book, as I told him, was not yet in the hands of the public), and that too with honourable mention by name of Lee, who had put me right. He refused. We took the question to Atensis.[21] He shuffled, no doubt scenting serious trouble ahead.

I replied to Lee.[22] He was followed by a pamphlet from Latomus,[23] the purpose of which is not clear to me, which attacked me with devious tricks. My reply was polite, and even, as some read it, humble. You know how impossible it has always been to force me into a controversy with Dorp,[24] for whose natural gifts I had a very special affection. My feelings towards Latomus were much the same, for at that time he seemed to me on the side of both the Graces and the Muses. But some evil genius did not allow our friendship to mature.

In the mean while I was the object of attacks from time to time in sermons delivered to mixed audiences. Eventually Atensis in a very crowded lecture belaboured me[25] with such abuse that people generally expected to see Erasmus die of resentment or go into hiding. An appeal was made to laymen in high places[26] in order to prejudice them against me. Men were sent out to rant against me everywhere. The campaign was so intensely offensive that the mildest of men might have been driven mad with fury.

At length, in an evil hour, appeared several pamphlets by Luther,[27] and at this the whole storm broke out afresh. Suspicion hardened among them that these pieces were written with help from me, because two or three of the prefaces were in rather better Latin.[28] The bachelors were given the task of collecting my errors. Soon everything was full of error; whole sackfuls of errors were collected in no time. And meanwhile I was not told of one of them! At the college drinking-parties Erasmus' errors were the only topic. As there was no end to this, I exacted from Atensis that he and two or three other scholars should list some passages to which they took objection. Atensis listed a very few, and none of any importance; Dorp listed some, which were less important still. Atensis testified that he had no doubt my intentions were excellent, and only asked that I should give explanations for the weaker brethren. I explained, and gave the book to him and to Dorp. Atensis approved of everything. He only wished it to be added that confession,[29] as now practised, was instituted by Christ. For this dogma, as its truth was not yet clear to me, I was unwilling to take responsibility. Then, when Atensis refused to be responsible for this business and the objections had already died down, it seemed best even to him to let the matter drop.

Again, when this sorry business of Luther was daily getting worse, and it was already obvious that they were planning serious trouble for me, I protested to some of the leading men and inquired what sort of monster they were hatching. Egmondanus alone, who is more outspoken – that is one good quality in him, at any rate – admitted that suspicion about Luther's books was at the bottom of it. I was astonished that such men should raise such an offensive attack on so slight a foundation, and told them the truth – that in Luther's books there was no syllable of mine,[30] nor any written with my knowledge or concurrence. Meanwhile the most worthless pamphlets were pouring out everywhere[31] – things in which the Germans take extraordinary pride;[32] and whatever appeared, they fathered it on me. At length Atensis, realizing, I suppose, that their suspicions were groundless, made moves through the rector[33] of the university and through my host, Jan de Neve of Hondschoote, to patch up peace and concord. I showed the greatest willingness, although while being wronged in so many ways I had not wronged a fly myself. Peace was concluded in Falcon College,[34] on terms that the past should be entirely forgotten; they would do all they could to repair the damage to my reputation, which they had injured in so many ways, and I would restrain the pens of my learned friends as far as I could. Would you believe it? – shortly afterwards there appeared the *Farrago* of my letters,[35] which had been selected from various bundles and published in Basel by certain German friends in whose loyalty I had often trusted with the most unfortunate results for me, and for whom I had done too much to comply with their wishes, which showed more zeal than discretion. Among these there were a few lines which gave great offence, particularly to the Carmelite.[36] Lo and behold, another storm all on a sudden, more violent than the first! And yet that volume of letters had been printed some six months before we had begun to treat of making peace.

You see, my excellent Barbier, that I have been far from despising the opinion of the theologians of Louvain, although I had no reason to choose them rather than other men as censors of my work. You see that it was not my fault if Christian friendship has not been maintained between us. And then, when this sorry Luther business was steadily getting worse, some people tried surprisingly enough to involve me in it. I have gone on record, in a thing actually published two years before,[37] that I have nothing whatever in common with Luther, and recognize no party except Christians, if party is the word for them. And all the time I was having stones thrown at me with surprising vehemence in public sermons and public lectures by a Carmelite and certain Dominicans,[38] sometimes even by name. To endure this was, I judged, better than a contest with the whole swarm.

Furthermore, when you say in your letter that in your part of the world the suspicion that I support Luther is extinct, this does not surprise me; but it is surprising that it should ever have arisen. I only wish I were as free from all faults as I am clear of this business! I should not hesitate to die even unshriven. At the outset it is hard to express the number and the quality of the men who supported Luther. For my part, after sampling a few short pages I seemed to detect that the business would end in uproar. And my hatred of controversy is such that I dislike even truth that is subversive. I was the very first person to warn him, in a letter,[39] to handle the business of the Gospel with the gentleness and moderation that the Gospel teaches. So far was I from giving him any encouragement that I wrote frequently to Luther himself and to Luther's friends to deter them from proceeding as they had begun.[40] And in this I was so active that certain people wrote and warned me,[41] if I did not like what Luther was about, at least to conceal the fact, for fear of arousing against myself the animosity and the pens of so many noblemen and men of learning. If Luther has in fact written in the spirit of the Gospel, as very many still maintain, there was nothing irreligious in my anxiety for the public peace; and if not, I was the very first person to try with all my might to stop the publication of his books.[42] Were I to tell you of the men who have appealed to me to join Luther's cause and the methods they have used[43] – the tricks with which some have tried to lure me and the virulence with which some have tried to drive me in that direction – you would really understand how I detest these feuds. I perceived that I should suffer the loss of the friends, numerous and uncommonly learned as they are, whom I had in Germany;[44] I was not unaware of the persistent enmity with which some among our own people pursued me in their hatred of the humanities; I saw clearly that it was safer to join the other party. But my resolution is, and shall be, unshaken to be torn in pieces rather than encourage discord, especially in business that concerns the faith.

Luther's supporters din into my ears the words of the Gospel 'I am not come to send peace, but a sword.'[45] For my part, though I seem to see some things now accepted in the church which could be altered to the great profit of the Christian religion, I can approve no reforms pursued with this sort of uproar. If learned men had once pooled their ideas and submitted sealed opinions to the leaders of both church and state on the things they judged to pertain to the gospel teaching in its purity, I might perhaps have been one of them[46] and would have given the most careful advice I could. But as it is, what could be more raving mad than to debate a question of such importance with scandalous pamphlets and lunatic uproar? In this matter the first point is that both sides have gone wrong, in my opinion, and too much passion has been brought to bear in both directions. A book has lately appeared by the cardinal of San Sisto,[47] which abstains entirely from personal abuse, avoids all scurrility, and proceeds by plain arguments and citations from authorities, an equally careful and able performance. I wish we had hundreds of such pieces written against Luther, which throw light on the subject instead of arousing discord. Everyone would like to be better informed. The other side may lose sight of moderation, but it was our duty to bear it in mind.

Indeed it is not a question of moderation but of common prudence, to avoid what would harm our cause and help the cause of our opponents. Had this been done at the outset, unless I am wrong, things would not have reached such a pitch of disorder. They can lay nothing at my door except that I was the first to oppose the choice of subversive clamour as a weapon against Luther, especially before the public; but if I did oppose that, I still left them free to protest as loudly as they would. With some of the learned men who now pass as not wholly out of touch with Luther,[48] I had already formed ties in the name of our common studies, before the world had ever heard Luther's name.

And again, he is said to have drawn to some extent on my books.[49] But I could not guarantee that no one in future will misuse what I write, any more than the evangelists and apostles could do the same. I wrote at that time what then seemed to contribute to the moral standards of the day; maybe I would have phrased some things more cautiously,[50] had I seen that a different time was coming as fraught with tragedy as the present. The standard topics out of which I virtually built my harangues were directed against those who neglect the springs of Holy Scripture and cleave too closely to the paltry problems of academic philosophy rather than theology; who neglect what belongs to true religion and put too much trust in ceremonies, displaying more of Judaism than of Christianity;[51] who with an inverted sense of values think those things most important which matter least, and think nothing of what really matters. Often I did battle with pen and ink against the wars[52] which for many centuries now have periodically set the world by the ears, which equally lower the standards of morality and disgrace the name of Christian. And thus far no one has been found who has been made one hair's breadth worse[53] by any book of mine. Many express their thanks as they begin to awake to the feeling for true religion. Subversion and indecency I have taken special pains to avoid in all I write. I refrain from laying down the law, for I would rather purvey good advice than dogma. In the points which are condemned in Luther's book I find nothing in which he agrees with me,[54] except perhaps that what I have stated with moderation and in its proper context he utters without restraint. For example: I may have written somewhere that less profit is to be gained from Dionysius than from Origen or Chrysostom, and he writes that Dionysius as an author is a pestilent ass.[55] If this is agreement, wine and vinegar will agree.

But you will say 'Hitherto you have not written a word against Luther.'[56] For my not doing so there have been two principal reasons, lack of leisure and the consciousness of my own ignorance.[57] I was distracted by my own researches, so much so that excessive labours often threatened my health. And I saw that it was one thing to encourage men to study good literature, to call them to a high standard of conduct, and to write down notes as I read the Holy Scriptures; and something quite different to discuss the essentials of the faith before a world-wide theatre. I saw feeling run so high in both parties that one side could not be satisfied by anything less than roaring at the top of its voice, while the other was so well furnished both with manpower and with two-edged pamphlets that I would rather be exposed to the lances of the Swiss[58] than cut to pieces by their sharp-pointed pens. For they have many men whose writings seem likely to live to posterity. All the same, I admit that where the faith is at stake one should think nothing even of one's life,[59] if only my abilities had answered my desires. At any rate, I cannot allow Latomus to say that he hates to see the world divided more than I do, especially as like some ferment this has turned the sweetness of our studies almost everywhere to vinegar. It would be mad to approve of all that Luther has written or will write in future; but dislike of an author is no reason to condemn what is true or distort what is accurate. If he can be said to write against Luther who calls him at different times donkey, blockhead, beast, devil, and Antichrist,[60] nothing would be easier than to write against him. Personally, I have read of all his works hardly a dozen pages; I have not the time, and if I had, I would rather invest my leisure in reading ancient authors. And yet I have hardly as yet found anyone who admits that he is sorry to have read his books, although there are many things that he dislikes.

Need I say more? The question is such that it is most difficult to satisfy men without ever betraying the truths of the Gospel. The subject demands not only impeccable learning but exceptionable wisdom, and one must speak with authority. And I foresee no shortage of men both able and willing to shoulder this task, bishops, cardinals, and even kings.[61] Whatever can be achieved by burning or by the decrees of princes has been fully attained; and I only wish this were as effective in changing men's minds as it is in stopping their tongues. If it is a pious act to damage Luther's cause, I have perhaps done him more damage than any of those who have declaimed against him most offensively and who have flayed him with their scandalous pamphlets. In the first place, his violent and rebellious style of writing has been opposed by me unflinchingly and right from the start, openly and in the presence of Luther's friends and enemies alike. I have not ceased to urge many people both in conversation and by writing letters to keep clear of his faction. No enthusiasm has been able to bring me, even for a moment, to involve myself in his affairs. This, I believe, has done more to weaken his party than the uproar aroused by some people I could name. This fact is so far from unknown in Germany that for a whole year now not one of those who pass for Luther's supporters has written me a line,[63] not one has come to see me or sent me greetings, although in the old days they almost did me to death with these polite attentions.[64] Indeed, as I learn from letters from my friends, Luther's party sometimes attack me in their public lectures,[65] and call me a Pelagian.[66] They would have good reason to be angry with me, had I ever been in their camp or encouraged all this business. As it is, they are angry without a cause, because I have always tried to recall them from their stormy style of writing to the mildness of the Gospel.

Nor do I listen to those, great men in other respects, who say that the disease was too severe to be cured by mild physic;[67] the body must be thrown into confusion by some powerful remedy, in order that health may follow in due course. If this is right, I would rather others were the agents in it than myself. If the corrupted morals of mankind need some such treatment, God will not lack a Nebuchadnezzar[68] by whose hand he can scourge his people. I do not find that any such action was taken by the men of the apostolic age, and like them I do not believe in doing things by violence. Christ cast out those who sold and bought in the temple,[69] but he never gave such instructions to his followers, to whom he delegated the duty to teach, not to fight. I am, in short, always on the side of concord, and here too I would rather have peace with some injustice than war however just.[70] How I wish feelings on both sides would cool down, that we might all devote ourselves to finding common ground in the truth of the Gospel before we hurry on to propagate religion! But this would be best done, not by issuing pamphlets to the general public but by taking counsel under the seal of secrecy. We ought to find out where this passion comes from that has so widely fastened on men's minds. Maybe it would be easier to remove this evil if we removed the springs from which it flows. But the initiative must lie with monarchs. For myself, when I have finished what is to appear at the next fair,[71] I shall try my hand at something which will be not so much an attack on Luther, who has had quite enough abuse thundered at him if abuse could get us anywhere, as an attempt to heal our present discords.[72]

Now I know you will say: 'This is the way to go to war.' I only wish, my dear Barbier, this could truly be said of me. But I fear that I have still come almost prematurely; so thickly are the devoted squadrons massing, and they do not yield their ground. And I, to be sure, shall be handsomely rewarded for my labours all this time, in being pelted with stones by both sides. On our side I am most falsely maligned as Luther's man;[73] in Germany I am abused as an opponent of his faction. If only the sacrifice of my life, and not merely of my reputation, would enable me to convert this most perilous storm into a calm! Personally, I see no way out, unless Christ himself, like some god from the machine,[74] gives this lamentable play a happy ending. And all the while, though I have almost grown deaf to this word Lutheran, I do not yet really understand what it means. If anyone is a Lutheran who has read Luther's books, Latomus has read them too. If he is not a Lutheran who reads them in order to refute them or condemn them, how pray can he be a Lutheran who reads them with the intention of extracting whatever makes for edification and rejecting any errors with disgust? If he is a Lutheran who maintains and approves all he has written and will write hereafter without exception, I have never yet met such a man, nor do I think any man's brains are so diseased. I at least would not wish to be devoted to that degree to Jerome or Augustine – hardly to Paul himself, if you will allow a little exaggeration.

In any case, how can I, who neither read his books nor defend anything in them, be represented as a Lutheran? If everyone is orthodox who speaks ill of Luther, the people of Christendom are to be congratulated. But I fear, my excellent Barbier, there are many people who attack some unimportant things in what he writes – such as 'whatever the just man does is sin'[75] – with execration, though they themselves do not believe what is the basis of all our faith, that the soul survives the death of the body. All the same, I perceive two ways in which I might seem to be a Lutheran. First, if that man is a Lutheran from whose books he has taken a starting-point for error (if indeed he has taken anything out of my books), I could be called one; and in the same way the apostle Paul will be a Lutheran too, from whose books he has taken far more than from mine. Whence did the heretics of old time get the seeds of their errors, if not from Scripture? Yet no one blames the writers of Scripture for this. Besides which, if he is a Lutheran who wishes Luther well in any way, as he certainly does who urges him towards better things, and wishes to see him set right, under that heading I was certainly a Lutheran once and still am, and so I think are all true Christians. Who would not rather see his brother corrected than destroyed?[76]

But it is more than time to bring this nonsense to an end. How much longer will you torment us with the desire for your society?[77] When will you give us another chance to see you? How I wish I could behold you in a mitre in that Paria of yours![78] My life upon it, I would rather live over there among tribes utterly unknown than here amid this mad passion for denigration, a disease that used to be at home in the lurking-holes of monks and has now made its way into the very courts of kings. There is not a drinking-party without passionate arguments about Luther; and then the disputation deviates onto Erasmus. In heaven's name! They will say anything, these men who know as much of the question as a camel does of painting. And it is they make the loudest clamour. This trouble I owe to my German kinsmen.[79] For my part, I am heartily in favour of Germany: one can hardly describe how it blossoms more day by day with the most gifted minds, who are much more devoted to me than I either deserved or desired. But I could wish that the friendship of some of them had been rather more of an unmixed blessing. England commonly has a bad reputation where loyalty is concerned. But there I have found such friends, so loyal, so unchanging, so well judged in their support of me, that I could not even have wished for anything better.

Farewell, my dear Pierre, and mind you come and see me as soon as you can, your pockets full of Spanish ducats. For here there is a great thirst for gold; indeed I perceive that those gold nuggets that you habitually promise me in Paria are very like the mountains of gold in Persia.

Bruges, 13 August 1521

1226 / To Hieronymus Froben — Bruges, 14 August 1521

Probably in December 1520 the Basel printer Johann Froben sent his son, Hieronymus, to the Low Countries, primarily, it seems, to consult Erasmus about the publication of Polidoro Virgilio's *Adagiorum liber* (cf Epp 1175 introduction and lines 124–9, 1210:7–8). On c 13 January 1521 Johann expected his son to be with Erasmus in Louvain (cf AK II Ep 764). Presumably Hieronymus returned soon thereafter, taking Virgilio's work back with him to Basel, where it was published in July. This visit was not the first of its kind (cf Ep 903:3n, and for the possibility of a more recent trip, Ep 1209 n4). It may well have furthered the growth of a close and trusting relationship between Erasmus and the young Froben, as is reflected in this letter. Hieronymus' lively interest in learning, in this case Hebrew, which he had to sacrifice to the family business, is also mentioned in the dedication to him of Sebastian Münster's *Epitome hebraicae grammaticae* (Basel: J. Froben August 1520).

This letter was printed in the *Epistolae ad diversos*.

ERASMUS OF ROTTERDAM TO HIERONYMUS FROBEN, GREETING

You thank me, my dear Hieronymus, because you say my letter[1] has made your father less unsympathetic to you. But to make him very sympathetic indeed is entirely in your own power. The way to do this is to show yourself a true son to him, and help in your father's business because you really want to. No wonder if paid workmen are sometimes idle. But you, when you help your father, are helping yourself too. You are now at an age when all labour comes easily. Spend it on things that are worth doing. When you are given any free time,[2] spend it on studies worth pursuing and on reading good books. Avoid the company of spendthrifts and idlers; detach yourself from pleasures that only young men enjoy, and acquire endowments of real value. If you do this, you will never want for money or reputation; but if not, my recommendation to your father will be wasted, and you will find you have been very ill advised. I hope this will not happen. I am confident, my dear Hieronymus, that you will turn out the sort of person that both you and I would wish. Farewell, and give my love to your little Erasmius,[3] who is, I hear, a very promising child.

Bruges, eve of the Assumption 1521

1227 / To Richard Pace — Bruges, 23 August 1521

Pace did not, as Erasmus had hoped he would (cf lines 34–5) show up in Bruges among Cardinal Wolsey's following (cf Ep 1223 introduction). In consequence he was sent this letter, which, like the following Epp 1228–30, was no doubt given for conveyance to Erasmus' friends among Wolsey's party. All were printed in the *Epistolae ad diversos*.

ERASMUS OF ROTTERDAM TO THE HONOURABLE RICHARD PACE, DEAN OF ST PAUL'S, LONDON, GREETING

No news of my notebooks,[1] my dear Pace, and this torments me worse than the time when all the money I had in the world was lost at one blow on the beach at Dover.[2] Whom I should blame for this loss, I do not know; but certainly that it was intentional on your part, I will not and cannot believe.

The book[3] his Majesty has written against Luther I have only seen in the hands of Marino,[4] the papal nuncio. I greatly long to read it, for I have no doubt that it is worthy of that very gifted mind, which shows such extraordinary powers, whatever the topic on which it is exercised. In olden time it was evidence of miraculous piety, and qualified him for the calendar of saints, if a prince freed the necks of his Christian subjects from the yoke of their enemies with armaments and armies. But the eighth Henry does battle for the Bride of Christ with his intellectual gifts and with his pen, showing clearly enough what he will achieve if matters come to open fight. Though his achievement meanwhile is, to my thinking, more difficult, and will win him renown more lasting and more truly his own. For glory in war is shared by Fortune between many men, and often she claims much the largest portion for herself; but in this field the campaign is fought solely with the forces of the spirit, and all the credit is due solely and properly to Henry. All those of us who have any respect or love for good literature should be most ungrateful, did we not feel reverence and devotion towards such a gifted mind, which is a wonderful ornament and advertisement of our studies. Nor have I any doubt that his distinguished example, excessively rare as it may be, will spur on many princes to be his rivals. Surely the priests, the monks, the bishops will be ashamed to be so ignorant of theology, when they see so great a monarch, so young, so much preoccupied with business, making such progress in the knowledge of divinity that he can even publish books to champion the Christian religion in its peril. Nor do I doubt that in this he will prove somewhat more successful than others who have previously tried their strength in the same field.[5]

But I will write more definitely about this when I have devoured the book, for I have a very great desire to read it. His Grace of York[6] has promised to let me have access to a copy. It was a great blow to me that you were not a member of this party, and I could have borne it more patiently if you had at least visited me by letter. Do not forget, my dear Pace, to whose office you have succeeded,[7] and the promises you have made me. For I expect you to see to it that I do not miss Colet over much, and you promised even more than that. You will more than satisfy my wishes and your promises, if thanks to you I am able to recover the bits and pieces I left with you at Ferrara.[8] Farewell, my excellent friend.

Bruges, 23 August 1521

Marcus Laurinus, the dean of St Donatian's, my host and a great admirer of yours, asks me to send you his warmest greetings.

1228 / To William Warham — Bruges, 23 August 1521

The text of this letter has an interesting history. The letter was printed in the *Epistolae ad diversos* (cf Ep 1206 introduction), but in re-editing it, Allen normally gave preference to the variant readings of a contemporary manuscript copy in the Öffentliche Bibliothek of the University of Basel (MS Ki.Ar. 25a no 97). He argued that, its blunders notwithstanding, the copy might have derived from Erasmus' rough draft. His conjecture was confirmed in 1924–5 when two copies of a rare print of Epp 1203, 1228 turned up: *Erasmi Roterodami duo epistolia de causa Lutherana* (n p, n d [Leipzig: M. Landsberg c October 1521]). Two later reprints were derived from the *Epistolae ad diversos*; cf Ep 1227 n3.

A comparison between the Leipzig pamphlet and the *Epistolae ad diversos*, supplemented by evidence of the early circulation of the two letters, leaves no doubt that the Leipzig text was based on Erasmus' original drafts, which may have been copied secretly before dispatch and sent to Saxony as evidence of Erasmus' hardening stance against Luther. On 7 March 1522 Erasmus complained about the circulation of Ep 1228 (cf Allen Ep 1263:18n), but he may have realized the indiscretion somewhat earlier and perhaps felt that he had no choice but to publish edited versions of both letters in the *Epistolae ad diversos*, although he did not hesitate to include Epp 1225 and 1236 in that collection, neither of which can have pleased Luther's friends. This translation follows the Leipzig text, but it does include significant sections (lines 30–51 'Luther ... when he was down'; lines 58–61 'Here ... Hungary'), which are found only in the *Epistolae ad diversos*. Presumably at least some of these additions were already part of the letter as sent to Warham, for one cannot see why they should have been inserted at the time of printing.

It should be noted that this letter first circulated in German Lutheran circles in a form that was substantially shorter and lent accordingly greater emphasis to Erasmus' pledge to participate in the religious controversy, evidently not on the side of Luther (lines 53–8); see Allen VI xx–xxi and H. Holeczek 'Die Haltung des Erasmus zu Luther nach dem Scheitern seiner Vermittlungspolitik 1520/21' *Archiv für Reformationsgeschichte* 64 (1973) 85–112.

ERASMUS OF ROTTERDAM TO THE MOST REVEREND WILLIAM WARHAM, ARCHBISHOP OF CANTERBURY, PRIMATE OF ALL ENGLAND, GREETING

When I heard that his Eminence the cardinal was to meet the emperor at Bruges,[1] I went to Bruges myself in hopes of seeing several friends there and conversing with them, who are among the most dear and pleasant of my possessions. My mind was possessed by a lively hope that the bishop of Rochester[2] would be there too; but this proved false.

The book which the king of England has written against Luther[3] I have seen, but have not yet received a copy, although his Eminence of York often promised he would send one. I suspect this is due to the negligence of the man who was given the task. Who would not feel enthusiasm at the gifts of such a prince, who sheds lustre in this way upon our studies, and champions our religion? In olden time it was thought the height of piety if kings defended the peace of Christendom by force of arms. He does battle for it with his intellectual gifts and with his pen, showing clearly enough what he would achieve if matters demand the sword. I am confident that he will set a splendid example, which other princes will be eager to follow. Surely priests and monks will now at last be ashamed to be quite ignorant of sacred studies, when they see that a great prince like this has made such progress in this field that he can even publish books to champion the Catholic religion. Some of his nobles, Mountjoy especially, have given me to understand beyond doubt that the book is, as the saying goes, the achievement of his own bow and spear;[4] nor do I doubt that it will prove fully worthy of that most gifted mind, which shows such extraordinary powers, whatever the topic on which it is exercised. But I will write more fully on this when I read the book.

The outlook seems to me as full of dangers as it well could be, and I see that I must navigate my course in such a way that I neither abandon Christ's business by seeking favour with men, nor plunge myself into some peril to no purpose. Luther has cast an apple of discord into the world, and I can see no part of it anywhere that is not in confusion. All men agree that the morals

Christian II of Denmark
Portrait by Jan Gossaert van Mabuse
Fondation Custodia (Coll. F. Lugt), Institut Néerlandais, Paris

of the church had gone too far downhill and that some powerful remedy was needed; but it seems to me we have almost come to such a pass that the medicine,[5] clumsily administered, does not drive out the virulence of the disease but makes it even more violent. I wish that remark were true which the invincible King Christian[6] of Denmark once made to me (in jest, as I suppose) when I said something of the sort to him; that mild medicines have no effect, and it is the mark of a drug that does you good that first it rattles the whole body. I am sure I see no good way out, unless Christ himself bring all our passionate folly to a favourable outcome, just as they say that Minerva habitually brought success to the imprudent counsels of the Athenians.[7] To me, who have always been a lover of tranquillity, this uproar in the world cannot be other than most disagreeable. Besides which, this business of Luther, far removed as it is from liberal studies, even so burdens the work of people like myself with considerable unpopularity. There is an element of chance in this: before Luther arose, I had long been fighting a bitter campaign against the sort of people who are now Luther's chief opponents. They are certain monks and theologians whom I could name, who give this ill-nourished and disordered doctrine[8] more importance than it deserves. And now they all vie with one another in attacking Luther, as the Greeks of old attacked Hector when he was down.[9] We must avoid him like Scylla, and yet make sure we are not swept into Charybdis.[10]

Some people are very urgent that I should write something against Luther. Once I have disentangled myself from the tasks which distract me at the moment – and this will not take long – I shall devote myself to reading all the works of Luther[11] and his opponents. It is not a task to be lightly undertaken. My object will be to be seen to be doing all I can to support the dignity of the Roman pontiff and the peace of Christendom. Here we are making great preparations for war against the French.[12] The pope is thoroughly provoked by his old friends, and has joined our side.[13] And all the time the Turks in arms are devastating Hungary.[14]

I pray that Christ the Lord may preserve your Grace for our benefit in good health. The rest of our news you will hear from the right reverend Thomas Halsey,[15] bishop of Elphin, whom I have always found a sincere well-wisher.

Bruges, 23 August 1521

1229 / To Thomas Lupset — Bruges, 23 August [1521]

Lupset was now at Oxford in possession of one of the readerships endowed by Cardinal Wolsey (cf Ep 967:40n). This letter was published in the *Epistolae ad diversos* with an incorrect year date; cf Ep 1227 introduction.

ERASMUS OF ROTTERDAM TO THOMAS LUPSET, GREETING

The rumour of your illness, my dear Lupset, gave me pain, and I am correspondingly delighted to hear that you are restored to us. I have written a life of Colet,[1] the whole in the form of a letter. If you wish it had been set forth more vividly, you will be partly to blame, for you did not give me a full enough account of the man in his true colours,[2] which no one could have done better than you. You say you are modelling your life on the style and pattern, as it were, of his, and this I am bound to approve most emphatically, provided you exercise a certain choice. The example you set before you is indeed a good one; but even in the best things we should imitate the outstanding features only, and even then only those that are suitable; for everything does not suit everybody. In him the outstanding thing was the way he drew the genuine philosophy of Christ from the pure well-head of the Gospels, and spread it abroad without money and without price among the multitude, so that we may think there was a touch of Providence in his family name, for Coheleth is the Hebrew word for 'preacher,' the Greek 'ecclesiastes.' Devote yourself to this same object with all your powers, and, unless I am quite wrong, you will end up as great as Colet.

At the same time, to follow his example and entirely deny yourself dinner[3] is a thing I do not approve, nor did I approve it in him. If you feel the need in the prime of life to bridle your bodily appetites, in my opinion this would be better achieved by a moderate use of food and drink than by severe and continuous fasting.[4] A large part of self-discipline consists in a definite resolve to wish to abstain. If you add to this the vigorous and uninterrupted study of the Scriptures, there will be no need to torment yourself by fasting, which may perhaps keep the luxuriance of youth in check, but at the price of bequeathing an enfeebled constitution to your old age, and may restrain the fires of the body only to enfeeble the powers of the mind.

I hope the patron deity of commerce will smile upon your excellent mother,[5] while she battles single-handed and in her own language with these strange creatures speaking foreign tongues. If only I had here ten female champions such as she, I should sleep the sleep of the just. I really think she, above all women, deserves to grow young again. Give my warmest greetings to your excellent father.[6] Look after yourself, my dearest Lupset. And remember me to those two frank and friendly Williams, Gonnell and Dancaster;[7] yes, and Master Gerard,[8] Colet's steward.

Bruges, 23 August [1520]

1230 / To Thomas Linacre Bruges, 24 August 1521

This letter was printed in the *Epistolae ad diversos*; cf Ep 1227 introduction.

ERASMUS OF ROTTERDAM TO THOMAS LINACRE, PHYSICIAN-IN-ORDINARY TO HIS MOST SERENE HIGHNESS THE KING OF ENGLAND, GREETING

It was with great distress that I heard from my friends that your health had not been good, for you of all people surely deserve to be untouched by old age or illness of any kind. But such is our condition from our birth, nor are the Fates amenable to any prayer; and so we must work hard in order to survive ourselves by such means as even fate allows. Furthermore, you will have noticed how parents depart this life with greater resignation if they have lived to see their children in some established position; and in the same way it is something, by publishing the fruit of our night-watches, to gain, as it were, a foretaste for the time being of the verdict which posterity will pass on us. But you (if you will allow me to speak freely) continually suppress your own works,[1] which are second to none in learning, so that there is some risk of your caution and modesty being mistaken for hardness of heart, if you will torment the scholarship of this generation with the long drawn-out expectation of your results, and so long deprive us of the enjoyment of your books, which we all are eager to see. Perhaps you take fright at my own example.[2] But do be careful, I beg you, while you are so anxiously avoiding my mistakes, not to fall into the opposite extreme. If there is any assistance you dare count on receiving from me, I assure you I shall always be most ready to help. Farewell, my excellent and excellently learned friend.

Bruges, St Bartholomew's day 1521

1231 / To Pieter Wichmans Bruges, [c 29 August] 1521

This letter, published in the *Epistolae ad diversos*, was written shortly before Erasmus' return from Bruges to his host at Anderlecht, Pieter Wichmans (d 1535), canon and scholaster of St Peter's. So shortly in fact that if we are to accept the date of Ep 1232, it would have reached its destination barely ahead of its writer (cf n1). It suggests that Wichmans gratified his guest not only with his charming hospitality (cf Ep 1208 introduction) but also with an outlook that was quite compatible with Erasmus' own. Thus the letter may have been written for publication, to honour Wichmans.

ERASMUS OF ROTTERDAM TO THE ESTIMABLE PIETER WICHMANS, CANON OF ANDERLECHT, HIS HOST, GREETING

You used to lament how sadly the faith has been shaken by the Lutherans, and you ought to rejoice with it when it happily regains its strength. On St Augustine's day[1] we had a sermon here from a man in very splendid priestly vestments. He spoke at length, doubtless under divine inspiration, and among other things restored in a surprising way the old standing of the four orders of mendicants,[2] as they call them, and of confession; both of which seemed to have suffered somewhat lately from the attentions of Luther's party.

The standing of the order he reinstated thus. Augustine, he said, was that spring in the midst of paradise whence came the four rivers,[3] that is, the four mendicant orders, who by their learning and holiness of life water the whole surface of the earth, that is, the whole church, and make it fertile. If he had said that Christ was the spring and the four rivers the four Gospels, the allegory would not have been wholly absurd. But as it is, what has Augustine to do with the four orders? And as for what he added about watering and making fertile, many men of good standing wished it were the truth, and a very great many men grinned broadly.

As for confession, he restored it as follows. 'Augustine,' he said, 'wrote a work on confession in many books, in which he confesses some almost ridiculous things, such as how he once watched, not without a certain pleasure, a spider hunting a fly.[4] This proves,' says he, 'that nothing is so small that there is no need to confess it.' In the first place Augustine is there using the word confession, which has a double meaning, both for the offering of thanks and for the confession of a fault. And in that work he rather gives himself credit than confesses faults; nor does he confess to a priest, but to God. And yet the preacher in saying this was using the word in its current sense, which means nothing to ordinary people except what theologians call 'sacramental confession.'[5] They say many things like this in public before large crowds, and are disappointed not to be treated as gods.

A third point was perhaps to my address, for I am thought in a prize speech[6] to have given too much importance to matrimony. 'Some people,' he said, 'condemn celibacy. Yet unless we had been celibate, the Christian faith by now would have been extinct.' In ancient days hardly anyone preached a sermon without posting secretaries to take down what he said.[7] If that were the practice today, heavens! what stories we should hear. Men who say things like that in the famous city of Bruges, which contains so many educated men, and so many men of lively wits and sound judgment even without academic education – what do you suppose they say in the villages, and across the dinner-table? And these are our pillars of orthodoxy.

I thought you ought to know this, so that you cannot say you never hear any news of what happens here; but you shall hear more by word of mouth. Farewell.

Bruges, 1521

1232 / To Nicolaas van Broeckhoven — Anderlecht, 31 August [1521]

With this letter Erasmus welcomes the appearance in print of Tertullian, one of the earliest Latin Fathers. The first edition of his works by Beatus Rhenanus (cf n1) was in fact a companion volume to Erasmus' Cyprian (cf Ep 1000) in the great enterprise of the Basel patristic editions (cf the preface). Both editions were provided with an index by the Franciscan Conradus Pellicanus (cf *Das Chronikon des Konrad Pellikan*, Basel 1877, 78).

Erasmus addressed this letter to one of his Antwerp friends, who apparently shared with him an intellectual, and in some way even a commercial, interest in the Tertullian edition (cf Epp 1507, 1696). Nicolaas van Broeckhoven, like other Antwerp friends (cf Ep 1188 n5), sympathized with Luther's ideas – a fact which is discreetly permitted to show in Erasmus' approach (cf lines 23, 33–5, 43–5). The letter was, none the less, printed in the *Epistolae ad diversos* (with an incorrect year in the date).

Later in the year Broeckhoven was arrested and charged with heresy, but managed to escape from his jail in Brussels (cf Fredericq IV 83). It is possible that Erasmus' advice to him not to relinquish his post despite stormy days (cf lines 109–14) points to the growing resolve to restrain the advocates of reform. Primarily, however, this letter seems designed to encourage the study of the Christian Fathers, thus pointing to Erasmus' own way of escape from the religious conflict.

ERASMUS OF ROTTERDAM TO NICOLAAS OF 'S HERTOGENBOSCH, HEADMASTER OF THE GRAMMAR SCHOOL IN THE FAMOUS CITY OF ANTWERP, GREETING

May all the blessed ones rain blessings on Beatus, our friend who has given us Tertullian,[1] that author so much beloved by Cyprian and so much praised by Jerome! If only he could have given us a complete and corrected text! But we owe a great debt to his industry for doing all that he could.[2] So far I have only been able to sample it rather than read it. Tertullian has of course a style of his own, which was I suppose admired at that date in Africa, though it seems somewhat harsh to us. My beloved Jerome made no attempt to conceal this; he credits him with close-packed epigrams, but also notes his difficulties in expressing himself.[3] All the same, who would not marvel at that ever-ardent heart, that exact knowledge of the Scriptures, and that ready memory? – and all this in those early days, when there was still no regular profession of theology, when there were no universities, no learned disquisitions, almost no commentators on the sacred books. When I think on this, dear Nicolaas, I feel our own times should do better.

Yet he has this fault, which Jerome condemns in Origen:[4] he sometimes does violence to the Scriptures, and does it with an effrontery that leaves Origen behind. For he as a rule is all argument and inquiry, while Tertullian is absolute and combative. An example is that passage where Christ says, 'He that putteth away his wife and taketh another, committeth adultery,'[5] which he interprets as no condemnation of divorce, except in cases where a wife is rejected for the purpose of marrying another woman who is more attractive. And further, his leaving the church, which ought not to be and cannot be excused, is yet palliated by Jerome:[6] 'having remained a priest of the Church,' he says, 'into middle life, he was then driven by the hostility and slanderous attacks of the clerics of the Roman church to fall into the heresy of Montanus.' The man who makes an honest mistake is deserving of mercy; but all heresy which is combined with obstinacy that will not learn must be abhorred by pious minds. And yet, as one poison is more deadly than another, so some heresies are more pestilent than others.

And those heresies seem least far removed from true religion which, from some excessive zeal for the full rigour of the Gospel, demand more of men than is right. Of this class were the people who expected a man who had once been baptized to maintain such a high standard of freedom from all contamination that they would never take back into the bosom of the church those who had once relapsed into any serious crime,[7] with the idea that the severity of this ecclesiastical censure should deter others from offending. For they did not hold, I think, that they must be banned from the kingdom of heaven because they had been put outside the portals of the church – which are entered frequently by those whom God will exclude from his presence. But the remedy of penance, which other and less severe authorities allowed to last for a given period only, they held to be perpetual, and supposed that this helped to maintain the rest of the flock in its obedience. Their view was very close to that held by St Augustine,[8] who opens the gate of the church to a man who has lapsed once after due penance, but does not open it to one who lapses a second time lest the church's discipline should be watered down. In the same way the early Fathers, moved by the example and language of Christ and the apostles, who speak so highly everywhere of chastity, disapproved of second marriage[9] and demanded continence, though St Paul gave instructions that a man should be received into the fellowship of the church who had married his father's wife,[10] and Christ does not require celibacy of his disciples, but says, 'He that is able to receive it, let him receive it.'[11]

With these I include the people who, reflecting what an impious and monstrous thing war is, and seeing peace and concord praised so highly everywhere in the Scriptures, have determined that no war can be lawful between Christians.[12] This sort of exaggeration is almost allowable even in the orthodox, whenever they either seek to deter us from different faults or encourage us to actions far removed from those which they wish us to avoid. They act like those who, given a curved stick, do not bend it until it is straight but curve it right back in the opposite direction, that it may end up by returning to the straight. And this, it seems to me, is the form taken by most of Tertullian's errors.

Some people's errors were so grotesque that the very men who held the doctrines were ashamed of them. Such were the views – not so much heresy as madness – of Simon and Menander,[13] who declared themselves the supreme power of God; of Basilides with his monstrous Abraxas;[14] and then of the Nicolaites,[15] whose dogma was community of wives. To these we may add the Ophites,[16] who worshipped the serpent that tempted Eve, and the Judaites,[17] who attributed the salvation of the human race to Judas, who betrayed Jesus. Soon faded were the delusions of Cerinthus and Valentinus,[18] faded the ravings of Manichaeus,[19] faded Montanus and his Paraclete.[20] And the Artotyrites[21] left a name of which scarcely anyone has heard.

Now heresies arose which were in themselves most pestilent, but could not strike deep roots because they conflicted openly with the authority of Scripture, which has always been unshaken, always accepted in perfect unison by churches all the world over. Such is the view of those who denied that Christ had a human body or, conversely, refused him a human soul; who denied that he had really suffered, or that he was born of a Virgin; who declared that the resurrection was complete when Christ rose from the dead, and that no other resurrection of the dead was to be looked for.[22] But no heresy roused greater disorders in the world than that of the Arians,[23] for it did not put forward monstrous things which were palpably absurd, and appeared to rest (for the Arians were not bad scholars) on the evidence of Scripture. The heresy of the Pelagians,[24] as far as concerns free will, has left traces which can be detected even now. But a good part of all the heresies seems to have taken its rise from the teaching of philosophers – which makes it the more surprising that we are now told that heretics cannot be refuted without the assistance of Aristotle's philosophy.[25] Either his philosophy is, we must suppose, a very holy business, or they are distinguished practitioners who know how to use it for such a purpose. In our own day there are even certain heresies of the philosophical schools, on which it were perhaps well not to debate so obstinately as to throw the whole world into confusion, especially as they neither contribute much to the good life nor stand in the way of Christ's glory.

But there is one heresy which is not thought worthy of the name, but does the greatest harm to our human life and is a major obstacle to the authority of the Gospel: when those who profess the philosophy of Christ and behave as the supreme leaders and chiefs of all Christian people openly in all their way of life, all their purposes, and all their efforts teach nothing but ambition of a more than theatrical sort, insatiable greed, inexhaustible appetite for pleasures, mad love of war, and all the other things which are an abomination to Holy Scripture and are rejected even by the philosophers of paganism. They do not speak of such things, of course, but example is more effective than precept.

In our conversation the other day you indicated that you were thinking of resigning from your despotic rule. I do not approve this idea. You have come on the stage; you must play out the part which the producer has allotted to you. If you are a man of high character, as I have no doubt you are, you will not resent your situation because it is beneath you; you will be satisfied with it for this reason, that it gives you such a chance to serve the community. You dislike the stormy days in which we live. Yes; but meanwhile, like a good ship's captain you must obey the winds until fair weather returns – for this tempest will not last long, or so I hope. Farewell, dearest Nicolaas.

From Anderlecht, 31 August [1520]

1232A / From Arsenius Apostolius — Florence, 31 August 1521

The text of this letter was discovered in Apostolius' letter-book, a Greek manuscript of the Biblioteca Vallicelliana in Rome: MS F 40 ff 46 verso–47 recto. It was first published by W.J.W. Koster 'Ein brief van de humanist Arsenius an Erasmus' *Hermeneus* 11 (1938–9) 17–20, and subsequently (with other letters by the same author) by M.I. Manousakas '*Ἀρσενίου Μονεμβασίας τοῦ Ἀποστόλη ἐπιστολαὶ ἀνέκδοτοι* (1521–34),' *Ἐπετηρὶς τοῦ Μεσαιωνικοῦ Ἀρχείου* 8–9 (1958–9) 5–56. The text translated is that of Manousakas, which differs in a few places from that of Koster.

Arsenius (or Aristoboulos) Apostolius (c 1468–1535) was a Cretan, who had come to Italy by 1492. He was appointed archbishop of Monemvasia on the Peloponnese, then under Venetian domination, and installed in 1506. Two years later popular opposition forced him to abandon his see and he returned to Italy. In Venice he met Erasmus (cf lines 10–12) amid the circle of scholars collaborating with the press of Aldo Manuzio. After sojourns in Rome, Florence, Crete, and again Monemvasia, Apostolius eventually died in Venice.

ARSENIUS, ARCHBISHOP OF MONEMVASIA, TO ERASMUS, GREETING

Whatever mark or imprint is made on physical bodies must inevitably perish, since the substance on which it is inscribed is perishable; but it is reasonable to suppose that whatever is written and inscribed on the book of the soul will never perish, since it rests on that which is eternal. So, my dear friend, even if you are not present, I can still see you as though reflected in the mirror of my heart and soul, and I love and cherish you and try to keep that affection undiminished. Indeed how could I not love the learned Erasmus, whose fame has spread through many lands and cities and whose influence is felt in every gathering and assembly? I believe that your own feelings towards me have been very similar ever since the learned Muses brought us together at Venice: but you could show more clearly how you feel by writing to me as I am writing to you. There is a danger that we shall forget our friendship if we allow silence to become a habit.

The man who brings you this letter is a countryman of yours.[1] Since he was on his way back to your part of the world, he begged me for a few lines to take to you. I have given him what he asked for in the hope of receiving something from you in return. I am also sending you a copy of my *Apophthegmata*, [2] which I published recently at Rome. I offer it as a small token of the friendship we feel for one another. Farewell.

Florence, 31 August[3] 1521

1233 / To Guillaume Budé — Anderlecht, [c September] 1521

This letter was written after Erasmus' return from Bruges to Anderlecht (cf Ep 1223 introduction) and printed in the *Epistolae ad diversos*. Written under the invigorating impact of a recent meeting with Thomas More (cf lines 2–8, 155), the letter also reacts to the new threats posed to the humanistic ideals by the religious confrontation and the recent outbreak of war (cf Ep 1228 n12). It opens with a public expression of solidarity between scholars, now that their respective rulers were at war (cf lines 15–17), and then turns to More and the education of women, a concern for which More's household set a shining example (for another example see Ep 1247).

ERASMUS OF ROTTERDAM TO HIS FRIEND GUILLAUME BUDÉ, GREETING

When I was lately at Bruges in attendance on the emperor with a great many other people, I caught many hares in one field as the proverb has it,[1] being able to greet many friends on that one occasion; above all, one no less civilized than he is eminent – a person no less amiable than the cardinal of York,[2] who was present as his king's representative and was received by our Prince Charles so lavishly, it was really almost royal. Cuthbert Tunstall was there, and Thomas More, and William Mountjoy, as well as countless others whom I do not mention only because I know that they are still unknown to you. Thomas More had great hopes of greeting you at Calais in the French mission.[3] The cardinal's arrival delighted me the more for this reason; I was hoping that the disorders which now exist between the world's most eminent princes, to the great peril of the human race, might be pacified by his wisdom and his prestige. But as things now are, I see nothing to hope for, unless some god from the machine[4] turns our purposes to better effect. But these upheavals between monarchs do not disrupt the bonds drawn by the Muses.

There are people whose interests are well suited if the emperor and the king of France do not see eye to eye.[5] These men cultivate the seeds of discord with the skill of classical tyrants, letting us weaken our resources in mutual disagreements while they establish their own despotic power. You can guess, I imagine, of whom I am thinking. If only both princes might be on their guard, and not utter later on those words that testify to wisdom too lately and too dearly bought: 'I had not thought of that'![6]

More is to be congratulated. He neither aimed at it nor asked for it, but the king has promoted him to a very honourable post, with a salary by no means to be despised: he is his prince's treasurer.[7] This office in England is in the first rank of grandeur and distinction, but is not unduly exposed either to unpopularity or to tedious press of business. He had a rival for it,[8] a fairly influential man who wanted the office so badly that he would not object to holding it at his own costs and charges. But that admirable king gave the clearest proof of his high opinion of More, in that he went so far as to give him a salary when he did not want the post, rather than accept an official who did not need to be paid. Not content with that, this most generous prince has also knighted him,[9] nor can there be any doubt that some day he will honour him with yet greater distinctions when the occasion presents itself; for normally princes show a much greater tendency to promote bachelors.[10] But More is so deeply embedded in the ranks of married men, that not even his wife's death has given him his freedom. For having buried his first wife, who was a girl when he married her, the widower has now taken unto himself a widow.[11]

I am the more delighted for More's sake at this attitude of his prince towards him for this reason, that whatever increase in authority or influence accrues to him, accrues, I believe, to the study of the humanities, of which he is such a keen supporter that, were his resources equal to his wishes, the English would find their gifted minds in no lack of an open-hearted and generous Maecenas. The courts of princes usually behave like the physician who first evacuates the body of the patient entrusted to him and then fills it up and restores its energy;[12] and I do not doubt that our friend More has had some such experience hitherto. How it has gone in your case you know better than I do. And yet gifted men have enjoyed his bounty, in the days when not only was he far from having plenty to give away, he was burdened with debt.

But to be a good scholar himself and give generous support to all other scholars is not the only way in which he honours liberal studies. He takes pains to give his whole household an education in good literature, setting thereby a new precedent which, if I mistake not, will soon be widely followed, so happy is the outcome. He has three daughters,[13] of whom Margaret, the eldest, is already married to a young man who is well off, has a most honourable and modest character, and besides that is no stranger to our literary pursuits. All of them from their earliest years he has had properly and strictly brought up in point of character, and has given them a liberal education. To his three daughters he has added a fourth girl,[14] whom he maintains as a piece of generosity to be a playmate for them. He also has a step-daughter[15] of great beauty and exceptional gifts, married for some years now to a young man not without education and of truly golden character. And he has a son by his first wife,[16] now a boy of about thirteen, who is the youngest of his children.

About a year ago, More took it into his head to give me a demonstration of the progress of their education. He told them all to write to me, each of them independently. No subject was supplied them, nor was what they wrote corrected in any way. When they had shown their drafts to their father for criticism, he told them, as though he took exception to their bad writing, to make a cleaner and more careful copy of the same words; and when they had done that, he did not alter a syllable, but sealed up the letters and sent them off to me. Believe me, my dear Budé, I never saw anything so admirable. In what they said there was nothing foolish or childish, and the language made one feel that they must be making daily progress. This charming group, with the husbands of two of them, he keeps under his own roof. There you never see one of the girls idle, or busied with the trifles that women enjoy; they have a Livy in their hands. They have made such progress that they can read and understand authors of that class without anyone to explain them, unless they come upon some word that might have held up even me or someone like me.

His wife, whose strength lies in mother-wit and experience rather than book-learning, controls the whole institution with remarkable skill, acting as a kind of overseer who gives each one her task and sees that she performs it and allows no idleness or frivolous occupations.

You are wont to complain in your letters from time to time that in your case classical study has acquired a bad name for having brought two bad things into your life, poor health and pecuniary loss.[17] The result of More's activity on the other hand, is to make it acceptable to everyone concerned on every count, for he says he owes to his literary studies his much better health, his popularity and influence with an excellent prince and all men both friends and strangers, his easier circumstances, his own greater happiness and the happiness he gives his friends, the services he can now render to his country and his relations and kinsfolk, his increased adaptability to court society, to life among the nobility, and to the whole way of life that he now leads, and a greater ease in pleasing heaven. At first liberal studies had a bad name for depriving their devoted adherents of the common touch. There is no journey, no business however voluminous or difficult, that can take the book out of More's hand; and yet it would be hard to find anyone who was more truly a man for all seasons and all men,[18] who was more ready to oblige, more easily available for meeting, more lively in conversation, or who combined so much real wisdom with such charm of character. The result is that, while only a few days ago a love of literature was thought to be of no practical or ornamental value, there is now hardly one of our great nobles who would reckon his children worthy of their ancestry if they had no education in liberal studies.[19] Monarchs themselves are thought to lack a good share of the qualities proper to a king if their knowledge of literature leaves much to be desired.

Again, scarcely any mortal man was not under the conviction that, for the female sex, education had nothing to offer in the way of either virtue or reputation. Nor was I myself in the old days completely free of this opinion;[20] but More has quite put it out of my head. For two things in particular are perilous to a girl's virtue, idleness and improper amusements, and against both of these the love of literature is a protection. There is no better way to maintain a spotless reputation than faultless behaviour, and no woman's chastity is more secure than her's who is chaste by deliberate choice. Not that I disapprove the ideas of those who plan to protect their daughters' honour by teaching them the domestic arts; but nothing so occupies a girl's whole heart as the love of reading.[21] And besides this advantage, that the mind is kept from pernicious idleness, this is the way to absorb the highest principles, which can both instruct and inspire the mind in the pursuit of virtue. Many have been exposed to the loss of their maidenhead by inexperience and ignorance of the world, before they know what the things are that put that great treasure at risk. Nor do I see why husbands need fear that if they have educated wives they will have wives who are less obedient, unless they are the kind of men who wish to demand from a wife what ought not to be demanded of respectable married women. In my opinion, on the other hand, nothing is more intractable than ignorance. At least, a mind developed and exercised by reading has this advantage, that it can recognize good and just reasons for what they are, and perceive what conduct is proper and what is profitable. Why, the man who has taught her the facts has almost converted her. Besides which, what makes wedlock delightful and lasting is more the good will between mind and mind than any physical passion, so that far stronger bonds unite those who are joined by mutual affection of minds as well, and a wife has more respect for a husband whom she acknowledges as a teacher also. Devotion will not be less because there is less unreason in it. Personally, I would rather have one talent of pure gold than three contaminated heavily with lead and dross.

We often hear other women returning from church quite ready to say that the preacher gave them a wonderful sermon, and they provide a lively account of his expression. Beyond that, they are quite unable to report what he said or what it was like. These young ladies recount nearly the whole sermon to you in order,[22] though not without some selection; if the preacher let fall anything foolish or irreligious or off the point, as we see not seldom happens nowadays, they know how to make fun of it or ignore it or protest against it. This, and only this, is what listening to a sermon means. One can really enjoy the society of girls like this. I differ profoundly from those who keep a wife for no purpose except physical satisfaction, for which half-witted females are better fitted. A woman must have intelligence if she is to keep her household up to its duties, to form and mould her childrens' characters, and meet her husband's needs in every way. Apart from that, when I was talking to More recently, I put the objection that if anything should happen, as the way of all flesh is, he would be the more tormented by grief for the loss of them, inasmuch as he had spent all that effort on their upbringing; and he replied, 'If anything inevitable were to happen, I would rather they died educated than uneducated.' And I was then reminded of that remark of Phocion,[23] I think it was, who was about to drink the hemlock, and when his wife cried out, 'O my husband, you will die an innocent man,' his answer was, 'What of it, my dear wife? Would you rather I died guilty?'

In the mean time the idea has come into my head of matching you two together as two outstanding leaders in this field, much as a man might compare Camillus and Scipio Africanus.[24] You have been fighting the enemies of good letters for more years and in an age more unfavourable to them, and in this respect at least you are ahead of More. At the same time, what you have been trying to do in your sons only and in your brothers, he does without hesitation in his wives and daughters too, with a brave contempt for the criticism excited by this new idea; and under this head, conversely, he is superior to you. Again, in published books you have done more for the supply in both languages than he has, and will do more still, I promise myself, in the future, if you can once start bringing forth the riches you have filed away and sharing them with the public. Not but what our younger men have great expectations of More too, for he is still a long way from old age and has a father aged, I suppose, not much less than eighty, whose old age is wonderfully green[25] – you could hardly find anyone who carries his years with a better grace. This allows one to hope for a ripe old age for More likewise. I perceive one thing in which you might render a very great service to Greek studies, if you were to make a really full lexicon,[26] not only listing the words but explaining the idioms and turns of speech peculiar to Greek when these are not generally known and obvious. It is a rather humdrum subject, I admit, and unworthy of your position; but I believe that a man of principle should be ready to demean himself to some extent for the public benefit, as Plato expects of his wise man.[27]

Aleandro[28] has now been here for some time, but up to now I have had little chance to see him, he has been so full of this Luther business, in which, to be sure, he has quitted himself like a man. When he has done with that, or more truly because he has now nearly done with it, it will be possible to enjoy his company sometimes, for I find him as pleasant as he is learned. Vives[29] is competing in the literary race with great vigour and equal success and, if I know his mettle, he will not slacken until he has left all the rest far behind. I think highly of you all for giving Brie advice which has made him change his mind,[30] and highly of him for trusting his friends' judgment. More will be so far from any hostile designs that he does not even bear in mind their earlier difference of opinion. I was delighted that he should be following your example and giving himself practice in letter-writing in both languages,[31] nor do I doubt he will be successful in an art which you were the first to attempt both in France and in our generation, with youthful audacity but the greatest success. His letter, which is as civil as it is learned, shall have an answer as soon as I have a spare moment.

I am writing this in my rural retreat at Anderlecht,[32] for I have taken your example and retired to the country myself; and I wish I could follow you in building too![33] In any case, the country has done me so much good that I mean to repeat the practice in future every year. Farewell.

1521

1233A / From Bonifacius Amerbach [Basel, September 1521]

The undated autograph rough draft of this letter is among the Amerbach papers in the Öffentliche Bibliothek of the University of Basel (MS C VIa f 354). It was first edited by Allen (Ep 1201) and subsequently by Alfred Hartmann (AK II Ep 813). Allen placed it at the beginning of May, but Hartmann showed that it belongs rather to September. Not until 5 September (AK II Ep 810), when he expected Erasmus' imminent arrival in Basel (cf Ep 1242 introduction), did

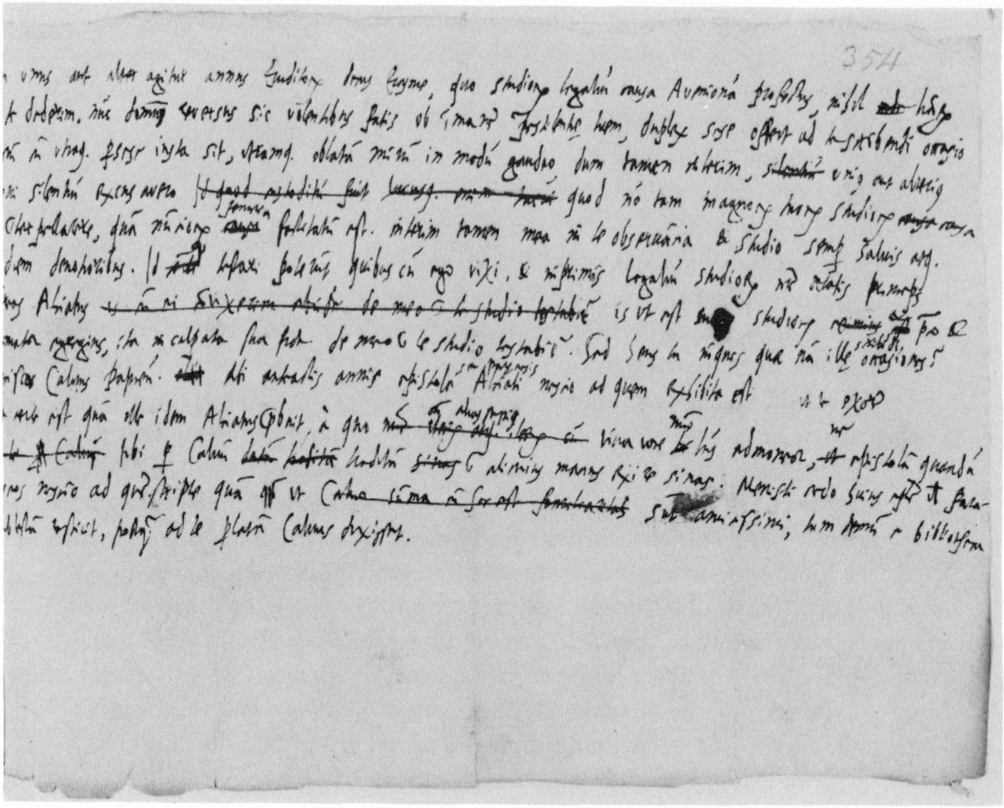

Autograph letter from Bonifacius Amerbach to Erasmus, Ep 1233A
Öffentliche Bibliothek, University of Basel

Alciati make the request which Amerbach passes on to Erasmus in lines 15–21. Erasmus replied to Alciati directly on 14 December (Ep 1250), but his reassuring, albeit ambiguous, declarations were also echoed in a letter from Amerbach (AK II Ep 830).

It is now a year or two, dear Erasmus, glory of the world of learning, since I set off for Avignon to pursue my legal studies,[1] and have not written you a letter. Now the appalling ravages of the plague have sent me home again,[2] since fate would have it so, and a twofold excuse presents itself for writing. Though either of them would be sufficient by itself, I am quite delighted to have the two excuses, provided I can secure forgiveness for my silence during this year or two, which was caused not so much by fear of interrupting your important researches as by lack of couriers. Yet all this time my respect and devotion have endured and grown greater day by day, as those whom I have lived with can testify, above all the leader of legal studies in our time, Andrea Alciati.[3] He is a champion of your work and a capital critic, and will testify with his unquestioned authority to the devotion which I feel for you.

Very well, you will say, but what are these reasons for writing of which you speak? Some years ago Francesco Calvo[4] of Pavia showed you a letter or advice to a friend,[5] I know not who, by Alciati. It is undoubtedly one that he had from Alciati, who has often asked me by word of mouth and now writes to ask that I should beg you not to let the letter given you by Calvo pass into the hands of anyone else. You remember, I expect, this letter or advice to I know not whom, which he knew to have been abstracted from his library only when Calvo told him (for they are great friends) that it had reached you …

1234 / To Johann Schudelin — Anderlecht, 4 September 1521

At a time when Erasmus felt that under the influence of Luther many German humanists were turning away from him (cf Ep 1225:302–6), the admiration (cf lines 5–7) even of an obscure schoolmaster proved gratifying and warranted this acknowledgment. Johann Schudelin, of Vaihingen north-west of Stuttgart, is known only as the headmaster of the Latin school of Memmingen, 1517–21. This letter was published in the *Epistolae ad diversos*.

ERASMUS OF ROTTERDAM TO JOHANN SCHUDELIN, SCHOOLMASTER OF MEMMINGEN, GREETING

Gabriel Stendelin,[1] a man whom I like for many reasons, induced me easily to take it in good part that you, though a stranger, should interrupt me with your letter. His influence over me went further still, and made me, very busy as I am, at least return the greetings, if I could not answer the letter, of a man who has made such friendly overtures. You say my works have much influence in your part of the world, and, if you speak true, I am glad that my nightly vigils should add some encouragement for men of good will to pursue a better life, now that they have so provoked many men to dislike me. Keep it up, my dear Johann; pursue with energy the calling in which I hear you have already earned so much praise. Concentrate not on doing battle with the henchmen of ancient ignorance but on planting the seeds of liberal education and simple piety in those whose years are unformed and teachable. If princes will not listen to wise advice, if leaders of the church prefer the honours of the world to the rewards offered by Christ, if divines and religious cannot give up those gatherings[2] of which they have so long been overfond, if the public will not be weaned away from its old habits, there remains this one way out, which still gives us good hope that the world may one day return to a more fruitful way of life: we must put new wine into the old bottles.[3] This new crop will one day spring up and will overwhelm even without a struggle these men who are not merely untaught but unteachable. If we bring up children on the right lines[4] and produce the writings of the Ancients in the light of day, we shall see a gradual fading away of a religion and education in which is neither piety nor culture. Here lies your course! Farewell.

Anderlecht, 4 September 1521

1235 / To Pierre Barbier — Anderlecht, 23 September 1521

This letter, which was printed in the *Epistolae ad diversos*, takes issue with a fresh attack by a Louvain theologian and was presumably again to be reported to Barbier's master, Cardinal Adrian of Utrecht, (cf lines 34–5 and Epp 1216, 1225). Barbier's answer is Ep 1245.

ERASMUS OF ROTTERDAM TO PIERRE BARBIER, GREETING

A faint ray of hope has dawned upon me here that you may sometime return to us;[1] and how I do trust that it may not prove false! As for my annuity, I hope your negotiations[2] prove as successful as they are protracted. Jan de Hondt[3] is still his old self.

My friend you know of, who is (I am sorry to say) as black-hearted as his frock is white,[4] surpasses himself day by day, and the man is now openly so mad that no one can endure him. Not to mention many other things, in a public lecture the other day, when he got to that passage 'We shall all sleep, but we shall not all be changed,'[5] 'At this point,' says he, 'Erasmus introduces a heresy, for he lays down the opposite of what is held by the church.' First of all, let us grant (false though it is) that a reading is heretical which is found in all the Greek copies, whose unanimity here is nowhere surpassed; I do not introduce a heresy when I only translate it, any more to be sure than Jerome did when he translated Origen's *Periarchon*.[6] As it is, though I explain in my *Annotationes*[7] that alternative readings existed even in Antiquity (which is made clear both by Jerome[8] and by the author of an extant short commentary on all the Pauline Epistles[9]), and though Thomas[10] in discussing both readings says that the reading followed by the Greeks contains no heretical meaning, yet this old man, who is a theologian and a Carmelite, was not ashamed to utter this crazy remark in an ordinary lecture and in the theological faculty, exactly as though his audience were blocks and not human beings. He cannot stoop to read what I have written,[11] and yet he is not ashamed to pronounce on a subject he knows nothing about. He had merely heard, over his wine,[12] I dare say, how I translated it. And he expects to be taken for a logician, because he has not forgotten his theory of contradictions.[13] Yet it was his duty to detect not what the words meant at first sight, but how they were to be understood and to whom they should be applied. Finally, granted that the reading is in doubt, the church is in no danger, even if there is something she does not know about the manner of the resurrection; just as she does not know if we shall all die, since it was not Christ's will that we should know the time of his coming.[14] What he is in his lectures, he is in all his teaching, with the result that many are driven away from theology by his spiteful nature. If only my lord of Tortosa[15] would return, and put an end to this disorder!

I have replied to Zúñiga;[16] the book is now printing in Louvain. What he wrote annoyed even Aleandro,[17] although at the start he had rather liked it. I regret that work,[18] to be quite frank. The New Testament,[19] revised and enlarged by me with incredible labour, is now printing a third time in Basel. But when will there be an end of these troubles? If nothing else, they certainly make impossible at the moment the serenity of mind of a true Christian, and the common run of students are alienated from theology. Mind you look after your health; otherwise, if you die (which God forbid), I shall sue you for damages, for you cannot die without my suffering great loss.[20]

Anderlecht, 23 September 1521

1236 / To Paolo Bombace — Anderlecht, 23 September 1521

This letter, which was published in the *Epistolae ad diversos*, answers Ep 1213 and perhaps a subsequent letter directed to Basel; cf line 49 and Ep 1213:67–9.

ERASMUS OF ROTTERDAM TO THE TRULY LEARNED PAOLO BOMBACE, GREETING

What is this I hear, my dear Bombace? Pope Leo, our supreme and lion-like

Leo, has read the letter which I wrote you in such a slipshod and colloquial fashion! What can have come over him, that he should turn his mind and his eye upon such trivial stuff? Not merely read it, but asked for it again, and shown it to men of learning! And did he read not only the letter I wrote to you, but letters to other friends as well? For my part, I normally disburden myself of everything, be it anxieties or gossip, freely and without a second thought in the sympathetic ear of friends like that. It is all up with me, if what you say is true, especially as I myself have no idea what nonsense I may have talked in such a letter. You say you thought I said too much about a certain person;[1] but I did not feel the need to discriminate when writing to such an old friend. In my letter to the pope himself,[2] at any rate, I said not a word about him. And apart from that, if you knew the facts, you would say that my complaints of him show great moderation. But whatever may have gone wrong under this head, I attribute it to the malicious gossip of certain persons I could name, who used incredible trickery in order to set us one against the other. Their criminal efforts did not escape my notice; but when we both saw them, it was too late.

So you have won yourself riches in Rome, riches which are free and not tied to any religious duties, and for which you have no one to thank but your own hard work; though your merits really deserved far more, yet, with things as they are, I rejoice in your success in having shaken off that most crushing of burdens, poverty. I imagine you now looking about you for an independent, peaceful way of life, a safe and quiet harbour to take refuge in. I have misgivings that you may suffer the same fate as the weasel in Horace,[3] which could not get out when full of food, having been skin and bone when it crept into the granary; yet I am sure you must try. Where could you hope for this better than in Rome? I am sure you should at all costs avoid Bologna, where (if nothing else) they will nibble your rope as you twist it.[4] Though my friend Scipio Carteromachus,[5] as you know, could not find even in Rome the freedom that he loved as much as anyone.

As for me, below your level of income though I am, I have ceased to complain of my luck. I have the wherewithal for a tidy way of life. I have means from which I can even spare a piece of gold now and then for a needy friend, so far am I from having to be a burden to anyone. For high position I have no desire, especially at the price one has to pay for it.[6] Had it come my way for nothing or at least at no great expense, and had it come my way in time, I would not think it should be utterly rejected, for this very reason, at least, that it has one advantage if no other: it protects us from the contempt of wretches, be they who they may. In this matter, as in all else, More has seen more clearly than I have myself. He is a knight; he is both councillor and treasurer[7] to an admirable king; and both these posts are reasonably independent and highly honourable, so that men of good will now love him all the more and wretches fear him. For in these days even such outstanding goodness of heart and such unparalleled charm cannot entirely escape all ill will.

The letter which you had sent to Basel[8] reached me safely. Cornelius,[9] to whom I had given letters of introduction to you and (if I mistake not) Aleandro, was stripped of his letters, his money, and his clothes at Alessandria[10] by the French outposts and then, with nothing, thrown into prison. In the end he was given the choice to depart as he was, with nothing, or to swing for it. And so he reached Basel in a linen shirt and nothing else. There he spent some days recovering, his nakedness was covered with German clothes, and a gold piece given him besides for his journey. In this state he came to me, and had to be provided a second time with journey-money. He said you had written at the same time to Cardinal Campeggi. If there was anything important in it, you must not mind writing it all out again.

The Spaniard of whom you write is one Diego Zúñiga, who has issued a most conceited book full of rant against the first edition of the New Testament.[11] You can see at once that he is showing off with astonishing ostentation, and when you look closer you will say it is all moonshine. I have published a laconic defence in reply[12] – an undertaking which I already regret; for his work is such that even Aleandro does not like it, nor will it do any harm to my reputation, at least among fair-minded, educated people. And yet my reply was not only brief but even courteous – not that he deserved this, but I have kept up a good name hitherto for moderation, and should be sorry to lose it.

I am well aware, my dear Bombace, nor do I forget how much I owe to Leo's attitude towards me, of which I have already so many proofs. Nor have I been as silent on his side of the question as you suppose. To begin with, I did my utmost to prevent this uproar from breaking out, and then when it did break out, to lull it to rest again; finally, when the blaze was already widespread, to make good the damage with the least possible disturbance of the public peace.[13] For I thought this would be most conducive both to the dignity of the Roman pontiff and to the ending of this tragic business in such a way that the evil once suppressed should not break out again. When that did not really succeed either, thanks to certain persons who thought more of their private interests than of the public weal, I held back many people,[14] partly by correspondence and partly by what I said to them, from taking part in this play.

Apart from that, if up to now I have published nothing in opposition to Luther,[15] there are many reasons. These I need not here recount, but the chief reason has been, that I have simply not had the time to read what Luther writes, so busy am I with revisions of my own work. And you see how prolific he is.[16] Nor is he by himself; he has a hundred hands. Nor would it be enough to run through his books once; they would have to be read over and over again. Even that would not suffice. Many people everywhere publish attacks on him, every one of which I should have to look into if I wished to do my job properly. Not to mention at the same time that to invite me to do this takes little account of the proverb 'let the horsemen scour the plain.'[17] It is a most perilous subject, and all my experience lies in other fields of study. Besides which it would now be reasonable, after all the books I have published, to give me my freedom and let me hereafter enjoy my studies at leisure. This was demanded by the growing burden of years and deserved by the efforts I have expanded hitherto on the cause of learning in general. This task is such that, if I once enter on it, I must work like a slave for the rest of my life.

My dear Bombace! It is easy enough to say 'Why not write against Luther?' But to do this means having even more materials at hand than it takes to make Hesiod's wagon.[18] I see how different and hard to please men's judgments are, particularly in our generation, which is more difficult than almost any other. On many points the universities on one side of the Alps differ from those on the other; and indeed theologians of the same university take one view in their public lectures and their books and another in genuine conversation. Besides which it is very hard to control one's pen in such a way as to respect the dignity of men without somehow infringing the glory of Christ, and to satisfy princes who are but mortals without at some point displeasing Christ our heavenly Prince. If pamphlets could suppress this trouble, every day fresh swarms of books appear, so that a mere Erasmus has no place; if clamour could do it, we have no lack of stentorian voices.[19] Of bonfires[20] everywhere we have had our fill. In public edicts no portentous threat has been passed over. But I fear that by these measures the evil may be suppressed for a time rather than extinguished, only to break out yet more perilously. The prospect appalls me, and I pray heartily it may not happen. No part of the world upholds the papal dignity more strongly than this land of ours; but it has suffered grievously from some most unpopular support.[21] Had they not behaved so madly, things would not have come to this pass. In fact, if even now they would hold their peace for three months, Luther with all his pamphlets would lose his appeal, and not the smallest change in human affairs would be made on his account.

I am entirely engrossed in revising the New Testament and some other works of mine,[22] slowly licking into shape the crude offspring of my brains like a she-bear.[23] But soon, I hope, I shall be blessed with a little more leisure.

I took particular trouble with Girolamo Aleandro[24] to get permission from him to read what Luther has written; for nowadays everywhere is full of informers and spies.[25] He denied absolutely that he could do this without obtaining leave specifically from the pope. I beg you therefore first of all to get me permission in a brief of some sort.[26] I should not like to give an opening to the wicked; it is all they ask. I have always been a sincere supporter of the public peace; very few more so. To strengthen the position of the gospel truth I would gladly give even my life.[27] Nor am I ignorant how much I owe to the pope's unheard-of kindness to me personally. If I am granted three or four more years of life, I will either die in the attempt or I will make him agree that I was not wholly ungrateful. His exceptional goodness deserves to be honoured in print by all the learned world. Others no doubt will do this with more skill than I, but at least none with more zeal. Nature may deny me eloquence, but the enthusiasm of a grateful heart will take its place. Some think they have done all they can for him if they have made him an object of fear; I shall strive to make the world love Leo rather than fear him.

But unless he himself keeps me safe to do him service in this way, I do not see how I can be preserved; such is the determination with which certain accursed individuals campaign against me. They prate against me by name; they vilify me before the public in open lectures and in sermons; they give a sinister account of me to princes. They suborn men to publish scandalous pamphlets which tear my reputation to shreds, they even threaten dagger and poison. Nor can anyone fail to see what they would do if they dared. I should call down all possible curses on my head with no hesitation if there is even one small pamphlet of Luther's which I have read right through;[28] if in all the pieces ascribed to him or circulated in his defence there is one syllable written by me or with my connivance;[29] if I have ever tried to defend any opinion of his. And some men are so perverse that they attribute to me even the things that Luther at his meeting with the emperor admitted were his own.[30]

The other day at a crowded dinner-table someone asked me what were the first words of *De captivitate Babylonica*.[31] This question I found extremely difficult to answer. Nothing was further from my thoughts. Then, when I inquired the reason for this question, he confessed that some people supposed it to be my work, because it begins with the words 'Whether I will or no,' which is not far from the beginning of the panegyric I wrote to celebrate Philip's return from Spain, which begins 'Whether you will or no.'[32] An elegant guess, you will agree! Aleandro gave me to understand that two pamphlets are attributed to me, one called *Eubulus*[33] and the other the *Lamentationes Petri*.[34] My life upon it if I had ever heard either title before he produced them. The first I have not yet been able to obtain. In the other I am treated in such a fashion that, if I knew who the author was, I should show him a little less than gratitude. And yet in works of this kind I would rather be abused than praised.

Some people are trying to persuade the public that the Lutheran plague started in this part of the world;[35] which I know to be as false as anything could be. Already some with nothing better to do have collected passages[36] from my books where Luther can be seen, they think, to have found the origin of his errors. They would be better employed in collecting them from the Gospels and the apostolic Epistles, from Augustine and Bernard and even Thomas himself. Where did most of the heretics in old days collect the sources of their errors? Was it not from the Holy Scriptures, when wrongly understood? I will challenge the whole of Germany without the slightest hesitation, and any supporters Luther may have in other places: let them show that he has had assistance from me in one single word in all the books he has published hitherto; nay, let them produce the letters I wrote to him on these subjects even in the days when there was still some hope that Luther's gifts and his pen might be at the service of Christ's glory. Those letters will make clear how I strove in every way to prevent this tragic tumult from arising. Though I did not entirely approve the steps his adversaries had taken, and I saw that much was accepted which it would be better to reform. My friendship with Aleandro, which was already no new thing, had almost been extinguished by their poisonous tongues; for these are the arts in which they show what gifts and wits they have. Now all is discovered and Aleandro has changed his mind; but the recall of words once uttered he finds easier to wish than to achieve. And so, dear Bombace, my most learned friend, if his Holiness will uphold my innocence against these impudent slanders, I shall not be found unfaithful,[37] so far as in me lies, either to the purity of the Christian religion or to his own exalted position.

I am still in two minds whether to go to Basel.[38] For whole years now I have been going there, but something always crops up to keep me here. Just now, I had quite made up my mind to take to the road, with the idea of finishing what I wished to do in Basel, and then migrating entirely to Rome,[39] there to devote what time is left me to the society of great scholars and the resources of great libraries. I had already set out on my journey – for my life in the country this summer has given me rather more strength[40] – but this cruel war which spreads more widely every day has deterred me. Yet this is what I still long to do, and perhaps I shall find courage to risk a throw, especially as I am urged to this course by Aleandro, whose counsel in the affairs of life I value no less than his opinion on things literary. In the meanwhile, make the most of your new wealth, and look forward to my company, if only these disputes between princes will settle down. Give my particular greetings to his Eminence Cardinal Campeggi and to your patron the cardinal of Santi Quattro.[41] Farewell, most faithful of patrons and most sincere of friends. Remember me to Francesco Chierigati.[42]

From the country. 23 September 1521

1237 / To Bernard Bucho van Aytta — Anderlecht, 24 September 1521

This letter, printed in the *Epistolae ad diversos*, is addressed to Bernard Bucho van Aytta (1465–1528) of Zwichem in Friesland, whose nephew, Viglius Zuichemus, was later to occupy a special place in Erasmus' heart. Born of a distinguished family, Bernard graduated MA from Louvain in 1487 and entered the church. In 1499 he was named to the Council of Friesland, and after the county had been ceded to the future Charles V, was appointed president of the council in July 1515.

While nothing is known about his previous connections with Erasmus, this letter shows that he had approached the scholar in search of a suitable tutor for the sons of an unidentified 'friend' (line 51), who were to be educated at Louvain. Bernard also took care of Viglius, who was then being educated in Leiden but would move to Louvain in the autumn of 1522 and become a student of Rescius and Goclenius; cf lines 35, 38.

ERASMUS OF ROTTERDAM TO THE MOST WORTHY BERNARD BUCHO OF FRIESLAND, DEAN OF THE HAGUE, GREETING

Honoured sir. After a long spell of ill health in Louvain, when I was setting my mass of papers in order with the intention of moving into the country[1] to restore my health, not a page escaped my scrutiny, and yet I did not find the small work which you entrusted to me, though I know I carefully put it on one side to keep it safe. And safe I do not doubt it is, but it is not to hand; for which I am sorry. I find this often happens: those things are most sure to be lost which I have taken special pains not to lose. Soon, I suppose, I shall again become a townsman instead of a rustic, and I will again go through my possessions. I should certainly be sorry for you to lose something you are fond of, when I have no further use for it.

That the Frisian people would welcome the humanities is, to be sure, nothing new, for long ago they gave us Rodolphus Agricola, Langen, and the Canters.[2] That men of eminent wealth and lineage should consider their children unworthy to inherit their estates and name unless they have developed their intelligence by humane studies[3] is indeed new, and we must heartily rejoice at the happy times we live in.[4] At Louvain the climate is most agreeable,[5] and there could not be a more peaceful place for study anywhere. Nowhere do the young show more enthusiasm for good literature, and many of them make wonderful progress, while the devotees of ancient ignorance protest in vain. Would that my advice might prove as fruitful for you as it is readily and carefully given. I will but indicate the names, and the choice is yours.

There is in Louvain at the moment Jacobus Ceratinus,[6] excellent scholar in both languages, and in character upright and unspoilt, which I know you think now less important than his qualifications. Plague and the wars,[7] the two greatest evils of human life, have driven him from Tournai, where he used to teach in the college of languages which is now being started.[8] There is also Hermann of Westphalia,[9] who lives in the College of the Lily, an excellent young man and an all-round scholar, but above all untiring as a teacher and guide and guardian of the young. In the same college there is Adrien of Soissons,[10] who is not only a capital scholar in Greek and Latin but knows some philosophy and is not ignorant of civil law, and is a very charming man. Then there is Rutgerus Rescius,[11] who lectures in Greek in the new college[12] founded by Jérôme de Busleyden, and who sets off learning above the common with incredible modesty; in fact he is almost as shy as a girl. Conradus Goclenius also,[13] who has keen judgment, unusual learning, untiring industry, and a lofty intelligence; he is a most courteous and delightful man and absolutely reliable, and also very sensible in matters of everyday business, which cannot usually be said of men in academic life. And Adrianus Barlandus,[14] a man without guile, a sincere and friendly person with a ready flow of fluent and classical Latin and many years' experience in that field. There is also Melchior of Trier[15] in the College of the Castle, a man of most blameless character almost worn out by his studies in philosophy and a student of theology of some years' standing; but to these gifts he adds no common skill in the two tongues. And there is Luis Vives, an all-round scholar; but I rather think he is averse from the kind of thing you want. Besides these there are many other men; but not so well known to me. Those I have listed I would underwrite without hesitation. Whichever of them you choose, you will have placed your friend's boys in good hands.

Please give the honourable Nicolaas Everaerts,[16] president of Holland, my greetings in return. May fate preserve that man for our benefit as long as possible, for he if anyone was born to be a blessing to the community! I will write to him shortly; for at this moment I am writing a load of letters[15] for two men, one bound for Spain and the other for Rome. Farewell, my honoured friend in the Lord.

Anderlecht, 24 September 1521

1238 / To Nicolaas Everaerts Anderlecht, [c October] 1521

Printed in the *Epistolae ad diversos*, this letter was dated from Anderlecht, apparently towards the end of Erasmus' stay there (cf lines 9–14). Thus this may well be the letter promised in Ep 1237:54–5.

ERASMUS OF ROTTERDAM TO THAT MOST ACCOMPLISHED DOCTOR OF CIVIL AND CANON LAW, NICOLAAS EVERAERTS, PRESIDENT OF HOLLAND, GREETING

Even if affection for my native land carried little weight with me, a warm feeling for you could easily attract me of itself, I will not say to Holland, but to any distant country you might choose. But though I have long been disposed to travel[1] and have got ready to set out from time to time, some fresh restraint has always arisen which does not allow me to be torn away from here. Nor is it my intention to visit that island of yours except in the summer months.[2] But the summer with us is so short that sometimes we have none at all, and we are aware that it is leaving us before we have seen it has arrived. Never before was it so clear to me that climate and not food dictates our life. This whole summer I have spent in the country,[3] and never was anything a greater success. I have become so much more lively under this clearer sky that you would think me a different person. Not that I am any less attached to my native Holland because the climate agrees with me so badly.[4] In fact I feel a wonderful satisfaction when I perceive that country, so fertile as it is in other things, now growing rich in men of distinguished abilities who will deserve to be remembered by posterity. How often have I thought it fortunate in the possession of Maarten van Dorp,[5] the one theologian among our countrymen to have united school divinity and a familiarity with good literature, or solid wisdom and true eloquence. But in the last few days I have been visited by Herman Lethmaet,[6] a native of Gouda who, if I mistake not, will equal or even surpass van Dorp – except that by unceasing study van Dorp every day surpasses himself.

Herman, although before he began to study theology he had made a successful start on a knowledge of Greek and what they call liberal subjects, conducted himself so well in this course of theology at the Sorbonne[7] that by a unanimous vote he obtained first place, and that too in a school which beyond dispute has always held the front rank in this field of studies. Nor is he merely well equipped in the verbal niceties with which they skirmish in the schools; there is nothing in the way of worldly wisdom or history or the ancient theologians which he has not read, and he has it at his fingertips. His intellect is quick and lively, his passion for knowledge is insatiable, his judgment ready and untramelled, and, what is unusual in men of this type, he has no arrogance, no ill temper, no conceit. His courtesy is remarkable, and so is his modesty. He gives everyone a patient hearing; makes way even for his inferiors. So many men, when they have reached the end of that course at the Sorbonne, sink into idleness just as though they had learnt all there is to learn, or they neglect their books and keep a sharp look-out, collecting benefices. This man, having won his laurels in theology with such distinction, devotes himself as eagerly to reading the best authors as though he had not finished his course of study but was now admitted to serious studies for the first time. But his welcome for these more humane authors does not mean that he has deserted his proper subject. And so I am full of hopes that if anyone will be the man to make such a well-judged mixture of the old and the new learning as may be perfectly satisfactory to the old friends of both.[8] For he has scarcely reached thirty and he enjoys excellent health, which gives promise of a long life, all the more because he himself is of most temperate habits – if only any mortal man is allowed to keep this up among the Hollanders. Nor do I doubt that more men like him will appear, if only this region can learn to do honour to outstanding abilities and understand how much more true and lasting glory it will earn from this.

I do not recommend Herman to you, for no doubt you know him better than I do, nor do I forget how keenly it is your habit to cultivate men of this kind. I only ask you to take trouble to recommend him to the other leading men in our native Holland. The quickest way for him to acquire a widespread reputation is to have the leaders of society on his side and be approved by the judgment of those who themselves enjoy universal approval. He has no desire for fame himself, and for this he deserves it all the more. And it is in the public interest that ordinary people too should have a high opinion of men of the highest merit.

The humanities were making pretty good progress everywhere, let the frogs croak as they will, had not this sad business of Luther arisen to throw everything into confusion. And as though this was not bad enough, I fear that unless some god from the machine[9] can lay to rest the tumult of war that gets worse every day, it will be not so much confusion for them as extinction. The whole Christian world, as though it were cut into two halves, is committed to a disastrous war.[10] Two princes, both eminent and both young, in whom obstinacy born of a noble spirit is greater than the wisdom that comes from experience of affairs, and both of them devotedly intent on mutual destruction, drag the world down to destruction with them; and all this time, immortal gods, where is the authority of the Roman pontiff? When some business of profit commends itself to him, he can command angels and devils too; and is he powerless when it comes to restraining his sons from such a destructive war? Where now are those preachers whose voices we hear so much? Either they are silent, or they have a fawning tongue. Someday perhaps our Charles will be heard to say 'I never thought that war was such a poisonous thing.' That lesson of his will cost us dear. In any case, we can do nothing in all this but pray that heaven may send us better times. If our court had but ten men like you, human affairs would be in better case.

But to return to the future of the humanities: now that Luther's business is settled (and I only hope it has been settled rightly), they are back where they started. Openly, in sermons and public lectures, they condemn the ancient languages and liberal studies, and some of them I could mention are ranting against Erasmus by name with preposterous falsehoods. Nor can I see at all what their aim is. If they intend to make the public understand that the orders in question[11] contain some brazen masters of abuse, the public is already more truly seized of that than may be expedient for them. If the object is to attract young men with no leanings towards good literature into the study of their pet theology, they could not scare them away more effectively than by such behaviour. In Paris and in Cambridge[12] the study of theology flourishes as it never has anywhere. And why? Because they adapt themselves to an age that is turning another way; because when these liberal studies even try to make their way in by force, they do not repel them as invaders but welcome them courteously as guests. If in Louvain the theological schools are unpopular (for such complaints are made), they cannot lay this at my door,[13] for I never said a word to discourage anybody. It is a few men whose capacity for abuse is as rabid as it is uneducated who scare away honourable minds. And what is done by a few is ascribed by the public to the whole body, when they see it happen so often with such impunity, and when they have aroused such tragic commotions on account of one word spoken by the professor of Greek,[14] which casts no aspersions on anybody.

I heartily approve their using the emperor's proclamation[15] as a weapon against scandalous pamphlets, though none of them complains of the infamous pamphlets of which, they tell me, a stream is produced in Cologne by Pfefferkorn;[16] nor is it hard to see who puts him up to this. But they ought at the same time to have used some imperial proclamation of the kind against these scandalous tongues,[17] which are more criminal than any libellous pamphlets. Otherwise honest men will be in a pretty plight, if such buffoons, with nothing in them but impudence and a malicious tongue, are allowed to attack a man's reputation in public with impunity, and others are not allowed to defend their reputations by the accepted method of publishing a book. They are furious if someone complains in a letter to a friend of what they publicly denounce before the multitude. Personally I would prefer to defend myself in such a way as not to hurt others; but if one man attacks another so that he cannot save his own life except by taking the life of his attacker, the laws lay the guilt upon the aggressor.[18] You will say, 'Take them to law.' Where can I go? They recognize the jurisdiction of neither prince nor bishop. The theologians, who govern things at their own sweet will, behave as though they were in these men's pay. Their priors either support them or have no control over them. So I must find what they call their vicar;[19] and meanwhile the man who ranted before the public today will be dining somewhere else tomorrow. This state of affairs gives the rascals courage to do anything. You would hardly believe how this behaviour estranges the public from them, and especially the principal men and intelligent people. When they notice this, of course they hold me responsible for trouble they have brought upon themselves in their own horse and cart.[20] I am prepared actually to laugh at the uproar they make, only I am sorry that human error should get theology a bad name, that this spoilt leaven should embitter the sweetness of our studies, and that public morality should suffer. Farewell, my distinguished friend.

From Anderlecht, 1521

1239 / To Gabriël Ofhuys — Anderlecht, 14 October [1521]

This letter is found printed in the *Epistolae ad diversos*, but as in the case of Epp 1206, 1225, a contemporary copy is preserved in the Gouda MS 1324; the differences between the two versions are negligible. No year was added to the date until the *Opus epistolarum* of 1529. The date, as it then appeared, needs to be corrected, since on 14 October 1520 Erasmus was in Antwerp (cf Ep 1153:101–2).

Gabriël Ofhuys (cf Ep 480A introduction) had, like Erasmus, joined the canons regular of St Augustine in his youth. Subsequently he became a Carthusian and when this letter was written lived in the charterhouse of Scheut at Anderlecht; cf Ep 1196 n58.

ERASMUS OF ROTTERDAM TO FATHER GABRIËL OFHUYS, MONK OF THE CHARTERHOUSE, GREETING

Study and business scarcely leave me leisure, as they say, to scratch my ears,[1] but I send you your verses;[2] I should not like you to complain that in any way you had not had what you wanted from your friend Erasmus, who is truly yours in Christ. I know how much evil idleness puts in men's heads; so I would rather see you spend on trifles of this kind the time left over from your religious duties, than lapse into something worse. All the same, it would be far better to impress an image of Christ and of Paul, a lively and effective image drawn from Scripture, upon your inmost heart, than to depict them with blacklead and copper plate and sheets of paper. But this I think you really do, my dear Gabriël; and that other activity is no more than the overflowing of a gifted mind, the kind of thing even Jerome approves in his friend Nepotianus.[3] I suppose that since the birth of Christ there has never been a generation more wicked than ours; so much the less ought you to regret your religious calling. As for me, my fate has swept me into these stormy waters. I may not keep silence, nor can I speak about Christ as I ought. Christ cries, 'Be of good courage; I have overcome the world.'[4] The world, I think, will soon be crying 'I have overcome Christ'; so true is it that for the heritage of the Gospel we see the open ascendancy of ambition, pleasure, greed, effrontery, vanity, shamelessness, jealousy, and ill will, even among those who profess themselves the light of this world and its salt.

I will come and see you again as soon as I can. Meanwhile give my greetings to your excellent prior,[5] and to the cellarer and the man who greeted me in passing in such a friendly way, I thought. May all go well with you, and as you aspire fervently towards heavenly things may Christ, the only hope of holy souls, prosper and bless you, dearest brother in Christ.

Anderlecht, 14 October [1520]

1240 / To Rutgerus Rescius — Anderlecht, [October?] 1521

Shortly after his appointment as professor of Greek in the *Collegium Trilingue* of Louvain, Rescius had suffered the ignominy of an unjustified arrest instigated by Jan Calaber (cf line 22), who was then rector of the university (cf Ep 1046 introduction). Rescius probably had to await the end of Calaber's rectorate in the spring of 1520 before he could go to law. This letter suggests that the litigation between them – conceivably refuelled by additional incidents, cf Ep 1238:100–4 – still continued, though by this time Erasmus had difficulty taking it seriously and urged Rescius to be more flexible.

This letter was first printed in the *Epistolae ad diversos* but the year in the date, 1521, was not added until the *Opus epistolarum* of 1529. Henry de Vocht (CTL I 476–7) argued that the letter belongs to the second half of August 1520, when Erasmus spent a few days in Brussels (cf Ep 1136 introduction) and might also have been visiting nearby Anderlecht. That is speculation, however, whereas in 1521 Erasmus wrote many letters while he was in Anderlecht (cf Ep 1208 introduction). Allen placed the letter here because of the resemblance between lines 9–11 and Ep 1238:100–4; cf also n1.

ERASMUS TO HIS FRIEND RUTGERUS RESCIUS, GREETING

If the affront were not so outrageous, my learned Rescius, I should most strongly advise you to accept peace even on unfair terms. As it is, the outrage is of such a kind that no one could fail to be appalled if a master had given his bought slave the kind of treatment which was planned by a malignant conspiracy of the very men whose business it was to protect deserving teachers from wrong of every kind; and I would not dare persuade you to overlook it, much as I might hope for your own sake that you could. What astonishing bullies they are! They would not endure a word of any criticism of themselves, but expect that you should remain silent in the face of such scandalous treatment, and almost go out of your way to ask their pardon, for fear that their dignity might suffer in the least. The story deserves to be recorded for posterity; but I think it a nobler sort of reaction to do as you have done up to now, and win as much good repute as you can for your calling as a teacher of Greek by your impeccable character and the trouble you take with your teaching.

If you cannot bring yourself to abandon the struggle (which I should be reluctant to ask of you, since your reputation may be at stake), mind you continue your litigation in the spirit in which it has been conducted hitherto. For when I was last in Louvain,[1] you had put on weight and looked so ruddy and vigorous that you seem to me to get fatter and not thinner by going to law. And you have a worthy opponent in Jan Calaber[2] the physician, who is as pale and thin as you are – so far from unlike you except in point of age, that there is a risk someone will think you are going to law with your own father. Though the man erred in my opinion by being not wicked but too obliging. Farewell, dearest Rescius.

Anderlecht, 1521

1241 / From Wolfgang Faber Capito [Halle?], 14 October 1521

The only source for this letter is Paulus Merula's *Vita Des. Erasmi* (Leiden 1607). Several gaps show that Merula had to contend with a defective manuscript. The authenticity, however, need hardly be questioned, as the text reflects Capito's known preoccupations at the time and also those of Erasmus, expressed no doubt in a letter, now lost, to which Capito is replying.

This letter was probably written from Halle an der Saale, which like Erfurt belonged to the ecclesiastical principality of Mainz. Capito's master, Cardinal Albert of Brandenburg, reinstituted on his return from the Diet of Worms (cf Ep 1197 introduction) a special indulgence available to those visiting a collection of relics preserved at Halle, although on Capito's advice he avoided otherwise antagonizing the Lutherans and had not published the Edict of Worms in his states. Luther and Capito exchanged threats over the Halle indulgence (cf Luther w *Briefwechsel* II Ep 433, end of September–beginning of October 1521), and Capito also reminded Luther of his continued efforts to protect him (cf Luther w *Briefwechsel* II Ep 447, 20–1 December). At the same time Albert himself wrote an exceptionally meek answer to an aggressive letter from Luther (cf Luther w *Briefwechsel* II Ep 448, 21 December, in reply to Ep 442) and succeeded in preventing the publication of a tract Luther had written 'Wider den Abgott zu Halle'; cf G. Krodel in *Luther's Works*, Philadelphia-St Louis (1955–) XLVIII 344–50. In another attempt to find a modus vivendi with the Lutheran camp, Capito, accompanied by Heinrich Stromer (cf Ep 1125 n5), visited Wittenberg on 30 September and 1 October. Luther was at the Wartburg (cf Ep 1203 n2), but in his absence Melanchthon and Jonas held constructive talks with Albert's emissaries (cf *Melanchthons Briefwechsel* I Ep 175).

FABRITIUS CAPITO TO ERASMUS OF ROTTERDAM, AN ALL-ROUND SCHOLAR AND A GOOD CHRISTIAN, GREETING

I wrote you lately a fairly long and perhaps fairly roundabout letter[1] – on purpose, for I have to be careful in this way among so many hidden dangers. My model in this is you, who are so prudent and circumspect in everything you send me; your policy I gladly adopt, but reproduce your gifts I cannot. I am also as a rule not in the best of health, and worn out by an amazing amount of business; for I belong to the court.[2] Luther's party are crazier and more insolent and more self-assertive in everything; they fix their teeth in anyone, no matter whom, and abuse everyone to his face with barbarous impertinence, such is their public contempt for all brains except their own. I appealed to them long ago, I begged them not to be so violent in everything and so grossly offensive in maintaining their cause; above all I urged them to give up this picking of small points in authors to find fault with; for men's good will is violently estranged by such overweening conceit. I hope that in future they will be more respectful in their references to you. There is no declaration in which they do not criticize you[3] when they are by themselves, and in public they set you up as the leader of their party in the most preposterous fashion. I freely confess, they have made me very angry, passionately devoted as I am to your reputation. As I said, they will treat you more discreetly sometimes, so far as I can see. King Charles will one day see things very differently.[4] Glapion's remark[5] seems to me very good. Christ will put an end to these troubles, beyond a doubt. For the reading of the Gospel, both in public and private, is a thing no one will be able to forbid; burning books gets nowhere.[6] And not a few people want just this – that the leaders of the church should set about their destruction[7] for the truth's sake; for then, they say, their cause, which looks dubious meanwhile, as though it needed the support of bloodshed, is strengthened. Scandalous pamphlets I utterly abhor. They will arouse the world to take steps against them once and for all, and I do not want this to happen quickly, for fear it happens in the wrong way. On Karlstadt I know the king has changed his mind.[8] Priests are

Girolamo Aleandro
Portrait engraving by Agostino Veneziano
Bibliotheca Apostolica Vaticana

marrying[9] wives in our part of the world, and monarchs approve, or at least overlook it.

My master on his return from Worms has undertaken to read the Scriptures.[10] He said the other day that he perceived the faith is not at risk, but that in finance and in authority there must be some loss, and promised generously that he would aid the common cause. And he is young, and a prince. Many people however perceive none of this, and so they rage all the more furiously.[11] Not a day passes without ... of a rapprochement with you.[12] For he begins to detect the force of the hidden truth, which you first brought into the light. Write,[13] more than once, and say what he ought to do; for it seems ... is anxious now for a book as much as anything else, as the surest remedy for the evil.[14] He has perceived that most regulations are perfectly shameless, and would see that they are altered, so far as this lies in his power, provided ... although he is a prince, and exposed to the most insolent toadies, and besides that, brought up as princes usually are. He told me to make excuses for his neglect of you, which he blamed on shyness and respect, not insincerity. He has a surprising fear of scurrilous pamphlets, by which he is so driven into the arms of the monkish party; so I do all I can to warn everyone to let him alone. If you love me, I beg you to let me know what you wish me to attempt while I have the prince so ready to listen to me; I shall leave him the moment he shows himself unfavourable to humane studies. I too will do my part for the public good. Farewell – and leave Aleandro alone.[15] We have to swallow a good deal, I think. The Fates will find a way.[16] Farewell, 14 October 1521.

1241A / From Girolamo Aleandro [Louvain? c 20–5 October 1521?]

This short, undated letter, together with Ep 256 and two subsequent letters, comes from Aleandro's copy-book in Rome (Biblioteca Apostolica Vaticana MS lat 8075 f 73 verso). It was first published by Jules Pasquier in 1895 (cf Allen Ep 2638 introduction). In Allen's edition it is printed as Ep 2680, but the editors abandoned an earlier assumption that it was a postscript to the preceding Ep 2679. It does not provide sufficient clues to date it with confidence, but no other moment in the relations between Erasmus and Aleandro seems to fit its content nearly so well as October 1521. Following some friendly meetings at Brussels (cf Ep 1233 n28), Erasmus returned to Louvain after 14 October and stayed for six days in an inn called the Wild Man, where Aleandro had also taken quarters. Sometimes they talked together until midnight. After a short trip to Antwerp, Erasmus met the nuncio again in Louvain, when both were ready to leave. Erasmus actually set out for Basel on 28 October (see Allen Ep 1342:100–10, 124, 133–4; cf Ep 1242 introduction). It is tempting to assume that Aleandro was writing from Louvain when Erasmus had gone to Antwerp and was thus looking forward confidently to seeing him once more before their ways parted. The copy-book provides no address, only the heading 'Eidem Erasmo,' which could be open to question.

I sent you a fairly long letter yesterday by the emperor's couriers in reply to the letter you sent me by Charles,[1] for I thought mine would reach you more quickly that way, especially as Charles had not made up his mind whether to visit his parents before returning to you. As it is, though there is no reason why I should give him a letter for you, I thought I would write just these few words, partly that he might not leave me entirely empty-handed and also to give you confidence to trust what he will report to you in my name. If I have kept him here for two days, the reason was the mass of business that almost overwhelms me every day, and because I had much to write to you, and have now changed my mind, and think it would be safer to keep it until I can report by word of mouth. Farewell.

1242 / To Stanislaus Thurzo [Basel, c 20 November 1521]

No sooner had Erasmus returned to Louvain from Cologne (cf Ep 1155 introduction) than he wrote again about visiting Germany in the spring of 1521 (cf Ep 1165:56). Similar announcements were frequently repeated (cf Epp 1203:37–8, 1209, 1236:197–204) and in view of his well-known difficulties at Louvain (cf Ep 1174 n1) they were readily believed. In January 1521 Johann Froben expected his arrival in Basel before Easter (cf AK II Ep 764). To please him and protect him from the tenacious illness that had plagued him on his last visit (cf Ep 847:7n), Froben had soon thereafter an open fireplace built in the room destined to house the great man (cf Ep 1248 n5; Zwingli *Werke* VII Ep 175). In June his Basel friends expected him any day (cf AK II Ep 791), while in Rome and Wittenberg it was assumed that he had moved there (cf Ep 1213:67–9, 1236:49; *Melanchthons Briefwechsel* II Epp 159, 164). Erasmus himself joked about the endless delay (cf Ep 1236:197–8), attributing it to pressing work and other causes, among which were no doubt the rural delights of Anderlecht and the desire to meet his English friends again (cf Epp 1208, 1223 introductions). On the other hand, it was above all the third edition of the New Testament that called for his presence at Basel (cf Ep 1174 n6), but Froben also delayed other books to await his arrival and final directions (cf Epp 1206 introduction, 1235 n5). He may also have hoped that by moving to Basel he could somehow escape from those urging him to write a book against Luther (cf Ep 1228 n11), although he did not at first expect to prolong his stay there beyond the winter (cf Epp 1209, 1236:200).

In his headnote to this letter Allen attempted a detailed reconstruction of Erasmus' journey and his movements immediately preceding it, based for the most part on information Erasmus himself supplied in Epp 1302, 1342. His last dated letter from Anderlecht (Ep 1239) is of 14 October. He then returned to Louvain for six days, made a trip to Antwerp to attend to financial matters, went back to Louvain, and from there set out for Basel on 28 October (cf Ep 1241A, Allen Epp 1302:23–4, 1342:102–10). He followed roughly the route of his earlier trips, especially that of September 1518 (cf Ep 867 introduction). For safety's sake he travelled from Tienen to Speyer in the company of a troop of disbanded soldiers, apparently responsible and disciplined men (cf Ep 1248 n1). On 15 November he reached Basel (cf AK II Epp 826, 828, 830; *Melanchthons Briefwechsel* I Epp 182, 191).

This letter is evidently the one mentioned in Ep 1243:3 and thus the first one extant following Erasmus' move to Basel. It is answered in Ep 1272 and was printed in the *Epistolae ad diversos*. Erasmus is answering a letter from Thurzo, which had been left at Basel to await his arrival (cf line 43). Thurzo's letter is missing, but lines 20–3 below suggest that it was a reply to Erasmus' Ep 1137, which he had sent Thurzo's brother, Johannes, in ignorance of his death.

Stanislaus Thurzo belonged to a family that owed its prominence to political skill as well as wealth derived from mining and other business ventures, often undertaken in partnership with the Fuggers of Augsburg. He was bishop of Olomouc in Moravia from 1497 to his death in 1540, and his administration of the diocese was worthy of the praise Erasmus gives him here. Together with his late brother, he had been introduced to Erasmus' works by Jacobus Piso (cf Ep 1206 n4), while attending the royal court of Buda.

ERASMUS OF ROTTERDAM TO THE RIGHT REVEREND STANISLAUS, BISHOP OF OLOMOUC, GREETING

I was greatly devoted to your brother Thurzo, bishop of Wrocław,[1] who had offered me his friendship in a most charming letter, although neither of us had ever set eyes on the other; in fact, he had found a reflection of me in my writings,[2] and in his turn had given me an idea of his generous heart in several letters.[3] His death was therefore all the more of a grief to me, not only because I myself had lost such a benefactor and a friend (though I think no loss in human affairs more serious than the loss of a good friend), but much more because his untimely death had removed from the scene such a pillar of the church. In old days it was 'few feel the god, though many bear the wand,'[4] and in our own time not all are bishops who wear the mitre. And yet this is the surest hope for the future prosperity of the kingdom of Christ, for the coming of which we all pray every day, if men like yourself, distinguished not only by ancient lineage but by the gifts of Christ, are promoted to be helmsmen of the church and contribute all their fortune, their high position, and their natural endowments to the advancement of the flock entrusted to them and to his advantage to whom all must render their account.

This sense of loss has been, if not removed, at least lightened for me by a letter from your Highness, which makes clear that like a second Thurzo, with the same learning and the same character a close family likeness, you have replaced your departed brother as a kind friend to my humble self. I rejoice to see the loss made good as best it can; but would it were possible to duplicate this most precious of all possessions, so that you might not mourn an excellent brother and I might enjoy two benefactors instead of one. The news of his death first reached me in Brussels through Jarosz Łaski,[5] the Polish envoy, a very cultured young man. For all his assurances I was reluctant to believe him. Then Sander,[6] the provost of Wrocław, gave me fresh courage, assuring me that he knew for certain from letters written by his friends that Thurzo had recovered. Shortly afterwards the same man received letters of another kind, and instead of baseless satisfaction plunged me in sincere and well-founded grief. But we all know already how unkind the Fates can be, giving the earth but a glimpse of what is highest, and leaving the second-rate with us until we sicken of it.

When you so generously offer me your kind help, I ought rather to be offering to do what I can for you, as the least of his followers for so great a patron. Your interest and support I welcome, for I need them now as never in my life before, against certain persons who conspire in an unpleasant way against liberal studies, while I long to see a fresh growth of ancient and genuine theology. Such is their wickedness that sometimes I almost regret the nights I spend in toil. Velius,[7] whom in many ways I need very much, I have not yet been allowed to see. He left your letter with friends; the present which you sent to be a pledge of your feelings towards me he will give himself when we can meet. As I cannot kiss your anointed hands, I have often put to my lips the letter which was written, you say, with your own hand. May Christ the almighty long preserve your highness for the benefit of us all.

1243 / To Stanislaus Thurzo — Basel, 22 November 1521

This is the latest letter to be published in the *Epistolae ad diversos* (cf Ep 1206 introduction); it was answered in Ep 1272.

ERASMUS OF ROTTERDAM TO THE RIGHT REVEREND STANISLAUS, BISHOP OF OLOMOUC, GREETING

Scarcely had I sealed my last letter[1] to you when Velius, hearing the rumour of my arrival, came speeding back to Basel (for, as it happened, he had already moved to Freiburg) and showed me your Highness' present;[2] and he went on to recommend it to me in so many ways that it was as welcome as if it had been of far greater value. Velius himself I learned to like far more than I had before, when I had only dipped into the output of his intelligence, for his extremely attractive character, though men of that kind are usually somewhat remote from ordinary human feelings. He also seemed to me much more fortunate than I had supposed. For one thing, the elegance and finish of his turn-out suggests that he must be reasonably well off. And then his personal appearance indicates that by a rare stroke of providence a most gifted mind is lodged in an equally gifted body. He has good reason to praise your Highness and speak so highly of you as he does; for he reveres you as a deity and sings your praises at some length. And indeed that you should attach such a man so closely to you and treat him so generously does your judgment as much credit as your generosity. So I feel bound to hold each of you much blessed in the other, you in such a protégé who can publish your virtues to the world,[3] and him in such an exceptional benefactor. My best wishes once more to your Lordship, to whom I present my humble duty.

Basel, 22 November 1521

1244 / To Willibald Pirckheimer Basel, 29 November 1521

This letter was first printed in *Billibaldi Pirckheimeri … opera* (Frankfurt 1610; repr 1969) 272.

Greeting, most honoured friend. Your last letter was delivered to me while I was talking with Aleandro.[1] As we happened to be staying in Louvain in the same inn, he often spoke to me of you, and in such terms that he seemed to be on your side. He showed me a diploma intended to free you from your troubles.[2] Your grievance, my dear Willibald, you share with many other people. For me they are planning destruction of a complicated kind. I cannot help wondering what god[3] swayed Luther's mind so that, while so many friends tried to deter him[4] from provoking the pope, he has written always with more and more asperity. I am still more surprised at the malignant zeal of certain men who willy-nilly have tried to drag some people into their way of thinking, as though they wished to perish in good company. For what other objects have they pursued with pamphlets like that, if not their own destruction? Men who write like this and utter these threats should have had troops at their disposal, had they wished to remain unharmed.[5] But see what results they have achieved! They have distorted humane studies with a burden of unpopularity, and every man of good will who is seriously attached to the truths of the Gospel is within range of perilous suspicions.

They have opened a great rift which divides the world everywhere, which will last maybe for many years and get steadily worse. In return for a clumsy attempt at liberty[6] slavery is redoubled, to such a degree that it is forbidden even to maintain the truth. A weapon is put into the hand of certain dastardly criminals with which to get their own back on all men of good will. A slur of no light kind is branded on the honour of Germany, for the rashness of a few firebrands is always imputed to the whole country. We[7] were supposed to lack wisdom and common sense; and now, formidable as we usually are, at least in arms,[8] we shall be despised even by the most despicable for having neither sense nor skill in arms. Some nobles in these parts are threatening the wealth of the clergy,[9] as though the end of Luther's tragedy might issue in that; and so they drive all religious institutions into the arms of the opposite party. Against me no moves have been made openly as yet, except that in Louvain especially certain Dominicans[10] abuse me in front of the people in sermons full of lies, and malign me on various charges in the ear of princes. Some whom I could name try to compel me to write against Luther,[11] though I have no leisure even to read his books. I see no better course in all this than to hold my tongue. I would advise you in support of your own case to write to Leo himself. He has a very kindly nature and favours learned men. I have spoken to Aleandro on the subject in a way that I think will be to your advantage, and that I believe to be the truth. Farewell.

Basel, St Andrew's eve 1521. In haste

Certain Germans[12] in whom I had entire confidence have proved quite untrustworthy.

Your sincere friend Erasmus

To the honourable Willibald Pirckheimer, senator of Nürnberg and a member of his Imperial Majesty's council

1245 / From Pierre Barbier — Vitoria, 29 November 1521

The original letter, autograph throughout, was among the manuscripts collected by Johann Friedrich Burscher formerly in the University Library of Leipzig but lost in the second world war (cf Ep 1067 introduction). It was first published in *Briefe an Desiderius Erasmus von Rotterdam* ed J. Förstemann and O. Günther (Leipzig 1904) 3–5.

Barbier's letter deals primarily with two legal transactions affecting Erasmus' annuity from Courtrai. The first concerned Erasmus' fear of losing his annuity in case Barbier were to die (cf Ep 1235:42–4, where his concern is barely concealed by one of the jokes with which the letters to Barbier usually end). As the annuity was settled upon benefices that Erasmus had resigned to Barbier and Barbier in turn to Jan de Hondt, the resident canon, Barbier's consent was needed each time that Jan de Hondt paid Erasmus his annuity (cf Ep 1094 n6) and Barbier's death might completely jeopardize his rights. This could be prevented by means of a papal reservation, but reservations were expensive and unless Erasmus were to survive the younger Barbier, the money would be wasted. Barbier therefore proposed that he sign a statement of consent, duly prepared by his attorneys, that would enable Erasmus, following Barbier's death, to secure a papal bull protecting his annuity. As for legal reasons the Courtrai prebend itself could not be subjected to such a substitution arrangement, Barbier proposed to exchange it (with the annuity settled on it) for another benefice that could. Despite Erasmus' impatience (cf Ep 1235:3–4), the matter dragged on, and by May 1522 Barbier's consent still had not reached him (cf Allen Ep 1287:10–11). For Erasmus' similar worries with regard to his English living see Ep 1176 n1.

The second transaction resulted from Barbier's desire to provide for his brother Nicolas. Perhaps as his reward in the original substitution arrangements, Barbier had retained for himself some benefices attached to the Courtrai prebend, including the parish church of St Gillis in the Waas (cf Ep 1094 n8). This he now wished to transfer to his brother, offering Erasmus adequate safeguards lest he lose the portion of his annuity settled upon St Gillis, or merely fear such a loss and therefore refuse his consent to the transfer. The safeguards included sending to Erasmus, rather than directly to Nicolas, the document that would enable his brother to complete the transaction.

Greeting, dear Erasmus, most learned master. Two letters[1] from you reached me together a few days ago, one dated 23 September, the other the twenty-fourth, and both written from Anderlecht. The confusions of the war,[2] from which we suffer here, will prevent me, I fear, from paying you a visit, at any rate as quickly as you suggest. But to stand by what I promised you in my other letter, that I would either visit your part of the world[3] before Christmas or look out for some way of getting the annuity made over to you, I laid the matter before some people with experience in business of your sort in Rome, and was told that our most Holy Father, if my consent is forthcoming, will readily reserve to you the fruits of the benefices which I received from you, dear Dr Erasmus, in return for the annuity. The result of which is that, whether I live or die, you cannot be deprived of the customary fruits. You will say perhaps 'This is likely to cost me a pretty penny'; my answer to that is that to put through this business at the Holy See I will appoint attorneys to agree on my behalf to an annuity of this kind, and from this moment, with the same effect as from that moment, I make a fully binding proposal that on the bare sight of the warrant, without waiting for the dispatch of the bulls, I will pay the annuity of which I speak.[4] And in that way there will be no need for you to face any expense beyond a single ducat, at any rate for the term of my life; and if it should happen that I die before you, it will be within your rights in accordance with the wording of the warrant to have the bull sent you without fresh consents from me or anyone else. But since it cannot be done this way in respect of the annuity of six pounds and a half gros[5] charged on the Courtrai prebend, I have decided to take some benefice or chaplaincy either here or in Flanders instead of that, and then in the same way I will give my consent to a similar annuity, just as I have already said I will consent in respect of the other benefices. But since notaries apostolic are scarce here, especially those who can write Latin, please do not think I am not keeping faith with you if I do not send a power of attorney to that effect in my letter; what I cannot do by this courier, I will do by the next.

Apart from that, you told me in another letter[6] that you would be content if I were to relinquish part of these benefices to my brother;[7] and so I am writing to him at the same time as this and sending him a power of attorney for the cession to him of the church of St Gillis in the Waas, asking him immediately to appoint attorneys to give consent to an annual payment of all the fruits of your benefit, as you have received them hitherto. This I am sending to you, to make him understand that he has you to thank more than anyone else for this gift; at the same time so that, if you are not satisfied, you can refuse to exhibit the power unless he first appoints satisfactory attorneys who, if he should by any chance be provided to the said church, can consent on his behalf to an annuity of the same amount as the sum that you have been accustomed to receive annually from the church aforesaid; and equally that, if you and your advisers in this matter think fit, you should not give a power of attorney of this kind until I have consented to the said annuity. And, as I have already said, the result of this will be that you can have no doubts about my brother; for after the consent by me of which I have spoken, he himself, once he has received the benefice, will not be able to escape an obligation to pay the annuity. Not indeed that I have any doubts about my brother's keeping faith with you or your losing confidence in him, but to remove all occasion of uncertainty, so far as this can conveniently be done. For if it were to be released to him before I consented to an annuity of this kind, he might die in the mean while, and so you would be deprived of your annuity and I of the benefice itself.

Of the events that have happened here I will write nothing, for fear of giving you an opportunity of making fun of my style, which is so unlike Livy's. If only I could write like my master Erasmus, I would certainly sing the praises of my own Charles,[8] as far as truth and honour would permit. There is no point in my giving you advice now about those troubles of yours in Louvain, since I see that I do more harm than good.[9] One thing I can do, and that I will: I will pray God so to direct you and all that is yours that what I am confident you are doing may turn to his glory and honour and your salvation and the profit of us all; and I beg you, dear master Erasmus, to do the same.

Farewell, from Vitoria[10] 29 November 1521.

Your devoted servant Pierre Barbier

To that most learned and most enlightened man Dr Erasmus of Rotterdam, his ever-to-be-respected master

1246 / From William Tate — Richmond, 4 December 1521

The letter actually sent, presumably in Tate's hand, is in the University Library of Wrocław, MS Rehdiger 254 no 149 (covering both sides of the sheet, each side headed with an 'IHS'). It was first published in *Briefe an Desiderius Erasmus von Rotterdam* ed L.K. Enthoven (Strasbourg 1906).

William Tate (d 1540), of York, had met Erasmus first in England and, probably in 1500, in Orléans (cf line 6). In 1505 he went to Rome with Erasmus' former pupil, Robert Fisher. After his return he was appointed rector of Everingham in Yorkshire (1508) and subsequently canon of York (1520). He also joined the court of Henry VIII – hence the dating of this letter from the palace of Richmond – and in July 1521 he was again sent to Rome, with twenty-eight copies of Henry's *Assertio* against Luther (cf lines 29–30), among them one bound in cloth of gold, which was presented to Leo X on c 14 September. The pope responded on 11 October with a bull praising the book and conferring upon the king the title of 'Defender of the Faith' (cf lines 24–5; LP III 1450, 1574, 1659). Tate was also asked to send Erasmus a copy, which presumably he did with this letter (cf lines 30–1). In Allen Ep 1342:858–65 Erasmus stated that the book, inscribed with his name by the king himself, had been sent in August 1521 but did not reach him until February 1522. However, he may have been thinking of the copy Cardinal Wolsey had promised him back in August; cf Ep 1228:8–11.

TO MASTER DESIDERIUS ERASMUS OF ROTTERDAM, DOCTOR OF TRUE PHILOSOPHY AND SACRED THEOLOGY, FROM WILLIAM TATE, LEAST AMONG DOCTORS OF LAWS, GREETING

I am moved to write to you now, most learned of men, partly by the ancient friendship between us which started here in Britain and was renewed in the French city of Orléans, partly because, as I strive to acquire the wisdom of philosophy (I mean, the philosophy of Christ), you show me the true path, or shall I say the royal road, more clearly day by day. Thus I should find it difficult to say what great benefits you are like to bring to all who fight Christ's battles. Blessed beyond a peradventure is the generation in which you were born, and I too am filled with exceeding joy that I have survived to see your day. I should rejoice however more exceedingly, if the distance between us allowed me at the present time occasionally to enjoy your society under my roof. In spirit I dwell secretly with you in your country, although my body is not a little wearied of the company of some men here, malicious, barking dogs who use their teeth continually on men of good will and scholars. All the same, when they attack others with their tongues, it is themselves they tear to pieces. Hence comes that utterance of the sage:[1] 'For the stirrings of envy are blows upon the back of the jealous man.' But pray be of good cheer; when they open their mouths sops are thrown to them, and their gaping jaws are soon shut.

You will have heard already,[2] I expect, that that most potent and elegant prince, our King Henry the Eighth, who is second to none in gifts of both body and mind and has deservedly been named most valiant Defender of the Faith throughout the whole round world not only by the Roman church but in light of the facts, has put together with his own pen a brilliant book against the Lutheran heresy – the argument, I mean, by which he rashly tries to undermine almost all the sacraments. Nor is this book without a name, for it has, if I may so express it, a most Christian title, to wit, *Assertio septem sacramentorum*.[3] Of this book, with the king's Majesty's approval, I have arranged to send you a copy. Pray read it; for I think you will find it the work not only of a prince as intelligent as he is learned but of an eminent theologian. And so, dearest Erasmus, do let your old friend Tate know as soon as you can what you think of this divine work; I ask this of you with some force, and wait day by day for your opinion on the point.

Farewell, leading light of our age. From Richmond[4] near London, 4 December in the year of our Saviour 1521

Your sincere friend, William Tate of York

1247 / From Konrad Peutinger — Augsburg, 9 December 1521

The letter actually sent, in Peutinger's own hand, with an enclosure written by his wife, is in the University Library of Wrocław, MS Rehdiger 254 nos 119–20. It was first published by L.K. Enthoven in 1906; cf Ep 1246 introduction.

TO DESIDERIUS ERASMUS OF ROTTERDAM, BEST WISHES FOR HEALTH AND TRUE FELICITY FROM KONRAD PEUTINGER OF AUGSBURG

I wish your Excellency joy of your return to Basel,[1] and I wish Upper Germany joy on her welcoming you once again, as we sincerely and entirely hope, to her great profit. If she enjoys the very great honour of your distinguished company, this means that you are ready to help all who desire to learn, all men of good will. You always outshone all other men by your singular wisdom, your virtue, and your consummate knowledge, and this becomes all the more true in proportion to the exceptional courtesy and kindness with which you greet everyone. This I experienced to my great joy in Bruges last year.[2] I have not forgotten the entertaining and at the same time authoritative opinions expressed in conversation by yourself and by the Englishman Thomas More,[3] that distinguished paragon of every virtue; so much so that as I read Jerome the presbyter restored by your exquisite scholarship and your other very learned works, to the perusal of which I am wonderfully addicted, if I am ever allowed any leisure from the law, my imagination is active and I seem to see and hear you teaching me, although I am so far away.

This is what happened yesterday. It was the second Sunday in Advent. I was enjoying the holiday, and amusing myself with my coins[4] and with reading the history of the emperors by Cornelius Tacitus. My wife[5] Margarethe was sitting near me, but at another table. She was reading your Latin translations of the New Testament, and at the same time she had in her hands a German version of it, very old and not particularly scholarly. Soon she recalled me from my favourite studies by saying 'I am reading the twentieth chapter of St Matthew, and I see that our friend Erasmus has added something to the text.' 'What can it be?' I said. She said again, 'Why, he gives things which are not in the German either.' I soon had Matthew's Gospel,[6] on which that same Jerome wrote a commentary, open before me, and the words 'And ye shall be baptized with the baptism that I am baptized with' were not there. I took refuge in your *Annotationes*,[7] from which I was immediately instructed by you that besides Mark[8] these words are also read in Matthew by Origen and Chrysostom and the Vulgate.[9] Then my wife insisted that we should read Origen's twelfth homily and Chrysostom's sixty-sixth on Matthew,[10] from which we understood clearly what you had restored from the Greek. I hope you will enjoy the thought, most noble of teachers, that you are still instructing daily not only me but my wife as well.

Our city, though it was attacked to some extent by the plague, is now recovering; the earth was white with snow and seared by the hoarfrost and hard with frost and ice, but the traditional mildness of our climate is reasserting itself. Our house however has so far remained untouched. How I wish the opportunity would offer of seeing your Excellency once again in our own country face to face! The note I enclose was written by my wife. Please let me know what you have thought worth printing. My best wishes to your Excellency. My wife greets you in Christ.

From Augsburg, 9 December 1521
To the revered and right learned Master Desiderius Erasmus of Rotterdam etc, my most honoured lord and teacher, in Basel

'Can you drink[11] of the cup that I am about to drink, and be baptized with the baptism that I am baptized with?' They say unto him, 'We can.' He saith unto them: 'Ye shall drink indeed of my cup, and be baptized with the baptism that I am baptized with; but to sit' etc.

'Mögend ir trincken den kelch den ich wird trincken vnd mit dem tawf, darin ich getawft, ir getawft werden?' Sy sprachen, 'Wir mögen.' Vnd er sprach zu yn: 'Wan meinen kelch werden ir trincken vnd mit dem tauf, darin ich getauft, ir getauft werden; aber zu sitzen' ecz. The common German version has this only: 'Mögend ir trincken den kelch den ich wird trincken?' Sy sprachen, 'Wir mögen.' Vnd der Herr sprach: 'Ja, mein kelch werden ir trincken' ecz. Here there is nothing about the baptism.

Margarethe Peutingerin of Augsburg

1248 / To Matthäus Schiner — Basel, 14 December 1521

This letter was printed at the end of the first edition of Erasmus' *Paraphrasis in Matthaeum* (Basel: J. Froben 15 March 1522; cf Ep 1255) and reprinted in the following Froben editions. Cardinal Schiner had encouraged Erasmus repeatedly to pursue the paraphrasing of the New Testament; cf n7 and Ep 1171 introduction.

TO THE RIGHT REVEREND MATTHÄUS, CARDINAL OF SION, FROM ERASMUS OF ROTTERDAM, GREETING

I have at last dared to risk a journey into Germany, though the whole route was everywhere full of soldiers[1] – so contemptuous was I of their large numbers, when I should have been afraid of a few. I was dreadfully anxious to assist at the birth of the New Testament,[2] which is now appearing for the third time. The Greek poet thought it better to stand in the battle-line and risk the chances of war three times than to bring forth once.[3] How much greater my own ill luck, who have to bring forth the same bantling so many times! But as the donkey,[4] they say, will go through fire and flame to rescue its young, it is not surprising that I should be willing to pass through so many dangers from time to time to assist my offspring. But it almost befell that my perilous and tiresome journey was in vain; for I soon began to feel ill from the stink of the stoves,[5] and when I had barely recovered I had another attack of the illness which brought me within peril of my life.[6]

Nevertheless, half dead as I was, I finished in the meantime a paraphrase on Matthew's Gospel, a work which I promised you in Brussels,[7] and which you promised to Germany in my name as you set out for Milan. Your Eminence is well aware how pitilessly she demands that promises be kept.[8] And so I have tried in this same work to pay both my debt and your own. The subject suited my state of health, for even if one must die in such a task, death would be holy and desirable. We are both entirely, I am sure, immersed in business, whether similar or not, I do not know. I only wish that what each of us is engaged on may be successful, or rather that what we are all engaged on may tend equally to the glory of Christ. Some baleful star, I know not what, or evil demon[9] must rouse these great tumults among mortal men. Nor is it enough that kingdoms and cities should thus be racked with civil war[10] and the greatest monarchs of the world meet in collision, but humane studies and the religion and the faith of Christians have to be shaken by these perilous rivalries. For my own part, if I can produce no remedy for such great evils, at least no one shall turn rebel with encouragement from me.

This generation, I perceive, is evil and perilous. What certain persons plan, or what the world is in travail with, I do not know. I for my part shall not cease to wish well, as I have always done, to the glory of Christ. I am a poor, weak man, who can do less than nothing; yet it is my joy to see the doctrine of the Gospels flowering again and as it were kindling into flame. If only I could put as much strength behind that movement as I wish! At least I try my hardest in good faith. My conscience is clear, and Christ is my witness: I seek neither wealth, which I have never found desirable, nor honours, which I have always abhorred; pleasures still less, which, if I had a mind to enjoy them, do not suit my years, and which I know I must soon leave behind. My desire is rather to get ready some provision to support me as I make a prosperous journey hence towards Christ, the goal of all my efforts. If only I could be successful in this enterprise as I have been in the apostolic Epistles! – for they are thumbed everywhere, even by laymen.[11] If only the stormy tempest of affairs would allow your Eminence to devote yourself to the one thing worth pursuing! And yet I know you do all you are allowed to do to promote Christ's cause – and will therefore, I doubt not, do the same for your Erasmus.

I have dedicated my work to our excellent prince, Charles,[12] partly as I foresaw, knowing his singular piety, that it would give his Majesty great pleasure, and partly that the blessing of such a name might recommend it to the hearts of a larger public. Rumours have begun to spread here about our Leo which I greatly desire may prove false.[13] No one had a more generous nature, and he was an especial patron of the humanities. To me he was particularly well disposed; but he was mortal. If it has pleased God to call his shepherd away to more secure felicity, I pray we may be given someone most like you – if indeed anyone can be more like you than you are yourself. May the Lord Jesus long preserve your Eminence in health and wealth.

Basel, 14 December 1521

1249 / To Matthäus Schiner — Basel, 14 December 1521

This letter is for the most part a shorter version of Ep 1248. While the larger version appeared in the *Paraphrasis in Matthaeum*, this one was presumably sent to Schiner as a letter. It was not printed until the *Opus epistolarum* of 1529.

ERASMUS OF ROTTERDAM TO MATTHÄUS, CARDINAL OF SION, GREETING

We are both of us entirely immersed in business. And I only wish that what we are engaged on may be successful. Or rather that what we are all engaged on may tend equally to the glory of Christ. The Paraphrase on Matthew which you encouraged me to undertake you will see printed come the next fair,[1] if only Christ lets me live so long. I am busy also on the New Testament, which is coming to birth for the third time.

This generation, I perceive, is evil and perilous. What plans others have, I know not; I personally should wish, if I might, to satisfy everybody. In this business of Luther I have perhaps done more good than some who boast that they have done great things. Among us certain persons, in great place but with tongues too ready to wag, have spread it abroad that I am a chorus-leader of the Lutheran faction;[2] the Germans themselves think very differently,[3] which makes things not too safe for me. Poor creature, miserable sinner as I am, I yet wish well to the glory of Christ, and for his sake to those who would promote his glory. I desire neither wealth nor honours; pleasures still less, which I know, however much I loved them, I must soon leave behind. If only the stormy tempest of affairs would allow you to devote yourself to the one thing worth pursuing! And yet I know you do all you are allowed to do for the cause of Christ – and will therefore do the same for your Erasmus.

Rumours have begun to spread about Pope Leo which I sincerely hope may prove false. Germany has given me its usual welcome: the stink of her stoves has almost finished me off. May the Lord Jesus long preserve your Holiness in health and wealth.

Basel, 14 December 1521

1250 / To Andrea Alciati

Basel, 14 December 1521

This is the first letter of Erasmus' correspondence with the leading Italian jurist, Andrea Alciati (1492–1550), of Milan. From the autumn of 1518 he taught for four years at the University of Avignon, where Bonifacius Amerbach was among his students. An outbreak of the plague induced him to interrupt his lectures by the end of February 1521 and to return to his native Milan (cf Ep 1233A:3; AK II Ep 780n). Although he went back to Avignon in November (cf AK II Ep 829), the news had not yet reached Basel, so that this letter and an accompanying one by Amerbach (AK II Ep 830) were directed to Milan. This letter, which was published in the *Opus epistolarum*, is answered in Ep 1261.

ERASMUS OF ROTTERDAM TO ANDREA ALCIATI, GREETING

Most learned sir, Bonifacius Amerbach, a frank and by no means tongue-tied herald of your virtues,[1] has told me much of you, and all of it very greatly to your honour and glory. He has moreover shown me your publication,[2] one of his favourite books, and so has caused me to entertain a high respect for your scholarship – almost incredible in one so young – and your spotless character, rich in graces of every kind.

The death of our friend Pyrrhus[3] was a great grief to me; I loved him as a person more than I did almost anyone, for I had known him since he was a boy. For his sake I particularly longed to visit Milan,[4] if that blockhead the god of war[5] did not reduce everything to chaos with his furious uproar. He had written to tell that he possessed some trifling pieces of mine, which I myself should have forgotten I had ever written; and I definitely wanted to carry these off, with no other purpose than to destroy them. For some of these Germans nowadays have a most foolish policy of publishing everything,[6] however much harm they may do to a man's reputation.

You make an urgent request in your letter to Bonifacius about your declamation.[7] I had already taken great care of it, to the extent of letting no one read it, except one close friend who can be absolutely trusted. So, as far as that goes, you can sleep the sleep of the just. Farewell.

Basel, 14 December 1521

1251 / From Johannes Sapidus [Sélestat], 30 December 1521

The autograph letter is in the University Library of Wrocław, MS Rehdiger 254 no 132. It was first edited by L.K. Enthoven in 1906 (cf Ep 1246 introduction). Sapidus was the headmaster of the famous Latin school at Sélestat in Alsace.

JOHANNES SAPIDUS TO ERASMUS OF ROTTERDAM, GREETING

The bearers of this letter,[1] my dear Erasmus, dearest of all the friends I ever had or shall have, have heard on good authority that you are restored to us and are now living in Basel;[2] and so they have been attracted and driven to come by one cause alone, and that an admirable one, the desire to see you, leaving their kindred, their country, and their homes and thinking nothing of the journey, which the severe cold and other things make unattractive, or even of the expense. It must be something important that gives them such an urge to visit you. For in hopes of making such a visit more easily (as they themselves supposed) both possible and permissible, they turned aside some miles from the direct road upon which they were set to see me, in order to secure a letter of introduction from one who had formerly been their tutor and whom they supposed to have great influence with Erasmus. And so, my dear friend, unwilling as I am to disturb you with a trifling request of my own, especially at this time when you are so fully occupied, and that with serious and difficult business, and though my own occupations do not leave me much leisure for the purpose, yet I could not refrain from obliging these young men, whose character and intelligence are alike excellent and who show such devotion to you, when they make such an honourable request, well urged if not well timed. In this matter I recognize my own lack of courtesy, for I had no right to make such a request on my own behalf, but I recognize also your own kindness, which is too great to take my request other than in good part. So the decision is in your hands; or rather, I hope that your decision will be that as they have prevailed with me for your sake I may in turn prevail with you for theirs. You will do so if you allow them to come and see you, which is all they ask for. Their haste to be going forbids me to write more. Please give my greetings to all friends in your part of the world.

Farewell. 30 December 1521

To Master Erasmus of Rotterdam, most learned of men, his great and valued teacher

THE VERGARA-ZÚÑIGA CORRESPONDENCE

translated by Alexander Dalzell and Erika Rummel

annotated by Thomas B. Deutscher

The five letters translated here were exchanged by Juan de Vergara of Toledo (1492–1557; cf Ep 1277) and Diego López Zúñiga (d 1531; cf Ep 1128) between 1521 and 1523. They have been included here because of the information they provide about the controversy then raging between Erasmus and Zúñiga, who in 1520 had published a critique of Erasmus' first edition of the New Testament (1516): *Annotationes contra Erasmum Roterodamum in defensionem tralationis Novi Testamenti* (Alcalá: A.G. de Brocar). Zúñiga, an accomplished scholar in Greek and Hebrew, was a member of the team assembled by Cardinal Francisco Jiménez de Cisneros to produce the Complutensian Polyglot Bible; as such he was perhaps the most competent critic of Erasmus' New Testament scholarship. His *Annotationes*, coming on the heels of the attacks of the Englishman Edward Lee, and occurring at a time when Erasmus was under mounting pressure to take a stand against Luther, caused the Dutch humanist considerable stress and anxiety, as is evident in the first letter. Erasmus' fears were well founded, for his first *Apologia contra Stunicam* did not silence the Spaniard but helped provoke him to extend the struggle to more dangerous ground, the question whether Erasmus was the source of the new ideas of Luther and his followers. Between the two protagonists stood Vergara, who represented the new generation of Spanish humanism, respectful towards Zúñiga but favoring Erasmus and trying in vain to play the peacemaker.

The most thorough accounts of the controversy between Erasmus and Zúñiga are Marcel Bataillon's *Erasmo y España* 2nd ed (Mexico City-Buenos Aires 1966) 91–102 and 115–32 and H.J. de Jonge's introduction to his edition of Erasmus' first *Apologia contra Stunicam*, ASD IX-2 3–57. The works published by Erasmus and Zúñiga during the course of their controversy are listed in Allen IV 622 and by de Jonge in ASD IX-2 41–2. The text of all five letters can be found in Allen IV 620–32.

The first four letters form part of what Allen has named the 'Heine Collection.' The collection consisted of twenty-four letters gathered by Doctor Gotthold Heine of Berlin at Madrid in 1846–7. Seven were copied in his own hand, and seventeen in the hand of an unknown copyist, probably a seventeenth- or eighteenth-century Spaniard. In the latter group are the first four letters translated into English here, as well as Epp 1277, 1312, 1554, 1684, 1864, 2003, 2562 between Erasmus and Vergara and other Spanish correspondents. The originals of only two of these seventeen letters could be located by Allen. The fifth letter comes from a manuscript in the Biblioteca Nacional at Madrid. It was first printed by Adolfo Bonilla y San Martín in *Clarorum Hispaniensium epistolae ineditae* (Paris 1901) 19ff and *Revue Hispanique* 8 (1901) 193–6.

TBD

1 / From Juan de Vergara to Diego López Zúñiga [Brussels, 10 October 1521][1]

About a year and a half ago I sent you in Spain a copy of the *Annotationes* of a certain Englishman called Lee,[2] which was an attack on Erasmus' edition of the New Testament; I also included a copy of Erasmus' reply;[3] I thought you would be interested to see a scholar fighting in the same field as yourself and to watch his adversary defending himself from the opposite point of view and erecting a barricade as it were in anticipation of your own attack. Unfortunately you had left for Rome[4] at the time and so it seems my trouble was in vain. Now Erasmus' *Apologia* has appeared, in which he replies to your *Annotationes*;[5] as soon as I noticed this, I felt, even more strongly than before, that I should send you a copy. So you will receive the book along with this letter; I have folded it into as small a parcel as I could, for I was afraid that if its size proved a nuisance to the courier, there would be less chance of its being safely delivered. So please let me know at the first opportunity if the book has reached you.

But I know you are interested in learning what Erasmus said to me on the subject; so let me tell you briefly. As soon as I put in at Bruges on my way from Spain,[6] the man met me and told me that for a long time he had been awaiting my arrival with the keenest interest, and he asked me for a copy of a work known as the *Annotationes*, which was an attack on his edition of the New Testament produced by someone with the name of Zúñiga, one of those prickly sophists from the University of Alcalá; he said he had been advised by a Flemish friend[7] who lived in Spain that I would have the book with me, as indeed I had promised when I met this friend some time before. When he heard that I had inadvertently left it behind (which was the truth), he expressed deep disappointment, particularly since he was getting ready to publish a third edition. 'For,' he said, 'the second edition has been out for some time;[8] so I can hardly doubt that it was spite on Zúñiga's part which made him conceal the existence of this edition, in which I had corrected many of the errors in the earlier version, and choose instead to attack the first edition as providing more ample material for his satirical pen.' I gave him my solemn word that the second edition had not yet reached Spain; I told him you are no prickly sophist, but a man who has devoted himself unceasingly to the study of the good authors, Greek and Latin, sacred and profane, that you know Hebrew also, and that from you he would have reason to fear not just the chaff of the sophists but a well-aimed and pointed attack. I told him also that you stood out among the members of your circle both by birth and talent, and I added whatever seemed likely in the circumstances to further and enlarge your reputation. One thing I forgot to mention – that you were admitted to holy orders – for I thought this could be taken for granted, but I see he has got it wrong, since he addresses you in his *Apologia* as a layman. Then he asked me if there was much venom in your book; he told me that this was the reason he had been so offended by Lee, since this sort of behaviour was something he could not bear. I replied that the book was not altogether lacking in candour, though you had restrained yourself fairly well, seeing that you are a naturally outspoken person who does not find it easy to be tolerant. So much for our first meeting. Later I learned from a mutual friend[9] that Erasmus suspected me of hatching some monstrous plot;[10] he thought I had indeed brought the book, but had decided to give it instead to one of his rivals who supported Lee, or at any rate that I was suppressing it to make it more difficult for him to write his *Apologia*.

After a few days had passed, I was invited by Erasmus to dine with him. I managed to clear myself of the latest of his suspicions, but no sooner had I done so than he began to revive his old fears that you had pretended not to have seen his second edition; for he thought it inconceivable that a work written before his second edition would not have appeared much earlier than in fact it did; he was sure you had deliberately chosen the version which offered the greater scope for criticism. This, he said, was what Lee had done, as indeed it is the general practice of all who are on the look-out for any target to attack. I tried to clear his mind of these nagging doubts, and I explained that I could almost claim to be an eyewitness[11] to the fact that you started your reply just as soon as the first edition arrived in Spain and that you were about to publish your *Annotationes* with a dedication to our common patron, his Eminence the cardinal,[12] when that good and pious man, who gives such generous support to scholars from every quarter, tactfully suggested that you write to Erasmus[13] and draw his attention to any mistakes you detected in his work rather than publish a polemical attack upon him. You acceded to his wishes and held up publication for several days;[14] consequently there was considerable delay before the work appeared, though you had finished it much earlier. I think he accepted this explanation, and we parted after I had undertaken to see that a copy was sent to him from Spain.

I then had to leave for Germany.[15] It was many days later when I returned,[16] and I understand that by then a copy of your *Annotationes* had reached Erasmus, whether by the good offices of that Flemish friend[17] of his or someone else, I do not know. I did not see the man for a long time, but then recently I noticed him taking something to the printers at Louvain which turned out to be this very *Apologia*, a copy of which I purchased straight off the press and am sending to you now. I asked him why he did not include the text of your *Annotationes*, as he had done in his reply to Lee, for it is more satisfactory if the reader can examine and judge the arguments of both prosecution and defence together. He replied that you had circulated your *Annotationes* widely enough and there was no need of a second edition. He told me also that he had learned in a letter from a friend in Rome called Bombace[18] that the pope[19] had issued an edict forbidding you to attack Erasmus or any of his editions of the New Testament, to which he had given his formal approval.

These are the matters I thought important for you to know. But to speak of Erasmus himself, so far as I am able to understand him, he is a man of exceptional intellect and judgment, with an ease and facility of style which may sometimes betray him into hasty and ill-considered publication; but this is a matter for scholars to judge; I should add that he is indefatigable, a man of almost immeasurable energy. He enjoys a reputation such as no one, I believe, has enjoyed during his lifetime for many generations past. He holds a unique position of respect, admiration, and esteem among that great host of scholars who are to be found throughout Germany, Belgium, and Britain; they compete in singing his praises, and while they themselves are sometimes brought low by the wounds which they are prone to inflict on one another with their pens, Erasmus sits *en dehors de la mêlée*, watching the gladiators from a ringside seat, while he is acclaimed by both sides with compliments and shouts of approbation. Nowadays no one produces a book or a speech or a page without, at the first opportunity, working in a complimentary reference to Erasmus' name, which is set in capital letters and adorned with the most flattering eulogies, with the object, presumably, of gaining the favour of the public. Nothing is more likely to win customers for the booksellers than to have the name of Erasmus on the title-page of all their publications, whether as expert reader, redactor, or annotator; and there is no book so expensive or so cheap and insignificant that it does not receive some added dignity and authority from the mention of Erasmus' name. Need I say more? You may take my word for it that he stands supreme in the judgment of learned and unlearned alike. The only person who dared to challenge him in print was Lee, but perhaps his courage and his sense of justice were not matched by his success. He was received like some Zoilus attacking Homer[20] or Momus attacking Venus.[21] He had no sooner issued the book than there was a flood of invectives, dissertations, lampoons, dirges,[22] which tore the wretched Lee apart so mercilessly that it looked as though he would be run through by the pens of his critics if ever he ventured into public.

To bring this to a conclusion, I must leave to better scholars and to men like yourself the more expert assessment of his literary work: I have the deepest respect and admiration for his tireless energy, remarkable in a man of his years,[23] for his extraordinary devotion to literature, and for a life lived in the service of learning. And, if you listen to me, you will seek to re-establish your friendship with him, the friendship of one scholar with another. If I can be of any assistance in bringing this about, I am ready to help, just as I am ready to serve you in any other matter where I see an opportunity to defend and promote your reputation.

2 / From Diego López Zúñiga to Juan de Vergara Rome, 9 January 1522

Most reverend sir. Here in Rome on 16 December I received your dispatch sent from Brussels on 10 October. Enclosed in the said dispatch was a letter[1] of yours, written in Latin, and the *Apologia*[2] of the renowned Erasmus, which I had long had a great desire to see; Paolo Bombace,[3] secretary to my lord of Santi Quattro,[4] who is Erasmus' advocate and patron here, showed me a letter[5] addressed to himself by the aforementioned Erasmus, in which he said, *inter alia*, 'The Spaniard who made such an insolent attack on my *Annotationes* is Zúñiga; I have answered him quite civilly in a brief *Apologia*.' So I have been most anxious to see a copy, and you have been good enough to satisfy my wishes by your thoughtfulness in sending the aforementioned *Apologia*. For this I am particularly indebted to you. I only wish that Lee's *Annotationes* and Erasmus' reply[6] had reached me at the same time – you tell me, sir, that you sent them to me in Spain, but I never set eyes on them until I arrived in Genoa[7] a year ago. It was about that time that a learned gentleman there[8] pointed them out to me along with the second edition[9] of Erasmus' New Testament. This was all quite new to me, for before that I had never seen any of this material, nor imagined that anyone would have anticipated me in goading this wild bull; I would very much have liked to have had that glory for myself.

Some time later I saw Lee's *Annotationes* and Erasmus' reply being bound here for the Portuguese ambassador;[10] but I have never seen any other copies at Rome, nor are there any available. For this reason, sir, please send them[11] by the first messenger who leaves for Rome, so that I may keep them with the other pieces you sent and see exactly what this Lee is saying; for I read his work very hastily in Genoa. As for Erasmus' *Apologia*, he did answer me, if I am not mistaken 'quite civilly,' though not in the sense he intended, but according to the meaning of the word in good plain Castilian.[12] I did not think that he was quite so ignorant as he has now shown himself to be in this *Apologia* of his; for although he admits to having made some errors, I see that he blatantly defends others which are graver still, excusing his ignorance as far as he can and defending himself with empty words.

Although at the time I was greatly saddened, as was to be expected, by the death of our good pontiff and lord, Pope Leo,[13] I could not contain my laughter when I read his *Apologia*.

Moreover I have come to realize from reading this work that Erasmus has no high opinion of me, and he is quite right, since until now no one has known whether I existed or not. But I have resolved to make my reply of such a nature that he will be compelled to take me seriously; for besides the material which I have in my own possession I have the great advantage here of the Greek libraries,[14] which offer much that is useful in my efforts to crush this barbarian. Here is how I propose to answer him. First, I shall try to show how ill informed was the reply which he made in the *Apologia*, in which, to mention just one thing, he deliberately suppressed points which I had made and which are available in print; next I shall reveal the errors into which he fell in his second edition – the third edition[15] has not been seen here to date and is not available; then I shall purge his notes on the *Letters* of St Jerome:[16] all this will make a fine book – enough to make Erasmus' ears ring. But since this is less than a man of such impious and blasphemous views deserves, I have planned a second book,[17] which is more or less in order, though it has not yet been published; in it I point out to the pope (in whose interest it is to take this matter in hand) how important it is to punish this Dutchman and compel him to recant, since I can show that among his impious teachings there are ten passages[18] in which he openly attacks the primacy of the Roman church. The Lutheran heretics have seized upon this as the plainest support for their own heretical beliefs. Master Erasmus will find this a more disagreeable tune than my having written a reply to his *Annotationes*. You will do well therefore to warn him to be on his guard in the future; for I am not the only one to raise a fuss about these matters – there are many others, and among them is a member of the ecclesiastical court, a learned Italian,[19] who has read all the works of Erasmus with this one purpose in mind – to seek out any blasphemous ideas which they contain and to dislodge the snakes, so to speak, from their pit. I have discovered that he has noted more than a hundred passages, and has copied them out and presented them to Pope Leo; the pope in turn gave them to a certain scholar at court,[20] whom I have not been able to identify, with instructions to prepare a response. I assure you all this is going on and will continue until Erasmus is obliged to come to Rome and do penance and recant

Or he will burn in a coat of pitch,
Like those who, fastened by the throat,
Stand amid flame and smoke.[21]

But enough on this subject. Erasmus, it appears, has published three editions of the New Testament, though it would have been better for him if he had not published any or taken it upon himself to make such disturbing innovations, as he will find out soon, perhaps in the very near future. I have only seen the edition at Alcalá to which I wrote my reply, and another printed in March 1519. Of the latter I have seen only two copies, one at Genoa and the other here at Rome in the house of my lord of Santi Quattro[22] – they say that this is the second edition. In the *Apologia* Erasmus often mentions a third edition, and you tell me that, when you arrived from Spain, he was preparing a third edition for publication. I beg you, sir, please write to me and identify the first, second, and third editions,[23] that is, let me know the day, month, and year when each of these was printed and why he published a third edition when there were still so many copies available of the second. I should also like to know if he saw my *Annotationes* before the publication of the third edition and why they do not send the second and third editions to Rome or, I am given to believe, anywhere else – I suppose their aim is to sell off the first editions. If there were any way of sending me here the third edition, I would be most pleased to have it.

Although the Roman booksellers have sent my *Annotationes* against Erasmus[24] and Lefèvre[25] to every city in Italy and have also dispatched copies to Lyon for distribution throughout France and Germany, there are still some left, since I brought a large number with me; some of these I should like to have delivered to Louvain so that Erasmus' friends there might see them and make up their minds about them. So please write to me and let me know if copies have arrived there and how many, and in what form you think fifty copies could be sent there.

Two months before Pope Leo's death, a German theologian called Eck,[26] who was the first person to launch an attack on Luther, arrived here and is still here. He brought fifteen pamphlets,[27] in German, composed recently by fifteen Lutheran heretics who have formed a conspiracy against the Roman church, though they do not have the courage to identify themselves. In three of them Erasmus is depicted with his doctoral cap, and each of the three spreads its impious doctrines beneath a quotation from the *Moria* of Erasmus. They evidently consider him one of their own tribe. The same opinion is held in Rome, and it was the opinion of Pope Leo also, who, if he were still alive, would give him his due deserts, for he had received information from Germany that Erasmus was secretly in league with Luther and was editing and polishing his works,[28] and, although Erasmus wrote to him[29] to justify himself, the pontiff was not satisfied. This is why he was so pleased when he saw my *Annotationes* against Erasmus and why he read and praised them. So you can see how much truth there was in the report which, according to Erasmus, Bombace had communicated to him.[30] It is all very well for him to comfort himself with empty words, but in the end he will see how much good they will do him.

The news from here is that Pope Leo died on 1 December at midnight. His funeral took place on the ninth of that month. The cardinals entered the conclave on the twenty-seventh. There were about forty in number altogether. On the fourteenth day of the conclave the most reverend the cardinal of Tortosa was elected *in absentia* and publicly proclaimed pope.[31] There was great joy in Rome over his election because of his great reputation for virtue and sanctity; within an hour his arms and the papal insignia, that is, the mitre and the keys, were displayed throughout the city. This is the Lord's doing, and this the day which the Lord has made.[32] Blessed be his name for providing so fine a shepherd for his church at a time of such great need. I have nothing more to write except to express the wish that the Lord will preserve you, most reverend Father.

Rome, 9 January 1522, the day of the election of the new pope

I am, sir, at your command, Diego López de Zúñiga

To the most reverend Doctor Vergara, canon of Alcalá, at the court in Flanders. Postage, two reales; I repeat, two reales

3 / From Diego López Zúñiga to Juan de Vergara Rome, 26 March 1522

The books[1] which you sent me along with your letter[2] could not have come at a better time. I had just finished my reply to Erasmus[3] a few days before – it does not differ much in substance or scope from my previous work – and the only thing which was holding up its publication was the fact that I could not lay hands on Erasmus' *Apologia* to Lee, to which he refers me in several places.[4] So the arrival of the book was a great help to me in my labours. I had come to the conclusion that, however much I might wish to do so, it would be wrong for me to rush into print; for I was afraid that instead of bringing into the world the sort of work which people perhaps expected of me, I might appear to have suffered a miscarriage; or I might fall victim to the fate which so frequently and deservedly besets my opponent because of his impatience to get his work in print. I was amused to discover what those friends of Erasmus[5] thought about his reply[6] to my *Annotationes* – that the force of my argument had not just been blunted, but completely demolished. I am afraid these people do not appreciate our Spanish mettle or realize that we are a nation which would sooner be robbed of life than of honour. That Erasmus is a learned man, I do not contest; in fact, if I had not thought him so, I am not so faint-hearted as to have taken him for my antagonist when there were so many men of letters to choose from. So let him regard it as a special compliment or as striking evidence of his own standing as a scholar that I thought him worth taking on in scholarly debate. As for his *Apologia*, now that I have read it, far from discouraging me from my purpose, it has made me all the more eager for the attack; for the feebleness of his defence has provided me with a much easier target to aim at. My reply, I think, has not turned out too badly, but whatever its merits, it will leave Erasmus in no doubt that I am not so poor a scholar as his *Apologia* suggests. This is not my only purpose in attacking him; there are other matters of greater moment,[7] which will enable the reader to see that this fellow Erasmus, who has been making such a noise throughout the world for many years, does not reign in the citadel of letters, as some people in this innocent and foolish world appear to have thought.

But perhaps I have said more than enough on this topic. I have read Lee's *Annotationes*[8] and I consider it a work of scholarship and not altogether devoid of literary merit. I am not surprised that Erasmus was upset by its publication, since in passage after passage Lee exposes his abysmal ignorance. It was this, I am sure, which bothered Erasmus, not Lee's venomous attacks, as you suggest in your letter. I do not find his reply to Lee very satisfactory, since he seems to be using all his ingenuity simply to drown his opponent in a flood of eloquence. How like Erasmus this is! For him it is less important to proclaim the truth than to ensure that he does not slip from the pedestal on which an ignorant public has placed him. As for your offer to send me the third edition of Erasmus' New Testament, there is no need to trouble yourself about it: it is easier for me to procure a copy from Basel, since Basel is closer to Italy than to Belgium. Please send me, as you promised in your letter, the rest of Erasmus' polemical writings against Lee,[9] also Latomus' *Dialogus* against Erasmus with Erasmus' *Apologia*[10] in reply.

I am pleased to send you my *Itinerarium*,[11] which records my journey to Rome from the town of Alcalá; I enclose also the letter which I recently wrote to the new pope;[12] they have won everyone's approval here in this unique and wonderful city, so I feel sure they will be welcomed also in your part of the world. I propose to send you shortly a little work[13] which I have written as an introduction to the three volumes in which I refute the impieties and blasphemies of Erasmus. The fact that it is not being sent to you now must be blamed on the printers: these people, with their remarkable talent for procrastination, are capable of dawdling over the simplest task. This will be followed by another short work[14] giving the actual texts of Erasmus' impious doctrines with only a preface from my pen. After this will come the indictment, to be followed in turn by a refutation[15] of his impieties; this was read some time ago by Pope Leo x and would now be in general circulation if he had not been taken from us. The fifth volume in the series will expose some fantastic and shocking lapses in Erasmus' commentary on the *Letters* of Jerome.[16] It is this work which is occupying my time at present. In this way I hope to make myself better prepared to review the long-awaited third edition of Erasmus' New Testament. With this work, unless I am mistaken, I shall prove to the reader my competence in a field which Erasmus impudently claims as his own. I enclose also some letters from the new pope[17] which were recently brought here from Spain. If anything turns up in your part of the world which might interest or amuse me, I know that you will be good enough to pass it on. Farewell.

Rome, 26 March 1522
Your friend, Zúñiga
To the most reverend Doctor Vergara, canon of Alcalá, in Flanders

4 / From Diego López Zúñiga to Juan de Vergara — Rome, 4 May 1522

I wrote you recently in Latin; for in your letter you had pressed me very strongly to do so. I also sent you my *Itinerarium*[1] and a copy of my letter to the pope;[2] all of which, I imagine, will be in your hands by the time you read this. Here now is something new, a work hot off the press,[3] which I have brought out in this gracious and benevolent city; it describes the 'blasphemies and impieties of Erasmus' and will help you to understand his mind and thoughts and attitude to religion. You will find him openly siding with Arius,[4] Apollinaris,[5] and Jovinian,[6] and also with the Wycliffites[7] and the Hussites[8] and indeed with Luther himself; for it was Erasmus and Erasmus alone who armed and equipped and trained Luther with these blasphemous notions of his, turning him against the true religion. So I wish those northerners joy of their Erasmus; I do not care if they call him the sun and the moon and the glory of Germany, or if they call him, as some do, 'Panerasmius,' the 'beloved of all,' so long as Italy calls him 'the enemy of religion' and Rome, which is queen and mistress of the world, knows him as a blasphemer who deserve the same penalty as Luther, that is, to be declared a public enemy of the Roman church. And unless he comes to his senses and recants his impious opinions, this is what will happen to him by the authority of our most Holy Father the pope[9] when he returns to the city – let the Erasmians have no doubts about this.

This is the substance of the book which is now on its way to you. There is nothing else which I ought to tell you for the moment. Write to me as soon as you can and let me know what those among whom you are living feel on this subject.

Rome, 4 May 1522
Your friend, Zúñiga
To Juan de Vergara, theologian and canon of Alcalá

5 / From Juan de Vergara to Diego López Zúñiga Valladolid, 7 May 1523

After my voyage[1] I was suddenly seized by a deep longing for my native land, which made me leave the court and return home;[2] I understand that at the same time you were driven from Rome by a severe outbreak of the plague; so it is almost a whole year since either of us has been in touch with the other by letter. But now that you have returned to your place at the papal court and I to the emperor's, it is time we resumed the steady tempo of our correspondence. Erasmus will give both of us enough to write about. Shortly before I sailed from Belgium, I wrote to him at Basel[3] and sent him a copy of Miranda's book.[4] He sent me a brief note[5] in reply, which reached me at Alcalá; in it I learnt that the sale of your works was prohibited at Rome by decree of the college of cardinals. I could scarcely believe this was true until that illustrious knight, your brother,[6] showed me a letter you had written in which you expressed regret on this very point; but you also said that you expected great things from the pope and hoped that your fortunes would improve when he arrived in Italy. So please let me know how you fared after the pope's arrival and if those polemical works of yours were ever published: you issued *un ouvrage préliminaire*,[7] which your brother allowed me to glance at. The book you sent me on the subject of 'blasphemies'[8] did a great deal of damage to the reputation which you had previously established with your *Annotationes*,[9] as I learnt from discussions with many people[10] when I was in Belgium. For to speak candidly, as a friend should, there is a widespread impression that you sometimes criticize as blasphemous what is sound Catholic doctrine; moreover you impute to the author statements which he put in the mouth of others, even those which he attributed to Folly, while you defend as gospel truth what many consider as old wives' tales and silly superstitions; some held that these lapses were the result of ignorance, but many, including those who wished to be more charitable, put them down to blind prejudice. Although I always try, wherever I am, to defend your reputation, on this occasion I felt completely inadequate to counter the resentment you had stirred up; and so this is why I thought it important to write to you and give you this unvarnished account of the situation. But if I may judge from the great calm which has followed the storm, there is now peace, or at any rate a truce,[11] between you – I should like to think it is peace. You have given enough rein already to anger and spleen; now it is time for gentleness and Christian charity. Whatever it may be, I should like to know. Farewell.

Your brother left here not so long ago on a commission for the emperor[12] to the queen of Lusitania.[13]

Valladolid, 7 May 1523

MONEY AND COINAGE OF THE AGE OF ERASMUS

A The coinage of the Burgundian-Hapsburg Netherlands before and after 1521

B Official coinage rates in February and August 1521

JOHN H. MUNRO

On 20 February 1521, Charles v authorized the first significant change in the Netherlands' coinage since the monetary reforms of 1496–9: the striking of new gold réals, demi-réals, and Carolus florins; and new silver réals (double Carolus), demi-réals (single Carolus), and patards (or stuivers). No debasement was officially intended, all the former Burgundian-Hapsburg coins were left in circulation at their 1499–1500 rates, and the exchange rates on most foreign gold coins were similarly left unchanged. But the new silver patard (stuiver) in fact contained 3.2 per cent less silver than the former issues. That change, and more particularly the French silver debasement of 1519 and the current central European silver-mining boom (then approaching its peak) inevitably raised the gold:silver ratio and thus market prices of gold coins. Charles v was finally forced to authorize higher rates on gold coins in a monetary ordinance of 15 August 1521. Minor adjustments followed in 1523, 1525, and 1526, but the 1521 rates were restored in March 1527. The Hapsburg gold coinages remained unchanged in value until July 1548; the silver coinages, until March 1553.

TABLE A
The coinage of the Burgundian-Hapsburg Netherlands before and after 1521

year and coin	fineness[1]	per cent purity	number struck to the marc[2]	weight in grams	pure metal content in grams	value in Flemish gros (d) in February 1521
1500–20: gold						
toison d'or	23 carats 9.5 grains	99.13%	54½	4.491g	4.452g	100d
St Philip florin	15 carats 11 grains	66.32%	74	3.307g	2.193g	50d
1500–20: silver						
réal (from 1505)	11 deniers 5 grains AR	89.51%	71¼	3.435g	3.074g	6½d
double patard	8 deniers AR	63.89%	79	3.098g	1.979g	4d
patard (stuiver)	4 deniers AR	31.94%	80	3.059g	0.977g	2d
gros (groot)	3 deniers 6 grains AR	25.95%	134	1.827g	0.474g	1d
1521–56: gold						
réal d'or	23 carats 9.5 grains	99.13%	46	5.321g	5.274g	120d
demi-réal	18 carats	75.00%	70⅛	3.490g	2.618g	60d
carolus florin	14 carats	58.33%	84	2.914g	1.700g	40d
1521–56: silver						
réal (double carolus)	11 deniers 5 grains AF	93.40%	80	3.059g	2.857g	6d
demi-réal (single carolus)	5 deniers 12 grains AF	45.83%	78½	3.118g	1.429g	3d
patard (stuiver)	3 deniers 17 grains AF	30.90%	80	3.059g	0.945g	2d

NOTES

1 For gold coins, fineness was measured in terms of 24 carats = 100%, with 12 grains per carat of gold; for silver coins, fineness was, until 1520, measured in terms of *argent-le-roy* (AR) = 23/24ths or 95.833% pure; after 1520, it was measured in terms of *argent fin* (AF) = 100.0% pure. In both systems, full fineness, AR or AF, consisted of 12 deniers, with 24 grains per denier.

2 Weight was measured in terms of the number of prescribed coins to be struck to the mint-weight unit, the *marc de Troyes* (8 Paris *onces*), which contained 244.753g. That system reflected the relative crudity and consequent inexactitude of minting techniques, which also allowed a certain tolerance or *remède* – a few coins or fractions thereof above or below the prescribed number per marc. The weights given in grams, therefore, are merely a theoretical, ideal mean.

TABLE B
Official coinage rates in February and August 1521

coin	February 1521		August 1521	
gold coin				
réal	120d	10s 0d	127d	10s 7d
demi-réal	60d	5s 0d	63d	5s 3d
carolus florin	40d	3s 4d	42d	3s 6d
ducat	79d	6s 7d	80d	6s 8d
écu au soleil	72d	6s 0d	76d	6s 4d
silver coin				
réal	6d		6½d	
double patard	4d		4d	
patard	2d		2d	

SOURCES

Louis Deschamps de Pas 'Essai sur l'histoire monétaire des comtes de Flandre de la maison d'Autriche (1482–1556)' *Revue belge de numismatique* 32 (1876) 49–124

H. Enno Van Gelder and Marcel Hoc *Les monnaies des Pays-Bas bourguignons et espagnols, 1434–1713* (Amsterdam 1960) 75–96

Algemeen Rijksarchief (Belgium), Rekenkamer, registers 18.124–45 and 17.882–3 (Bruges and Antwerp mint accounts)

Herman Van der Wee *The Growth of the Antwerp Market and the European Economy, Fourteenth–Sixteenth Centuries* 3 vols (The Hague 1963)

Notes

Preface

xi

1 Cf Ep 1221 n8.
2 Cf Ep 1144:70–3.
3 Cf Epp 1155:20–3, 1162 n36.
4 Cf Epp 1113 n15, 1186 n7.
5 Cf Epp 1001, 1009, 1030 and CWE 7 preface.
6 Cf Ep 1106 introduction.
7 Cf Epp 1155 and 1197 introductions.
8 Cf Ep 1228 n12.
9 Cf Ep 1161 n8.
10 Cf Ep 1228 n13.
11 CF Epp 1223 introduction, 1233 n3.
12 Cf Ep 1194 n1.
13 Cf Ep 1250 n5.
14 Cf Epp 1155 introduction, 1203 n2.

xii

15 Cf Epp 1186 n3, 1202 n10.
16 Cf Ep 1141 n11.
17 Cf Epp 1197 introduction, 1216 n19.
18 Cf Epp 1225 n52.
19 Cf Epp 1233:18–24, 1238:78–9.
20 Ep 1233:15–17
21 Cf Epp 1162 n36, 1167 n22.
22 Ep 1167:82–3
23 Cf Ep 1167 n20.
24 Cf Ep 1241 n9.
25 Cf Ep 1195 n3.
26 Cf Ep 1166 n24.
27 Cf Ep 502 introduction; CWE 27 156–60.
28 Cf Epp 1162:215–18, 1196 n42.
29 Cf Ep 1202:237–61.
30 Cf Epp 1174 n6, 1213 n16, 1247 n9.
31 Cf LB VI 64.

xiii

32 Cf Ep 1225 n29.
33 Cf Epp 1166 n30, 1216 introduction.
34 Cf Epp 1217 n29, 1225 n47.
35 Cf Ep 1233 n28.
36 Cf Ep 1228 n11.
37 Cf Ep 1216 n19.
38 Cf Ep 1202:300–1.
39 Ep 1119:45–6
40 Ep 1202:62–5, 73–154
41 Ep 1202:323–4; cf Epp 1167:182–4, 1195:120–36, 1219:109–11.
42 Ep 1155:17–18
43 Cf Ep 1219:140–3.
44 Epp 1167:386–90, 1155:18–19

xiv

45 Albano Biondi 'La giustificazione della simulazione nel cinquecento' in *Eresia e Riforma nell'Italia del Cinquecento: Miscellanea* I (Florence-Chicago 1974) 5–68.
46 Cf Ep 1143:16–21, 73–82.
47 Cf Ep 1166 n13.
48 Cf Epp 1174 n6, 1206:42–5, 1225 n29.
49 Cf Luther w *Briefwechsel* II Ep 490.
50 Cf Ep 1196 n42.
51 Cf Epp 1161 introduction, 1202, 1211.
52 Cf Allen Ep 1278:10–13.
53 Ep 1202:323–5
54 Cf Epp 164, 745 introductions.
55 Cf Ep 1218 n14.
56 Ep 1183:147–51; cf Ep 1195 n9.

xv

57 Cf Ep 1232 introduction.
58 Cf Ep 1206:143–6.

Notes to Letters

1122

1 decimarius] *Decimarius* or *Zehntner* was the title of fiscal officials in various mining centres of Saxony.
2 Albert] Albert of Saxony (1443–1500), the father of Duke George, was the founder of the *Albertiner* branch of the house of Wettin. In 1488 he went to the rescue of Maximilian I, who was in danger of losing the inheritance of his Burgundian wife, and was appointed governor of the Netherlands. In 1493 his services were rewarded with the regency and revenues of Friesland, but he could not establish full control over the territory. His interest in the silver production of Schneeberg is shown by Georgius Agricola (*Ausgewählte Werke* II 123–4), who tells of a banquet Duke Albert held underground in the mine, joking that he dined on a table of pure silver.

3 chancellor] Albert's chancellor in Friesland, 1512–15, was Simon von Reischach, doctor of law, whom Erasmus had probably met in 1511 in London. Reischach belonged to a Saxon embassy negotiating a renewal of the trade agreement between England and Friesland concluded in 1505. The ambassadors arrived on 29 April 1511 and apparently were still in London on 10 July, when Erasmus presumably returned there from the continent (cf Ep 225 introduction). See LP I 729, 804.14, 811; *Akten und Briefe zur Kirchenpolitik Herzog Georgs von Sachsen* ed Felician Gess (Leipzig 1905–17) I 351, 831.

4 letter ... sent me] Ep 963; for the medal which Frederick the Wise sent as a present see Epp 872:27n, 1001:46–57.

5 Eppendorf] Heinrich Eppendorf (c 1490–after 1551) was born in Eppendorf near Freiberg (Saxony). He was probably the son of the hereditary reeve, who also kept an inn. He matriculated at the University of Leipzig in 1506, graduated BA in 1508, and subsequently received a scholarship from Duke George. After this visit to Louvain he registered at the University of Freiburg on 26 September 1520. In 1522 he went to Basel and attached himself to Erasmus. In the ensuing conflict between Hutten and Erasmus Eppendorf took Hutten's side, and his relations with Erasmus ended in bitter animosity. From 1523 onwards he lived in Strasbourg and worked for the printers, translating Plutarch and the Elder Pliny into German. His claim to noble birth rests on shaky foundations, but Erasmus, like others, accepted it at the time. He put 'ab Eppendorf' when revising the letter for the *Epistolae ad diversos*, but subsequently in the *Opus epistolarum* the 'ab' was removed; see Ep 1437 and Werner Kaegi in *Historische Vierteljahrsschrift* 22 (1924–5) 469–79.

6 three lumps of native silver] In his *Bermannus* Georgius Agricola discusses at length the various types of silver found in the Erz mountains and in Bohemia; see *Ausgewählte Werke* II 114–19, and cf Ep 1125 n9.

7 myself in lead] Erasmus had recently had a portrait medal struck; the design is attributed to Quinten Metsys; see Ep 1092 n2.

1123

1 your letter was printed] Ep 911 was published in Erasmus' *Farrago* of October 1519. Meanwhile Mosellanus may have realized that the approach chosen in that letter was inappropriate (cf Ep 948 introduction); more specifically he probably referred to one sentence (cf Ep 911:63n), which was deleted when Ep 911 was reprinted in the *Epistolae ad diversos* (cf lines 8–10). Naturally, Erasmus also suppressed the letter in which Mosellanus had lodged his complaint; for a clue to its contents see Ep 1125 n4.

2 these Germans] In this case, the Basel editors of the *Farrago* (cf Ep 1009 introduction). There are many such expressions of discontent with German publishing (cf Ep 1186 n13) and with the temper Erasmus thought was typical of the Germans (cf Epp 967:115–23, 998:72–8, 1155:31–3, 1167:198–204, 1173: 90–2). Heinrich Eppendorf later expressed his irritation when reading this passage and similar ones (see Ep 1206 introduction; Allen IV 617).

3 archbishop of Mainz] The unauthorized publication of Ep 1033, addressed to Albert of Brandenburg, had caused embarrassment to both the recipient and the author.

4 second edition ... correspondence] The *Epistolae ad diversos*; see Ep 1206 introduction.

5 letter I wrote to Luther] The first printing of Ep 980 had probably been arranged by Mosellanus himself (cf Ep 948 introduction). It was also reprinted repeatedly in combination with Ep 1033 (cf above n3). For the Roman reaction to Ep 980 see Ep 1143 introduction, and for its circulation in the Netherlands thanks to Jacob of Hoogstraten and others cf Ep 1030 n7.

6 Oecolampadius] Johannes Oecolampadius, the future reformer of Basel, had informed Erasmus of his intention to retire to a monastery; cf Epp 1102 introduction, 1139:122–3.

7 your duke] See Ep 1125.

8 for Germany] See Ep 1155 introduction.

9 Lee] Edward Lee had gathered together critical notes on Erasmus' New Testament and caused him grave worries for many months (see the prefaces to CWE 6 and 7). In particular he had been concerned lest the quarrel cause his English friends to turn against him (cf Epp 1026 n3; 1083 n12). During a recent meeting with the English court at Calais Erasmus sought and received reassurance in this regard (cf Epp 1106 introduction; 1127A:2–7). Three years later he recalled that he also met Lee himself (who was then probably on his way home to England; cf Ep 1140 introduction) and shook hands with him to show that their war was ended; see ASD IX-1 160, cf Epp 1100 introduction, 1132:17–24, 1175 n28.

10 Hephestius] 'The little Vulcan.' Erasmus is referring to the Louvain theologian Jacobus Latomus (cf Ep 934), who limped (cf Ep 1088 n8), like the ancient god. An oration of Mosellanus' had given him cause to launch an attack against Erasmus and the reconciliation which followed (cf Ep 1022) had been short-lived. Erasmus came to consider him as his principal, if discreet, enemy at Louvain, especially after the death of 'Noxus,' to whom he had previously attributed the same role; cf Epp 1113:13–15, 1127A:50–1, 1804.

11 Noxus] Jan Briart of Ath, who was until his recent death (8 January 1520) 'vice-chancellor' of the University of Louvain; see Ep 1029 n2.

12 epigrams attacking Lee] *In Eduardum Leum ... epigrammata*, Mainz 1520 (cf Epp 1083, 1122 introductions). The collection combines vilification of Lee with extravagant praise for Erasmus. Mosellanus himself may also have intended to attack Lee; cf Ep 1083 n9.

1124

1 pour cold water ... competition] Not to discourage them – the modern sense of the phrase – but to stimulate them to fresh efforts; cf *Adagia* I x 51.

2 old subjects ... amity] Cf Ep 1125 introduction.

3 as Livy puts it] Livy 21.4.1, quoted from memory, as here, in *Adagia* I vi 28, IV iii 44

1125

1 Albert] See Ep 1122 n2.

2 chancellor] Simon von Reischach; cf Ep 1122 n3.

3 Frederick] Frederick the Wise, elector of Saxony, was George's cousin. In 1502 he had founded the University of Wittenberg; cf Epp 871:20n, 939.

4 Mosellanus] There is reason to think that the following lines (28–37) are based on information contained in Mosellanus' recent letter (cf Ep 1123 n1).

In a note in the margin of his copy of the *Epistolae ad diversos* (cf Ep 1206 introduction; Allen IV 617) Heinrich Eppendorf claimed that such was the case and that he had seen Mosellanus' letter in the course of his visit to Louvain; cf Ep 1122 introduction.

5 Stromer] Stromer was now physician to Duke George and also taught medicine at the university. After his return to Leipzig, he became a citizen in February 1520 and was also elected to the city council; cf below lines 34–5.

6 Pistoris] Simon Pistoris (1489–1562), son of a Leipzig physician and professor, had studied in Italy and Leipzig, where he received a doctorate in law in 1514. As professor ordinarius he headed the faculty of law from 1519 to 1523 and was afterwards chancellor to Duke George. He became a reliable supporter of Erasmus, and also a correspondent.

7 Breitenbach] Georg von Breitenbach (d 1541) was born in Leipzig, where he studied from 1501 and received a doctorate in law. In 1524 he succeeded Pistoris as professor ordinarius. He was also in the service of Duke George, after whose death he became in 1540 chancellor to the elector Joachim II of Brandenburg.

8 Eppendorf] See Ep 1122 n5.

9 nugget] Erasmus uses here the Latin term 'massa,' whereas in Ep 1122:13 he spoke of three 'massulae,' using the diminutive. It seems that he is referring to two separate gifts.

10 Attic talent] The same figure of speech, based on Athens' standard unit of weight, is used in Ep 1119:7.

1126

1 book] Lee's *Annotationes* on Erasmus' New Testament; see Ep 1037.

2 kinsmen] Cf Ep 1053 n21.

3 even those] The conservative theologians of Louvain; cf Ep 998 introduction.

4 an abbot … stupidity] Richard Kidderminster or Bartholomew Linsted; see Ep 1061 n23, n24.

5 Standish] Henry Standish, bishop of St Asaph and warden of the London Franciscans, had been critical of Erasmus for years (cf Epp 481:44, 608:15n). Throughout this letter Erasmus presents him as an ignoramus and a stubborn opponent of the new learning. Perhaps Erasmus' judgment was more objective on the second point than on the first. Standish left a fine library and bequeathed a sum of money for the Oxford Franciscans to buy more books.

6 He was preaching … London.] The following incident is also reported at the beginning of Erasmus' *Apologia de 'In principio erat sermo'* (LB IX 111E–12C; cf Ep 1072), where Standish's name is not mentioned. Ep 1127A:25–47 repeats, with some variations, the episodes concerning Standish which are told in this letter. They may have occurred shortly after the second edition of the New Testament (cf Ep 864) had reached England in the spring of 1519. If so, the lord mayor of London mentioned in line 39 was Sir James Yarford, for whom see *Acts of the Court of the Mercers' Company, 1453–1527* ed L. Lyell (Cambridge 1936) 200 and passim.

7 Augustine … *verbum* rather than *ratio*] See perhaps *De trinitate* 15.16 (CC 50A 500), where Augustine notes that the Son is called the *verbum* rather than *cogitatio* of God.

8 off the point] Literally 'nothing to do with Bacchus'; cf *Adagia* II iv 57.
9 bachelor] No doubt the royal chaplain John Stokesley; cf lines 86–91, 168–9 and Epp 855:47–9, 1127A:11–14.
10 married man] Thomas More, who is also mentioned in lines 57, 80–1, 116–19 and identified in Ep 1127A:29
11 St John] John 1:1, LB VI 335–7
12 what Augustine says] Cf above n7.
13 'Thine ... Lord'] Wisdom 18:15
14 official document] See Epp 338:27n, 835 introduction, 864.
15 queen] Cf below n25.
16 upon his knees] The incident related in this paragraph and the following ones (to line 193) is resumed more briefly in Epp 1162:167–78, Allen Epp 1581: 340–7, 2045:65–84, and also in the *Apologia de loco 'Omnes quidem'*; cf LB IX 433C–34B and Ep 1235 n5.
17 counting the points ... fingers] Of the three charges Standish made the first is answered in the next paragraphs to line 155; the second is treated briefly in lines 210–17, but had recently been answered fully in a letter (Ep 1006:179–252), which is found, like the present one, in the *Epistolae ad diversos*; the third accusation is taken up in lines 217–20, 263–81, 338–68.
18 "We shall all rise ... changed"] 1 Cor 15:51. The same criticism was voiced by Nicolaas Baechem Egmondanus, and Erasmus finally answered with the *Apologia de loco 'Omnes quidem'*; cf Ep 1235 n5.
19 my annotations] See LB VI 740–3; cf Ep 1235 n7.
20 continuous text] Erasmus' Latin translation of the Greek New Testament
21 mere women] Cf Ep 1196 n2.
22 Lucian's principle ... hold one's tongue] In *Adagia* II vii 4 Erasmus ascribes this, in different wording, to Lucian's *Rhetorum praeceptor*, perhaps recalling paragraph 20. Here he gives the first two words of a line from the lost *Philoctetes* of Euripides (fragment 796, Nauck), which were proverbial in Antiquity.
23 throw in the sponge] Literally 'to proffer grass'; cf *Adagia* I ix 78.
24 out of the Hebrew] Cf Ep 843:23n.
25 the queen] Here as in line 101 and Ep 1127A:24–5 it is suggested that Queen Catherine of Aragon followed the theological debate attentively; for her learning cf Ep 855:34n.
26 capital offence] Cf Ep 1053 n62.
27 in Louvain in a public lecture] See Ep 946 introduction.
28 elsewhere] In the New Testament; see Ep 1006:179–252.
29 the eucharist] Cf below lines 338–68.
30 laws of the Caesars ... guilty] *Codex Iustinianus* 9.46.10
31 he must have talked] Reading 'deblaterarit'
32 Ajax' example ... pigs] Cf *Adagia* I vii 46. For Ajax' madness see Sophocles *Ajax* and Ovid *Metamorphoses* 13.
33 Reuchlin] For the controversy around the Hebrew scholar Johann Reuchlin see Epp 290, 694 introductions, Ep 1155 n5.
34 the man's name ... for the moment] He was the Dominican Vincentius Theoderici; see Ep 1196, which repeats the four episodes narrated in the following paragraphs to line 368. For the many feuds involving Erasmus and members of the Dominican and Carmelite orders cf the indexes of CWE 5–8.

35 passage] See below lines 338–68, where the account of this episode is completed.

36 pamphlet ... on this very subject] It is not known to exist.

37 business of nothing down ... their teeth into] Erasmus is presumably referring to the examination of his works undertaken by some junior members of the Louvain faculty of theology (cf CWE 7 preface). Coinciding with the time of this examination, Theoderici received, at the beginning of the winter term 1519–20, authority to lecture in the university. For the two preceding years he had taught in the *studium* of his order; see de Vocht CTL I 465.

38 he did not deserve] As the Latin term here is 'indignus,' Erasmus may perhaps be referring to his note on 1 Cor 13:4 (LB VI 725–6), which first appeared in the 1518/19 edition. This note, however, is frankly critical of Thomas, stating that he would have deserved to do better ('indignus') than insert into a commentary on Scripture rubbish gleaned from unscholarly sources. Another account of this exchange is given in Ep 1196:45–51, and other assessments of Thomas are in Ep 1211:467–83. It may be noted that Luther was also accused of irreverence with regard to St Thomas (cf Ep 1033:243–4) and that Theoderici's own work was in the field of Thomistic scholarship; cf Ep 1196 introduction.

39 letter ... to Thomas Lupset] Ep 1053:486–7; cf above n26 and lines 224–6.

40 a passage ... without original sin] Erasmus refers to his note on Matthew 12:47 (LB VI 69–70), which first appeared in 1518/19. The inference of the sentence quoted verbatim is, as he states here, that Mary was not free of original sin. But the remainder of his note, and also a second account of this incident in Ep 1196:58–67, leave no doubt that Erasmus himself favoured the opposite view, and this is presumably what Theoderici had maintained. The immaculate conception of Mary became a dogma of the Catholic church in 1854. Thomas Aquinas (d 1274), after much hesitation, finally concluded against it, but a Franciscan general chapter in 1263 bound all members of the order to observe the feast of her immaculate conception, which was also celebrated by all eastern churches, and the Franciscan John Duns Scotus (d 1308) offered a series of arguments in favour of the immaculate conception which was decisive in the long run. In Erasmus' day, however, both Dominicans and Franciscans were still divided on this question, and Erasmus' personal view on the issue agrees with his general preference for the Franciscan order; cf Epp 1033 n36, 1173:144–5, 1174 n5.

41 a passage ... than any other] Erasmus refers to the first of his two notes on 1 Cor 11:24 ('This is my body, which is for you; do this as a memorial for me') (LB VI 716–18). Even in the final version both appear to cast some doubt on the degree of support that Scripture can give to any dogmatic tenet concerning the eucharist. To that extent Theoderici's apprehension is understandable. The following summary is a fair reflexion of Erasmus' text in the 1518/19 edition (page 342) although the direct quotation (lines 350–7) is not entirely literal. It was removed in the edition of 1527 and replaced with an admission of the incompetence of human reason in matters of faith.

42 'Note how dangerously ... so often'] Evidently a handwritten marginal note in the copy of the New Testament *Annotationes* (1518/19) which Theoderici had before him

43 'poetry'] Cf Ep 1153 n42.

44 no more than moles] Cf *Adagia* I iii 55.
45 rabbis] Erasmus continues to use such terms as 'rabbis,' 'Judaism,' 'Jewish ceremonial' in a denigrating manner to characterize the scholastic theologians and preachers and the narrowly legalistic and despotic vision of the church he believed them to advocate; cf Epp 541:149–70n, 694 introduction, 858:71, 1137:26, 1153:160, 1183:41, 1225:242, 1234 n2.
46 the salt of the earth, the light of the world] Matthew 5:13–14
47 on absolute power] Cf Epp 872:20n, 1039:114–22, 281–6.
48 your host] Marquard von Hattstein, canon of Mainz; cf Ep 1109:32–6.
49 Nesen] The German scholar and lampoonist Wilhelm Nesen had failed to obtain authority to lecture at Louvain (cf Ep 1046 introduction) and by now had left Louvain for good, evidently planning to revenge himself on his opponents (cf Ep 1165 n17). With Buschius he had worked to coordinate the German response to Lee's attack upon Erasmus (cf Epp 1083 introduction, 1088 n4). On 14 September he engaged himself for three years as head of a new Latin school at Frankfurt; cf de Vocht CTL I 467–8.
50 Dorp] Maarten van Dorp was a member of the Louvain faculty of theology.

1127

1 elsewhere] Cf Ep 1125 introduction.

1127A

1 from his books] Cf Ep 872:14n.
2 Lee] Cf Ep 1123 n9.
3 king and queen] For Erasmus' recent interview with Henry VIII and Catherine of Aragon at Calais cf lines 66–9 and Ep 1106 introduction.
4 Spanish Franciscan] No identification has been suggested. In Ep 1126:33–85 a similar attack is attributed to Henry Standish, who is likewise identified in both letters as the hero of the episodes described hereafter to line 47.
5 Scotus] Cf Epp 1126 n40, 1211 n69. A survey of Oxford college libraries shows that there was demand – although not an exceptional one – for Scotus' works throughout the century; see N.R. Ker 'Oxford College Libraries in the Sixteenth Century' *Bodleian Library Record* 6 (1957–61) 459–515.
6 King's chaplain] Most likely John Stokesley; cf Ep 1126 n9.
7 gold chains] The ambiguity may be intentional; cf Ep 999:80–1.
8 in such a fix] Literally 'stuck in the water'; cf *Adagia* I iv 100.
9 Standish] See Ep 1126:100–93 and n5.
10 Thomas More] Cf Ep 1126 n10.
11 Jan Turnhout] Jan Nys Driedo (d 1535) of Turnhout near Antwerp matriculated at Louvain in 1491. His friend Adrian of Utrecht encouraged him to study theology. After obtaining his doctorate in 1512 he was appointed professor ordinarius of theology about 1515. He was a biblical scholar of note, warmly supported the Collegium Trilingue, and was unsympathetic to Luther from the beginning; cf Ep 1163 n3 and de Vocht CTA II 505–8.
12 Latomus] Cf Ep 1123 n10.
13 off the mare] Cf *Adagia* I viii 95.
14 peace in your university] Cf Ep 1125 introduction.
15 'new learning'] 'Nova doctrina' is not a term Erasmus normally uses when he

refers to humanistic studies. Perhaps he meant 'religious reform,' or, more likely, an integral approach consisting of both.

16 Guillaume Petit] There is no indication at this time that Petit, the royal confessor, had already taken a stand against Luther. He supported Lefèvre d'Etaples and perhaps Reuchlin too; cf Augustin Renaudet *Préréforme et humanisme à Paris* 2nd ed (Paris 1953) 646–7, 659–60, 736. Erasmus was suspicious of him for other reasons; see Epp 744:21n, 778:21–4.

17 Hoogstraten] Jacob of Hoogstraten had paid repeated visits to the Netherlands in recent years and campaigned against Reuchlin, Luther, and Erasmus himself; see Epp 1006 introduction, 1030 n7, 1040.

18 He asked me ... you.] During their meeting at Calais (cf Ep 1106 introduction). Another report of this is contained in a letter from Osvaldus Myconius to Rudolphus Collinus (Clivanus, Am Bühl) in Milan, dated from Lucerne, 20 November 1520; it is printed in [Salomon Hess] *Erasmus von Rotterdam nach seinem Leben und Schriften* (Zürich 1790) I 607–8. Myconius probably owed his information to Erasmus' friends at Basel, and thus indirectly to Erasmus himself. His account may be somewhat biased; it also raises the possibility that the last statement here attributed to Henry VIII reflects Erasmus' own view (cf Ep 1127:18–20). According to Myconius the king patted Erasmus on the shoulder and asked him why he did not defend [!] Luther. Erasmus allegedly answered that to do so was not for him as at Louvain he was now counted among the philologists rather than theologians (cf Ep 1173:87–90). The conversation apparently continued, but Myconius merely reports that the king finally dismissed Erasmus with a compliment and a gift of fifty ducats.

19 your answer ... at Louvain and Cologne] See Epp 1113 n15, 1186 n7.

20 *Julius exclusus*] Cf Epp 502, 961:41–3.

21 bishop of Liège] Erard de la Marck; cf Epp 980, 1038 introductions.

22 set his heart ... cardinal's hat as well] For the fulfilment of these ambitions cf Ep 1166 n14, n31.

23 he] Erard de la Marck; cf Allen Ep 1482:6–8.

24 Aleandro] In 1524 Erasmus recalled that the prince-bishop himself had shown Aleandro's letter to Erasmus (cf Allen Epp 1482:6–8, 1496:17–23; see also Ep 1167:134–7). For friendly contact between Erard and Erasmus towards the end of 1519 see Ep 1038. Since Erasmus later thought that Aleandro's letter had turned Erard temporarily against him (cf Allen Ep 1482:11–12; Balan no 89), it was perhaps rather in the summer of 1520, when attending the court of Charles V (cf Ep 1129 n1) that he was shown Aleandro's letter; cf Ep 1123:10–13.

25 letter ... the cardinal of Mainz] Ep 1033, addressed to Albert of Brandenburg; cf Ep 1123 n3.

26 controversies with Eck] See Epp 769, 844, 872:25n. With the Leipzig disputation (cf Ep 948 introduction) Johann Maier of Eck had emerged as Luther's most visible opponent in Germany.

27 commentary on the psalter] The reference apparently is to the later parts of Luther's *Operationes in Psalmos* (cf Ep 980:59–61). The date of 1520 is given at the end of the second part.

28 to whom ... the other day] Ep 1113

29 Karlstadt] Andreas Karlstadt was professor of theology in Wittenberg and a participant in the Leipzig disputation.

1128

1 Lee] Cf Ep 1123 n9, n12.
2 Zúñiga] Diego López Zúñiga (d 1531) belonged to a distinguished family of scholars and prelates. He was educated, and subsequently taught, at the University of Alcalá, where he worked on the Complutensian polyglot (cf CWE 3 220). His critical *Annotationes* against Lefèvre d'Etaples (Alcalá: [A.G. Brocario] 1519) were followed by his *Annotationes … contra Erasmum Roterodamum* (Alcalá: A.G. Brocario 1520), both of which defended the Vulgate. At the time Erasmus was writing this letter, Zúñiga, basing his critique on the *Novum Instrumentum* of 1516 (cf Ep 384), attacked primarily Erasmus' Latin translation of the Greek text. He was preparing to go to Rome, where he arrived after a long journey on 9 February 1521 (see below 337, Letter 1 n4). A friend of Zúñiga, Juan de Vergara, (cf Ep 1277) had recently arrived in the Netherlands, and when Erasmus met him at Bruges (cf Ep 1129 n1), their conversation was about Zúñiga. In a letter to Zúñiga (Brussels, 10 October 1521; below 337–40) Vergara recalls that Erasmus had already heard of Zúñiga's book from a Flemish friend in Spain, perhaps Pierre Barbier (cf Ep 1216), who had written Erasmus to say that he was giving Vergara a copy to take along. Vergara assured Zúñiga that he spoke the truth when he told Erasmus he had forgotten to bring the book. He also told Erasmus that his opponent was a serious scholar, knowledgeable both in Greek and Hebrew, and, upon Erasmus' question, that Zúñiga's criticism was quite frank. Vergara's further observations are confirmed by the present letter. Erasmus judged the situation in the light of his traumatic experiences with Edward Lee and was convinced that he was purposely denied access to Zúñiga's *Annotationes* while they would be shown to his enemies behind his back; cf Ep 1216:2–4 and Marcel Bataillon *Erasmo y España* 2nd ed (Mexico City 1966) 92–7.
3 cardinal of Toledo] Francisco Jiménez de Cisneros died on 8 November 1517. Vergara, his former secretary, had come to the Netherlands to report to the new archbishop of Toledo, Cardinal Guillaume de Croy (cf Ep 628:70n). Jiménez was mentioned to Erasmus by Vergara (see his letter to Zúñiga, n2 above), who failed to persuade Erasmus that Zúñiga had not deliberately ignored the revised New Testament of 1518/19; cf Ep 864.
4 that offences come] Cf Matt 18:7, Luke 17:1, Ep 1113:28–30.
5 conspirators] Cf Epp 1126, 1127A.
6 Philippus] Philippus Melanchthon had been invited to join the University of Ingolstadt where his great-uncle, Johann Reuchlin, had recently taken up an appointment (cf Ep 1129 introduction). Melanchthon, however, was committed to remain in Wittenberg; see *Melanchthons Briefwechsel* I Epp 77, 99–100.
7 Oecolampadius] Cf Ep 1123 n6.
8 letters] Not known to exist

1129

1 Bruges] Charles V was at Bruges between 25 and 29 July (Gachard II 28). Erasmus too was at Bruges, having perhaps accompanied his monarch from Calais (cf Ep 1106 introduction), and met with friends old and new (cf Epp 1141:3, 1145:5–7), among them Konrad Peutinger (cf Ep 1247:10–14), councillor to Maximilian I, who fits the following description very well; but perhaps Erasmus meant Salzmann; see the introduction.

2 Württemberg] For Duke Ulrich see Epp 747:81n, 923:27n.
3 you ought to know this] For the first of many indications of Fisher's interest in Reuchlin see Ep 457.
4 outburst of pamphlets] See Ep 1083 introduction.
5 do as I ask] Cf Epp 1100 introduction, 1123, 24–7 and n9.
6 become a Frenchman] Cf Ep 1165 n21.
7 war] Erasmus' remarks may well have been prompted by his recent meeting with Hutten (cf Ep 1114 introduction), where Hutten in a jocular mood developed the idea that the German knights could take up their arms against the Roman church and its supporters. In a letter of 4 June he conveyed to Luther Sickingen's offer of a safe refuge, and not until January 1521 did Luther reject their military plans unequivocally, denouncing the idea of shedding blood in the name of the Gospel (Luther w *Briefwechsel* II Ep 368). The Dominicans participated significantly in the Roman proceedings against Luther and had long been the protagonists in the feud with the Reuchlinists. In August 1519 Hutten's patron, Sickingen, threatened to use violence against the German friars and frightened them sufficiently to send a peace delegation to Reuchlin; cf Ep 1182 n4 and Geiger *Reuchlin* 444–51.
8 Bohemians] Cf Epp 1021:186–97 and n14, 1156:58–62.

1130

1 three Magdalens] Erasmus' reference recalls the title of Lefèvre's rejoinder to his critic, John Fisher, *De tribus et unica Magdalena disceptatio* (Paris: H. Estienne 1519; cf Ep 1030 n2), but in Ep 766:26 and elsewhere he used the same words to refer to Lefèvre's *De Maria Magdalena et triduo Christi* (Paris 1517), which was reprinted in 1518 and 1519. The preceding correspondence with Lips refers to several other books Erasmus had presented to the monks of St Maartensdal.

1131

1 Deloynes, Ruzé, and Du Ruel] Members of the Paris humanist circle gathered around Budé
2 note to Bérault] Cf Ep 1117 n4.
3 things ... already finished] For More's *Epistola ad Germanum Brixium* see the introduction and Ep 1087 introduction.
4 1521] Wrong date added in the *Opus epistolarum* of 1529

1132

1 offering of a book] The paraphrase of the Epistles of Peter and Jude; see Ep 1112.
2 pamphlets] Cf Epp 1083 introduction; 1123 n9, n12.
3 Palaeologus] Christophorus is perhaps identical with the Clemens Palaeologus who in 1517 had visited Switzerland on a similar errand; see Ep 594:5–11.
4 Hesiod's dictum] Cf Hesiod *Works and Days* 346; *Adagia* I i 32.

1133

1 passage ... father] See Ep 1087 n26; cf Ep 1117:71–2. The text has been amended to read 'father' where Erasmus by mistake had written 'son.'
2 Jupiter] A similar comparison between the king of the gods and Henry VIII is implied in Allen Ep 2040:41–2.

1134

1 knight] Presumably as a complimentary formula Erasmus uses here the term *eques auratus* 'golden knight.' For other occurrences see Ep 1220 n1; as he used this term quite seldom, the special emphasis should not be overlooked.

2 letter] It is missing, but may have reached Erasmus together with Ep 1109, which he had recently answered with Ep 1126.

3 in your society ... in Mainz] For Erasmus' visits to Mainz in 1518 see Epp 843, 867 introductions. He could, however, have met Rotenhan in the course of an earlier journey along the Rhine in 1515 or 1516; cf Epp 337, 410 introductions.

4 'Twere death ... his spite'] Cf Virgil *Eclogues* 3.15.

5 some people] Cf Epp 1126, 1127A, 1128.

6 whole month and a half] Cf Ep 1080 introduction.

7 least satisfaction ... his success] Erasmus was convinced that Lee was primarily a tool in the hands of his opponents, the Louvain theologians (cf Ep 998 introduction). His quiet departure from Louvain (cf Ep 1140 introduction) and their failure to write anything in his defence did not weaken this conviction; cf Ep 1139:16–17.

8 Seneca] Allen suggests that Rotenhan might have adapted lines 503–8 of Seneca's *Oedipus*; cf Ep 39:48–9.

9 throes ... birth] For the significance of this metaphor, which is used very often by Erasmus, cf Bietenholz *History and Biography* 21–2.

1135

1 a legate ... at Charles' court] The nuncio attached to the court of Charles V since January 1520 was Marino Caracciolo, who had earlier been accredited to Maximilian I (cf Ep 865:72n). It is probably he who is meant here (cf Ep 1188:29), although he was soon to be joined by a special legate more eminent than himself. Girolamo Aleandro had left Rome on 27 July, entrusted with the publication and execution of the papal bull against Luther (cf Ep 1141 n11). One set of instructions for him is dated 16 July (Balan no 3). But travelling by way of France, he did not reach Cologne until 22 September and was in Antwerp on 26 September for his first audience with the emperor (see Pastor VII 417–20; cf Ep 1157 n2). Hutten subsequently refers to Aleandro in similar terms; see Ep 1161:30–3.

2 weakness] Cf Epp 694 introduction, 1006:81–6, 160–2, 1033:40–4, 210–27, 1041:12–20. Meanwhile, on 23 June 1520 Rome had ruled against Reuchlin; cf Epp 622:36n, 1155.

3 all you could to persuade] Apart from Epp 1033, 1041 cf Epp 939:69–71, 126–7, 961:36–8, 967:86–114, all published in the *Farrago* of October 1519; cf the introduction.

4 letters ... other people] In addition to Epp 1033, 1041, cf perhaps Epp 622, 939, 980.

5 slit the throat ... *Epistolae obscurorum virorum*] Cf Epp 622, 636, 808, 961:34–6; for a slight indication of initial support see Ep 363:5–7.

6 Camarina] A Greek city in Sicily, whose history gave rise to the proverb 'Move not Camarina, for it is not to be moved'; cf *Adagia* I i 64.

7 stronghold of the Hutten family] The castle of Steckelberg near Fulda

1136

1 not to breed ill will ... more attractive] Cf Ep 1125 introduction.

2 hornets' nest] Cf *Adagia* I i 60.

3 after the funeral] Literally 'from the pyre.' Erasmus used the same phrase in Ep 867:294; cf perhaps *Adagia* II vii 11.

4 most consistently unfortunate ... ever lived] Erasmus frequently expressed similar feelings; cf Epp 1102 n2, 1178:2, 1196:473–7, 1206:87–90.

1137

1 the second I have received] Ep 1047, following Ep 850

2 Jewish ceremonies] Cf Ep 1126 n45.

3 rich householder ... things new and old] Cf Matt 13:52.

4 'Make haste slowly'] Cf *Adagia* II i 1.

5 proverb] Cf *Adagia* II ix 60.

6 gold coin] According to Allen's note, this was a 'rather mysterious, but not uncommon' gold coin, struck by the Dacian or Getic king Coson between 40 and 29 BC. The three figures are explained as a consul marching between two lictors, and the bird as an eagle. The subscription in Greek capitals is ΚΟΣΩΝ.

1138

1 as the proverb has it] Cf *Adagia* I i 34.

2 Mountjoy] William Blount, Lord Mountjoy, was one of Erasmus' first patrons in England.

3 Lovell] Thomas Lovell (d 1524) is documented at Cambridge in 1500–1 as a student of civil law and by 1513 received a doctorate in canon law. In the same year he was given a canonry at Wells. From 1516 to his death he was subdean of Wells and frequently acted as vicar-general for the nonresident bishops, cardinals Adriano Castellesi and Thomas Wolsey. His love of learning and generosity towards Erasmus are reflected in Ep 1491; see Emden BRUC. He is not identical with Sir Thomas Lovell (d 1524), for whom see *Dictionary of National Biography* ed S. Lee (London 1885–).

4 Toneys] Robert Toneys (d 1528) was probably educated at Cambridge (1479–81), as were Lovell and Burbank, his colleagues in Wolsey's service. He was canon of Sarum (1494–9) and subsequently held prebends in Wolsey's dioceses of Lincoln and York. After 1514 his signature appears under many documents, in later years sometimes together with that of Burbank. In December 1520 he was a clerk to the court of chancery. See Emden BRUC; LP I 3101, III 1083; Ep 1492.

5 Philippi] Perhaps, as Allen suggested, Francisco Felipe or Felipez, who is said to have come to England in the retinue of Catherine of Aragon in 1501. He remained among her trusted servants and in 1527–9 he made two or more trips to Spain for interviews with Charles V, conceivably as a double agent, serving Henry VIII as well as Queen Catherine. His royal pension was last paid in 1540. If he is intended here, Erasmus may have had a somewhat mistaken impression of his age. Also, unlike those mentioned before and after him, he is not known to have been connected with Wolsey's household; see Allen's note and Garrett Mattingly *Catherine of Aragon* (Boston 1941) 253–4, 276.

6 Francis the physician] John Francis was one of the founders of the London College of Physicians in 1518 and was still prominently associated with it in 1523. In December 1520 he cured the aged Christopher Urswick, patron of many humanists. In 1524–6 he is documented as a physician in Wolsey's household. There are no clues for the beginning of his friendship with Erasmus, nor for his later life and death. See Epp 1532, 1759; LP II 4450, III 1103, IV 2397.

7 Sampson] Richard Sampson was a chaplain to Wolsey; cf Ep 388:38n.

8 Gonnell] William Gonnell (cf Ep 274 introduction) had been a good friend of Erasmus at Cambridge. Mention of him here could suggest that he was now at court and perhaps in Wolsey's service.

9 Clement] John Clement, a protégé of More and Wolsey, was at this time studying medicine (cf Ep 1087:685–8). He was to arrive in Louvain before Erasmus left for Basel; cf Ep 1242 introduction.

10 Pace] Richard Pace (cf Epp 1210, 1218, 1227), is compared to Pylades, the proverbial friend and companion of Orestes.

11 Tunstall] Cf Ep 1146 introduction.

1139

1 join the madman in his lunacy] Cf *Adagia* IV vii 14.

2 Apostle's teaching] Cf Rom 12:21.

3 despised even by his own party] Cf Ep 1134 n7.

4 his *Annotationes*] See Ep 1037.

5 even among those .. well] Cf Epp 750, 1026 n3, 1053 n21, 1123 n9.

6 the month and a half] Cf Ep 1080 introduction.

7 from Cain] Cf Gen 4:15.

8 never having blackened ... anything I have written] Cf *Adagia* I viii 4; Epp 1007 n10, 1053 n62.

9 as a boy] Thomas More, for example; cf *The Correspondence of Sir Thomas More* ed E.F. Rogers (Princeton 1947) Ep 75:116–17.

10 light of the world and the salt of the earth] Cf Ep 1126 n46.

11 like a fishwife] Literally 'speaking from a wagon,' Ep 1153 n20.

12 dog or viper] Cf Horace *Epistulae* 1.17.30; *Adagia* II ix 63.

13 your story] See Ep 1095:121–49.

14 very good fun] Cf Ep 1095:153–7.

15 a certain abbot] See Ep 1126 n4.

16 given them to no one to read] Lately perhaps (cf Epp 1100 introduction, 1157:2–3), but for Erasmus' initial reactions see Ep 1083 introduction.

17 your threat] Cf Ep 1095:160–2.

18 set out for Germany] See Ep 1155 introduction.

19 Callipides] A man who fails to carry out his projects; cf *Adagia* I vi 43.

20 Oecolampadius] See Ep 1123 n6.

1140

1 Origen] For projects of Origen editions involving Erasmus cf Ep 1017 n3; for a request to send him another manuscript from St Agnietenberg cf Ep 504.

2 Prior of St Agnes] Gerard of Kloster, prior of St Agnietenberg near Zwolle; cf Epp 504, 1116.

3 brothers at Zwolle] The Brethren of the Common Life had a monastery at Zwolle and the school directed by Listrius was closely connected with it; cf R.R. Post *The Modern Devotion* (Leiden 1968) 580 and passim.
4 wife] Justina; cf Ep 1013A n2.
5 dropping of Greek] Latin 'omissis Graecis literis': perhaps the omission of Greek letters in a printed book or possibly the suspension of Greek instruction in Listrius' school; cf Ep 500:23–5.
6 Augustine] The prior was not alone in feeling that Erasmus was lacking in esteem for the patron of the order to which they both belonged; cf Epp 769:57–114, 1994. For a similar objection concerning St Bernard see Ep 1142.
7 not so prickly] Cf Ep 1076 n1.
8 praise St Thomas enough] Cf Ep 1126 n38.

1141

1 Bruges] Cf Epp 1129 n1, 1145 n1.
2 his Lordship] Philip of Burgundy, bishop of Utrecht
3 I had told him ... prebends] Perhaps in August 1519 when he met Philip in Mechelen (cf Ep 1001:10–11). Mostly because of residence requirements, offers of prebends (cf Ep 456:184–7) were not attractive to Erasmus, unless perhaps he could resign them to a substitute and receive an annuity from him, as in the case of the Courtrai canonry (cf Ep 1245 introduction). He seems to have wished for further negotiations about Philip's offer.
4 my advice ... seditious stuff] Cf Ep 1167: 173–210.
5 new attack against Reuchlin] Cf Epp 1129 n7, 1155 n2.
6 his own business] Encouraged by Spalatinus and Melanchthon, Luther often expressed his support of Reuchlin from 1514 onwards. In a famous and well publicized letter to him of 14 December 1518 he spoke of Reuchlin as the forerunner who had to spend himself so that others could rise in defence of the Gospel; much later he understood his own work as a continuation of Reuchlin's (cf Geiger *Reuchlin* 353–4; Luther w *Briefwechsel* I Ep 120). Although he did not mention Reuchlin specifically in Epp 980, 1113, 1127A, Erasmus may have thought that these warned Luther sufficiently against confusing his attack upon the church with the advocacy of biblical scholarship; but cf Ep 1155 n5.
7 Eck ... disputation] Johann Maier of Eck opposed Luther and Karlstadt in the Leipzig disputation. Judgment was referred to the theological faculties of Paris and Erfurt; cf Epp 948 introduction, 1020 n9.
8 Hoogstraten ... syllogisms] It is not clear to what project Erasmus is referring.
9 Louvain] Cf Epp 1070 n1, 1164:75–8.
10 University of Paris] Following the condemnation of Luther's errors by the theologians of Cologne and Louvain, a similar verdict had long been expected from Paris, but it was not delivered until 15 April 1521. It was then printed at once: *Determinatio theologicae facultatis Parisiensis super doctrina Lutheriana* (Paris: J. Bade n d); Cf Epp 1167:430–3, 1202 n49.
11 a bull and a cloud of smoke] Erasmus plays on the word 'bulla,' the original meaning of which is 'bubble' (cf *Adagia* III vi 98). The papal bull *Exsurge, Domine*, dated 15 June 1520, was publicly posted by Eck in Meissen, Merseburg, and Brandenburg on 21, 25, and 29 September respectively, and also officially proclaimed in the Netherlands by Aleandro (cf Ep 1135 n1). It

threatened Luther with excommunication unless he recanted (cf Ep 1192 n8). Using the special authority granted to him by the papal court, Eck extended this measure to some others including Karlstadt, Egranus (cf Ep 1122 introduction), Lazarus Spengler, and Willibald Pirckheimer (cf Ep 1182 n2), adding their names to the bull. Like the preceding articles of condemnation issued by the universities of Cologne and Louvain (cf Ep 1070 n1), the papal bull also prescribed the burning of Luther's books. Formal burnings were staged by Aleandro in Louvain and Liège on 8 and 17 October, and there were many others (cf Epp 1113 n10, 1157:7–9, 1166:57–61, 1186 n8; AK II Ep 761); see Boehmer *Luther* 351, 355, 365 and Fredericq IV 33–4, and for Erasmus' reaction to the bull and the burnings cf Epp 1164 n17, 1166 n13.

12 a bishopric waiting for me] Perhaps this reflects new rumours (rather than a revival of schemes previously discussed at the court of Charles; cf Epp 475:5n, 1117 n11). Erasmus may be speculating on an offer from Rome to be conveyed to him by the nuncio Aleandro, his old friend, who was now on his way to the Netherlands (cf Ep 1135 n1). Leo X himself may be hinting at a favour of this kind in Ep 1180:11–16, and there is a curious echo in a text attributed to one Heinrich, Prior of Gund, and printed with the first edition of Erasmus' *Axiomata pro causa Lutheri* (cf Ep 1155 introduction). It speaks of a fat bishopric offered to Erasmus (in Cologne) by the papal legates (cf Ep 1167 n20), provided he were prepared to write against Luther, and has Erasmus reply that Luther was too great for him to understand, let alone refute (quoted in Allen's note on this passage); cf Epp 967:89–91, 1143:56–60.

1141A

1 visit to Holland] In the spring of 1519 Erasmus had written of such a project; cf Ep 1092 n1.

2 library] In 1530/1 Jan gave his magnificent library to the court of Holland at The Hague in exchange for a prebend. His books helped lay the foundations of the Royal Library at The Hague.

3 Gerard] Probably Gerard Geldenhouwer, the recipient of Ep 1141, who had published a number of metric compositions, or conceivably Cornelis Gerard (cf Ep 17 introduction), a poet laureate who had been many years before a close friend but is not mentioned in more recent letters in Erasmus' preserved correspondence

1142

1 Moses … horned] Cf Exod 34:29–35 (Vulgate). The 'horns' of Moses were traditionally interpreted as beams of light.

2 Germans … belongs] Cf Ep 1244 n7.

3 wine … the heart of man] Cf Ps 103:15 (Vulgate).

4 Philip of Macedon … Aristotle the philosopher] The king appointed Aristotle to be the teacher of his son Alexander; cf Plutarch *Alexander* 7.1–2, Diogenes Laertius 5.4.

5 questionists] Many works of scholastic philosophy and theology are arranged as a series of questions and answers.

6 passage … Bernard] The passage concerning St Bernard appeared first in the *Ratio verae theologiae* of 1518 (cf Ep 745 introduction; LB V 129A). It offers

mild criticism of the saint for having sometimes quoted Scripture playfully and out of context, 'with elegance, but irresponsibly' (cf lines 107–9 below), mostly because he had it so much at his fingertips; cf Ep 1140 n6.

7 my blood froze in my veins] Cf Virgil *Aeneid* 3.259–60.

8 his life] The following is a literal quotation from the earliest and most important life of St Bernard, composed by William of Saint-Thierry, Geoffrey of Auxerre et al (*Vita* 1.4; PL 185:241).

9 St Augustine on Psalm 48] *Enarrationes in Psalmos* 48.1 (CC 38:550). Schirn quotes the text with insignificant omissions and variants.

10 the story of the prophet] Cf 2 Kings 4:39–41.

11 Sant'Ambrogio ... the abbot or the cellarer] The same directions are given in the letter to Beatus Rhenanus (cf introduction), but there is no trace of any answer. The abbot at this time was one Angelo Piatti.

12 Chiaravalle] The abbey of Chiaravalle, four miles south of Milan, was founded by St Bernard in 1135 and became the foremost house of the Cistercian order in Italy.

13 a German ... Cîteaux] In the letter to Beatus Rhenanus, Schirn in this place describes himself as 'the last in the order of theologians.'

1143

1 attempted to connect ... with the case of Luther] Cf Ep 1155 n5.

2 always maintained ... published] Cf Ep 1141 n6.

3 I do not know] Cf Epp 939:69–71, 1167:219–21. For indications of Erasmus' acquaintance with some of Luther's writings cf Epp 872:16–18, 939:105n, 967:104–6, 980:59–61, 1033 n15, 1127A:78–9, 100–2, 1183:100–3, 1186 n3, 1202 n10, 1203:30–1; cf also Ep 1236:127–31.

4 expositor ... ancient manner] Cf Epp 980:59–61, 1119:39–41, 1127A:98–9, 1167:140–2. In 1524 Erasmus specified the *Operationes in Psalmos* (cf Ep 980:60n) as one of the works of Luther he liked best (cf Allen I 31), while Luther's commentary on Galatians (1519, Luther W II 436–618) contained several friendly references to Erasmus (482, 553, 589, 601).

5 almost the first person ... public strife] Cf Epp 872:22–3, 980:45–56, 1113:27–8, 1202:33–6, Allen Ep 1526:24–9.

6 dissuade Johann Froben ... his works] For Erasmus' steps see Epp 904:20n, 1033:52–5, 1167:305–7, 1195:143–4. His concern was shared by Rome, and in October 1520 the papal nuncio Antonio Pucci (cf Ep 860) presented to the Swiss diet a letter from Aleandro and demanded action against the printers (cf Zwingli *Werke* VII Ep 161). Four months earlier, on 23 June, when Johannes Egranus (cf Ep 1122 introduction) had arrived in Basel, presumably with a fresh supply of Lutheran copy for print, Caspar Hedio wrote from Basel to Capito in Mainz (British Library, London, Add MS 21524 f 5). Hedio said that the printers were under pressure not to print Luther any longer, adding that he had done for Egranus what he could.

7 to friends] The description that follows could apply to Epp 872:15–23, 947:32–43, 983:11–18, 1113:24–7, 1119:31–6, 1127:20–3, 1139:95–8, and no doubt other letters, now missing; cf Ep 1202:36–9.

8 writing to me two years ago] Ep 933, of 28 March 1519

9 that letter] Ep 980; cf introduction.

10 'I write … already'] See Ep 980:59, a statement which repeatedly required an explanation. In Ep 1162:195–6 it appears in the same paraphrase as is used here, while in Ep 1167:251–2 a literal quotation is preferred. As late as 1525 Nicolaas Baechem Egmondanus used this sentence as a crucial argument in his attacks on Erasmus; see de Vocht CTL II 270.

11 phrase I added … supporters] See Ep 980:42–3, referring to support for Luther in the Netherlands.

12 Bishop of Liège] Erard de la Marck; cf Epp 980, 1038 introductions, 1041 n7.

13 Leipzig … Basel] Cf Epp 1123 n5, 1202:228–9. The contrast is with Erasmus' own edition of Ep 980 in the *Farrago*, printed at Basel.

14 nearly two years ago] On 30 May 1519 (cf lines 27–8 above). The Leipzig disputation began four weeks later; cf Ep 948 introduction.

15 Luther's supporter] 'Lutheranus' in the Latin text; cf Ep 1162 n36.

16 beyond the limits … my brains] Cf Epp 967:89–91, 1141 n12, 1167:224–50, 1183:33–9

17 universities … engaged on it] Cf Epp 1033 n21, 1141 n10.

18 my own … bishop] Erasmus was a priest of the diocese of Utrecht, whose bishop was then Philip of Burgundy; cf Ep 1167:471–2.

19 hatred of … liberal studies] Cf Ep 1167:82–3.

20 first refuted … men's minds] Cf Ep 1144 n3, and for the burning of Luther's books cf Ep 1141 n11.

21 A free and generous mind … compulsion] Cf Ep 1153 n34.

22 Rome] Erasmus often expressed hopes, and sometimes plans, for a return to Italy, and Rome in particular: in 1514–15 (cf CWE 3 index), in 1517–18 (cf Ep 770 introduction), and again at this time when he was specifically eyeing the treasures of the Vatican Library (cf Epp 1167:3–6, 1176:11–14) in view of his work on the third edition of the New Testament (cf Ep 1174 n6) and perhaps on Augustine (cf Ep 1144:80–1 and n17). In subsequent letters Erasmus seems to have dampened the expectations of his Roman friends that he might visit them soon. In June 1521 Paolo Bombace only expected him to go to Basel (cf Ep 1213:67–9), but the idea of ending his life in Rome still appealed to him; cf Ep 1236:199–207.

23 conferences of princes … delayed me] The Calais meeting (cf Ep 1106 introduction) and subsequent attendances at the court of Charles V; cf Epp 1129 n1, 1132, 1136, 1146, 1155 introductions.

1144

1 English doctor of civil and canon law] These words, originally part of the salutation, were removed in the *Opus epistolarum* of 1529, perhaps an indication that Erasmus then believed them to be inconsistent with the facts. Chierigati apparently held a doctoral degree in civil and canon law from the University of Siena (cf B. Morsolin in *Atti, Accademia Olimpica … Vicenza* 3, 1873, 132). Allen suggested that Chierigati might have received an honorary degree when he was in England as a papal nuncio, perhaps in connection with the ceremonial opening of St John's College, Cambridge on 29 July 1516; cf Ep 432:3n.

2 ill-starred beginning] Allen noted a similar statement in the *Consilium* (*Opuscula* 353:20–1; cf Ep 1149 introduction).

3 prove Luther wrong] Erasmus was aware of many polemical replies to Luther

but did not think that they had succeeded in refuting his views; see Epp 872:25n, 1033:84–7 and n23, 1070 n1, 1141:21–5, 1143:78–81, 1153:110–13, 160–72, 1166:65–8, and cf Ep 1164 n15.

4 bull ... preach against Luther] The reference must be to *Exsurge, Domine* (cf Ep 1141 n11), although it had yet to be officially published and did not instruct the clergy to preach against Luther (cf Epp 1153:143–6, 1192 n8). Rumours about its contents were evidently circulated from the pulpit, partly perhaps based on a confusion with the condemnations of Luther by the theologians of Cologne and Louvain (cf Ep 1030 n7). The *Acta contra Lutherum* (cf Ep 1166 n24) speak of the bull as 'born in Cologne and Louvain, and printed before it was published, the text as printed differing from that brought by Aleandro' (*Opuscula* 322–3; cf below lines 33–5, Ep 1166 n13). The same source refers to the two sermons Nicolaas Baechem Egmondanus (cf lines 31–3) preached at Louvain on 9 and 14 October, after Aleandro's arrival (cf Ep 1153). In the second 'he held up the bull for the people to see and said, "Behold the seal!" ... And as if the bull had not been enough he also produced an order from the rector of the university, adding, although no such thing is found in the bull, that no pamphlets were to be sold that attacked the reputation of the university and good men' (*Opuscula* 320–1).

5 in their cups] Cf Ep 1162 n19.

6 a certain Preacher here] Evidently Vincentius Theoderici (cf Ep 1196 introduction), who is described in similar terms in Ep 1186:20–3.

7 Morychus] Properly a name of the god Bacchus, Morychus became to the Ancients the proverbial measure of stupidity; cf *Adagia* II ix 1.

8 A second man ... black heart] The Carmelite Nicolaas Baechem Egmondanus, frequently mentioned by Erasmus with a pun on the white habit of his order; cf the index.

9 Lefèvre d'Etaples] Cf Ep 1196 n76.

10 two members] Cf Ep 1147:96–101.

11 Antwerp] Cf Ep 1188 n5.

12 Minorite] Erasmus repeated the following story several times until 1528; cf Ep 1183:136–40. In Ep 1192:34–45 he identifies the church as St Donatian's, and in Allen Epp 1967:140–6, 2045:150–63 he supplies enough additional information about the magistrate (line 48) to make it clear that he was Frans van Cranevelt (cf Ep 1145; de Vocht *Literae* Epp 246, 248). He also protested the incident to the bishop of Tournai, Louis Guillard (cf Ep 1212). The suffragan bishop of Tournai with title to the see of Sarepta was Nicolas Bureau (Burellus), who was appointed on 2 December 1519 and held the office until his death in Bruges in 1551. He was greatly concerned about heretical books and in 1527 attacked Juan Luis Vives in much the same fashion as he did Erasmus on this occasion. Vives thought no better of him than did Erasmus; see de Vocht *Literae* Ep 246.

13 beasts, donkeys, storks, and blockheads] Cf Epp 1183 n28.

14 advice ... world at large] This sentence and the preceding one bring to mind the title of the *Consilium*; cf Ep 1149 introduction.

15 careful to conceal their views] Cf the preface.

16 through what channels ... this business of Luther] Cf Epp 1183:144, 1195:29–30, 138–43, 1213:55–7, 1217:118–20, 1225:193–9.

17 Augustine] Although the great edition of St Augustine did not appear until

1528–9, frequent references indicate to what degree it already engaged Erasmus' mind and time; cf Epp 844:275n, 1174:19–21, 1204:29–33, 1212:45–7, 1218:20–1, 1222:28–32, 1309.

18 I shall display … to the see of Rome] See Ep 1228 n11, and for a preliminary realization of this intention cf the *Consilium*.

19 Your letter] It is missing; in view of Erasmus' fear of indiscretion it can be assumed that Chierigati had mentioned criticism of Erasmus in Rome; cf Ep 1143 introduction.

20 in Rome] Cf Ep 1143 n22.

21 Worcester] Silvestro Gigli; cf Ep 1080.

1145

1 More] For Thomas More's embassy to Bruges cf Ep 1106 introduction. Erasmus visited Bruges, where he met More and also Gerard Geldenhouwer, a childhood friend of Cranevelt (cf Epp 487 introduction, 1141:3), at the end of July (cf Ep 1129 n1). Henry de Vocht (*Literae* 313–14) argues that Erasmus visited Bruges again in the second half of August.

2 Sicilian dinners] Cf *Adagia* II ii 68, referring to the rich and sophisticated cuisine of the Syracusans.

3 Flemish habits] For recent attacks upon Erasmus cf Ep 1144:37–46; for his earlier criticism of the Flemish attitude towards learning cf Epp 412:62–3, 421:149–50.

4 gold ring] Allen refers to a fifteenth-century English gold ring in the British Museum with the motto 'al is god wele.' See also Joan Evans *English Posies and Posy Rings* (Oxford 1931) 18; cf William Shakespeare *As You Like It*, 3.2.287–9: 'You are full of pretty answers. Have you not been acquainted with goldsmiths' wives and conned them out of rings?'

5 two ancient coins] For More's interest in this matter cf his verses 'On Ancient Coins Preserved in the Home of Jérôme Busleyden': *The Yale Edition of the Complete Works of St Thomas More* (New Haven-London 1961–) III-2 no 250.

6 Fevijn] Jan van Fevijn, canon of Bruges, was a good friend of Erasmus.

1146

1 crown of bay] The earliest reference to Brassicanus' title of poet laureate is found in a letter of 4 March 1518; cf A. Horowitz *Analecten zur Geschichte der Reformation und des Humanismus in Schwaben* (Vienna 1878) Ep 1.

2 praise] The reference is perhaps to Brassicanus' Πᾶν: *Omnis* ([Haguenau]: T. Anshelm for J. Knobloch April 1519) a short collection of verse with honorific mentions of Erasmus in the preface and the poem *Omnis*.

3 reproduce him entire] In a similar way Erasmus was to oppose the exclusive imitation of Cicero in his *Ciceronianus* of 1528; see CWE 28 357–8.

4 'many … teachers'] A Greek line of unknown authorship, quoted in the *Adagia* III v 23 after Cicero *Ad familiares* 9.7

5 outstripped in this field] Cf Ep 1107 n1.

6 grievous vices of character] An unusually sweeping statement. As specific examples Erasmus often mentioned Poggio Bracciolini and Giovanni Pontano; see eg Ep 337:352–6.

1147

1 as Ovid puts it] *Metamorphoses* 1.654

2 Dorp … public sermon] Erasmus' term (*concio*) means a public oration or sermon. When visiting Holland in October–November 1519 Dorp had given a much-noted speech before the Council of Holland (cf Ep 1044 n4). It may be noted that the name of Dorp's first patron was also Man. For Meynard Man, abbot of St Adalbert's, Egmond, cf Epp 304:178n, 676:38–40, 1044:61–4.

3 by France] Cf Epp 321:16n, 926:37n; and for Erasmus' own appraisal cf Epp 421:34–6, 928:40–4, 1111:95–6, 1165:52–3.

4 Batavia … part of Germany] In 1514–15 a learned discussion had erupted as to whether the ancient geographers were right when they included Batavia among the regions of Gaul (cf lines 46–50, Ep 534:32) and whether the Batavia of Caesar and Tacitus was identical with modern Holland. Around the time of this letter Gerard Geldenhouwer, who denied the two propositions, had resumed the discussion in *Lucubratiuncula de Batavorum insula* (Antwerp: M. Hillen 19 September 1520; NK 978). Erasmus, who had recently met Geldenhouwer (cf Ep 1141:3) and had moreover just returned from Antwerp (cf Ep 1146), was evidently aware of this treatise, in the preface of which he himself is described as 'immortal glory of Batavia and Germany.' Perhaps this called the letter of Manius back to his attention. Johan Huizinga has suggested that in his eagerness to state his opinion on the matter Erasmus probably invented Manius and his letter; cf *Gedenkschrift zum 400. Todestag des Erasmus von Rotterdam* (Basel 1936), especially 40–2. Erasmus often spoke about his own Hollanders with ironical praise, as he does here, (but cf Ep 1216:46–52), and by and large he did not hesitate to identify himself with the Germans in the wider sense of the word; cf Ep 1244 n7.

5 the great Peripatetic] Aristotle *Rhetoric* 4.1 (1388a)

6 not wish … intelligible to the first comer] Cf Epp 744:16n, 24n, 778:24n, 886:61n, 911:63n, 954:10n; see also *De Copia*, CWE 24 317–18 and E. Rummel 'The Use of Greek in Erasmus' letters' *Humanistica Lovaniensia* 30 (1981) 55–92, esp 69–70.

7 your order and … the Carmelites] For attacks upon Erasmus by individual Dominicans and Carmelites cf the indexes CWE 4–8; for what follows cf also Ep 1196 n42.

8 indiscriminate attacks] Erasmus uses a familiar tag from Virgil *Aeneid* 9.595, literally 'things deserved and undeserved.'

9 two of your brethren here] The aspirant is clearly Laurens Laurensen (cf Ep 1166 n6); the other Dominican is either Vincentius Theoderici (cf Ep 1196) or the prior of the Louvain house (cf Ep 1164 n12); for both alternatives cf Epp 1144:27, 37–41, 1165:7, 19.

10 a certain Carmelite] Nicolaas Baechem Egmondanus; cf Ep 1153.

11 bad influences … against me] The reference is probably to Jan Briart and Jacobus Latomus; cf Epp 337:394–5, Allen 1804:216. For Dorp's attack on the *Moria* see Ep 304.

1148

1 Zasius] Udalricus Zasius, a distinguished professor of law at Freiburg, had composed Ep 1120 on behalf of the two abbots.

2 elephant] Cf *Adagia* I ix 69.
3 various factions] Cf Ep 694:6–9, also Epp 628:19–20, 1004 n30.
4 roll of councillors] Cf Ep 370:18n, and for Erasmus' attendances at court, which had been quite frequent of late, cf Epp 410, 596 introductions, 926–7, 1143 n23.
5 the man ... trouble] Gangolf I von Geroldseck; cf Ep 1120 n4.

1150

1 inheritance of those ancestral virtues] These words may have struck a sympathetic note in Gattinara, who was strongly advocating the resumption of Maximilian's policy of Italian intervention; cf K. Brandi *Kaiser Karl V.* (Munich 1937–41) II 104–7 and *Staatspapiere zur Geschichte des Kaisers Karl V.* ed K. Lanz (Stuttgart 1845) 1–9.
2 position ... under Maximilian] As councillor and confessor; cf Ep 1149 introduction.
3 Le Sauvage] Cf Epp 410, 852:72n. Gattinara took over the seals on 15 October 1518. For Le Sauvage's support of Erasmus cf Epp 597:30n, 608:19n.

1151

1 annuity ... from the prince] Erasmus is perhaps referring to a payment received on account of his councillor's pension (cf Ep 370:18n). Two hundred florins (money-of-account) were due to him annually, but no payments are recorded in his correspondence after one received in the summer of 1517 (cf Ep 621 introduction). Another semi-annual payment was made in the spring of 1521; cf Ep 1205:21–4.
2 curbed] Erasmus seems to be referring to his opponents among the Louvain theologians; cf Epp 1123 n9, 1144:33, 40–1.

1152

1 Cologne] See Ep 1155 introduction.
2 letter] Ep 1033
3 Punic treachery] Cf *Adagia* I viii 28.
4 Faber] Cf Ep 1149 introduction.

1153

1 your instructions ... papal diploma] Cf Epp 1141 n11, 1144 n4.
2 St Denis' day] Tuesday, 9 October 1520
3 subject of charity] Cf Ep 1126:21–2.
4 maintained from the beginning] Cf Epp 939:69–85, 1033:40–77. Erasmus insisted on this point, cf Epp 1143:13–21, 1162:33–5, 1183:109–11, 1191:36–7, 1192:7–8.
5 in published books] Cf Ep 980, published in the *Farrago*.
6 set right ... destroyed] Cf Ep 1033:74–5, 1195:21–2, 93–4, 1196:229–30, 1217:23–4, 1225:371–2 and the *Consilium*, for which cf Ep 1149 introduction.
7 space of time] In the bull *Exsurge, Domine* (cf Ep 1141 n11) Luther was given sixty days to recant before his excommunication would take effect.
8 Luther had written] Cf Ep 1033 n15.

9 malignant slanders] Cf Ep 1053 n62.
10 In a letter ... cardinal of Mainz] Ep 1033:87–92; if Erasmus' recollections in the *Spongia* (ASD IX-1 147–8) can be trusted, the point came up again in the confrontation before Rosemondt.
11 leading member of your faculty] Perhaps Maarten van Dorp; cf Ep 1162:87–9.
12 as they say ... cover] Cf *Adagia* III v 35.
13 my pen as an instrument] Cf Ep 1164 n15.
14 left the track] Literally 'outside the olive-trees'; cf *Adagia* II ii 10.
15 not by Christ] Cf Ep 1225 n29.
16 defence ... to Lee] Cf LB IX 255–62, where Erasmus answers Lee's criticism of his note on Acts 19:18.
17 white habit] Cf Ep 1144 n8.
18 following Sunday] 14 October
19 Antwerp] Cf Ep 1199 introduction.
20 drunkard on a wagon] Cf Ep 1162 n19; Erasmus uses an adage referring to itinerant actors, *Adagia* I vii 73.
21 eminent theologians] Cf Ep 1144 n3.
22 two letters] Epp 980, 1033
23 several supporters here] Ep 980:42–3; cf Ep 1162 n11.
24 Jacobites] This term is derived from the Dominican priory of Paris, situated amid university colleges in rue Saint-Jacques. Erasmus uses the term frequently for the Dominicans in general. Here he is also alluding to their role as inquisitors. Since papal inquisitors were first appointed in 1231, this task had most often been given to Dominicans; cf Ep 1182 n4.
25 the bull smacks more ... Leo's kindly nature] Cf Ep 1166 n13.
26 allowed him time] Cf above n7.
27 my advice was] Cf Ep 1164 n15.
28 rabbis] Cf Ep 1126 n45.
29 Silvester] Silvestro Mazzolini called Prierias; cf Epp 872:19n, 1006:154, 1033:159–61, 236–8.
30 some Minorite] Augustin Alveldt; cf Ep 1167 n72.
31 the third anonymous] Isidorus de Isolanis (d 1528), a Dominican of Santa Maria delle Grazie at Milan, who taught theology in several houses of his order. His *Revocatio Martini Lutheri Augustiniani ad Sanctam Sedem* was published anonymously (n p, n d), but it is dated from Cremona, 22 November 1519 (cf Luther w *Briefwechsel* I Ep 221). King Francis I, who held the duchy of Milan, is praised towards the end of the book.
32 others too] Cf Ep 1165:16–17.
33 cardinal of Tortosa] The Louvain faculty of theology did not publish its condemnation of Luther (cf Ep 1030 n7) before consulting Cardinal Adrian of Utrecht, the future Pope Adrian VI, who did not apparently resign the university chancellorship (coupled with the deanship of St Peter's) until later in 1520. His supporting letter, dated 4 January 1520, headed the printed volume (Louvain: D. Martens, February 1520; cf Ep 1070 n1) and provided its title; cf de Jongh 43*–46*.
34 A noble nature ... donkeys] Paralleled almost literally in the *Consilium* (*Opuscula* 357:90–1; cf Ep 1149 introduction). For similar expressions cf Epp 1143:81–2, 1167:287–8, 1173:54–6.

35 The burning … men's hearts] Cf Ep 1173 n8.
36 a cardinal … good to me] Albert of Mainz, recipient of Ep 1033
37 'my friend'] This incongruous addition of the possessive 'noster' to Luther's name, which Erasmus here reports on hearsay, has not been traced in the early printings of Ep 1033; cf Ep 1217:27–9.
38 Greek in Rome] Cf Ep 1062 n13.
39 Leo x approved … my industry] With Ep 864
40 *Glossa ordinaria*] Cf Ep 1112 n6.
41 our prince … flourish] The foundation of the university was authorized by the pope on 9 December 1425 at the request of Duke John IV of Brabant, the chapter of St Peter's, and the city council of Louvain; see de Jongh 30.
42 *poetria*] This awkward and quite unclassical form is also ridiculed in Epp 1110:19, 1126:370, 1196:487, 604. As here, it is attributed to Baechem in the *Epistola de magistris nostris Lovaniensibus* and the *S. Nicolai vita* (see de Vocht CTL I 589–90, 601 and cf below Ep 1165 n17). It was evidently used to refer to humanistic studies in general.
43 crooked wedge … knot] Cf *Adagia* I ii 5.
44 Tomorrow] It would seem from lines 59–60, 132–3 that such a meeting was already under consideration and from Ep 1162:10–15 that it eventually took place, perhaps on a somewhat later date, as the one attended by Baechem as well and described in Ep 1162. It appears, however, that by 23 October Erasmus was already in Cologne; cf Ep 1155 introduction.
45 if … your health permits] Cf Ep 1162:45.

1154

1 Majesty] King Louis II
2 manifesto and rule] Arkleb probably sent with this letter the *Apologia sacrae scripturae* edited by Mikuláš Klaudyán (Nürnberg 1511), or perhaps a composite volume starting with that treatise. At least the *Apologia* appears to have been the book earlier given to Erasmus by Klaudyán himself and Laurentius Voticius when they visited him in the summer of 1520 (cf Ep 1039 introduction). When answering this letter, Erasmus stated that he had received another copy of the same book from the two envoys of the Czech Brethren but had not read it as yet; see Ep 1183:8–10.
3 Brethren] Cf Ep 1021 n14, n20.
4 Luther … much read] An indication of Luther's popularity may be found in the number of Czech translations of his writings published in 1520–2; see Benzing *Lutherbibliographie* nos 204, 514–15, 682, 769, 799, 889, 918, with addenda and corrections in H. Claus and M.A. Pegg *Ergänzungen zur Bibliographie der zeitgenössischen Lutherdrucke* (Gotha 1982). The following sentences would seem to refer to the works of Luther alone, and not to those of Erasmus. Like other Utraquists, Arkleb was sympathetic to Luther's message.
5 Romanist] Augustin Alveldt (cf Ep 1167 n72), whose attack was answered by Luther with *Von dem Papsttum zu Rom wider den hochberühmten Romanisten zu Leipzig*, twelve editions known, all of 1520; see Luther W VI 277–324 and Benzing *Lutherbibliographie* nos 655–66.
6 the seed you sow] Contrary to the first two and the last paragraphs of this letter, where Erasmus alone is addressed in the second person singular,

this part (to line 64) is in the plural, evidently intending Luther and Erasmus together.
7 trampled under foot and suffocated] Cf Luke 8:5–7.
8 the Fuggers] Cf Ep 1183 n2.
9 Znojmo] Near the Moravian border with Austria, fifty miles north-west of Vienna
10 Boskovice and Czernahora] Boskovice is in Moravia, 20 miles north of Brno; Czernahora lies to the south-west of Boskovice.
11 Vranov] Just west of Znojmo

1155

1 cardinal of Sion] Matthäus Schiner, an old patron of Erasmus, had left Zürich on 6 August to join the train of Charles v. Due to his influence both at Rome and among the Swiss he was treated as a power in his own right by friend and foe alike. His presence in Cologne is recorded for 5 November and in the course of their renewed contacts he apparently urged Erasmus to continue his work on the paraphrases. Cf Ep 1171 n11; AK II Ep 745; Büchi II nos 751, 754, 757.
2 console you … bitter feelings] Reuchlin's trial at Rome had ended on 23 June with a qualified condemnation; cf Ep 623:36n.
3 Jacobites] The Dominicans; cf Ep 1153 n24.
4 unspoken judgments of men of good will] Cf Epp 1167:389–90, 1171:85–6; for the significance of these statements see the preface.
5 your cause … the humanities] It may be noted that the cause of Reuchlin is here (and also in Epp 1143:10–13, 1167:82–92) seen to be identical with that of the humanities, which is to say Erasmus' own cause. Erasmus reacted to Reuchlin's condemnation with feelings of generosity and solidarity. When he met Aleandro in Cologne, he seems to have expressed the fear that Rome would follow up its previous verdict by condemning all of Reuchlin's books, and his own too (cf Balan no 36). On the other hand, when he thought of Reuchlin as a student of the Talmud and the Cabbala (as in Epp 967:77–83, 1033:40–2, 1041:9–11), Erasmus had refused to be associated with his cause. Above all, when he remembered that Reuchlin and Luther were capable of using immoderate language, it seemed to him that both were jeopardizing the progress of the humanities and that he must emphasize the distance that separated him from both (cf Epp 967:76–9, 85–6, 1167:105–14, 1188:5–8, 1217:104–5). The friendly stance of this letter coincides with a softening of his view of the Cabbala; cf Ep 1160 n1.
6 civil restraint … urged them to adopt] Cf Ep 1123 n2.
7 English bishop] John Fisher, who may in the mean time have answered Ep 1129. For earlier expressions of his desire to meet Reuchlin see Epp 324:20–2, 457:9–17.

1156

1 Cicero's words … just war] Cicero *Epistulae ad familiares* 6.6.5
2 when doctors … infected matter] Cf Ep 1219:116–19.
3 German mentality] Very similar words are used in the *Consilium*, also with regard to the religious situation of Bohemia; see *Opuscula* 358.

4 Luther was told … his violence] Cf Ep 1167:172–89.
5 'in civil war … general'] Cf *Adagia* II ii 91. Androclides stands for any humble soldier.
6 'The Lord … own'] 2 Tim 2:19
7 on papal bulls] Cf Ep 1141 n11.
8 says Faber] There is no close parallel in the *Consilium*. What follows is hard to reconcile with an information related by Peutinger himself, according to which Faber had played an active role in the burning of Luther's books at Louvain on 8 October (cf *Peutingers Briefwechsel* 329). On the other hand, the papal court and Aleandro received critical reports of his funeral sermon for Guillaume de Croy (cf Ep 1184 n2), preached three months later in Worms. According to these reports he had savagely attacked Rome, speaking in German. Cf Balan nos 15, 62; below Ep 1161 n8.
9 Scylla … Charybdis] Cf Ep 1186 n5.
10 arbitration … above all suspicion] According to the *Consilium* (*Opuscula* 359) the conciliators were to be named by Charles V, Henry VIII of England, and Louis II of Hungary and Bohemia.
11 Diet of Worms] Cf Ep 1197 introduction.

1157

1 letters attacking Lee] It seems that the Erfurt circle had composed some letters against Edward Lee which were excluded from Froben's *Epistolae aliquot eruditorum virorum*, cf Epp 1083, 1088 introductions.
2 Aleandro has arrived] He was in Louvain with the imperial court from 1 to 8 or 9 October (cf Gachard II 28); for Erasmus' contacts with him cf Ep 1167 n20.
3 burnt … Luther's books] Cf Ep 1141 n11; for details on the tumultuous burning in Louvain see de Jongh 230–5. In Cologne the books were burnt on 12 November; cf Ep 1166:57–61.
4 in silence] Cf Ep 1155 n4.
5 a letter-carrier presented himself] Paul Kalkoff, and following him others, have speculated about this unidentified man, who is not mentioned anywhere else. He was made out to be an official courier or guardsman sent by the elector Frederick the Wise to accompany Jonas and Kaspar Schalbe on their visit to Erasmus in May 1519 (cf Ep 963:6n), which would thus have received a semi-official diplomatic character. Accordingly, the man's contact with Erasmus mentioned here was interpreted in a similar fashion; see Paul Kalkoff *Erasmus, Luther und Friedrich der Weise* (Leipzig 1919) 33–6, 58, 62.
6 Schalbe, Draconites, Hessus] For Schalbe see above n5; Johannes Draconites (cf Ep 1122 introduction) and Helius Eobanus Hessus were other members of the Erfurt humanist circle.

1158

1 old enough … what that life is like] Cf Ep 1183 n32.
2 your letter] Presumably a letter Oecolampadius had sent prior to the ones acknowledged in lines 3–4. It was answered in Ep 1102 and is also mentioned in Epp 1123:15–16, 1139:122–3.

3 Pharisees] Cf Ep 1102:21.
4 *Metaphrasis* … has come] *In Ecclesiastem Solomonis metaphrasis divi Gregorii Neocaesariensis* (Augsburg: S. Grimm and M. Wirsung 1520). This is Oecolampadius' Latin translation of a paraphrase by St Gregory called Thaumaturgos, bishop of Neocaesarea (third century). In his preface, dated from Altomünster, 1 July 1520, Oecolampadius stated that he had translated the paraphrase before his departure from Mainz.
5 Capito] Wolfgang Faber Capito had left Basel on 28 April 1520 to take up his new appointment as preacher of the cathedral of Mainz. He accompanied the elector of Mainz, Cardinal Albert of Brandenburg, to Aachen for the coronation of Charles V and was appointed councillor to the elector (cf Zwingli *Werke* VII Ep 157). It was partly due to him, and to Erasmus' influence, that Cardinal Albert refused to publish the bull against Luther in his dioceses and to have Luther's books burnt (cf Ep 1141 n11). Capito was at this time in Cologne with his master (cf Ep 1155 introduction). In a letter to Luther of 20–1 December 1521 (cf Luther w *Briefwechsel* II Ep 447) he recalled how Erasmus had advised him there to keep to the 'middle of the road' and how he himself had laboured to prevent any harsh measures against Luther; see J.M. Kittelson *Wolfgang Capito* (Leiden 1975) 57–60, and cf below Ep 1217 n16.
6 courtier] After reading this sentence in the *Epistolae ad diversos*, Capito lodged a bitter protest; see Allen Ep 1374:5–20, and cf Ep 1241:8.

1159

1 the poem … Louvain] Allen suggested that this was a *Carmen in quosdam theologastros Lovanienses sycophantas extemporale*, which he found printed in *Flores sive elegantiae ex diversis libris Hochstrati … per Nicolaum Quadum Saxonem collectae* and in a reprint of Erasmus' *Apologia de 'In principio erat sermo,'* both n p, n d. The former, which may date from 1520, is described in Hutten *Operum supplementum* II 104–6; Sbruglio's *Carmen* ends with a praise of Erasmus.
2 old maxim … Roman lawyers] Cf *Adagia* II iv 16, which quotes the jurist Ulpian, who used the saying to urge restraint in the acceptance of gifts.
3 receive praise … himself] Erasmus recalls a line from a lost Roman tragedy (Naevius *Hector proficiscens* fragment 2, Ribbeck), which Cicero was fond of quoting.
4 one hair's breadth] Cf *Adagia* I viii 4.
5 in the shade] Cf Ep 1107 n1.

1160

1 not notably hostile] This statement has an apologetic ring, for Erasmus had earlier expressed frank hostility (for examples cf Epp 798:20–6, 967:79–80, 1006:170–1, 1033:40–2). Just at the time he apparently became acquainted with Ricius' book, however, he also wrote a warm and generous letter to Reuchlin (cf Ep 1155, especially n5). There may well be a connection between the two letters, both written at Cologne; conceivably this letter might have been intended to serve as a commendatory epistle when the *Apologeticus sermo* was going to be printed.

1161

1 the place … more unpopular than anywhere else] Louvain; cf below lines 118–21, 132 and n4. There is no reason to assume with Allen that Cologne was meant, where not only Aleandro, but also Frederick the Wise, Sickingen, and Capito were present; cf Epp 1155 introduction, 1158 n5.

2 Number Ten] Pope Leo x

3 'I never thought … here'] Cf *Adagia* I v 8.

4 cardinal of Tortosa] Adrian of Utrecht, who continued to have great influence in Louvain (cf Ep 1153 n33). No letter of his to the pope concerning Erasmus has been found, but despite Erasmus' critical remarks in Ep 1166:116–18, it seems possible that Adrian actually recommended Erasmus in view of his stated desire to go and work in Rome; cf Epp 1143 n22, 1225 introduction.

5 Aleandro] Cf Ep 1167 n20.

6 Franz's policy] Franz von Sickingen had rendered valuable service to the Hapsburgs at the time of the imperial election and afterwards been appointed councillor to Charles v. Right up to the time of his recent attendance of Charles' court at Cologne (cf Ep 1155 introduction) he hoped to win over the emperor for a united stand of the German nation against the Roman church; cf Ep 1166:79–81.

7 Slavonic scoundrel] Aleandro, who was born in Friuli of a family that traced its descent in part to the marquises of Pietrapilosa in Istria. Hutten's derogatory use of the term is similar to the claim that he was a Jew; cf Ep 1166:94 and Balan no 23.

8 offering the crown to Caesar] Crowned King of the Romans at Aachen (cf Ep 1155 introduction) and consequently authorized by the pope to use the title emperor-elect, Charles still had to undertake the traditional journey to Rome to receive the imperial crown from the hands of the pope. The papal coronation emerged as a topic for discussion at the Diet of Worms (cf Ep 1197 introduction), where Aleandro accused Guillaume de Croy, lord of Chièvres, of offering concessions to the Lutherans in order to obtain their backing for the expedition, and the Dominican Johannes Faber urged Charles to his face in a public sermon to expel the French from Northern Italy and purge the papal court (see Balan nos 12, 15; cf Ep 1156 n8 and *Reichstag zu Worms* 137–8, 261). Not until 1530 was Charles crowned by Pope Clement VII.

9 myself … the price] Cf Ep 1135 introduction.

10 approve my design] Cf Ep 1114 introduction and lines 13–14.

11 proclamation … intervenes] Cf Ep 1166 n20.

12 countless examples … trusted] Hutten was just then collecting material for his *Anzeige, wie sich die Päpste gegen die deutschen Kaiser gehalten*. Benzing *Hutten und seine Drucker* lists five anonymous editions of 1521 (nos 162–6); cf Hutten *Opera* v 363–95.

13 Your friends in Basel … to see you] Cf Ep 1242 introduction.

14 enjoy more liberty] This compliment to Swiss liberty comes at a time when the notion became commonplace and Swiss chroniclers adopted the mythical figure of William Tell as its incarnation; see R. Feller and E. Bonjour *Geschichtsschreibung der Schweiz* (Basel 1962) I passim. Two years later Hutten himself found in Switzerland a safe refuge for the last months of his life.

15 by what Luther writes] Basel publishers had a significant stake in the dis-

semination of Luther's writings and anonymous Lutheran pamphlets. Cf Ep 904:20n; Benzing *Lutherbibliographie* 470 and passim; Holeczek *Erasmus Deutsch* I 336.

16 a poem ... in German] *Klag und Vermanung gegen dem übermässigen unchristlichen Gewalt des Papstes*. Benzing *Hutten und seine Drucker* lists three anonymous Strasbourg editions of late 1520 (nos 144–6). Hutten had recently visited Strasbourg (cf BRE Ep 182); for his popularity in Basel at just this time cf AK II Epp 749, 751.

17 Ebernburg] Franz von Sickingen's principal castle, south of Kreuznach in Rheinland-Pfalz, now restored as a conference centre

18 Mainz, or Cologne] Cf Ep 1155 introduction. For a rumour of Erasmus' presence in Mainz at this time cf BRE Ep 182. He expected to visit Cardinal Albert of Brandenburg on his way south; cf Epp 1101:3–4, 1165:54–6.

1162

1 I had written ... pulpit] Ep 1153

2 no lasting good ... come of it] Cf *Adagia* I viii 38.

3 supporter of Luther] Cf Ep 1167 n22.

4 glittering bile] Cf Horace *Satires* 2.3.141.

5 'Thou fool'] The Latin text has 'racha,' a Hebrew invective used in Matt 5:22.

6 in the doctor's hands] Cf Ep 1153:255.

7 of women too] Cf Ep 1196 n2.

8 right to preach] Priests and deacons are qualified to preach, but to do so they require specific permission from the bishop of the diocese, monks from their superior as well. Erasmus had preached some sermons during his days in Paris in 1495–6; see Allen I 37, 146.

9 having said ... letter to the rector] Cf Ep 1153:220–3.

10 formal brief] Ep 864

11 'Dorp, indeed!'] This passage suggests some hostility to Dorp on the part of Baechem. There is some evidence (see Luther w *Briefwechsel* II Epp 273, 281) that Dorp refused to endorse the condemnation of Luther by the Louvain faculty of theology (cf Ep 1153 n33); at least he once refused a request by his colleagues to state solemnly that the decision had been unanimous. See de Jongh 45*; cf de Vocht MHL 234–43 and here Epp 1153:109–13, 1167:428–30.

12 condemns Luther] Cf Ep 1141 n11.

13 venomous attacks ... before I set foot in Louvain] At Brussels in the autumn of 1516; cf Epp 948:141–8, 1196:128–30, 1225:59–63.

14 your acts] For Erasmus' participation in faculty meetings cf Epp 637:12n, 695:20–2.

15 reconciliation ... between us] Cf Ep 1022.

16 Gospel teaches us to do] Cf Matt 5:44, Luke 6:27.

17 wine-party in Falcon College] Cf Ep 1022 introduction. It appears that as an exercise of supererogatory devotion Baechem refrained from eating meat on Wednesdays as well as Fridays and Saturdays; Erasmus said so again in his *Apologia de loco 'Omnes quidem'* (LB IX 440E, cf Ep 1235 n5), and the point was also made in the *Epistola de magistris nostris Lovaniensibus* and the *S. Nicolai vita*; see de Vocht CTL I 591, 600–1, and cf Ep 1165 n17.

18 principal] Nicolas Coppin (d 1535), of Mons, principal of the Falcon, succeeded Adrian of Utrecht as dean of St Peter's in 1520 (cf Ep 1153 n33). He had been rector for the summer term of 1520, preceding Rosemondt. He did not become hostile towards Erasmus until 1525.
19 we drink too much] Erasmus was in fact quick to make suggestions of this kind; cf above lines 26–7 and Epp 1144:25–7, 1153:106–7, 1192:36, 1196:448–9, 497, 586–7, 627, 1225:379–81.
20 in writing] In the *Apologia invectivis Lei* (*Opuscula* 292; cf Ep 1080 introduction).
21 about Lefèvre and me] Cf Ep 1196 n76.
22 sermon ... grinning] Cf Ep 1153:20, 96–8.
23 *Epistolae* ... tribute] Cf Ep 1196 n86.
24 John Standish] Actually Henry Standish, bishop of St Asaph; for the episode here related see Ep 1126:99–193.
25 declamation] The *Encomium matrimonii*; see CWE 25 129–45, and cf Ep 604:12n.
26 put a spell ... everything] Erasmus frequently charged the friars with such practices; cf his colloquy *Funus* (ASD I-3 537–51) and *De praeparatione* (ASD V-1 380). It was also brought against Baechem in the *Epistola de magistris nostris Lovaniensibus*; see de Vocht CTL I 588, and cf Ep 1165 n17.
27 letter ... to Luther] Ep 980
28 having added ... doing now] Cf Ep 1143 n10.
29 by burning ... men's minds] Cf Epp 1141 n11, 1173 n8.
30 hard inside ... walnut] Cf Horace *Epistles* 2.1.31, proverbial example of an untenable view; cf *Adagia* I ix 73.
31 drinking-party] Cf above lines 118–19.
32 my letters] The *Farrago*, which was the latest edition of Erasmus' letters, (cf Ep 1009 introduction) bears out Baechem's complaint; cf for instance Epp 539, 936, 946, 951, 980, 991, also Ep 1196 n42.
33 *synceres*] This blunder is also attributed to Baechem in Ep 1196:670. The correct form required is *synceros*.
34 against him] Cf the preface and Ep 1164 n15.
35 on many grounds] The following points are treated very fully in Ep 1173:44–101.
36 member of Luther's party] The Latin term here used is *Lutheranus*. Erasmus continued to react vigorously against those who thought that the term applied to him; cf for instance Epp 1164:70, 82, 1167:439, 1196:674–6, 1217:149, 1219:69–76, and especially 1225:339–72.
37 more criminal than he is] Erasmus may have been thinking of Vincentius Theoderici and Jacobus Latomus; cf Epp 1123:21–4, 1196 salutation.
38 sty in the eye] Cf *Adagia* II viii 65.

1163

1 reprint the *Farrago*] See Epp 1009, 1206 introductions.
2 Dirk] Dirk Martens, the Louvain printer, was a friend of both Erasmus and Barlandus. Erasmus apparently thought that in refusing to print the book in question, Martens had shown his sympathy for Luther too openly. In fact Martens printed this letter, and although he stocked Luther's books for sale, he had later to print the condemnations of the Cologne and Louvain theologians and also the Edict of Worms; cf Epp 849:32n, 1030:11–15 and n4, 1070 n1, 1216 n19.

3 Turnhout's book] Jan Driedo of Turnhout (cf Ep 1127A n11) had been designated by the faculty of theology to deliver the inaugural lecture of the new winter term on 1 October 1519. It may have been on this occasion that he took issue with Luther's Ninety-five Theses. In his subsequent lectures he continued his scholarly critique of Luther's tenets and also prepared a pamphlet on the topic. Despite Erasmus' efforts, his propositions were apparently never printed in this form. See Ep 1167:460–6, de Jongh 158–60, and *Acta contra Lutherum* in *Opuscula* 325; cf Ep 1166 n24.
4 refuted ... reasons] Cf Ep 1164 n15.
5 the pope's bull ... weight] Cf Ep 1141 n11.

1164

1 Frisian Dominican] Laurens Laurensen; see Ep 1166 n6.
2 *Antibarbari*] Cf Ep 1110 introduction.
3 cardinal of Sion] Erasmus had recently dined with Cardinal Matthäus Schiner (cf Ep 1155 n1). In a letter of 1516 Erasmus reported on Schiner's authority an outrage committed in a Dominican monastery, the cardinal having told it 'at the dinner-table in the hearing of many people' (Ep 447:660–4). Allen assumed that this was the incident here alluded to and speculated that the passage in Ep 447 could have been added in 1529 when that letter was first printed.
4 always avoided names ... orders] This is, at least in part, a self-deception; cf Ep 1196 n42.
5 Jerome] Cf Ep 1167 n7.
6 on the wagon] Cf Ep 1153 n20.
7 *Antibarbari* ... liberal education] See Jacob Batt's discourse, CWE 23 28:16–33, 33:13–17 and passim.
8 in his briefs ... deserves the name] See Epp 338:37–8, 339:3–6.
9 Lateran Council] In its eighth session of 19 December 1513 the Fifth Lateran Council decreed that no one in orders, after completing the elementary course in grammar and dialectic, should go on to study only philosophy and literature for more than five years. It was permitted, however, as Erasmus here states, to pursue the liberal arts beyond that term in combination with theology or canon law; see *Conciliorum oecumenicorum decreta* ed G. Alberigo et al, 2nd edition (Freiburg, etc 1962) 582.
10 Cologne] Cf Ep 1155 introduction.
11 Maximilian of Middelburg] Maximilian of Burgundy (d 1535) was a son of one of the many bastards of Duke Philip the Good. In 1506 he matriculated at the University of Louvain. In 1518 he was appointed abbot of the Premonstratensian abbey of Middelburg on the island of Walcheren, where he resided from 1520 on, having previously spent much time in attendance at court. Among the books of Jan de Hondt, in St Martin's church, Courtrai, Allen found a copy of Erasmus' *Adagia* (Basel: J. Froben [1515]), which had belonged to Maximilian, who gave it in June 1521 to one 'Johannes Largus, decretorum scriba.'
12 prior of the Dominicans] He has not been identified; in the light of Ep 1166:51–2 it seems that he had come to Louvain from a monastery in Holland, perhaps The Hague.
13 St Catherine's day] Sunday, 25 November

14 opening lecture on St Paul] No doubt at the beginning of October; the incident is also mentioned in Epp 1173:130–4, 1192:53–6, 1196:631–4. It was apparently in another lecture of that same course that Baechem also attacked Jacques Lefèvre d'Etaples; cf Epp 1153:103–5, 1192:56–8, 1196:618–24.

15 my unwavering support] Erasmus often repeated that he wished to see Luther refuted by serious arguments derived from Scripture (cf Epp 1033:95–6, 1163:15–17, 1167:445–8). He was ambiguous, however, concerning his own co-operation. Without refusing altogether to take up his pen to make himself the mouthpiece of the faculty (cf Ep 1153:73–4), he normally found many reasons for declining to do so (cf Epp 1143:56–63, 1162:230–41, 1173:44–101), at least for the time being; see further Ep 1228 n11.

16 Turnhout] Cf Ep 1163 n3.

17 no one saw me downcast] For the controversy surrounding the burning of Luther's books at Louvain (8 October) see de Jongh 230–5, and cf Ep 1156 n8. In contrast to the present statement Erasmus often deplored the burnings; cf Epp 1153:179–81, 1166:57–65, 1186:18–23.

18 Vincentius] The Dominican Vincentius Theoderici; cf Epp 1165:7–13, 1196.

19 1519] The year added in the *Opus epistolarum* of 1529 is clearly wrong.

1165

1 rejected ... from the pope] For the bull see Ep 1141 n11. The popularity of the reformation throughout the Netherlands and especially Holland is noted by Girolamo Aleandro in his dispatch to Rome, dated from Mainz, 28 February 1521. According to Aleandro Luther's doctrine is preached there in public and 'all this happens because of the Hollander Erasmus' (Balan no 32). For the subsequent development cf Ep 1216 n19.

2 president] Nicolaas Everaerts; cf Epp 1092, 1186.

3 proclamation from the prince] Cf Ep 1166 n20.

4 bishop of Utrecht] Philip of Burgundy

5 Vincentius] The Dominican Vincentius Theoderici; the incident here reported is likewise mentioned in Epp 1164:85–8, 1186:20–3, 1196:159–65.

6 Camelite] A nickname for the Carmelite Nicolaas Baechem frequently used by Erasmus (cf line 31, Ep 1173:125) and also in such pamphlets as the *Epistola de magistris nostris Lovaniensibus* and the *Hochstratus ovans*; cf below n11, n17.

7 Latomus] Jacobus Latomus did publish a treatise in defence of the condemnation of Luther by the Louvain faculty of theology, *Articulorum doctrinae fratris Martini Lutheri per theologos Lovanienses damnatorum ratio* (Antwerp: M. Hillen 8 May 1521; NK 1329).

8 Turnhout] Cf Ep 1163 n3.

9 second Dominican] Laurens Laurensen (cf Ep 1166 n6) was called by Erasmus a 'theologiae candidatus' in Ep 1147:97. The reference here ('baccalaureus currens') refers to a student who has completed one or more of the baccalaureates prerequisite to the award of the licence in theology.

10 pamphlet ... attacking me] The *Apologia* of the Dominican Jacques Hasard (Louvain: D. Martens 1520; NK 3142) which according to the colophon was written by the hand of his brother, the Carmelite Julien Hasard. This is a very short and curious treatise; rather than attacking Erasmus, it defends biblical philology, provided the Vulgate text is always retained in the liturgy.

11 dialogue ... mentioned] Erasmus expected Capito to recognize the piece from

this description; therefore – and contrary to Allen's suggestion – it can hardly be the well-known *Hochstratus ovans: dialogus* or an excerpt of it (see Hutten *Operum supplementum* I 461–88). It is true that the anonymous dialogue was printed and began to circulate at just this time, but Cardinal Wolsey is not mentioned; there is only a passing reference near the beginning to a 'learned English bishop' (466). Erasmus evidently assumed that Capito might perhaps know the author; thus he may be referring to one of the tracts produced by German humanists in defence of himself against Edward Lee and the Louvain theologians. Erasmus was now anxious to suppress these and in some cases he clearly succeeded; cf Epp 1083 introduction, 1139:108–16, 1157:2–5.

12 Lee in England] Cf Ep 1140 introduction.

13 with Polidoro] For Polidoro Virgilio and Erasmus' suspicion see Ep 1175 introduction and n28.

14 Dorp] Cf Ep 1162 n11.

15 pastor of the Groote Kerk] Hendrik Hoevelmans, curate of the collegiate church of Notre Dame, Antwerp, had three years earlier received a licence in theology from the University of Louvain. The little information available about him ceases after 1521.

16 Mechelen ... grain] These riots are also mentioned by Gerard Geldenhouwer in his *Collectanea* ed J. Prinsen (Amsterdam 1901) 2, 56–7.

17 Nesen] Wilhelm Nesen already had considerable experience in the publishing of pamphlets directed against Erasmus' opponents in Louvain (cf Epp 1083 introduction, CWE 7 329–47). Erasmus' statement here was no doubt intended to encourage Nesen to continue, although with due care lest Erasmus himself be compromised. In fact about this time Nesen published anonymously the *Epistola de magistris nostris Lovaniensibus* followed by *S. Nicolai vita* ([Sélestat: L. Schürer 1520]; reprinted with commentary in de Vocht CTL I 575–602 (with omissions) and Zwingli *Werke* VII 378–420). The *Epistola* is addressed to Huldrych Zwingli and signed with Nesen's initials, G.N.N. It reviles the Louvain theologians primarily for their condemnation of Luther (cf Ep 1153 n33) and mentions Erasmus in passing. The *S. Nicolai vita* is a spirited attack on Nicolaas Baechem presented in the style of traditional hagiography. Erasmus evidently knew about it and the date of this letter (line 49) may be another humorous allusion to it. Nesen probably wrote the two pieces late in 1519 when he was in Louvain; not surprisingly there occur a number of parallels with statements Erasmus made in his letters of that time, but the only close analogy is to Ep 1033, already published.

18 pressure ... in print] Cf Ep 1164 n15.

19 Dorp] Did the dialogue mentioned in line 25 above refer to Dorp in connection with the Louvain condemnation of Luther (cf Ep 1162 n11)? Nesen, by contrast, could be trusted not to repeat his earlier attack on Dorp (cf CWE 7 331); the latter is not mentioned in the *Epistola de magistris nostris Lovaniensibus*; cf above n17.

20 nearer ... than the Luther business] Capito, who had taken part in the great campaign of German humanists against Edward Lee (cf Ep 1083) can hardly have failed to interpret this passage as a suggestion that Aleandro might deserve similar attacks; cf Ep 1167 n20.

21 become a Frenchman] Cf Epp 926:37, 1129:23, 1147 n3.

22 Carinus] Ludovicus Carinus, a young Swiss humanist, had recently been in Cologne and may well have met both Erasmus and Capito there (cf Ep 1155 introduction). By this time he had become Capito's secretary in Mainz; cf Ep 1215:12–14.
23 Hartmann] Hartmann von Hallwyl (cf Ep 561:68n) had also joined Capito in Mainz.
24 attitude ... towards me] After the embarrassing publication of Ep 1033 Erasmus had written Epp 1101, 1152 in efforts to appease Cardinal Albert of Brandenburg, but apparently had received no answer. Subsequently Capito's remark in Ep 1241:39–43 must have given Erasmus great satisfaction.
25 appear again] Cf Ep 1242 introduction.
26 Neuenahr] Hermann von Neuenahr had recently been Erasmus' host in Cologne (cf Ep 1155 introduction). This letter was evidently sent to him for forwarding to Mainz.

1166

1 three years ago now] Erasmus' appointment as a councillor to the future Charles V probably took effect on 1 January 1516 (cf Epp 370:18n, 392:17n). The following passage appears to be written quite carelessly; in conjunction with Ep 1174:12–15 it may be interpreted as follows. Chancellor Jean Le Sauvage had personally taken charge of the handling of Erasmus' appointment and on one occasion, in 1517 (ie three years ago), had even arranged for the payment of his salary arrears (cf Ep 621 introduction). But Le Sauvage had died on 7 June 1518, and not until quite recently through personal attendance at court had Erasmus succeeded in having another instalment paid (cf Ep 1151 n1). In preparation for his travels (cf Ep 1174 n1) he had also been able finally to formalize the terms of his councillorship. There is no trace now of the patent that was apparently issued at this time.
2 not much ... court] Cf Ep 1148:8–16.
3 bellies] Cf Epp 1171:97, 1174:6, 1177:42, 1191:31, 1205:33.
4 attacks ... lectures] Cf Epp 1153 introduction, 1164:66–9.
5 old man] Age supposedly connotes wisdom; cf Ep 1173:38. Baechem was then about fifty-eight.
6 Laurensen] Laurens Laurensen (d 1533) of Friesland joined the Dominican monastery of Groningen, where he was lector 1516–18 and from 1523 prior. When he attacked Erasmus, he was studying in Louvain for his licence in theology (cf Ep 1165 n9) and no doubt living in the Dominican house there.
7 officially silenced ... university] By the rector, Godschalk Rosemondt, and subsequently by the papal nuncio, Girolamo Aleandro; cf Allen Ep 1581:377–85 and ASD IX-1 152.
8 to stimulate ... flags] For the adage used in the Latin text cf Ep 1124 n1.
9 Vincentius] Vincentius Theoderici (cf Ep 1196 introduction) was born in Beverwijk, between Haarlem and Alkmaar.
10 approached him] Cf Ep 1196:36–102.
11 prior] Cf Ep 1164 n12.
12 burning at Louvain] Cf Epp 1141 n11, 1164 n17.
13 produced the bull] Much the same words are used twice in the *Acta contra*

Lutherum (*Opuscula* 320:16, 322:56–7, and cf also 328:135; for the *Acta* see below n24). The context there suggests that a forged version of the bull *Exsurge, Domine* was set in circulation by the theologians of Cologne and Louvain before Aleandro brought the official version from Rome. Aleandro himself stated that Erasmus challenged the authenticity of the bull to his face (cf Ep 1167 n20). Luther too found it expedient at first to claim that the bull was not authentic (see Luther w VI 576–629). The condemnations of Cologne and Louvain (cf Ep 1030 n7) had in fact been used for the drafting of the papal bull. Erasmus also expressed his disappointment and doubts about the bull in Epp 1153:142–5, 1156:93–9, 1167:449–50; cf Ep 1196 n13.

14 bishop] Erard de la Marck was created cardinal on 9 August 1520, but the promotion was not made public until a year later.

15 Cologne] Erasmus may have witnessed the burning; cf Epp 1155 introduction, 1157 n3.

16 Latomus ... Turnhout] Cf Epp 1163 n3, 1165 n7.

17 pamphlets ... hitherto] Cf Epp 1144 n3 1153:160–7.

18 nuncio] Girolamo Aleandro; cf Ep 1167 n20.

19 Sickingen] Sickingen, whose Latinized name is here spelled 'Singlius' (cf Ep 999 n57) had evidently talked to Erasmus when both were at Cologne, probably over the dinner-table of Frederick the Wise; cf Epp 1155 introduction, 1161 n6.

20 proclamation ... issued] Although the burning of Luther's books in Louvain on 8 October 1520, when Charles V was in town, cannot have occurred without the emperor's placet (cf Balan no 23; Fredericq IV 33–4), no evidence has been found of a formal document issued at that time. Although such a step had been variously expected, or feared, for months (cf Epp 1161:75–6, 1165:3–5, 1192:73–4) a proclamation in the name of Charles V was not forthcoming until 20 March 1521. It ordered the burning of Luther's books; for the text see Fredericq IV 43–5, but cf also Ep 1192 n8.

21 brief ... case] Balan no 1; cf Ep 1155 introduction.

22 Diet of Worms] Cf Ep 1197 introduction.

23 bull] Cf Ep 1141 n11. Erasmus' allegation is proven wrong by the instructions issued to Aleandro for his nunciature; see Balan nos 2–3.

24 Jew] This allegation is particularly prominent in the preface of an anonymous tract entitled *Acta academiae Lovaniensis contra Lutherum*, published anonymously, perhaps in Cologne at the time of Erasmus' visit (cf Ep 1155 introduction). When this preface was reprinted separately in an edition of the *Hochstratus ovans* (cf Ep 1165 n11), the date of Cologne, 4 November 1520 was added to it (see W.K. Ferguson in the introduction to his edition of the *Acta* in *Opuscula* 304–28). It is often assumed that the *Acta* are wholly or in part the work of Erasmus. For a number of close parallels between the *Acta* and Erasmus' letters see the index under 'Erasmus'; but cf also Ep 1218:23–4. At least, Aleandro's allegations were not entirely far-fetched when he claimed that Erasmus was responsible for some of the anonymous pamphlets circulating everywhere (cf Epp 1195:8–9, 1218:14–17, 1236:165–7; Balan nos 14, 21). As for the rumour of Aleandro's Jewish descent, the nuncio apparently accused Erasmus to his face of having started it when they subsequently met at Brussels (cf Ep 1233 n28), and Hutten repeated the allegation in his

Expostulatio against Erasmus (see ASD IX-1 150 and Hutten *Opera* II 207; cf also Ep 1161 n7).

25 scurrilous pamphlets] Cf above n24, Epp 1165 n11, n17, 1168 n5, 1186 n13.

26 civil strife ... discouraged by me] Cf Ep 1143 n5, n7; see also Ep 1127A.

27 He writes] In his missing answer to Ep 1127A; see the introduction to that letter.

28 Staupitz] In August 1520 Johann von Staupitz had resigned from his office as vicar-general of the German friars of St Augustine. Subsequently the cardinal of Gurk, Matthäus Lang, had attracted him to Salzburg. Erasmus may well have received the information here related at Cologne from Rudbert von Mosham, if not from the cardinal himself (cf Ep 1155 introduction). It is confirmed by a letter of Staupitz himself of 4 January 1521, in which he reports that Lang was ordered to make him abjure Luther's heresies. Staupitz refused on grounds that he had never embraced them in the first place; cf Luther w *Briefwechsel* II Epp 366, 375.

29 faults ... curia] Cf Ep 872:19–21.

30 Adrian of Utrecht] Cf Epp 1153 n33, 1161 n4. Erasmus' severe judgment here agrees with his disapproval of Adrian shown in some preceding statements (cf Epp 608:12–15, 713:18–22, 969:21–3). For a shift in Erasmus' opinion cf the preface and Ep 1216 introduction.

31 abbey in Antwerp] Erard de la Marck became commendatory abbot of St Michael's, Antwerp, in 1520.

32 a letter from Hutten] See Ep 1135:2–5.

33 declared war] Cf Ep 1129 n7.

34 'The Fates ... way'] Virgil *Aeneid* 3.395; cf Ep 1199 n1.

35 Observant Franciscans ... keep their mouths shut] The Observant Francesco Licheto (d 15 September 1520), general of the reformed Franciscan order, visited the monasteries of the German province shortly before his death and saw to it that Luther's books were burnt.

1167

1 in Rome] Erasmus' wish to spend a winter in Rome was no doubt genuine (cf Ep 1143 n22). How seriously he wished to remain there for the rest of his life (cf lines 9–10) is less certain; cf Ep 1166:111.

2 much ... besides pagan authors] Cf, however, Ep 770.

3 conferences ... monarchs] Cf Ep 1143 n23.

4 native rudeness] Cf Ep 1123 n2.

5 best for both] The same point, put partly in identical terms, was added in the revised Ep 1062:60–4. For other pleas for peaceful coexistence between humanism and scholasticism, especially in the universities, cf Ep 1125 introduction.

6 Leo himself] Cf Ep 1062 n13.

7 St Jerome ... Eustochium] Erasmus may have remembered, among others, some passages in such famous letters of Jerome's as Epp 22.13ff, 27, and 125.16ff. St Paula and her third daughter, St Eustochium, followed Jerome from Rome to the Orient and in 386 settled permanently in Bethlehem, setting up four monasteries. A number of Jerome's letters to Eustochium survive, including the famous Ep 22, but no replies are extant.

8 I never attack … by name] Cf Epp 1164:9–15, 1196 n42, also Ep 1162:215–18 and n32.

9 fountain-head … humane studies] This statement is closely paralleled in the *Acta contra Lutherum* (*Opuscula* 324:79–80; cf Ep 1166 n24. Cf also Ep 1143:74–6.

10 one man's resentment] Johann Pfefferkorn is intended; cf Ep 694 introduction, where he is wrongly said to have been a Dominican, and *Acta contra Lutherum* in *Opuscula* 324:71–80.

11 the tongues … bargain] Cf Ep 1155 n5.

12 in his briefs] Cf Ep 1164 n8.

13 nothing in common … Reuchlin] Cf Ep 1155 n5.

14 discussions] In 1515 at Frankfurt; cf Ep 967:81n.

15 elegant] Reading 'politioris' in place of 'peritioris.'

16 evidence to satisfy them … pieces] Erasmus refers to the examination of his works undertaken by the theological faculty of Louvain with an aim of finding heresies; cf CWE 7 preface and Epp 1217:64–6, 1225:117–23.

17 letter … to Luther] Ep 980

18 another to the cardinal of Mainz] Ep 1033, addressed to Albert of Brandenburg

19 in circulation here] Cf Epp 1030 n7, 1040.

20 in a letter … it had reached the pope] The letter here mentioned must be either an unknown letter from Aleandro to Erasmus or, more likely, Aleandro's letter to Erard de la Marck, which the bishop himself had shown to Erasmus (cf Ep 1127A n24). The conversation with Aleandro did not take place until some time later. When the nuncio first attended Charles V's court at Antwerp and Louvain (cf Epp 1135 n1, 1155 introduction), he was, according to Erasmus' accounts, inveigled by Jacob of Hoogstraten and avoided his old friend (cf Allen Ep 1482:8–11; ASD IX-1 150). Aleandro, however, said that Erasmus did not want to see him (Balan no 36). Thus it was not until Erasmus' visit to Cologne that they faced one another, and even then there was hesitation. Erasmus refused the nuncio's invitation to dinner for fear of poison (cf Ep 1188:35–42). Even his Polish and Hungarian diplomat friends had warned him of Aleandro's hostility (cf Allen Ep 1482:13–15). Aleandro was equally nervous; in Cologne he was publicly lampooned and subsequently during the Diet of Worms (cf Ep 1197 introduction) he feared assassination (cf Balan nos 12, 22, 24). They finally met on c 9 November for five or six hours amid outward manifestations of affection and even kisses when they parted (Balan no 36, also for the following points; ASD IX-1 150). Erasmus defended Reuchlin (cf Ep 1155 n5) and according to Aleandro questioned the authenticity of the bull *Exsurge, Domine* (cf Ep 1166 n13), while Aleandro invited him to Rome in view of his desire to work at the Vatican Library (cf lines 3–4). Their show of affection, however, was simulated (cf the preface). Aleandro continued to think that Erasmus was probably more dangerous than Luther and bitterly resented the respect he still commanded at Rome (cf Balan nos 14, 21, 36), while Erasmus felt maligned and persecuted and missed few opportunities to attack the nuncio in turn; cf the index and Ep 1233 n28.

21 expound the mysteries … classical manner] Cf Ep 1143:16–19.

22 I thought well of Luther] Here and in many other places Erasmus attempts to explain and qualify the term 'favere Luthero,' which he had used in Ep 980:41–3; cf Epp 1033:59–77, 176–7, 1041:32–3, 1143:19–21, 42–6, 1144:20–2, 1153:23–6, 39–45, 1162:33–5, 1219:30–2, and here lines 134, 283–99, 410–21.
23 writing to me] Ep 933, answered by Erasmus in Ep 980
24 Pray consider] Allen noted that Erasmus here lapsed into the plural (*videte*), probably an indication that this letter was intended for circulation at the Roman curia.
25 I warned him … majesty of princes] Cf Epp 980:47–9, 1127A:70–4, 1143 n7.
26 expedient to conceal it] Cf the preface.
27 Plato … clearly] Cf *Republic* 3.389B, 459C–D; cf Ep 1195:131–6.
28 not to condemn … mere asseveration] Cf Epp 980:50–3, 1127A:51–6.
29 German temperament] Cf Ep 1123 n2.
30 not to answer … another] Cf Epp 980:53–8, 1127A:68–70.
31 sultan] Cf Epp 1033:122–3, 1041:31–2, 1192:84–6, 1202:274–8, 1219:66–7.
32 panel of judges] Cf the *Consilium* (Ep 1149 introduction).
33 superficial scholar] Erasmus often repeated that he was not sufficiently grounded in formal theology to attack Luther; cf Epp 1143:59–60, 1153:62–5, 1217:152–6, 1225:259–74, and below lines 224–9.
34 from ancient sources] Cf Ep 1153:209–13.
35 universities] Cf Epp 1030 n7, 1141 n10, 1143:60–1.
36 for adding … what you do always] Ep 980:59; cf Ep 1143 n10.
37 Minerva and the sow] Cf *Adagia* I i 40.
38 my adding … books] Ep 980:41–2
39 judge … prosecutor … counsel] Cf Epp 1033:63–4, 1183:103–4.
40 my letter … cardinal of Mainz] Ep 1033
41 Noble nature … for tyrants.] Cf Ep 1153 n34.
42 Cyprian … views] Cf Ep 1000:165–7.
43 Jerome … condemned] See *Vita Hieronymi* in *Opuscula* 151–2, and cf Epp 844:274, 1211:27–33.
44 Augustine … distance.] Tychonius or Ticonius was a dissident Donatist theologian of the late fourth century. St Augustine took issue with him in various writings, recording some of his views and even using them against other Donatists. Erasmus may here have been thinking of Augustine Ep 93.43–4 and *De doctrina christiana* 3.92–133 (30–7); see CSEL 34-2:485–7, 80:104–17.
45 printing in Basel] Cf Ep 904:20n. The assertion that Erasmus had discouraged the printing of Luther's works already during his visit to Basel in the summer of 1518 can be true only in a general sense at best.
46 through friends] Cf Ep 1143 n7.
47 friends warned me] Cf Epp 1225:298–308, 1241:8–19.
48 proved him wrong] This sentence too is repeated almost verbatim in the *Acta contra Lutherum* (*Opuscula* 326:105–6).
49 unnecessary to confess … capital sins] Cf Epp 1033 n15, 1153:49–58, 1202:252–5.
50 advent of Antichrist is upon us] Luther could be thought to have expressed

this conviction most recently in *Adversus execrabilem Antichristi bullam* ([October] 1520); see Luther w VI 604, 612.

51 Augustine ... Donatists] Cf Epp 858:268n, 939:121n, 1202:120–4.

52 penalty ... community of the orthodox] In accordance with Titus 3:10–11. Erasmus' views in this matter greatly influenced the toleration debates of the sixteenth century; cf *Supputatio*, LB IX 580–3.

53 one hair's breadth] Cf Ep 1159 n4.

54 Roman name] Cf Ep 1156:62.

55 Paul ... infancy] Cf 2 Cor 11:13–15, 1 Tim 1:20, 3:5–9, 2 Tim 2:17–18.

56 from men's minds ... libraries too] Cf Ep 1173 n8.

57 by those qualified ... integrity] Cf Epp 1163:12–16, 1164:75–8.

58 unspoken judgments of learned and pious individuals] Cf Ep 1155 n4.

59 Dominicans themselves] No doubt Erasmus here thought above all of Johannes Faber and the *Consilium* (cf Ep 1149 introduction); cf below lines 500–4.

60 Leaders in this business] Cf Ep 1182 n4.

61 Moses ... father-in-law] Cf Exod 18:19–24 and Ep 1006:378–9.

62 only two ... opinions] Cologne and Louvain; cf Ep 1030 n7.

63 theologians ... among themselves] Louvain; cf Ep 1162 n11 and analogous statements about opposing theologians in Louvain, perhaps referring to Dorp, in the *Acta contra Lutherum* in *Opuscula* 322:46–51, 325:97–9.

64 University of Paris] Cf Ep 1141 n10.

65 supporter for Luther] Cf Ep 1162 n36.

66 first person ... Luther's books] Cf Ep 1143:21–8.

67 written in wine] Cf *Adagia* I vii 1.

68 always urged ... against Luther] Cf Ep 1164:75–8 and below lines 460–6.

69 terrifying bull] Literally repeated in the *Acta contra Lutherum* (*Opuscula* 320:16); cf Ep 1141 n11.

70 more melancholy] Cf Ep 1164:78–9.

71 Silvester Prierias] For this Dominican see Ep 1153 n29. He is mentioned with Alveldt and Radini in the *Acta contra Lutherum* in *Opuscula* 327.

72 Augustin the Minorite] The Franciscan Augustin Alveldt, of Alfeld near Hildesheim, was lector in the Leipzig monastery of his order when he attacked Luther in his *Super apostolica sede* (Leipzig: M. Lotter 1520). For Luther's reply see Luther w VII 277–324.

73 Thomas Rodaginus] Tommaso Radini Tedeschi (1488–1527), of Piacenza, had joined the Dominican order in his youth. He was living in Rome when he wrote *Ad principes et populos Germaniae* (Rome: J. Mazochius August 1520) against Luther. Melanchthon replied to him, using the name of Didymus Faventinus (cf Ep 1199 n6; *Melanchthons Briefwechsel* I Epp 109, 126, 135).

74 Jan Turnhout] Cf Ep 1163 n3.

75 my own diocesan bishop] Cf Ep 1143 n18.

76 Those who admit ... within reach.] This comparison appears to be inspired by Erasmus' native Holland, where much cultivated land lies below sea level.

77 court martyrdom] Cf Ep 1218 n14.

78 one of Luther's party] Cf Ep 1162 n36.

79 fed and fattened ... public] The friars

80 bring me under suspicion] Cf Epp 1180, 1195 introductions.

1168

1 Thersites] An unpleasant character in Homer's *Iliad* (2.212–75), who reviles Agamemnon, the leader of the Greeks, until silenced by Odysseus; cf *Adagia* IV iii 80.

2 a wife] On 25 November Melanchthon married Katharina Krapp (1497–1557), daughter of a Wittenberg cloth merchant who was then the burgomaster of the city. Erasmus' formulations here appear to betray his awareness of Melanchthon's agonizing over the decision to get married. In August he became engaged at the urging of his friends, who hoped that marriage would tie him to Wittenberg and improve his frail health, but in letters following the wedding he continued to express uneasiness about his decision; cf *Melanchthons Briefwechsel* I Epp 102, 105–8, 118, 123, 126.

3 what Eck is doing] Proclaiming the bull against Luther and burning his books; cf Ep 1141 n11.

4 'The fates ... way.'] Cf Ep 1166 n34.

5 placards] Placards against Eck appeared in the streets of Leipzig on 29 September; in the night of 3–4 October he fled from the city (cf Luther w *Briefwechsel* II Ep 340). A good idea of the virulent campaign against Eck is afforded by the witty lampoon *Eccius dedolatus*, which was printed in the summer of 1520; see *Eccius dedolatus: a Reformation Satire* tr T.W. Best (Lexington 1971). For Erasmus' often professed dislike of smear tactics see Ep 1053 n62, but cf also Ep 1166 n24.

6 warlike valour] Cf Epp 919:38–9, 939:27–30, 1244:24–7.

7 settled without disturbance] Cf Ep 1149 introduction.

8 hornets] Cf *Adagia* I i 60.

1169

1 back here] Back from Cologne (cf Ep 1155 introduction) by way of Aachen. As the imperial court was in Cologne at the time of Erasmus' visit he may well have seen Marliano and Scarpinelli.

2 queen of Aragon] Germaine (d 1538), daughter of Jean de Foix, Viscount of Narbonne. After the death of her first husband, Ferdinand II of Aragon, she married on 17 March 1519 Margrave John of Brandenburg-Ansbach (1493–1526), a brother of the ruling Margrave Casimir and of Albert, the Master of the Teutonic Order. John attended the court of the future Charles V in Spain. He was appointed viceroy of Valencia and created king of Bogya in Africa in order that his wife might retain her royal rank (cf LP III 130). The couple accompanied the monarch to the Netherlands in 1520 and subsequently to Aachen for his coronation and to Cologne.

3 Leonardus Priccardus] See Ep 1170.

4 Sunday] Presumably 18 November; cf Ep 1155 introduction.

5 German stoves] Cf Ep 1248 n5.

6 Cicero] Nothing appears to be known of Scarpinelli's study of Cicero.

7 like Jerome] See Jerome's Ep 22.30; cf Ep 906:330n.

8 your society] Erasmus expected to go to Worms at the time of the diet; cf Ep 1197 introduction.

9 Saeverus] An unidentified man connected with Marliano and Scarpinelli; cf Epp 1195:171, 1198:57 and CEBR III.

1170

1 Aristophanes puts it] *Plutus* 885
2 a letter ... to Beatus Rhenanus] Ep 867
3 prolonged far into the night] Cf Ep 867:118–21. In the *Epistolae ad diversos* the references to 'their usual potation' and 'drinking till late' have disappeared and it is merely stated that dinner was served late according to local custom.
4 drinking-party] See above n3; cf Ep 1162 n19.
5 dean's] Perhaps Johann Schoenraid; see Ep 867:117–18, 130–1.
6 to stay all night] Cf Luke 24:29.
7 vice-provost] Werner Huyn van Amstenrade; cf Ep 867:123n.
8 Plato] Cf *Laws* 1.639D–641D.
9 Vlatten] Johann von Vlatten died in 1562 as chancellor of the duchies of Jülich-Cleves-Berg; cf introduction and Ep 1390.

1171

1 count of the Valais] In 999 King Rudolph III of Upper Burgundy gave the Valais in perpetuity to the bishops of Sion. As its counts the bishops became vassals of the emperor.
2 Peter's ... Jude] Cf Ep 1112.
3 involved in darkness] In need of clarification
4 Hebrews] Cf Ep 1181 introduction.
5 John] Cf Ep 1179.
6 Augustine] Cf for instance Augustine's *De peccatorum meritis et remissione* 2.3.3 (CSEL 60:73). For Erasmus' interest in this passage of James cf also his note on James 2:13 (LB VI 1030), quoting several works of Augustine.
7 'Whose ... all'] James 2:10, according to the Vulgate, which Erasmus also follows in his translation of the Greek New Testament.
8 he says ... without works] Cf James 2:17, 20.
9 Paul ... friend of God] Cf Rom 4:1–4.
10 gaps] Erasmus' commentary, as given in LB VI 1025–38, refers to many difficulties, but not to gaps.
11 your voice ... onto the course] Presumably this refers to Erasmus' recent meeting with Schiner at Cologne; cf Ep 1155:3.
12 bedevilled] The play on words is based on *Adagia* I v 74.
13 with both hands] Cf *Adagia* I ix 16.
14 blacker by a single hair] Cf Epp 1007 n10, 1159 n4.
15 Thomas] St Thomas Aquinas, the model of scholastic theology; for recent criticism of Erasmus' assessment of him cf Ep 1126:289–97.
16 Hugo and Lyra] Hugo of Saint-Cher and Nicholas of Lyra; cf Ep 843:588n.
17 silent criticism of educated men] Cf Ep 1155 n4.
18 fewer recruits ... flock] Cf Ep 1183:131–4.
19 horse and cart] Cf *Adagia* I i 50.
20 wedge ... knot] Cf *Adagia* I ii 5.
21 potbellies] Cf Ep 1166 n3.

1172

1 second Jacobite] Cf Epp 1153 n24, 1173 n24.
2 previous rascal] No doubt the Dominican Laurens Laurensen, who had been

silenced temporarily by the rector, Rosemondt; cf lines 37–9, Ep 1166:25–32.

3 'vain talker'] Erasmus habitually used the Greek term 'mataeologus,' which recalls 1 Tim 1:6 and Titus 1:10 and could serve as a pun on 'theologus'; see eg Ep 1173:125 and the *Apologia de loco 'Omnes quidem,'* LB IX 440C; cf Ep 1235 n5.

4 Christmas play-acting] Throughout Europe Nativity plays were traditionally performed in or outside the churches; see *Enciclopedia dello spettacolo* (Rome 1954–66) under 'Natale.'

5 discussion with Egmondanus ... at all] Cf Ep 1162.

6 moral maxim] Literally 'mime'; Erasmus cites a line from a short collection of aphorisms in verse attributed to Publilius Syrus, a writer and actor of mimes for the stage in the first century BC, which he had earlier published (cf Epp 298, 678). This is a variant form of A 12 in the numeration of W. Meyer's edition (Leipzig 1880).

7 warned off ... penalties] Cf Ep 1166 n7.

1173

1 proverb ... daughter] Cf *Adagia* I vii 4.

2 Petrus ... Amicus] Pieter de Vriendt (d 1556), of Tholen in Zeeland, had matriculated at the University of Louvain in 1515. Following this recommendation, Cranevelt approached Louis Guillard, bishop of Tournai (cf Ep 1212) and de Vriendt was in fact appointed teacher at the chapter school of Tournai. In 1530 he was promoted doctor of laws at the University of Louvain and appointed to a chair of civil law there in 1533.

3 Gilles de Busleyden] Gilles was a brother of Erasmus' friend Jérôme de Busleyden, founder of the Collegium Trilingue.

4 my doing ... they would like] Cf Epp 1162:192–5, 1164:70–2.

5 throws a stone ... lecture] Cf Epp 1153, 1185 n4.

6 before the rector ... university] Cf Ep 1162.

7 honourable theologians ... Luther to pieces] Cf Ep 1162:219–37.

8 fixed in their hearts] The passage from line 48 bears a close resemblance to the *Consilium* (*Opuscula* 357:81–5; cf Ep 1149 introduction) and the *Acta contra Lutherum* (*Opuscula* 328:138–40; cf Ep 1166 n24). Similar expressions occur in Epp 1153:179–81, 1162:203–5, 1167:379–85.

9 noble natures ... rule] Cf Ep 1153 n34.

10 empty the mortar ... in it] Cf *Adagia* I i 85, quoting words attributed to Phormio; cf below n21.

11 why should I ... rather than anybody else] Cf Ep 1164 n15.

12 hay on his horns] Cf *Adagia* I i 81; hay was tied to the horns of a dangerous bull as a warning to passers-by.

13 schoolmaster] Cf Epp 1127A n18, 1167:233–6, 1219:81–7.

14 anger of the Germans] Cf Ep 1123 n2.

15 two universities] Cf Ep 1167 n62.

16 by the pope] Cf Ep 1141 n11.

17 Latomus and Turnhout ... now] Cf Epp 1163 n3, 1165 n7.

18 defeated ... Louvain] Cf Ep 1162:236–7.

19 at Calais ... monarchs] Cf Ep 1106 introduction.

20 Jacobite] The Dominican Laurens Laurensen; cf Epp 1166 n6.
21 Phormio] The parasite in Terence's play of that name
22 vituperative sense] Erasmus uses the nonce-word 'cacological,' parodying 'tropological' and the other senses of the text recognized by the interpreters of Scripture.
23 *Antibarbari*] Cf Epp 1110 introduction, 1164:6.
24 another Jacobite] This Dominican, who attacked Erasmus in his Sunday sermon (16 December) in St Peter's church, has not been identified; cf Ep 1172:4–7, Allen Ep 1581:380–1.
25 'vain talker'] Cf Ep 1172 n3.
26 Camelite] Cf Ep 1165 n6.
27 lectures on the Pauline Epistles] Cf Ep 1164 n14.
28 order] Erasmus repeatedly insisted that he had always liked the Dominican order, which is meant here (cf Epp 1006:5–6, 1192:84), because of its relative indifference to ritual; cf Ep 1196:293–5.
29 conception ... Mother of God] Cf Ep 1126 n40.
30 Savoronella ... more abandoned] For Savonarola and the Jetzer affair in Bern cf Ep 1033 n35, n36.
31 Hoogstraten] Cf Ep 1127A n17.
32 letters] Cf Ep 300:23–7.
33 collecting their cheeses] Cf Ep 877:19n.
34 in a letter] For this missing letter cf Ep 1078 introduction.
35 personal reflection] Cf Ep 1167:55–9.
36 Chrysostom] The following citations are taken from a series of sermons (*Ad populum Antiochenum* nos 22–80) no longer attributed to St John Chrysostom. In Erasmus' edition of Chrysostom in Latin (Basel: H. Froben 1530) they are found in volume IV 569, 571, 573 (Sermons 55 and 56); subsequently in volume V of the Froben edition of 1547, which was revised by Sigismundus Gelenius, it was recognized that they did not belong to the sermons Chrysostom had given in Antioch.
37 Jerome and Bernard] In a number of treatises and letters Jerome and Bernard exalted the true monastic vocation and at the same time denounced the vices that stood in its way; see eg Bernard's *De praecepto et dispensatione* (PL 182:859–94) and Jerome's letters to Eustochium; cf Ep 1167 n7.

1174

1 Sheer madness] This sigh of despair comes among many other indications that the hostility of the Louvain theologians was proving unbearable to Erasmus (cf Epp 1172–3, 1175:42–4, 1176:15–17, 1185 n4, 1196 and 1217 introductions). For some time he had planned to revisit Basel (cf Ep 1242 introduction) and Rome (cf Ep 1143 n22). Even the thought of moving permanently to the Eternal City crossed his mind (cf Ep 1167:9–11). His efforts to regularize his claims to an annuity from the imperial court (cf lines 12–15) also point to the anticipation of a prolonged absence. Although he did not now consider leaving Louvain for ever (cf Ep 1209 n1), his days there were numbered; cf Epp 1199, 1208 introductions.
2 potbellies] Cf Ep 1166 n3.
3 patent was never issued] Cf Ep 1166 n1.

4 both Testaments in Greek] Erasmus refers no doubt to his own copy of the Aldine Greek Bible (cf Ep 770). As he had given Lips a copy of the second edition of his New Testament (cf Ep 955), Lips presumably required the 'Septuagint' translation of the Old Testament. He had earlier been looking for the Hebrew text (cf Ep 1048). But as Erasmus points out, the Old Testament in Greek was not separately available in the Aldine edition. Nor was any copy of the Aldine Bible in stock in Antwerp, so Erasmus eventually lent Lips his own (cf Ep 1189:6–9). The scarcity of that expensive volume in the Netherlands is illustrated by Juan Luis Vives in a note for his edition of *De civitate Dei*, written between 1 April and 14 July 1522 (see Epp 1271, 1303). Vives deplored the fact that he had to work without access to the Septuagint, as no copy was available in the entire region after Erasmus had departed for Basel, taking his own with him; see Augustine *De civitate Dei* (Basel: J. Froben 1522) 603–4. Before long, the Complutensian polyglot became available to scholars; cf Ep 1213 n17.

5 Franciscans] Although some Franciscans sided with Erasmus' critics in the Dominican and Carmelite orders, he evidently thought well enough of some scholars in the Franciscan house of Louvain to lend them a precious volume (cf Ep 1189:9–11). For further evidence of friendly contacts with the Franciscan monasteries in his neighbourhood see Epp 749, 1044:35–41. Another Franciscan, Johannes Mahusius of Oudenarde, even published an *Epitome* of Erasmus' *Annotationes* on the New Testament (Antwerp: J. Steels 1538; NK 1455). It is possible that this measure of mutual sympathy was influenced by the traditional rivalries between the Franciscans and the Dominicans; cf Epp 1126 n40, 1166:125–9.

6 revision of the New Testament] The second edition of 1518/19 (cf Ep 864) was selling so well that the printer Johann Froben was planning a third as early as the autumn of 1519 (cf Epp 1029:34, 1030:28), but it was not until a year later that Erasmus' correspondence shows him seriously engaged in revising the text and even envisaging a trip to Rome for this purpose (cf Ep 1143 n22). In the end he had to be content with asking his friend Bombace for some of the information he had hoped to extract from the Vatican Library (cf Ep 1213 n14). A first part of the revised copy was sent to Basel before 27 May 1521 (cf Ep 1206:71–3), while the remainder probably accompanied Ep 1206, dated from that day (cf AK II Ep 791). Erasmus continued to check some points after that date, however, (cf Epp 1212:44–6, 1214 n4) and to make additions, at least to the annotations, such as those resulting from his visit to Bruges in August 1521, where he consulted four New Testament manuscripts in Latin belonging to the chapter of St Donatian's (cf Ep 1223 introduction; LB VI 5C, 21F–22B, 1080D). Meanwhile Froben pressed ahead, although Basilius Amerbach declined to assist him (cf Epp 1207:20–5, 1235:38–9), and the text volume was printed before Erasmus' arrival in Basel (cf Ep 1242 introduction). As with the preceding edition, however, he did not permit the *Annotationes* to be completed in his absence (cf Allen Ep 1342:90–5). The colophon of the *Annotationes* is dated February 1522, and on 21 March Erasmus announced that the New Testament had appeared (cf Allen Ep 1267:29–30). An expression of deference to the ultimate judgment of the church was printed prominently on the title-page of the text volume and Erasmus later hinted at changes introduced for prudence's sake (cf

Allen Ep 1418:40–3). The most significant of these were due to Edward Lee and Diego López Zúñiga (cf Ep 1213 n16; *Vadianische Briefsammlung* II Ep 247). See also Allen Ep 373 introduction.

7 Augustine ... let me know] This initiative seems to have been successful; see Ep 1189:10–11, and cf Ep 1144 n17.

1175

1 Lee ... New Testament] Cf below n28.

2 half-Christian book] Froben's edition of Polidoro's collection (July 1521) was enlarged by a newly added section of 431 adages derived from Christian sources or otherwise suitable for religious prose. This section is prefaced with a second letter to Pace, dated like the first (cf the introduction) from London, 5 June 1519.

3 most elegant type and paper] The volume, with a title frame by Urs Graf, certainly is handsome. Its accuracy, however, left much to be desired, and when copies reached England Polidoro had a sheet of corrections printed for insertion; see Allen Ep 1702:1n.

4 for so long] From lines 39–42 below it follows that Erasmus did not meet Polidoro until his second visit to England in 1505–6.

5 in the shade] Cf Epp 1107 n1, 1146:23–5.

6 first edition] Of Erasmus' *Adagia*, 1500; cf Ep 126.

7 character in tragedy] At the outset of the Trojan war, King Priam sent his youngest son Polydorus with much of his treasure to safety in Thrace, where he was murdered for the gold by the local prince Polymnestor. The story comes at the beginning of Euripides' *Hecuba*, but Erasmus' quotation is from the retelling of it by Virgil *Aeneid* 3.55–6.

8 dissembling] An analogous term was actually used in Polidoro's preface; cf below n19.

9 preface ... printed yours] Schürer reprinted Erasmus' *Adagia* with the colophon date of Strasbourg, July 1509. In his preface to the reader, dated 18 June, he mentioned Polidoro's collection, of which he had published a reprint in December 1508. Polidoro had evidently assumed that Schürer's was the first edition of Erasmus' *Adagia*.

10 Philippi] Johannes Philippi, of Kreuznach in the Rhineland, is documented in Paris 1483–1519, from 1494 as a printer. After his first edition of Erasmus' *Adagia* (cf lines 59–61), he reprinted them in 1505.

11 'white line on a white stone'] It is invisible; cf *Adagia* I v 88.

12 at dinner] They both agreed that the exchange at dinner was 'in jest' (cf lines 71–2). Polidoro mentions it in his preface (cf the introduction), but he adds that afterwards Erasmus claimed pointedly and publicly that he had been the first Latin writer to tackle the subject; cf Ep 269:62–3.

13 Cologne ... Paris] Cf Ep 172:9n.

14 Louvain] In September 1502; cf Ep 171 introduction.

15 I now ... understand] Cf Ep 1174 n1.

16 Lukas] Lukas Walters; cf Ep 531:462–6.

17 Busleyden] Jérôme de Busleyden (cf Ep 1173 n3) evidently owned Polidoro's collection in its second edition (Venice: C. de Pensis 6 November 1500), which Erasmus assumed to be the first.

18 letter of Fausto] Fausto Andrelini; see Ep 127.

19 theft or plagiarism] In his preface (cf the introduction) Polidoro mentioned that others had charged Erasmus with deliberate failure to admit his 'imitation,' which was adding 'nothing except bulk' to the *Adagia*. For himself, however he accepted that Erasmus had had no knowledge of his own collection when producing the *Adagia*.

20 Beroaldo] For Filippo Beroaldo the Elder see CEBR I. Polidoro had been his student and owed much to his inspiration.

21 Poliziano] Cf eg *Adagia* I iv 8 and 39, II ii 65 and ix 1, III vii 3.

22 you say ... bulk] See above n19.

23 *Collectanea*] The title of the first edition was *Paroemiarum, id est adagiorum, collectanea* (cf CWE 1 256 illustration). For the editions printed by Josse Bade (Paris 1506) and Aldo Manuzio (Venice 1508) cf Epp 194, 211 introductions.

24 Johannes Anglus] Giovann'Angelo Scinzenzeler, son of an immigrant from Zinzenzell in Bavaria, took charge of his father's press in 1500; he is last mentioned in 1526. He reprinted Polidoro's collection in 1506 and again in 1512 for the Da Legnano brothers of Milan; cf CEBR III.

25 Perotti] After its first appearance (Venice 1489) Niccolò Perotti's *Cornucopiae* had been reprinted many times and had gradually been enlarged to become a standard reference work for Latin composition.

26 'truth ... afar'] Quoted from Polidoro's preface; cf introduction.

27 *De rerum inventoribus*] Cf introduction.

28 mention of Lee] 'Edward Lee, my friend' is mentioned in Polidoro's second preface (cf above n2) among many other Englishmen deserving praise. But the connections between Lee and Virgilio (cf Ep 1165:28–9 and above lines 2–3) do not seem to have alarmed Erasmus unduly, as the controversy with Lee was now over; cf Ep 1123 n9.

1176

1 he will survive me ... enfeebled state] Allen was no doubt right to discern a note of jest in Erasmus' request for a 'fat prebend,' but his desire to protect the income from his living at Aldington (cf Ep 255 introduction) against the chances of Warham's death and political change was not new (cf Ep 702 introduction). Ep 1205:44–51 confirms Warham's concern for Erasmus' freedom from financial worries and his offer to reserve for him another benefice, which had still to fall vacant. Erasmus reacted to this offer with some scepticism, and in fact Aldington remained his only living in England (cf LB V 811E). The annuity was paid after Warham's death, as late as Michaelmas 1533, as is shown by Erasmus' autograph statement of his income (Öffentliche Bibliothek of the University of Basel, MS C VIa 71 f 1). For a similar concern with regard to Erasmus' Courtrai living cf Ep 1245 introduction.

2 again ... in advance] As was done in 1518–19; see Ep 823 introduction.

3 revisit Italy] Cf Ep 1143 n22.

4 congress of princes] This is perhaps another indication that Erasmus thought about attending the Diet of Worms; cf Ep 1197 introduction.

5 St Paul ... once only] Cf 2 Cor 11:25 and Ep 1185 n4; for Erasmus' predicament at Louvain cf Ep 1174 n1.

6 Dr Welles] Thomas Welles (1466–c May 1524), of Alresford, Hampshire, ob-

tained his BA and MA at Oxford and afterwards apparently went to Turin to receive a doctorate in divinity there in 1503 (as Erasmus did three years later). In 1521 Welles' doctorate was incorporated at Oxford. Ordained a priest in 1498, he became Warham's chaplain and received many benefices.

7 Pylades] The proverbial friend of Orestes

1177

1 three letters … me] None is known to exist.

2 in Cologne] Cf Ep 1155 introduction.

3 Ruthenians] This name normally applies to the Ukrainians, but sometimes also to the Russians in general. It is not clear in what sense Erasmus is using it. Lines 31–2 below suggest that he believed many Ruthenians were Christians who had broken away from the Church of Rome; perhaps he meant Orthodox Christians; cf below n5.

4 honest in Athens] Cf *Adagia* IV i 53, assuming corruption to be the norm in that state.

5 his neighbours are heretics] In lines 37–9 below Erasmus speaks of heretics abiding by the teachings of the Gospel in terms reminiscent of his recent assessment of the Czech Brethren (cf Ep 1039:163–82). See also Ep 1154 introduction and lines 18–21. Perhaps Ep 1154, which he would answer before long, had recently arrived; cf Epp 1183:11–13, 1186:11.

6 paraphrases] See Ep 1171 introduction, and cf Epp 1112, 1179, 1181.

1178

1 elephant out of a gnat] Cf Ep 1148 n2.

2 Fortune … unkindly] Cf Ep 1102 n2.

3 one scratches another] Cf *Adagia* I vii 96.

1179

1 business of the empire] Cardinal Schiner had recently gone to Worms in preparation for the diet (cf Ep 1197 introduction). For his business there cf Büchi nos 761, 766–8; Balan no 20 and passim; *Reichstagsakten* J.R. II 507, 520–1, and passim.

1180

1 certain persons] Among them no doubt Aleandro; cf Ep 1167 n20.

2 products of your pen … in circulation] Among these Ep 980 appears to have been the most objectionable; cf Epp 1143 introduction, 1167:111–23.

3 loyalty … Christendom] Cf Ep 1143:67–71. It is tempting to connect this statement with the *Consilium* (Cf Ep 1149 introduction), but nothing seems to be known about Rome's reaction to the latter.

4 suitable reward] Cf Ep 1141 n12.

1181

1 done for me] Cf Epp 447, 521, 567, 649, 1079.

2 as Varro puts it] Cf *Adagia* II iii 48, where Erasmus quotes 'Man is but a bubble' from the preface of Varro's *Res rusticae*.

1182

1 A letter ... arrived] Since the 'long reply ... printed in Basel' can only refer to Ep 856, Erasmus may either here recall (inaccurately) Pirckheimer's complaints in Ep 1095:7–9, a letter answered already in Ep 1139, or, barring some other confusion, Ep 1139 may have failed to reach Pirckheimer. A fresh complaint in a recent letter now missing might then have been related by Erasmus to Ep 856, perhaps in error.

2 summoned to Rome] When Johann Eck was lampooned in the anonymous *Eccius dedolatus* (cf Ep 1168 n5), he believed that Pirckheimer had composed it, an assumption shared by many modern authors. As a result Pirckheimer was, as he had anticipated (cf Ep 1095:93–5), among those threatened by Eck with excommunication when Eck published the bull *Exsurge, Domine* (cf Ep 1141 n11). Pirckheimer did not share Luther's dogmatic views and after repeated appeals and a request for absolution that amounted to a recantation Eck eventually absolved him. But in the mean time the Roman curia had prepared a second and final bull against Luther, dated 3 January 1521 (cf Ep 1192 n8). On the same day new instructions were issued to the legates in Germany in which Pirckheimer, Hutten, and Lazarus Spengler were included in the condemnation of Luther and their absolution reserved to the Holy See alone (Balan no 8). The matter was then taken to the papal nuncio Aleandro, who wrote to Rome on 3 August 1521 requesting authority to absolve Pirckheimer and Spengler. He did so without enthusiasm, however, in response to pressure from the imperial court (Balan no 109). He was granted the requested authority in a brief dispatched from Florence on 3 August (Balan no 113). It was probably this document he showed to Erasmus in October; see Ep 1244:4 and Willehad Paul Eckert and Christoph von Imhoff *Willibald Pirckheimer* (Cologne 1971) 272–4.

3 stones thrown ... in their sermons] Cf Ep 1185 n4.

4 harm to the pope ... popularity for Luther] Erasmus frequently repeated in various forms the charge that certain Dominicans and their allies harmed the pope's cause more than Luther's and that their excesses were motivated by ambition and greed; cf Epp 1033:157–61, 1153:125–8, 1167:450–60, 1183:60–8, 104–9, 1188:8–11, 1191:37–41, 1192:14–21, 1192A:7–10, 1195:38–47, 1196:488–591, 730–33, 1199:14–19, 1236:111–17.

1183

1 brief reply] Perhaps this had been Erasmus' original intention, but when he reached the topic of Luther's revolt against the church, many thoughts came effortlessly to mind that he had formulated before on other occasions. At any rate, no further reply is ever mentioned again.

2 the Fuggers] The use of their services had been proposed by Arkleb (cf Ep 1154:69–71). Fugger representatives were regularly present at the imperial court (cf Ep 1148 n4) and the firm had extensive business interests in Hungary and Bohemia. But although Erasmus already had contacts with the Thurzo family (cf Ep 850), principal partners of the Fuggers in central Europe, his correspondence does not reveal the use of the Fuggers for the conveyance of mail until 1529.

3 the book] Cf Ep 1154 n2.

4 two Bohemians] Mikuláš Klaudyán and Laurentius Voticius visited Erasmus in the summer of 1520; cf Ep 1039 introduction.
5 Šlechta] Ep 1021
6 prophet ... witness] Cf eg Zeph 3:17.
7 contracted ... limits] In recent times on account of the Turks; cf Ep 729:56n.
8 Campeggi] Cf Epp 1025 n3, 1062.
9 nuncio] Perhaps Marino Caracciolo, whom Erasmus could have met on several occasions (cf Epp 1135 n1, 1148 n4); or possibly this topic arose in Erasmus' conversation with Aleandro at Cologne (cf Ep 1167 n20). Allen referred to Ep 1144, addressed to Francesco Chierigati, but he was not at this time a nuncio. No answer is known to Erasmus' letter to him.
10 as they should] Cf Epp 1167:386–8, 1182 n4.
11 nor ... knowledge] Cf Epp 1143:59–60, 1153:63–7.
12 Jewish ceremonial] Cf Ep 1126 n45.
13 deeply sunk ... minor problems] A similar statement occurs in the *Consilium* (*Opuscula* 359:114–18; cf Ep 1149 introduction).
14 left undecided ... the Gospel] Cf the preface.
15 the best part of the realm] Cf Ep 1021:106–9.
16 Nicolaites] Cf Ep 1021:100–1.
17 Pyghards] Cf Ep 1021 n20.
18 entrust this question ... beyond doubt] The proposal for a panel of scholars to deal with the heretics in Bohemia bears a close resemblance (even literal in parts) to the proposal made in the *Consilium* to treat with Luther and his followers; see *Opuscula* 359:129–33 and cf 358:104–6.
19 the men ... other motives] Cf below lines 104–9 and Ep 1182:10–14.
20 merciful shepherd of his people] Cf Epp 1199:37–8, 1203:27–8.
21 Peter ... powers that be] Cf 1 Pet 2:13–18.
22 preside in Rome] Cf Ep 950:61–3.
23 needs be that offences come] Cf Matt 18:7, Luke 17.1.
24 wont to do myself] Despite the caveat in lines 114–15, this statement clearly contradicts Erasmus' many assurances that he never read Luther's writings (cf Ep 1143:15–16). Cf also Ep 1167:145–6 and the *Consilium* (*Opuscula* 358:103–4): 'No one denies he is a better man after reading Luther's books, despite certain things one might perhaps justly dislike.'
25 Dominicans and Carmelites] Cf above lines 60–2.
26 often said so] Cf Ep 1153 n4.
27 patron ... advocate ... judge] Cf Ep 1167 n39.
28 donkey ... stork ... blockhead] Cf Epp 1144:45–6, 1192:38–9, 1225:280–1.
29 a bull has appeared] Cf Ep 1141 n11.
30 on occasion ... divine wisdom] Cf for instance Epp 456:253–5, 274–5, 858:89–97.
31 differ ... from Thomas] In the *Annotationes* on the New Testament; cf Ep 1126 n38.
32 young men ... life of religion is] See Ep 858:521–5; cf Epp 1171:90–2, 1196:343–5, 1202:250–2, 1211:34–43, and for Erasmus' personal experience cf Ep 447:344–6.
33 not read them] Cf Ep 1200 n10.
34 solid rock] Cf Matt 7:24–5, Luke 6:48, also Matt 16:18.

35 To the honourable … Moravia] Allen placed here the address he had found, in Erasmus' own hand, at the bottom of the original of Ep 1154, immediately below Arkleb's signature. A first attempt at spelling Arkleb's unfamiliar name is scratched through.

1184

1 company of Williams] Cf Ep 1003 n6.

2 Croy] Cardinal Guillaume de Croy died at Worms on 6 January 1521 after a fall from his horse. Cardinal Albert of Brandenburg celebrated the funeral mass for him, with the Dominican Johannes Faber preaching the sermon (cf Ep 1156 n8). Charles v attended; cf Balan no 15.

3 book] *De contemptu rerum fortuitarum* had recently been published; cf 1073 n16.

4 uncle] Guillaume de Croy, lord of Chièvres (cf Ep 532:30n) was also to die at Worms (27/8 May 1521), of the plague.

5 Vives] Juan Luis Vives had been the cardinal's tutor at Louvain; cf Ep 957 introduction.

6 recent letter to him] Cf Ep 1185 n1.

7 More's letter] The reply to Germain de Brie's *Antimorus* (cf Epp 1087, 1131 introductions). More had met Budé at the celebrated gathering on the Field of the Cloth of Gold, prior to meeting Erasmus at Calais; cf Ep 1106 introduction.

8 Hutten] Ulrich von Hutten and Budé had met at Paris in September 1517; cf Ep 744:52n.

9 lost to literature] Cf Ep 1129 n7.

10 The man … friends of mine] This William has not been identified; line 7 above may suggest that he had come from Paris and was now ready to go back.

11 fish-eating] Lent had begun on 13 February.

1185

1 Budé's letter to Vives] Dated from 10 January [1521], this letter clearly was intended to be read by Erasmus and to please him. Budé expresses fear that he may have succeeded less in restraining Germain de Brie (cf Ep 1087 introduction and lines 485–8) than Erasmus in restraining More. But already on 28 January Budé could write to Brie himself, expressing his satisfaction that Brie did not intend to continue his quarrel with More; see Guillaume Budé *Opera* (Basel 1557; repr 1969) I 327–30, 414–15.

2 to Hué] Ep 1003, addressed to Guillaume Hué, dean of Paris

3 fanatical opposition … here] Cf Ep 1174 n1.

4 the first of martyrs] In many letters of this period Erasmus repeated that he was being stoned, like St Stephen, the protomartyr (cf Acts 7:58–60) and St Paul (cf Ep 1176:15–16); see eg Epp 1173:30, 1182:10–11, 1196:518–20, 1203:17–20, 1216:78–80.

5 Ruzé and Deloynes] Cf Ep 1131 n1.

6 Budé] Ep 1184

7 Herman of Friesland] Cf Ep 1131.

1186

1 liberal studies … Christianity] For the following cf Ep 1185:22–5.

2 I warned him ... ill feeling.] In Ep 1127A:68–74; cf Ep 1167 n25.
3 *De captivitate Babylonica*] Martin Luther *De captivitate Babylonica ecclesiae praeludium* (Wittenberg: [M. Lotter c 6 October 1520]; Luther w VI 484–573). For the quick succession of reprints and translations, including a Dutch one, see Benzing *Lutherbibliographie* nos 704–17. Whether or not Erasmus had himself read Luther's critique of the sacramental teachings of the Roman church, he was certainly aware of its decisive impact (cf Ep 1217:43–5). In June 1521 Albrecht Dürer received a copy of it at Antwerp from Cornelius Grapheus (see Dürer *Diary* 98). Henricus Glareanus at Paris owned a copy and avidly read it three times (cf Zwingli *Werke* VII Ep 183). Johann Bugenhagen attributed his conversion to Lutheranism to this work, after concluding at first that its author was the worst of heretics (cf Luther w VI 496). Erasmus was soon accused of being that author; see Epp 1218:18, 1236:158–65.
4 Bohemians] Cf Epp 1039, 1154 introductions, 1183. In *De captivitate Babylonica* Luther answered those who charged him with the 'heresies' of Wycliffe and Hus; see Luther w VI 508–9.
5 Scylla ... Charybdis] Cf *Adagia* I v 4 and Ep 1156:106–7. If Luther is equated with Scylla, Charybdis evidently is the onslaught of conservative theologians (cf Epp 1174 n1, 1185:30–2). The saying is used again in this sense in Epp 1191:43–4, 1195:99–100, 1205:31–2, 1216:82–3, 1228:51–2.
6 horse in the fable] The horse had a quarrel with the wild boar, enlisted the help of man, and found himself committed to serving in harness for ever. This story is found in the Latin collection of Aesopic fables made by Phaedrus 4.4; for the story of the he-goat, see Phaedrus 4.9.
7 like the he-goat ... to get out] Tit for tat. Erasmus was aware of a sentence in Luther's *Responsio* to the theologians of Louvain and Cologne, where the reformer had likened him to a 'ram with his horns entangled in a thornbush'; cf Epp 1113 n15, 1127A:77–9.
8 burn Luther's books] Such burnings are recorded in Ghent on 24 June 1521 and in Antwerp on 13 July, both in the presence of Aleandro and Nicolaas Baechem Egmondanus (cf Ep 1216 n19), and in Amersfoort, east of Utrecht, on 19 August (cf Fredericq IV 76, 78, 80, V 400–7). It may be more than coincidence that no similar act is recorded for The Hague, the seat of Everaert's Council of Holland (cf Ep 1165:1–6).
9 Vincentius] Vincentius Theoderici; cf Ep 1165 n5.
10 Silvester, Augustin, Todischius] Prierias, Alveldt, and Tommaso Radini Tedeschi; cf Ep 1167:456–60.
11 Eck] Cf Epp 1141 n11, 1182 n2, n4.
12 with his own weapons] Cf Ep 1195 n11.
13 Germans publish everything] Cf Epp 904:20n, 1166 n25, 1193. Erasmus expressed himself in similar terms in Epp 1188:47, 1217:45–6, 1225:143–5, 1250:14–16.

1187

1 here ... with Longueil] In October 1519 (cf Ep 1011 n1). Christophe de Longueil (cf Epp 914, 1144 introduction) was in Padua at the time this letter was written.
2 'knew ... men'] Horace *Ars poetica* 142, echoing Homer *Odyssey* 1.3

1188

1 fate thought otherwise] Cf Epp 1186:1–8, 26–7, 1199 n1.
2 to Reuchlin] Cf Epp 1143:10–13, 1155 n5.
3 in collusion with him] Cf Ep 1182 n4.
4 Jacobites] Cf Ep 1153 n24.
5 Antwerp] In what follows, in repetitions of this same story (cf Epp 1192:45–52, 1196:269–73), and also elsewhere (cf Epp 1144:41–2, 1196:588–91, 677–9), Erasmus insisted that the civic authorities of Antwerp had advised the clergy to 'preach the Gospel' and refrain from polemics. While no such instructions appear to be known (but cf Fredericq IV 36), there cannot be any doubt about the strong appeal Luther's works exercised upon the town clerk, Cornelius Grapheus, a friend of Erasmus (cf Ep 1186 n3) and upon Jacob Proost, the prior of the Augustinian friars (cf Ep 980:62n). The papal nuncio Aleandro complained in his dispatches about Luther's popularity in this metropolis of international commerce. He reported that Luther's works were shipped from Antwerp to England and Spain, and even that they were printed there in Spanish at the expense of Iberian Jews only superficially converted to Catholicism; see Balan nos 12, 32, 120 and Paul Kalkoff *Die Anfänge der Gegenreformation in den Niederlanden* (Halle 1903) I 38–64.
6 Matthias] Matthias Weynsen (d 1547), of Dordrecht in Holland, was appointed warden of the Franciscan monastery of Antwerp in 1518. A firm opponent of Luther, he later rose to be provincial. For his view as here reported cf Ep 1211 n77.
7 cut off … they receive] Cf Ep 1173:158–60.
8 imperial proclamation … papal bull] Cf Epp 1166 n20, 1141 n11.
9 Cajetanus] Tommaso de Vio, Cardinal Cajetanus; cf Epp 1006 n21, 1033:157–61, 1182 n4, but also Ep 1225 n47.
10 Miltitz] Karl von Miltitz (c 1490–1529), a Saxon noble, had joined the papal court in 1514. In 1518 he was sent on a good-will mission to Saxony and presented a sacred 'golden Rose' to Frederick the Wise. At the same time he involved himself in negotiations about the case of Luther, in the course of which he exceeded his authority to propose compromises, but in the end achieved nothing.
11 Marino] Marino Caracciolo; cf Ep 1135 n1.
12 Aleandro] Cf Ep 1167 n20.
13 childish principle] See 1 Kings 12:10, 2 Chron 10:10.
14 Pucci] Cf Ep 860 introduction.
15 Duchesne] Guillaume Duchesne (de Quercu), of Saint-Sever in Calvados, was from 1493 a member of the Collège de Sorbonne and received a licence in theology in 1496. Luther held him responsible, together with Noël Béda, for the Paris *Determinatio* against himself (cf Ep 1141 n10); so also did Henricus Glareanus in Paris, who added that Duchesne was also wont to lash out against Lefèvre d'Etaples and Erasmus; see Luther w *Briefwechsel* II Ep 425 and Zwingli *Werke* VII Ep 183.
16 Béda of Standonck] This appears to be Erasmus' earliest known reference to his most unrelenting critic in Paris (cf Ep 1571). Noël Béda (c 1470–1537), had been principal of the Collège de Montaigu, founded by Jan Standonck, until 1513–14 and continued to be associated with it.

17 in Paris ... out of the way] This rumour, which has not been found in other sources, appears to have no substance.

18 In Cologne ... I refused.] Cf Ep 1167 n20.

19 indulgences] For Erasmus' condemnation of the practice cf Epp 786:25–6, 858:215–17, 1211:173–84.

20 the Germans publish ... get hold of] Cf Ep 1186 n13.

21 Mauritszoon and ... Sasbout] Jacob Mauritszoon and Joost Sasbout, colleagues of Everaerts in the Council of Holland, were also greeted in Ep 1092:19.

1189

1 my journey] To Germany (cf Epp 1197, 1242 introductions) and perhaps to Rome; cf Ep 1143 n22.

2 three philippics] Gold florins of St Philip, struck in the Burgundian-Hapsburg Netherlands from 1496 to 1521, with a nominal value of 50d gros Flemish (= 3s sterling; cf 348–9 above and CWE 1 318, 327, 336–9).

3 Greek Bible ... ten florins] Cf Ep 1174 n4. The same price was asked in 1520 for the Aldine Bible by Johann Froben in Basel; cf Zwingli *Werke* VII Epp 133, 156. Presumably the florins are the Burgundian-Hapsburg money-of-account (the gulden or livre d'Artois): at 40d per florin, a sum worth 33s 4d gros Flemish, or about 23s sterling. Cf CWE 1 323, 347.

4 Easter] 31 March 1521

5 Minorites ... to have it] Cf Ep 1174 n5.

6 *Contra Faustum*] There is no reference to a manuscript of *Contra Faustum* associated with St Maartensdal in either Erasmus' edition (Basel: H. Froben 1528/9) VI or CSEL 25:249–797.

1190

1 three philippics] Cf Ep 1189 n2.

2 Aerts] Jan Aerts (Arnoldi), of Nossegem between Brussels and Louvain, was elected prior of the Augustinian canons at St Maartensdal, Louvain, in January 1493. He resigned in 1497 for reasons of health, but was prior again from 1509 until his death in 1537, providing sound management to the monastery at a time when this was badly needed.

3 paraphrases ... yet] Erasmus probably refers to Froben's collection of March 1521; cf Epp 1171, 1181 introductions.

4 from Worms] For the Diet of Worms and Erasmus' plans for a visit cf Ep 1197 introduction.

1191

1 Clava] Antonius Clava was a civic magistrate of Ghent and a friend of long standing (cf Ep 175:13n). This passage shows that they continued to correspond, although no letters are extant between April 1518 and July 1523 (Epp 841, 1373).

2 ancient promise] Made perhaps during one of Erasmus' visits to Ghent; cf Epp 596, 841 introductions.

3 as the fable has it] The limbs complain that the stomach does nothing but eat and decide to stop working for it; they soon find themselves the chief

sufferers. The famous parable is best known from its use by Menenius Agrippa in the revolt of the common people in Rome, assigned to 494 BC; see Livy 2.32.9–12, and cf also 1 Cor 12:12–27.

4 bellies] Cf Ep 1166 n3.
5 with any fellow-Christian] Cf Epp 1153:25–6, 1192:7–8.
6 No one ... command] Cf Ep 1182 n4.
7 wound himself ... every day] Cf Ep 1195 n11.
8 Scylla, Charybdis ... for us] Cf Ep 1186 n5.
9 last spark of gospel teaching] Cf Ep 1205:34–5.
10 Willem de Waele] A prominent citizen of Ghent; cf Ep 301:39n.
11 list of Williams] Cf Epp 1003 n6, 1184:3.
12 cardinal de Croy] Cf Ep 1184 n2.

1192

1 count of Nassau] Henry III of Nassau-Dillenburg, a great favourite of Charles V and now governor of Holland and Zeeland; for Erasmus' connections with him cf Ep 1092:20–1.
2 kinsman of mine] In the absence of more tangible information on Erasmus' kin Allen mentions here one Gerard Gregorisz (Guerard Gregoire Hollandois), an obscure painter who lived and worked in 1522 at Tournus, between Dijon and Lyon. The claim that he was a relative of Erasmus is made by Pierre de Sainct-Julien *De l'origine des Bourgongnons* (Paris: N. Chesneau 1581) 536. Allen suggested that Gerard could have tried to enlist the help of his famous kinsman in order to obtain commissions for paintings.
3 fellow-Christian] Cf Ep 1191 n5.
4 set right ... altogether] Cf Ep 1153 n6.
5 put it there] Like the scorpion; cf Ep 1196 n6.
6 roast or boiled] Cf Epp 1192A:14–16, 1195:51–2.
7 these monks] Cf Ep 1182 n4.
8 bull ... against Luther] Such instructions are given in two documents that might be intended here. One was the papal bull *Decet Romanum pontificem* of 3 January 1521. This was issued after the sixty days accorded to Luther for a recantation in *Exsurge, Domine* (cf Ep 1141 n11) had expired, and implemented the ban with which he had been threatened in the earlier bull. The extent to which the new bull became public knowledge prior to the autumn of 1521 is, however, subject to controversy (cf *Reichstag zu Worms* 250–1). The other document was a proclamation issued by Erard de la Marck, bishop of Liège, and Girolamo Aleandro on 17 October 1520. This proclamation ordering the burning of Luther's books has been plausibly identified with Balan no 60, edited there under a misleading date; see L.-E. Halkin 'Le plus ancien texte d'édit promulgué contre les Luthériens' *Revue d'histoire ecclésiastique* 25 (1929) 73–83, but cf also Epp 1144 n4, 1166 n20.
9 They say] The following charges may have been derived from the list of Luther's errors included in the bull *Exsurge, Domine*; cf Ep 1141 n11
10 Jacobite ... black art] This Dominican (cf Ep 1153 n24) has not been identified.
11 Carmelite ... Erasmus in Brabant] Erasmus repeats this story in Ep 1212:29–34, adding that he had learnt it in 'letters from friends.' Neither his source nor the identity of the Carmelite preacher appear to be known. In a letter to

Henricus Cornelius Agrippa dated from Annecy, 10 September 1521, the episode is reported in much the same terms, except that Luther is named in place of the Minorite, and the statement is attributed to a Dominican (cf H. Cornelius Agrippa *Opera*, Lyon, n d; repr 1970, II 626). Allen also drew attention to an anonymous *Misocacus: civis Utopiensis Philaletis ex sorore nepotis dialogi tres* [Paris: Pierre Vidoue c 1526], attacking the Paris theologians for their condemnation of Luther (cf Ep 1188 n15). They are credited with saying that Charles V was Antichrist and Erasmus, Lefèvre d'Etaples, Reuchlin, and Luther were his evangelists.

12 suffragan of Tournai] Nicolas Bureau; cf Ep 1144 n12.
13 over their liquor] Cf Ep 1162 n19.
14 storks ... Antichrists] Cf Ep 1183 n28.
15 educated man] Frans van Cranevelt
16 in Antwerp] Cf Ep 1188 n5.
17 Matthias] Matthias Weynsen; cf Ep 1188:11–15.
18 Egmondanus] Nicolaas Baechem Egmondanus; cf Ep 1164 n14.
19 Charles ... peace of Christendom] Cf Ep 1192A:10–13.
20 proclamation by Charles] Cf Ep 1166 n20.
21 supporter of ... Preachers] Cf Ep 1173 n28.
22 Grand Turk] Cf Ep 1167 n31.
23 count] Henry of Nassau
24 Ysselstein] Floris van Egmond, an old patron (cf Ep 178:48–54), had also accompanied Charles V to Worms; cf *Reichstagsakten* J.R. II 787, 797.
25 son] For Erasmus' connection with Maximiliaan van Egmond cf Ep 1018.

1192A

1 attracted to Luther] Cf Ep 1192:70–3.
2 Jacobites and Carmelites ... popularity] Cf Epp 1153 n24, 1182 n4.
3 Leo ... Charles too] Cf Ep 1192:61–4.
4 the loss ... serious] Identical Latin words were used in Ep 1192:12, but the formulation of the thought was modified in consideration of the recipient.
5 Lent as well] 13 February–30 March 1521

1193

1 publish ... important enough] Erasmus evidently refers to unauthorized editions.
2 method of letter-writing] Erasmus refers to *Brevissima ... conficiendarum epistolarum formula*, based on an early version of what eventually was to become *De conscribendis epistolis* (cf Epp 71, 909:19–20, 34n; ASD I-2 152–579). For the *Formula*, see CWE 25 255–67; for *De conscribendis epistolis*, see CWE 25 1–254. It can be conjectured that the *Formula* was first edited in 1519–20 by Ulrich Hugwald in Basel. This unauthorized edition was reprinted several times before Erasmus returned to the topic and composed the much larger *De conscribendis epistolis* (Basel: J. Froben August 1522; cf Ep 1284). It is possible that the decision to do so was taken at about the time of this letter.
3 Paludanus] The unauthorized editions of the *Formula* were prefaced with a letter closely resembling Ep 71 and allegedly addressed by Erasmus to one Petrus Paludanus; see Allen XI 366–7 and CEBR III.

4 published once or twice] The three elegies included in the *Progymnasmata* had first been edited in Erasmus' absence (cf Allen I 5–6) by his friend Reyner Snoy (cf Ep 190:14n) in the *Herasmi Roterodami silva carminum* (Gouda 1513; NK 871). There is no trace, however, of any other unauthorized edition; cf Reedijk no 23 headnote.

1194

1 so much blessed] Erasmus refers to the progress made by humanistic learning and writing in his own lifetime, which had prompted him earlier to hail the arrival of a new Golden Age (cf Epp 541:13, 964:85n). References to the great promise of the age have by the time of this letter become rather rare (cf Epp 1223:19–20, 1237:15–19), while pessimistic assessments dominate; cf for instance Epp 1205:32–5, 1239:14–22.

2 exquisite taste] Cf *Adagia* II viii 59.

3 Theodoricus] In the title of *De contemptu mundi* this monk is called Theodoricus of Haarlem. No identifications have been proposed either for him or for his nephew Jodocus; for the question whether they were fictitious characters see CEBR III.

4 a word here and there] It is possible that the changes made at this time included most or all of the final chapter 12 of *De contemptu mundi*; cf Ep 1196 n52 and Sem Dresden in ASD V-1 30–4.

1195

1 several friends] In September 1524 Erasmus recalled that Wolfgang Faber Capito (cf Ep 1158:22–3) had written to him and that the emperor's confessor Jean Glapion (cf Ep 1275) had warned him of Aleandro's agitation at court (cf Allen Ep 1482:17–18). Both attended the Diet of Worms (cf Ep 1197 introduction). In Ep 1199:26–8 Erasmus found it advisable to say that the man who had written him a warning letter – perhaps Capito – had exaggerated.

2 supporter of Luther] Cf Ep 1167 n22.

3 scandalous pamphlets … to me] In his dispatch to Rome from Worms dated 12 February 1521 (Balan no 21) Aleandro affirmed that many weighty members of the imperial court, and especially the bishop of Tuy, believed Erasmus to be the author of some books attributed to Luther, and that the books he published under his own name were full of dangerous errors. The issue came to a head in July when Aleandro and Erasmus met in Brussels (cf Epp 1218:14–17, 1236:165–8). For other recent pamphlets that might well have been attributed to Erasmus see Ep 1166 n24, also Epp 1165 n11, n17, 1168 n5, 1199:28–35.

4 you warned me] Cf Ep 1198:17–22.

5 preaching to the converted] Cf *Adagia* I ii 12, literally 'reminding someone who had not forgotten.'

6 I urged … learned men.] Cf Epp 1033:95–6, 1164 n15.

7 put right … put down] Cf Ep 1153 n6.

8 lure me … camp] Cf Ep 1144 n16.

9 disagree … from Christ] For the proviso contained in this formulation cf below lines 118–20, Epp 1167:470–1, 1183:144–5, 1217:161–3, and the preface.

10 destiny] Cf below lines 146–9, Ep 1199 n1.

11 No one does Luther more harm than himself] Cf Epp 1186:26, 1191:41–2, 1202:292–5, 1218:2–4, also Ep 1186:8–10.
12 damage the pope's cause] Cf Ep 1182 n4.
13 boiled or roast] Cf Ep 1192:11–12.
14 very close friends] In one of his dispatches from Worms (Balan no 36) Aleandro confirmed that they had shared a room together at Venice for some six months (in 1507–8) and added that Erasmus had then attended his daily lectures on Plutarch's moral writings. Erasmus also recalled their association in Epp 1219:18–19, 2644.
15 in print] In *Adagia* II i 34 Erasmus acknowledged Aleandro's help with that adage in a passage first printed in Froben's edition of October 1520.
16 his instructions ... Luther's party] This is in fact borne out by Leo X's letter to Aleandro of 16 July 1520; see Balan no 3.
17 other people I could name] Cf Epp 1218:8–12, 1219:12–20.
18 an opponent] The reference is to Luther.
19 drawn heavily on my books] Cf CWE 7 preface and Epp 1196:558–60, 1218: 25–8, 1219:59–61, 1225:233–4, 362–6, 1236:174–8.
20 first of his articles] Erasmus appears to be referring to the list of Luther's errors included in the bull *Exsurge, Domine* (cf Ep 1141 n11). These sentences, or as Luther too calls them, articles, are repeated and reaffirmed in Luther's *Assertio omnium articulorum ... per bullam ... damnatorum* (cf Ep 1203 n9). The first article posits spontaneous justification by faith in a formulation to which Erasmus would hardly have subscribed (cf Ep 1196 n51). He may also be thinking here of the second article, which posits that it is utterly contrary to Christ's teaching to maintain that a newly baptized child is free of sin; cf also article 32, and below Ep 1225:359–61.
21 familiar] Marliano had been attached to the court of the Netherlands since 1506 or earlier; thus Erasmus may have had early opportunities to meet him. Allen also draws attention to Marliano's friendship with Andrea Ammonio, who was close to Erasmus during his stays in England; see Allen Ep 218 introduction.
22 put right ... put down] Cf above lines 21–2.
23 Scylla ... Charybdis of the opposite faction] Cf Ep 1186 n5.
24 honour of the Roman pontiff ... peace of Christendom] Cf Ep 1149 introduction.
25 read right through] Cf Ep 1143 n3.
26 the order I condemn] Mostly the order of St Dominic; cf Ep 1173 n28.
27 Time ... into the open] Cf *Adagia* II iv 17; Ep 974:10n.
28 one hair's breadth] Cf *Adagia* I v 6.
29 conceal the truth] Cf above lines 79–81 and the preface.
30 Plato's opinion] Cf Ep 1167 n27.
31 rule of faith] Cf Epp 1154:25–8, 1183:27.
32 wrote back ... Catholic church] Cf Ep 1183:33–5, 144–5.
33 resist ... printing] Cf Ep 1143 n6.
34 an approach to him] In Ep 980:45–50
35 superstitious fear] Cf above line 39.
36 libellous pamphleteering] Cf Ep 1053 n62.
37 Hutten] Having given Hutten Ep 1114 as an introduction to Marliano, Eras-

mus was content even now to remember him to the bishop of Tuy; cf the introduction. For Hutten's current situation Epp 1135 introduction, 1182 n2.

38 resulting burden … no one else's] Cf Ep 1165 n17 and above n3.

39 Ferdinand] On 2 April 1521 (cf LP III 1223) Archduke Ferdinand arrived in Worms from the Netherlands, remaining there until 30 April (cf *Reichstagsakten* J.R. II 779, 870, 985). For Erasmus' unconvincing explanation of his failure to join Ferdinand's party cf Ep 1197 introduction.

40 Scarpinelli … some time ago] Ep 1169

41 Severus] Cf Ep 1169 n9.

1196

1 to Louvain] From Paris in 1517

2 habit of women] The commonplace of women's propensity to slander and 'bitching' is also used below in lines 514–15, 656–7 and Epp 1144:29–30, 1162:51–2, 1217:92–4, but the qualifications here and elsewhere should be noted; on another occasion Erasmus praised the dexterity of female eloquence (cf Ep 1229:29–32) and in general he had a high opinion of educated women; cf Ep 1233 introduction and Elisabeth Schneider *Das Bild der Frau im Werk des Erasmus von Rotterdam* (Basel 1955).

3 tumbrel or hoy] Cf *Adagia* I iv 19 and below lines 226, 564, 573–4.

4 Augustinian house] Either the monastery of the Augustinian eremites on the Fish-market, incorporated into the University of Louvain in 1447, which had offered the newly founded Collegium Trilingue (cf Ep 691 introduction) temporary facilities (cf de Vocht CTL I 295), or St Maartensdal, the house of the Augustinian canons, which Erasmus visited from time to time; cf Epp 1000B, 1048, 1190.

5 for Holland] If Erasmus' account is, as he claims (lines 136–7) roughly chronological, Theoderici must subsequently have paid another visit to his native Holland; cf line 160.

6 scorpion … tail] Cf Pliny the Elder *Naturalis historia* 29.29.91. Erasmus was fond of this idea; cf Epp 1013:4–5, 1192:9–11, 1212:27–9 and CWE 23 271.

7 in your lodgings] Erasmus' report of that meeting extends to line 114 (cf line 98, and also Ep 1166:47–50), but he also mentions a subsequent conversation; cf line 96.

8 did not deserve] Cf Ep 1126 n38.

9 another place] In Ep 1053:458–96; cf Ep 1126:302–26.

10 Blessed Virgin] Cf Ep 1126 n40.

11 I had cited] Cf Ep 1126:338–68.

12 old principle … a good thing] Cf *Adagia* I ii 49.

13 the bull … against Luther] *Exsurge, Domine* was first proclaimed in the Netherlands on 28 September (cf Ep 1141 n11). Theoderici had presumably accused Erasmus of doubting the bull's authenticity; cf Ep 1166 n13.

14 individual … white] Nicolaas Baechem Egmondanus, the Carmelite; cf Ep 1144 n8.

15 Paul … effect] Cf 1 Tim 1:20, Titus 3:10.

16 'charity … all things'] 1 Cor 13:7

17 letter … your order] Ep 1033, addressed to Cardinal Albert of Brandenburg

18 declaimed … had edited] Cf Ep 1162 n13.

19 never read it] Cf Ep 1200 n10.
20 return to the letter] In lines 224–62
21 Faber] Cf Ep 1149 introduction.
22 ready to make up a quarrel] Cf Ep 1022 introduction.
23 man advanced in years] Faber was born c 1470.
24 at Dordrecht] Apparently on another visit to Holland (cf n5). The same incident is related in Ep 1165:7–12 and must thus have occurred before 6 December 1520.
25 in Holland] Cf Ep 1165 n1.
26 St Thomas Aquinas' day] 7 March; the young eulogist is not identified.
27 Horace's ... *montes*] *Odes* 2.10.11–12, misquoted by the preacher so as to wreck both metre and sense. His second mistake suggests an ignorance of elementary Latin. The two parallel examples of rustic ignorance are from Plautus *Truculentus* 691 and 689–90.
28 Plutarch comparing ... counterparts] In his parallel *Lives* Plutarch paid generous homage to the greatness of the Romans.
29 an ant and a camel] Cf *Adagia* I v 47.
30 we heard you ... answers] Presumably in an academic disputation. Just at the time that Erasmus arrived in Louvain, Theoderici earned his licence (31 June 1517) and doctorate (13 October 1517) in theology; see de Jongh 41*–42*.
31 Lindos] At Lindos, on the island of Rhodes, sacrifices in honour of Hercules were accompanied by curses and abuse; cf *Adagia* II v 19.
32 *Moria* ... *Antibarbari*] Cf Ep 1164:5–7.
33 letter ... to the cardinal] Ep 1033; cf above lines 125–6.
34 boats, and wagons] See above n3.
35 set right ... extinguished] Cf Ep 1153 n6.
36 honour ... tranquillity of Christ's people] Cf Ep 1149 introduction.
37 Bern] Cf Epp 1033 n36, 1173:146–7.
38 despotic rule] Cf Ep 1033:133–6.
39 Savaronella] Girolamo Savonarola; cf Epp 1033 n35, 1173:145–6.
40 a certain monk] Matthias Weynsen, a Minorite; cf Ep 1188 n5, n6.
41 Jerome's books ... virgins] Cf Ep 1167 n7.
42 never mentioned ... by name in my books] In Epp 1164:12–13, 1167:76–7 Erasmus had extended this claim to cover individual monks as well as orders, while in Ep 1225:154–60 he offers a partial contradiction. Although he had never shown much restraint in identifying his opponents as Dominicans, Carmelites, or members of other orders, it is true that in the *Farrago* (cf Ep 1009 introduction) the names of some individuals were withheld (eg in Epp 483, 948). The subsequent *Epistolae ad diversos* (cf Ep 1206 introduction) are quite uninhibited in this regard (cf the indexes of CWE 7–8, under 'Dominicans,' 'Carmelites') and do little to bear out Erasmus' contention in lines 341–3, below; cf also Ep 1006 n1.
43 Dominican order ... above the rest] Cf Ep 1173 n28.
44 Neuenahr] Cf Epp 1078 introduction, 1173:158–63; the letter here mentioned is missing.
45 Buschius] In the *Spongia* Erasmus makes it clear that the following lines refer to Buschius' *Vallum humanitatis* (Cologne: N. Caesar 12 April 1518); see ASD IX-1 138.

46 another man] Perhaps Ulrich von Hutten, whom Erasmus had urged to show restraint (cf Epp 636:29–30, 951:45–6). Allen suggested that here the anonymous *Hochstratus ovans* (cf Ep 1165 n11) which has been attributed to Hutten, among others may be meant. In the *Spongia* Erasmus stated that it might seem to have been written in support of him, but that he had always condemned it and done his best to have it suppressed; see ASD IX-1 142.
47 poisoning] Cf Ep 1188:37–40.
48 Vincentius] Theoderici's name was suppressed in print throughout this letter except here. Its retention was probably an oversight and in the corrigenda of the *Epistolae ad diversos* (cf Ep 1206 introduction) an effort was apparently made to correct the lapse by changing 'Vincentius' to 'Vucenta'; this induced the editors of the *Opus epistolarum* to put 'Bucenta' here and in the other places where the name is missing. 'Bucenta' means oxherd, rustic ploughman.
49 my books] Cf Ep 858:395–8.
50 in several places] Such as Ep 858:353–6
51 works of charity] This emphasis is difficult to reconcile with justification by faith as taught by Luther; cf Epp 1195 n20, 1202:174–5. For Erasmus' view see also LB IX 1241C–D.
52 profession] The passage from 'The most sacred vow …' is very similar to the closing passage of *De contemptu mundi* (ASD V-1 85–6), except that there the comparison is specifically with the cowls and vows of the Dominicans and the Carmelites; cf Ep 1194 n4.
53 warned … to be found] Cf Ep 1183 n32.
54 correct the Magnificat … Lord's Prayer] Cf Ep 948:108–13.
55 Gospel of St John] Cf Epp 1072, 1126 n6.
56 over the wine] Cf Ep 1162 n19.
57 'Blessed … hate you'] Luke 6:22
58 Carthusian houses too] For Erasmus' friendly contacts with the Brussels monastery about this time, especially with Gabriël Ofhuys, who was a monk there, cf Ep 1239. Other Carthusians among his friends were Gregor Reisch, Johannes and Levinus Ammonius, and Jan of Heemstede. At the beginning of his *Apologia adversus Petrum Sutorem* (LB IX 740) he wrote of his admiration for the order.
59 in despite of Fortune] Cf Ep 1102 n2.
60 *poetria*] Cf Ep 1153 n42.
61 gentile prince] We are unable to suggest an identification.
62 Saul] The future apostle Paul, who attended and approved the stoning of St Stephen; see Acts 7:57–60, and cf Ep 1185 n4.
63 earth and heaven] Cf *Adagia* I iii 81.
64 theologian … deserves the name] Perhaps Herman Lethmaet (cf Ep 1238:22–30). Allen proposed Gillis van Delft; for both cf Allen Ep 1581:299–301. It is not known what other theologians (lines 544, 547) took part in the dinner conversation afterwards reported to Erasmus; perhaps Maarten van Dorp?
65 Jacobite … honey] The Antwerp Dominican Petrus Mellis (Melis) must be meant, whose name equals the Latin word for honey. He is documented from 1507 to 1528. On 26 August 1517 he received a doctorate in theology at Cologne, with Jacob of Hoogstraten as his promoter. Afterwards he lived

at the Antwerp monastery, but eventually ran away and left the church of Rome; see CEBR III and Wolfs *Acta capitulorum* 25–6, 94.
66 from Erasmus' teats] Cf Ep 1195 n19.
67 barge or wagon] Cf n3 and below lines 573–4.
68 Franciscans ... wagoners] Cf Epp 1173 n28, 1174 n5.
69 Bacchanalia] Cf Ep 1162 n19.
70 Antwerp] Cf Ep 1188 n5, and above lines 269–73, 552–7.
71 support ... for Luther] Cf Ep 1182 n4.
72 Egmondanus ... little sense] Cf above lines 128–35.
73 *poetria*, as he called it] Cf above line 487, Ep 1153 n42.
74 overtures for peace] For the short-lived agreement of 13 September 1519 cf Epp 1022, 1162:110–23.
75 defence ... be made] The *Apologia* preceding the New Testament, followed in the 1518/19 edition and thereafter by *Capita argumentorum contra morosos quosdam ac indoctos*; for both see the preliminary pages of LB VI.
76 Lefèvre and I ... depths of hell] Erasmus had strong feelings about this incident. He first mentioned it about February 1520 in his *Apologia invectivis Lei* (*Opuscula* 292; cf Ep 1080) stating that the dictum had occurred during a course of lectures on the Psalms, in which Baechem had frequently returned to this topic. The dictum is also reported more briefly in Epp 1144:35–6, 1162:143–6; cf also Ep 1192:29–33.
77 after dinner] Cf Ep 1162 n19.
78 camel dancing] Cf *Adagia* II vii 66.
79 opening lecture ... Epistles] In October 1521; cf Ep 1164 n14.
80 Attic wit] Cf *Adagia* I ii 57.
81 mud-slinging ... dunghill] It is not possible to reproduce the play on words in the Latin text between *cavilli* (abuse) and *cauli* (fold-yards).
82 When he was publishing ... Luther himself.] Cf Ep 1144:33–5, n4.
83 presence of Godschalk] Cf Ep 1162.
84 Balatro] He is a buffoon, and Nomentanus a parasite, at an absurd dinner-party described by Horace *Satires* 2.8.
85 forgeries] Cf Ep 1162:83–5.
86 *Epistolae eruditorum virorum*] The reference is to the two collections of letters in support of Erasmus against Edward Lee (cf Ep 1083 introduction). For the suppression of other pieces cf Ep 1165 n11.
87 'Imagine I ...'] Cf Ep 1162:53–5.
88 rhetorical use of courtesy] Cf Ep 1162:197–200; cf also above lines 482–6.
89 Stesichorus] This early Greek lyric poet was according to legend struck blind as a punishment for insulting Helen of Troy, and cured when he recanted in verse, with a 'palinode'; cf *Adagia* I ix 59.
90 *synceres*] Cf Ep 1162 n33.
91 Luther's party] Cf Ep 1162 n36.
92 prior of Antwerp] The prior of the Antwerp Carmelites was Sebastian Craeys; for his hostility against Erasmus cf Ep 948:114–40. Erasmus' claim that he was a doctor of theology has not been confirmed.
93 story of Standish] Cf Ep 1126:15–193.
94 why number ... sand] Cf *Adagia* I iv 44.
95 'pestilent'] Cf above lines 558–9.

96 Sileni turned inside out] Cf *Adagia* III iii 1.
97 truth in jest … shouting] Cf Ep 1182 n4, Allen Ep 1397:27–8.

1197

1 a hair's breadth] Cf Ep 1195 n28.
2 books I could name] Allen suggested the *Consilium* (cf Ep 1149 introduction) which was both anonymous and orthodox, but Gattinara's assertion that the books were free of heresy is perhaps no more than a reassuring gesture, worthy of the great diplomat; cf introduction and Epp 1195 n3, 1199:28–35.

1198

1 in Spain] Marliano had accompanied the future Charles V to Spain, 1517–20; cf Ep 596, 1106 introductions.
2 I arranged with … Barbier, to write and tell you] See Erasmus' reply directly to Marliano, Ep 1114.
3 Brussels] Cf Ep 1136 introduction.
4 never said anything of you] Cf Epp 1165 n1, 1167 n20.
5 two speeches against Luther] One of these – no doubt the 'fairly mild' one – was addressed to Charles V and ostensibly published in Rome, 'apud aedem divi Marci' n d; [Strasbourg: J. Prüss? 1520–1]; also several editions n p (see Lauchert and cf the copies in the British Library, and the Öffentliche Bibliothek of the University of Basel). The second speech was perhaps addressed to Duke George of Saxony and published or reprinted at Leipzig in 1522; see Friedrich Lauchert *Die italienischen literarischen Gegner Luthers* (Freiburg 1912) 224–9, Balan no 12.
6 as you say you have] Erasmus had sent greetings to Severus, but only said that he had written to Scarpinelli (cf Ep 1195:170–1), referring probably to Ep 1169, which may thus have failed to reach its destination.

1199

1 to fate] In Erasmus' letters of this period, fate, sometimes called the 'god from the machine' (cf *Adagia* I i 68) is often held responsible for the dramatic and disastrous events of the day, especially those involving Luther; cf Epp 1186:26–7, 1188:4–5, 1195:39, 147–9, 1202:41–2, 1203:26–7, 1218:1–2, 1219:62–3, 1225:343–4, 1238:65–6, 1244:6–7, 1248:25–7.
2 the girdle of the Graces] A phrase recollected from Horace *Odes* 3.21.22. The Graces are sometimes represented clasping one another's hands and can stand as a symbol of the civilized social intercourse which binds men together.
3 putting the pope … unfortunate position] Cf Ep 1182 n4.
4 Tunstall] As the English ambassador (cf Ep 1146 introduction), Tunstall followed Charles V and probably had last seen Erasmus when they both were at Cologne in October–November 1520 (cf Ep 1155 introduction; LP III 1043, 1050). Tunstall also attended the Diet of Worms, until he was recalled by Henry VIII. He left soon after 11 April and was at Mechelen on 23 April; cf LP III 1224, 1248.
5 the man who wrote to warn me] Probably Wolfgang Capito; cf Ep 1195 n1, Allen Ep 1482:13–17.
6 Didymus Faventinus] Philippus Melanchthon replied to Tommaso Radini Tedeschi (cf Ep 1167 n73) with an *Adversus Thomam Placentinum pro Mar-*

tino Luthero theologo oratio (Wittenberg [February 1521]); see *Melanchthons Werke in Auswahl* ed R. Stupperich (Gütersloh 1951–) I 56–140. It was published under the name Didymus Faventinus, but at the end Melanchthon's own name is given in Greek.

7 *Consilium*] Cf Ep 1149 introduction.

8 clemency] Cf Ep 1183:72–4.

9 books ... Luther] Cf Ep 1203:30–2.

10 a certain Dominican] Johannes Faber; cf Ep 1149 introduction.

1200

1 Willem] In the *Epistolae ad diversos* the pastor's name had originally been given as Pieter, perhaps an indication that Erasmus' acquaintance with him was rather slight. The mistake was corrected in the corrigenda appended to the *Epistolae ad diversos*.

2 young man] He is plausibly identified by Heinrich Eppendorf in a manuscript note in the margin of his personal copy of the *Epistolae ad diversos* (cf Ep 1206 introduction). According to Eppendorf he was Frederiks' son. When the letter was published this fact was perhaps concealed in view of the father's clerical status. Jeroen Frederiks (d 1558) studied in 1522 at Freiburg and obtained subsequently a doctorate of laws. He became director of finance of the city of Groningen. How Erasmus had helped him is not known.

3 gilt cup] This was described as Willem's gift in a list of Erasmus' belongings dated 10 April 1534, where it figures among the lesser gilt cups (see Öffentliche Bibliothek of the University of Basel, MS C VIa 71 ff 2–3). It was also listed in the inventory made after Erasmus' death and was given to Bonifacius Amerbach. Nothing is known of it after that; see Emil Major *Erasmus von Rotterdam* (Basel [1925]) 53, 59.

4 Gozewijn] Gozewijn of Halen was the head of the house of the Brethren of the Common Life at Groningen. It seems that he visited Louvain from time to time; cf Ep 838:3n.

5 prompted you] Literally 'pulled your ear'; cf *Adagia* I vii 40.

6 preachers] Erasmus was referring to monks (cf below lines 50–63) and thinking no doubt primarily of his troublesome critics among the Preachers or Dominicans.

7 holding ... by the ears] Cf *Adagia* I v 25.

8 a library ... church] Willem's books, which he left to St Martin's, are now in the library of the University of Groningen; they include eight incunables. For details see Allen's note.

9 two men ... preachers of the Gospel] Cf above n6; for a Dominican from Groningen who had recently attacked Erasmus see Ep 1166 n6.

10 never done so] Erasmus reported analogous answers in various contexts; cf Ep 1144 n12, 1183:136–40, 1196:132.

1202

1 support at Worms] When Luther went to the diet (cf Ep 1197 introduction), Jonas accompanied him from Erfurt to Worms and subsequently left with him. He was close to Luther throughout the visit; cf *Jonas Briefwechsel* Epp 47–8 and *Reichstag zu Worms* 278, 419–21, 427.

2 the best men] Cf Ep 1217 n16.

3 good and bad fish … tares mixed with the wheat] Cf Matt 13:24–30, 47–8.
4 Jerome … Babylon of the Apocalypse] See his letter 46.12 (CSEL 54:341).
5 St Bernard … *De consideratione*] In this work, addressed to Pope Eugenius III, St Bernard of Clairvaux attacked some corrupt practices of the Roman curia and the negligence of recent popes; see 1.9–11, 4.2 (PL 182:739–42, 772–5).
6 end in uproar] Cf Ep 1143 n5.
7 warning letters … friends of his] Cf Epp 980, 1143 n7.
8 what god … heart] Cf Ep 1199 n1.
9 Luther's books … to read] Cf Ep 1143 n3.
10 paradoxes] The most famous of Luther's paradoxes probably occurs at the beginning of his *Tractatus de libertate christiana* (c December 1520) and is given special emphasis in the typographical arrangement; cf Luther W VII 21, 49; Benzing *Lutherbibliographie* nos 755–63 (nine Latin editions 1520–1) and nos 734–46 (thirteen of the German version). For possible hints of Erasmus' acquaintance with the work at this time cf below lines 172–5, Epp 1203:9–14, 1244:19–21.
11 husband the truth] Cf below lines 53–5, 124–5, 142–8, and see the preface.
12 Aristotelian system] Erasmus may have thought of Luther's *De captivitate Babylonica* (Luther W VI 508, 510; cf Ep 1186 n3), but the analogies are not specific; cf below n49, and also Luther W I 650, II 396, VI 29.
13 bids his followers … kingdom of God] Cf Matt 10:7, Mark 6:7–12, 16:15–16, Luke 24:47.
14 multitude … to the church] Cf Acts 2:41.
15 urging them … untoward generation] Cf Acts 2:40.
16 drunk with new wine] Cf Acts 2:13–15.
17 testimony of Joel] Cf Acts 2:16–21, Joel 3:1–5 (2:28–32).
18 just man … authority of God] Acts 3:14, 17–26
19 'Men and brethren … David'] Acts 2:29
20 Paul … for Christ] Cf I Cor 9:22; below Ep 1233 n18.
21 'And the times … winked at'] Acts 17:30
22 'men of Athens'] Acts 17:22
23 worship of demons] Cf Acts 17:16.
24 inscriptions on an altar] Cf Acts 17:23; Paul's cunning is explained more fully in Erasmus' corresponding note to the New Testament, where he quotes Jerome; see LB VI 501E.
25 but a man] Cf Acts 17:31.
26 Aratus] Cf Acts 17:28; Aratus, a Stoic philosopher of the third century BC, is identified as Paul's source in Erasmus' note on this passage; see LB VI 502D–E.
27 Festus … Agrippa] Cf Acts 26.
28 Augustine … charity] Cf Ep 1167:347–57.
29 not their destruction] Cf below lines 330–1, Ep 1153 n6.
30 Paul … gentiles] Cf Rom 13:1, Titus 3:1.
31 recantation … high priest] Cf Acts 23:2–5.
32 servants … than they did before] Cf Eph 6:5, Col 3:22, 1 Tim 6:1, Titus 2:9.
33 wives … of the Gospel] Cf I Cor 7:13–16.
34 Brutus] Cf Cicero *Epistulae ad Brutum* 25.
35 Plato] Cf Ep 1167 n27.

36 reliable physicians … overwhelm] Cf Ep 1219 n21.
37 as the Greek proverb has it] Cf *Adagia* I i 62.
38 Paul … to the flesh] Gal 5:13–14
39 encouraged … than that] This argument was probably written with Hutten in mind; cf Ep 1129 n7.
40 he-goat in the fable] Cf Ep 1186 n6.
41 unless Christ … public good] Cf Ep 1205 n10.
42 burden Reuchlin … ill will] Cf Ep 1155 n2, n5.
43 sent Luther … Leipzig] Ep 980; cf Ep 1123 n5.
44 a letter under seal] Ep 1033, addressed to Albert of Brandenburg
45 Willibald … letter to me] Willibald Pirckheimer's letter appears to be lost. As a plausible example of a printed letter that may not actually have been sent Pirckheimer, Allen suggested the preface of the *Epistolae duae* by Heinrich Stromer and Gregor Kopp; see Ep 1083 introduction.
46 selection of tendentious statements … in German translation] Erasmus' concern is understandable in view of the copious material collected by Heinz Holeczek in his *Erasmus Deutsch*, esp I 81–108. In particular Holeczek describes no less than thirty anonymous editions, all dated 1521, of individually selected texts from Erasmus' *Annotationes* to the New Testament of 1518/19. They include eg a translation of Erasmus' note on Matt 16:18 ('*Tu es Petrus*'), in which he argues that with these words Christ was laying the foundations of the Christian faith rather than the papal office, and on Matt 11:29–30, in which he comments critically on vows, oral confession, the papal ban, and Aristotelian philosophy. In writing to Jonas, Erasmus may well have guessed what circles stood behind these anonymous pamphlets. Holeczek suggests that the translator was Georgius Spalatinus, and Jonas, who was then preparing to move to Wittenberg, was in close contact with Spalatinus.
47 Santiago] Santiago de Compostela, famous centre of pilgrimage; cf Ep 858:433–8.
48 young men … what that life is] Cf Epp 858:521–5, 1183 n32.
49 Luther] Allen suggested that the following statements attributed to Luther were derived from the *Determinatio* of the theological faculty of Paris (cf Ep 1141 n10). It lists passages deemed to be heretical, which in fact mention Aristotle and Dionysius the Areopagite. But there is not otherwise a verbal resemblance to Erasmus' text here, and in the absence of an adequate critical edition of the *Determinatio* (cf Luther w VIII 267–90) further study is required.
50 burden of confession] Cf above n46, Ep 1225 n29, and also Ep 1167 n49 for similar criticism of Luther.
51 books of Dionysius … seem to promise] Here and in Ep 1225:235–7 Erasmus is perhaps referring to his note on Acts 17:34 (*Annotationes* 1518/19, 225; LB VI 503), which argued against the identity of Dionysius the writer with the biblical Areopagite and also mentioned Origen and Chrysostom.
52 kicks over the traces] Literally 'leaps over the fence'; cf *Adagia* I x 93.
53 Paul … Peter] Cf 2 Pet 3:15–16.
54 Pamphlets … depicted] One perfect example of the kind of illustrated pamphlet so irritating to Erasmus – what others may have perished we do not know – is the earliest Reformation pamphlet printed by Christoph Froschauer in Zürich, *Die göttliche Mühle* (1521). The unnamed author is thought to have been Martin Seger, while Zwingli arranged the publication. A woodcut

(reproduced on page 208 above) shows God's mill restored to a proper working order. Christ pours the wheat of the Gospels, Erasmus bags the flour, and Luther kneads the dough, which is being distributed to the clergy in the form of books. The pope, a cardinal, and a bishop refuse to receive their copies. A bird crying 'ban' is charging towards Luther, but 'Karsthans,' the type of the gallant peasant, is intercepting it; see Joachim Staedtke *Anfänge und erste Blütezeit des Zürcher Buchdrucks* (Zürich 1967) 44–5 and Holeczek *Erasmus Deutsch* I 12–13.

55 Ruthenians] Cf Ep 1177 n3.
56 Turks] Cf Ep 1167 n31.
57 broken reeds] Cf *Adagia* I vii 85.
58 our native Germany] Cf CWE 7 preface.
59 Luther ... end in strife.] Cf Ep 1195 n11.
60 disputations ... not free] Cf Ep 1163:12–18.
61 Hutten ... tumults] Cf Epp 1135, 1161 introductions.
62 Melanchthon] Ep 1113 to Melanchthon seems to be inspired by the same concern.
63 leave them to their Lord and Master] Cf Ep 1183:146–7.
64 Philippus] Melanchthon; cf introduction.
65 put down] Cf above n29.

1203

1 liberty of the Gospel] Cf Ep 1202 n10.
2 safe keeping] When Erasmus wrote this Luther had been at the Wartburg for just ten days, having been carried off on his return from Worms (cf Ep 1197 introduction), on orders from Frederick the Wise, elector of Saxony, who at Worms denied any knowledge of Luther's fate. In view of the wild rumours about Luther's disappearance circulating everywhere (cf Ep 1221 n8) Erasmus proved to be remarkably well informed. See Herbert von Hintzenstern *300 Tage Einsamkeit. Dokumente und Daten aus Luthers Wartburgzeit* (Berlin 1967).
3 vent their fury here ... best people] Cf Ep 1174 n1.
4 Stephen himself] Cf Ep 1185 n4.
5 evil spirit] Cf Ep 1199 n1.
6 in Cologne ... clemency] Cf Epp 1149, 1155 introductions.
7 burns the decretals] Cf Ep 1197 introduction.
8 *De captivitate Babylonica*] Cf Ep 1186 n3.
9 assertions] *Assertio omnium articulorum M. Lutheri per bullam Leonis X novissimam damnatorum* (Luther W VII 91–151; Benzing *Lutherbibliographie* nos 779–83: five editions 1520–1); cf Ep 1195 n20.
10 in collusion with Luther] Cf Ep 1182 n4.
11 your way] To Basel; cf Ep 1242 introduction.

1204

1 as Plato ... says] See Plato *Epistles* 9.358a.
2 Florus] He produced an epitome of Livy's history of Rome.
3 not everything] Barlandus published no more than short abstracts of the adages he had selected.
4 St Augustine] Cf Ep 1144 n17.

1205

1 Zacharias of Friesland] Little is known about Zacharias Deiotarus (Diotorus) of Friesland. He seems to have settled in England by 1519 and to have remained there until his death in 1533. Apart from this letter there is no record of his earlier service with Erasmus, nor of his entry into Warham's household. A loyal friend and admirer, he continued to write to Erasmus; see Epp 1990, 2237, 2496.

2 that Italian] Perhaps Benedetto de' Fornari, Antwerp banker and agent for Raffaele Maruffo, another Genoese banker established in London (cf Ep 892:21–2). Both had previously been involved in the payment of the annuity from the living of Aldington, which Warham had given Erasmus (cf Epp 255, 823 introductions). His 'deputy' (line 14) could be Maruffo, or possibly vice versa.

3 stuivers] The current Burgundian-Hapsburg silver double gros (2d), also known as the patard. Cf CWE 1 327, 331, and Table A, 349 above.

4 I lose fifteen florins] The transaction discussed here concerns a recurrent remittance (cf lines 16–18), no doubt Erasmus' annuity from Aldington (for payments of which in 1517/18–1519/20 see Ep 823 introduction). From what is stated here one may assume that Erasmus had been remitted the sum of 150 florins (money-of-account) or £25 gros Flemish, as the supposed equivalent of one year's Aldington annuity, £20 sterling. But in fact those 150 florins were worth only £17 or £18 sterling at best. Erasmus might have expected to receive, after the deduction of all charges, around 160 florins (and £20 sterling should have been worth around 175 florins). Cf Ep 823:7n; CWE 1 347. This payment may have been for the year ending on Lady Day (25 March) 1522, as requested by Erasmus in Ep 1176:9–11. If so, only the remittance of the preceding year (to Lady Day 1521) seems to have left no record in his correspondence.

5 deputy ... itch too] Cf above n2.

6 complaint] Erasmus plays on words by using here again the Latin word '*scabies*,' previously translated as 'itch.'

7 hot spell ... fever] Cf Ep 1208 introduction.

8 labour I cannot escape] Right then Erasmus was probably struggling to complete the revision of the New Testament (cf Ep 1174 n6). Another 'great object' was the edition of St Augustine; see Ep 1204:29–32.

9 annuity] It seems that Erasmus had now received another half-yearly instalment of his annuity as councillor (cf Ep 1151 n1), no doubt as a result of his patient lobbying at court (cf Ep 1143 n23), which also netted a patent confirming his appointment (cf Ep 1166 n1). In 1517 it had been proposed that one of two semi-annual payments be made at Pentecost (cf Ep 565:17), which in 1521 was 19 May.

10 unless Christ converts ... folly] Cf Ep 1202:197–9, 1228:39–41. The saying about the owl rescuing the Athenians is in *Adagia* I viii 44.

11 Scylla ... Charybdis] Cf Ep 1186 n5.

12 bellies] Cf Ep 1166 n3.

13 thoughtful enquiries ... need] Apart from the missing letter from Deiotarus (cf lines 1–2), see also Ep 1176:3–5.

14 two servants] Johannes Hovius and Lieven Algoet; cf Epp 1091, 1209 n4.

15 benefice] Deiotarus' letter may have repeated an offer earlier made through Thomas Bedyll (cf Ep 1176 n1). Conceivably one should also assign to this period Warham's offer of a substantial cash gift on arrival in England, which is presented in Allen and CWE as Ep 214. That offer was reported by Gerard Geldenhouwer on a page of his *Collectanea* apparently written in 1521. Erasmus did not, however, consider a return to England in the foreseeable future; cf below lines 51–3.

16 carcass] Cf Job 39:30, Matt 24:28, Luke 17:37.

1206

1 my friends in Germany ... unpopular] Cf Ep 1186:27–9.

2 first edition] The *Auctarium* of August 1518 (cf Ep 886:57n), followed by the *Farrago*; cf Ep 1009 introduction.

3 furiously angry] Apart from the many critical reactions to Ep 980, addressed to Luther, cf Epp 1123 n1, 1170, 1225:154–60.

4 Piso] Jacobus Piso, then Polish ambassador to the papal court, met Erasmus at Siena in 1509; cf Ep 216.

5 making some things explicit ... had been put] Cf Epp 948, 966, 973 introductions, 999 n10, n28, n32.

6 removing ... offence] Cf Epp 287:15n, 1123 n1, 1170 n3.

7 paraphrases] Probably the collection of March 1521; cf Ep 1171 introduction.

8 misguided ... often is] Cf Epp 885 introduction, 886:30.

9 New Testament] The printer's copy for the third edition; cf Ep 1174 n6.

10 whole expense ... charged to me] For the financial arrangements between Erasmus and the Froben press cf Ep 885 introduction. By stating this point in public Erasmus no doubt wished to impress upon the readers that he had done all he could to prevent the printing of offensive statements.

11 satisfy all men] Cf Epp 1202:101–2, 1233 n18.

12 evil genius of mine] Cf below lines 136–8, Ep 1136 n4.

13 Brutus and Phalaris] As Erasmus rightly detected, the letters attributed to them, in Greek, are the spurious productions of some later rhetorician.

14 Paul and Seneca] The correspondence, in Latin, of St Paul and Seneca is a forgery of unknown date; cf Ep 325:78–81.

15 Aeneas Pius] Enea Silvio Piccolomini, Pope Pius II, 1405–64

16 as Horace says] *Odes* 2.1.6

17 Tiro] Marcus Tullius Tiro, eventually freed by his master, was Cicero's slave and secretary, who edited his correspondence after his death.

18 St Bernard's ... black mark] See, for instance, St Bernard of Clairvaux's epistolary campaign against Pierre Abélard in *Opera* VII–VIII ed J. Leclercq and H. Rochais (Rome 1974–7) Epp 188–93 and passim.

19 1520] This year, which is wrong of course, was added in the *Opus epistolarum* of 1529.

1207

1 by mention ... works] See Epp 334:132–3, 335:327–31, 396:295–300.

2 supervising ... New Testament] Cf Ep 864. According to Ep 904:42–3 Basilius did not, however, read any of the proofs for the second edition of the New Testament.

3 Glaucus and Diomede] They exchanged armour in Homer, one suit being of gold and the other of bronze, and so became proverbial for any unfair exchange; cf *Adagia* I ii 1.
4 Delphian oracle] Using the adage *'ex tripode,'* I vii 90.
5 New Testament] The third edition; cf Ep 1174 n6.
6 go abroad] A letter of 30 June 1521 from Albert Burer to Basilius (AK II Ep 797) suggests that Amerbach had intended to leave Basel in Burer's company for a visit to Wittenberg but had subsequently changed his mind.
7 no stone unturned] Cf *Adagia* I iv 30.
8 Bonifacius] For Basilius' brother cf Ep 1233A. On 22 May 1521 Udalricus Zasius wrote from Freiburg, encouraging Bonifacius to visit him in the near future (AK II Ep 785:21).

1208

1 Leonard] He is not identified; Allen suggested Leonard Casembroot (1495–1558), who started his career as a tutor of highly-placed youths. He was a protégé of Erasmus' friend Marcus Laurinus and later a correspondent of Erasmus; cf Ep 1594.
2 son] Presumably the eldest son, Hendrik, born after 1504, or the second, Maarten, born in 1509. The boy and his tutor may have been staying in Anderlecht, or perhaps in Gaasbeek (cf the introduction) or Brussels.
3 gather] Reading *'colligo'* for *'cogito'*

1209

1 a house for me] When leaving for Anderlecht (cf Ep 1208 introduction), Erasmus had given up his lodgings in the College of the Lily (cf Ep 643:14n). Although he expected to be away for about a year, he intended eventually to return to Louvain (cf Allen Ep 1257:10). For further details of Erasmus' residence in the Lily see Allen's note.
2 New Testament] Accepting Allen's tentative emendation, 'Novum Testamentum,' for an incomprehensible 'nomen, tamen'; cf Allen Ep 1342:89–93.
3 Rutgerus] Rutgerus Rescius; cf Ep 1240.
4 Swiss friend] He is not identified; conceivably Johannes Hovius, of whose origins no more is known than that he had entered Erasmus' service at Basel (cf Ep 867:189n) or a messenger recently sent by Johann Froben (cf Ep 1210), conceivably Froben's son Hieronymus (cf Ep 1226). Allen's suggestion that Hieronymus was at this time in Erasmus' service is contradicted by Ep 1205:48.
5 rascal] Erasmus uses the German term 'Schnapphahn' (prowler). He must be referring to the messenger who had taken Ep 1203 to Basel (cf Ep 1207 introduction) and on his return had probably just then arrived in Anderlecht en route to Louvain, carrying the shirt sent by Gertrud Lachner, Johann Froben's wife.

1210

1 proverbs] The *Adagiorum liber* of July 1521; cf Ep 1175 introduction, n3.
2 *De rerum inventoribus*] Reprinted by Froben with the *Adagia*; cf Ep 1175 introduction.

3 Hieronymus] Cf Epp 1175 introduction, 1226.
4 treasurer] More was knighted (cf Ep 1220 n1) and also appointed under-treasurer of the exchequer in May 1521. While his duties in that office were light, the annual salary of £173 6s 8d sterling (worth about 1500 florins Flemish or £250 gros) was considerable; cf Epp 1223:50–2, 1233:25–7, and J.A. Guy *The Public Career of Sir Thomas More* (New Haven 1980) 24.
5 seeing him ... in August] Cf Ep 1223 introduction.
6 notebooks ... Rome] In the winter of 1508–9 Erasmus had left some manuscripts with Pace at Ferrara; Pace in turn left them behind in Rome; cf Epp 211:53n, 1110:41–6, 1224 introduction, 1227:3–6, 39–41.
7 *Antibarbari*] Cf Ep 1110 introduction.

1211

1 portrait in miniature] Cf Ep 999:20–1, 28–9.
2 Saint-Omer] In May 1501; cf Ep 153 introduction.
3 Mountjoy] William Blount, Lord Mountjoy, had been Erasmus' pupil in Paris.
4 Vitrier] Jean Vitrier, born c 1456 at Saint-Omer, an Observant Franciscan (cf Ep 163:5n). Despite the pioneering efforts of André Godin, who discovered and published Vitrier's book of homilies (Geneva 1971), Vitrier's life is not well known. For many of the following details Erasmus' account is the only source known to date.
5 tall and well-built] The same Latin adjectives are used to describe Colet; see line 290.
6 Scotist philosophy] Cf below n69.
7 Origen] Cf Epp 165:9–12, 1167:296–7 and for Erasmus' own tendency to concur with Vitrier's view cf Ep 844:272–4. See André Godin *Erasme lecteur d'Origène* (Geneva 1982) 26–7 and passim.
8 ignorance of youth] Cf Ep 1183 n32.
9 sleep again] Cf Epp 296:19–20, 447:439.
10 Paul] Cf 1 Cor 8:9, 9:20, 22.
11 knew his fingers and toes] Quoted from Juvenal 7.232; cf *Adagia* II iv 91. Erasmus uses the same expression with regard to Origen (see LB VIII 438B).
12 divide his sermons ... preachers do] 'Divisio' was a well-established norm in the medieval art of preaching; see J.J. Murphy *Rhetoric in the Middle Ages* (Berkeley 1974) 310–11, 324, and passim.
13 noisy ranting] A passage in Erasmus' *Ecclesiastes* (LB V 987C) further emphasizes the contrast between preachers seeking cheap popularity and a Franciscan modelling himself after Paul (paraphrasing again 1 Cor 9:22; cf above n10, Ep 1233 n18). Vitrier is identified as the Franciscan in question in the alphabetical index of the third edition of the *Ecclesiastes* (Basel: H. Froben and N. Episcopius August 1536).
14 Scotus or Thomas or Durandus] Cf below n69, n70. Durand of Saint-Pourçain was a fourteenth-century representative of the school of Nominalism.
15 house of ... nuns] The convent of St Margaret's at Saint-Omer
16 Jacobite ... bishop] Jean Vasseur (cf Ep 130:75–9). There is evidence that Vasseur was the driving force later on behind Vitrier's enforced resignation from his wardenship at Saint-Omer; see below lines 248–50 and CEBR III.
17 bishop of Thérouanne] Cardinal Philippe de Luxembourg (1445–1519), a

prelate attached to the royal court of France, whose mother was an aunt of Louis XI. In 1476 he was bishop of Le Mans and in 1498 he was confirmed as bishop of Thérouanne. He also held several other sees at one time or another.

18 a mule or a horse as he went] The point Erasmus wishes to make is that Vitrier cheerfully broke certain rules of his order. The statutes of the Observant Franciscans, as ratified at the general chapter of Barcelona, 1451, renewed older prohibitions for the brethren to travel other than on foot and especially condemned an evasion by which a mule was substituted for the horse specifically forbidden by the older rules. The statutes of Barcelona also laid down that whenever possible the brethren should travel in pairs; cf below lines 153, 169, 201. See *Monumenta Franciscana* II ed Richard Howlett (London 1882) xxiv, 95.

19 swans … die] Cf *Adagia* I ii 55.

20 Ghisbert] The town physician of Saint-Omer; cf Ep 95:13n.

21 mighty works … people] Cf Matt 13:58, Mark 6:5.

22 anxious … confessions he openly abominated] The same is said of Colet (see below lines 533–5). Cf also *De concordia*, LB V 502B.

23 God delights … cheerful giver] Cf 2 Cor 9:7.

24 at the time] In the winter of 1501–2; cf Epp 163:5–6, 169 introduction.

25 companion … layman] Cf above n18 and line 153.

26 two jubilees out of one] The interval between holy years had been reduced to twenty-five from fifty (1343) and thirty-three (1389) by Pope Paul II in 1470. Erasmus probably recalled the indulgence offered in Alexander VI's bull of 1 June 1500, inaugurating the jubilee of that year.

27 Tournai] Erasmus probably meant to say 'Thérouanne'; cf above n17, below line 200.

28 foolish confidence … free from sin] Cf Ep 1188 n19.

29 new church] Consecrated on 12 June 1502

30 'the accursed … gold'] Virgil *Aeneid* 3.57

31 the man concerned] He has not been identified, but is described, as Allen noted, in terms reminiscent of Johann Poppenruyter, to whom Erasmus dedicated the *Enchiridion*, which was written at the time of his close contacts with Vitrier (cf Allen I 19–20, Ep 164). On the other hand, if the episode belongs to that period and consequently to the region of Saint-Omer, one might seek the courtier at the castle of Courtebourne, perhaps among the family of Antony of Burgundy, 'le Grand Bâtard.'

32 which he did] In 1502, after two years in office

33 a man … whom I know] He is not identified.

34 Courtrai] There were several nunneries in and near Courtrai.

35 short books in French] Only his book of homilies is known today; cf above n4.

36 father … lord mayor] Sir Henry Colet (d 1505) was lord mayor of London in 1486 and 1495.

37 mother] Dame Christian Knyvet, who died in 1523, was fondly remembered by Erasmus as late as 1532; cf Allen Ep 2684:74–80.

38 sons … daughters] Lupton has identified one son, Thomas (d 8 September 1479). In his annotated translation (cf introduction) he mentions a stained glass window showing ten sons and ten daughters.

39 title ... arts] Colet is often thought to have taken his MA at Oxford c 1490; cf below n48.
40 Plato] Cf Ep 118:24–5.
41 France ... Italy] Colet was at Rome in March–May 1493 and visited Orléans and perhaps Paris on his return from Italy, 1494–5; cf Epp 106:4, 480:224–6.
42 so unfair as Augustine] The Latin '*iniquior*' probably should be taken here to mean unfair in the sense of 'partial to, showing undue preference for' (cf the analogy in lines 29–33 above). Colet quoted Augustine more often than any other Father and without any sign of disapproval (cf Lupton's annotated translation 22, and his *Life of Colet* 57). As this account is written with great care, it is unlikely that Erasmus would have rashly generalized upon any odd incident where Colet might in fact have criticized Augustine.
43 Scotus and Thomas] Cf below n69, n70.
44 authors who did ... for the Italians] Here and in an enlargement of this thought in the *Ecclesiastes* (LB V 856AB) Erasmus fails to name the English writers he offers for comparison with Dante (1265–1321) and Francesco Petrarca (1304–74). This is probably an indication that he was not so familiar with such names as John Gower (c 1330–1408) and Geoffrey Chaucer (c 1340–1400).
45 without fee] Cf below line 375, Ep 1053 n72.
46 St Paul] Cf Ep 108:76n.
47 first knew him] In the summer of 1499, when Colet was thirty-three or perhaps thirty-two. For Erasmus' own age cf Ep 940:8n.
48 theology ... no degree whatever] For Colet's academic studies there are no sources that are prior to or clearly independent of Erasmus' letters; cf above lines 291–3, below lines 318–22, and for details see CEBR I.
49 title of doctor] Probably in 1504; cf Ep 181:20n.
50 dean of St Paul's] Colet was certainly dean by May 1505; cf Ep 181:21n.
51 given up supper entirely] Cf below lines 433–5. Thomas Lupset followed this example, of which Erasmus disapproved (cf Ep 1229:19–20). Archbishop William Warham was likewise accustomed to go without supper; cf the *Ecclesiastes* (LB V 811C).
52 conversation ... serious people] According to *Adagia* I x 74, Colet used to say that one's daily conversation was the measure of a man; cf the importance properly attached to Luther's table talk, recorded by a number of contemporaries and first edited by Johannes Aurifaber in 1566; cf Luther w *Tischreden* I–VI.
53 of Christ] Cf below line 360, Ep 1027:7–8.
54 on pilgrimage] Their pilgrimage to Canterbury is described in the colloquy *Peregrinatio religionis ergo*, ASD I-3 470–94; cf also *Modus orandi Deum*, ASD V-1 154.
55 new school] Although schooling facilities for the choirboys of St Paul's had existed previously, Colet's foundation, established in 1508–12, was truly new both in enrolment and in scope; see M.F.J. McDonnell *The Annals of St Paul's School* (Cambridge 1959) 1–57.
56 boy Jesus ... teacher] Erasmus wrote some epigrams suitable as an inscription for this picture, which were first printed in 1511 (cf Ep 175 introduction and Reedijk nos 86–90). His *De puero Iesu* was also written for Colet's school

(cf Allen I 21). In the elementary grammar (accidence) Colet composed for the teaching of Latin in his new school there is a Latin prayer to 'the boy Jesus, head of this school'; see Lupton *Life of Colet* 290.

57 'Hear ye him'] Matt 17:5, Luke 9:35

58 immensely expensive ... burden] Cf Ep 260:30–5.

59 his bishop] Richard Fitzjames (d 1522) had spent thirty years in Oxford when he was appointed bishop of Rochester in 1497. In 1503 he was transferred to the see of Chichester and in 1506 to that of London. He undertook important renovations at St Paul's cathedral. For Erasmus' frank assessment of him see below lines 575–80.

60 used the money ... cathedral] Colet defended the practice of assigning bequests to another purpose, provided it was more consonant to the will of God and the spirit of charity; see his *Opuscula quaedam theologica. Letters to Radulphus* ..., ed J.H. Lupton (London 1896; repr 1966) 112–13, 244–5.

61 in charge of the finances] A more detailed discussion of these arrangements is found in Erasmus' *De pronuntiatione* (ASD I-4 24). It was in fact the Mercers' Company which Colet appointed trustees of his foundation; see *Acts of Court of the Mercers' Company, 1453–1527* ed L. Lyell and F.D. Watney (Cambridge 1936) 360–4.

62 married citizens of approved reputation] Cf below lines 495–9.

63 splendid house] Colet called it his 'nest' in Ep 314:12. In Lent 1530 it was occupied by Cardinal Wolsey after he had been forced to relinquish the chancellorship (see Allen's note). Richmond is south-west of London; cf below n102, Ep 287.

64 sweating sickness] Perhaps during the momentous epidemic of 1517 (cf Epp 623, 639:3n). Cardinal Wolsey had no less than four attacks within a month; see Sebastiano Giustiniani *Four Years at the Court of ... Henry VIII* tr R. Brown (London 1854) II 120, 127.

65 IOAN. COL.] No doubt Colet himself had asked that no more be written on his tomb, which probably disappeared around 1680 in the course of renovations in St Paul's. An epitaph in verse by William Lily was placed near the tomb, but before 1633 another, in prose, was engraved on the stone. In his *Life of Colet* (ch 13) Lupton compares it to Ep 1053:581–6 and argues that it may have been composed by either Erasmus or Thomas Lupset.

66 love of money] Cf Ep 270:28–43.

67 Christ calls ... imitate] Cf Matt 18:1–4.

68 second topic] Cf above line 421.

69 Scotists] Erasmus had pointed out earlier that Colet's low opinion of John Duns Scotus and other scholastic philosophers was not uninformed (cf lines 302–4). Vitrier's seems to have been only a little more favourable (cf lines 24–7). So was Erasmus' own (cf lines 576–80, and Epp 1127A:11–13, 1183: 128–31), although in recent years he had been anxious to avoid any confrontation with scholastic theologians, as long as they did not attack him; cf Epp 1002 n4, 1125 introduction.

70 praised Thomas] St Thomas Aquinas; cf Ep 1126:289–93.

71 *Catena aurea*] The 'Golden Chain' is a gloss of continuous commentary on the four Gospels, based on a variety of authors. Even in modern times it has retained some of its popularity.

72 among the Italians ... wise and pious] In view of Colet's interest in contemporary Florentine Platonism, one is reminded of the abbey of Camaldoli, south-east of Florence, and in particular of abbot Mariotto Allegri, 'a man of proven piety and scholarship,' who is thus introduced, together with Marsilio Ficino and others, in Cristoforo Landino's *Disputationes Camaldolenses* (printed in Florence 1478); cf *The letters of Marsilio Ficino* (London 1975) Ep 119; Sears Jayne *John Colet and Marsilio Ficino* (Oxford 1963).

73 certain Germans] Cf perhaps Ep 423:26–8.

74 married couples] Cf above lines 398–403.

75 Dionysius] Probably during his years at Oxford (c 1495–c 1503) Colet composed a condensed paraphrase of the *Hierarchiae* of Dionysius then usually thought to be the Areopagite; cf below n80.

76 adoration of images] Well before the beginning of the Protestant reformation, this position had led to trouble for Colet; see lines 589–91.

77 a priest ... sacramental function] Allen's note quotes evidence to show that Vitrier was among those who doubted whether a sinning priest could efficaciously administer the sacraments. Colet's qualified sympathy for this position, which is at variance with orthodox theology, was shared by Erasmus; cf Epp 1053:458–60, 1188:11–15.

78 colleges] In *De pronuntiatione* (ASD I-4 24) Erasmus refers in a similar context to *collegia canonicorum* 'chapters of canons.' Some of these, however, were closely connected with medieval universities and colleges.

79 anxious ... just as much] Cf above n22.

80 a book] Lupton and Allen draw attention here to a *Breviloquium* of the sayings of Christ, which was first listed among Colet's writings by Konrad Gesner in 1551; nothing is known of it today. For Colet's penchant for arranging notions into groups of three cf his *Super opera Dionysii* ed J.H. Lupton (London 1869; repr 1966) 99, 104–5, 191–2 and his marginalia to his copy of Ficino's letters, see Jayne (above n72) 86, 97–9.

81 a splendid thing] Lines 535–42 above show that for Colet what mattered was the 'lively feeling' of the celebrating priest, which might be dampened by the repetitive mechanism of 'long prayers every day.'

82 a hindrance to good writing] This point is borne out by Colet's accidence (cf above n56, Lupton *Life of Colet* 291–2). In editing Colet's *Super opera Dionysii* (above n80), Lupton noted in Colet's 'a certain inaccuracy of diction' (page xiii). For Erasmus' own view cf Ep 1115:31–6.

83 refrained from writing books] Colet's known writings, all of minor scale, probably date from his years at Oxford and were not printed until 1869–76. The exception is one sermon published in 1512; cf CEBR I.

84 storms ... shaken] Cf above lines 421–2.

85 his diocesan] Bishop Fitzjames; cf above n59.

86 Scotist] Cf above n69.

87 was he] Colet

88 Eastminster] This is quite an unusual way to refer to St Paul's, chosen no doubt to establish an analogy with Westminster Abbey. There was a Cistercian abbey (St Mary de Graces) near the Tower, but St Paul's was never the location of a monastery.

89 weapon ... destroy someone] Recent parallels were the lists of Luther's errors

inserted in the condemnations of the universities of Cologne, Louvain, and Paris as well as the bull *Exsurge, Domine*, and also the scrutiny of Erasmus' own works by the theologians of Louvain; cf the preface of CWE 7.

90 archbishop of Canterbury] William Warham did not proceed with the action against Colet, but Erasmus at one time accused him of siding with Colet's accusers; cf Ep 414:6–7.

91 not worship images] Cf above lines 520–2.

92 Paul ... hospitality] Cf Rom 12:13, Titus 1:8.

93 passage] John 21:15–17

94 unjust peace ... most just of wars] Cf Cicero *Epistulae ad familiares* 6.6.5. The dictum is also reported by Richard Pace in his *De fructu* (repr and tr. Frank Manley and R.S. Sylvester, New York 1967, 104–5; cf Ep 776:4n). Colet's initiatives at the outset of the campaigns of 1512 and 1513 (cf below n97) are discussed in R.A. Adams *The Better Part of Valor* (Seattle 1962) 66–71.

95 two Minorites] Edmund Birkhead (cf below n103) and Henry Standish, who succeeded Birkhead at his death as bishop of St Asaph. For Standish's powerful voice cf *Adagia* II v 98.

96 poets] Cf Ep 1153 n42.

97 expedition ... against the French] The campaign against Courtrai and Thérouanne in the spring of 1513.

98 Good Friday] 25 March 1513. Allen's note presents evidence that from 1510 to 1517, with the possible exception of 1514, Colet preached each Good Friday before the court. The English expeditionary force against France set sail from Plymouth on 20 April.

99 Julius and Alexander] Julius Caesar and Alexander the Great, but Colet and his audience in 1513 would also recall the warrior popes, Julius II and Alexander VI.

100 like birds mobbing an owl] Cf Ovid *Metamorphoses* 11.24–5.

101 house of Franciscans] This house was built on a site granted to the Observant Franciscans c 1480 and maintained close connections with the royal family. Henry VIII and Catherine of Aragon were married in its chapel, and the princesses Mary and Elizabeth were baptized there; for details see Allen's note.

102 palace at Greenwich] Contrary to Henry VII, who preferred Richmond (cf above n63), Henry VIII in this period normally chose Greenwich when he wished to be near London. The manor of Greenwich had fallen to the crown at the death of Humphrey, Duke of Gloucester in 1447.

103 Bricotus] Edmund Birkhead or Bricotus (d 1518), a Franciscan, lived in the Cambridge house of his order 1501–3 while earning a doctorate in theology. From 1511 to 1516 he was regularly one of the Lenten preachers at court. In 1513 he was named to the bishopric of St Asaph, which he held until his death.

104 never be a just war] Cf Ep 1232:56–60.

105 proverb] Cf *Adagia* II iii 58.

1212

1 Pieter de Vriendt] Cf Ep 1173 n2.

2 your suffragan] Nicolas Bureau; cf Ep 1144 n12.

3 scorpion ... venom] Cf Ep 1196 n6.
4 a certain monk] Cf Ep 1192:29–33.
5 New Testament] Cf Ep 1174 n6.
6 St Augustine] Cf Ep 1144 n17.
7 Clichtove] Clichtove (cf Ep 594:15n) was now Guillard's secretary.

1213

1 studious life of long ago] At Bologna in 1506–7
2 return to teaching] At Bologna Bombace had taught the humanities from 1505 to 1512.
3 four hundred ducats] This sum, worth £133 6s 8d gros Flemish or 800 'florins,' almost £92 sterling, was far in excess of the salaries of seventy and one hundred ducats offered to Greek professors in Louvain and Venice respectively, then thought to be substantial; cf Epp 836:8n, 854:60–1, and Table B, 350 above.
4 Hercules ... free] There was a legend that he had descended to the nether regions to bring back Theseus.
5 last letter to me] It thus seems that Bombace had heard from Erasmus more than once in the not so distant past. Letters to Bombace could have been sent with Epp 1143–4, 1167 and possibly with an answer to Ep 1180 (cf Ep 1236:14). Aleandro was under the impression that Erasmus communicated frequently with Rome (cf Balan nos 21, 36). For the contents of his messages cf below lines 55–61.
6 my master] Cardinal Lorenzo Pucci; cf Ep 1000.
7 Sadoleto] For Jacopo Sadoleto cf Ep 1180 introduction.
8 a certain person] Erasmus' answer suggests that he did not feel free to complain about this critic to the pope directly (cf Ep 1236:12–15). No doubt he was Aleandro; cf Epp 1167 n20, 1218:11–17, 1219:18–20.
9 Spaniard] Diego López Zúñiga (cf Ep 1128 n2). At the time of Leo X's death (cf Ep 1248 n13), the injunction was apparently in danger of being revoked; see Allen Epp 1260:188–94, 1268:70–5, and cf Ep 1180 introduction.
10 take up arms ... vigorously] Cf Epp 1180 introduction, 1228 n11.
11 offending many people] The supporters of Luther; cf Epp 1144:70–3, n16, 1162:72–6, 1225:268–72.
12 certain idiots ... on purpose] Perhaps an echo of Erasmus' own words about some of Luther's opponents; cf Epp 1167:449–55, 1195:43–52, also Ep 1182 n4.
13 reached Basel] Cf Epp 1143 n22, 1242 introduction.
14 Vatican library] When Erasmus no longer hoped to visit Rome (cf Ep 1143 n22) in time to make changes in the third edition of his New Testament (cf Ep 1174 n6), he must have asked Bombace to consult for him the Greek manuscripts in the Vatican Library. The following citations come from the famous codex Vaticanus B. Although Erasmus answered Bombace's letter at a time he was still revising the *Annotationes*, it was not until after the third edition that he added a reference to Bombace's help and the readings of the Vatican manuscript; see LB VI 1080E.
15 chapter 4] 1 John 4:1–3; Erasmus' text represents the reading commonly accepted today, whereas Bombace's differs from it in two minor points.

16 chapter 5] 1 John 5:7–11; Bombace's text represents the reading commonly accepted today, whereas the Latin Vulgate adds to 5:7–8 the only explicit reference to the Trinity of Father, Son, and Holy Spirit found in the New Testament (the so-called *comma Johanneum*). In the second edition of 1518/19 (cf Ep 864) Erasmus still ommitted this addition, stating merely that he had not found it in the Greek text. In his second *Responsio* to Edward Lee (cf Ep 1080 introduction) he explained that he would have accepted the passage had he been able to find it in a single Greek manuscript (cf LB IX 275B). As a result he was presented with the evidence of what is now MS Trinity College Dublin A 4.21. This manuscript was said to be an old codex, but was actually written about 1520 by a Franciscan at Oxford, who translated the *comma* from Latin into Greek. Erasmus stood by his earlier statement and added it at first to a separate edition of the Latin translation (Basel: J. Froben June 1521) and subsequently to the third edition (1522) of the entire New Testament, but in a note added to the third edition he expressed his suspicion that the manuscript was a fabrication (cf LB VI 1080D). Today no Greek manuscript dating from before the sixteenth century is known to contain the *comma Johanneum*; see ASD IX-2 12, 258–9 and B.M. Metzger *The Text of the New Testament* second ed (Oxford 1968) 101–2.

17 printed editions] The New Testament had been printed five times in Greek. Apart from Erasmus' own two editions (1516, 1518/19), there were two others, based on his text: the Aldine of February 1518 (cf Ep 770) and one edited by Nikolaus Gerbel (Haguenau: T. Anshelm March 1521). Finally, copies of the New Testament volume of the Complutensian polyglot (cf CWE 3 220), which had been printed as early as January 1514, could by then just have reached Rome, where Diego López Zúñiga, one of its editors, now lived. Erasmus did not see it until after his third edition was completed.

1214

1 Cornelis] Erasmus' reference to his profession ('advocatus a fisco') appears to correspond to the functions exercised at Ghent by Cornelis van Schoonhove (d 1528). Ep 1594 provides evidence that Erasmus and Schoonhove were friends.

2 Ghent and Termonde] Erasmus would pass through Termonde and Ghent on his way from Louvain to Bruges. In view of lines 26–8 Allen suggested that he had travelled with the abbot from Ghent to Termonde on return from one of his visits to Bruges, perhaps that of July 1520; cf Ep 1129 n1.

3 Laurinus] An old friend at Bruges; cf Ep 651.

4 St Jerome's commentary on the Psalms] The authenticity of the *Breviarium in Psalmos* attributed to Jerome was a matter of some importance to Erasmus, partly because it included a passage lending support to Lefèvre's attack upon his *Annotationes* on the New Testament (cf Epp 597:37n, 778:203n). Perhaps he wished to examine this question afresh in the course of his current revision of the New Testament (cf Ep 1174 n6). Whatever the response he received from St Bavo's, he saw no need to change the passage in question (on Heb 2:7) in the third edition of his *Annotationes*. According to Allen, the second edition of Jerome (Basel: J. Froben 1524–6) also fails to show whether or not Erasmus used such a manuscript.

5 return to Bruges] Cf Ep 1223 introduction.

1215

1 country retreat of mine] Cf Ep 1208 introduction.
2 beggar-bullies] The friars, especially the Dominicans and the Carmelites; cf Epp 998:71, 1144:25.
3 Carinus] Erasmus had met Ludovicus Carinus in the company of Wilhelm Nesen (cf Ep 994 n1), who was now at Frankfurt, but Carinus had meanwhile become the secretary of Capito at Mainz (cf Ep 1165 n22). After Erasmus' move to Basel (cf Ep 1242 introduction) Carinus joined his household, conceivably in consequence of the letter here mentioned.

1216

1 At last] For the delay incurred cf Ep 1128 n2, and for early traces of the circulation of López Zúñiga's book in central Europe see BRE Ep 204, AK II Ep 789 and Allen's note. It did not become known outside Spain until after the author's arrival in Rome, February 1521 (cf Ep 1213:36–41). Erasmus' answer, the *Apologia respondens ad ea quae Iacobus Lopis Stunica taxaverat in prima duntaxat Novi Testamenti aeditione* was published by Dirk Martens ([Louvain c September 1521]; NK 2851; LB IX 283–356); cf Epp 1235:36–8, 1236:61–70.
2 horn of plenty] Cf *Adagia* I vi 2.
3 elephant … fly] Cf Ep 1148 n2.
4 distinguished pedigree] Erasmus' information probably came from Juan de Vergara; cf Ep 1128 n2.
5 Cardinal of Toledo] Francisco Jiménez de Cisneros, d 8 November 1517; cf Ep 1128 n3.
6 Croy] Cardinal Guillaume de Croy, had recently succeeded Jiménez as archbishop of Toledo and had died on 6 January 1521; cf Ep 1184.
7 the moment … dead] López Zúñiga did not publish his book until 1520, three years after Jiménez's death; the second edition of Erasmus' New Testament was published in 1518/19. Erasmus' mind again (cf above lines 2–4) seems to associate him with Edward Lee, who had eventually published his critique of the first edition of Erasmus' New Testament after he had seen the second; cf Ep 1037 introduction.
8 Let him … convince us] Cf below n14.
9 Jerome … indexes] Oecolampadius' pioneering *Index* to the great Basel edition of Jerome was published in May 1520 (cf Ep 1102 n1). For the first edition of the *Enchiridion* cf Ep 164.
10 'with a mind … controversy'] Cf below n14.
11 Oecolampadius] The corrector of the first edition of the New Testament; cf Ep 354.
12 statement] In the *Annotationes* on Acts 16:11 and Rom 15:24 (cf LB VI 495E, 649C). In an outburst of patriotism López Zúñiga had objected that Naples was not so much 'occupied' by Spain as rather possessed of right, but he had also expressed an opinion as to the location of 'Neapolis' referred to in this verse of Acts, which Erasmus eventually accepted after the third edition of 1522 (cf Ep 1174 n6). A reference to Erasmus' Dutch origins (cf Epp 770:65n, 1147 n4) occurs in that same note of Zúñiga's.

13 Sogdiana] The region of Asia between the rivers Jaxartes and Oxus
14 introduction] Zúñiga's book is prefaced by a 'Prologus ad lectorem,' which begins with a commendation of Erasmus' translations from Lucian and Euripides and his *Adagia*, but implies that this is no basis on which to tackle the problems of Scriptural texts. Other passages of this preface are criticized by Erasmus – rather harshly – in lines 4–5, 30–41, 59–60.
15 his translator] The translator of the Latin Vulgate
16 expectation] More than once Erasmus had some reason to expect Barbier's return to the Netherlands (cf Epp 1114:5, 1245:5–7), but he stayed abroad. Erasmus' eagerness to see him (cf also Epp 1225:391–2, 1235:2–3) no doubt reflects sincere friendship, but there were also financial considerations involved, as Barbier exercised some control over Erasmus' annuity from Courtrai; cf Epp 1094 n6, 1245.
17 My own departure] To Basel; cf Ep 1242 introduction.
18 bombarded ... by the abuse] Cf Epp 1174 n1, 1217 introduction.
19 finished ... here] After Erasmus' earlier remarks on the progress of Lutheranism in the Netherlands (cf Epp 1165 n1, 1188 n5), this statement reflects the hardening of the Catholic reaction with the return of Charles v and the papal nuncio Aleandro from the Diet of Worms (cf Ep 1197 introduction). Aleandro was then in Louvain, having arrived there on c 21 June (cf Balan nos 101, 105–6). Dirk Martens (cf Ep 1163 n2), who had earlier had his stock of Lutheran books confiscated by the nuncio, found himself compelled to print the Edict of Worms for him (NK 3298; cf Ep 1221:51–2), which Aleandro published over the next few weeks in Antwerp, Ghent, Brussels, and Bruges, burning heretical books wherever he could find any (cf Ep 1186 n8; Balan nos 102, 108–9, 120). For Erasmus' personal reaction to the changing climate see the preface.
20 Scylla ... Charybdis] Cf Ep 1186 n5.
21 countryman] Cf Ep 1208 introduction.

1217

1 Vincentius] The Dominican Vincentius Theoderici
2 letter ... order] Ep 1033, addressed to Albert of Brandenburg
3 plan ... Luther] The *Consilium*; cf Ep 1149 introduction.
4 before ... promulgated] Cf Epp 1070 n1, 1141 n11.
5 put Luther right] Cf Epp 1033:75, 79, 1153 n6.
6 member ... household] Ulrich von Hutten; cf Epp 1033, 1161 introductions.
7 'my friend Luther'] Cf Ep 1153 n37.
8 condemnation ... Paris authorities] It had been published with the date of 15 April 1521; Erasmus had expected it for some time; cf Ep 1141 n10.
9 No religious order ... dislike.] Cf Ep 1196 n42.
10 Dominican theologian ... learning] Johannes Faber
11 a certain prince] Probably Albert of Brandenburg; cf Ep 1149 introduction.
12 *De captivitate Babylonica*] Cf Ep 1186 n3.
13 policy ... nothing dark] Cf Ep 1186 n13.
14 at that stage] At Cologne, prior to the publication of the *Consilium*
15 a religious man ... unimpaired] This sentence repeats the title of the *Consilium*.
16 men of the highest reputation] The context here and also in Ep 1202:7–10

suggests that Erasmus perceived the spirit of the *Consilium* behind some efforts undertaken at the Diet of Worms (cf Ep 1197 introduction) to enter into a dialogue with Luther and his supporters, all the more so as Johannes Faber, the instigator of the *Consilium*, was present at Worms (cf Ep 1184 n2). Among the men with an open mind Erasmus would probably have ranked Capito and also Charles v's confessor, Jean Glapion, who talked at length to the Saxon chancellor Gregor von Brück, and together with the imperial chamberlain Paul von Armerstorff, visited the Ebernburg on 6–7 April for talks with Hutten, Sickingen, and Martin Bucer. No doubt Erasmus had also heard of the negotiations on 24–5 April between Luther himself and Richard von Greiffenklau, archbishop of Trier, assisted by Johannes Cochlaeus and Konrad Peutinger. Cf *Reichstag zu Worms* 99–101, 110–11, 277–92; *Reichstagsakten* J.R. II 477–94, 599–632.

17 groundless suspicion] Cf Ep 1167 n16.
18 manslaughter ... reputation] Cf Ep 1196:52–5.
19 like stones] Cf Ep 1185 n4.
20 women] Cf Ep 1196 n2.
21 neither Reuchlin's nor Luther's] Cf Ep 1155 n5.
22 done more ... than any mortal man] Cf Ep 1143:22–9.
23 honourable silence] Cf Ep 1155:18–19.
24 spiteful pamphlets ... everywhere] Cf Ep 1195 n3.
25 nothing of mine] Cf Ep 1166 n24.
26 approached by many men] Cf Ep 1144 n16.
27 with every fibre of my being] Literally, with hands and feet; cf *Adagia* I iv 15.
28 in the Falcon] It was in the Falcon, an arts college of the University of Louvain, that on 13 September 1519 a reconciliation had taken place between Erasmus and his critics in the theological faculty; see Ep 1022 introduction.
29 Atensis] This passage shows that Erasmus was now prepared to take a more detached view of the deceased 'vice-chancellor' Jan Briart of Ath (cf Epp 946, 1029 n2), while inclining to see in Nicolaas Baechem Egmondanus the driving force of opposition against him; cf Ep 1225:18–21 and preface.
30 no holds barred] Literally, with the spirit of a gladiator (who will take any risk); cf *Adagia* I iii 76.
31 Luther's party] Cf Ep 1162 n36.
32 lack of skill in theology] Cf Ep 1167 n33.
33 three universities ... Luther] Cologne, Louvain, and Paris
34 the emperor has added his] The Edict of Worms (cf Ep 1197 introduction) was just then printed in Louvain; cf Ep 1216 n19.
35 while this is possible] For this proviso cf Ep 1195 n9 and the preface.
36 before Rosemondt] Cf Ep 1162.

1218

1 god from the machine] Cf Ep 1199 n1.
2 He himself ... wound] Cf Ep 1195 n11.
3 constantly warned ... under control] Cf Epp 980, 1127A, 1143 n7.
4 Jacobites] The Dominicans; cf Ep 1153 n24.
5 the Louvain people ... against me] For this passage cf Ep 1217 introduction.
6 poisonous pamphlets ... everywhere] Cf Ep 1195 n3.

7 heard ... from him] This is the first indication that Erasmus had met the nuncio again at Brussels; cf Ep 1233 n28.
8 Luther has acknowledged ... before the emperor] At Worms, on 17 April; cf Ep 1197 introduction.
9 he] Aleandro; cf Ep 1186 n3.
10 New Testament] Cf Ep 1174 n6.
11 Augustine] Cf Ep 1144 n17.
12 anything to do with] Cf, however, Ep 1166 n24.
13 out of my books] Cf Ep 1195 n19.
14 risk my life for the truth] The significance of this statement, and a similar one in Ep 1167:488–9, should perhaps not be overrated; both were made in an effort to contrast Erasmus' caution with Luther's rashness. Erasmus said at the same time that he would gladly give his life for the faith and the 'gospel truth'; see Epp 1225:272–4, 1236:133–4.
15 like Peter] Cf Matt 26:69–75, Mark 14:66–72, Luke 22:56–62, John 18:25–7; also Gal 2:11–13.
16 pamphlet about Julius] The *Julius exclusus*; cf Ep 502 introduction, CWE 27 156–60.
17 Luther is in ashes] For the burning of his books cf Epp 1141 n11, 1216 n19.
18 More's letter] Cf Ep 1220 introduction.
19 cardinal] Thomas Wolsey

1219

1 whose friendship ... enjoyed] Cf Ep 1195 n14. It may be noted that this letter and Ep 1195, both released forthwith for publication, emphasize the old friendship between Erasmus and Aleandro and attribute the nuncio's departure from it to the influence of the Louvain theologians. Ep 1218:10–14, which was not meant to be published, is less sparing.
2 scandalous pamphlets ... both sides] Cf Ep 1195 n3, 1218:14–18.
3 Sibyl's leaves] Palm leaves, on which she wrote her oracles; cf *Adagia* I vii 91.
4 not one syllable ... my connivance] Cf Epp 1218:22–4, 1225:141–2, 1236:181–3.
5 Nor have I supported him] Cf Ep 1167 n22.
6 to prevent ... his books] Cf Epp 1143 n6, 1217:107.
7 No one can fail ... every kind.] This sentence closely resembles a statement in the *Consilium*; see *Opuscula* 356:69–72, and cf Ep 1149 introduction.
8 I have hated war] Cf Ep 1225 n52.
9 done away with] Cf Ep 1125 introduction.
10 taken ... from my books] Cf Epp 1195:72–84.
11 some deity ... on its way] Cf Ep 1199 n1.
12 even the Turks] Cf Ep 1167 n31.
13 Luther man] Cf Ep 1162 n36.
14 critic you speak of] Erasmus is referring to information contained in Mountjoy's letter; the critic, mentioned again in lines 88–91, has not been identified.
15 most accomplished theologian among you] Could John Stokesley be meant? Cf Epp 855:47–9, 1126:50–3.
16 schoolmaster] Cf Ep 1173 n13.
17 Luther acknowledged ... emperor.] Cf Ep 1197 introduction and the identical

statement in Ep 1218:17–18. In view of Ep 1195:79–80 Allen argued that despite some analogies the present letter could not be contemporary with Ep 1195.

18 never published ... my name to it] Whatever the authorship of the *Julius exclusus* (cf Ep 1218:41–3), the *Consilium* (cf Ep 1149 introduction), and the *Acta contra Lutherum* (cf Ep 1166 n24), Erasmus may be correct in claiming that he was not directly involved with their publication.

19 always submitted ... the church] Cf Epp 1174 n6, 1225 n29.

20 before Herod] Cf Luke 23:9.

21 careful physicians ... come back] Cf Epp 1156:21–5, 1202:148–51, 1225:312–15, 1228:33–9 (where Christian II of Denmark is said to have contradicted Erasmus on the point that mild medicine was preferable), 1233:47–9. In Ep 914:32–8 Longueil uses the metaphor of lenient and severe treatments to compare Erasmus and Budé.

22 others ... success] Cf Ep 1186:23–6.

23 go to Basel] Cf Ep 1242 introduction.

24 in hand] Cf Ep 1212:44–6.

25 attempt something ... heal this discord] Cf Ep 1228:53–8 and the preface.

26 men of great learning] Cf Epp 1163 n3, 1165:16–18, 1225:215–18.

1220

1 right honourable] Here and in Epp 1223:50, 1233:35 Erasmus refers to More's knighthood, using the complimentary term *eques auratus* 'golden knight.' This special emphasis is explained by the fact that More's knighting was quite recent; it seems to have occurred by the middle of May 1521. See Ep 1210 n4 and cf Ep 1134 n1.

2 imitation gems] A good-humoured reminiscence of an episode (told by Erasmus in the *Moria*, ASD IV-3 132–3) when More in the course of educating his young wife had deceived her with sham jewels.

3 delight in gaming] Cf Ep 999:108–10.

4 college of the three tongues] Cf Ep 1221 n3.

5 Attic wit] See Ep 1196 n80, cf Ep 999:117–23.

6 prose ... poetry] Cf Ep 999:269–71.

7 for friendship ... made] Cf Ep 999:98–108.

8 averse from filthy lucre] Cf Ep 999:216.

9 his children taught in liberal subjects] For examples cf Epp 737, 957–9, 1018, 1192:91–4, 1237.

10 none is at home in literature] Cf Ep 1004:165–7.

11 Halewijn] Cf Epp 641, 1115.

12 Cranevelt] Cf Ep 1145.

1221

1 Brussels] Cf Ep 1218 introduction.

2 Gilles de Busleyden] Brother of Jérôme de Busleyden, the founder of the Collegium Trilingue. Gilles continued to represent the family in its management; for his unselfish support see below n6.

3 Agathius] Presumably Agazio Guidacerio (1477–1542), of Rocca, a priest and at this time professor of Hebrew at the Sapienza, the University of Rome. His appointment to the Collegium Trilingue, as envisaged in this letter, did

not come to pass, but in 1530 he went to Paris as a royal lecturer in Hebrew. The following assessment of conditions at the Trilingue is quite accurate (cf de Vocht CTL II 76–80). The president was Jan Stercke, the Latin professor was Conradus Goclenius and the Greek professor was Rutgerus Rescius, while the chair of Hebrew was vacant; cf Ep 691 and the preface of CWE 7.

4 this climate of ours] For Erasmus' liking of the climate of Louvain cf Epp 881:8–10, 883:20–1, 1111:89–90, 1224:10–11, 1237:18–19.

5 salary] Cf Ep 1213 n3.

6 depriving ... share] According to Henry de Vocht (CTL I 292–3) Jérôme's brothers were 'deprived' of his inheritance in the sense that they did not claim it (when according to the will they could have done so) in view of the university's initial refusal to accept the new college; cf Ep 691.

7 good luck go with him] In a play on words on Agathius' name Erasmus puts ἀγαθῇ τύχῃ in Greek.

8 Luther ... ambushed and killed] The most famous reaction to this wide-spread rumour came from Albrecht Dürer, then also in the Netherlands, who called in his diary for Erasmus to take Luther's place (Dürer *Diary* 90–3; cf also the preface, Balan nos 95, 97, and *Melanchthons Briefwechsel* I Epp 139, 159. For Luther's detention at the Wartburg cf Ep 1203 n2.

9 burnt at Worms] On 29 May 1521, the eve of Corpus Christi. For the preparations cf Balan no 97.

10 printed at Louvain] Cf Ep 1216 n19.

1222

1 Laurentius] Marcus Laurinus, dean of St Donatian's, Bruges, whose name was perhaps misread by the editors of Vives' *Opera* of 1555.

2 Etienne Lecomte] Lecomte, of Bailleul (d around 1544) had been appointed secretary to the chapter of St Donatian's in 1520.

3 as the man says] Cicero *Epistulae ad familiares* 3.9.2

4 regent of the College of the Lily] Jan de Neve

5 proverbs] Perhaps in preparation for the next edition of Erasmus' *Adagia* (Basel: J. Froben January 1523); cf below lines 39–40.

6 Johannes] Johannes Hovius; cf Ep 1205 n14.

7 I got no better] In the preface of his edition of Augustine's *De civitate Dei* (Basel: J. Froben 1522) Vives confirmed that he had fallen ill soon after the death, on 6 January 1521, of his patron, Cardinal Guillaume de Croy, and recovered in June at Bruges.

8 the king and More] More was expected at Bruges with Cardinal Wolsey for a meeting with Charles V in August; cf Ep 1223 introduction. The following sentences seem to indicate that Vives had already secured some support from the English queen, Catherine of Aragon, and that he looked especially to More in the hope that he would help him obtain an appointment at the court of England. His letter to More (line 20) is not extant.

9 as Appius said] The phrase is cited in a spurious letter from the historian Sallust to Caesar (1.1.2) as having been read by the early Roman statesman Appius Claudius; see *Fragmenta poetarum Latinorum* ed W. Morel (Leipzig 1927) 6.

1223

1 Busleyden College] Cf Ep 1221 n3.
2 Happy are those ... this generation!] Cf Ep 1194 n1.
3 'between ... rich'] Hesiod *Works and Days* 23–4
4 the two of you] Goclenius and Rutgerus Rescius; cf Ep 1221 n3.
5 soured with falsehoods] Cf Ep 1174 n1.
6 a picture of you] In Ep 1220
7 knighted] Cf Ep 1220 n1.
8 treasurership] Cf Ep 1210 n4.

1224

1 list of Williams] Thale's name does not, in fact, figure among Erasmus' enumerations of friends of that name; cf Epp 1003 n6, 1184:3.
2 Ferrara] In December 1508; cf Epp 211:53n, 216A.
3 climate of Louvain] Cf Ep 1221 n4.
4 British plague] The occurrence of plague in England at this time is confirmed by a letter from Richard Pace of 28 August to Cardinal Wolsey in Calais; see LP III 1516.

1225

1 urging me ... time] Barbier's letters of this period have not survived with the exception of Ep 1245 (in part no doubt for the reason stated there in lines 54–6). His admonitions were perhaps issued with the encouragement of Cardinal Adrian of Utrecht, who had retained strong links to his former university (cf Epp 1153 n33, 1216 introduction) and apparently also pressed the other side to show restraint; cf below lines 39–40.
2 as the saying goes] Cf *Adagia* I ii 46, 47.
3 Archbishop of Canterbury] William Warham
4 cardinals ... Rome] Such as Raffaele Riario, Domenico Grimani, Lorenzo Campeggi, Lorenzo Pucci
5 Atensis] Jan Briart of Ath (cf Ep 1217:135–8); the generous praise Erasmus finds for him (below lines 46–50) may also have been intended for the ears of Cardinal Adrian, his great friend.
6 theologians ... faction] Nicolaas Baechem Egmondanus and Vincentius Theoderici
7 Dorp] Cf Epp 304, 337, 347 of 1514–15.
8 to Louvain] In July 1517; cf Ep 596 introduction. The claim that Erasmus followed the wishes of Charles V was earlier made in his *Apologia invectivis Lei*; see *Opuscula* 237–8.
9 efforts of Atensis] In September 1519; cf Ep 1217:132–9.
10 until ... Three Tongues] The latent conflicts first came to a head in the autumn of 1518; cf Ep 934 introduction.
11 Nicolaas the Carmelite] Nicolaas Baechem Egmondanus
12 cardinal of Tortosa] Adrian of Utrecht; cf above n1.
13 correcting it] For the second edition, 1518/19; cf Ep 864.
14 Nicolas of Mons] Nicolas Coppin; cf Ep 1162 n18.
15 first conversation ... Egmondanus] After Erasmus' move to Louvain; cf Ep 1196:129–32.
16 to Basel] In May 1518; cf Ep 843 introduction.

17 invited me to supper] Erasmus had earlier related this episode more fully in his *Apologia invectivis Lei*; see *Opuscula* 248–9.
18 rather be corrected than commended] Cf Ep 1076 n1.
19 I returned] In September 1518; cf Ep 867.
20 plague] Cf Ep 867:224–77.
21 to Atensis] Cf Epp 998 introduction, 1053 n14.
22 replied to Lee] In March–April 1520; cf Ep 1080 introduction.
23 pamphlet from Latomus] In March 1519 (cf Ep 934). The chronology of Erasmus' account is garbled; cf below n25.
24 controversy with Dorp] Cf Ep 475:28–31.
25 Atensis ... belaboured me] In February 1519; cf Ep 946 introduction.
26 laymen in high places] In the autumn of 1519; cf Ep 1038.
27 pamphlets by Luther] The Froben collection of his Latin works (cf Ep 904:20n). The significance of the following account of an investigation of Erasmus' works by the Louvain theologians has been noted in the preface of CWE 7. It is not clear what book (line 129) Erasmus gave Briart and Dorp to read. Perhaps it was a short collection – he calls it 'libellum' – of revised notes to the New Testament, some of which might subsequently have been incorporated in the third edition; cf Ep 1174 n6.
28 prefaces ... better Latin] Erasmus refers to three anonymous prefaces to the reader (two of them very short), probably written by Capito and inserted at various points in the Froben collection.
29 confession] In the first edition of the New Testament (1516) Erasmus' note on Acts 19:18 referred to occasional occurrences in ancient times of the practice of voluntary public confession. In the 1518/19 edition he added that the modern custom of secret ('auricular' or 'sacramental') confession appeared to have developed from bishops counselling in private some persons afflicted by a troubled conscience. In subsequent editions he left it at that (cf LB VI 507–8). His views on this point were also criticized by Lee (cf LB IX 255–62) and Baechem (cf Ep 1153:80–3). In compliance with the Index of Trent (1564) most of the passage was later deleted by Catholic editors; see Allen's note.
30 no syllable of mine] Cf Ep 1219 n4.
31 worthless pamphlets ... everywhere] Cf Ep 1195 n3.
32 Germans take ... pride] Cf Ep 1186 n13.
33 rector] The Latin term *gymnasiarcha* used here referred in Louvain to the regents of arts colleges. The reference here is no doubt to Nicolas Coppin, who was at that time regent of the Falcon; cf Epp 1022 introduction, 1162:118–19.
34 Peace ... Falcon College] On 13 September 1519; cf Epp 1022, 1162:115–21, 1217:133–9.
35 *Farrago* of my letters] The *Farrago* (cf Ep 1009 introduction) included letters from August 1519 and was published in October. Thus Erasmus' claim that it was printed in spring 1519 (lines 161–2) is untenable.
36 Carmelite] Nicolaas Baechem; see Ep 1162:215–18, and cf Ep 1196 n42.
37 published two years before] Ep 1033; cf its introduction and lines 40–6.
38 a Carmelite ... certain Dominicans] Nicolaas Baechem Egmondanus, Vincentius Theoderici, and Laurentius Laurentii.
39 in a letter] Ep 980:45–58.

40 wrote frequently ... begun] Cf Epp 1127A, 1143 n7.
41 certain people ... warned me] Hutten did so; cf Ep 1135:18–44.
42 stop ... books] Cf Ep 1143 n6.
43 to join Luther's cause] Cf Ep 1144 n16.
44 loss of the friends ... in Germany] Cf below lines 302–11.
45 'I am not ... sword'] Matt 10:34; cf Ep 1129 n7.
46 perhaps have been one of them] Erasmus did offer such private advice to Albert of Brandenburg (cf Epp 1033, 1217:25–6) and Frederick the Wise (cf Ep 1155 introduction), and was to do so again at the request of Pope Adrian VI; see Adrian's biography in CEBR I.
47 the cardinal of San Sisto] Tommaso de Vio, Cardinal Cajetanus *De divina institutione pontificatus Romani pontificis* (Rome: M. Silber 22 March 1521). In the preface to his excellent critical edition (Münster 1925, xiii–xiv) Friedrich Lauchert concurs with Erasmus' judgment here, which presents a marked change in Erasmus' views on Cajetanus (cf Ep 1188:28–9) and the issue at stake (cf Ep 1202 n46), perhaps again in consideration of Cardinal Adrian of Utrecht.
48 learned men ... with Luther] Erasmus could be thinking of Beatus Rhenanus, Capito, Hutten, Spalatinus, Mutianus Rufus.
49 drawn ... on my books] Cf Ep 1195 n19.
50 more cautiously] Cf Ep 1219:59–66.
51 ceremonies ... Judaism ... Christianity] Cf Ep 1126 n45.
52 against the wars] Faced with the reality of a new war (cf Ep 1228 n12), Erasmus repeatedly emphasized his consistent abhorrence; cf below lines 322–3, Epp 1232:56–61, 1233:18–24, 1238:68–79, 1248 n10, and for references to his earlier books and passages of letters denouncing war see Ep 603 introduction and Allen 1219:41n.
53 one hair's breadth worse] Cf Ep 1159 n4.
54 in Luther's books ... agrees with me] Cf Epp 1195:72–84, 1202:237–58.
55 less profit ... pestilent ass] Cf 1202:255–8.
56 'Hitherto ... against Luther'] Erasmus' arguments (to line 339 below) are repeated – sometimes amplified and sometimes modified – in Ep 1236:84–143.
57 consciousness of my own ignorance] Cf Ep 1167 n33.
58 the Swiss] Cf Ep 855:4n.
59 even of one's life] This statement is repeated without qualification in Ep 1236:133–4; cf Ep 1218 n14.
60 donkey ... Antichrist] Cf Ep 1183 n28.
61 cardinals ... kings] Cf above lines 215–18, Ep 1227 n3.
62 burnings ... decrees of princes] Cf Epp 1166 n20, 1186 n8, 1192 n8, 1216 n19.
63 for a whole year ... a line] This is perhaps an indication that Hutten's Ep 1161 had not reached Erasmus. On the other hand, he cannot be expected to have saved, or even published, any compromising letters; cf above lines 193–8, Ep 1206:146. Ep 1211:2–3 appears to contradict the statement he makes here.
64 polite attentions] Cf Epp 870 introduction, 963:6n, 1122 introduction.
65 attack me ... lectures] Cf Ep 1241:15–19.
66 a Pelagian] The followers of the fifth-century heretic Pelagius were accused of excessive reliance on human morality and will, underrating the importance of grace in salvation (cf Ep 1232:88–9). This charge against Erasmus (cf Allen

Epp 1259:14, 1275:27) was apparently based on some passages in the *Enchiridion*. This at least is what Albert Burer told Beatus Rhenanus in a letter from Wittenberg, 30 June 1521 (BRE Ep 206). Allen noted that Luther had in his first communication invited Erasmus to read Augustine's books against the Pelagians; see Ep 501:55–8.

67 those … mild physic] One of whom, apparently, was Christian II of Denmark; cf Epp 1219 n21, 1228:33–9.

68 Nebuchadnezzar] Cf 2 Kings 24:10–15.

69 Christ … temple] Cf John 2:14–16, Matt 28:19.

70 peace … however just] Ep 1211 n94; cf above n52.

71 next fair] Both the third edition of the New Testament (cf Ep 1174 n6) and the *Epistolae ad diversos* (cf Ep 1206), and probably also the *Apologiae omnes* (cf Ep 1235 n5) were at one time expected to be launched by Froben at the Frankfurt book fair of autumn 1521, but were held back in the end until the spring fair of 1522.

72 I shall try … to heal our present discords] Cf Ep 1228:53–8.

73 Luther's man] Cf Ep 1162 n36.

74 god from the machine] Cf Ep 1199 n1.

75 'whatever … sin'] Cf Ep 1195:72–4.

76 rather … corrected than destroyed] Cf Ep 1153 n6.

77 desire for your society] Cf Ep 1216 n16.

78 that Paria of yours] Cf below lines 391–4, Ep 913:6n.

79 German kinsmen] Apparently the editors of the *Farrago* and *Epistolae ad diversos* (cf Ep 1206 introduction) were among those Erasmus had in mind; cf Ep 1244:41–2, Allen Ep 1278:10–13.

1226

1 my letter] Not extant

2 given any free time] Hieronymus, aged twenty, is thus viewed as a printer and the eventual successor to his father's business. In the case of Erasmius, his little brother, Erasmus later advised against a premature involvement in the printing firm; cf Allen Ep 2231.

3 Erasmius] Cf Ep 635:26n.

1227

1 my notebooks] Cf below lines 39–41, Ep 1210 n6.

2 Dover] Cf Ep 119:9n.

3 the book] Henry VIII's *Assertio septem sacramentorum adversus Martinum Lutherum* (London: R. Pynson 12 July 1521; STC 13077). Among the reprints Allen noted two Strasbourg editions (J. Grüninger 9 August and 7 September 1522), with an appendix containing Epp 1219, 1228, reprinted from the *Epistolae ad diversos*. Grüninger's second edition is a German translation by Thomas Murner. For Erasmus' own copy see Ep 1246 introduction. Whereas Luther suspected Edward Lee of having written the king's book (cf Luther w *Briefwechsel* II Ep 511 and some Lutherans apparently attributed it to Erasmus (cf Allen Ep 1290:16–19), he was himself satisfied that the author was Henry; cf Ep 1228:21–3.

4 Marino] Marino Caracciolo (cf Epp 865:72n, 1188:29); the meeting is described in Allen Ep 1342:848–57.

5 more successful … same field] Cf Ep 1153:163–7.
6 York] Cardinal Thomas Wolsey; cf Ep 1123 introduction.
7 to whose office … succeeded] The deanship of St Paul's, London, formerly held by John Colet
8 Ferrara] Cf Ep 1224 n2.

1228

1 at Bruges] Cf Ep 1223 introduction.
2 bishop of Rochester] John Fisher
3 the book … against Luther] Cf Ep 1227 n3.
4 bow and spear] Cf *Adagia* I vi 19.
5 medicine] Cf Ep 1219 n21.
6 King Christian] Christian II of Denmark (1481–1559), husband of Charles V's sister Isabella, visited the Netherlands from June to September 1521. Erasmus met him at Bruges (cf Ep 1223 introduction) and was delighted to find that the monarch greatly appreciated his company (cf Allen Epp 1342:78–80, 1381:35–8). Christian's popular appeal is confirmed by Albrecht Dürer, who took his portrait at Antwerp in July (cf Dürer *Diary* 99–100, plate 63). Erasmus was evidently aware of Christian's ambiguous policy in religious matters (cf Ep 1241 n8) but he did not betray any knowledge of the political motives of the king's visit, nor of his previous campaign in Sweden, which he had followed up with a scandalous trial and mass executions at Stockholm, 8–9 November 1520.
7 unless Christ … Athenians] This is a slight variation of Ep 1205:27–9.
8 ill-nourished … doctrine] Scholastic theology is meant.
9 attacked Hector when he was down] Cf Homer *Iliad* 22.369–71.
10 Scylla … Charybdis] Cf Epp 1186 n5, 1205:31–2.
11 all the works of Luther] There is no reason to disbelieve Erasmus' many assurances that his acquaintance with Luther's writings was on the whole slight (cf Epp 1143 n3, 1225:281–3). Recently, however, he had begun to have second thoughts (cf Epp 1144:81–2, 1219:135–7, 1225:331–4) about his previous refusal (cf Epp 1164 n15, 1180 introduction) to write and publish something in defence of the Roman faith. While his recent pledges to do so were cautious, conditional, and addressed to correspondents who would receive them with satisfaction, they were also allowed to go out in print. At the same time they emphasized that his aim was not so much to attack Luther as to pursue the approach suggested by the *Consilium* (cf lines 57–8, Ep 1149 introduction). In promising to make his voice heard, he was no doubt encouraged by a report that Pope Leo X had shown great interest in his recent letters to Rome (cf Epp 1213:28–33, 1236:3–8). He was never fully resolved, however, and after his move to Basel (cf Ep 1242 introduction), he did not pursue the project (cf Ep 1244:33–5). Later he even claimed that he had gone to Basel to escape from the pressing admonitions of the emperor's confessor, Jean Glapion, that he write against Luther; cf Allen Ep 2792:17–19.
12 war against the French] Since the end of 1520 the French king had been engaged, first through such allies as Robert de la Marck (cf Ep 1065 introduction), but soon afterwards also directly, in campaigns against the emperor in the frontier regions of the Pyrenees and the Netherlands (cf Ep 1192

introduction). Fighting broke out also in Italy (cf Ep 1236 n10). Erasmus followed these developments with anguish and particular concern about the dire consequences for culture; cf Epp 1237:27–8, 1238:68–79, 1248:25–30.
13 The pope ... our side.] Leo X had initially supported Francis I in his efforts to become emperor (cf Ep 1009 introduction), but in May 1521 he concluded after lengthy negotiations an alliance with Charles V (cf Pastor VIII 35). Erasmus sharply criticizes his position in Ep 1238:72–6.
14 Hungary] In the spring of 1521 Sultan Suleiman I launched his first campaign in the Balkans, crowning his successes against the Hungarians with the conquest of Belgrade on 29 August; cf LP III 1376, 1471–2, 1532, 1561.
15 Halsey] Cf Ep 254; he was apparently present at the Bruges meeting; cf Ep 1223 introduction.

1229

1 life of Colet] Ep 1211
2 you did not give me ... true colours] In response to Ep 1026:2–5
3 deny yourself dinner] Cf Ep 1211 n51.
4 continuous fasting] Cf Erasmus' own dispensation with regard to Lent and other fast days, Ep 1542.
5 mother] Alice Lupset (d 1545). Allen suggested that the context here implies that she was by then in charge of her husband's business; Ep 1196 n2.
6 father] William Lupset (d 1522), a London goldsmith. It may be noted that in the *Epistolae ad diversos* the text read 'step-father,' which was changed to 'father' in the *Opus epistolarum* of 1529.
7 Gonnell and Dancaster] Common friends; see Epp 274, 1027, and cf Ep 1003 n6.
8 Gerard] William Garrard; cf Ep 1027 n3.

1230

1 suppress your own works] This is another expression of the impatience Erasmus had shown for years to see Linacre's works in print and accessible to him (cf Epp 755:32n, 868:73–82). Linacre followed up his earlier translations with a Latin rendering of Galen's *De temperamentis* (Oxford: J. Siberch 1521; STC 11536) which was nearly ready when this letter was written. Its preface is dated 5 September 1521 and addressed to Leo X, reminding him of their studies together.
2 my own example] Perhaps Erasmus realized that the ease with which he wrote and published could be dangerous (cf Epp 914:11–14, 57–62) or, more likely, he recalled the many controversies caused by some of his books.

1231

1 St Augustine's day] 28 August
2 mendicants] Franciscans, Dominicans, Carmelites, and Austin friars
3 that spring ... four rivers] Cf Gen 2:10–14.
4 spider hunting a fly] See Augustine *Confessions* 10.35.57.
5 'sacramental confession'] Cf Ep 1225 n29.
6 prize speech] The *Encomium matrimonii*; cf Epp 604:12n, 1006 n32.
7 take down what he said] Allen in his note gives an example for this practice,

which was widespread in the later Middle Ages; another well-known case is the German sermons of Master Eckhart; cf also Ep 1233:145–9.

1232

1 Tertullian] Tertullian *Opera* (Basel: J. Froben July 1521), a first edition. The very title of the work, echoing Jerome (cf below n6) emphasizes that Cyprian used to read Tertullian every day; cf Ep 1000:165–70.

2 all that he could] Beatus Rhenanus' preface (BRE Ep 207), addressed to Stanislaus Thurzo (cf Ep 1242), emphasizes the poor quality of his manuscripts, which came from the abbeys of Payerne on the Lake of Neuchâtel and Hirsau in Baden-Württemberg.

3 Jerome … expressing himself] In his Ep 58.10 (CSEL 54:539); cf Ep 1000:62–5.

4 Jerome condemns in Origen] Cf Jerome's Ep 98.10 (CSEL 55:194); cf also Ep 1167:296–7.

5 'He that putteth … adultery'] Matt 19:9, Mark 10:11, Luke 16:18. Tertullian's interpretation is quoted by Erasmus in the *Annotationes* to the New Testament (LB VI 693F); cf also Ep 1006 n23.

6 Jerome] *De viris illustribus* 53 (PL 23:663); cf below n20.

7 people who expected … serious crime] Especially the Montanists, partly under the influence of Tertullian himself, and the Novatians, another third-century heretical movement.

8 Augustine] Cf for instance his Ep 153.3.7 (CSEL 44:401–4). This view was generally held by the western Fathers, including Tertullian in *De poenitentia* (CC 1:319–40).

9 disapproved of second marriages] As did Tertullian in *De monogamia* (CC 2:1227–53).

10 St Paul … wife] Cf 1 Cor 5:1, 13; 2 Cor 2:5–8.

11 'He that … receive it'] Matt 19:12

12 no war … between Christians] In *De corona* (CC 2:1037–66) Tertullian argued that Christians must not serve as soldiers; cf Ep 1228 n12.

13 Simon and Menander] This paragraph is largely inspired by a short treatise *Adversus omnes haereses*, which was printed in Beatus Rhenanus' edition of Tertullian, but is not now attributed to him. For Simon and Menander, early Gnostics, see *Adversus omnes haereses* 1.2–3 (CC 2:1401).

14 Basilides … Abraxas] For Basilides, another Gnostic, and his divine principle called 'Abraxas' see *Adversus omnes haereses* 1.5 (CC 2:1402).

15 Nicolaites] See Rev 2:6, 15 (cf Ep 1021:101–2), *Adversus omnes haereses* 1.6 (CC 2:1402–3).

16 Ophites] See *Adversus omnes haereses* 2.1 (CC 2:1403).

17 Judaites] Cf Ep 1039:69–71, *Adversus omnes haereses* 2.5–6 (CC 2:1404).

18 Cerinthus and Valentinus] For these Gnostics see *Adversus omnes haereses* 3.3, 4.1 (CC 2:1405–6).

19 Manichaeus] Manichaeism, founded by the Persian Mani in the third century on the basis of the traditional Iranian dualism between the powers of good and evil, posed a major threat to early Christianity.

20 Montanus and his Paraclete] Montanus, who claimed to be the Paraclete, was the founder of the Montanist sect, which originated in Phrygia towards the middle of the second century. Their orientation was vigorously eschato-

logical; Tertullian was a Montanist from c 205 on. See *Adversus omnes haereses* 7.2 (CC 2:1409).

21 Artotyrites] A Montanist sect, said to use bread and cheese to celebrate communion; see e.g. Augustine *De haeresibus* 28 (CC 46:303).

22 those who denied ... looked for] Tertullian argued in *De carne Christi* and *De resurrectione mortuorum* (CC 2:871–917, 919–1012) against the Docetists, who denied Christ's human body, and against Gnostic sects who denied the resurrection of the dead. Christ's human soul and birth from the Virgin were denied by the Arians; see below n23.

23 Arians] Following the Council of Nicaea, 325, Arianism, opposing some central aspects of the Catholic doctrine of the Trinity, developed into the most dangerous heresy of the fourth century.

24 Pelagians] Cf Ep 1225 n66.

25 without ... Aristotle's philosophy] Cf Ep 1202:69–72, n49.

1232A

1 countryman of yours] He has not been identified.

2 *Apophthegmata*] Arsenius had recently edited a large collection of Greek proverbs gathered mostly by his father, Michael Apostolius: Ἀποφθέγματα ... *Praeclara dicta philosophorum, oratorum et poetarum* (Rome: at the Greek Gymnasium 1519). When reworking his *Adagia* in Venice, Erasmus had used this collection in manuscript.

3 31 August] Literally 'the last day of the third decade of Boedromion.' This is interpreted by Manousakas as 30 September and by Koster as 16 August (cf introduction), but neither can be correct. Greek dates in this period followed the Roman calendar, but the Roman names of the months were often replaced with Greek names borrowed from classical antiquity. Various attempts had been made by Greek scholars to establish a correspondence between the Greek and Roman calendars and to assign appropriate Greek equivalents to the Roman months. The system which Arsenius is likely to have followed is that proposed by Theodorus Gaza in 1495, whose *De mensibus* went through several editions in the first half of the sixteenth century and which Jean Lange asked Erasmus to translate (Allen Ep 1407:60). In this system Boedromion is August; see Paul Tannery 'Les noms de mois attiques chez les Byzantins' *Revue archéologique* 3rd series, 9 (1887) 23–36, repr Tannery *Mémoires scientifiques* IV (Paris 1920) 223–39. In the Greek calendar 'the last day of the third decade' is the last day of the month.

1233

1 as the proverb has it] Cf *Adagia* III vi 63.

2 cardinal of York] For the negotiations with Cardinal Wolsey and his delegation cf Ep 1223 introduction. One of the English diplomats was Thomas More; Allen's note on this passage quotes evidence that he had conversations at Bruges with Gasparo Contarini and Juan Luis Vives.

3 at Calais ... French mission] A French delegation headed by Chancellor Antoine Duprat arrived in Calais on 4 August to meet Cardinal Wolsey and, in view of the outbreak of war between France and the emperor (cf Ep 1228 n12), to prevent the collapse of Anglo-French friendship. Wolsey, of course,

kept his cards close to his chest, but after his return from Bruges the French soon realized that their mission had failed (cf LP III 1463, 1467, 1478, 1498, 1513). Budé had met More on the Field of Cloth of Gold in June 1520 (cf Ep 1106 introduction), but was not now a member of Duprat's team.

4 god from the machine] Cf Ep 1199 n1.

5 people ... eye to eye] The De la Marck family is a case in point; cf Epp 1065 introduction, 1225 n52.

6 'I had not thought of that'] Cf Ep 1161 n3.

7 treasurer] Cf Ep 1210 n4.

8 a rival for it] He is not identified.

9 knighted him] Cf Ep 1220 n1.

10 bachelors] Ecclesiastics, who can be rewarded with church benefices and whose families are less likely to claim an inheritance

11 girl ... widow] Jane Colt, Alice Middleton; cf Ep 999 n27, n29.

12 physician ... its energy] Cf Ep 1219:116–20. For More's loss of income when first entering the king's service cf Ep 999 n25; cf also Ep 1236:37–44.

13 three daughters] Cf Ep 999 n28.

14 fourth girl] Margaret Giggs

15 step-daughter] Alice Middleton, named for her mother and married to Sir Giles Alington

16 son by his first wife] John More, b 1508 or 1509

17 complain in your letters ... pecuniary loss] Cf Epp 435:132–9, 583:104–5.

18 for all seasons and all men] Cf *Adagia* I iii 86 and 1 Cor 9:22, a verse that had great significance for Erasmus; cf Epp 1202:101–2, 1206:85–6, and Bietenholz *History and Biography* 86–9, 93.

19 hardly one ... liberal studies] Cf Ep 1220:49–53.

20 free of this opinion] Cf Ep 1196 n2.

21 love of reading] On this subject Erasmus wrote later his colloquy *Abbatis et eruditae* (first printed in March 1524, ASD I-3 403–8), commending especially More's daughters, the sisters of Willibald Pirckheimer, and Margarete Blarer.

22 recount ... in order] Cf Ep 1231 n7.

23 remark of Phocion] This story is told of Socrates and his wife Xanthippe in Diogenes Laertius 2.35.

24 Camillus and Scipio Africanus] The saviour of Rome, who defeated the Gauls in 387/6 BC, and the conqueror of Carthage, 202 BC

25 father ... wonderfully green] John More, born c 1451; cf Ep 999 n11.

26 lexicon] In a detailed note on Greek dictionaries in the sixteenth century Allen here refers to Erasmus' preface (Ep 1460) for the Ceratinus-Froben lexicon of 1524, to Budé's *Commentarii linguae Graecae* (Paris 1529), and to material for a Greek dictionary collected by Budé towards the end of his life and put to good use in the dictionaries published under the name of Jacques Toussain (Paris 1552) and Budé himself (Geneva 1554).

27 Plato ... wise man] Cf Plato *Republic* 7.519.

28 Aleandro] His previous relations with the nuncio (cf Ep 1167 n20) and also Aleandro's visit to Louvain in late June had filled Erasmus with anxiety (cf Epp 1216 n19, 1217 introduction). More recently, however, a measure of rapprochement, or at least more frequent and ostensibly friendly contact, had developed. Aleandro arrived in Brussels c 28 June (cf Balan no 102) and

stayed at the imperial court except for various trips to other cities in Flanders and Brabant. A first meeting between them took place before 5 July (cf Ep 1218:14–17), and more talk is reflected in Epp 1235–6, although deeply rooted suspicions were not easy to overcome (cf Ep 1236:12–20, 189–93). The present statement addressed to Budé, who had been friendly with Aleandro in Paris (1508–13), also is in marked contrast with the earlier diatribes, even when considering that, like Epp 1235–6, it was composed with an eye to being shown around and quickly published. Before he left Anderlecht, Erasmus had another interview with Aleandro at Brussels, on Sunday, 6 October, which lasted for nearly five hours (cf ASD V-1 150) and, as the nuncio reported to Rome with studied malice, led to a heated discussion of the evidence for St Peter's presence in Rome (Balan no 126; cf Ep 1202 n46). After 14 October Erasmus returned to Louvain and stayed for six days in the Wild Man inn, where Aleandro had also stopped. When Erasmus returned from a short trip to Antwerp, Aleandro was still there. Presumably this was the last they saw of each other, and their meetings there may well have been the friendliest in a long while (cf Ep 1244:1–4, Allen Ep 1342:102–10, 134–48). Before leaving Louvain, Aleandro seems to have sternly admonished Erasmus' stubborn critic, Vincentius Theoderici (cf Allen Ep 1342:133–47). Aleandro's Ep 1241A probably also reflects the ease of these encounters, which was not destined to last; cf Aleandro's biography in CEBR I.

29 Vives] Juan Luis Vives was also a friend of Budé's. Erasmus had recently met him at Bruges (cf above n2). He was now completing his edition of Augustine's *De civitate Dei*; cf Ep 1309.

30 giving Brie advice … change his mind] Cf Epp 1131 introduction, 1185 n1.

31 letter-writing in both languages] This reference presumably is to a letter from Brie, partly in Greek, that Erasmus had recently received (cf lines 196–201). It is now missing.

32 rural retreat at Anderlecht] Cf Ep 1208 introduction.

33 in building too] Cf Epp 435:146–7, 568:14–15.

1233A

1 for Avignon … legal studies] Amerbach was in Avignon from May 1520 to February 1521 and returned to Basel between 24 April and 9 May (cf Ep 1020 n6, AK II Epp 779–82). He had written to Erasmus before his departure (Ep 1084).

2 plague … home again] Cf Ep 1250 introduction.

3 Alciati] Cf Ep 1250.

4 Calvo] The humanist and publisher Francesco Giulio Calvo was repeatedly in contact with Erasmus. Until 1521 he was a major importer of Lutheran books into Italy.

5 letter … to a friend] In his youth Alciati had written a bold letter (or declamation, as Erasmus calls it in Ep 1250:18) against the monastic way of life. Now he was afraid that it might be printed in Basel or Germany and damage his reputation at home. His pressing inquiries, especially with Amerbach, continued until 1531 when he finally seems to have felt satisfied that it had been destroyed. It survived, however, and was eventually published: *Contra vitam monasticam, ad collegam olim suum Bernardum Mattium*, ed Antonius

Matthaeus (Leiden 1695). As the manuscript can be traced back to Petrus Scriverius, a seventeenth-century Leiden professor, who possessed many papers connected with Erasmus (cf Allen I 46, 575, 581, 598), it seems probable that the Alciati manuscript in Erasmus' possession was not destroyed after all, although Erasmus clearly thought in good faith that it was.

1234

1 Stendelin] He may perhaps have visited Erasmus at this time, taking Schudelin's letter and securing this reply. Afterwards he has been traced only once, in 1531, as a friend of Henricus Cornelius Agrippa mentioned in a letter addressed to the latter.

2 gatherings] Erasmus uses the Greek term *synagoge*, which recalls his frequent comparisons between Judaism and scholasticism; cf Ep 1126 n45.

3 new wine ... old bottles] Cf Matt 9:17.

4 bring up children on the right lines] Cf Ep 1233 introduction, and for encouragement to another schoolmaster at just this time cf Ep 1232:109–12.

1235

1 return to us] Cf Ep 1216 n16.

2 negotiations] Cf Ep 1245 introduction.

3 Jan de Hondt] He was the canon of Courtrai responsible for the payment of Erasmus' annuity, which was always done promptly.

4 My friend ... white] The Carmelite Nicolaas Baechem Egmondanus (cf Ep 1144 n8); his attack here reported parallels an earlier one by Henry Standish; cf Ep 1126:135–51.

5 'We shall ... not all be changed'] 1 Cor 15:51. Erasmus here cites Baechem quoting the Vulgate, whereas the Greek manuscripts had the reading now considered to be authentic: 'we shall not all sleep, but we shall all be changed.' The Vulgate reading is taken to refer to the resurrection and divine retribution, whereas the Greek reading points to the immanence of the author's eschatological expectation: not all of us will be dead by the time the world ends. Following the defence presented in this letter, Erasmus wrote a short *Apologia de loco 'Omnes quidem'* (LB IX 433–42), which was published in his *Apologiae omnes* (Basel: J. Froben February 1522). In this edition the *Apologia de loco 'Omnes quidem'* and an enlarged version of the first *apologia* against López Zúñiga were added on preliminary quires without pagination to copies of a volume of *apologiae* produced by Froben in October/November 1521. As this earlier volume appears to be exceedingly rare (cf L.-E. Halkin in *Bibliothèque d'Humanisme et Renaissance* 45, 1982, 343–8), it may have been quickly removed from circulation pending Erasmus' arrival in Basel; cf Ep 1242 introduction.

6 *Periarchon*] Origen's most important theological work (in Latin *De principibus*) was translated into Latin both by Rufinus and Jerome, but the latter's version – no doubt much the better of the two – is lost except for a few fragments.

7 *Annotationes*] A fairly full discussion of this passage, in the light of the patris-

tic commentaries, is first given in the 1518/19 edition of the New Testament (*Annotationes* 355–6; cf Ep 864 introduction). Further material was added in the 1522 edition; cf Ep 1174 n6 and LB VI 740–3.

8 Jerome] Cf LB VI 740F, IX 435C–E.

9 author ... Pauline Epistles] According to Allen's notes here and in VII xxii, the author of this commentary is none other than the heretic Pelagius (cf Ep 1225 n66). Erasmus had recognized that it was not by Jerome, although he regarded it as orthodox, and printed it in the Jerome edition of 1516 (IX ff 131–90); cf LB VI 741E–F, IX 435C–D, 437C–D.

10 Thomas] Thomas Aquinas; cf LB VI 741F–742A, IX 437D.

11 read what I have written] Cf Ep 1200:53–6.

12 over his wine] Cf Ep 1162 n19.

13 theory of contradictions] Such as, for example, Pierre Abélard's method in *Sic et non*

14 time of his coming] Cf Matt 24:36, Acts 1:7.

15 my lord of Tortosa] Cardinal Adrian of Utrecht

16 replied to Zúñiga] Cf Ep 1216 n1.

17 Aleandro] Cf Ep 1233 n28.

18 that work] Having to answer Zúñiga; cf Ep 1236:64–6.

19 New Testament] Cf Ep 1174 n6.

20 you cannot die ... great loss] Cf Epp 1094, 1245 introduction, lines 11–12.

1236

1 a certain person] Girolamo Aleandro

2 letter to the pope himself] Ep 1143, and perhaps subsequently an answer to Ep 1180, if *literis* refers to more than one letter; cf Ep 1213 n5.

3 the weasel in Horace] Cf *Epistles* 1.7.29–33.

4 nibble ... twist it] To twist a rope of hay, and have it immediately eaten by a donkey, was a proverbial image for labour wasted (cf *Adagia* I iv 82–3). If Bombace were to return to his native Bologna, relatives and friends would make demands upon him.

5 Carteromachus] Scipione Fortiguerra called Carteromachus; cf Ep 217:4n.

6 price ... pay for it] Cf Ep 1233:47–51.

7 knight ... treasurer] Cf Epp 1210 n4, 1220 n1.

8 Basel] Cf Ep 1242 introduction.

9 Cornelius] He has not been identified. Allen suggested Cornelis, the son of Erasmus' old friend Jacob Batt; cf Epp 573, 839–40.

10 Alessandria] The loss of this strategic fortress on the crossroads between Milan, Turin and Genoa, late in January 1521, was a severe blow to the French; cf Ep 1228 n12, LP III 2017, 2035.

11 Zúñiga ... New Testament] Cf Ep 1128 n2.

12 laconic defence in reply] Cf Ep 1216 n1.

13 public peace] Cf Ep 1149 introduction.

14 held back many people] Cf Ep 1143 n7.

15 nothing in opposition to Luther] The following text to line 143 is closely reminiscent of Ep 1225:261–339, and elaborates on a number of points made in the earlier letter.

16 how prolific he is] Cf Ep 1173:95–8.
17 'let the horsemen … plain'] Cf *Adagia* I viii 82, meaning 'let people do what they will do best.'
18 Hesiod's wagon] In *Works and Days* 456 Hesiod says it takes a hundred pieces of timber to make a farm wagon; cf *Adagia* IV iii 88.
19 stentorian voices] Stentor, a Greek herald in the *Iliad*, was famous for his loud voice; cf *Adagia* II iii 37.
20 bonfires] Cf Epp 1216 n19, 1218:45.
21 unpopular support] Cf Epp 1182 n4, 1188:24–8.
22 revising … works of mine] Cf Ep 1225 n71.
23 she-bear] Cf Pliny *Naturalis historia* 8.126; Erasmus *Parabolae* CWE 23 252.
24 Aleandro] Cf Ep 1233 n28.
25 spies] Cf *Adagia* I ii 44.
26 a brief of some sort] No such brief is known to have been issued.
27 give even my life] Cf Ep 1218 n14.
28 even one … read right through] Cf above lines 85–7, Ep 1225:281–3.
29 one syllable … my connivance] Cf Ep 1219 n4, below lines 180–5.
30 admitted were his own] In Worms before the assembled diet; cf Epp 1197 introduction, 1219:97–8.
31 *De captivitate Babylonica*] Cf Ep 1186 n3.
32 'Whether you will or no'] For the *Panegyricus*, published in 1504, see CWE 27 xiii–xix, 2–75.
33 *Eubulus*] *Oratio Constantii Eubuli Moventini de virtute clavium et bulla condemnationis Leonis decimi contra Martinum Lutherum* ([Sélestat: L. Schürer 1521?]; repr in Hutten *Opera* V 350–62). It is addressed to Charles V. Aleandro was told by Jakob Spiegel that the author was Paulus Phrygio (see Aleandro's dispatch from Worms, 6 February 1521, Balan no 19); cf *Short-Title Catalogue of Books Printed in Germany* … (London 1962).
34 *Lamentationes Petri*] *Lamentationes Petri, autore Esdra scriba olim, modo publico sanctorum pronotario, cum annotationibus seu additionibus Iohannis Andreae* (n p, n d [Zwolle: S. Corver 1521], NK 2985). Allen suggested that it might have been written in Friesland. Esdras and Iohannes Andreae are pseudonyms. For hypotheses about the author see NK.
35 Lutheran plague … this part of the world] Cf Ep 1165 n1. Well before Luther certain heretics in the Netherlands opposed some of the teachings of the church concerning the sacraments; for these, and for Erasmus' own position in this regard, see G.H. Williams *The Radical Reformation* (Philadelphia 1962) chapter 2.
36 collected passages from my books] Cf Ep 1225:117–22.
37 not be found unfaithful] Cf Ep 1228 n11.
38 Basel] Cf Ep 1242 introduction.
39 Rome] Cf Ep 1143 n22. In the event, however, his plans for the future took a different course (cf Ep 1209 n1), and the war in Italy ruled out even a visit to Rome; cf Ep 1250:10–11.
40 life in the country … strength] Cf Ep 1208 introduction.
41 cardinal of Santi Quattro] Lorenzo Pucci
42 Chierigati] Cf Ep 1144.

1237

1 into the country] Cf Ep 1208 introduction.

2 Agricola, Langen, and the Canters] Rodolphus Agricola, Rudolf von Langen, and Jan Canter and his family, outstanding representatives of early humanism north of the Alps; cf CEBR I and II.

3 their children … humane studies] Cf Ep 1220 n9.

4 happy times we live in] Cf Ep 1194 n1.

5 climate … agreeable] Cf Ep 1221 n4.

6 Ceratinus] After meeting Erasmus at Louvain in the summer of 1519 (cf Ep 992 introduction), Ceratinus began to teach Greek at Tournai, but he had moved to Louvain shortly before this letter was written.

7 wars] Cf Ep 1228 n12.

8 college of languages … started] Erasmus' friend, Robert de Keysere, and the vicar-general of Tournai, Pierre Cotrel, attempted to establish in Tournai a Collegium Bilingue for the study of Greek and Latin, but many difficulties had to be overcome until a regular programme could be offered from 1525 to 1530, when the college was forced to close for good.

9 Hermann of Westphalia] Hermann Stuve (died c 1560), of Vechta, had studied in Cologne and taught in Zwolle under Gerardus Listrius, extending hospitality to his former teacher, Johannes Murmellius (cf Ep 697). He was now in Louvain, earning his living as a private tutor, and would end his life as a Lutheran pastor in his native Westphalia.

10 Adrien of Soissons] Adrien Amerot (d 1560), of Soissons, was in 1512 one of Aleandro's students at Paris. In 1513 he went to Louvain, where he lived in the College of the Lily, as Erasmus did from 1517. Even before earning his MA in 1516, he was tutoring other students in Greek. In 1520 he published an excellent Greek grammar and in 1545 he succeeded Rutgerus Rescius (cf line 35) as professor of Greek at the Collegium Trilingue.

11 Rescius] Cf Ep 1240.

12 new college] Cf Ep 1221 n3.

13 Goclenius also] Cf Ep 1209.

14 Barlandus] Cf Epp 1163, 1204.

15 Melchior of Trier] Melchior Matthaei of Vianden in Luxembourg, north-west of Trier (died c 1535), went to Louvain in 1508 and subsequently taught there at the College of the Castle. In 1522 Erasmus wished to see him settled in a good position (cf Ep 1257). From 1525 he taught at the Collegium Bilingue of Tournai.

16 Everaerts] Cf Ep 1238.

17 load of letters] Only Ep 1235, directed to Spain, and Ep 1236, directed to Rome, seem to have survived.

1238

1 disposed to travel] Erasmus had earlier announced his intention to visit Holland in the summer of 1520; cf Ep 1092:4.

2 that island … summer months] Walcheren, where Everaerts was born and no doubt owned property. For a daunting account of its climate in the autumn cf Ep 663:1–36.

3 in the country] Cf Ep 1208 introduction.
4 agrees with me so badly] Cf Ep 296:68–9, 221–2.
5 Dorp] He was a native of Naaldwijk in South Holland and a protégé of Everaerts; cf Ep 1044:23–7.
6 Lethmaet] Lethmaet (born c 1492), of Gouda, was from 1522 canon of St Mary's, Utrecht. He corresponded with Erasmus; cf Ep 1320.
7 course of theology … Sorbonne] A recent MA, Lethmaet entered the Collège de Sorbonne in 1510 at the age of nineteen. Three years later he was appointed to a fellowship there, and in 1520 he completed his doctorate in divinity.
8 mixture … friends of both] Cf Ep 1125 introduction.
9 god from the machine] Cf Ep 1199 n1.
10 war] On the war between Charles V and Francis I of France and the role of Pope Leo X cf Ep 1228 n12, n13.
11 orders in question] The Dominicans and Carmelites, in particular; cf the index.
12 Cambridge] Cf Epp 730:19–21, 1111:32–38.
13 at my door] Cf Ep 1196:356–91.
14 professor of Greek] Rescius; cf Ep 1240 introduction.
15 emperor's proclamation] The Edict of Worms; cf Epp 1197 introduction, 1216 n19.
16 Pfefferkorn] Johann Pfefferkorn still kept up the struggle against Johann Reuchlin, after whose condemnation (cf Ep 1155 n2) he triumphantly published *Ein mitleydliche Claeg … gegen … Reuchlin* ([Cologne] 21 March 1521); see Hutten *Operum supplementum* II 114–15.
17 against these scandalous tongues] For Erasmus' earlier efforts to bring about legal checks against denigratory pamphlets cf Ep 1053 n62.
18 the laws … aggressor] Already in Roman law the principle of self-defence was well established; see, for instance, *The Theodosian Code* 9.14.2, tr C. Pharr (Princeton 1952) 236.
19 priors … vicar] In various orders of monks and friars (cf Ep 1231 n2), priors directed the individual monasteries, whereas the provinces of the order were headed by a father provincial. The Dominicans and Franciscans were also subdivided in congregations headed by a vicar (of the general). Erasmus may here have equated vicars and provincials.
20 horse and cart] Cf Ep 1171 n19.

1239

1 scratch my ears] Cf *Adagia* II iii 15.
2 your verses] It appears that Ofhuys was working on an engraving of some biblical scene and had asked Erasmus for a metrical inscription to accompany it. The verses for Ofhuys may have been enclosed on a separate sheet (for a similar case cf Ep 1130). They are not known to exist now; cf Reedijk 400.
3 Jerome … Nepotianus] Cf Jerome's Ep 60:12 (CSEL 54:563–4).
4 'Be … the world'] John 16.33
5 prior] Jan Meerhout (d 1550), appointed prior to the Scheut Carthusians in 1517

1240

1 last in Louvain] Cf the introduction. The words do not sound as if written at a time when Erasmus lived in Louvain but had gone away for just a few days, as he had in August 1520. However, during his stay at Anderlecht (May-October 1521) he repeatedly paid short visits to Louvain; cf Allen Ep 1342:19–22.

2 Jan Calaber] Jan Calaber (d 1527), of Louvain, received a doctorate in medicine from Louvain in 1489. He continued to teach in the university and was three times elected rector for a term, the last one being winter 1519–20.

1241

1 I wrote … letter] The letter is missing.

2 belong to the court] For Capito's misgivings cf lines 50–3, Ep 1158 n6. Not until after his departure from the court of Mainz did he again find some time for his studies.

3 criticize you] Cf Ep 1225:306–8.

4 Charles will … differently.] Erasmus too predicted that Charles v might come to regret his current policies (cf Ep 1238:78–9), but he was referring to the war with France, while Capito here intends the Edict of Worms.

5 Glapion's remark] Capito is presumably referring to Erasmus' letter. For contacts between each of them and the confessor of Charles v cf Epp 1217 n16, 1228 n11.

6 burning books gets nowhere] Cf Epp 1141 n11, 1186 n8, 1216 n19.

7 set about their destruction] We translate *perditum*, not *perditos*.

8 Karlstadt … his mind] In the spring of 1521 Andreas Karlstadt (cf Ep 1127A n29) had gone to Denmark upon the invitation of King Christian II, who was prepared to use reforming ideas in his efforts to control the bishops and nobles. But the king could not afford to antagonize the imperial court with his religious policies (cf Ep 1228 n6), and in June the disappointed Karlstadt returned to Wittenberg (cf Luther w *Briefwechsel* II Ep 407; BRE Ep 206).

9 Priests are marrying] On some cases in Saxony see Aleandro's complaint (Balan no 107) and Luther's challenge to Albert of Mainz (Luther w *Briefwechsel* II Ep 442). On 26 May 1521 Christian II of Denmark ordered his bishops to get married.

10 read the Scriptures] Writing to Luther (Luther w *Briefwechsel* II Ep 447), Capito said that he had induced Cardinal Albert to study the Gospels and St Paul on the question of good works, an exercise to which the cardinal was little accustomed; cf Ep 661:22n.

11 rage all the more furiously] Anton Philipp Brück (in *Reichstag zu Worms* 257–70) emphasizes the contrast between Albert's cautious restraint and the popular tendency to see in him one of Luther's principal enemies. In the bull *Decet Romanum pontificem* (cf Ep 1192 n8) he was named as one of the executors of the ban against Luther and in April he was threatened in an anonymous poster affixed to some public places in Worms, both matters of considerable concern to him; cf Aleandro's dispatches, Balan nos 74, 93.

12 rapprochement with you] Cf Ep 1165 n24.

13 Write] Erasmus is not known to have done so.

14 a book ... remedy for the evil] Cf Ep 1228 n11.

15 leave Aleandro alone] Capito continued to make friendly overtures to Aleandro (cf lines 4–6), who in turn treated him cautiously as a Lutheran in disguise (see Balan nos 19, 37; cf the preface). On 29 March 1521 Capito wrote to Aleandro, describing how he had publicly asserted that the nuncio 'was on excellent terms with Erasmus, and as a proof I produced his letter to me, in which he mentions you with distinction'; see Paul Kalkoff *W. Capito im Dienste Erzbischofs Albrechts von Mainz* (Berlin 1907) 135.

16 The Fates ... way.] Cf Ep 1166 n34.

1241A

1 Charles] If this letter belongs to October 1521, Charles may well be Karl Harst (cf Ep 1215), who accompanied Erasmus from Louvain to Koblenz, perhaps en route for his parental home at Wissembourg in Lower Alsace.

1242

1 your brother ... bishop of Wrocław] Johannes Thurzo (d 2 August 1520).

2 reflection ... writings] Cf Ep 850:5, 24–32, 46–8.

3 in several letters] Epp 850, 1047

4 'few feel ... wand'] Cf *Adagia* I vii 6.

5 Łaski] Hieronim (or Jarosław) Łaski (1496–1541) was with his brothers Jan and Stanisław brought up at the court of their uncle, Jan Łaski, archbishop of Gniezno. After a grand tour of Europe and the Holy Land, he was in 1520 appointed Polish envoy to visit Francis I of France and the new emperor, Charles V, who was preparing to return from Spain to the Netherlands. On this mission he was accompanied by his younger brother Jan, the future reformer. They met Erasmus at Brussels (cf Ep 1136 introduction) and after attending the coronation at Aachen, met him again at Cologne; cf Ep 1155 introduction and Allen I 33:3–10.

6 Sander] Michael Sander (d 1529), doctor of civil and canon law of the University of Bologna, became by 1512 secretary to Cardinal Matthäus Schiner, who was one of Erasmus' patrons. He was provided with a number of benefices and was commendatory abbot of San Cristoforo, near Bergamo, and dean (rather than provost) of the Wrocław chapter. On 29 June 1521 Schiner sent him from Brussels to Cardinal Wolsey and in July and August he was with Charles' court at Antwerp and Ghent; cf LP III 1375, 1419 and Büchi II nos 783, 786, 788.

7 Velius] Caspar Ursinus Velius (cf Ep 548:6n) had arrived in Basel in August, carrying Thurzo's letter and gift for Erasmus. Recently he had moved on to Freiburg, where he was to spend the winter, publishing meanwhile with Froben at Basel a collection of his Latin verse, *Poemata* (March 1522). They contain many pieces in praise of the Thurzos; cf AK II Ep 817–20.

1243

1 my last letter] Ep 1242

2 present] We do not know what Thurzo had sent, but his next gift to Erasmus, delivered together with Ep 1272, was four gold coins.

3 publish your virtues to the world] Cf Ep 1242 n7.

1244

1 with Aleandro] Cf Ep 1233 n28. Pirckheimer's letter is missing.

2 diploma ... from your troubles] Cf Ep 1182 n2.

3 what god] Cf Ep 1199 n1.

4 friends tried to deter him] So did recently Capito; see Ep 1241 introduction and lines 11–16, and cf also Ep 1143:25–9.

5 remain unharmed] Erasmus may be thinking of Hutten, struck by the papal ban (whereas Pirckheimer had now been rehabilitated; cf Ep 1182 n2), and Luther, additionally struck by the Edict of Worms; cf Epp 1197 introduction, 1203 n2.

6 attempt at liberty] Conceivably Erasmus may be thinking of Luther's *De libertate christiana*; cf Ep 1202 n10.

7 We] Erasmus identifies himself with the Germans, as he did in Epp 1110:72–3, 1111:95–7, 1202:284; cf Ep 1142:13–14.

8 in arms] Cf Ep 1168 n6.

9 some nobles ... the clergy] Cf Epp 1120, 1148, 1161 introduction.

10 Dominicans] Cf Epp 1196, 1217:17–19, and the index.

11 Some ... to write against Luther] Among them Jean Glapion; cf 1228 n11.

12 Certain Germans] Cf Ep 1225 n79.

1245

1 Two letters] Ep 1235 and another letter now missing. Perhaps it was not released for publication because it dealt with Barbier's advice concerning the Louvain theologians, which Erasmus evidently had not liked; cf lines 58–9.

2 war] Cf Ep 1228 n12.

3 your part of the world] No doubt the Netherlands (cf Ep 1216 n16); Barbier was not as yet aware of Erasmus' move to Basel (cf Ep 1242 introduction). His other letter is also missing.

4 I will pay ... I speak] It appears that Jan de Hondt's remittances were nominally payable to Barbier, who in turn paid Erasmus.

5 six pounds and a half gros] In Flemish money-of-account; this was equivalent to 39 Flemish florins or livres d'Artois, and worth about £4 10s 0d sterling, or 19 Italian ducats.

6 another letter] Not known to exist

7 my brother] Nicolas Barbier; cf Ep 613.

8 Charles] He has not been identified; conceivably Karl Harst (cf Ep 1215, Allen Ep 1621:1–2). Allen suggested the Emperor Charles v.

9 I see ... than good] Cf above n1.

10 Vitoria] Presumably Vitoria in the Basque country

1246

1 utterance of the sage] We are unable to suggest an identification.

2 heard already] Cf Epp 1227:7–8, 32–4, 1228:8–11.

3 *Assertio septem sacramentorum*] Cf Ep 1227 n3.

4 Richmond] Cf Ep 1211 n63, n102.

1247

1 to Basel] Cf Ep 1242 introduction.
2 in Bruges last year] Cf Ep 1129 n1.
3 More] Cf Ep 1145:6–8.
4 my coins] Peutinger was a passionate collector of coins and other old and curious objects. See the description of his coin collection given in his will quoted in *Jahres-Bericht des historischen Kreis-Vereins ... Schwaben und Neuburg* 15/16 (1849–50) 65.
5 wife] Margarethe Welser (1481–1552) was descended from one of the great merchant families of Augsburg, second only to the Fuggers. By the time she married Peutinger in 1498 she had learnt Latin. She is perhaps the housewife eager to discuss the Epistle to the Romans mentioned by Urbanus Rhegius a month later (cf Allen Ep 1253:24–7). For other women knowledgeable in Latin cf Ep 1233 introduction and lines 62–84, n21.
6 Matthew's Gospel] Matt 20:23, checked by Peutinger in the Vulgate
7 *Annotationes*] The edition of 1518/19; cf Ep 864 introduction, below n9, n11.
8 besides Mark] Mark 10:39, where the words in question appear in the Vulgate
9 and the Vulgate] This last reference was added only in the 1518/19 edition of the New Testament, evidently in error, as the Vulgate text of Matthew does not have the clause in question. Perhaps as a result of Margarethe's query Erasmus eliminated the words 'and the Vulgate' from the third edition of the New Testament of 1522; cf LB VI 105E and Ep 1174 n6.
10 Origen's ... Chrysostom's ... on Matthew] Following up the reference given by Erasmus in his note on Matt 20:23
11 Can you drink ...] Cited again after the 1518/19 edition, whose translation of this passage does not entirely agree with the preceding first and following third editions; cf LB VI 106A.

1248

1 full of soldiers] On his way to Basel (cf Ep 1242 introduction), Erasmus travelled from Tienen to Speyer in the company of German soldiers, who had been dismissed from the imperial troops in the Netherlands and were returning home, transporting their booty on wagons (cf Allen Ep 1342:148–54). They appear to have been contented and disciplined, unlike the bands of soldiers Erasmus had feared so often on his previous journeys between the Netherlands and Basel; cf Epp 412:4–8, 829:9–12, 832:14–16, 867:29–30.
2 New Testament] Cf Ep 1174 n6.
3 Greek poet ... to bring forth once] Cf Euripides *Medea* 250–1.
4 donkey] Cf Pliny *Naturalis historia* 8.68.169.
5 stoves] For Erasmus' dislike of the customary central-European stoves cf Epp 867:17–21, 1169:19, and other letters listed in Allen's note here. Johann Froben had a fireplace built specifically for Erasmus (cf Ep 1242 introduction), and so did also Johann von Botzheim in Constance; cf Allen Ep 1382:60–1, BRE Ep 227.
6 illness ... my life] It continued to the end of 1522; cf Ep 1311, BRE Ep 216, and Allen's note here.
7 Brussels] Erasmus had often gone to Brussels during the summer he spent at Anderlecht (cf Epp 1208, 1218 introductions). In Allen Ep 1255:24–9 he

recalled that Schiner had urged him to tackle Matthew when they first met at Brussels, after the cardinal's return from Worms (in the train of Charles v). On 30 June Schiner set out from Brussels for Switzerland (cf LP III 1357, 1375, 1388) and on 25 September he reached the region of Como with the Swiss mercenaries he had recruited for the papal army; cf Büchi II no 798 and below Ep 1250 n5.

8 how pitilessly she demands … kept] Cf Allen Ep 1255:80–1.

9 baleful star … evil demon] Cf Ep 1199 n1.

10 civil war] In their war against Charles v and Leo x (cf Ep 1228 n12, n13) the French had Italian, Netherlandish, and even Spanish allies; moreover, both sides were employing Swiss mercenaries. But Erasmus might have termed all wars between Christians 'civil wars' (*bella intestina*); cf Ep 1238: 68–9.

11 thumbed everywhere … laymen] There were many reprints of the paraphrases of individual epistles as well as collections in Latin and also a German translation by Leo Jud, sold either individually or with a collective title-page (Zürich: C. Froschauer 1521); see Holeczek *Erasmus Deutsch* I 296, and cf also Ep 1171 introduction.

12 Charles] Cf Ep 1255.

13 Rumours … false] Pope Leo x died on 1 December 1521.

1249

1 next fair] The spring book fair at Frankfurt; cf Ep 1225 n71.

2 certain persons … Lutheran faction] Among them Girolamo Aleandro; cf Epp 1165 n1, 1167 n20.

3 Germans themselves … differently] Cf Ep 1225:301–8.

1250

1 herald of your virtues] Cf Epp 1020:57–64, 1233A:10–14.

2 your publication] Alciati's *Paradoxa*, a work of legal erudition, first printed in Milan, 1518, was being reprinted just then at Basel in a revised version (cf AK II Epp 766, 830), but did not appear until 1523.

3 Pyrrhus] Jean Pyrrhus d'Angleberme had in 1501 been Erasmus' pupil in Paris (cf Ep 140:37–9). After a career as professor of law in Orléans (cf Ep 725) he was appointed to the administration of French-occupied Milan and he died there in the course of 1521.

4 visit Milan] On his way to Rome; cf Ep 1236:200.

5 god of war] Cf Ep 1228 n12. Milan was captured on 19 November by the imperial and papal armies led by Ferdinando Francesco d'Avalos, marquis of Pescara, and Cardinals Giulio de' Medici (the future Clement VII) and Matthäus Schiner, who had secured Swiss mercenaries for the pope; cf Ep 1248 n7 and Büchi II no 802.

6 these Germans … publishing everything] Cf Ep 1186 n13.

7 declamation] Cf Ep 1233A n5.

1251

1 the bearers of this letter] They have not been identified.

2 Basel] Cf Ep 1242 introduction.

The Vergara-Zúñiga Correspondence

1

1 Brussels, 10 October 1521] The date and place of this letter are given in Letter 2.

2 *Annotationes* of ... Lee] Edward Lee (cf Ep 765 introduction) published his *Annotationes in Annotationes Novi Testamenti Desiderii Erasmi* in February 1520 (Paris: G. de Gourmont for K. Resch). It contained 243 notes on Erasmus' first edition of the New Testament (Basel: J. Froben February 1516) and 25 on the second edition (Basel: J. Froben 1519).

3 Erasmus' reply] Erasmus' *Apologia invectivis Lei* (*Opuscula* 236–303) was first published at Antwerp by Michaël Hillen in early March 1520 and reprinted by Eucharius Cervicornus at Cologne later that month. It was followed by the *Responsio ad annotationes Lei* (April 1520; LB IX 123–200) and the *Liber tertius quo respondet reliquis annotationibus Ed. Lei* (May 1520; LB IX 199–284).

4 left for Rome] Zúñiga set out for Rome from Alcalá in August 1520 with the intention of visiting the curia and possibly of trying to convince the pope that the time had come to curb Erasmus. Having travelled along the coast, he arrived in Rome on 9 February 1521, and later that year published an account of his voyage, the *Itinerarium ab Hispania usq[ue] ad urbem romanam in quo multa varia ac scitu dignissima continent[ur]* (Rome: M. Silber). At Rome Zúñiga enjoyed the protection of Cardinal Bernardino López de Carvajal (cf Ep 239) and later obtained a position at the University of Rome.

5 *Apologia ... Annotationes*] Zúñiga began to write his *Annotationes contra Erasmum Roterodamum* soon after receiving a copy of Erasmus' first edition of the New Testament in the second half of 1516. Cardinal Jiménez de Cisneros (cf Ep 541) discouraged immediate publication, but two and one half years after the cardinal's death in November 1517 the work was printed (Alcalá: A.G. de Brocar 1520). A volume of fifty-eight folios (115 pages), it contained 212 notes on Erasmus' New Testament, in which Zúñiga tried to demonstrate the superiority of the Vulgate translation of the New Testament on philological grounds. Erasmus replied one by one to Zúñiga's criticisms in the *Apologia respondens ad ea quae Iacobus Lopis Stunica taxauerat in prima duntaxat Novi Testamenti aeditione* (ASD IX-2 58–267) published at Louvain by Dirk Martens between 23 September (Ep 1235) and 10 October 1521, the date of this letter.

6 from Spain] Vergara travelled to the Low Countries with the imperial court in the spring of 1520 to inform Guillaume (II) de Croy (cf Ep 647), recently appointed archbishop of Toledo, about conditions in the archdiocese. His first encounter with Erasmus occurred at Bruges between 25 and 29 July (cf Epp 1128, 1129).

7 a Flemish friend] Almost certainly Pierre Barbier (cf Ep 443) who travelled to Spain in 1517 in the retinue of Jean Le Sauvage and later entered the service of Adrian of Utrecht, elected Pope Adrian VI (cf Ep 171) in January 1522. In Ep 1114 of 21 June 1520 Erasmus mentioned receiving letters from Barbier, now lost, which may have informed him about Zúñiga's *Annotationes*. In Ep 1216 of 26 June 1521 Erasmus informed Barbier that he had finally obtained Zúñiga's book.

8 third edition ... second edition ... for some time] The second edition of the New Testament by Erasmus was published by Froben in 1518/19 and the third in 1522.

9 mutual friend] Possibly Alfonso de Valdés (Ep 1807), who also travelled to Flanders with the imperial court in 1520, or Juan Luis Vives (cf Ep 927), who was tutor to Vergara's patron, Guillaume (II) de Croy

10 monstrous plot] Erasmus had earlier accused Edward Lee of trying to conceal his criticisms in order to maximize their damage to his reputation (cf Allen Ep 1037 introduction); he evidently thought that Zúñiga had similar plans.

11 eyewitness] Vergara, a fellow of the College of San Ildefonso from about 1514, assisted in the Polyglot project, helping prepare the interlinear translations of the Greek text of Wisdom, Ecclesiastes, and Job. In 1516 or 1517 he became secretary to Cardinal Jiménez.

12 the cardinal] Jiménez de Cisneros

13 write to Erasmus] Zúñiga did not do so.

14 for several days] Vergara's statement that Zúñiga delayed publication 'for several days' was not accurate, for the *Annotationes* were only printed two and one half years after Jiménez de Cisneros' death. Vergara may thus have been responsible for Erasmus' claim that Zúñiga rushed to publish his work 'at once' on the death of Jiménez (cf Allen Ep 1216:21).

15 for Germany] Vergara accompanied Guillaume de Croy to Germany. Croy was at Cologne in November 1520 and then travelled to Worms to attend the diet. He died there on 6 January 1521 following a riding accident.

16 when I returned] Vergara returned to the Low Countries in the summer of 1521.

17 that Flemish friend] Barbier

18 Bombace] Paolo Bombace (cf Ep 210) was then secretary to Cardinal Lorenzo Pucci (cf Ep 860). For Bombace's remarks to Erasmus see Allen Ep 1213 of 18 June 1521, lines 33–7.

19 the pope] Leo X

20 Zoilus attacking Homer] Zoilus of Amphipolis was a cynic philosopher of the fourth century BC notorious for the bitterness of his attacks on Homer.

21 Momus attacking Venus] Momus was a Greek mythical figure personifying mockery, often critical of his fellow gods and goddesses.

22 invectives ... dirges] There were a number of attacks on Lee, notably the *Epistolae aliquot eruditorum*, first published at Antwerp by Michaël Hillen in May 1520 with expanded versions appearing later in the year at the presses of Hillen and Froben in Basel. The collection came to include contributions by Thomas More, Wilhelm Nesen, Beatus Rhenanus, and Ulrich von Hutten, among others. Cf Allen Ep 1083 introduction. Heinrich Stromer and Gregor Kopp also published letters defending Erasmus against Lee (Leipzig: M. Lotter the elder 1520; cf CWE Ep 1083 introduction), while the humanists of Erfurt published a volume of *Epigrammata* against the English scholar (Erfurt: H. Knappe 1520) and Johannes Gertophius a *Recriminatio* (Basel: A. Cratander 1520); cf Allen Ep 998.

23 a man of his years] Erasmus was in his early to mid-fifties in 1521.

2

1 a letter] Letter 1

2 *Apologia*] Cf Letter 1 n5.

3 Paolo Bombace] Cf Letter 1 n18.

4 my lord of Santi Quattro] Cardinal Lorenzo Pucci

5 a letter] Allen Ep 1236 of 23 September 1521, lines 53–6

6 Lee's *Annotationes* and Erasmus' reply] Cf Letter 1 n2 and n3.

7 arrived in Genoa] Zúñiga travelled to Rome via Genoa in 1520–1; cf Letter 1 n4.

8 a learned gentleman there] Perhaps Battista Fieschi (d after 1535), a doctor of civil and canon law who helped Agostino Giustiniani (cf Ep 810) publish a polyglot psalter (Genoa: P.P. Porro 1516) and was mentioned by Giovanni Angelo Odoni as an admirer of Erasmus in 1535 (Ep 3002). Agostino Giustiniani, a Dominican monk named bishop of Nebbio in Corsica in 1514, taught at Paris between 1517/18 and 1522, so it is unlikely that he would have met Zúñiga at Genoa.

9 second edition] Cf Letter 1 n8.

10 the Portuguese ambassador] Not identified

11 send them] Cf Letter 3:1.

12 in good plain Castilian] Literally 'quite civilly.' The phrase is in Latin; in Castilian 'quite civilly' can mean 'like a layman' or 'in the manner of someone of low rank.'

13 Pope Leo] Leo x died on 1 December 1521; see below, line 117.

14 Greek libraries] In addition to the Biblioteca Apostolica Vaticana, Rome boasted the libraries of a number of wealthy cardinals, several of which were open to scholars. According to Ludwig von Pastor, Giovanni de' Medici made his personal library available to scholars, continuing to maintain it as a separate collection even after his election as Pope Leo x (cf *The History of the Popes* ed and trans R.F. Kerr et al, 3rd ed (London 1938–53) VIII 263).

15 second ... third edition] Cf Letter 1 n8.

16 notes on the *Letters* of St Jerome] Erasmus edited the letters of Jerome, which filled the first four volumes of the works of Jerome published by Johann Froben at Basel in 1516 and reprinted in 1524–6. Cf Allen Ep 396 introduction.

17 a second book] In 1521 Zúñiga had circulated in Rome the manuscript of a book entitled 'Erasmi Roterodami blasphemiae et impietates ex eiusdem Annotationum libro in Novum Testamentum excerptae, cum Stunicae confutatoriis contra eundem annotamentis,' which contained passages from Erasmus' works followed by an extensive commentary by Zúñiga designed to show that Luther and Erasmus shared the same ideas. Although the work was dedicated and presented to Leo x (cf Ep 1260), the pope forbade its publication, and it survives only in manuscript at the Biblioteca Nazionale at Naples – perhaps the very copy presented to Leo. After Leo's death, and before his successor, Adrian VI, arrived in Rome, Zúñiga published an abridged version, fifty-five pages in quarto, of this work, containing only the excerpts from Erasmus' works and entitled *Erasmi Roterodami blasphemiae et impietates nunc primum propalatae ac proprio volumine alias redargutae* (Rome: A. Bladus [7 April to 4 May] 1522). Cf H.J. de Jonge in ASD IX-2 22–3 and below, Letter 3:2.

18 ten passages] Zúñiga raised several of these points in the published version of the *Blasphemiae et impietates*. For example, he accused Erasmus of impiety because he referred to the pope as the 'vicar of Peter' rather than the 'vicar of Christ' and because he had written that the words 'You are Peter' (Matthew 16:18) applied to the universal body of Christians. For Erasmus' response see LB IX 361D–E, 365C–D.

19 a learned Italian] A remote possibility here is Girolamo Aleandro (cf Ep 256), who was Erasmus' most prominent Italian critic at this time. However, Aleandro had been in the Low Countries and in Germany since the summer of 1520, trying to enforce the papal bulls against Luther. Further, according to Erasmus, Aleandro once rejected a book by certain monks of Louvain and Cologne drawing parallels between Luther and the Dutch humanist (LB IX 378D), and he was unsympathetic towards Zúñiga's work (Ep 1235). Other possibilities include Silvester Prierias, Battista Casali, and Alberto Pio. Prierias (cf Ep 872) was the Dominican master of the sacred palace who as censor reviewed Luther's theses on indulgences of 1517 and became the first Italian literary opponent of the German reformer. Although Prierias remained on friendly terms with Erasmus and invited him to Rome, Erasmus indicated (Ep 1412) that the Dominican took issue with passages in at least one of his letters, perhaps Ep 1342. Casali (cf Ep 1479), who wrote an 'Invectiva in Erasmum Roterodamum' (Biblioteca Ambrosiana MS G 33 inf II ff 82–7) in 1524, would seem to be ruled out by the fact that in the spring of 1522 he sent the highly favourable Ep 1270A to Erasmus, although it is possible that this letter masked his true feelings. Alberto Pio, prince of Carpi (cf Ep 1634), wrote a *Responsio* to Erasmus in which he, like Zúñiga, accused the Dutch humanist of affinities with Luther. However, Erasmus only heard of his criticisms in 1524 or 1525 (Epp 1479, 1576) and it was only in May 1526 that Pio completed and signed his *Responsio*, published in 1529 (Paris: J. Bade).

20 a certain scholar at court] Perhaps a reference to Sancho Carranza de Miranda (cf Ep 1277), another scholar of Alcalá, who was at Rome on a mission for the Spanish church between 1520 and 1522. He was soon to publish a critique of Erasmus' New Testament scholarship entitled *Opusculum in quasdam Erasmi Roterodami annotationes* (Rome: A. de Trino 1 March 1522). However, it seems unlikely that Zúñiga failed to meet this fellow Spaniard before January 1522. Zúñiga may have been concealing Carranza's identity in order to heighten the fears of Vergara and Erasmus. It is also possible that this reference may be to one of the Italians mentioned in n19 above.

21 flame and smoke] Juvenal 1.155–6. The reference is to the *tunica molesta*, or shirt of pain, made of pitch and set on fire as a punishment for criminals.

22 my lord of Santi Quattro] Lorenzo Pucci

23 first, second, and third editions] Cf Letter 1 n5 and n8.

24 *Annotationes* against Erasmus] Cf Letter 1:8–9.

25 and Lefèvre] A reference to Zúñiga's *Annotationes contra Iacobum Fabrum Stapulen[sem]* (Alcalá: A.G. de Brocar 1519), against the commentary on the Epistles of Paul by Jacques Lefèvre d'Etaples (cf Ep 315)

26 Eck] Johann Maier of Eck (cf Ep 769) was at Rome between October 1521 and February 1522 (cf Allen Ep 1260:78n).

27 fifteen pamphlets] This reference is to a single publication, *Die xv Buntgenos-*

sen [Basel: P. Gengenbach 1521] by Johann Eberlin of Günzberg (d before 13 October 1533), a Franciscan who had embraced the Lutheran reform. The work, published anonymously, consisted of fifteen parts, two of which were based on passages from the *Moria* which ridiculed friars and the veneration of the saints. The title-pages of three parts, including these two, bore a woodcut based on Metsys' medallion of Erasmus (Allen Ep 1092), with the date changed to 1521. Cf Allen Ep 1481, NDB IV 247–8, and Gottfried Blochwitz 'Die antirömischen deutschen Flugschriften der frühen Reformationszeit (bis 1522) in ihrer religiös-sittlichen Eigenart' *Archiv für Reformationsgeschichte* 27 (1930) 145–254, esp 159–60, 227–8. In 1522 Erasmus wrote that he knew nothing of this work or its author (LB IX 378F–379A).

28 editing and polishing his works] Erasmus was frequently accused of writing works of Luther. Cf Epp 961, 967, 1225, 1342. Erasmus claimed that Aleandro and his circle suspected him of being the author of *De captivitate Babylonica*, Luther's attack on the seven Catholic sacraments, even after Luther acknowledged it as his own work at the Diet of Worms in 1521 (cf Allen Ep 1218:15–16n).

29 wrote to him] Perhaps Ep 1143 of 10 September 1520

30 which ... Bombace had communicated to him] Allen Ep 1213:33–7

31 proclaimed pope] Adrian of Utrecht was appointed bishop of Tortosa on 18 August 1516 and elected pope on 9 January 1522, taking the name of Adrian VI.

32 This is ... the day which the Lord has made.] Ps 118:23–4

3

1 The books] Lee's *Annotationes* and Erasmus' *Apologia invectivis Lei*, referred to in the following lines; cf Letter 1 n2 and n3.

2 your letter] Vergara had written to Zúñiga on 28 February 1522, but that letter is now lost. Cf Allen's introduction to Letter 2, IV 625.

3 my reply to Erasmus] Probably a reference to the 'Erasmi Roterodami blasphemiae et impietates' a manuscript copy of which Zúñiga had presented to Pope Leo late in 1521 (see Letter 2 n17). Although Zúñiga states that this work did not differ much in scope or substance from his previous work, the *Annotationes contra Erasmum Roterodamum*, it in fact extended his argument by attempting to link Erasmus to Luther.

4 several places] Cf ASD IX-2 82, 92 and passim.

5 friends of Erasmus] Possibly Barbier and Bombace are intended here, as well as Jakob Ziegler, who had met Zúñiga at Rome in the fall of 1521 and expressed his dislike of him in Ep 1260 to Erasmus. Ziegler wrote a defence of Erasmus entitled *Libellus ... adversus Stunicae maledicentiam* (Basel: J. Froben April 1523).

6 his reply] Cf Letter 1 n5.

7 matters of greater moment] A reference to the new line of attack taken in the 'Blasphemiae et impietates'; see above n3.

8 Lee's *Annotationes*] Cf Letter 1:1–2.

9 polemical writings against Lee] Cf Letter 1 n3.

10 Latomus' *Dialogus* ... Erasmus' *Apologia*] Jacobus Latomus (cf Ep 934), a theologian of Louvain, opposed the idea that the classical languages were neces-

sary for the study of theology and wrote the dialogue *De trium linguarum et studii theologici ratione* (Antwerp: M. Hillen 1519) in reaction to Petrus Mosellanus' *Oratio de variarum linguarum cognitione paranda* (Leipzig: V. Schumann 1518), and indirectly to Erasmus' *Ratio verae theologiae*. Although Latomus did not mention Erasmus by name, Erasmus decided to reply with the *Apologia contra Latomi dialogum* (Antwerp: J. Thibault [1519]: LB IX 79–106).

11 *Itinerarium*] Cf Letter 1 n4.

12 letter ... to the new pope] The *Epistola ad pontificem noviter electum* [Rome 1522] was sixteen pages in quarto. The recently elected pope was Adrian VI.

13 a little work] The *Libellus trium illorum voluminum praecursor, quibus Erasmicas impietates ac blasphemias redarguit* (Rome: A. Bladus 1522) was a short work of fifty-eight pages intended as a warning that Zúñiga still intended to publish the complete text of the 'Blasphemiae et impietates.' The *Libellus* was published between the date of this letter and July 1522, since Erasmus' reply to it was published by Johann Froben with *De interdicto esu carnium* on 6 August 1522. In LB IX 375–81 Erasmus' reply is given the title *Apologia ad Prodromon Stunicae*, although it first appeared simply as an appendix to Erasmus' *Apologia adversus libellum Stunicae cui titulum fecit Blasphemiae et impietates Erasmi* (LB IX 355–75), also published with *De interdicto esu carnium*.

14 another short work] The abridged *Blasphemiae et impietates*, the publication of which Zúñiga announces in Letter 4.

15 indictment ... refutation] A reference to the original 'Blasphemiae et impietates,' a manuscript of which had been presented to Leo X

16 Erasmus' commentary on the *Letters* of Jerome] Cf Letter 2 n16. Zúñiga prepared annotations or scholia on Erasmus' editions, and a copy of these were sent to Erasmus after Zúñiga's death (cf Ep 2705), but they are now lost.

17 letters from the new pope] Letters from Adrian VI, who was still in Spain in March 1522

4

1 *Itinerarium*] Cf Letter 1 n4.

2 letter to the pope] Cf Letter 3 n12.

3 a work hot off the press] The abridged *Blasphemiae et impietates*. Cf Letter 2 n17 and, for Erasmus' reply, Letter 3 n13.

4 Arius] Arius (c 250–336), was a priest of Alexandria in Egypt who denied the divinity of Christ and of the Holy Spirit. Zúñiga had first insinuated that Erasmus was tending to Arianism in his *Annotationes*, when, for example, he took issue with a statement by Erasmus that Christ was referred to as God only two or three times in the New Testament. For Erasmus' reply see ASD IX-2 124–5.

5 Apollinaris] Apollinaris (c 300–c 390), bishop of Laodicea, in reaction to Arius developed the unorthodox view that Christ was divine but did not possess a human nature. In his *Annotationes* Zúñiga had tried to implicate Erasmus in this heresy because of his interpretation of the application of the word 'servant' to Christ in Acts 3:26. Cf ASD IX-2 142–5.

6 Jovinian] Jovinian was a heretic of the fourth century who attacked Christian forms of asceticism including virginity and fasting. He was vehemently

denounced by Jerome and was condemned in 390. Evidently Zúñiga was alluding to Erasmus' criticisms of monasticism and attacks on monastic abuses.

7 Wycliffites] Followers of John Wycliffe (c 1330–84), the Oxford theologian whose views on church property, papal authority, and the Eucharist were condemned by the Council of Constance (1414–18). In the *Blasphemiae et impietates* Zúñiga accused Erasmus of reviving his attacks on papal authority. For Erasmus' response see LB IX 365C.

8 Hussites] Followers of Jan Hus (c 1369–1415), the Czech reformer burnt as a heretic by the Council of Constance. Again, Zúñiga appears to have felt Erasmus was following them in undermining papal authority (cf LB IX 383D).

9 the pope] Adrian VI, elected in January 1522, arrived in Rome only in August.

5

1 my voyage] Vergara refers to his travels to the Netherlands and Germany, which began in 1520; see Letter 1:16 and n16.

2 leave the court and return home] After the death of Guillaume de Croy, archbishop of Toledo, in January 1521, Vergara entered the service of the emperor Charles V. He returned to Spain in 1522.

3 wrote to him at Basel] Ep 1277 of 24 April 1522

4 Miranda's book] Sancho Carranza de Miranda's *Opusculum in quasdam Erasmi Roterodami annotationes*; see Letter 2 n20. Carranza had dedicated the book to Vergara in the hope that he would explain its scholarly purpose to Erasmus (cf Ep 1277).

5 brief note] Ep 1312 of 2 September 1522

6 your brother] Perhaps Juan, to whom Zúñiga dedicated his *Itinerarium ... ad urbem romanam* (ASD IX-2 13)

7 *un ouvrage préliminaire*] The *Libellus trium illorum voluminum praecursor*, mentioned by Zúñiga in Letter 3:51–3; see n13.

8 'blasphemies'] The *Blasphemiae et impietates*, which Zúñiga sent to Vergara with Letter 4

9 *Annotationes*] The *Annotationes contra Erasmum Roterodamum*, Zúñiga's original attack on Erasmus

10 many people] This group almost certainly included Vives, to whom Vergara had shown Zúñiga's vehement Letter 2 (cf Allen Ep 1271:74–82), possibly Valdés, and a certain Herman (cf Vergara's Ep 1277 to Erasmus), possibly Herman Lethmaet of Gouda (cf Ep 1320), who was with the Hapsburg court in the Netherlands by November 1522.

11 a truce] The truce at this point was probably the result of Adrian VI's injunction that Zúñiga not publish against Erasmus. In the year following Adrian's death the Spaniard published a series of pamphlets against Erasmus, including the *Conclusiones principaliter suspectae et scandalosae quae reperiuntur in libris Erasmi Roterodami* (Rome: [A. Bladus?] between 14 September and 19 November 1523), the *Loca quae ex Stunica annotationibus in tertia editione Novi Testamenti Erasmus emendavit* (Rome: n pr 1524), and the *Assertio ecclesiasticae translationis Novi Testamenti* (Rome: n pr 1524). Erasmus replied to the *Conclusiones* with another *Apologia* (LB IX 381–92), printed by Froben with the *Exomologesis* in March 1524. His reply to the *Assertio* took the form of a

letter to Hubertus Barlandus of 8 June 1529 (Ep 2172; LB IX 391–400). After 1524 Zúñiga had continued to work on Erasmus' editions of the New Testament and of St Jerome, but without publishing his annotations. Indeed his attitude toward Erasmus seems to have moderated, for before his death in 1531 he made arrangements to have his notes copied and sent to Erasmus by Cardinal Francisco de Quiñones (Epp 2637, 2701). The task was eventually completed by Iñigo López de Mendoza, bishop of Burgos (Epp 2705, 2905, 2951).

12 the emperor] Charles v

13 queen of Lusitania] Eleanor, sister of Charles v, married Manuel I of Portugal in 1518. Although Manuel died in December 1521 his successor, John III, did not marry until 1525; his bride was Catherine, another sister of the emperor.

TABLE OF CORRESPONDENTS

WORKS FREQUENTLY CITED

SHORT-TITLE FORMS

INDEX

TABLE OF CORRESPONDENTS

THE VERGARA-ZÚÑIGA CORRESPONDENCE

WORKS FREQUENTLY CITED

This list provides bibliographical information for works referred to in short-title form in this volume. For Erasmus' writings see the short-title list, pages 470–3. Editions of his letters are included in the list below.

Agricola *Ausgewählte Werke*	Georgius Agricola *Ausgewählte Werke* ed Hans Prescher (Berlin 1955–)
AK	Alfred Hartmann and B.R. Jenny eds *Die Amerbachkorrespondenz* (Basel 1942–)
Allen	P.S. Allen, H.M. Allen, and H.W. Garrod eds *Opus epistolarum Des. Erasmi Roterodami* (Oxford 1906–58) 11 vols and index
ASD	*Opera omnia Desiderii Erasmi Roterodami* (Amsterdam 1969–)
Balan	Pietro Balan ed *Monumenta reformationis Lutheranae ex tabulariis secretioribus S. Sedis 1521–1525* (Regensburg 1884)
Benzing *Hutten und seine Drucker*	Josef Benzing *Ulrich von Hutten und seine Drucker. Eine Bibliographie der Schriften Huttens im 16. Jahrhundert* (Wiesbaden 1956)
Benzing *Lutherbibliographie*	Josef Benzing *Lutherbibliographie* (Baden-Baden 1966)
Bietenholz *History and Biography*	P.G. Bietenholz *History and Biography in the Work of Erasmus of Rotterdam* (Geneva 1966)
Boehmer *Luther*	Heinrich Boehmer *Martin Luther: Road to Reformation* (Meridian Books, New York 1957)
BRE	A. Horawitz and K. Hartfelder eds *Briefwechsel des Beatus Rhenanus* (Leipzig 1886, repr 1966)
Büchi	Albert Büchi ed *Korrespondenzen und Akten zur Geschichte des Kardinals Matth. Schiner* (Basel 1920–5) 2 vols
CC	*Corpus Christianorum: Series Latina* (Turnhout 1953–)
CEBR	P.G. Bietenholz and T.B. Deutscher eds *Contemporaries of Erasmus: A Biographical Register of the Renaissance and Reformation* 3 vols (Toronto 1985–7)
CSEL	*Corpus scriptorum ecclesiasticorum Latinorum* (Vienna-Leipzig 1866–)
CWE	*Collected Works of Erasmus* (Toronto 1974–)
Dürer *Diary*	Albrecht Dürer *Diary of His Journey to the Netherlands, 1520–1521* ed J.-G. Goris and G. Marlien (Greenwich, Conn 1971)
Emden BRUC	A.B. Emden *Biographical Register of the University of Cambridge to AD 1500* (Cambridge 1963)
Epistolae ad diversos	*Epistolae D. Erasmi Roterodami ad diversos et aliquot aliorum ad illum* (Basel: J. Froben 31 August 1521)
Farrago	*Farrago nova epistolarum Des. Erasmi Roterodami ad alios et aliorum ad hunc: admixtis quibusdam quas scripsit etiam adolescens* (Basel: J. Froben October 1519)

Fredericq — P. Fredericq ed *Corpus documentorum inquisitionis haereticae pravitatis Neerlandicae* (Ghent 1889–1906) 5 vols

Gachard — L.P. Gachard and C. Piot eds *Collection des voyages des souverains des Pays-Bas* (Brussels 1874–82) 4 vols

Geiger *Reuchlin* — Ludwig Geiger *Johann Reuchlin* (Leipzig 1871; repr 1964)

Holeczek *Erasmus Deutsch* — Heinz Holeczek *Erasmus Deutsch* (Stuttgart-Bad Cannstatt 1983–)

Hutten *Opera* — E. Böcking ed *Ulrichi Hutteni equitis Germani opera* (Leipzig 1859–61; repr 1963) 5 vols

Hutten *Operum supplementum* — E. Böcking ed *Ulrichi Hutteni equitis operum supplementum: Epistolae obscurorum virorum* (Leipzig 1864–9; repr 1966) 2 vols

Jonas Briefwechsel — Gustav Kawerau ed *Der Briefwechsel des Justus Jonas* (Halle 1884–5; repr 1964) 2 vols

de Jongh — Henri de Jongh *L'ancienne faculté de théologie de Louvain au premier siècle de son existence* (Louvain 1911)

LB — J. Leclerc ed *Desiderii Erasmi Roterodami opera omnia* (Leiden 1703–6; repr 1961–2) 10 vols

LP — J.S. Brewer, J. Gairdner, et al eds *Letters and Papers, Foreign and Domestic, of the Reign of Henry VIII* (London 1862–1932; repr 1965) 36 vols

Lupton *Life of Colet* — J.H. Lupton *A Life of John Colet* 2nd ed (London 1909; repr 1961)

Luther w — *D. Martin Luthers Werke: Kritische Gesamtausgabe* (Weimar 1883–)

Matricule de Louvain — E. Reusens, A. Schillings, et al eds *Matricule de l'Université de Louvain* (Brussels 1903–)

Matricule d'Orléans — C.M. Ridderikhoff, H. de Ridder-Symoens, et al eds *Premier livre des procurateurs de la nation germanique de l'ancienne Université d'Orléans, 1446–1546* (Leiden 1971–)

Melanchthons Briefwechsel — Heinz Scheible ed *Melanchthons Briefwechsel: Kritische und kommentierte Gesamtausgabe* (Stuttgart-Bad Cannstatt 1977–)

NK — W. Nijhoff and M.E. Kronenberg eds *Nederlandsche Bibliographie van 1500 tot 1540* (The Hague 1923–71)

Opuscula — W.K. Ferguson ed *Erasmi opuscula: A Supplement to the Opera omnia* (The Hague 1933)

Opus epistolarum — *Opus epistolarum Des. Erasmi Roterodami per autorem diligenter recognitum et adjectis innumeris novis fere ad trientem auctum* (Basel: Froben, Herwagen, and Episcopius 1529)

Pastor — Ludwig von Pastor *The History of the Popes from the Close of the Middle Ages* ed and trans R.F. Kerr et al, 3rd ed (London 1938–53) 40 vols

Peutingers Briefwechsel — Erich König ed *Konrad Peutingers Briefwechsel* (Munich 1923)

PG — J.P. Migne ed *Patrologiae cursus completus ... series Graeca* (Paris 1857–1912) 162 vols

PL — J.P. Migne ed *Patrologiae cursus completus ... series Latina* (Paris 1844–1902) 221 vols

RE — L. Geiger ed *Johann Reuchlins Briefwechsel* (Stuttgart 1875; repr 1962)

Reedijk — C. Reedijk ed *The Poems of Desiderius Erasmus* (Leiden 1956)

Reichstagsakten J.R. II — Adolf Wrede ed *Deutsche Reichstagsakten* Jüngere Reihe II (Gotha 1896)

Reichstag zu Worms — Fritz Reuter et al eds *Der Reichstag zu Worms von 1521: Reichspolitik und Luthersache* (Worms 1971)

STC — A.W. Pollard, G.R. Redgrave, and W.A. Jackson eds *A Short-Title Catalogue of Books Printed in England, Scotland, and Ireland and of English Books Printed Abroad* (London 1926; 2nd ed 1976–)

Vadianische Briefsammlung — E. Arbenz and H. Wartmann eds *Vadianische Briefsammlung* Mitteilungen zur vaterländischen Geschichte 24–5, 27–30, and supplements (St Gallen 1890–1908)

de Vocht CTL — Henry de Vocht *History of the Foundation and the Rise of the Collegium Trilingue Lovaniense 1517–1550* Humanistica Lovaniensia 10–13 (Louvain 1951–5) 4 vols

de Vocht *Literae* — Henry de Vocht ed *Literae virorum eruditorum ad Franciscum Craneveldium 1522–1528* Humanistica Lovaniensia 1 (Louvain 1928)

de Vocht MHL — Henry de Vocht *Monumenta humanistica Lovaniensia* Humanistica Lovaniensia 4 (Louvain 1934)

Wolfs *Acta capitulorum* — S.P. Wolfs ed *Acta capitulorum Germaniae Inferioris ordinis Fratrum Praedicatorum ab anno MDXV usque ad annum MDLIX* (The Hague 1964)

Zwingli *Werke* — Emil Egli et al eds *Huldreich Zwinglis Sämtliche Werke* Corpus Reformatorum 88–101 (Berlin-Zürich 1905– ; repr 1981)

SHORT-TITLE FORMS FOR ERASMUS' WORKS

Titles following colons are longer versions of the same, or are alternative titles. Items entirely enclosed in square brackets are of doubtful authorship. For abbreviations, see Works Frequently Cited.

Adagia: Adagiorum chiliades 1508, etc (Adagiorum collectanea for the primitive form, when required) LB II / ASD II-5, 6 / CWE 30-6
Admonitio adversus mendacium: Admonitio adversus mendacium et obtrectationem LB X
Annotationes in Novum Testamentum LB VI
Antibarbari LB X / ASD I-1 / CWE 23
Apologia ad Fabrum: Apologia ad Iacobum Fabrum Stapulensem LB IX
Apologia ad Caranzam: Apologia ad Sanctium Caranzam, or Apologia de tribus locis, or Responsio ad annotationem Stunicae ... a Sanctio Caranzam defensam LB IX
Apologia ad viginti et quattuor libros A. Pii LB IX
Apologia adversus Petrum Sutorem: Apologia adversus debacchationes Petri Sutoris LB IX
Apologia adversus monachos: Apologia adversus monachos quosdam hispanos LB IX
Apologia adversus rhapsodias Alberti Pii LB IX
Apologia contra Latomi dialogum: Apologia contra Iacobi Latomi dialogum de tribus linguis LB IX
Apologiae contra Stunicam: Apologiae contra Lopidem Stunicam LB IX / ASD IX-2
Apologia de 'In principio erat sermo' LB IX
Apologia de laude matrimonii: Apologia pro declamatione de laude matrimonii LB IX
Apologia de loco 'Omnes quidem': Apologia de loco 'Omnes quidem resurgemus' LB IX
Apologia invectivis Lei: Apologia qua respondet duabus invectivis Eduardi Lei *Opuscula*
Apophthegmata LB IV
Appendix respondens ad Sutorem LB IX
Argumenta: Argumenta in omnes epistolas apostolicas nova (with Paraphrases)
Axiomata pro causa Lutheri: Axiomata pro causa Martini Lutheri *Opuscula*

Carmina varia LB VIII
Catalogus lucubrationum LB I
Christiani hominis institutum, carmen LB V
Ciceronianus: Dialogus Ciceronianus LB I / ASD I-2 / CWE 28
Colloquia LB I / ASD I-3
Compendium vitae Allen I / CWE 4
[Consilium: Consilium cuiusdam ex animo cupientis esse consultum] *Opuscula*

De bello turcico: Consultatio de bello turcico LB V
De civilitate: De civilitate morum puerilium LB I / CWE 25
De concordia: De sarcienda ecclesiae concordia LB V
De conscribendis epistolis LB I / ASD I-2 / CWE 25

De constructione: De constructione octo partium orationis, or Syntaxis LB I / ASD I-4
De contemptu mundi: Epistola de contemptu mundi LB V / ASD V-1
De copia: De duplici copia verborum ac rerum LB I / CWE 24
De immensa Dei misericordia: Concio de immensa Dei misericordia LB V
De libero arbitrio: De libero arbitrio diatribe LB IX
De praeparatione: De praeparatione ad mortem LB V / ASD V-1
De pueris instituendis: De pueris statim ac liberaliter instituendis LB I / ASD I-2 / CWE 26
De puero Iesu: Concio de puero Iesu LB V
De ratione studii LB I / ASD I-2 / CWE 24
De recta pronuntiatione: De recta latini graecique sermonis pronuntiatione LB I / ASD I-4 / CWE 26
De tedio Iesu: Disputatiuncula de tedio, pavore, tristicia Iesu LB V
De virtute amplectenda: Oratio de virtute amplectenda LB V
Declamatio de morte LB IV
Declamatiuncula LB IV
Declarationes ad censuras Lutetiae vulgatas: Declarationes ad censuras Lutetiae vulgatas sub nomine facultatis theologiae Parisiensis LB IX
Detectio praestigiarum: Detectio praestigiarum cuiusdam libelli germanice scripti LB X / ASD IX-1
[Dialogus bilinguium ac trilinguium: Chonradi Nastadiensis dialogus bilinguium ac trilinguium] *Opuscula* / CWE 7
Dilutio: Dilutio eorum quae Iodocus Clithoveus scripsit adversus declamationem suasoriam matrimonii
Divinationes ad notata Bedae LB IX

Ecclesiastes: Ecclesiastes sive de ratione concionandi LB V
Elenchus in N. Bedae censuras LB IX
Enchiridion: Enchiridion militis christiani LB V
Encomium matrimonii (in De conscribendis epistolis)
Encomium medicinae: Declamatio in laudem artis medicae LB I / ASD I-4
Epigrammata LB I
Epistola ad Dorpium LB IX / CWE 3
Epistola ad fratres Inferioris Germaniae: Responsio ad fratres Germaniae Inferioris ad epistolam apologeticam incerto autore proditam LB X
Epistola ad graculos: Epistola ad quosdam imprudentissimos graculos LB X
Epistola apologetica de Termino LB X
Epistola consolatoria: Epistola consolatoria virginibus sacris LB V
Epistola contra pseudevangelicos: Epistola contra quosdam qui se falso iactant evangelicos LB X / ASD IX-1
Epistola de esu carnium: Epistola apologetica ad Christophorum episcopum Basiliensem de interdicto esu carnium LB IX / ASD IX-1
Exomologesis: Exomologesis sive modus confitendi LB V
Explanatio symboli: Explanatio symboli apostolorum sive catechismus LB V / ASD V-1
Expostulatio Iesu LB V

Formula: Conficiendarum epistolarum formula (see De conscribendis epistolis)

Hymni varii LB V
Hyperaspistes LB X

Institutio christiani matrimonii LB V
Institutio principis christiani LB IV / ASD IV-1 / CWE 27

[Julius exclusus: Dialogus Julius exclusus e coelis] *Opuscula* / CWE 27

Lingua LB IV / ASD IV-1
Liturgia Virginis Matris: Virginis Matris apud Lauretum cultae liturgia LB V / ASD V-1

Methodus: Ratio verae theologiae LB V
Modus orandi Deum LB V / ASD V-1
Moria: Moriae encomium LB IV / ASD IV-3 / CWE 27

Novum Testamentum: Novum Testamentum 1519 and later (Novum instrumentum for the first edition, 1516, when required) LB VI

Obsecratio ad Virginem Mariam: Obsecratio sive oratio ad Virginem Mariam in rebus adversis LB V
Oratio de pace: Oratio de pace et discordia LB VIII
Oratio funebris: Oratio funebris Berthae de Heyen LB VIII

Paean Virgini Matri: Paean Virgini Matri dicendus LB V
Panegyricus: Panegyricus ad Philippum Austriae ducem LB IV / ASD IV-1 / CWE 27
Parabolae: Parabolae sive similia LB I / ASD I-5 / CWE 23
Paraclesis LB V, VI
Paraphrasis in Elegantias Vallae: Paraphrasis in Elegantias Laurentii Vallae LB I / ASD I-4
Paraphrasis in Matthaeum, etc (in Paraphrasis in Novum Testamentum)
Paraphrasis in Novum Testamentum LB VII / CWE 42–50
Peregrinatio apostolorum: Peregrinatio apostolorum Petri et Pauli LB VI, VII
Precatio ad Virginis filium Iesum (in Precatio pro pace)
Precatio dominica LB V
Precationes LB V
Precatio pro pace ecclesiae: Precatio ad Iesum pro pace ecclesiae LB IV, V
Progymnasmata: Progymnasmata quaedam primae adolescentiae Erasmi LB VIII
Psalmi: Psalmi, or Enarrationes sive commentarii in psalmos LB V / ASD IV-2
Purgatio adversus epistolam Lutheri: Purgatio adversus epistolam non sobriam Lutheri LB IX

Querela pacis LB IV / ASD IV-2 / CWE 27

Ratio verae theologiae: Methodus LB V
Responsio ad annotationes Lei: Liber quo respondet annotationibus Lei LB IX
Responsio ad collationes: Responsio ad collationes cuiusdam iuvenis gerontodidascali LB IX

Responsio ad disputationem de divortio: Responsio ad disputationem cuiusdam Phimostomi de divortio LB IX
Responsio ad epistolam Pii: Responsio ad epistolam paraeneticam Alberti Pii, or Responsio ad exhortationem Pii LB IX
Responsio ad notulas Bedaicas LB X
Responsio ad Petri Cursii defensionem: Epistola de apologia Cursii LB X
Responsio adversus febricitantis libellum: Apologia monasticae religionis LB X

Spongia: Spongia adversus aspergines Hutteni LB X / ASD IX-1
Supputatio: Supputatio calumniarum Natalis Bedae LB IX

Vidua christiana LB V
Virginis et martyris comparatio LB V
Vita Hieronymi: Vita divi Hieronymi Stridonensis *Opuscula*

Index